# DISQUISITIONS AND NOTES

## ON

## THE GOSPELS.

MATTHEW.

BY

JOHN H. MORISON.

Second Edition.

*Wipf & Stock*
PUBLISHERS
*Eugene, Oregon*

Wipf and Stock Publishers
199 W 8th Ave, Suite 3
Eugene, OR 97401

Disquisitions and notes on the Gospels: Matthew
By Morison, John H.
ISBN: 1-59244-818-6
Publication date 8/26/2004
Previously published by Walker, Wise, and Company, 1861

# PREFACE.

THE object of this work is to assist in the interpretation of the Gospels. It does not seek to go beyond the authority of Jesus. It does not undertake to show what the Evangelists ought to have said, and to force their language into accordance with it. If in any case it may seem to go beyond them, it has been only to meet the honest sceptic of our day on his own ground, and show either that he has misinterpreted the words and acts of Christ, or that those words and acts are in accordance with the great principles of reason, which reach alike through the realms of physical and moral being. The one all-sufficient answer to the unbelief of our age is still the same that Jesus addressed to the Sadducees, who represented the refined and philosophical scepticism of his day: "Ye do err, not knowing the Scriptures, nor the power of God." A true understanding of the Scriptures, with the insight which is gained from them in the light of the highest philosophy into the ways and works and character of God, is the most effectual remedy for scepticism, whether it be a disease going on through moral infidelity to intellectual unbelief, or an honest antagonism to doctrines which falsely call themselves Christian or Evangelical.

The best antidote to scepticism and to a narrow religious dogmatism, is the same. Both believers and unbelievers read too much *about* the Gospels in the works of their favorite guides, and study the Gospels themselves too little. We have never known a diligent and thorough study of the New Testament to end either in bigotry or unbelief. There is a truthfulness breathing through its writings which cannot but affect the ingenuous mind that puts itself freely and constantly into communication with them, and there is a freedom, a breadth of moral purpose, a largeness of thought, a catholicity of sentiment, about them, which must give something of its own generous and liberal spirit to those who place themselves habitually and unreservedly within their influence.

In preparing this work I have sought to avail myself of such helps as have been furnished by the scholarship of past ages; to take advantage of the improved methods of investigation which have been recently adopted, and to borrow liberally from the varied stores of information which have been gained through the enterprise, the laborious researches, the intellectual culture, and the conscientious love of truth for which many of the Biblical scholars of our day have been so honorably distinguished. For example, the text which is here followed in all the variations which are of consequence enough to warrant a departure from the reading in our Common English Version, is Tischendorf's Stereotype Edition of the New Testament, published in 1850. This work, which, we believe, stands higher than any other edition of the New Testament in the estimation of those most competent to judge, was prepared by a careful comparison of all the most ancient manuscripts of the New Testament to which the editor could gain access. Many years were spent upon it, and no labor or expense was spared which promised any useful results. In regard to the Geography of the Holy Land, and the topography of Jerusalem and its environs, so important in order to a correct understanding and a vivid perception of many incidents in our Saviour's life, almost everything that we know with clearness and certainty has been gained since Dr. Robinson began his Biblical Researches in Palestine, less than thirty years ago. Within less than forty years, since Winer first published his " Grammar of the New Testament Diction" in 1822, a revolution hardly less remarkable has taken place in this department of Biblical knowledge, and commentators have been called back from their freaks of utter lawlessness to the orderly rules and principles of grammatical construction. It is a matter of regret, that, in the only English version that we have of Winer's Grammar, the text, without any notice of the alterations being given, has been tampered with and changed by the translator for doctrinal reasons. But the promptness with which this act has been exposed and rebuked in this country, not only by the Christian

Examiner, but by the Bibliotheca Sacra, is a cheering evidence of the candor as well as vigilance which guards the integrity of sacred learning. Indeed, within the lifetime of the present generation, a more generous spirit has been infused into these studies. They have been taken out from the darkened cell of monkish or sectarian exclusiveness, into the light of the world's advancing intelligence. Critical works, like those of Stanley, Jowett, Trench, and Alford, Schleiermacher, Olshausen, De Wette, Winer, and Meyer, Stuart, Norton, Noyes, Palfrey, Furness, Hackett, and Nichols, show that the finest artistic taste and moral sensibilities, the severest inductions of logic, the nicest discriminations of philological science, the most scholarly attainments and accomplishments, together with habits of profound and original thought, may be worthily employed in throwing light on the sacred writings, and in bringing out the great and momentous truths which they contain. This branch of learning is, therefore, indicating its liberal tendencies, and beginning once more to gain a hearing from classes of men who formerly looked upon it with indifference or contempt. A thorough knowledge of the Gospels is found to enrich the mind and enlarge the heart. While the most effective means of controlling a congregation, in or out of the church, — the arts of rhetoric, and the attractive but superficial attainments which go to furnish the intellectual wardrobe of a popular preacher, — tend towards bigotry and conceit, the study of the Bible, the habit of throwing one's self into the heart of one after another of its great subjects, with the intellectual helps which are essential to it, can hardly fail to quicken the intellect, refine the moral sentiments, and make one's sympathies wider and more generous. The study of the Gospels, pursued in such a spirit, must at least conduce to humility, and that is closely allied to charity. I think that we may see some evidence of this liberalizing tendency in theological seminaries, where the greatest attention is paid to Biblical studies, as well as in the tone of works, like the Bibliotheca Sacra, which treat such subjects most thoroughly. Ecclesiastical history, dogmatic theology, the speculative doctrines of metaphysics and of morals, may be enlisted in the service of a party; but the Gospels more than anything else refuse to be confined within a sect, to serve its exclusive purposes, or to do its work.

This volume was begun more than five years ago, at the suggestion of the Rev. Henry A. Miles, D. D., to meet what was supposed to be a want in this department of religious instruction. In its plan it differs materially from Livermore's Commentary, leaving more room for the extended discussion of subjects, and following each verse of the text less closely in its remarks. If I could be sure that in my Notes I have made as faithful and intelligent a use of the materials accessible to scholars now, as Mr. Livermore did of those which were within his reach in the preparation of his work twenty years ago, I should give it to the public with comparatively few misgivings. If this volume should be favorably received, it will probably be followed by another on the three remaining Gospels, though this forms a complete work in itself. Nearly all the difficult questions which are likely to come up in Mark and Luke have been already considered. But the Gospel of John will require an extended preparation, and, in many respects, a distinct and original mode of treatment. In the mean time, and as a most important part of the same series with this, our readers will be glad to learn that a volume on the other books of the New Testament may be expected from the Rev. A. P. Peabody, D. D.

J. H. M.

MILTON, February 14, 1860.

# CONTENTS.

|  | PAGE |
|---|---|
| INTRODUCTION | 11 |
| The Gospel according to Matthew | 31 |

### CHAPTER I.

| | |
|---|---|
| The Lineage or Genealogy of Jesus | 33 |
| Miraculous Conception | 35 |
| Prediction of Christ's Birth | 39 |

### CHAPTER II.

| | |
|---|---|
| Visit of the Wise Men, or Magi | 45 |
| Murder of the Children in Bethlehem | 50 |
| Quotations from the Prophets | 52 |

### CHAPTER III.

| | |
|---|---|
| John the Baptist | 60 |

### CHAPTER IV.

| | |
|---|---|
| The Temptation in the Wilderness | 70 |
| Makes his Home in Capernaum | 78 |
| The Call of Simon Peter and Andrew his Brother, and of John and his Brother James | 79 |

### CHAPTER V.

| | |
|---|---|
| Introduction to the Sermon on the Mount | 85 |
| The Beatitudes | 87 |
| Fulfilling the Law and the Prophets | 88 |

### CHAPTER VI.

| | |
|---|---|
| General Design | 101 |
| Lord's Prayer | 102 |
| Perfect Trust in God | 107 |

## CHAPTER VII.

Analysis . . . . . . . . . . 117

## CHAPTER VIII.

Gospel View of Miracles . . . . . . . 126
Healing the Leper . . . . . . . . 135
Healing the Centurion's Servant . . . . . . 141
Bearing our Infirmities . . . . . . . 143
Let the Dead bury their Dead . . . . . . 147
Stilling the Tempest . . . . . . . . 148
Angelic Existences and Agencies . . . . . . 152
Evil and Disorderly Spirits . . . . . . 157

## CHAPTER IX.

Christ's Way of viewing Death . . . . . . 174

## CHAPTER X.

Directions to the Apostles . . . . . . . 183
The Coming of the Son of Man . . . . . . 186
Further Directions to the Apostles . . . . . 188
Life or Soul . . . . . . . . . 191
Different Degrees of Reward . . . . . . 193

## CHAPTER XI.

John the Baptist and his Message . . . . . . 201
Great Privileges unimproved visited by a heavier Condemnation 207
Christ's Thankfulness, and his Call to the Heavy Laden . 208

## CHAPTER XII.

Christ's View of the Sabbath . . . . . . 216
Hatred of the Pharisees against Jesus . . . . . 219
Casting out Satan by Satan . . . . . . 219
The Unpardonable Sin . . . . . . . 222
Further Remarks of Jesus . . . . . . . 223
Jesus and his Mother . . . . . . . 224

## CHAPTER XIII.

Parables . . . . . . . . . . 232
The Parable of the Sower . . . . . . . 237
Teaching in Parables . . . . . . . 238
The Tares and the Wheat . . . . . . . 240
The Wicked One . . . . . . . . 245

## CHAPTER XIV.

Herod Antipas . . . . . . . . . . 260
Feeding the Five Thousand . . . . . . . 264
Jesus walking on the Water . . . . . . . 266

## CHAPTER XV.

Jesus and the Jewish Traditions . . . . . . 273
Fulfilment of Prophecy . . . . . . . 274
The Syro-Phœnician Woman . . . . . . . 278
Feeding the Four Thousand . . . . . . . 279

## CHAPTER XVI.

A Sign from Heaven . . . . . . . . 288
On this Rock I build my Church . . . . . 289
The Keys of the Kingdom of Heaven . . . . . 290
The Humiliation and Sufferings of the Messiah . . . 292

## CHAPTER XVII.

The Transfiguration . . . . . . . . 305
The Coming of Elijah . . . . . . . . 312
The Tribute-Money and the Fish . . . . . . 313

## CHAPTER XVIII.

The Primitive Church of Christ . . . . . . 320

## CHAPTER XIX.

The Christian Law of Divorce . . . . . . 332
Christ Blessing the Children . . . . . . 335
The Young Man who came to Jesus . . . . . 336
Hard for the Rich to enter Christ's Kingdom . . . 338
Gaining by Renouncing . . . . . . . 340

## CHAPTER XX.

The Laborers in the Vineyard . . . . . . 348

## CHAPTER XXI.

Reckoning of Time . . . . . . . . 361
Triumphal Entry into Jerusalem . . . . . . 364

## CHAPTER XXII.

The Wedding Feast . . . . . . . . 376
Paying Tribute to Cæsar . . . . . . . 377
The Resurrection from the Dead . . . . . . 379
The Two Great Commandments . . . . . . 381
Christ the Son of David . . . . . . . 382

CONTENTS.

### CHAPTER XXIII.

| | |
|---|---|
| Christ's Denunciation of the Pharisees | 391 |
| The Cumulative Guilt of a Nation | 394 |

### CHAPTER XXIV.

| | |
|---|---|
| Our Saviour's Gift of Prophecy | 401 |
| The Coming of the Son of Man in Judgment to the Jews | 407 |
| The Coming of the Son of Man in Judgment to All | 418 |
| Conclusion | 422 |

### CHAPTER XXV.

| | |
|---|---|
| Purpose of these Parables | 432 |
| Parable of the Virgins | 432 |
| Parable of the Talents | 434 |
| Parable of the Sheep and the Goats | 434 |
| The General Resurrection and Day of Judgment | 437 |

### CHAPTER XXVI.

| | |
|---|---|
| The Supper at Bethany.—Judas | 444 |
| The Last Supper | 445 |
| Warning Peter | 449 |
| The Agony of Gethsemane | 450 |
| The Apprehension of Jesus | 458 |
| Jesus taken before the High-Priest | 460 |
| Peter's Denial | 461 |

### CHAPTER XXVII.

| | |
|---|---|
| Preliminary Trial of Jesus before the Sanhedrim | 479 |
| Repentance and Death of Judas | 480 |
| Jesus before Pilate | 481 |
| The Crucifixion | 483 |
| Precautions against his Resurrection | 488 |

### CHAPTER XXVIII.

| | |
|---|---|
| The Gospel Narratives of the Resurrection | 503 |
| The Different Accounts not Contradictory | 505 |
| The Different Times of his Appearance | 508 |
| Each Account Independent of the Rest | 511 |
| The Resurrection of Jesus | 512 |
| The Formula of Baptism | 515 |
| Concluding Remarks | 519 |

| | |
|---|---|
| INDEX | 537 |

# INTRODUCTION.

### HOW TO STUDY THE GOSPELS.

WE are more and more convinced that the Gospel of Christ is to be the great source of moral and religious instruction and improvement to the world. The writings of the New Testament stand apart from all others. No works of man's genius pretend to an equal fellowship with them. They reach now, as they always have done, above the highest thought and experience of our race. As the sky rises as far above us when we are on the loftiest mountain as in the lowest valley, so they rise as far above the ideas and civilization of the world now, as they did in the days of Tiberius and Nero. There can hardly be a more convincing proof of their Divine authority than this; we mean, in the words of a profound and original thinker, Dr. Nichols, "the Gospel's sun-like solitude in the moral firmament. The vast space around it is clear of all light but its own."

And this suggests a most important principle of interpretation. As these writings rise above all others, and shine in a vast space "clear of all light but their own," so it must be in that light, more than by any helps drawn from inferior sources, that we are to learn and to apply their truths. It is wonderful how our Saviour imbued with the universality of his own mind every transient incident and word into which his thought or life passed, so that it has become, like himself, to us "the same yesterday, to-day, and forever."

## INTRODUCTION.

"The grass which to-day is and to-morrow is cast into the oven," "the sower" who "went forth to sow," "the fields" "white already to harvest," "the light and gladness of the marriage feast" contrasted with "the outer darkness" where "shall be wailing and gnashing of teeth," the "grain of mustard-seed," the children at their sports in the market-place, "I was thirsty and ye gave me no drink," his taking little children into his arms, his inspection of the tribute-money, are, by means of the virtue which went into them from him, taken up from the sphere of limited and transient expressions or incidents, and stand out forever as emblems of universal and undying truths. He who could thus imbue the most ephemeral forms of speech with an imperishable life, and who could place a slight act of grateful reverence, or a casual conversation with a sinful woman by the side of a well, among the memorable events in the world's history, must have been charged with life and power beyond all others. And his language, passing from its earthly uses into a medium for the communication of divine and heavenly truths, and of an influence more subtile and life-giving than any truths in their naked presentation to the intellect, can borrow little from subsidiary illustrations and analogies. We have only to open our souls to it, as we do our eyes to the light, and it will come in. If we give ourselves up to it, we shall not be left in darkness or in doubt. It speaks with its own authority, and explains and enforces its own decisions. Often when we try to explain it, we shall only turn the attention away from it, or darken and obscure it by our words of inferior wisdom. A great part of our Saviour's language, and most of the lessons taught by his life, are of this character. He is the one Mediator between God and man, and it is worse than vain for us to interpose ourselves as his interpreters.

This is one of the reasons why all commentaries are read with a sense of disappointment. They are expected to throw new light on the great essential teachings of Christ;

and that is what no commentators can ever do. They might as well hope to throw new light upon the sun. Happy are they if they can to some extent remove from his teachings the obscurations which men have thrown over them. They are expected to give new efficacy to the "virtue" that goes out from them; and that they can never do. We may hope to clear up some of the obscurities which obsolete customs, or modes of speech foreign to our habits of thought, have caused. We may analyze our Saviour's discourses, and show the underlying principles by which the different parts are united. We may bring together expressions, such as "the kingdom of Heaven," "the coming of the Son of man," "the end of the world," which with slight modifications are scattered through the accounts of his ministry, and, by a careful comparison of the different conditions and circumstances under which they were used, may detect the differences of meaning which were put upon them, and the central idea which gives a unity to these different meanings. We may free some of the fresh and beautiful expressions of Scripture from their subjection to the canting phraseology of a formal piety, and some of its sublime enunciations of truth from their cruel bondage to the "decrees" of metaphysical speculations or ecclesiastical councils. We may compare the different narratives of the same events, and by combining them into one may harmonize what to the superficial reader seem to be contradictions. We may bring out the relations of time and space to the Gospel narratives, and thus make the acts and words of Jesus more consistent with one another, and more real to the reader. Above all, we may come back to the simple and natural methods of inquiry which are employed in the interpretation of all other writings. What Bacon and Newton, and other great philosophers, have done for the study of the mind of God in the book of nature, by breaking loose from arbitrary and unnatural methods of investigation, and applying the most direct and simple processes, is what the ablest religious

14     INTRODUCTION.

thinkers and scholars must do, and to some extent are doing, for the study of the mind of God in the volume of that other book, in which he would reveal himself to us with greater fulness and a more affecting power. As what Bacon and Newton did most of all was to call men back to nature itself, as it exists in the world around us, so what we have to do most of all is to call men back to the Gospel itself, as it lies before us, dimly prefigured in the Old Testament, and embodied in the New.

There are two things essential in order to a right understanding of the Gospels;—1. A fitting preparation of heart; and, 2. A mind free from all preconceived opinions which may bias or mislead us in our investigations. The first is a moral and spiritual preparation; the second is that, but it is also and mainly an intellectual preparation.

1. There is the fitting preparation of heart. This is what our Saviour meant by the faith, which he always regarded as essential to salvation. It was not an intellectual belief such as men have made it since, but a disposition of heart, a readiness to receive and to obey him in whatever he might teach or command. With this faith in the heart showing itself by obedience and fidelity in the life, our Christian consciousness will be enlarged, and we shall take in more and more of the truth. All that is most essential in the Gospels may be received. Its holiest precepts will direct us in our lives; its richest promises will be fulfilling themselves in our experience. Its great words of comfort and of power, which lie beyond the reach of criticism or commentary, will take up their abode in us, and become to us spirit and life. It is through this preparation of heart that the family Bible gains such a hold on the affections, instils into the soul its divinest influences, guides us in our duties, and teaches us how to turn sorrow and weariness and pain, and even sin itself, into the means of deliverance and triumph. Thus it is that Jesus introduces himself to us as our Teacher and Saviour. The Holy Spirit enters our souls, and renews

them with a perpetual influx of life. And God reveals himself to us in whatever is great or beautiful in nature, in the dear and sacred relations which bind us to one another, and in all the gracious and merciful, though to us often mysterious and painful orderings of his providence. This use of the Bible — its daily and familiar companionship, its confidential communications to us in our retired moments — is worth more than all its more elaborate and learned lessons.

2. But there is also to be a preparation of the intellect, and in order to this, first of all, we must allow no preconceived opinions to stand in the way of a perfectly free and fair investigation. We must remember that, as students of the New Testament, one is our Master, even Christ, and that as no want of faith can be an excuse for setting aside anything that he has taught, so neither should any preconceived opinions of ours, or creeds drawn up and established by human authority, stand as a barrier between his words and us. If our views are not broad enough to take in any doctrine that he has taught, then we must make them broad enough. There is a freedom, a greatness, not merely an elevation but a breadth of thought, in his instructions, strangely in contrast with the narrow and enslaving opinions which metaphysical divines have elaborated " in order to satisfy the demand of unity in the Christian consciousness and in the activity of the dialectic reason," or which ambitious rulers in the Church have established as an engine of administrative authority. Christ has set our feet in a large place, and our allegiance to him requires that, in the study of his words and life, we should jealously assert and exercise the liberty wherewith he has made us free.

A mournful spectacle, in this respect, has been presented by the Christian world. Advantage is taken of the new convert, in the most impressible moment of life, when he has no time or heart to examine for himself, when he is rejoicing in the advent of new hopes and a new experience, and his whole nature is fluent with emotion,—advantage is taken of him, in the unsuspecting confidence of his first enthusiasm, to impose upon him the sectarian stamp which is to fix his theological opinions, and be henceforth a bar, on the right hand and the left, in all his Biblical and theological investigations. Assuming those opinions to be true, he must study the Scriptures, not as a disciple of Jesus, but as the partisan of a sect. The word of God is in bondage. It can teach only what a human creed allows it to teach. In this respect, the Church of Rome, if it has a wider despotism than all the rest, is more consistent with itself. It does not profess to leave the people free to read for themselves. It claims for itself the right and the authority to be the sole interpreter of the Scriptures. But in most of the Protestant denominations, while there is professedly the greatest reverence for the Scriptures and the rights of the individual reason and conscience, no man is allowed to study the Scriptures freely under the guidance of his own reason and conscience. If he finds in them doctrines not in accordance with "the standards" or "articles" of his church, he is called to account. If he continues so to read the Scriptures, and see those doctrines there, he is excommunicated, and shut out from the ordinances of his religion. — A generous and catholic faith, which would leave the Bible open to all, that they may read it as they do the book of nature, in perfect freedom, accountable only to God, — this faith in Christ and his instructions rather than in man and his traditions; — if the Son of man should come now, would he find it on the earth?

Yet none the less is it our duty so to learn and so to speak. In all branches of the Church we hear generous voices from men seeking a larger liberty for others, and using it themselves. Some, like Henry Ward Beecher, without any great amount of learning or any remarkable fitness for critical studies, take up the great truths of the Gospel into their capacious souls, and speak them out with

## INTRODUCTION.

a power that breaks through sectarian restraints and finds an earnest response from thronging multitudes. Others, like Dr. Bushnell, with a riper scholarship, finer powers of analysis, and the same hearty devotion to Christ, not as he lies bound up corpse-like in church creeds, but as he reveals himself through the writings of Evangelists and Apostles, and to the Christian consciousness of each individual soul, are preaching a more generous and living Gospel. Others again, like Jowett and Stanley and Williams and Archbishop Whately, from the great centres of religious intelligence to our Anglo-Saxon race, from Oxford and Cambridge and the metropolis of Ireland, are using a larger liberty, and in works of Biblical criticism or religious inquiry are giving to the world examples of a freer thought, and a more faithful exposition of writings, which rise above and pass beyond the limitations of scholastic theologians and sectarian creeds, as the heavens, which shine on all, rise above and stretch beyond every earthly distinction of individual proprietorship or national domain. It is a comfort to be able to quote language like this from a sermon preached before the University of Oxford by the author of the Life of Dr. Arnold: "The true creed of the Church, the true Gospel of Christ, is to be found, not in proportion as it coincides with the watchwords or the dilemmas of modern controversy, but rather in proportion as it rises above them, and cuts across them. . . . . . The very peculiarity, the very proof of the divinity of his doctrine, was that they could not square it with any of their existing systems. . . . . . And it is both a confirmation and illustration of this character of Evangelical doctrine, that, if we look into some of the earthly representations of it which have met with most universal acceptance, they also share in this freedom from the bonds in which the world is anxious to confine us." (Stanley's Canterbury Sermons, pp. 113 – 115.) There is a healthful ring in these words, which is full of encouragement and hope.

Not only are we, in the study of the Gospels, to beware

of every human authority that would interpose itself between them and us, but we must also take heed to ourselves. We may be as much enslaved to our own way of viewing things, or to the personal feelings by which we are led in one direction or another, as to the established creed of a church. Whatever the motive, we must be careful not to twist and torture our Saviour's words to bring them into harmony with our ideas. A single example will illustrate what we mean. A writer, speaking of Christ in his mediatorial humiliation, says (Huntington's "Christian Believing and Living," p. 364): "Voluntarily, to this end, and for the time, things which only the Father knoweth are veiled from the Son, and he says (in language which we have only to suppose put into the mouth of any other being to find it in fact a proof of his divinity), 'My Father is greater than I.'" By the divinity of Christ the writer has just explained that he means his equality with the Father. To say then, that his declaration, "My Father is greater than I," is in fact a proof of his divinity, that is, a proof that his Father is *not* greater than he, is flatly to contradict the Saviour. To assert that we have only to suppose this language " put into the mouth of any other being to find it in fact a proof of his divinity," is to assert that in *our opinion* the language of Jesus, in its simple and obvious meaning, is so extravagant that we can accept it only in a sense directly opposite to what it says. Is this honoring Christ? St. John (1 John iii. 20) uses a form of expression precisely like this of Jesus, "God is greater than our heart." Is his language therefore a proof of *his* or of *our* divinity? In Job xxxiii. 12 we find it asserted, with no appearance of impiety or extravagance, "that God is greater than man." We are not arguing, or speaking even by implication, against the doctrine in support of which this delaration of our Saviour is so distorted from its plain and natural meaning. We quote the passage simply as an illustration of what seems to us a vicious, arbitrary, and most dangerous method of interpretation. Our reverence for Christ is shocked by such a way of dealing with his words.

We solemnly believe that, except from a perversion of the moral sentiments, there is no greater bar in the way of a true understanding and application of the Gospels, than this habit of forcing them into conformity with our preconceived ideas. We must remember that they are to guide us, and not we them. If our capacity for Divine truth is to be the measure of what we receive, it must not be, even in our own minds, the measure of what Christ has taught, so that all his teachings must be forced into conformity with it. We must not let the limitations of our human thought turn aside from its only direct and natural meaning any clear and explicit statement of his. If we find ourselves tempted to do this, we may be sure that there is something wrong, not in his instructions, but in our opinions. We are, then, with all humility before him, to re-examine our opinions, and see if we cannot readjust *them* in such a way as to make them harmonize with the text. A less violent wrench than that which is here applied to the words of Christ would probably bring our views into accordance with his words. But if our opinions are fixed as one of the immutable terms in this controversy, then let us remember that so plain a declaration of his cannot be altered for our accommodation; and, without attempting to make it mean precisely the opposite of what it says, as plainly as language can say anything, let us leave the two — his assertion and our opinion — confronting one another, and acknowledge that it requires a higher wisdom than ours to bring them into harmony. But, after all, as a matter of interpretation not less than of Christian faith, our human inference is more likely to be wrong than the words of Christ. The opinion of overwhelming majorities in his Church can have no weight against his decisive and unqualified declaration. We, — all men, — the doctrine "which always, everywhere, and by all men" has been maintained, if any such *contro-*

*verted* doctrine can be found, — may be wrong, but HE CANNOT.

We must then be on our guard against this forced method of interpretation, which has prevailed in past centuries almost as extensively as forced methods of interpreting the phenomena of nature before the time of Bacon and Galileo, and which has its influence still, though the ablest Christian scholars and thinkers are protesting against it more and more. It has its influence just where it will be most widely disseminated and most fatal. It enters into the apparently superficial, but nevertheless powerful and lasting, means of religious education for the young. The creed is taught first, and then the Bible in conformity with the creed. In some churches, at the end of every chapter that is read, and of every Psalm that is rehearsed, a doxology, which is in fact a creed in miniature, is repeated, as if the words of Scripture could not be trusted without it. How much more in harmony with nature and with truth, as well as with Christ's method of teaching, is that suggested by the generous and manly Robertson in a Confirmation Lecture. "Let the child's religion," he says, (Sermons, 1st Series, pp. 73, 74,) "be expansive, — capable of expansion, — as little systematic as possible; let it lie upon the heart like the light, loose soil, which can be broken through as the heart bursts into fuller life. If it be trodden down hard and stiff in formularies, it is more than probable that the whole must be burst through, and broken violently and thrown off altogether, when the soul requires room to germinate. And in this way, my young brethren, I have tried to deal with you. Not in creeds, nor even in the stiffness of the catechism, has truth been put before you. Rather has it been trusted to the impulses of the heart; on which, we believe, God works more efficaciously than we can do. A few simple truths: and then these have been left to work, and germinate, and swell. Baptism reveals to you this truth for the heart, that God is your Father, and that Christ has encouraged you to live as your Father's children. It has revealed that name which Jacob knew not, — Love. Confirmation has told you another truth, that of self-dedication to Him. Heaven is the service of God. The highest blessedness of life is powers and self consecrated to His will. These are the germs of truth: but it would have been miserable self-delusion, and most pernicious teaching, to have aimed at exhausting truth, or systematizing it. We are jealous of over-systematic teaching. God's love to you, — the sacrifice of your lives to God, — but the meaning of that? Oh! a long, long life will not exhaust the meaning, — the name of God. Feel him more and more, — all else is but empty words."

In all our studies, and especially in all our religious teachings, we must leave room for growth, and be more earnest to implant the principles of righteous living, and a reverence for the truth as it is in Jesus, than to prove any doctrines on which the Christian world is divided to be true. And if at any time, we are to hold our dogmatic theology in abeyance, it is when we are engaged in interpreting for ourselves, or teaching to others, the words and the acts of Christ.

---

Perhaps the forced methods of interpretation have for no single purpose been carried to a more unwarrantable extent than in the attempts which have been made to produce a literal conformity between different accounts of the same event by the different New Testament writers, so as not to violate the doctrine of a plenary verbal inspiration. But now that doctrine is no longer held to be respectable among enlightened Biblical critics and scholars. Dr. Cureton, the learned Canon of Westminster, in the preface to his "Syriac Gospels," p. lxxxix., speaks of "the verbal inspiration of the Gospels" as "a theory long since abandoned by all scholars and critics, which, indeed, could only be maintained by those who are entirely ignorant of the way in which the New Testament has been transmitted to our own times, and which, if persisted in, must involve very serious objections against these inspired writings, and tend to infidelity." Alford, in the Prolegomena to his learned and valuable Commentary on the New Testament, thus speaks of the theory of verbal inspiration: "Much might be said of the *à priori* unworthiness of such a theory as applied to a Gospel whose character is the freedom of the spirit, not the bondage of the letter; but it belongs more to my present work to try it by applying it to the Gospels as we have them. And I do not hesitate to say, that being thus applied, its effect will be to destroy altogether the credibility of our Evangelists. . . . . . The fact is, that this theory uniformly gives way before intelligent study of the Scriptures themselves; and is only held, consistently and thoroughly, by those who have never undertaken that study."

But the same violence which has been employed in forcing the language of the Gospels into harmony with a creed or an unnatural theory of inspiration, has also been used to force their statements into accordance with some favorite theory of the writer. Thus Paulus has endeavored to explain the miracles of Christ in accordance with a theory which excludes all miraculous influences, and according to which neither the ruler's daughter nor Lazarus was actually dead. The great value of Dr. Furness's charming writings on the Gospels is, we think, in some cases, seriously impaired by the restraint that is put upon him, and which he imposes upon the accounts of the Evangelists, in consequence of his favorite theory in regard to the manner in which miracles must be wrought.

The same unnatural perversion of the language of the Gospels has been effected by sceptics and unbelievers, who exercise as much ingenuity in forcing the accounts of the different Evangelists into a contradiction, as the old commentators did in forcing them away from it. They find it easier thus to discredit the authority of the sacred writings altogether, than to explain them away in such a manner

## INTRODUCTION. 23

as to confirm their naturalistic theories. The critical writings of Strauss and Baur are of this sort. They begin with theories about the Gospels, to which the Gospels themselves are forced to submit. There is no question in regard to the learning, the ability, or the consummate generalship of the men who lead the movement from within against the authority of the Gospels. And they have been of immense service in calling the attention of sensible and educated men to the Gospels, and inducing them to examine them for themselves, not through the perverse optics of these framers of theories, but with their own calm and unbiassed judgment. This of itself is a great gain. All that is needed in order to establish the truthfulness of the Gospels is that they should be thus examined.

And here we cannot too earnestly urge the great body of intelligent men and women to refuse to take any one's theory about the Gospels without first studying, not specious writings in support of it, but the Gospels themselves. Let them test every assumption of the theorist by a careful reference to the record, and not admit this or that assertion in regard to what is found in them, until they see it there with their own eyes. The study of the Gospels is a simple thing. The knowledge which has a direct and important bearing on the most important subjects in them is contained within a small compass. The comparison of one narrative with another, in order to satisfy ourselves in regard to their true relations, is easily effected by a little care, and the application of a reasonable amount of intelligence. There is a vast deal of humbug in the pretensions of our modern neologists. The cloud of words thrown round their theories, like the cloud of mysticism which enveloped the old doctrines of the Church in its pretensions to an infallible inspiration and authority, has only to be tried in the light of reason and common sense by the truthful words of the Evangelists, and it will vanish away.

Extraordinary pretensions, however, have always, for a

season, an influence altogether disproportionate to the real power that is in them. A sceptical thought is easily lodged in the mind. Delicate and sensitive natures, who wish to believe, are afraid to examine, lest the foundations of their faith should sink under them. Strong-minded, efficient men, who ought to study into these things, and thus satisfy themselves, as they easily might, are deterred from so doing by a secret misgiving lest the grounds of their faith should not bear investigation. Some retreat into the straiter sects, from a less to a more rigid form of Congregationalism, from Congregationalism to Episcopacy, from Episcopacy to the Church of Rome, or directly, for extremes meet on the other side, from the Absolutism of Rationalism to the Absolutism of Romanism. There is everywhere, even in the Roman Catholic communion itself, a sentiment of unrest, coming from an inward unbelief, which men try to cover up and hide from themselves by stricter articles of faith, by more imposing forms of worship, by Church authorities, instead of healing it by letting in upon it the simple truths of the Gospel, as examined in the light of reason, and tested by conscientious and faithful lives. But change of position is not change of heart. The inward unrest, the hidden unbelief, which durst not trust God's truth unless guarded by human defences, clings to them still. These make-believe methods of finding a religious faith, and with it health and peace of mind, answer no good end. The sudden and unnatural marriages which are sometimes sought in the desperation of disappointed affections are seldom blessed. There is a hidden element of falsehood, or self-deception, at the centre of them all.

If we have doubts, we must meet them fairly and honestly for ourselves. If they are practical doubts, relating to the essentials of Christianity, the efficacy of prayer, the presence and the power of God in the soul, the mediatorial office of Christ between God and, men, we must read the Gospels for practical guidance, and, seeking to give ourselves up entirely to their instructions by prayer, by humility of heart, by a warmer charity towards others, by more faithful and obedient lives, with the help which God will certainly give to us if we seek it thus, in our renovated affections, and the deeper, purer life of the soul, we shall find the faith, and with it the inward tranquillity and repose, which we crave. That is, we shall find enough of them to serve as a foretaste and pledge of the perfect love and peace which shall be fulfilled to us only in the kingdom of Heaven. And this is all that has been gained by the greatest saints, — by Madame Guyon and Fénelon, Archbishop Leighton and Baxter, Charles Wesley and Channing and William Croswell, as we see when we are admitted to a knowledge of their interior lives. "The perfect," we once heard Dr. Channing say, "is what we must always seek, but never hope to gain." If, on the other hand, our doubts are of an intellectual character, we must meet them fairly on intellectual grounds, and not push them aside for others, whether sceptics or bigots, philosophers or Christian believers, to do our work for us. It is better to read the Gospels ourselves, not through the creed of a church or a philosophical dogma, but with our own eyes and minds, such as God has made them, and judge of them by the principles of reason and common sense. If they give way under the examination, let us meet the facts of the case like brave and honest men, and not like children, who blind their eyes from fear of seeing a ghost. But they will not give way. They only ask to be tried on their own merits. The reason why they seem to us so unsubstantial is, that we do not rest our weight upon them. They are like the bridge across the St. Lawrence at Montreal, which sensitively vibrates to the slightest breeze, and therefore the timid traveller may fear to trust himself upon it; but ten thousand tons of human beings and costly merchandise resting upon it, only show how firm and strong it is. The more severely we test the Gospels, the more securely shall we find ourselves sustained by them. "Come, and see, and know for yourselves," is their appeal to us. Only let us examine them as they are in themselves, giving ourselves up to their great thoughts, opening our souls to the holy spirit which is proceeding from them, and the divine life which is embodied in them, and which by an eternal generation is born from them into the heart and life of our race. If we have doubts or fears, let us search the Scriptures till we are satisfied in regard to them. We have never known a man to have his faith shaken by a thorough and impartial investigation of the New Testament; but thousands have in this way had it confirmed and established.

It does not require any great amount of learning to study the Gospels intelligently. The deepest thought and the widest amplitude of knowledge may find room for exercise, if we undertake to explore them in all their fulness, and in all the curious details connected with them. We may lose ourselves amid the wonders and mysteries of the Divine nature, if we undertake to fathom them in our speculations. But a clear mind, faithfully applying itself to the study of the Gospels in a truthful spirit, is all that is required in order to gain from them the knowledge that is most valuable to us. An acquaintance with ancient customs, with oriental productions, modes of living, and forms of speech, may give us a more precise idea of what is meant in some cases. But even then, except in a very few instances, the essential truth is not affected. It may be pleasant to us, and may gratify a reasonable curiosity, to know precisely what were the lilies of the field and the fowls of the air to which our Saviour called attention, as emblems and proofs of the paternal providence of God, — to know that it was the fruit of the carob-tree, "with a hard, dark outside, and a dull sweet taste," and not husks, which the Prodigal longed to eat as he fed it enviously to the swine, while he was perishing with hunger, — to know how the houses were constructed so that the paralytic might be taken up by an outside staircase to the flat roof, and let down through it on his bed into the inner room or open court, where Jesus sat surrounded by a throng of people. But the lesson taught, in each one of these cases, to our minds and hearts, is wholly independent of such knowledge. And there is danger lest, in seeking for the adventitious information, we should have our interest absorbed in that which was intended only as an illustration, and drawn away from the vital truth which it was employed to convey.

The geography of Palestine is intimately connected with our Saviour's ministry. As we follow him back and forth, from place to place, on the map, events start up before us, distinct and alive, each one with its own individuality upon it. Almost any person may learn enough of the geography of Palestine for this purpose. In getting a clear view of his life, and in comparing the different Evangelists with one another, it will be a great help to connect each event with the spot where it occurred, and thus make it real to us. It will give the Gospels a firmer hold on our minds, and free us from the indistinct and dreamy notions with which we regard them, and through which they are so easily turned into myths. We are thus enabled to feel and handle them, and see that they are not bodiless apparitions, but substantial facts. But we may study the geography of Palestine so as to know all about the various localities in their relation to the Gospels, and yet be all the while so absorbed in the geography itself as to have no perception of the moral influences which have made those places holy and immortal in the affections of mankind. Much of our Sunday-school teaching, we fear, is of this sort.

One difficulty in the way of our studying the Gospels arises from the fact that we are so familiar with them that their words pass through our minds without making any impression. This difficulty may be obviated by reading them in some foreign language, or, if we cannot do that, in some translation different from our common version. Norton's or Campbell's translation, or even Sawyer's, notwithstanding the severe criticisms which it has called out, will sometimes reveal to us a sentiment or a thought which had escaped us in our daily reading. We have endeavored in this work to assist the student by analyzing in some cases, e. g., in the Sermon on the Mount, our Saviour's discourses, and thus bringing out the depth, the affluence, the comprehensiveness and completeness of the thought. After such an analysis we may come back to the familiar language with new interest; and while we see in it a deeper and richer meaning than before, we may find in the old words an aroma of Christian sentiment which had escaped in the process of analyzing the thought, and which can be embodied in no other words but those around which the religious associations of our own lifetime, and of centuries before, have been gathering.

We would ask the attention of those who have a taste for such investigations, and particularly, if it may be done without presumption, the attention of men of a legal training, to the narratives which we have constructed from the different Evangelists, of the events connected with the last days of our Saviour's life, and the morning of the Resurrection. No external evidence has ever produced such undoubting confidence in our mind as the way in which these four distinct narratives, now approaching and now diverging from one another, — now almost united in one, and now apparently inconsistent with each other, — keep on, each one in its independent course, while all combine to set forth the same great facts with no real inconsistency even in their minutest details. We would particularly ask that the accounts of the denials by Peter, the trial of Jesus, and the events on the morning of the Resurrection, may be subjected to the severest test of a judicial investigation, by the aid of a topographical plan of Jerusalem and its vicinity, and of a Jewish palace, with a careful attention to the precise words of the original Greek (disregarded in our English version), by which the writers denote the different parts of a palace, — the house itself, the inner court or hall, the gateway or entrance to the court, and the tessellated pavement in front of the palace, on which Pilate erected the judgment-seat, from which he unwillingly pronounced the sentence of death on the Saviour of the world. Those who may be inclined to follow out this interesting and conclusive method of inquiry under the guidance of a powerful, discriminating, and appreciative mind, are referred to the very able work entitled "Hours with the Evangelists," by I. Nichols, D. D. "The more," says Da Costa, "we examine the Gospels in detail, as with a microscope, the more diversities will multiply under our eyes; but the more also shall we find these diversities consistent, and so consistent that they constitute in each of the four Gospels a particular and distinctive character. And when once we have found this special character of each Gospel, we have also found the way to bring all these *real diversities* and *apparent contradictions* into one final and harmonious unity."

But after all, even in an intellectual point of view, the most effective method of studying the Gospels is with a direct application of their precepts to the duties and circumstances of life. The philosophy of our day is experimental. Its truths and their value in each case are tested by experiment under the guidance of known facts. So the precepts of Christ, both in regard to their truthfulness and their value, are to be tested by being applied and carried out in practice. The great interior principles of faith and love must be tried in our hearts; and they must be carried out in our fidelity to the precepts and commands by which our external lives are to be regulated. In this way, the intellectual study of the Gospels, which often turns aside into eccentric vagaries or degenerates into lifeless and heartless speculations, is tested by our own experiences, and the truths which it places before us as abstractions are filled out with the warmth and enthusiasm which are essential to them, and without which we can no more see them as they are, than we can understand the beauty of the flowering fields as they are in June, from the dried specimens in the hands of a botanist, or the diagrams in his book. There is a spiritual life flowing through every part of the Gospels, which have been created as living organisms, and not put together as pieces of mechanism; and when in our own souls we have experienced that inward life, we see it in them and them in it. Every word that our Saviour spoke, every act that he did, has an organic completeness in itself, and is endowed with the power of perpetuating its own life in the lives of others. Every portion of the Gospels has this essential vitality, a living and perpetual witness, to the soul which receives it, of the source from which it came. Cut off any one precept, and it grows out again from the parent stock. You cannot make it dead, so long as you test its vitality in your own soul.

The separation of the intellectual study of the Gospels from the life in which their truths live and bloom, is a sad necessity, if it be a necessity, in the scientific education of theological students. It leads them, like the wandering spirit of old, into dry and desolate places, and opens before them the dreariest visions of holiness and faith. He who studies our Saviour's precepts about prayer, and never prays, can have, even intellectually, but a meagre idea of the subject. He who studies the great law of pre-eminence among his disciples (Matt. xx. 26) will make poor work with the doctrine until he has sought to realize it in himself, not only by an outward show of obedience, but an inward subjection of his whole nature to its spirit. It is only by the union of study and practice that the highest ends of religious teaching can be gained. Then the marriage between the intellect and the heart will be completed, and from it will be born a life of faith and holiness and charity, which will grow up as the true and worthy offspring of such a union.

# THE GOSPEL ACCORDING TO ST. MATTHEW.

It does not enter into the design of this work to determine the authenticity or genuineness of the Gospels. We take that for granted, referring those who may wish to examine the matter thoroughly to Mr. Norton's "Genuineness of the Gospels" for the external evidence, and to Dr. Nichols's "Hours with the Evangelists" for the internal evidence. We suppose the Gospel of St. Matthew to have been written by him in the language which was then spoken in Palestine and which is usually called the Aramæan or Aramaic, and to have been afterwards translated into Greek, either by the Apostle himself or by some other competent person. In the year 1842 a copy of the greater part of the Gospel of St. Matthew in the Syriac language was obtained by Archdeacon Tattam from a Syrian monastery in the valley of the Natron Lakes, which was published in 1858 by William Cureton, D. D., Canon of Westminster, &c., which is regarded by the very learned editor as among the oldest manuscript copies of the Gospel now known, and respecting which he does not hesitate to express his belief, that " it has, to a great extent, retained the identical terms and expressions which the Apostle himself employed; and that we have here, in our Lord's discourses, to a great extent, the very same words as the Divine Author of our holy religion himself uttered in proclaiming the glad tidings of salvation in the Hebrew dialect to those who were listening to him, and through them to all the world." (Cureton's Syriac Gospels, Pref., p. xciii.) The precise time when the Gospel was written is uncertain. "Were we," says Davidson (Introduction to the New Testament, p. 136), "to express an opinion, we should be inclined to adopt A. D. 41, 42, or 43 as the most probable." "The place where the Gospel was written is uniformly said to have been Judæa." Davidson supposes it to have been written in Hebrew, and that the Greek version "must have been made before the close of the first century; probably before the appearance of the Gospel of John." It is one of the traditions respecting it, and it bears internal evidence to the same effect, that it was written particularly for the Jews. We see marks of this intention, especially in the first chapters; but throughout the Gospel there is evidently a peculiar adaptation to the Jewish mind, particularly when speaking of events as necessary in order to the fulfilment of the prophecies, and in the pains which are taken to set forth the new religion as a fulfilment, while the traditions of the Pharisees were only a perversion and abuse, of the Law and the Prophets.

# MATTHEW.

## CHAPTER I.

### 1-17.—THE LINEAGE OR GENEALOGY OF JESUS.

THE Gospel of Matthew bears internal evidence of having been written by a Jew, and with particular reference to his own countrymen. We see marks of this design especially in the first chapters, which open the whole subject from a Jewish point of view, and in a manner particularly adapted to the feelings and habits of thought then existing among the Jews. The writer is not, as has been charged against him, imbued with their prejudices and their erroneous ideas respecting the Messiah. But he has been educated as a Jew, and in sympathy with the Jewish mind. If he has also been introduced into a higher realm of spiritual life and thought, he is able to enter, as no one but a person born and brought up in a Jewish atmosphere could, into the views and feelings of his countrymen. By his appreciation of their state of mind, and his sympathy with them in their religious expectations, he is able to gain a hearing from them, while he turns in the direction of their strongest expectations, and shows how the prophetic writings find their fulfilment in Jesus. His quotations and allusions, his local and historical references, his mode of presenting what they would regard as objectionable subjects, his forms of expression and methods of appeal through their early religious associations, are all adapted to the Jewish mind, and fitted to lead them, without any needless shock to their prejudices, into a recognition of Jesus as the Messiah.

We have an instance of this in the opening words of the Gospel, "The lineage of Jesus Christ, son of David, son of Abraham." The term "son of David" seems to have been one held in the highest reverence among the Jews, even if it were not used, as it probably was, like the word Messiah, to designate "him who was to come," their great "deliverer" and "redeemer." By the use of this term, therefore, Matthew at the beginning appeals to a national expectation, which he still encourages when, in a genealogy, probably copied from public registers whose authority was recognized by the Jews of his day, he traces step by step the descent of Jesus from their most powerful monarch, and through him from their most illustrious ancestor. The prejudice which otherwise might have led them to put aside with contempt the claims of a poor young man from Galilee, is thus removed at the very outset. Though Jesus of Nazareth was despised and rejected of men, yet he was descended from a race of kings and patriarchs. We can scarcely conceive how this dry catalogue of hard words should rouse the national enthusiasm of a Jew by its roll of mighty names, and awaken his respect for one whose advent into the world had been prepared through such a line of ancestors.

In order that it should have any weight with the Jews, this table of names must have been copied from family registers which they recognized as authentic. Whatever view, therefore, we may take of the inspiration of the writer, our confidence in his accuracy cannot be affected by any omissions or mistakes that may be pointed out in the list of names. It is not on his authority as that of an inspired writer, but on their authority as records preserved and accepted by the Jews, that Matthew presents them to his countrymen. If he had been inspired to correct every mistake and supply every omission, every alteration that he made would serve only to destroy their authority with those for whom he was writing, and to excite their prejudices against him. This view of the matter takes away altogether the force of objections to the accuracy of the Gospels, which are drawn from apparent discrepancies between the genealogy here and that in Luke iii. 23–38. We have only to suppose them to be, as they unquestionably are, copies of different records, which had been kept in different places, and which varied from one another, either through want of exactness in the records, or in consequence of the different methods by which the line of ancestors was brought down from a common original. The labored attempts, therefore, to reconcile these two lists of names with each other, or with records found in the Old Testament, however interesting they may be to ingenious scholars, can have no important bearing on the trustworthiness of the Gospels.

### 18 – 25. — MIRACULOUS CONCEPTION.

The account of the birth of Jesus which is given here and in the second chapter of Luke, has been a stumblingblock to many sincere minds, and is rejected as in itself incredible by some who accept as authentic the other evangelical accounts of miracles. But is there anything in the nature of things incredible in what is here recorded? The great naturalists of our day recognize a succession of creative epochs, when higher types of physical life were introduced. The different orders of animals which have appeared from time to time were not slowly evolved by a process of development from lower orders previously existing, but one after another they have been introduced by separate and original acts of creation. Now, as the physical advancement of the world has thus been marked by distinct creative epochs, might we not expect something of the same kind in its spiritual advancement? "But how is it possible," we are asked, "that such an event as that recorded here and in the second chapter of Luke could take place?" How is it possible, we ask in reply, that a new order of animals should be introduced, or the first man created? We cannot understand these things, and our ignorance should make us slow in setting limits, not only to what is possible, but to what is probable, in the exercise of God's almighty and creative power. Within certain spheres of creative action, where facts enough are ascertained to determine what is the established order of development and progress, as, for example, in the sciences of natural history, chemistry, and astronomy, we may draw our inferences with a good degree of certainty, and foretell what is to be from our knowledge of what has been. But even here we are not competent to decide beforehand when a new creative epoch shall supervene upon the existing order of things in time to come, as it has in time past, or whether it shall come at all. Our knowledge does not reach far enough, — we have not ascertained facts enough, or with a sufficient degree of exactness, — to comprehend these widely separated and therefore apparently extraordinary interpositions, or to reconcile them with what we know of the laws of nature. There was a time when the motion of comets was supposed to be wholly eccentric, and inconsistent with the laws of planetary motion. It only required a wider and more precise knowledge of facts to reduce them all to the same law. So, unquestionably, it is in regard to the widely separated creative epochs in the physical universe.

And have we not a right to infer, at least as not impossible or in itself extremely improbable, something of the same kind in regard to those apparently anomalous interventions by which a higher spiritual life has from time to time been brought into the world? Is it the part of a true philosophy to deny the alleged fact, because we cannot see far enough to reconcile it with our preconceived and limited ideas of nature and the natural order of events? In regard to the miraculous conception of Jesus by an immediate creative act of the divine spirit, may we not regard it as analogous to those creative epochs when new orders of plants or animals are first introduced? As to the vulgar objection, that it involves an act which is in itself impossible, or at least utterly incredible, we may allow it to have some weight with us, when those who urge it show wherein the birth of a soul into the world by the immediate act of God, as here related, is in itself more impossible, or more utterly inexplicable to us, than the ordinary process by which a plant, an animal, or a human being is produced. The precise means by which life is perpetuated is just as much a mystery to us as the means by which it was originally introduced with the first plant, or man, or with Jesus, who stands at the head of a new and spiritual creation.

This much may be urged from their own stand-point against the conclusions of those who, on scientific grounds, reject this whole class of facts as lying outside of the order of nature. There are others, who believe in the Christian miracles, but reject the account of the miraculous conception as something plainly unnatural and improbable. Among these, perhaps at the head of this class of writers, is Dr. Furness, in the views which he has taken of this matter in the fresh, original, and beautiful works which he has published on Jesus of Nazareth. He lays great emphasis on the naturalness of the Christian miracles, — the ease with which they were evidently performed by Jesus in the natural exercise of his own faculties. But why were they so easy to him, unless because of the extraordinary powers with which he was endowed? He came to introduce a new epoch of spiritual life; and, that it might be in conformity with the order of nature, must it not have been by a new act of creation? He who stood at the head of this new era, by the natural exercise of his own powers uttering thoughts and doing deeds man never had done before, must have been endowed as man never had been before. And could these extraordinary endowments have been bestowed upon him in any way more in accordance with the order of nature than by the method here indicated, i. e. by a new act of creative power?

When speaking of nature as containing within itself all the powers and agencies of the universe, we must not confine ourselves to the limited operations which take place within our ordinary experience, but must leave room for those great secular interpositions which are equally a part of the divine system of nature, and which, at widely distant intervals in the fulness of time, bring in new orders of beings and new eras of life. Immeasurably the greatest religious epoch since the creation of man was that which was introduced by Jesus. When we speak of it merely as of a new revelation, we fail utterly to express either its character or its greatness. Matthew and Luke, in their account of the conception of Jesus by an immediate act of God's creative spirit; the introduction to the Gospel of John respecting *the word made flesh;* the language of Paul, as, e. g. in Col. i. 15 – 20, where he speaks of Christ as the first-born of every creature, and, not the revealer alone of divine truth, but the creator of new worlds of spiritual life and power, — are in this way brought into harmony with one another, with the account of his miracles, and with the otherwise extraordinary language which he applied to himself. The Gospel account of the conception of Jesus comes as the fitting and natural introduction into the world of a divine life, which, growing up under the laws of our mortal and human condition, should, as a new creation, stand at the head of a new era in man's history. Here, at its beginning on the earth, is a fountain high and large enough to fill all the streams of action, thought, and life which flow through the Gospel narratives. The knowledge, holiness, and power of Jesus, so far transcending all that man had known or been or done, are only on the same high level as his birth. The beginning is needed, in order to account for that which follows. Without it, the miracles, and still more the terms in which Jesus constantly spoke of himself, would seem to us unnatural and monstrous.

We accept, then, the account of the miraculous conception, not only because it is an undisputed part of the Gospel narratives, but because something of the kind is required by the higher and broader analogies of nature, and in order to the completeness of the Gospels themselves.

### 22, 23. — PREDICTION OF CHRIST'S BIRTH.

The account of the miraculous conception of Jesus by a virgin would undoubtedly appear harsh and offensive to the Jewish mind. To soften this impression, the writer introduces from one of the most honored among the Jewish prophets language which so exactly describes the case before them that the whole matter presents itself as a fulfilment of the ancient prediction. The passage quoted from Isaiah vii. 14 is taken from the Septuagint version, where the word παρθένος, *virgin*, is used instead of a literal translation of the less decisive Hebrew word, which means *damsel*, or *a young and unmarried woman*. This particular word, in the connection in which it is here given, is just the one to meet the Jewish feeling caused by the account of the birth of Jesus, and meet it all the more effectively because the purpose for which the passage is introduced is not stated. It is as if the writer, seeing how his Jewish readers were likely to be affected by an account so extraordinary, had said, "Here we may apply the words of the prophet, 'A virgin shall conceive and bear a son,'"— thus, in the very language of their sacred writings, describing that feature in the birth of Jesus which must have been most offensive to them. We are to regard the quotation as primarily brought forward less for the purpose of arguing from a prophecy fulfilled, than to soften their prejudices by the literal application to the objectionable features of the case before them of language which they held sacred.

Is the passage here quoted from Isaiah a prediction of the Messiah? To answer this question we must examine it in its original connection. There we find that Syria and Samaria have combined against Ahaz, king of Judah, who is greatly terrified and discouraged. The prophet announces, as a sign to Ahaz, that a woman then unmarried shall bear a son, and call his name Immanuel (God-with-us, in token of God's presence), and before the child shall be old enough to know good from evil, the land whose two kings so terrified Ahaz should be desolate. This, as any one who reads the whole chapter (Noyes's Translation) must see, is the only application required or suggested by the language.

May it not, however, in accordance with the divine intention, be taken up out of its original surroundings, and as a prophetic declaration find its highest and truest fulfilment in some remote and entirely different class of events? "Often," says Bengel, "predictions are quoted in the New Testament which the original hearers were undoubtedly required by *the divine purpose* to apply to events then taking place. But the same divine purpose, looking farther on, so framed the language that it might fit more exactly the times of the Messiah, and this divine purpose, the Apostles teach, we are readily to accept." "The difficulty," says Olshausen, (Commentary on Gospels, Matthew i. 22, 23,) "can be removed by our acknowledging in the Old Testament prophecies a twofold reference to a present lower subject and to a future higher one. With this supposition, we can everywhere adhere to the immediate, simple, grammatical sense of the words, and still recognize the quotations of the New Testament as prophecies in the full sense. And it belongs to the peculiar adjustment and arrangement of the Scripture, that the life and substance of the Old Testament were intended as a mirror of the

New Testament life, and that in the person of Christ particularly, as the representative of the New Testament, all the rays of the Old Testament ideas are concentrated as in their focus."

We may admit the general principle here stated. The only objection to applying it in the case before us is the want of sufficient evidence that this particular passage was intended, either by the prophet or the evangelist, to be so understood. On reading carefully the whole passage in Isaiah, from the beginning of the seventh chapter to the eighth verse of the ninth chapter in Dr. Noyes's Translation, we cannot free ourselves from the impression, that though the seventh chapter standing by itself might indicate no allusion to the Messiah, yet the extraordinary passage beginning with the last verse of the eighth and reaching through the first seven verses of the ninth chapter can hardly be understood in any other way than as pointing on to the times of the Messiah; and if so, as giving some countenance to those who interpret vii. 14 as in a secondary sense applying to the same distant event. For the opposite view, see Dr. Palfrey's able, ingenious, and elaborate work on "The Relation between Judaism and Christianity."

## NOTES.

THE book of the generation of Jesus Christ, the son of Da-
2 vid, the son of Abraham. —— Abraham begat Isaac; and Isaac begat Jacob; and Jacob begat Judas and his brethren.

1. **Jesus Christ**] In the body of the Gospel, where Jesus is spoken of as present and acting, he is never called by his official title, *Christ, the Messiah*, or *the anointed*, though he is constantly so called in the Acts and the Epistles. This is one of the slight but unmistakable marks of truthfulness in the writers of the New Testament. **the son of David**] i. e. the true Messiah. "For by no more common or more proper name did the Jewish nation point out the Messiah, than by *the son of David*. See Matt. xii. 23, xxi. 9, xxii. 42 ; Luke xviii. 38 ;

And Judas begat Phares and Zara of Thamar. And Phares begat Esrom; and Esrom begat Aram; and Aram begat Aminadab; and Aminadab begat Naasson; and Naasson begat Salmon; and Salmon begat Booz of Rachab. And Booz begat Obed of Ruth. And Obed begat Jesse; and Jesse begat David the king. And David the king begat Solomon of her that had been the wife of Urias. And Solomon begat Roboam; and Roboam begat Abia; and Abia begat Asa; and Asa begat Josaphat; and Josaphat begat Joram; and Joram begat Ozias; and Ozias begat Joatham; and Joatham begat Achaz; and Achaz begat Ezekias; and Ezekias begat Manasses; and Manasses begat Amon; and Amon begat Josias; and Josias begat Jechonias and his brethren, about the time they were carried away to Babylon. — And after they were brought to Babylon, Jechonias begat Salathiel; and Salathiel begat Zorobabel; and Zorobabel begat Abiud; and Abiud begat Eliakim; and Eliakim begat Azor; and Azor begat Sadoc; and Sadoc begat Achim; and Achim begat Eliud; and Eliud begat Eleazar; and Eleazar begat Matthan; and Matthan begat Jacob; and Jacob begat Joseph the husband of Mary, of whom was born Jesus, who is called Christ.——So all the generations from Abraham to David are fourteen generations; and from David until the carrying away into Babylon are fourteen generations; and from the carrying away into Babylon unto Christ are fourteen generations.

Now the birth of Jesus Christ was on this wise: when as his mother Mary was espoused to Joseph, before they came together, she was found with child of the Holy Ghost. Then Joseph her husband, being a just man, and not willing to make

---

and everywhere in the Talmudic writers." Lightfoot.   8. **and Joram begat Ozias**] Ozias was not the son of Joram, but there were three kings between them, — Ahaziah, Joash, and Amaziah. In the Syriac version edited by Dr. Cureton, these names are supplied. In these genealogical tables it was not unusual to omit several generations, and to reckon the legal grandson or great-grandson as if he were a son. Ozias is the Greek name for Uzziah, as Achaz is for Ahaz, Ezekias for Hezekiah, Manasses for Manasseh, &c.   17. **from Abraham to David are fourteen generations**] Only thirteen are here given. One name may have slipped out of the account; but, as Lightfoot states, literal exactness in numbers was not regarded by the Jews.   19. **Then Joseph her husband**] It was the custom among the Jews for a man to be betrothed to a woman some time before he actually took her from her father's house to live with her as his wife. During this interval she was considered his wife,

her a public example, was minded to put her away privily.
20 But while he thought on these things, behold, the angel of the
Lord appeared unto him in a dream, saying: Joseph, thou son
of David, fear not to take unto thee Mary thy wife; for that
21 which is conceived in her is of the Holy Ghost. And she shall
bring forth a son, and thou shalt call his name JESUS; for he
22 shall save his people from their sins. (Now all this was done,
that it might be fulfilled which was spoken of the Lord by the

---

and was legally liable for any misconduct, the same as if they had actually *come together* in marriage. If Joseph, therefore, had instituted proceedings against Mary for conjugal infidelity, the legal penalty, a disgraceful divorce or perhaps death, would have been exacted. The word translated *just*, δίκαιος, does not bear the meaning *merciful*, which is sometimes put upon it. A paraphrase closer to the original would be : " But Joseph, her husband, though a just man, [and therefore unable to countenance what seemed to him a violation of the law,] yet not wishing to expose her [to unnecessary shame or suffering], had made up his mind to put her away privately;" not, however, without a writing of divorce, as that would have been unlawful. For the law of divorce, see Deut. xxii. 23, xxiv. 1. 20. **in a dream**] This mode of divine communication, i. e. through a dream, is mentioned nowhere in the New Testament but here and in the next chapter, unless we regard the dream of Pilate's wife, xxvii. 19, as of the same character. 21. **and thou shalt call his name Jesus**] i. e. SAVIOUR, — in Hebrew, the same name as Joshua. **for he shall save his people from their sins**] The true character of his salvation, namely, salvation from sin rather than from its penalties, is here distinctly set forth.

**his people**] not the Jews alone, but all who accept him as their Saviour. 22. **that it might be fulfilled, &c.**] ἵνα, *that*. " It is impossible," says Alford, " to interpret ἵνα in any other sense than ' in order that.' The words ' all this was done,' and the uniform usage of the New Testament, in which ἵνα is never used except in this sense, forbid any other." We are surprised at so unqualified a statement. Winer, the ablest writer on the Grammar of the New Testament, though he insists on *design* as the primary and almost uniform meaning of the word, is yet obliged to allow that there are cases (e. g. John i. 27, iv. 34, vi. 7, xv. 8, xvi. 7; Matt. xviii. 6; Luke xi. 50, xvii. 2, &c.) where " the original import of the particle of design entirely disappears." Winer, xliv. 8, c. (Masson's Tr., Am. ed. p. 354). Sophocles, in his learned work, " A Glossary of Later and Byzantine Greek," Introduct., § 95, says: " In later and Byzantine Greek, ἵνα often denotes a result; that is, it has the force of ὥστε, *that, so that, so as.*" And this he proves by many examples. *Purpose* or *design* is not then necessarily implied by the word ἵνα. On the contrary, it is also used to denote result as well as purpose; e. g. Luke ix. 45: " But they understood not this saying, and it was hid from them, *that* [ἵνα, *so that*] they perceived it not." This passage, we think, furnishes the key to the passage here, and to the same form of expression, Matt. ii. 15, iv. 14, xxi. 4, xxvii. 35. In every one of these instances, *so that* is a better translation of ἵνα than *in order that*. It is equally in conformity with the grammatical usage of the Greek word, and evidently better describes the use that is made of the prophecies. The Evangelist does not mean to say, these events occurred *in order that* the words of the prophet

prophet, saying: "Behold, a virgin shall be with child, and 23 shall bring forth a son, and they shall call his name Emmanuel;" which, being interpreted, is, God with us.) Then Joseph, 24 being raised from sleep, did as the angel of the Lord had bidden him; and took unto him his wife, and knew her not till 25 she had brought forth her first-born son; and he called his name Jesus.

---

might be fulfilled," but "they occurred in such a manner that as a result the words of the prophet were fulfilled in them." 22. **might be fulfilled**] πληρωθῇ. What is meant by *fulfilled?* The literal meaning of this word is *filled*, or *filled out.* Thus Matt. v. 17: "Think not that I come to destroy the law or the prophets: I come not to destroy, but to fulfil;" i. e. I come to carry out to its complete and spiritual fulfilment the law whose burdensome forms, once a help, are now a hindrance to the work for which it was given. To fulfil, in this case, is not, therefore, a literal fulfilment, — for in the literal sense of the words, Jesus did come to destroy the law; but it was to fulfil the law in a different and higher sense than had previously been thought of. The same, we suppose, is also true in regard to the prophets. Not always in a literal sense, but in their deepest and highest meaning, in the divine truth and life, the spiritual redemption and deliverance towards which they were pointing, their words are fulfilled in Jesus. So, in other ways, in an inferior sense, even one which though literal may never have occurred to them, specific words which they used may have been fulfilled in particular incidents connected with his life, i. e. may be used to describe them, as in the passage before us. See also Notes on ii. 5, 15, 17, 23; xxi. 4. For a fuller exposition of the subject of Prophecy, see xxiv.

23. **Behold, a virgin**] The first clause of this sentence is the emphatic one. The name *Emmanuel,* which is found nowhere else in the New Testament, was not given to Jesus. He was not so named by his parents. He never assumed the name himself, and was never so called by his disciples. It was directed to be given to a child mentioned in Is. vii. 14, who was to be born in the reign of Ahaz, and who was to be to him a sign that God was with him. "The mere use of such a name," says Dr. Barnes, "would not prove that he had a divine nature," especially, we might add, when there is no evidence that he ever bore the name. It does, however, unquestionably describe the mission of our Saviour, in whom God was with us, manifesting himself in the flesh, and reconciling the world to himself. The Jews were in the habit of giving significant titles to their great men. Thus the original name of Joshua was *Oshea* or *Saviour,* and Moses, Num. xiii. 16, called him *Jehoshua,* which means *the salvation of God. Eli* means *My God; Elijah, My God Jehovah; Elisha, God the Saviour.* 25. **her first-born son**] Tischendorf, in conformity with the reading in some of the best manuscripts, leaves out the word *first-born;* but Alford retains it, with the remark that the omission "was evidently made from superstitious veneration for Mary." The perpetual virginity of the mother of Jesus, as held by the Roman Catholic Church, is not implied or intimated here by either reading.

## CHAPTER II.

### 1-12.—VISIT OF THE WISE MEN, OR MAGI.

THE remarkable event in this chapter, at least that which gives the greatest trouble to those who would understand in all its bearings every particular connected with the Gospel narratives, is the visit of the Magi, or wise men, under the guidance of a star, or some extraordinary luminous appearance in the heavens. A vast deal of learning has been expended upon the subject without coming to any satisfactory results. It has never been definitely ascertained who these wise men were, or what was the precise appearance in the heavens that brought them to Bethlehem. All that can be learned is, that there was at that time a widely extended expectation in the East of the birth, in that part of the world, of some one who was to have an extraordinary influence on human affairs. Jews, in their various national misfortunes, and the migrations consequent upon them, had mingled as permanent residents with the people beyond their eastern borders. They had undoubtedly carried with them their religious notions, and particularly the prophetic expectations of the Messiah, which had entered so deeply into the heart of the nation. Their ablest and wisest men would naturally be brought into connection with the corresponding classes whom they might meet in foreign lands, and in the interchange of ideas with one another whatever was most remarkable in the science or religious systems of either would become the common property of all. Thus there may have been in those Eastern regions men of devout and earnest hearts, waiting anxiously for some new manifestation from Heaven, and for some new and higher agency to go forth amid the confused and otherwise hopeless affairs of the world. When the fulness of time had come, a sign was given to them. As, to the shepherds at Bethlehem, who as Jews were accustomed to the idea of angelic ministrations, a vision of angels announced the birth of the Messiah, so to the Magi, who were accustomed to look to the heavenly bodies for portents of earthly changes, a star or other brilliant light in heaven was given as an indication of the great event for which they had been waiting. Probably they had already fixed on Judæa, and of course on Jerusalem, the capital of Judæa, as the scene of the long-expected events. The often quoted passages from the Roman historians, Suetonius and Tacitus, both refer to Judæa as the place from which, according to expectations generally prevalent in the East, a man was destined, about that time, to come and obtain the empire of the world. Pliny not improbably had reference to something of the same kind in calling Jerusalem (II. N., l. 5, c. 15) "by far the most illustrious city, not only of Judæa, but of the East," since in outward splendor it was greatly inferior to other Eastern cities. The place, therefore, was fixed and known. When the unusual appearance in the sky was seen, which the wise men accepted as a signal to announce the birth of the expected deliverer, they knew at once to what place it would lead them. Carrying the gifts which, with their Eastern ideas and habits, they regarded as most worthy to be offered on such a visit, they hastened to Jerusalem, and made known the object of their journey.

The inhabitants of Jerusalem were deeply moved by the report of their coming. The hoary-headed monarch, whose long reign of cruelty and blood was soon to find a fitting termination in the horrible and loathsome disease which closed his miserable life, had, of course, his cruel suspicions excited by any reference at that time to the birth of a king. Only a short time before, more than six thousand of the Pharisees (Josephus, Ant. 17. 2. 4) had refused the oath of allegiance to him, and foretold "how God had decreed that his government should cease, and his posterity be deprived of it." He put to death their leading men; but, sitting on a throne to which as a foreigner he could have no rightful claim, the Idumæan Herod was not the man to forget their predictions, or anything else that might stand in the way of his regal power and its continuance in his family. But it would not do to let his fears be known. Cloaking, therefore, his murderous intention under an affectation of reverence for the predicted Messiah, he called together the chief priests and the scribes, who as teachers of the law were most thoroughly versed in the sacred writings, and asked them where the Christ, or the Messiah, was to be born.

The inquest which he made, and the manner in which it was received and answered, prove how general and how strong among the Jews the expectations of the Messiah were. The leading minds of the nation evidently felt themselves to be on the eve of the extraordinary series of events which had been foretold by their prophets centuries before, and which had always been kept up in the expectations of the people.

Having learned the particular place of the Messiah's birth, the wise men set out for Bethlehem. While on their way, they were gladdened exceedingly by seeing again the star which they had seen while in the East, and which now showed itself in such a direction that it seemed to be leading them forward, till on their reaching the place it appeared to stand over the spot where the young child was. The expression, "to stand over a place," in its application to a heavenly body, was not foreign to ancient modes of speech. Josephus, in enumerating the portents which went before the destruction of Jerusalem, speaks of a comet which "stood over the city," in precisely the same form of words that is here applied to the star.

Bethlehem was a small town six or seven miles south of Jerusalem, but endeared to the Jewish heart by many precious historical associations. Within its limits, on the way to Jerusalem, Rachel, the favorite wife of Jacob, had died and was buried. There was the scene of most of the affecting events recorded in the beautiful pastoral of Ruth. There was the residence of Jesse, and there the genius and the devotions of David had been called out while tending his father's flocks amid its hills. There, by the consecrating oil of the aged Samuel he had been set apart for the kingly office. And there, five hundred years later, according to Jewish traditions, but we know not on what authority, was the birthplace of Zerubbabel, who led back the captive Jews from Babylon, and rebuilt their temple.

Bethlehem abounds in high hills, from which the Dead Sea, and the mountains beyond its eastern shore, are visible. Some have supposed that the star which attracted the wise men in the East was the luminous appearance (the glory of the Lord shining round about them) which the shepherds, Luke ii. 9, saw on the night of the nativity, and which from those lofty hills might have been seen far to the eastward. But this will not account for the star which the Magi saw on reaching Bethlehem. Some have supposed that it was a comet; others, and Trench among them, have thought that it was a peculiar star, like that which shone out suddenly in Cassiopeia, November 11, 1572, and which, after surpassing in apparent size all the fixed stars, and even the planet Jupiter, being sometimes distinctly seen at midday, gradually decreased, till, sixteen months after it was first seen, it seemed to go out entirely, and no traces of it have been discovered since. This star was observed and reported by Tycho Brahe, the most illustrious astronomical observer of his day. Another star, yet more remarkable, appeared in 1604, at the same time with, and in the immediate neighborhood of, a remarkable conjunction of the planets Saturn, Jupiter, and Mars, — "such a conjunction," says Trench, (in his "Star of the Wise Men," p. 32,) "as, occurring at rarest intervals, must yet have occurred as regarded the first two planets in 747, and all three in 748 A. U. C.; in years, that is, either of them very likely to have been, and one of which most probably was, the true Annus Domini."

But these speculations, though they may possibly point to a true solution of the phenomena in question, do not seem to us of much consequence. With the birth of Christ we are introduced into a sphere of higher than material agencies. From the first inception of his earthly being, in the overshadowing power and spirit of the Most High, to the time when he "was taken up" from his disciples, "and a cloud received him out of their sight," Jesus was attended by powers which come not usually within the cognizance of the senses, and of which our natural philosophy, limited as it is by the observation of physical facts through the senses, can render no adequate account. They belong to a province of divine agencies into which we have not been permitted to enter far enough to be able to speak with any certainty of the conditions or the extent of their influence on human affairs or the material universe. When once we are brought, as we are by the life of Jesus, into the realm of miraculous manifestations, it is idle to attempt to explain them by principles drawn from the narrow and unwieldy phenomena of physical science.

The anniversary of the wise men offering their gifts to the infant Jesus has been celebrated in most Christian churches as the Epiphany, or manifestation of Christ to the Gentiles. The wise men are regarded by the Roman Catholic Church as kings who came from different parts of India, and to them has been applied the language of the seventy-second Psalm, "The kings of Sheba and Seba shall offer gifts," "and to him shall be given of the gold of Sheba." Each of the gifts also has its mystical signification, — the gold, a royal offering, indicating his kingly office, the frankincense denoting his heavenly origin, and the myrrh (in about a hundred pounds of myrrh and aloes his body afterwards was laid, John xix. 39) prefiguring his death. These are fanciful interpretations, but probably they come nearer to the reverential feeling which they were employed to express, than any meaning that we can arrive at through the researches of natural history. In all ages of the world, especially in those Eastern regions, the devout and lowly in heart have delighted in offering up whatever was most beautiful and precious, as a token of inward reverence and affection. In this way gold and gems and precious gums and ointments became invested with hallowed associations, and spoke to the soul with a grace and charm that we in our cold climate can poorly comprehend. A Judas might count the pecuniary cost of such gifts, and wise men in our day, whose wisdom is wholly absorbed in estimating their outward value, may exclaim about the waste in matters of sentiment. But the Saviour has recognized in such gifts a deeper and holier worth than any merely pecuniary value, even though it were to be expended upon the poor.

### 16 – 18. — MURDER OF THE CHILDREN IN BETHLEHEM.

The account of the murder of the innocents has been set aside as unhistorical, because it is mentioned by no other historian, and because it has been thought to be a crime too foolish and too atrocious even for the crafty and cruel Herod. But the craftiest men are often taken in their own craftiness. Their roundabout, underhanded, complicated plans for the accomplishment of what might be done so much more easily by some direct means, often fail of their purpose, and in the result appear like folly. "Any one," says Trench, "who is acquainted with, and calls to mind, the cruel precautions of Eastern monarchs, in times past and present, in regard of possible competitors for their throne, often making an entire desolation, even of their own kindred round them, will see in this what many an Eastern monarch would have done, — what certainly a Herod would not have shrunk from doing." His jealousy, which had been excited by the errand of the wise men, was changed to rage when he found that they had eluded, and, as he proudly considered it, "mocked" him. He determined therefore, in his wrath, to secure the destruction which he had designed for one of the children of Bethlehem by a summary act of vengeance on all. This was entirely in keeping with all that we know of Herod. "The man," says Trench, "who could put his wife and three of his own sons to death, who made a solitude round him by the slaughter of so many of his friends, who could kill, under semblance of sport, as he did, the youthful high-priest, Aristobulus; who, when he was himself dying by horrible and loathsome diseases, so far from being softened, or owning the hand of God, which every one else saw therein, could devise such a devilish wickedness as that narrated by Josephus, to secure weeping and lamentation at his death,* would have had little scruple in conceiving or carrying out an iniquity such as the sacred historian lays here to his charge." Nor would the crime be one of so remarkable a character that historians like Tacitus or Josephus would be unlikely to omit it in their

---

* According to Josephus, Antiq., Lib. XVII. c. 6, s. 6-8, "It troubled him greatly to anticipate the joy which there would be among the Jews at his death; and with the purpose of turning this joy into weeping, he got together from every city the chief personages of the land, whom he shut up in the Hippodrome of Jericho, where he lay dying. He then obtained a promise from his sister Salome and her husband, that, the instant he expired, these all should be slain, so that, although none wept and lamented him, there should yet be abundant weeping and lamentation at his death. His intentions were not better fulfilled than those of tyrants after their deaths commonly are."

imperfect catalogue of his crimes. The act was one of
no political importance. The number of children murdered has been greatly exaggerated in the popular mind.
" From two years old, and under," in the Jewish mode
of reckoning, probably means, downward from those who
have entered on their second year, or, as we should say,
under one year old. In a small place like Bethlehem
they could hardly have numbered more than ten or fifteen,
and these might have been put out of the way without
any public commotion by the practised and accomplished
agents of a tyrant like Herod.

## QUOTATIONS FROM THE PROPHETS.

6. The references to the Old Testament in this chapter are
worthy of notice. The quotation here from Micah v. 2
is given, not merely as an important historical fact in its
relation to the inquiries of Herod, but as showing that
the great Jewish council, or Sanhedrim at Jerusalem, composed of the chief priests and the men most learned in
the law, had fixed on Bethlehem, where Jesus had just
been born, as the birthplace of the Messiah. The ancient
prophet, therefore, as interpreted by the highest religious authority recognized among the Jews, accorded with
the writer as to the place of the Messiah's birth. This
must at the outset have had great weight with those whose
favorable attention Matthew wished particularly to gain.
It is not *his* opinion of the application of the prophecy
that is given, but the deliberately expressed opinion of
those whom they looked up to as their authorized teachers
in such matters. See John vii. 42.

15. The second quotation, " *Out of Egypt have I called
my Son,*" Hos. xi. 1, is given as one of the coincidences
in language and in fact which could not but strike those
who regarded both as sacred, and who thus through their
religious associations would be led on in the narrative

with less violent antipathies. Whether Israel, (whom God here calls his son,) coming up out of Egypt to receive and to perpetuate the knowledge of the true God through the laws and institutions appointed by him, was or was not held forth by the prophet as a type of that greater Son of God now coming from Egypt, who was to exercise a yet mightier influence in the advancement of God's kingdom through the earth, is of little consequence, so far as the writer's purpose or the pertinency of the quotation is concerned.

17, 18. The third quotation is from Jeremiah xxxi. 15. Jerusalem had been taken and destroyed by Nebuzaradan. The Jewish nobles had been slain, and after the sons of the king, Zedekiah, had been murdered in his sight, his own eyes were put out. The people were gathered together in chains at Ramah, a city of Ephraim, probably about six miles northward from Jerusalem, whence they were to begin their wearisome and sorrowful journey towards Babylon, the land of their long captivity. The prophet Jeremiah, who had been one of the captives, and who is now predicting the joyful return of his people from their bondage, contrasts their future gladness with the feelings of that dismal day when they were taking their departure frðm Ramah with such lamentation and bitter weeping, that it seemed as if Rachel, the wife of their common ancestor, were there, as a mother, weeping for her children, and refusing to be comforted because they were not. This striking and beautiful figure the Evangelist has transferred to Bethlehem, to represent the lamentation, weeping, and great mourning caused by the murder of the children. The image of Rachel rising from her tomb and weeping there is rendered more appropriate by the fact that her grave was near Bethlehem, in the midst of those who had been sacrificed by that barbarous act of cruelty. Whether Jeremiah used language which, besides describing the sorrows at Ramah and the joyful return of the Jews from Babylon, pointed on in prophetic vision to the sorrows of Bethlehem, and the more joyful deliverance which should thence ensue, is not clearly announced, though the chapter, taken as a whole, seems to abound in words expressive of a grandeur and magnificence too rich and vast to find their entire fulfilment in the restoration of the Jews from Babylon. There is nothing distinctly said in the Gospel beyond the application of the passage to the mourning at Bethlehem; but if the Jews regarded it as being in some sense one of their Messianic prophecies, the few words quoted might carry their minds unconsciously on, from the parallel between the sorrows at Ramah and at Bethlehem, to the higher coincidence between the joys of the deliverance from the captivity at Babylon and the grander deliverance for which they were looking forward to the Messiah. The force of such allusions comes through the fine but powerful associations which cannot be expressed in words, far more than through any direct or logical appeal to the understanding.

Dr. W. M. Thomson, in his work on Palestine, says (Vol. II. p. 503) in regard to this quotation: "The poetic accommodation of Jeremiah was natural and beautiful. Of course it *is* accommodation. The prophet himself had no thought of Herod and the slaughter of the infants." That is, in his opinion (and the facts of the case, as far as known, certainly go to sustain him in it), the language of Jeremiah is here quoted, not as a prediction of this event, but merely as furnishing words which describe the sharpness of the sorrow caused by Herod's cruelty.

23. The fourth apparent quotation from the Old Testament is of a different kind. "That it might be fulfilled which was spoken by the prophets, 'He shall be called a Nazarene.'" No such passage is to be found in the Old Testament. Dr. Palfrey supposes that the reference is to Judges xiii. 5, "He shall be a Nazarite." Tischendorf makes the reference to Isaiah xi. 1, where the word translated Branch is in Hebrew *Netser* or *Nazer*. But

the term Nazarene was one of contempt and disgrace, as the place, and everything belonging to it, John i. 46, were despised among the Jews. When, therefore, St. Matthew speaks of Jesus as dwelling in Nazareth, and of course bearing the despised name of Nazarene, he would soften the prejudice thus awakened, by intimating, though in obscure terms, that even thus he was fulfilling in himself what had been spoken by the prophets of the Messiah, as one despised and rejected of men. The form of speech, " by the prophets," is unlike that which occurs anywhere else in the Gospels when a quotation is made from a particular writer, and of itself would seem to imply that an idea expressed by different prophets, rather than the specific language of any one writer, was what was referred to as fulfilled in Jesus, when he was called by that mean and offensive name. This is the interpretation given by Kuinoel, Olshausen, Trench, and others, and seems to us more natural than any other. But we are too far removed from the times and habits of the writer, and those for whom he wrote, to speak with certainty of allusions which appealed so delicately to their finer sensibilities through the associations growing out of their religious culture

## NOTES.

Now when Jesus was born in Bethlehem of Judæa, in the days of Herod the king, behold, there came wise men from the east 2 to Jerusalem, saying, Where is he that is born King of the

1. **Herod the king**] " Herod the Great, son of Antipater, an Idumæan by an Arabian mother, made king of Judæa on occasion of his having fled to Rome, being driven from his tetrarchy by the pretender Antigonus, and confirmed in his office by Augustus Cæsar after the battle of Actium. He died miserably, five days after he had put to death his son Antipater, in the seventieth year of his age and the thirty-eighth of his reign, and the 750th year of Rome. The events here related took place a short time before his death." Alford. 2. **Where is he that is born King of the Jews?**] " There had prevailed in

MATTHEW II.

Jews? for we have seen his star in the east, and are come to worship him. When Herod the king had heard these things, he was troubled, and all Jerusalem with him; and when he had gathered all the chief priests and scribes of the people together, he demanded of them where Christ should be born. And they said unto him, In Bethlehem of Judæa; for thus it is written by the prophet: "And thou, Bethlehem, in the land of Juda, art not the least among the princes of Juda; for out of thee shall come a Governor, that shall rule my people Israel." Then Herod, when he had privily called the wise men, inquired of them diligently what time the star appeared, and he sent them to Bethlehem, and said: Go and search diligently for the young child; and when ye have found him, bring me word again, that I may come and worship him also. When they had heard the king, they departed. And, lo, the

---

all the East an ancient and constant expectation that, according to the fates, men coming from 'Judæa should rule the world,' *rerum potirentur*." Suetonius, Vesp. c. 4. "Many had been persuaded that it was contained in the ancient writings of the priests, that the East should prevail, and that men coming from Judæa should rule the world." Tacitus, Hist. V. 13.

**to worship him**] "To do homage to him in the Eastern fashion of prostration." Alford.

2. Some readers may be interested in the following statement, which is borrowed from astronomical calculations, by Alford: — "In the year of Rome 747, on the 20th of May, there was a conjunction of Jupiter and Saturn in the twentieth degree of the constellation Pisces, close to the first point of Aries, which was the part of the heavens noted in astrological science as that in which the signs denoted the greatest and most noble events. On the 27th of October, in the same year, another conjunction of the same planets took place, in the sixteenth degree of Pisces; and on the 12th of November a third, in the fifteenth degree of the same sign. On these last two occasions the planets were so near, that an ordinary eye would regard them as one star of surpassing brightness. Supposing the magi to have seen the *first* of these conjunctions, they saw it actually 'in the east;' for on the 20th of May it would rise shortly before the sun. If they then took their journey, and arrived at Jerusalem in a little more than five months, (the journey from Babylon took Ezra four months, see Ezra vii. 9,) if they performed the route from Jerusalem to Bethlehem in the evening, as is implied, the November conjunction in the fifteenth degree of Pisces would be before them in the direction of Bethlehem, coming to the meridian about eight o'clock, P. M. These circumstances would seem to form a remarkable coincidence with the history in our text."

4. **And when he** [Herod] **had gathered all the chief priests and scribes of the people together**] This was probably a meeting of the Jewish Sanhedrim, which consisted of seventy-one members, and was at that time the highest religious tribunal known among the Jews, being composed of priests, Levites, and Israelites. The scribes were the teachers and interpreters of the law.

6. **And thou, Bethlehem**] This free version of Micah v. 2 is given as the report or answer of the Sanhedrim

star, which they saw in the east, went before them, till it came
10 and stood over where the young child was. When they saw
11 the star, they rejoiced with exceeding great joy; and when
they were come into the house, they saw the young child with
Mary his mother, and fell down, and worshipped him; and
when they had opened their treasures, they presented unto
12 him gifts, gold and frankincense and myrrh. And being
warned of God in a dream that they should not return to
Herod, they departed into their own country another way.

13 And when they were departed, behold, the angel of the Lord
appeareth to Joseph in a dream, saying: Arise, and take the
young child and his mother, and flee into Egypt, and be thou
there until I bring thee word; for Herod will seek the young
14 child to destroy him. When he arose, he took the young child
15 and his mother by night, and departed into Egypt; and was
there until the death of Herod; that it might be fulfilled which
was spoken of the Lord by the prophet, saying: "Out of
16 Egypt have I called my Son." Then Herod, when he saw
that he was mocked of the wise men, was exceeding wroth;
and sent forth and slew all the children that were in Bethlehem, and in all the coasts thereof, from two years old and
under, according to the time which he had diligently inquired
17 of the wise men. Then was fulfilled that which was spoken by
18 Jeremy the prophet, saying: "In Rama was there a voice
heard, lamentation, and weeping, and great mourning; Rachel
weeping for her children, and would not be comforted, because
19 they are not." But when Herod was dead, behold, an angel
20 of the Lord appeareth in a dream to Joseph in Egypt, saying:
Arise, and take the young child and his mother, and go into
the land of Israel; for they are dead which sought the young
21 child's life. And he arose, and took the young child and his
22 mother, and came into the land of Israel. But when he heard

---

to Herod.    9. **the star**] "If it is to be understood as standing over the house, and thus indicating to the magi the position of the object of their search, the whole incident must be regarded as miraculous. But this is not necessarily implied, even if the words of the text be literally understood; and in a matter like astronomy, where popular language is so universally inaccurate, and the Scriptures so generally use popular language, it is surely not the letter, but the spirit of the narrative with which we are concerned." Alford.

14. **and departed into Egypt**] where, at no very great distance from Jerusalem, and within a Roman province, he would be

MATTHEW II.

that Archelaus did reign in Judæa, in the room of his father Herod, he was afraid to go thither; notwithstanding, being warned of God in a dream, he turned aside into the parts of Galilee. And he came and dwelt in a city called Nazareth; 23

safely beyond Herod's jurisdiction.
**22. Archelaus**] succeeded his father, and at first claimed to be a king; but he never had the title of king conferred upon him by the Roman Emperor. In the ninth year of his government he was removed from office. **23. And he came and dwelt in a city called Nazareth**] Had we only this Gospel, we should certainly infer that Joseph and Mary had previously lived in Bethlehem, and now went into Galilee to reside as in a strange place, while Luke (ii. 4, 39) speaks of them as coming up from Nazareth to Bethlehem immediately before the birth of Jesus, and returning again to Nazareth, apparently without any delay after the rites of purification had been performed, which, according to the law, would be forty days after his birth. How is this account of Luke's to be reconciled with Matthew's account of the flight into Egypt, which covered the whole time between the birth of Jesus and the death of Herod? It is impossible to determine how long a time that was, because it cannot be determined with certainty in what year Jesus was born. But on any hypothesis it is difficult to reconcile the accounts of the two Evangelists. The magi could hardly have reached Bethlehem before the purification in the temple; for the remarkable circumstances connected with that event (Luke ii. 22-39) must in that case have attracted the now awakened and jealous attention of Herod. Both the visit of the magi and the residence in Egypt then probably occurred after the purification and before the return to Nazareth. But if Luke had been aware of these events, would he have omitted all notice of them? Does his account, "And when they had performed all things according to the law of the Lord, they returned into Galilee, to their own city, Nazareth," leave room for the intervening residence in Egypt? The subject will be more fully discussed when we come to treat of the Gospel of Luke. In the mean time, it is well to remember, that, in these very brief and rapid sketches of events in our Saviour's life, there must, from the very character of the narrative, be abrupt transitions from one event to others which occurred at a wholly different time, and under entirely different circumstances. The Gospel of Matthew or Luke is not much longer than a eulogy on some eminent man. One Evangelist, in his brief sketch, having his mind particularly interested in one class of facts connected with the birth of Jesus, might speak of the visit of the magi, the cruelty of Herod, and the consequent flight to Egypt, while another might select a wholly different class of facts, and speak of the annunciation, the journey from Nazareth to Bethlehem, the vision seen by the shepherds, the circumcision, the purification, and the subsequent removal back to Nazareth, without giving any ground to infer that either was ignorant of what the other has recorded, or that because one has related one class of events, therefore the other class of events, which purports to have occurred at nearly the same time, could not have taken place. Both the Evangelists together fail to relate a hundredth part of the incidents which interested those then living in Palestine within two years of the birth of Jesus. Nothing is more unsafe than to infer a contradiction from a want of coincidence in two such narratives; for in each of them, from a great abundance of facts and sayings, — so many, says John, that the world could not contain them if they should all be written, — the writer makes such selections as may best suit his purpose, and uses them,

that it might be fulfilled which was spoken by the prophets, He shall be called a Nazarene.

---

generally without indicating the precise time to which they relate. We shall find, as we go on, that it will not do to take any one of the Gospels as a precise chronological statement of events; still less as an account intended to embrace all the facts belonging to any one period of our Saviour's life. As respects the birth of Jesus, Mark and John say nothing; Matthew relates one series of events intimately connected, and Luke another, while both, excepting a single incident, Luke ii. 41 – 52, pass over the whole period of his childhood and youth till he was about thirty years of age.

## CHAPTER III.

#### John the Baptist.

There was, as we have already seen, among the Jews, a general but indefinite expectation of the Messiah, which had only been strengthened by their national vicissitudes and misfortunes. While they were scattered through distant lands, mingling with other nations, and in some measure adopting their philosophical ideas, the particular form which this expectation assumed varied with the place of their sojourn and their individual habits of thought. "Each region," says Milman, "each rank, each sect: the Babylonian, the Egyptian, the Palestinian, the Samaritan; the Pharisee, the lawyer, the zealot, arrayed the Messiah in those attributes which suited his own temperament." Some one was needed in Judæa to give consistency to these varying expectations, and especially to give them new intensity and power by announcing as already at hand that kingdom of God to which they had been pointing forward through so many centuries. This was the office assigned to the Baptist. He was not a follower of Christ, but only the herald to announce his coming. It was not given to him as it was to the disciples of Jesus, (Matt. xiii. 11,) "to know the mysteries of the kingdom of Heaven," but "the least in the kingdom of God," (Luke vii. 28,) i. e. the humblest Christian, was declared by Jesus to be "greater than he." We must, therefore, be careful not to ascribe to him ideas which could be entertained only by those who had learned them from the Messiah himself.

He had been brought up among the mountains of Judæa,

about as far to the south as Jesus was to the north from Jerusalem. His habits of life were probably those of a religious recluse, with a conviction borne in upon him that he had been born and set apart for some great· and holy purpose. Like the mighty prophet Elijah of old, he was rude in dress, simple in diet, and severe in speech, dwelling in religious thought and prayer amid the solitudes of nature. When the time had at length arrived, he came down from the mountains to the valley of the Jordan. He announced the approaching kingdom of Heaven in terms of startling decision and severity. He warned men to flee from the wrath that was impending over the ungodly, and to prepare themselves, by change of heart and newness of life, to meet the Messiah at his coming. Crowds from all quarters gathered round him. Even Pharisees and Sadducees came to witness his baptism. He sees their national delusion in supposing that, because they are descended from Abraham, they must therefore be admitted into the Messiah's kingdom. This new kingdom, he tells them, is not thus easily to be entered. " Ye generation of vipers, who hath warned *you* to flee from the coming wrath ? Bring forth then fruit worthy of repentance, and do not think to say, .' We have Abraham for our father.' From these stones [that are lying round us] God can raise up children, or successors, to Abraham." And then, to impress them with a sense of the urgency of the occasion, as if not a moment were to be lost, he exclaims, with vehement and terrible earnestness, that the axe even now is lying at the root of the tree, and every tree that bringeth not forth good fruit is cut [chopped] down and cast into the fire. "I, indeed," he continues, "baptize you with water unto repentance," receiving none to my baptism but those who repent, and confess their sins; "but here is coming one mightier than I, who will subject you to a more searching ordeal, baptizing you, not in water alone, but in the holy spirit [wind] and fire," " for," he says, continuing the same thought still under the imagery of wind and fire, "with his winnowing instrument in his hand, he will clear up his threshing-floor, gathering the wheat into his storehouse and burning the chaff with unquenchable fire."

Some have supposed that John here, by these different kinds of baptism, describes the different degrees of spiritual attainment in his disciples and those of the Messiah. "Baptism with water," says Olshausen, "implies repentance, and purification from sin; baptism with the spirit refers to the inward cleansing in faith, (the Holy Spirit being conceived of as the regenerating principle,) and, lastly, baptism with fire expresses the glorification of the regenerated higher life into its own peculiar nature." But these ideas, however familiar they may be to us, belong, in the higher development of our Christian experience, to a plane of spiritual life and thought which we have reason to suppose that John, who was only the herald or forerunner of Christ, had never reached. As the humblest disciple of Jesus, he "who is least in the kingdom of God," knows more of its interior life and economy than he who was not only "a prophet, but more than a prophet," under the old dispensation, it would be a serious anachronism to assign to John, at that time, so profound a knowledge of the religion of Jesus. The same remark applies also, though with less force, to the interpretations by which the baptism of the Holy Ghost and of fire are referred to the tongues of flame on the day of Pentecost (Acts ii. 3, compared with Acts i. 5, xix. 2, 3). For this would be to ascribe to the Baptist, before the ministry of Jesus had begun, a degree of knowledge which the disciples of Jesus did not have till some time after its close. So also the explanation of the baptism of fire by a reference to the "much tribulation" of Acts xiv. 22, and "the fire" (1 Cor. iii. 13) which "shall try every man's work, of what sort it is," implies in John a sort of knowledge which we have no reason to suppose that he possessed. Besides, any one of these interpretations interferes with the straightforward, direct, and vehement earnestness of his speech.

Why did Jesus come, to be baptized by John? The question is one which we cannot fully and confidently answer. But as John had been raised up to announce the immediate coming of the Messiah, and by his preaching had excited such an expectation in the minds of thousands, the object of all this movement on the part of the Baptist would be lost to the cause, unless his predictions should in some way be connected with Jesus. Jesus, therefore, in the fulness of time, came to John at the Jordan. Whether they had previously had any personal acquaintance with each other is not quite certain. Though their mothers were related, the two families lived in the opposite extremities of Palestine, and probably their only opportunities of meeting would be in Jerusalem, at the great religious festivals. The extraordinary circumstances attending their birth would naturally draw their parents together. The probability, therefore, is that they had had some personal knowledge of each other, and that the expression of the Baptist (John i. 33), "I knew him not," means that he did not till then know him as the Messiah. But in order that the testimony of John should have its due weight with the people, it was important that it should come from him, not as a personal friend and companion of Jesus, but as an independent witness and prophet of God.

John, therefore, was brought up under the old dispensation, having only a slight personal acquaintance with Jesus, and came forth, as he was moved by the spirit of God, to herald the coming of that kingdom in which the law and the prophets alike were to find their fulfilment. Like Moses, he was to lead the people out of their ancient bondage through the wilderness to the very borders of the promised kingdom, seeing it near, pointing it out to his followers, indicating and setting apart their future and greater leader, but himself, for wise and weighty reasons, not permitted to enter within its borders. As he was the last, and in some respects the greatest of the prophets belonging to the ancient dispensation, Jesus, who submitted to all the requirements of that dispensation, came to receive from him its solemn sanctions, and it has been thought in the very place where Joshua, or Jesus (for the names are the same) led the tribes of Israel on dry ground through the Jordan, there he went down to its baptismal waters, and in his own person consecrated forever the rite which through all coming ages should stand as the sign, if not the seal of admission into his kingdom. As he went up from the water, and stood (Luke iii. 21) praying, his countenance we may suppose radiant with the emotions of the hour, behold, the heavens were opened to him, and he perceived the spirit of God, pure and peaceful as a dove (the sacred bird of Syria) descending, and (John i. 32) resting upon him; and behold, a voice from the heavens saying, 'This is my son, the beloved, in whom I am well pleased."

When John saw Jesus, he was awed by him as in the presence of a superior being, and shrunk from administering to him the rite of baptism. He felt his own inferiority. The "former things" to which he belonged were now to be fulfilled by passing away, through a species of dissolution, into the higher kingdom which is to be inaugurated. With the modest humility which becomes a true servant of God, he submits to the request of Christ, and in so doing receives from heaven the proof that the Messiah has come. He sees, that, like the star which has been the harbinger of a fairer day, he must decrease, (John iii. 30,) while the Sun of Righteousness which he has announced as rising upon the world must increase in brightness and power. In that new kingdom no office was assigned to him. It was appointed in the counsels of Infinite Wisdom that he should stand apart as the appointed herald, but not be a follower of the Messiah.

From that day the ministry of John was in fact ended.

"For this purpose," he said, (John i. 31,) "am I come baptizing with water, that he should be made manifest in Israel," and in proportion as he is made known must the Baptist retire before him. "I am," he said, (John i. 23,) "the voice of one crying in the wilderness," and now that voice having waked the solitudes of Judæa, and turned the expectations of the nation towards the Messiah, recedes again into silence. There is something very touching and very beautiful in the readiness with which this great man, so honored and reverenced among all the people as a prophet of God, humbled himself before Jesus from the first moment of his appearance. And, in all the circumstances of our Saviour's coming, in the blended dignity and humility which marked his personal deportment, and the tokens of divine love and approbation which came down to him from heaven, we see how befitting the work which had been given him to do was this his first entrance on the field of his labors.

## NOTES.

IN those days came John the Baptist, preaching in the wilderness of Judæa, and saying: Repent ye, for the kingdom of

1. **In those days**] An indefinite expression nearly corresponding to our *at length*, or *in the course of time*. In this case it refers to what took place nearly thirty years after the events spoken of in the paragraph next preceding it. In Exodus ii. 11 it is used as a form of introduction to events which occurred forty years after those described in the previous sentence.

**preaching**] proclaiming as a herald who goes before to announce the coming of a king. "When Ibrahim Pasha proposed to visit certain places in Lebanon, the emeers and sheiks sent forth a general proclamation, somewhat in the style of Isaiah's exhortation, to all the inhabitants to assemble along the proposed route, and prepare the way before him. The same was done in 1845 on a grand scale, when the present Sultan visited Brusa. The stones were gathered out, crooked places straightened, and rough ones made level and smooth." The Land and the Book, Thomson, II. 106. Sometimes they sent forward heralds to announce their approach, and to require the people to make this preparation for their coming.

**in the wilderness**] not strictly a desert, but compara-

heaven is at hand. For this is he that was spoken of by the 3
prophet Esaias, saying, "The voice of one crying in the wilderness, prepare ye the way of the Lord, make his paths
straight." And the same John had his raiment of camel's 4
hair, and a leathern girdle about his loins; and his meat was

---

tively an uninhabited region round the Jordan. **2. Repent ye**] The Greek word literally refers to a change of mind or thought, and implies a change so deep that it reaches the very fountain of thought, and therefore touches the inmost motives which give their shape and coloring to the life. Dr. Campbell and Mr. Norton translate it, *Reform;* but this to most minds conveys the impression of an external change rather than of one which, beginning in the soul, works outward through the conduct, till mind and heart and life alike are transformed. The word *Repent* is confined too exclusively to the inward feeling of sorrow, which is only the beginning of the change that is required. **2. the kingdom of heaven**] literally, *the kingdom of the heavens,*— a form of expression used only by Matthew, the other Evangelists using the term *kingdom of God.* Some stress has been laid, and perhaps not without reason, on this expression as indicating a plurality of *heavens,* corresponding to the many mansions in his Father's house which Jesus speaks of (John xiv. 2), and adapted to the sons of God in the different stages of their spiritual progress. The idea of the kingdom of Heaven or kingdom of God as synonymous with the Messiah's kingdom was probably familiar to the Jews, borrowed, perhaps, from passages like Daniel ii. 44. It is used in the New Testament with different shades of meaning to indicate the Messiah's kingdom: 1. as an inward principle of life in the soul (the kingdom of God is within you, Luke xvii. 21); 2. as a divine power extending through the world and changing its whole character (a little leaven which leaveneth the whole mass, Matt. xii. 33); 3. as an organized polity, like a net cast into the sea, Matt. xiii. 47, 48, and taking into itself the good and the bad till they shall at length be separated in the end of the world; 4. as the Messiah's kingdom when it shall take the place of the Jewish dispensation after the destruction of Jerusalem, Luke ix. 27; or, 5. as it shall appear in its consummation amid the brighter glories of a higher world, when the Son of man shall sit on the throne of his glory, Matt. xxv. 31, when it shall be fulfilled in the kingdom of God, Luke xxii. 16, or when through much tribulation we shall enter the kingdom of God, Acts xiv. 22. These different meanings melt insensibly into one another. We have no reason to suppose that John the Baptist understood the expression at all in its higher signification, but only as indicating an outward, visible kingdom, founded on the principles of righteousness, but exercising an earthly authority and power. **3. For this is he that was spoken of by the prophet Esaias**] The quotation is from the Septuagint. The whole passage should be read (Isaiah xl.) in order to understand the effect intended by the introduction of a few of the words here. The Baptist, in John i. 23, describes himself by these same words. **4. his raiment of camel's hair, and a leathern girdle about his loins**] The Jews expected Elijah as the forerunner of the Messiah, and this description corresponds to that of Elijah in 2 Kings i. 8, "He [Elijah] was an hairy man, and girt with a girdle of leather about his loins." Elijah was intimately associated in the Jewish mind with the Messiah as his forerunner, and Jesus himself xvii. 10 - 13, distinctly declares that this expected Elijah is none other than John the Baptist. The prophecy which probably gave rise to the

5 locusts and wild honey. Then went out to him Jerusalem,
6 and all Judæa, and all the region round about Jordan; and
7 were baptized of him in Jordan, confessing their sins. But
when he saw many of the Pharisees and Sadducees come to his
baptism, he said unto them: O generation of vipers, who hath
8 warned you to flee from the wrath to come? Bring forth

expectation is a remarkable one, and, from its place at the very end of the Jewish Scriptures, Malachi iv. 5, 6, must have attracted particular attention: "Behold, I will send you Elijah the prophet before the coming of the great and dreadful day of the Lord, and he shall turn the heart of the fathers to the children, and the heart of the children to their fathers, lest I come and smite the earth with a curse." This describes the influence of John in preaching his doctrine of repentance, and thus preparing the hearts of the people, parents and children, for the coming of Christ. **and his meat was locusts and wild honey**] Locusts, first boiled and then dried in the sun, and carried like parched corn in bags, are still sometimes used as an article of food by the Bedouin on the frontiers of Syria. The insects were grasshoppers, and not locusts, and should be so read wherever the word occurs in the Bible. Jaeger. *The wild honey* was not, as some have thought, a vegetable product exuding from trees, but honey made by wild bees. "Wild honey," says Thomson, "is still gathered in large quantities from trees in the wilderness, and from rocks in the wadies, just where the Baptist sojourned, and where he came preaching the baptism of repentance." 6. **And were baptized of him in Jordan**] "When *men* were admitted as proselytes, three rites were performed, — circumcision, baptism, and oblation; when *women*, two, — baptism and oblation. The whole families of proselytes, including infants, were baptized." Alford. "*Baptism*, symbolical or ceremonial washing, such as the Mosaic law prescribed as a sign of moral renovation, and connected with the sacrificial types of expiation. It was from these familiar and significant ablutions that John's baptism was derived, and not from the practice of baptizing proselytes, the antiquity of which as a distinct rite is disputed." Alexander on Mark. "It was in itself," says Stanley, "no new ceremony. Ablutions, in the East, have always been more or less a part of religious worship, easily performed and always welcome. Every synagogue, if possible, was by the side of a stream or spring; every mosque, still, requires a fountain or basin for lustrations in its court." 7. **Pharisees and Sadducees**] Josephus represents these two sects as originating about one hundred and fifty years before Christ. They overlaid the law and the prophets by their traditions, and, like all sects who trust to forms and traditions, they neglected the spirit of their religion, and became remarkable for their superstition and hypocrisy. They had great influence, as their representatives in all ages have among their own people, and, like their successors now, were the most malignant enemies of Jesus, as he appeared in the simplicity of his instructions and the purity of his life. The Sadducees, who were supposed to be so called from a Hebrew word, meaning righteousness, rejected *all* tradition, and, though it was not originally one of their distinguishing features, yet in our Saviour's time they denied the reality of a future life. By confining themselves to a bare, literal, moral conformity to the law of Moses, they lost all spiritual life, and with it all belief in spiritual influences or spiritual beings. They are the type of the carnal unbelief which prevails among the philosophical classes, and those

therefore fruits meet for repentance, and think not to say within yourselves, We have Abraham to our father; for I say unto you, that God is able of these stones to raise up children unto Abraham. And now also the axe is laid unto the root of the trees; therefore every tree which bringeth not forth good fruit is hewn down, and cast into the fire. I indeed baptize you with water, unto repentance; but he that cometh after me is mightier than I, whose shoes I am not worthy to bear; he shall baptize you with the Holy Ghost, and with fire. Whose fan is in his hand, and he will thoroughly purge his floor; and gather his wheat into the garner, but he will burn up the chaff with unquenchable fire.

Then cometh Jesus from Galilee to Jordan, unto John, to be

---

whose thoughts are "bound up in a materialistic prosperity."

**11. The Holy Ghost]** The word translated Ghost or Spirit means also air or wind, and the comparison is between water with which John baptized and the more searching elements wind and fire, by which the Messiah should try his followers. **Whose shoes, &c.]** In the Talmud it is said, "Every office a servant will do for his master, a scholar should perform for his teacher, except loosing his sandal thong." Milman's History of Christianity, Book I. Chap. 3. The office lower than that of a disciple to the Messiah, which the Baptist speaks of as still too high for him, is used to indicate, not only his reverence for that exalted being, but also his consciousness of the remarkable fact, that, in the purposes of the Almighty, it was not appointed for him to hold even the lowest place in the new kingdom which he had announced. According to Lightfoot, it was the token of a slave having become his master's property, to loose his shoe, to tie the same, or to carry the necessary articles for him to the bath. **and with fire]** "The double symbolic reference of fire, elsewhere found, e. g. Mark ix. 49, as purifying the good and consuming the evil, is hardly to be pressed into the interpretation of *fire* in this verse. the prophecy here being solely of that higher and more perfect baptism to which that of John was a mere introduction." Alford. **12. Whose fan]** the winnowing shovel with which the grain when thrashed was tossed into the air so as to separate the chaff from the wheat.

**he will thoroughly purge his floor]** The threshing-floor may sometimes have been a large, flat rock, but usually it was a level spot of earth trodden or rolled smooth and hard. The grain was beaten out by flails, or trodden out by oxen. **13. to Jordan]** "It was the one river of Palestine, —sacred in its recollections,—abundant in its waters; and yet, at the same time, the river, not of cities, but of the wilderness, — the scene of the preaching of those who dwelt not in king's palaces, nor wore soft clothing. On the banks of the rushing stream the multitudes gathered, —the priests and scribes from Jerusalem, down the pass of Adummim; the publicans from Jericho on the south, and the Lake of Gennesareth on the north; the soldiers on their way from Damascus to Petra, through the Ghor, in the war with the Arab chief Hareth, the peasants from Galilee, with ONE from Nazareth, through the opening of the plain of Esdraelon. The tall 'reeds' or canes in the jungle waved, 'shaken by the wind'; the pebbles

14 baptized of him. But John forbade him, saying: I have need
15 to be baptized of thee, and comest thou to me? And Jesus
answering said unto him, Suffer it to be so now; for thus it
becometh us to fulfil all righteousness. Then he suffered him.
16 And Jesus, when he was baptized, went up straightway out of
the water; and, lo, the heavens were opened unto him, and he
saw the Spirit of God descending like a dove, and lighting up-
17 on him. And, lo, a voice from heaven, saying, This is my
beloved Son, in whom I am well pleased.

of the bare clay hills lay around, to which the Baptist pointed as capable of being transformed into 'the children of Abraham'; at their feet rushed the refreshing stream of the never-failing river. There began that sacred rite, which has since spread throughout the world, through the vast baptistries of the southern and Oriental churches, gradually dwindling to the little fonts of the north and west; the plunges beneath the water diminishing to the few drops which, by a wise exercise of Christian freedom, are now in most churches the sole representative of the full stream of the Descending River." Stanley.

**to be baptized of him**] We know too little of the significance of this rite at that time among the Jews, and especially as it was administered by John, to understand why Jesus should himself have observed it. In addition to what we have suggested in our general remarks on the subject, it may also be true, as Alford says, that he did it "as bearing the infirmities and carrying the sorrows of mankind, and thus beginning here the triple baptism of water, fire, and blood, two parts of which were now accomplished, and of the third of which he himself speaks, Luke xii. 50, and the beloved Apostle, 1 John v. 8, where *spirit* stands for *fire*." Great stress is laid on the manner in which Jesus was baptized, whether it was by immersion, effusion, or sprinkling. The *coming up out of the water* seems to imply that he went down into the water, where he was either immersed, or had water poured upon him while he stood in the river near its bank. We have no certain knowledge on the subject. If it had been important we probably should have had it. But why should his precise mode of baptism be of consequence any more than the particular garment which he then wore? If it is essential to baptism that we should enter the water precisely as he did, why is it not essential to the Lord's Supper that in partaking of it we should recline upon a couch as he did? It is foreign to the whole tone of his instructions to lay any stress on the external and incidental adjuncts of a form. 15. **Suffer it to be so now**] Let it be so for the present, just now. It is fitting that we both of us should fulfil all righteousness, i. e. all requirements of the law. For the present, therefore, permit me as the fulfiller of the law to receive this rite while you as its agent administer it. 16. **and he saw the Spirit of God descending like a dove**] may have been a mental vision, open to the spiritual perceptions of Jesus and of the Baptist, John i. 32, or it may have been the actual bodily shape of a dove appearing to them as symbolical of the pure and peaceful spirit of God and of him who that day was first publicly set apart for his great and sacred work. We should translate the verse as follows: And the moment that Jesus, being baptized, was gone up out of the water, lo, the heavens were opened to him, and he saw the spirit of God, descending like a dove, coming upon him.

## CHAPTER IV.

### 1–11.— The Temptation in the Wilderness.

We suppose that very few able scholars of our day regard the account of the Temptation as an account of events which actually took place according to the letter of the narrative. Some — Schleiermacher, for example — look upon it as a parable by which Jesus would impress most important lessons on the minds of his disciples. "Three leading maxims of Christ," he says, in his Critical Essay on the Gospel of St. Luke, "for himself and for those who were invested by him with extraordinary powers for the promotion of his kingdom, are therein expressed: the first, to perform no miracle for his own advantage, even under the most pressing circumstances; the second, never to undertake, in the hope of extraordinary Divine aid, anything which, like the dropping from the pinnacle of the temple, as it does not lie in the natural course of things, would be merely prodigious; lastly, never, though the greatest immediate advantage were by that means attainable, to enter into fellowship with the wicked, and still less into a state of dependence upon them; and Christ could not express himself more strongly against the opposite mode of conduct than by ascribing it to Satan. . . . . . In such a sense, then, Christ delivered this parable to his disciples."

These undoubtedly are in part the lessons taught by the temptation in the wilderness. But it is doing violence to the language and spirit of the narrative to interpret it as applying in no way to the inward personal experience of Jesus. Jesus, "conceived of the Holy Spirit," had nevertheless been subjected to the mental as well as physical conditions of our human nature, and, instead of attaining at once, by reason of his divine origin, to "all the fulness of God," grew not only "in stature," but "in wisdom, and in favor with God and man." This sense of intimate union with God must have grown up in him with the unfolding consciousness of inward life and power, and have been dependent in some measure on the influences which usually affect our human sensibilities. In taking upon himself our infirmities, he was of course subject in some degree to our fluctuations of feeling, and exposed, as we find in his history, to periods of unusual elevation or depression of spirit. Though living "in the bosom of the Father," "not alone because the Father was with him," yet there were times when, under the pressure of severe mental or bodily anguish, his sense of oneness with God was for the moment disturbed or lost, and he prayed in agony of spirit that the cup might pass from him, or, as if wholly deserted, uttered his cry of complete desolation upon the cross.

At the time of his baptism Jesus seems to have been lifted up into a state of unusual spiritual exaltation, and being (Luke iv. 1) full of the Holy Spirit, he was led away, as by a divine impulse, — "led up of the Spirit," — into the solitary and mountainous regions about Jericho, and there gave himself to the thoughts suitable to his nature and condition, and to the great and solemn work on which he was now to enter. Mark describes the savage features of the country by saying that Jesus was there "with the wild beasts." He remained forty days. So Moses was in the mountain (Ex. xxxiv. 28) "forty days and forty nights," and "he did neither eat bread nor drink wine," and Elijah (1 Kings xix. 8) went in the strength of what he had eaten "forty days and forty nights unto Horeb, the mount of God." It is impossible to say how long without any natural or supernatural sustenance the body may continue, while the mind is withdrawn from outward interests and wholly absorbed in matters pertaining to its own sphere and life. By such an absorption of mind, the body may be thrown out of its normal condition, and as, in some extraordinary cases of swooning, may remain in what would seem almost a temporary suspension of the animal functions. However this may be, Jesus was in the wilderness forty days, either wholly without food, or with only such scant and insufficient nutriment as the mountain solitudes might offer, without thought or care on his part. The soul, abstracted from the body and material things, dwelt apart in a world of its own. But at last, the body, overcome by its long privations and the strain to which its finer organs had been subjected, sunk down, and the mind was called away from its own meditations and emotions to sympathize with the pangs of bodily suffering. The soul which had been lifted up to such heights of spiritual insight, and burdened with such a weight of duty and of glory, was now brought down to a keen and painful sense of earthly weakness, and the first thought that occurred to him was to employ the miraculous powers with which he had been gifted as the Son of God to turn the stones around him into loaves. From whatever source the thought may have come, it was probably entertained in that half-unconscious state, which we sometimes experience when the mind is so occupied with other matters that we mechanically assent to what is proposed for our physical comfort or relief. There was nothing of itself sinful in the act suggested. But when the attention of Jesus was awakened, he saw whither the suggestion tended, and that, in employing his miraculous powers to satisfy his personal wants, he should stoop from his perfect disinterestedness, and spend on a low and selfish object gifts bestowed on him for the highest good of all. No craving of hunger should make him forget the higher wants of his nature.

"Not by bread alone," he replies, in language borrowed from the great lawgiver of Israel (Deut. viii. 3), "but by every word that proceedeth out of the mouth of God, doth man live."

Having thus appealed from the exactions of hunger to the sources of a higher life in God, he is next tried by a suggestion of an entirely different character. He knew how gross and earthly were the expectations of the Messiah which prevailed among his countrymen, and how impossible it would be to overcome their prejudices, change all their ideas and habits of thought, by the life of humiliation and sorrow which he was to lead among them. Why shall he not seek to reach their hearts in some other way? Instead of shocking their most dearly cherished hopes, and repelling them forever from his kingdom, why shall he not enforce upon them the terms of his great mission by some public and extraordinary display of his miraculous endowments, and so overcome them with wonder and astonishment that they will hail him at once as the deliverer who had for so many centuries been foretold by prophets and longed for by patriarchs and kings? In thought, he is borne to the summit of a lofty wing of the temple, while hundreds of thousands are gathered there at one of the great national festivals. As they are gazing upward towards him he is tempted to ask why he shall not cast himself down, knowing that as the Son of God he will be upborne by his angels and permitted to come to no harm? Thus he would show his confidence in God, and at the same time inaugurate his kingdom on the earth under the most favorable circumstances. The thought evidently had power to move and disturb him. But instantly he detects the dark design which lies concealed under this specious proposal. He sees that, instead of showing confidence in God by this vain and presumptuous display of his powers, he would only be tempting his providence. As the temptation was enforced by words taken from the Psalms, so he replies in language taken also from the Scriptures (Deut. vi. 16), "Thou shalt not tempt the Lord thy God."

In the first temptation, the motive, the desire to appease his hunger, was innocent, but the object was unworthy the intervention of his miraculous powers. In the second temptation, the object, the speedy establishment of his kingdom, was worthy, but the motive which lay concealed under it, the love of immediate distinction, coupled with an unwillingness to wait God's time, was wrong. There yet remains another form in which the temptation may come. The question which might be supposed to be uppermost in the mind of Jesus was, how he might most effectually accomplish his work. The great changes which had been wrought, even in the religious ideas and institutions of mankind, had been accompanied, if not actually brought about and impressed on the common mind, by great political and social revolutions. It was so that Moses, placed in the exercise of his miraculous powers at the head of the Jewish people, led them out of Egypt, and established a higher worship and a more beneficent law. Why then may not Jesus, in establishing a still purer faith and worship, enlist on his side the powers of this world through the universal dominion to which he may attain by the exercise of his marvellous endowments? It was no dream of earthly ambition, no vulgar thought of royal or imperial magnificence, that could be permitted even to approach the mind of Jesus, still less to throw a momentary shadow over it, or awaken one disturbing emotion or desire. But by placing himself at the head of the nations, at that grand crisis of human affairs, might he not more speedily and more effectually establish the kingdom of God among men than through the ignominious path of weakness, sorrow, humiliation, and death? May he not in this way save his followers from the mortification and sorrows to which they must be exposed? For a moment the thought came over him. But then, how shall such power over the nations be gained? How secure the earthly throne through which his heavenly kingdom is to be advanced? There is but one reply. Only by falling down and worshipping the prince of this world, only by submitting to its spirit and maxims, only by stooping to such considerations and measures as may influence worldly minds, can he bring the powers of the world under him. The cross, which he has seen looming up in the divine majesty of humiliation and suffering at the very entrance into his kingdom, must be lowered before the ensigns of earthly greatness. The crown of righteousness, which shines with no earthly splendors and for no mortal eyes, must grow dim and pale before the dazzling glories of an earthly diadem. Those great words hereafter to be uttered, and to carry terror into the hearts of kings, "My kingdom is not of this world," the sublime and perfect trust, which in the very hour and power of darkness would not call in even the legions of obedient angels to enforce his authority or defend him from wrong, must give way to the appeal to human prejudices and passions, to the marshalling of hosts and the bloody caparisons of war, that so the Prince of Peace may establish his reign of peace upon the earth. The thought is one abhorrent to every principle of his nature and his religion. The motive appealed to was high and pure; the end was the very one for which he was born into the world; but the means were bad. Instantly the disguise of the tempter is torn off, and his dark purposes are unmasked. "If only thou wilt fall down and worship me." He repels alike the temptation and the tempter with an energy of expression which shows how much he had been disturbed by the thought, and how vehemently he abhors and detests the blasphemous condition which had been so artfully concealed within it. "Get thee hence, Satan; for it is written [Deut. vi. 13], Thou shalt worship the Lord thy God, and him only shalt thou serve." It is remarkable, that the only other instance in which our Saviour used this energetic expression of abhorrence occurred when, in reply to his prediction of the sufferings and shameful death which awaited him, Peter (Matt. xvi. 23) began to rebuke him in words which implied that the Messiah could not thus meanly and ignobly die. This was the one suggestion of evil, veiling itself in garments of light, which he met with the sharpest exhibition of sensibility and impatience.

Here the Devil left him, as St. Luke says, "for a season," and "behold, angels came and ministered unto him." There is nothing in either of the Evangelists to imply that the tempter came in bodily shape, or that such a presence was recognized in any other way than by the nature of the suggestions that were made. Whether there really is a prince of darkness, a malignant and mighty spirit, who had access to the mind of Jesus, with power to instil into it thoughts of evil under the guise of holiness and faith, is a question that we shall consider more fully hereafter. See xiii. 24–30. We know, however, too little of the unseen world of spiritual existences, and especially of the dark background of evil which lies behind all actual sin, to be able to speak with confidence on such a subject. How far that invisible realm of life may be peopled by spiritual beings good and bad, how far, if at all, the two orders of spiritual beings may be allowed to intermingle and carry on their various works, what limitations are assigned to their free action, and how the kingdoms of light and darkness may be arrayed one against the other, are questions which we cannot specifically answer. An evil man separated from the body is an evil spirit. There is then, so far as we can see, no more reason why evil spirits should not exist than that evil men should not. "There is nothing," says Mr. Norton, (Translation of the Gospels, Vol. II. pp. 61, 62,) "in the idea of dæmons being allowed to affect the minds and bodies of men irreconcilable with anything we see in the moral government of God. There is no proof *à priori* against such agency." It narrows down the world in which Jesus moved, far more than reason gives us any warrant for doing, to cut him off from connection with all existences, except God on the one hand, and man with the laws and forces of the material universe on the other. We cannot say how far the work of redemption in which he was engaged allied to itself the sympathy and employed the assistance and fellowship of angels, such as here came and ministered to him, or of holy men in their spiritual estate, such as Moses and Elijah who talked with him on the mountain of Transfiguration. Neither can we say how far his mighty work of redemption may have reached down through realms of spiritual darkness, and arrayed against him the active malignity of evil spirits as well as of wicked men. Without the recognition of such existences both above and below, passages in his life, such as the temptation, the transfiguration, the agony, the cry upon the cross, to which the wondering and trusting instincts of his followers have turned in all ages, lose much of their sublime moral significance, and their mysterious spiritual power. The victory which he gained in the wilderness was over something more than a passing thought of evil, which of itself could have had no power to shake his firm and sinless mind. It was the first of that series of struggles and victories through which he was to overthrow the very empire of darkness, and "destroy him that had the power of death."

While we thus view the temptation as one which actually occurred to Jesus in the suggestion of thoughts which for the time disturbed and agitated his spirit, we may see in it an epitome of the heaviest temptations that can assail his disciples, and of the way in which they should be overcome. There are the temptations of desire, — the love of enjoyment, the love of admiration, and the love of power, not presenting themselves to us in their coarse and selfish colors, as self-indulgence, vanity, and ambition, but clothing themselves in hues borrowed from heaven, and insinuating themselves into our hearts by false appeals to high and generous and holy ends. There is no sin in laboring to satisfy our bodily wants; but to concentrate our highest and best gifts on this work is to lose sight of the more essential truth, that we are to live not

by bread alone, but by all the influences and teachings of
God. In that way the soul will be impoverished by the low
and narrow acts to which it is devoted. On the other hand,
in a high and religious act, throwing ourselves as favored ones
of heaven on the special providence of God, that through the
wonder thus excited we may gain over advocates to his
cause, we may be led by hidden motives of personal vanity
unconsciously to tempt and provoke that Providence whose
leadings we ought to wait for and obey. Or while both the
end and the motive are right, in our impatient zeal to advance what we believe to be the cause of righteousness and
God, we may be tempted to stoop to unsanctified means, and
to consent for the time to worship even the Devil in his
disguise, if only he, with the powers which have been committed to him, will help us on in our work.

### 12–16. — MAKES HIS HOME IN CAPERNAUM.

From the way in which the narrative goes on, we should
suppose that the events recorded in the twelfth and following verses succeeded immediately to the Temptation. But
from the first five chapters of John, we find that a considerable period of time and some important acts here intervened.
Jesus, immediately after the Temptation, had come to John
the Baptist, who on seeing him pronounced to his followers
the remarkable words, "Behold the lamb of God, which
taketh away the sin of the world." Jesus then returned
to Galilee where his first miracle was performed, and afterwards came up to Jerusalem to the Passover. It was
probably while he was at Jerusalem that he heard of
John's imprisonment, which led him to hasten his return
to Galilee. On his way back to Galilee he had the conversation with the woman of Samaria, which is related in
the fourth chapter of John. He now left Nazareth and
took up his abode at Capernaum, which was near the
northwest corner of the Sea of Galilee, though its pre-

cise locality is not known with certainty. The quotation from the Old Testament is part of the remarkable passage already alluded to in the first chapter of Matthew, and might well be employed by the writer to call the attention of his Jewish readers to the extraordinary events which he is about to record as in some sense a fulfilment of the hardly less extraordinary prediction. Isa. viii. 22; ix. 1 – 7.

## 17 – 22. — THE CALL OF SIMON PETER AND ANDREW HIS BROTHER, AND OF JOHN AND HIS BROTHER JAMES.

The readiness with which this call was obeyed would indicate some previous knowledge of Jesus on their part, such as we find (John i. 35 – 42) that they actually had. The expectations excited by John the Baptist were kept intensely alive by Jesus, though he had not yet publicly declared himself to be the Messiah. His proclamation (iv. 17) is the same as that of the Baptist: " Repent; for the kingdom of heaven is at hand." But while he used and continued to use words familiar to the Jews as describing an earthly kingdom, he took them up, as he did so many other Jewish phrases, into a higher plane of thought, and gradually invested them with a higher meaning and a purer spirit. He did not institute a new religious language; but by a change of heart and life and thought through the great truths which he proclaimed, he would fill out old and familiar expressions with new ideas, and make them glow with the new light which he had thrown into them.

23 – 25. The nature of the diseases which are here specified, and the character of his miracles, will be more properly considered in the specific cases as they occur hereafter.

## NOTES.

THEN was Jesus led up of the Spirit into the wilderness, to be tempted of the devil. And when he had fasted forty days 2 and forty nights, he was afterward an hungered. And when 3 the tempter came to him, he said: If thou be the Son of God, command that these stones be made bread. But he answered 4 and said, It is written, "Man shall not live by bread alone,

---

**1. Led up of the Spirit**] Luke says: "And Jesus, being full of the Holy Ghost, returned from Jordan, and was led by the Spirit into the wilderness;" i. e. Jesus, filled with the spirit of God, and therefore desiring a season of solitude, was led up into the wilderness, where he might give himself up entirely to the thoughts and emotions which pressed upon him, and rapt him as it were in an ecstasy so absorbing that for the time all consideration of earthly things, even of his own bodily wants, was forgotten.

**the wilderness**] Probably the wild and mountainous region above Jericho, which, from the *forty days*, is called *Quarantaria*. Others suppose it to have been the Arabian desert of Sinai, where Moses and Elijah each fasted forty days. We do not think that Jesus attached any importance to such coincidences in time or place. His teachings and his life belong to a higher sphere of thought. **to be tempted**] *In order*, or *so as* to be tempted; the result put as if it had been the design. He was so filled with the spirit of God, that he sought for himself a solitary place where he might give himself up entirely to Him, and there, after his physical energies had become entirely exhausted, was a reaction in his mind.

**of the devil**] For this word see Dis. here and XIII., and Note xiii. 39. 2. **fasted forty days and forty nights**] In regard to the Oriental use of language in our day, Thomson, I. 132, says: "You may take this as a general canon of interpretation, that any amount much less than usual means 'nothing' in their dialect; and if you understand more by it, you are misled. In fact, their ordinary fasting is only abstaining from certain kinds of food, not from all, nor does the word convey any other idea to them." It *may*, however, be taken here in its stricter meaning. Luke says, iv. 2, "And in those days he did eat nothing."

3. **And when the tempter came to him**] He was hungry, and in his hunger the tempter came to him. Oppressed with hunger, his mind reverted to the words spoken at his baptism, "This is my beloved son;" and the thought was suggested to him, "If thou art really the Son of God, turn these stones into bread, and relieve thy necessities." But immediately he replies to the suggestion, from whatever source it may have come;

4. **It is written, Man shall not live by bread alone**] "*Even in bread* man lives not by bread only, for is not the life more than meat? Is not the word, the will, the power of God in everything; so that we do not inhale our very breath from the air [alone], but from the breath of God? . . . . . In the deepest meaning of the essential and only truth, all *things* in the world, after their kind, are only variously embodied words of the Creator, inasmuch as by his mighty word alone they are upheld in being. . . . . . What is man? Not the body with its earthly, animal soul, but the true and proper man, that is, the living spirit which came forth from God, which only lives in and by the spirit of God, which con-

MATTHEW IV. 81

but by every word that proceedeth out of the mouth of God."
5 Then the devil taketh him up into the holy city, and setteth
6 him on a pinnacle of the temple; and saith unto him, If thou
be the Son of God, cast thyself down; for it is written, "He
shall give his angels charge concerning thee; and in their
hands they shall bear thee up, lest at any time thou dash thy
7 foot against a stone." Jesus said unto him: It is written again,
8 "Thou shalt not tempt the Lord thy God." Again, the devil
taketh him up into an exceeding high mountain, and showeth
him all the kingdoms of the world, and the glory of them, and
9 saith unto him, All these things will I give thee, if thou wilt
10 fall down and worship me. Then saith Jesus unto him: Get
thee hence, Satan; for it is written, "Thou shalt worship the

---

tinually goes forth as *word* for the preservation of the creature. . . . . . But this leads us further and further; and '*not alone*' vindicates again the true life of man in God, against such as in their error cleave to any institution of the means of life, as if it was not God alone in them that gave them efficacy. As a general rule the word of God, externally written and preached, is given for the food of the inner man; but inasmuch as the living word of God in the word is the true word, thou mayest, if it be his will, without Scripture and preaching, live by his spirit; without intercourse with brethren be connected with the Church; even without the physical bread of the sacrament, receive, nevertheless, tho heavenly bread. Every manna given by God in the creaturely form is a witness that points beyond itself to the immediate outgoing of God's life for the life of man." Stier. 5.

**pinnacle of the temple**] πτε-ρύγιον, *wing*, "spoken of the highest point of the temple buildings, probably the elevation of the middle portion of the triple portico or colonnade along the southern wall, which at its eastern end impended over the valley of Kidron; so that if from its roof one attempted to look down into the gulf below, his eyes became dark and dizzy before they could penetrate the immense depth; Jos.

Ant. XV. 11. 5. The actual height above the bottom of the valley was probably not less than three hundred and ten feet." Robinson.

7. "Wherein consists the tempting of God on the part of man? It is the complete opposite of the seeking in faith, of the waiting upon God in the obedience and confidence of trust, a self-willed demand of the mighty help of God; and consequently unbelief, disobedience, and distrust are its innermost principles. . . . . Every sin in its innermost principle is, properly speaking, a tempting and challenging of God; since he who should obey tests the Almighty whether the way of his own self-will shall not prosper. But then, particularly, when the unbelief and disobedience of self-will presses forward in what is false presumption, though seemingly only a ·firm confidence in promised assistance, as if God must and should hearken to it; this is the marked aggravation of sin, to which Satan here allures." Stier.

10. **Get thee hence, Satan**] The term *Satan* may here be applied to the evil suggestion, as it is in xvi. 23. **and him only**] Deut. vi. 13; x. 20. The quotation, like most of the quotations in Matthew, is from the Septuagint, and not from the Hebrew, where the word meaning *only* is not to be found.

11. **Then the devil leaveth**

Lord thy God, and him only shalt thou serve." Then the devil 11
leaveth him; and, behold, angels came and ministered unto
him.

Now when Jesus had heard that John was cast into prison, 12
he departed into Galilee. And leaving Nazareth, he came 13
and dwelt in Capernaum, which is upon the sea-coast, in the
borders of Zabulon and Nephthalim; that it might be fulfilled 14

---

**him, and, behold, angels came and ministered unto him**] The presence of the evil spirit and the ministry of the angels rest here on the same authority. But we must not confound our popular idea of the devil with that of the Evangelist. Still less are we to confound with it the philosophical idea borrowed from the East, which makes the prince of darkness the almost equal antagonist of God. Whatever else they may teach on this subject, the Gospels lend no countenance to any such doctrine as this. The most that can be legitimately inferred from them is, that there are evil spirits, and one at their head, "the devil and his angels," xxiv. 41, who, within certain limits allowed by God, may have the power of suggesting evil thoughts. There is nothing in this chapter to show that Satan appeared in bodily form or to the outward eye, even if we suppose the language to mean that he was personally present. All that is implied, even on that supposition, is, that Satan, seeing our Saviour's helpless condition, —

"Ill wast thou shrouded then, O patient Son of God!"—

took advantage of his weariness, exhaustion, and consequent depression, and suggested to him the thoughts here recorded, as if they had been the spontaneous suggestions of his own mind. There is nothing which proves it to have been the writer's intention to say that he transported Jesus bodily to the temple and mountain. The most that can be inferred is, that he took him away in thought or in spirit, presenting to him these objects and suggestions so vividly that the whole transaction seemed as if it had actually passed before him. "The temptation of Jesus," says Olshausen, "stands as one of those decisive events, such as are met with in a lower degree in common life also, and which, by the determination that we take in them, give a direction to the whole after-life. The Saviour here appears as standing between the two worlds of light and darkness. As the hostile powers fled, heavenly powers surrounded him, and joined in celebrating the victory of good." "Since," he continues, "the temptation of Jesus took place in the depth of his inward life without witnesses, we must regard the narration of Jesus as the only source of information and testimony to its reality." 13. **And leaving Nazareth, he came and dwelt in Capernaum**] "Nazareth, Kefr, Kenna, Kânâ, and all the regions adjacent, where our Lord lived. and where he commenced his ministry, and by his miracles 'manifested forth his glory,' were within the limits of Zebulon; but Capernaum, Chorazin, and Bethsaida were in Naphtali. It was this latter tribe that was 'by the way of the sea beyond Jordan, Galilee of the Gentiles.' Zebulon did not touch the sea at any point, but the territories of these two tribes met at the northeast corner of the Büttauf, not far from Kânâ, and within these two tribes thus united our Lord passed nearly the whole of his wonderful life." Thomson, II. 122, 123. 14, 15. **which was spoken by Esaias**] The passage here following is a free quotation from Isa. ix. 1, 2. Dr. Noyes's translation from the Hebrew is as follows:—

15 which was spoken by Esaias the prophet, saying: "The land of Zabulon, and the land of Nephthalim, by the way of the 16 sea, beyond Jordan, Galilee of the Gentiles, the people which sat in darkness saw great light; and to them which sat in the 17 region and shadow of death light is sprung up."——From that time Jesus began to preach, and to say: Repent; for the kingdom of heaven is at hand.

18 And Jesus, walking by the Sea of Galilee, saw two brethren, Simon called Peter, and Andrew his brother, casting a net 19 into the sea; for they were fishers. And he saith unto them: 20 Follow me, and I will make you fishers of men. And they 21 straightway left their nets, and followed him. And going on from thence, he saw other two brethren, James the son of Zebedee, and John his brother, in a ship with Zebedee their father, 22 mending their nets; and he called them. And they immediately left the ship and their father, and followed him.

23 And Jesus went about all Galilee, teaching in their synagogues, and preaching the gospel of the kingdom, and healing all manner of sickness and all manner of disease among the 24 people. And his fame went throughout all Syria; and they brought unto him all sick people, that were taken with divers diseases and torments, and those which were possessed with

---

1 "But the darkness shall not remain where now is distress;
Of old he brought the land of Zebulon and the land of Nephtali into contempt;
In future times shall he bring the land of the sea, beyond the Jordan, the circle of the Gentiles, into honor.

2 "The people that walk in darkness behold a great light;
They who dwell in the land of deathlike shade,
Upon them a light shineth.

5 "For the greaves of the warrior armed for the conflict,
And the war-garments rolled in blood,
Shall be burned; yea, they shall be food for the fire.

6 "For to us a child is born,
To us a son is given,
And the government shall be upon his shoulder,
And he shall be called
Wonderful, counsellor, mighty potentate;
Everlasting father, prince of peace.

7 "His domain shall be great.
And peace without end shall rest Upon the throne of David and his kingdom.
He shall fix and establish it Through justice and equity,
Henceforth and forever."

It is difficult to suppose that this language was intended to express nothing more than the temporal prosperity of the land under any one of its kings. 23. **in their synagogues**] "Synagogues are not mentioned till after the captivity. See Jos. Ant., XIX. 6. 3; De Bel. Jud., VII. 3. 3. In the time of Jesus they were spread all over Palestine, as well as among the dispersed Jews; in Jerusalem there are said to have been four hundred and eighty of them." Olshausen. The officers of the synagogue appear to have been, —1. the ruler of the synagogue, Luke viii. 49; xiii. 14, who had the care of public order, and the arrange-

devils, and those which were lunatic, and those that had the palsy; and he healed them. And there followed him great multitudes of people from Galilee, and from Decapolis, and from Jerusalem, and from Judæa, and from beyond Jordan. 25

---

ment of the service; 2. the elders, who with the ruler formed a sort of council; 3. the substitute or angel of the assembly, — *legatus* or *angelus ecclesiæ*, — who was the reader of prayers, &c.; 4. the ὑπηρέτης, or chapel clerk, to prepare the books for reading, to sweep, &c. There were seats, the first row of which appear to have been coveted, Matt. xxiii. 6; a pulpit for the reader, lamps, and a chest for keeping the sacred book." From this account it is easy to see how the Christian Church, with its service, grew out of the Jewish synagogue.

## CHAPTER V.

INTRODUCTION TO THE SERMON ON THE MOUNT.

THE precise order of events is not observed by St. Matthew. He does not distinctly point out the time when the Sermon on the Mount was given. After a passage, iv. 23 – 25, which, in its general terms applying to Christ's manner of life and the extent of territory which he visited, may cover no small part of his ministry in Galilee, this particular discourse is specified; but, except what might be inferred from the part of the narrative in which it occurs, no reference is made to the time when it was given. It is very much as if the writer had said, Jesus went for a considerable period of time through an extensive region, performing miraculous cures and attended by great multitudes of people. On one occasion, when he saw an immense concourse of people who had come from Galilee and Decapolis, from Jerusalem and Judæa, and from beyond the Jordan, he went up into a mountain. Luke vi. 12 – 18, on the other hand, indicates the time and the circumstances. It was just after Jesus had chosen his twelve disciples. He had retired into a mountain to spend the night in prayer. And in the morning, having set apart his twelve disciples, he came down to a level spot on the mountain, and there, when great multitudes had come to him, and he had healed their sick, " he lifted up his eyes on his disciples," and, addressing himself particularly to them, uttered these words. The fact of his speaking particularly to his disciples must be borne in mind, in order to understand the extent and bearing of some of the directions. Though containing principles applicable to all his followers in all ages, they were primarily addressed to the Apostles, and have some specific rules which apply particularly to them and to those who may be situated as they were.

Jesus had as yet made no public proclamation of the character of his kingdom. The multitudes were gathering round him in eager expectation of the time when he would raise the standard under which they should march on to victory and universal dominion. They thought only of an outward, visible kingdom, whose throne should be established by overthrowing existing governments, and placing the Jewish people, under their divine leader, at the head of all the nations of the earth. The visions of warlike conquest, of earthly glory and power, which had attended them through so many centuries, sweetening the cup of present sorrow, defeat, and captivity with the hope of future triumph over all their enemies, were now about to be realized. The long-expected Messiah had made his advent at last. Thousands were thronging about him, anxiously awaiting from him the signal for their national deliverance. Under circumstances of extraordinary solemnity he was now about to inaugurate his kingdom. The excitement is intense and overpowering.

The terms used by the Evangelists Matthew and Luke would seem, as Tholuck and Olshausen say, to indicate the peculiar solemnity of the occasion. "He lifted up his eyes on his disciples," as if aware that the great crisis in man's history had come, and that he was now about to proclaim for the first time a kingdom such as never before had been established on earth. The expression, "having opened his mouth," implies a previous silence, in which the impatient expectations of the people were painfully suppressed. At last he opened his mouth, and what are the words which come to them? They are ready for deeds of violence. They would take up arms to throw off the Roman yoke. They have come to receive the benediction of their great deliverer before enlisting under his banner for the wars in which he is to lead them on to what the prophet Daniel had described when he said, vii. 14, "There was given him dominion and glory and a kingdom, that all people, nations, and languages should serve him: his dominion is an everlasting dominion, which shall not pass away, and his kingdom, that which shall not be destroyed."

### 3 - 16. — THE BEATITUDES.

But all these expectations, all their hopes of external dominion and glory, are thrown down and destroyed forever by the first words that fall from the lips of him to whom they had looked as their Messiah. His benedictions are not for the mighty men of war, for those who make their way to positions of wealth and power, and who are honored among men. But, "Blessed are the poor in spirit; Blessed are they that mourn; Blessed are they who hunger and thirst after righteousness; Blessed are the meek; Blessed are the merciful, the pure in heart, the peacemakers." And, as if this were not enough to crush all the worldly hopes with which they had come to him, he still more pointedly adds, "Blessed are ye when men shall revile you, and persecute you, and shall say all manner of evil against you falsely, for my sake." Here, in his prophetic mind, seeing as already present the spiritual victories which are to be gained through obloquy, persecution, and death, he breaks out, for the moment, into a lyric strain of exultation such as we find only on two or three other occasions in his life. He calls on his followers to rejoice, and be exceeding glad. He sees in them even now the grand conservative element of society, the salt of the earth, which, amid the general corruption and decay, shall save the world from death. Amid the almost universal darkness they are to be the light of the world, — a light so shining before men that they, seeing their good works, shall glorify their Father who is in heaven.

And from that day to this how true have these words of Jesus been in their application to those who have done most for the advancement of his kingdom! "Holy men," says Mr. Norton, Tracts on Christianity, p. 144, "have suffered and died to procure for us the privileges which we enjoy. . . . . . They have followed in the track of pure splendor, in which their great Master ascended to heaven. . . . . . There is something very solemn and sublime in the feeling produced by considering how differently these men have been estimated by their contemporaries, from the manner in which they are regarded by God. We perceive the appeal which lies from the ignorance, the folly, and the iniquity of man to the throne of Eternal Justice. A storm of calumny and reviling pursued them through life, and continued, when they could no longer feel it, to beat upon their graves. But it is no matter. They have gone where all who have suffered, and all who have triumphed, in the same noble cause, receive their reward; but where the wreath of the martyr is more glorious than that of the conqueror." This triumph through death, this crown of martyrdom more joyful and glorious than all the insignia of earthly greatness or success, was first announced by Jesus Christ in the Sermon on the Mount, and held up by him as the last and highest of the Beatitudes.

## 17–48. — FULFILLING THE LAW AND THE PROPHETS.

But this mode of teaching looks like an attempt to do away with the old dispensation, or to make it of no account. Such a purpose would prejudice against him, not Pharisees alone, but even the humble-minded and devout Jews who have been waiting for his coming. He therefore declares that he has not come to destroy, but to fulfil, the law and the prophets. "Till heaven and earth shall pass away, not one jot or one tittle [*jot*, the least letter in the Hebrew alphabet, and *tittle*, a slight mark or corner of a letter], not the smallest letter or stroke, shall pass away from the law, till all be fulfilled." But he did destroy the ceremonial law of Moses. In what sense then did he come to fulfil it? In that sense, we may reply, in which it was intended from the beginning that it should be fulfilled. It came from God. It embodied its holy principles and its prophetic life in outward ceremonies adapted to a rude and idolatrous age. It spoke to the coarse, dull minds it met, through such a language as they could understand, of symbols, types, and sacrificial observances. It went on from age to age, with judges and prophets, unfolding its deeper meaning with the advancing intelligence of the nation, writing out its expanding history of obedience and disobedience with their swiftly following retributions, in the progress of the race, pouring out its devotions in hymns and psalms and spiritual songs, giving utterance to its hopes in prophecies which flashed on with their sublime anticipations through distant centuries, till at length all law and history, hymn and prophecy, should be taken up into the life towards which they had always been pointing, and find their fulfilment in the spiritual religion, *the kingdom of God*, which Jesus came to establish on earth, and which in its saintly fellowship reaches up from earth to heaven. Thus, the law, according to its sacred and original design, was not destroyed but fulfilled, when in the fulness of time it left behind its now wearisome and ineffectual forms, and took up its sinless abode in Jesus Christ, condensing its instructions into his words, appealing to men through him as a divine life, and concentrating into his death the infinite treasures of divine love, mercy, and forgiveness, which had been poorly symbolized to the burdened heart of man by the ark of the covenant, the mercy-seat, and the sacrifices, in the wilderness or the temple, through so many centuries.

Jesus fulfils the law and the prophets first of all by taking up and condensing into his own words the life-giving spirit which pervaded them. Thus, as Cyprian long ago remarked, he has sometimes given one or two precepts, e. g.

Matt. vii. 12, or xxii. 37 – 40, on which, as he said, "hang all the law and the prophets." In this way he shows in the Sermon on the Mount how the law and the prophets are to be fulfilled, not by a literal, heartless, and formal observance; for unless their "righteousness," i. e. in this connection, their obedience to the law, should be something more than that of the Scribes who taught and the Pharisees who formally observed its precepts, they could not enter into the kingdom of the heavens.

Then, by a few illustrations which go to the very root of the matter, in a manner more masterly than anything else in the range of legal or metaphysical analysis, he seizes on the principle which underlies the form and gives its meaning to the enactment, and shows how the law, defeated often and made of none effect by an obedience which is confined to a literal observance of its precepts, is really to be fulfilled only by obedience to its spirit and intention.

The law, 21, forbids the act of murder. But do they therefore keep the law in its purest intention who observe this precept and yet cherish an angry, contemptuous, or malicious spirit, which is in itself the soul and essence of murder?

The law, 27, forbids adultery, and so far has respect to our human weakness and hardness of heart, xix. 8, as to allow the separation of man and wife, provided that certain legal forms are observed. But the true intention of the law, which looks to chastity as belonging to the soul as well as to the body, goes beyond the outward act. It would pluck out the eye that tempts to sin, cut off the offending hand, and allow nothing but death, or that violation of the great and essential law of conjugal fidelity which is in itself a dissolution of the marriage tie, to interfere with the permanency of that relation, which, as an Apostle has said, Eph. v. 32, "is a great mystery," which enters the inmost springs of social and domestic purity, and touches at its source the fountain of life to every child that comes into the world.

The law, 33, forbids perjury. But obedience to this negative precept does not answer the intention of the law, which finds its fulfilment only in such a state of inward integrity and reverence for God and the truth, that a man's word will be as sacred as an oath; and consequently oaths themselves in the dealing of Christians with one another will be superfluous, and therefore, according to the spirit of the third commandment, profane. Especially will this principle cut off those foolish forms of oaths then common among the Jews, which were made for evasion and dishonesty, and which, as Jesus declared in another place (Matt. xxiii. 16 – 22), are sacrilegious and profane. "If," says Philo Judæus, " a man must swear, and is so inclined, let him add, if he pleases, not indeed the highest name of all, and the most important cause of all things, but the earth, the sun, the stars, the heaven, the universal world," &c., &c., (Bohn's Philo Judæus, III. p. 256,) so as to evade the third commandment. There does not seem to be any reference here, in our Saviour's words, to judicial oaths.

The law, 38, *allows* retaliation, "an eye for an eye, and a tooth for a tooth." But he who has been wronged is not *bound* thus to avenge himself. The highest intention of the law, the principle of justice which by the injured party is to be blended with mercy, finds its fulfilment, not in a literal observance of the precept and the revengeful spirit thus cherished, but in that state of mind which would rather suffer evil than inflict violence in .return, and submit even to an unreasonable demand rather than forcibly to resist it. While the principle here involved is to be of universal application, the specific directions were undoubtedly intended particularly for the disciples. Nor even by them, as Jesus showed in his own conduct, John xviii. 23, when smitten on the face, were they to be literally observed.

The pure intention of the law, 43, which, in commanding to love our neighbor, would seem also to command us to hate our enemies, is fulfilled only in such an extension of the literal precept as may embrace all mankind, and lead us to love even our enemies, and pray for those who persecute and wrong us, that so we may strive to be perfect even as our Father in heaven is perfect, who causeth his sun to shine and his rains to descend on the evil and the good.

This train of thought runs through the whole Sermon on the Mount. There is no repeal of the old law, but a more thorough application and universal extension of its principles. If it left many of its forms and specific rules behind, it was only that it might be fulfilled, according to its original and divine intention, by being taken up into a higher realm, and, as a spiritual power and influence, establishing its kingdom in the heart, and reaching the fountains of thought and life. The Jewish altar and temple must be overthrown. The smoke of the morning and evening sacrifice shall no longer rise from Mount Moriah. The Jews shall be dispersed through all the nations, and the Mosaic observances, as living institutions, be swept away from the earth. But till heaven and earth pass away, not one iota of the law in its essential characteristics shall pass away, till all its purposes are fulfilled. It came from God. It is the source of all true order and harmony in civil communities, and in the souls of men. It would lead by its divine precepts and its divine life through all the constraints and oppositions and changes of our mortal condition to the attainment of peace and harmony and spiritual joy. This law of God Jesus found stifled beneath endless traditions and restraints, like Lazarus in his tomb. He called it into life. He loosed it from its grave-clothes, and sent it forth a free, beneficent, and living spirit, with words of holy benediction, forgiveness, life, and peace to weary, sorrowing, and sinful hearts, who were sitting in darkness, and waiting for the kingdom of God. And in whatever age the Pharisees among Christian sects have sought by their traditionary doctrines or forms to bind and bury it, and to build up in its place a system of ceremonial observances and articles of faith which lead to superstition and hypocrisy, the simple words and acts of Jesus, the Gospels in their simplicity and power, and especially this great Sermon on the Mount, are always the most terrible as they are the most effectual protest against them.

## NOTES.

AND seeing the multitudes, he went up into a mountain; and
2 when he was set, his disciples came unto him. And he opened
3 his mouth, and taught them, saying: Blessed are the poor in
4 spirit, for theirs is the kingdom of Heaven. Blessed are they

---

1. **a mountain**] This is supposed to be a mountain known as Keerun Hattin, the Horns of Hattin; but there is no certainty in regard to it. The place most probably was on the west side of the Lake of Galilee. 2. In regard to the disappointment caused to all the Jewish prepossessions and ambitious hopes by these Beatitudes, Dr. Palfrey says: "I think we may see that Jesus designed to break the force of the blow, by hinting that the view which he was presenting was not without warrant from those same Old Testament Scriptures which it seemed to oppose. To this end not a little of the phraseology employed by him on this occasion appears to have been assumed." Among the instances which he gives, compare Matt. v. 3 with Ps. li. 17; Isa. lxvi. 2, v. 4, with Ps. cxxvi. 5; Isa. lxi. 2, v. 5, with Ps. xxxvii. 11, v. 6, with Ps. xvii. 15, v. 7, with Ps. xxxvii. 25, 26, xli. 1. 3. **Blessed are the poor in spirit**] Not the poor in this world's goods, though the idea is founded on a reference to them, but they who so feel their spiritual wants as to long for the riches of God's spiritual kingdom; for theirs, in a peculiar sense, is the kingdom of God. It is not improbable, as has been suggested, that "our Lord may have had a reference to the poor and subjugated Jewish people around him, once members of the theocracy, and now expectants of the Messiah's temporal kingdom, and, from their condition and hopes, taken occasion to preach to them the deeper spiritual truth." 4. This verse carries on the same idea, and gives its benediction, not only to the poor, but to those who have such a consciousness of spiritual loneliness that they mourn as in a state of bereavement, "for they shall be comforted." To them the Comforter shall come. The solitude in which they mourn shall be filled by Him whose absence they lament. And as the poor and sorrowing, in opposition to the proud and self-satisfied, are blessed, so also, 5, *are the meek*, in opposition to the wilful and violent; for they (Ps. xxxvii. 11) shall inherit the earth, or *the land*. The expression " to inherit the land" originally applied to the promised land, became at length a common term to denote the full enjoyment of the Divine blessing. As the poor in spirit shall enjoy the kingdom of God spiritually present in their souls, so the meek, in the renunciation of wilfulness and violence, shall enjoy it also in its outward gifts. Meekness

that mourn; for they shall be comforted. Blessed are the 5
meek; for they shall inherit the earth. Blessed are they 6
which do hunger and thirst after righteousness; for they shall
be filled. Blessed are the merciful; for they shall obtain 7
mercy. Blessed are the pure in heart; for they shall see 8
God. Blessed are the peacemakers; for they shall be called 9
the children of God. Blessed are they which are persecuted 10
for righteousness' sake; for theirs is the kingdom of Heaven.
Blessed are ye, when men shall revile you, and persecute you, 11
and shall say all manner of evil against you, falsely, for my
sake. Rejoice, and be exceeding glad; for great is your re- 12
ward in heaven; for so persecuted they the prophets which
were before you.——Ye are the salt of the earth. But if the 13
salt have lost his savor, wherewith shall it be salted? It is
thenceforth good for nothing, but to be cast out, and to be trodden under foot of men. Ye are the light of the world. A 14
city that is set on an hill cannot be hid; neither do men light 15
a candle, and put it under a bushel, but on a candlestick; and
it giveth light unto all that are in the house. Let your light 16
so shine before men, that they may see your good works, and
glorify your Father which is in heaven.——Think not that I 17

---

is a quality of mind which disarms opposition, admits us to the confidence and affections of others, and thus, enabling us to enjoy whatever is most to be desired in the intercourse of life, leads us truly to inherit the land. The expression reaches on also to the period when the violent shall be put down, and the meek prevail and triumph.

**11. for my sake**] "Where selfishness prevails, there cannot be such suffering as bestows happiness. But where suffering is incurred for the faith's sake, and is borne in faith, it perfects the inward life, and awakens the desire for eternity." Olshausen. **13. if the salt**] If *you*, the very salt of the earth, should lose your virtue, how can the deficiency be made up? "It is a well-known fact that the salt of this country [Palestine], when in contact with the ground, or exposed to rain and sun, does become insipid and useless. It is not only good for nothing, but it actually destroys all fertility wherever it is thrown. "It is cast out" and "trodden under foot;" so troublesome is this corrupted salt, that it is carefully swept up, carried forth, and thrown into the street. There is no place about the house, yard, or garden where it can be tolerated." And so, our Saviour says, it is with those who, being teachers and preachers of righteousness, lose their zeal and fall away from the faith. **16. So**] As the city on a hill, as the candle on a candlestick, so, i. e. in like manner, let your light shine. **17. to fulfil**] One of the Fathers compares the law to a *sketch*, which the painter does not destroy, but fills out. It means to *complete* or *carry out*. So, xxiii. 32, "Fill ye up [fulfil] then the measure of your fathers," i. e. complete the work which they have begun. So here, to fulfil the law and the prophets is

am come to destroy the law or the prophets; I am not come to
18 destroy, but to fulfil. For verily I say unto you, till heaven
and earth pass, one jot or one tittle shall in no wise pass from
19 the law, till all be fulfilled. Whosoever therefore shall break
one of these least commandments, and shall teach men so, he
shall be called the least in the kingdom of Heaven; but whosoever shall do and teach them, the same shall be called great in
20 the kingdom of Heaven. For I say unto you, that, except your
righteousness shall exceed the righteousness of the Scribes and
Pharisees, ye shall in no case enter into the kingdom of Heaven.
21 Ye have heard that it was said by them of old time, "Thou
shalt not kill; and whosoever shall kill shall be in danger of
22 the judgment." But I say unto you, that whosoever is angry
with his brother, without a cause, shall be in danger of the

---

to complete their work, — to carry
out and finish their design, — though
such a fulfilment or completion
should be accomplished by leaving
their temporary provisions behind,
and absorbing their essential life
and truth into the higher dispensation for which they were intended
to prepare the way, and by which
they are apparently superseded.

20. **Scribes**] "Persons devoted to
the work of reading and expounding the law, whose office seems first
to have become frequent after the
return from Babylon. They generally appear in the New Testament
in connection with the Pharisees;
but it appears from Acts xxiii. 9
that there were Scribes attached
to the other sects also. In Matt.
xxi. 15 they appear with the chief
priests; but it is in the temple
where they acted as a sort of police.
. . . . . Their authority, as expounders of the law, is recognized
by our Lord himself, Matt. xxii. 1,
2; their adherence to the oral traditionary exposition proved, Matt. xv.
1; the respect in which they were
held by the people shown, Luke xx.
46; their existence indicated, not
only in Jerusalem, but also in Galilee, Luke v. 17; and in Rome, Josephus, Ant. XVIII. 3. 5." Alford.

22. **without a cause**] is omitted
by Tischendorf, and is undoubtedly
an interpolation. There are three
degrees of guilt here indicated: 1.
anger against a brother; 2. anger
venting itself in a term of contempt,
*Raca, thou vain, empty one;* 3. anger,
using a still more bitter term of reproach, $μωρέ$, either a Greek word
signifying "thou fool," or a Hebrew
word signifying "rebel," and the
very word for uttering which Moses
and Aaron were debarred from entering the land of promise; *Hear
now, ye rebels*, Num. xx. 10. The
punishment due to each of these
three degrees of guilt is graduated,
— 1. by "*the judgment*," or local and
inferior court; 2. by "*the council*,"
or Sanhedrim, the highest legal
Jewish tribunal; and 3. and severest
of all, by "*the Gehenna of fire*."
"the end of the malefactor, whose
corpse, thrown into the valley of
Hinnom, was devoured by the
worm, or the flame." *Gehenna*,
the valley of Hinnom, or Tophet,
running down from the west on the
southern border of Jerusalem to
the valley of Jehoshaphat. It has
been supposed that the allusion
here is to the offal from the city,
which was thrown out into this
valley to be consumed by fire. But
Dr. Robinson says that there is no
evidence of such fires having been
kept up in the valley. "Here," he
says, "the ancient Israelites estab-

judgment; and whosoever shall say to his brother, Raca, shall be in danger of the council; but whosoever shall say, Thou fool, shall be in danger of hell fire. Therefore if thou bring 23 thy gift to the altar, and there rememberest that thy brother hath aught against thee; leave there thy gift before the altar, 24 and go thy way; first be reconciled to thy brother, and then come and offer thy gift. Agree with thine adversary quickly, 25 whiles thou art in the way with him; lest at any time the adversary deliver thee to the judge, and the judge deliver thee to the officer, and thou be cast into prison. Verily I say unto 26 thee, thou shalt by no means come out thence, till thou hast paid the uttermost farthing. Ye have heard that it was said 27 by them of old time, "Thou shalt not commit adultery." But I say unto you, that whosoever looketh on a woman to lust 28 after her hath committed adultery with her already in his heart. And if thy right eye offend thee, pluck it out, and cast it from 29 thee; for it is profitable for thee that one of thy members should perish, and not that thy whole body should be cast into hell. And if thy right hand offend thee, cut it off, and cast it 30 from thee; for it is profitable for thee that one of thy members should perish, and not that thy whole body should be cast into hell. It hath been said, "Whosoever shall put away his wife, 31 let him give her a writing of divorcement." But I say unto 32 you, that whosoever shall put away his wife, saving for the cause of fornication, causeth her to commit adultery; and who-

---

lished the idolatrous worship of Moloch, to whom they burned infants in sacrifice. 2 Kings xxiii. 10; Jer. vii. 31. It was apparently in allusion to this detested and abominable fire that the later Jews employed the name of this valley (Gehenna) to denote the place of future punishment, or the fires of Tartarus."

23. "It is not what complaints we have against others that we are to consider at such a time, but what they have against us; not what ground *we have given* for complaint, but what complaints *they*, as matter of fact, *make* against us." Alford.

25. **thine adversary**] he to whom thou hast given offence.

**Whiles thou art in the way with him**] to the judge, i. e. before the case is brought before a public tribunal. This is the literal sense: it involves another and higher meaning; *the way of all the earth*, through which we are journeying to the judgments of eternity, and the word "*quickly*" alluding to the swiftness of the passage, and the shortness of life. 29, 30. **If thy right eye, ..... if thy right hand, offend thee**] i. e. tempt thee to sin. We are to destroy the first buddings of evil desire, though it should be by the sacrifice of what is most dear and useful to us. There must be no dallying or parleying with the temptations of passion. Whatever the sacrifice, we must turn away at the very beginning. He who hesitates is lost.

soever shall marry her that is divorced committeth adultery.
33 Again, ye have heard that it hath been said by them of old
time, "Thou shalt not forswear thyself, but shalt perform unto
34 the Lord thine oaths." But I say unto you, Swear not all;
35 neither by heaven, for it is God's throne; nor by the earth, for
it is his footstool; neither by Jerusalem, for it is the city of the
36 great King; neither shalt thou swear by thy head, because
37 thou canst not make one hair white or black. But let your
communication be, Yea, yea; Nay, nay; for whatsoever is

---

**32. causeth her to commit adultery**] How so? By putting her away for any other cause than the one herein specified, the man declares the whole previous marriage to have been unlawful, impure, and adulterous, and thus makes her guilty of adultery. Any other reason for divorce than the one specified, which is in itself a dissolution of marriage, would invalidate the whole previous marriage, and prove the parties living under its sanction to have been in that very act guilty of adultery. We do not find the difficulty by which most commentators, from St. Augustine downwards, are embarrassed in their interpretation of this passage. The man who unjustly repudiates his wife, does not oblige her to marry again, and therefore does not, in that way, cause her to commit adultery. And yet this is what is usually regarded as the true interpretation. **And whosoever shall marry her that is divorced, committeth adultery.**] The only person who, according to our Saviour, is properly and really divorced, is she who has been guilty of fornication, and he who marries *her* thereby incurs the guilt of adultery. The intention of this, and of the other passage in which Jesus speaks of divorce (see xix. 8, 9), is to render the marriage relation as indissoluble as possible,—1. by forbidding divorce except for a single cause; and, 2. by forbidding the woman who is thus put away, and the man who puts away his wife for any other cause than that, to marry again. But how is it with one who, through the criminal conduct of the other party, is divorced? There is no authority given for such an one to marry again, though it is not specifically forbidden. The Roman Church forbids such marriages; the Greek and Protestant churches allow them. The spirit, if not the letter, of our Saviour's instructions would seem to discountenance them. 33, 35. " Men had learned to think that, if only God's name were avoided, there was no irreverence in the frequent oaths, by heaven, by the earth, by Jerusalem, by their own heads, and these brought in on the slightest need, or on no need at all; just as now-a-days the same lingering half-respect for the Holy Name will often cause men, who would not be wholly profane, to substitute for that name sounds that nearly resemble, but are not exactly it, or the name, it may be, of some heathen deity." Trench. This whole matter of blasphemously trifling and evasive oaths is again powerfully brought forward in Ch. xxiii. 16–22; and that passage may be taken as the best commentary on this: "Ye say, whosoever shall swear by the temple, it is nothing;" but, in fact, "whoso shall swear by the temple, sweareth by it, and by Him that dwelleth therein. And he that shall swear by heaven, sweareth by the throne of God, and by Him that sitteth thereon." 36. Thou must not, then, swear even by thine own head; for it is not thine own: thou canst not change one hair white or black. It, also, is the " creature of God, whose destinies

## MATTHEW V.

more than these cometh of evil. Ye have heard that it hath 38 been said, "An eye for an eye, and a tooth for a tooth." But I 39 say unto you, that ye resist not evil ; but whosoever shall smite thee on thy right cheek, turn to him the other also; and if any 40 man will sue thee at the law, and take away thy coat, let him have thy cloak also; and whosoever shall compel thee to go a 41 mile, go with him twain. Give to him that asketh thee ; and 42

and changes are in God's hand; so that every oath is an appeal to God." **37. cometh of evil]** Among true men more is not needed, and whatever more than a simple affirmation is required by men is because of the wickedness among them. Among you, in your dealings with one another, this necessity ought not to exist. **38. an eye for an eye]** This rule, Ex. xxi. 24, as St. Augustine has said, was not intended as an incitement, but as a limit to private revenge; not as a command stimulating men to do so much, but as a command forbidding them to exact more. The command, however, in its original connection, is to the wrong-doer, "Then thou shalt give life for life; eye for eye." **39. That ye resist not evil]** τῷ πονηρῷ, the evil or wicked man, who is doing you a wrong. It is better to submit to a wrong-doer than to retort by violence. The literal turning of the left cheek, of course, is not intended. When Jesus, John xviii. 22, 23, was thus smitten, he made no violent resistance, but, without turning the other cheek, mildly remonstrated against the wrong. His example is the best possible commentary on his words. **40. sue thee at the law]** From personal violence, Jesus comes to a case of legal oppression, and applies the same principle there. Rather than resist the legal decision, which commands him to give up his *coat*, an inner and less costly garment, as a pledge for what he is charged with owing, the Christian is even to give up his cloak, the outer and more valuable garment, which, according to the law, Ex. xxii. 26, could not legally be kept over night, because it was used as a coverlet by the poor at night. **41. whosoever shall compel]** "This language is taken from a Persian custom. A courier travelling on the king's business could lawfully impress into his service men, horses, ships, boats, or any vehicle, to accelerate his journey. The same custom prevailed under the Roman governors or Tetrarchs." Livermore. The Jews complained of this practice, on the part of the Romans, as a heavy grievance. Jos. Ant., XIII. 2. 3. "We learn, from coins and inscriptions, that the couriers in the service of the Roman government had the privilege of travelling through the provinces free of expense, and of calling on the villagers to forward their carriages and baggage to the next town. Under a despotic government this became a cruel grievance. Every Roman of high rank claimed the same privilege; the horses were unyoked from the plough to be harnessed to the rich man's carriage. It was the most galling injustice which the provinces suffered. We have an inscription on the frontier town of Egypt and Nubia, mentioning its petition for a redress of this grievance ; and a coin of Nerva's reign records its abolition in Italy. Our Lord could give no stronger exhortation to patient humility than by advising his Syrian hearers, instead of resenting the demand for one stage's 'vehiculation,' to go willingly a second time." Eclectic Review. **42. Give to him that asketh]** The same spirit of kindness and submission, which is to be exercised toward the enemy

43 from him that would borrow of thee turn not thou away. Ye
have heard that it hath been said, "Thou shalt love thy neigh-
44 bor, and hate thine enemy." But I say unto you, love your
enemies, bless them that curse you, do good to them that hate
you, and pray for them which despitefully use you and perse-
45 cute you; that ye may be the children of your Father which is
in heaven; for he maketh his sun to rise on the evil and on the
46 good, and sendeth rain on the just and on the unjust. For if
ye love them which love you, what reward have ye? do not
47 even the publicans the same? And if ye salute your brethren
only, what do ye more than others? do not even the publicans

---

who subjects us to personal violence, and toward an unjust antagonist in the law, is to be extended to our neighbor in the less imperious and pressing claims that are made upon us. The command, which is not to be understood literally, but like those before it, as a Hebrew form of comparison, is this: Rather err on the side of charity than on the side of prudence. This method of interpretation is entirely in accordance with what is customary in Oriental, and indeed in our own forms of speech. When a father says to a credulous child, "My son, believe nothing that you hear reported," his meaning is plain enough. He would guard his child against the extreme to which he sees him exposed, by expressing very strongly his preference for the opposite extreme, where the danger to him is so much less. The commands here are of this sort. Jesus does not command us to exercise no discretion in complying with the requests of others. But in opposition to one extreme, he sets before us the other as that towards which we ought rather to incline. It would be a perversion of his meaning to give to every one whatever he might ask, — a sword to the madman, money to the intemperate or the impostor. "Ours should be a higher and deeper charity, flowing from those inner springs of love which are the sources of outward actions, sometimes widely divergent, whence may arise both the timely concession and the timely refusal."

45. **for he maketh his sun**] A similar expression is quoted from Seneca by Meyer: "If you imitate the gods, give benefits even to the ungrateful; for the sun rises even for the wicked, and seas are open to pirates." 46. **the publicans**] Tax-gatherers. This race of men, so frequently mentioned as the objects of hatred and contempt among the Jews, and coupled with sinners, were not properly the *publicans*, who were wealthy Romans, of the rank of knights, farming the revenues of the provinces; but their underlings, heathens or renegade Jews, who usually exacted with recklessness and cruelty." Alford.

47. **publicans**] *Gentiles.* Tischendorf. 48. **Be ye therefore**] "Wherefore ye shall be perfect." The future for the imperative, as in the Ten Commandments. "In Greek authors," says Winer, xliii. 5. c., "this mode of expression is considered softer than the imperative." **perfect**] Not partial and one-sided in your aims, but whole, entire, complete. Be not one-sided, like the publicans, who love only those that love them; nor like the Gentiles, who salute only those who salute them; but be ye perfect, even as your Father in heaven is perfect. Let no aim less comprehensive than this satisfy you. As to the technical doctrine

so? Be ye therefore perfect, even as your Father which is in 48 heaven is perfect.

---

about perfection in this life, it can be held only by those whose standard of perfection is very low and incomplete. There is no passage in the Bible more opposed to such a doctrine than this, in the comprehensive aim which it sets before us, to keep us always active and always humble, "asserting as it does, that likeness to God in inward purity, love, and holiness must be the continual aim and end of the Christian in all the departments of his moral life." This may be considered as the sublime conclusion of the second part of the Sermon, the first part ending with the sixteenth verse.

# CHAPTER VI.

### GENERAL DESIGN.

In the preceding chapter, Jesus has spoken of the higher fulfilment of the law of "righteousness" which he demanded in the relation of man to man through obedience to its principles, especially in those points where it had been impeded in its operation and curtailed in its requirements by the low intellectual, moral, and spiritual condition of the people. He now shows how this same "righteousness," vi. 1, (for "righteousness," not "alms," is the word in the best editions of the New Testament,) is to be fulfilled in the duties which were regarded as more immediately connecting man with God.

Here, as in the previous chapter, v. 17-20, he first, 1, states the general principle, and then, as he had done before, goes on to illustrate it by examples, which, in language that a child may understand, exhaust this whole branch of the subject. In your alms, which were justly regarded as religious duties, ("He that hath pity for the poor, lendeth unto the Lord," Prov. xix. 17; "They cannot recompense thee, but thou shalt be recompensed at the resurrection of the just," Luke xiv. 14,) in your prayers and fastings, Jesus says, in substance, you must take heed, lest, looking to the praise of man for your reward, you shall fail of being approved by God. Almsgiving, prayer, and fasting should be dear to you, not as securing the favor of man, but as solemn privileges to be used and duties to be performed in the sight of God, and from motives which He who is unseen, 6, "in secret," will approve and reward.

### 7–15. — LORD'S PRAYER.

Under the head of prayer without ostentation or vain and foolish repetition, Jesus gave his disciples an example of the sort of prayer which he would have them use. Not that exactly these words were always to be employed by them. The same prayer, as preserved by St. Luke, is not in precisely the same words as here, and in the recorded devotions of Christ and the Apostles there is no evidence that this or any other liturgical form made a part of the service. Yet it was undoubtedly intended by him to serve through all ages as a guide and help to his followers in their devotions. For in it he has condensed into a few simple words all that we should most earnestly ask of God in prayer.

"Whatever from the beginning," says Stier, "since men first, on account of sin and evil, lifted their hearts and hands to heaven, has been in their minds to ask, is here reduced, in the simplicity of the new and everlasting covenant, the last utterance of God to us in his Son, to one word, which will remain man's last utterance also to God, until heaven and earth are divided no more. All the cries which go up from man's breast upon earth to heaven, meet here in their fundamental notes; and are gathered into words which are as simple and plain for babes as they are deep and inscrutable for the wise, as transparent for the weakest understanding of any truly praying spirit as they are full of mysterious meaning for the mightiest and last struggles of the spirit into the kingdom and glory of God."

We may pray in secret; but it is no solitary or unsocial act in which we are engaged. By the word "*Our*" we are bound to one another more closely as we kneel to offer up our supplications not for ourselves alone, but for all with whom we are connected as children of a common Father. "We do not," says Cyprian, in his commentary or homily on the Lord's Prayer, "pray each one for himself alone; for we do not say, '*My* Father who art in heaven,' or, 'Give *me* this day my daily bread,' &c. He who is the God of peace, and the author of unity and concord, would have us pray each one for all." Prayer thus becomes a bond of union, not only with God, but with one another among all his people. Our affections are drawn out more earnestly towards our brethren, and we feel that we are all one community of souls, bound together by common sympathies and wants as we lift up our hearts in prayer to Him, whom we thus address as the common Father of us all.

While the expression "*Our Father*" gives warmth and strength to this feeling of fellowship and brotherhood towards man, it unites us to God in the closest and most endearing relation. Bringing him down to us as our Father, and binding us to him by all the tender and powerful associations connected with that name, it adds the expression, "*who art in heaven*," to lift us up into that purer realm with all the fond hopes and affections that cling trustingly and lovingly to him.

Being thus lifted up with Him into his heavenly kingdom, as children with their Father, we ask that his name, here put for Himself, the infinite source of all holiness, may be hallowed, — held sacred and holy by all his children, — that through his holiness perpetually renewing itself in our hearts by the progress of the divine life in the soul and throughout the world his name may be honored and revered as holy.

But it is not so now. Here is a world of sin and disorder, where injustice and cruelty and evil passions so widely prevail, and human governments and laws have not the power, and oftentimes have not the disposition, to restrain them and root them out. We ask therefore that God's kingdom may come, that in its outward, visible authority, with all its spiritual agencies and powers, it may come down from heaven and be established on the earth; that everywhere, in each soul and throughout all the world, its supreme authority may be recognized and its commands obeyed, and men give to it the allegiance which is due from loyal and obedient subjects to the divine kingdom which is placed over them.

But the kingdom of God — this reign of laws and government — does not sufficiently endear itself to us. It does not satisfy the *heart*. Even in the exercise of God's authority and the advancement of his kingdom, we long for a more intimate personal relation than any which can exist between the laws or the ruling institutions of an empire and its subjects. By the petition, "*Thy will be done in earth as it is in heaven*," God is brought into this personal relation with us. He is not an Almighty monarch, however righteous, enforcing laws however just, without any regard to the individual wants and personal feelings of his subjects. His personal will, as that of a Father, is brought into a thoughtful, compassionate, all-subduing connection with the souls of his children. Not merely do we say, "Thy purposes be accomplished in those great events, which, ordered by thine infinite wisdom, reach through kingdoms, worlds, or ages for their fulfilment, and before which we would bow down in awe and submission;" but, "May thy will, in all the minute and affecting incidents of life, enter into our hearts, control every thought and emotion there, and bring us into a cheerful, loving, childlike obedience to thee. May thy will, visiting us as a personal presence, and commending itself to all our dearest hopes and affections, be done among us on earth as it is among the angels of heaven, those prompt and willing messengers of his goodness, who delight to "do his commandments, hearkening unto the voice of his word." "Here," says Claudius, "I picture to myself heaven and the holy angels who do his will with joy, and no sorrow touches them, and they know not what to do for love and blessedness; and then I think, if it were only so here on earth!"

It is a great thing to pray that God's will may be done. This prayer was uttered by our Saviour in agony of soul, and we know not how deeply God in his answer to it may strike into the very heart of what is dearest to us. The petition certainly means that we should give up every unjust or unholy object of ambition or gain that we possess or desire to possess, and that we should strive to remove every little resentment and unworthy feeling, every darling habit and propensity which may in any way interfere with our moral and religious well-being. It may be also that in praying that his will may be done, we are asking him to take from us some of our dearest earthly friends or possessions; since the loss of these may be needed, in order that his will may be done in our hearts as it is among his angels in heaven. If we think of these things, and condense them all into this petition with perfect submissiveness of soul, not only as we kneel by a dying friend or child, but in our usual morning and evening prayers when all things are fair and bright around us, there will be no lack of feeling in our devotions, and our prayers will have a holy and uplifting influence on our lives.

"But he who knoweth our frame, and remembereth that we are dust," will condescend to our lowest wants. From these lofty subjects of contemplation and of prayer, the name, the kingdom, and the will of God, our Saviour lets us come down to a sense of our human wants, and teaches us to pray for "our daily bread." Thus, our daily food, asked and received from God, may become a daily motive for intercourse with Him, and a daily source of thankfulness and devotion. The more we learn to connect the thought of God with even the smallest of his gifts, the more constantly will the sense of his goodness and our obligation to him be kept alive in our hearts. But while we ask for our bodily food, our daily bread, in which words are included all our earthly wants, these same words may remind us of the bread from heaven, the spiritual food, which we also need and ask to have supplied to us day by day.

Not only are we dependent creatures, resting on God's daily bounty for our support, but as erring, sinful beings we turn to him in penitence, and ask to be forgiven, even as we forgive those who have sinned against us. There has always been danger lest religion should be separated from morality, and men's prayers to God stand apart from their sympathies with one another. But the most difficult and most affecting duty to others is woven into our daily prayer, and made the only condition on which we are permitted so much as to ask that God will forgive us our sins. And to bind this condition still more forcibly upon us, the Saviour adds as a comment to the prayer: "For if ye forgive men their trespasses, your Heavenly Father will also forgive you; but if ye forgive not men their trespasses, neither will your Father forgive your trespasses." We have no right to ask God's forgiveness, except so far as we are ready to forgive those who have injured us.

Not only have we sinned in times past, but as we call to mind our transgressions, we feel anew and more keenly the sense of our own liability to sin; and we pray therefore with renewed earnestness that our Father, in his great mercy, will so order events as not to lead us into temptation. Full of contrition for our former offences, with a sense of weakness aggravated by our consciousness of guilt, we turn, as helpless, erring children to their father, with the further, heartfelt petition, "And lead us not into temptation, but deliver us from evil." *From evil,* first and most of all, *from sin,* with the mournful train of griefs and pains which follow after it as its natural attendants. But in this petition we pray also to be delivered from every form of evil. "Here," says the author who has just been quoted from Dr. Hedge's Prose-Writers of Germany, "I still think of temptations, and that man is so easily seduced and may stray from the strait path. But at the same time I think of all the troubles of life, of consumption and old age, of the pains of childbirth, of gangrene and insanity, and the thousand-fold misery and heart-sorrow that is in the world, and that plagues and tortures poor mortals, and there is none to help. And you will find, if tears have not come before, they will be sure to come here." And from this vast accumulation and variety of evils we pray God to deliver us, and rest in the certain assurance and conviction that he will hear and answer our prayer.

Every element of devotion is here; — praise, confession, supplication, ascription, even without the last clause. There is no want of our spiritual or mortal nature which is not recognized and provided for. "The true Christian," says Luther, "prays an everlasting Lord's Prayer." What else indeed can he pray, either in act or word or thought? To pray the Lord's Prayer is not merely uttering the words. It is lifting the soul up, that it may be touched with love and reverence by the hallowed name of our Father who is in heaven. It is striving to bring heart and life into accordance with all that is divine, so as to realize the true union between human effort and the Divine will. To pray the Lord's Prayer in spirit and in truth is to live it all out as in God's presence and with his aid. This co-working of man with God, this union of earnest effort and earnest prayer, is the life of all that is best within us.

### 16 – 34. — PERFECT TRUST IN GOD.

Having thus lifted up the souls of his hearers into communion with God, Jesus carries them along on this high plane of thought, and continues to show how the "righteousness" of the first verse is still to be fulfilled by motives which look to God, and not to man. In their fasting, which he does not enjoin as a duty, he directs them so to demean themselves as not to attract the notice of men, but appear to their Father in heaven as fasting, — hungering and thirsting (v. 6) for his righteousness. But the love of praise is not the only influence that may come in to destroy our singleness of purpose, and weigh down our heavenly affections by its sordid and unworthy motives. The love of earthly gain must be overcome by the love that follows the richer treasures which we lay up for ourselves in heaven. For where the treasure is there the heart also will be; and if the mind is once corrupted by these inferior passions, it is as if the eye of the soul were diseased and clouded, so that the truth of God is shut out or perverted, and the very light that is in us turned into darkness. And if the *light* within thee be darkness, how great, the Saviour exclaims, "will the *darkness* be!" We can then, he adds, 24, safely owe no double allegiance to God and the world. If one master is loved and obeyed, the other will be hated, or at least neglected and despised.

But Jesus goes deeper than this into the secret motives of the heart. The same spirit which leads to avarice in the accumulation of wealth, may, by undue anxiety about the provisions necessary for our daily wants, interfere with the purity of our religious motives, and the simplicity of love and faith with which we are to look to God for our support, and to receive our food and raiment day by day as from his hands. Nothing can exceed the poetic beauty of this passage (25-34), the logical force of its reasoning, or the calm and sublime convictions of religious trust in which it rests. Are not the life, — the soul, — and the body, which God has freely created and bestowed, more than food or raiment? As he has provided these greater gifts, can ye not trust him in those which are the least? "Look at the birds of heaven;" [which may have been flying near them;] "for they sow not, neither do they reap, nor gather into barns; and yet your Heavenly Father feedeth them." Observe the exquisite tenderness in the mode of expression; — not *their* God or *their* Father, but *your* Heavenly Father. "And are not *you* far more to him than they?" While the reasoning proves the assertion to the understanding with logical power, these words bring it home with endearing emphasis to the heart. There is then no cause for anxiety; but if there were, of what use could it be? With all his anxiety, who among you could add one cubit to his life? "And as to raiment, why should you be anxious?" They were in the open field, and the flowers probably were near them. "Consider the lilies of the field, how they are growing: they toil not, they spin not; but I say unto you, that not Solomon in all his glory was arrayed like one of these." And if God so clothe these perishing things, — the grass of the field which flourishes to-day only that it may be consumed to-morrow, — will he not much more clothe you, O ye distrustful ones? Do not put yourselves on a level with the unbelieving Gentiles, who are anxious about these things. And then he adds, in words which bring the paternal providence of God tenderly and warmly home to them, even in the smallest matters, "Your Heavenly Father knoweth that you have need of all these things. But seek ye first his righteousness and his kingdom, and all these things will be given to you in addition." "Wherefore," — for all these reasons, especially as they are summed up in the last sentence, — "be not anxious about the morrow; for," — in addition to the reasons already given — "the morrow, like to-day, will have, and will make provision for its own trials." Live faithfully 'amid the duties of to-day, with a perfect trust in your Heavenly Father for all that lies beyond; for by so doing you will best prepare yourselves for the duties and the trials of to-morrow. The evils of to-morrow will be provided for, and will be enough in themselves when to-morrow comes, without being forestalled now, and adding their weight to the already sufficient burdens of to-day. The meaning of the passage, which closes the third division of the Sermon on the Mount, is, That we are to live as God's children in the present, giving ourselves up entirely to the duties which he assigns to us, with that perfect trust in him which leaves no room for anxiety in regard to the perishing things of time which we may need in the future.

It is impossible to describe the new life and meaning which these words about the birds and flowers throw into nature, whose creatures, perpetually fed and clothed by God, are objects of his care and proofs of his active, all-pervading presence, as they are the symbols of his goodness. The doctrine implies all that is valuable in pantheism, the all-pervading, efficient presence of God, while over the universe thus pervaded and sustained it throws the kind, intelligent providence of a personal God, and the thoughtful, benignant love of our Heavenly Father.

While our Saviour would here withdraw us entirely from earthly anxiety, creating in the soul a love and faith which cast out fear and distrust, there is nothing of Asceticism or Stoicism in his instructions. He recognizes the evils of life. He does not ignore or despise its good things. *Our Heavenly Father knows that we have need of them.* And because he knows our need of them, and will provide for it, we are to place them where they belong, as wholly subordinate to the heavenly treasures, and, without anxiety or care for them, seek first his righteousness and his kingdom.

## NOTES.

TAKE heed that ye do not your alms before men, to be seen of them; otherwise ye have no reward of your Father which
2 is in heaven. Therefore when thou doest thine alms, do not sound a trumpet before thee, as the hypocrites do in the synagogues and in the streets, that they may have glory of men.
3 Verily I say unto you, they have their reward. But when thou doest alms, let not thy left hand know what thy right
4 hand doeth; that thine alms may be in secret; and thy Father, which seeth in secret, himself shall reward thee openly. ——
5 And when thou prayest, thou shalt not be as the hypocrites are; for they love to pray standing in the synagogues and in the corners of the streets, that they may be seen of men.
6 Verily I say unto you, they have their reward. But thou, when thou prayest, enter into thy closet, and when thou hast

---

**1. Your alms**] Your *righteousness*, δικαιοσύνην, not ἐλεημοσύνην, is undoubtedly the true reading; and it is to be taken here in the same sense as in v. 20, where it is used by Jesus to show the sort of fulfilment of the law which he came to enforce. **2. do not sound a trumpet**] There is no good reason to suppose that this custom literally prevailed, though one of the Fathers mentions it as a tradition in his day, "that the hypocrites call the beggars together by the sound of the trumpet." But Lightfoot, in his comment on this passage, says: "I have not found, although I have sought for it much and seriously, even the least mention of a trumpet in almsgiving."
**they have their reward**] Have reward enough, — what they sought and bargained for, namely, the praise of man, and also, what they did not seek or bargain for, the disapprobation of God. **3. let not thy left hand**] Do it without any regard to what others may say or think, in such perfect simplicity of heart, that not even the left hand may know of the charity which the right hand is bestowing. Perhaps the fact that the alms-box in Jewish synagogues stood on the right hand of the passage into the house added to the force of the expression.
**4. in secret**] Unseen. **openly**] This word is omitted in the best editions of the Greek text, both here and in vv. 6 and 18.
**6. enter into thy closet**] This is not necessarily to be taken literally. We may, as St. Chrysostom has said, shut our closet doors, and yet leave the doors of the mind open to thoughts inconsistent with our devotions. The ostentation of the thing is what is condemned. He who anywhere, though it be in a public place, retires within the closet of his own mind, and there prays to God in the secrecy and simplicity of his soul, obeys this injunction of our Lord; while it is violated by him who willingly allows it to be understood that he often shuts himself up in his closet for secret prayer. The secret prayer that is talked about to others is no longer secret. In this particular the race of Pharisees is not yet extinct. There is a time and a place for our public devotions. But above all, in the secrecy of our own souls, by acts too sacred for man to see or to hear about, we are to keep up the habit,

shut thy door, pray to thy Father which is in secret; and thy Father, which seeth in secret, shall reward thee openly. But 7 when ye pray, use not vain repetitions, as the heathen do; for they think that they shall be heard for their much speaking. Be not ye therefore like unto them; for your Father knoweth 8 what things ye have need of, before ye ask him. After this 9 manner therefore pray ye: Our Father, which art in heaven, hallowed be thy name; thy kingdom come; thy will be done, 10

---

not merely of daily, but of constant communion with God, and thus keep alive the spirit of devotion within us. While Jesus here enjoins secret prayer, he does not forbid social or public prayer, in which he is known to have engaged more than once. Matt. xi. 25, 26; John xi. 41, xvii. 1-26. **7. vain repetitions**] Do not babble, or make unmeaning repetitions in your prayers. "What is forbidden in this verse," says Alford, "is, not *much* praying, for our Lord himself passed whole nights in prayer; nor praying in the same words, for this he did in the very intensity of his agony at Gethsemane; but the making number and length *a point of observance*, and imagining that prayer will be heard, not because it is the genuine expression of the desire of faith, but because it is of such a length, has been such a number of times repeated. The repetitions of Pater Nosters and Ave Marias in the Romish Church, as practised by them, are in direct violation of this precept."
**9. After this manner**] "We may place our little children's hands together, and teach them, say ye. Well for every one for whom this is early done; it is not too soon as early as the child can cry. My father and my mother, and lift up his eyes to heaven as a child of humanity. How perfect is the simplicity of this beginning of all prayer, descending to the root and principle, already naturally present in the heart, of all sense of love and trust for gift and help. . . . . . Further, what an inexhaustible meaning is there in the conjunction, in this first glance towards heaven, of the Father-name which is inborn and sweet to every child of man, with the universal compass of all things and the hosts of the universe. He whose are all the heavens, and not thy own earth merely, is the Father, is thy Father." Stier. "In the Lord's Prayer, which is prayer in its most perfect form, we are taught to acknowledge the Lord as the sole object of our worship; to revere his name or attributes; to desire at heart the restoration of his kingdom within us, and throughout the world; to resign our wills to his will in all his dispensations and in every act of his providence, till earth shall become as heaven within us; till the external form of our actions be one with the internal spirit which rules them, and the whole earth may be brought to the worship of the Lord in the harmony and peace of heaven." Arbouin.
**9. thy name**] "De Wette observes: 'God's name is not merely his appellation, which we speak with the mouth, but also and principally the idea which we attach to it, his Being, as far as it is confessed, revealed, or known.' 'The name' of God in Scripture is used to signify that revelation of himself which he has made to men, which is all that we know of him; into the depths of his being, as it is, no man can penetrate." Alford. 10. **as it is in heaven**] "As in the courses of sun and stars, so among the morning stars and sons of God, Job xxxviii. 7, there is the festal service of those who, active in rest, shout for joy in their ranks of blessedness. So should it be upon earth: vast is the meaning which carries the promise in this prayer far above all the stir and tumult of humanity,

11 in earth as it is in heaven; give us this day our daily bread;
12 and forgive us our debts as we forgive our debtors; and lead
13 us not into temptation, but deliver us from evil; for thine is
the kingdom, and the power, and the glory, forever. Amen.
14 For if ye forgive men their trespasses, your Heavenly Father
15 will also forgive you; but if ye forgive not men their trespasses, neither will your Father forgive your trespasses. ——
16 Moreover, when ye fast, be not, as the hypocrites, of a sad
countenance; for they disfigure their faces, that they may appear unto men to fast. Verily I say unto you, they have their
17 reward. But thou, when thou fastest, anoint thine head, and

---

inviting and urging all the children of God to restless wrestling in praying and receiving, and fervor in doing his will." Stier.

**11. our daily bread**] ἐπιούσιον. A great deal of learning has been expended on this word, but with no more satisfactory result than that in our English version. Its root may be two words, which mean *on-coming*, referring to the day now *coming on*, and well enough translated by our '*daily*.' But the most satisfactory analysis of the word is that adopted by most of the Greek Fathers, ὁ ἐπὶ οὐσίᾳ ἡμῶν, *what is needed for our subsistence*. By the word *bread* is meant everything that is required for our support,—all the needful things of time. This undoubtedly is the primary meaning of the petition; but it may also extend itself so as to include the higher nutriment,—those things which are requisite and necessary as well for the soul as the body.

**13. and lead us not into temptation**] There is a sense, and that a profound one, in which all actions and events proceed from God. With this comprehensive view of the Divine agency reaching through all things, these words mean, 'so order all events connected with us, and so assist us in the government of our own thoughts, that we may not be led into temptation.' The two clauses of the petition must be taken together: 'lead us not into temptation, but [on the contrary] deliver us from evil.' The first clause, growing out of our consciousness of weakness and exposure, gives force to the second. Feeling keenly our liability to evil, we ask with more intense earnestness that God will deliver us. It is said, James i. 13, 'God cannot be tempted with evil, neither tempteth he any man.' But this which implies direct personal solicitation to sin, is not inconsistent with the fact that, in the vast and manifold orderings of God's providence, he should sometimes give rise to contingencies which lead men into temptation, so that, with philosophical strictness of speech, he may be said to lead men into temptation. But that is an incidental result, growing out of complicated causes intended for other purposes, and therefore *allowed* by God; but not *designed* by him for the purpose of tempting us. The substance of the whole matter is stated by St. Paul, 1 Cor. x. 13; 'but God is faithful, who will not suffer you to be tempted above that ye are able; but *will with the temptation also make a way to escape* that ye may be able to bear it.

**For thine is the kingdom, and the power, and the glory, forever. Amen.**] There is no trace of this ascription in early times, in any family of manuscripts, or in any exposition. It is excellent in itself; but we have no reason to suppose that it originally formed any part of the Lord's Prayer.

**17. anoint thine head**] i. e. do as you are in the habit of doing; let there be nothing unusual in

wash thy face; that thou appear not unto men to fast, but unto thy Father which is in secret; and thy Father, which seeth in secret, shall reward thee openly.——Lay not up for yourselves treasures upon earth, where moth and rust doth corrupt, and where thieves break through and steal; but lay up for yourselves treasures in heaven, where neither moth nor rust doth corrupt, and where thieves do not break through nor steal. For where your treasure is, there will your heart be also. The light of the body is the eye. If therefore thine eye be single, thy whole body shall be full of light; but if thine eye be evil, thy whole body shall be full of darkness. If therefore the light that is in thee be darkness, how great is that darkness! No man can serve two masters; for either he will hate the one, and love the other; or else he will hold to

---

your appearance to attract attention. The disfiguring of the face, in v. 16, refers to the habit of covering the face with ashes, or leaving it unwashed and neglected in times of fasting. 19. **treasures upon earth**] No small part of the "treasures" in the East consisted of sumptuous and magnificent garments. "I had," says Bartolomo, "put my effects into a chest, and opening it afterwards, I discovered an innumerable multitude of termites (or ants). They had perforated my linen in a thousand places, and gnawed my books, my girdle, my amice, and my shoes."

**rust**] βρῶσις,— a more general term than rust: anything that corrodes, that eats into and consumes what is valuable. **break through**] Prof. Hackett, speaking of the unsubstantial character of many of the houses in the East, built as they are of small stones and clay, says that "the labor of digging through such walls cannot be difficult. Those who wished to plunder a house would be apt to select a place where the partition was apparently thin, and then stealthily remove the stones or clay, so as to open a passage. In some parts of our English version 'breaking through' should be changed to 'digging through.'" Illustrations of Scripture, p. 95. 22.

**single**] *clear*, with no foreign substance to obstruct the passage of the light through it. The eye, i. e. the medium through which the light passes, is put for the light itself, as in our common speech we use the word *cup* to express the wine which is contained in it. As the pure, clear eye is the medium through which the light finds its way into the body, and fills it with light, so the conscience, when it is clear of every foreign influence, lets the light of God's truth into the soul. But if, 23, thine eye be *evil*, i. e. the opposite of clear, no light can enter, and the whole body is full of darkness. And if the very *light* that is in you be darkness, how great must the DARKNESS be! Man's lower nature is enlightened, spiritualized, and sanctified by the spiritual light which comes into it through the eye of the soul; but if that light, through the perversion of the eye, be darkness, how great must the darkness of the sensuous life be. There are none so mournfully dark as they who, claiming to be Christians, thus distort, pervert, and turn into darkness the very light of God's truth. How many professed teachers of righteousness, their intellectual and spiritual perceptions clouded by their own preconceived opinions, refuse to receive the Gospel in its simplicity, and

the one, and despise the other. Ye cannot serve God and
Mammon. Therefore I say unto you, Take no thought for
your life, what ye shall eat, or what ye shall drink; nor yet
for your body, what ye shall put on. Is not the life more than
meat, and the body than raiment? Behold the fowls of the
air, for they sow not, neither do they reap, nor gather into
barns; yet your Heavenly Father feedeth them. Are ye not
much better than they? Which of you by taking thought can
add one cubit unto his stature? And why take ye thought for
raiment? Consider the lilies of the field, how they grow;

spend all their ingenuity and strength in turning its light into darkness! **24. Mammon**] According to Augustine this was a Carthaginian name for lucre or gain. The researches of scholars have thrown no further light upon it. **25. Take no thought**] This word, μεριμνᾶτε, from a root implying division, admirably expresses the divided and distracted state of mind which is here condemned as directly opposed to the entire consecration of the whole man to God, with perfect trust in him. The transition is a natural one from the single eye of v. 22, to the divided allegiance of v. 24, and from that to the distracted, anxious state of mind which is produced when the simple, trusting devotion of the soul to God is disturbed by too fond a regard for lower things: " This 'take no thought' is certainly an inadequate translation, in our present English, of the Greek original. The words seem to exclude and to condemn that just forward-looking care which belongs to man, and differences him from the beasts, which live only in the present; and most English critics have lamented the inadvertence of our authorized version, which, in bidding us 'take no thought' for the necessaries of life, prescribes to us what is impracticable in itself, and would be a breach of Christian duty, even were it possible. But there is no 'inadvertence' here. When our translation was made, 'take no thought' was a perfectly correct rendering of the original.

'Thought' was then constantly used as an equivalent to anxiety or solicitous care; as let us witness this passage from Bacon: 'Harris, an alderman in London, was put to trouble, and died with *thought* and anxiety before his business came to an end.' Or, still better, this from one of the 'Somers Tracts' (its date is that of the reign of Queen Elizabeth): 'In five hundred years, only two queens have died in childbirth; Queen Catherine Parr died rather of *thought*.' A better example than either of these is that occurring in Shakespeare's 'Julius Cæsar,' ('*take thought* and die for Cæsar') where 'to take thought' is to take a matter so seriously to heart that death ensues." Trench.

**for your life**] ψυχῇ, a word which has no equivalent in our language, and is translated *life*, in this place, ii. 20, x. 39, xvi. 25, and xx. 28, but is rendered *soul*, xi. 29, xii. 18, xvi. 26, xxii. 37, and xxvi. 38. It means the vital, sentient principle which constitutes our identity, and which may be thought of in its relation to our physical nature, as our physical, mortal life, or in its relation to our spiritual nature, as the soul. See x. 39, xvi. 25, 26. **27. one cubit unto his stature**] The primary meaning of the word here rendered *stature* is *age*, which is the more forcible term of the two. Who, by anxiety, can add a cubit to his term of life? **28. the lilies of the field**] We cannot tell precisely what flowers these were. "But if, as is probable, the name

they toil not, neither do they spin; and yet I say unto you that even Solomon in all his glory was not arrayed like one of these. Wherefore, if God so clothe the grass of the field, which to-day is, and to-morrow is cast into the oven, shall he not much more clothe you, O ye of little faith? Therefore take no thought, saying, What shall we eat, or what shall we drink, or wherewithal shall we be clothed? (For after all these things do the Gentiles seek;) for your Heavenly Father knoweth that ye have need of all these things. But seek ye first the kingdom of God, and his righteousness; and all these things shall be added unto you. Take therefore no thought for the morrow; for the morrow shall take thought for the things of itself. Sufficient unto the day is the evil thereof.

---

may include the numerous flowers of the tulip or amaryllis kind, which appear in the early summer, or the autumn of Palestine, the expression becomes more natural, — the red and golden hue fitly suggesting the comparison with the proverbial gorgeousness of the robes of Solomon." "Whatever was the special flower designated by the lily of the field, the rest of the passage indicates that it was of the gorgeous hues which might be compared to the robes of the great king." Stanley. "As the beauty of the flower is unfolded by the divine Creator-Spirit from within, from the laws and capacities of its own individual life, so must all true adornment of man be unfolded from within by the same Almighty Spirit." Alford. 30. **cast into the oven**] The slight annual plants, which are called grass, are still used for fuel in the East. The oven is a sort of earthen pot (the mouth downward, and tapering towards the top) in which a fire is kindled that heats it easily, and the bread, rolled out thin, is spread over the outside surface and quickly baked. 33. **the kingdom of God, and his righteousness**] Tischendorf has it: "But seek ye first his righteousness and his kingdom," which reading is sustained by the best manuscripts, and indicates the true order in which we are to seek, first, the righteousness, and then, through that, the kingdom of God. "By the kingdom of God," says Swedenborg, "in its universal sense, is meant the universal heaven; in a sense less universal, the true Church of the Lord; and in a particular sense, every particular person of a true faith, or who is regenerated by the life of faith; wherefore, such a person is also called heaven, because heaven is in him; and likewise the kingdom of God, because the kingdom of God is in him, as the Lord himself teacheth in Luke xvii. 20, 21."

34. **for the morrow**] For to-morrow will have cares and troubles enough of its own, just as to-day has. It has no claims to exemption from evil more than to-day, and therefore we are not to increase the burdens of to-day by uselessly forestalling the troubles of to-morrow. Do what we can, it will have trials enough of its own. Leave it, therefore, as you do whatever else is unavoidable, submissively and trustingly in the hands of God.

# CHAPTER VII.

### ANALYSIS.

MOST readers are accustomed to regard the Sermon on the Mount as made up of disconnected maxims and precepts. But on a critical examination, nothing perhaps strikes us more than the intimate relation of the parts, bound together as they all are, and making one orderly and consistent whole. After the benedictions in the fifth chapter, Jesus shows how the law is to be more strictly observed by obedience to the spirit rather than the letter. In the sixth chapter, he shows how improper motives may vitiate our religious acts, darken the light that is in us, break up our allegiance to God, and disturb our faith. The seventh chapter, after a few specific rules particularly applicable to the disciples, but involving principles of conduct which can never be out of season, closes with considerations of momentous interest and importance in their application to those who would be his followers in all coming times.

First, 1 – 5, he warns those who are going forth to regenerate and reform the world, that they must beware of cherishing a censorious temper or habit of mind, and especially be careful to have their own souls pure before they should dare to arraign the conduct of others or exhort them to cast out their sins; lest like hypocrites they should condemn in others faults which they themselves cherish in more aggravated forms. Only purity in their own hearts and lives will enable them to aid others in putting away their sins. Still, 6, they are to exercise their discretion in regard to others, and not waste their time and precious gifts on those who will listen only to what appeals to their impure, coarse, and sensual appetites. Lest, however, they should be discouraged by such persons, they are exhorted, 7 – 10, to look to One who will always hear, and never refuse to assist them. *Ask, seek, knock*, express the different degrees of earnestness in prayer, which will not be in vain. *Therefore*, 11 – 12, since God, even more than an earthly father, will give good things to them that ask him, they are in some measure to imitate his beneficence, and do to others as they would have others do to them. For here, in doing thus to others with a constant and prayerful reference to God, is the fulfilment of all that has been enjoined by the law, or taught by the prophets. See xxii. 40.

The question is sometimes asked, how far the Golden Rule is original in this place. Similar precepts have been quoted from other writers, but no one which has the same fulness of meaning as this. In Tobit iv. 15, we read, "Do to no man that which thou hatest." Kuinoel quotes from the Talmud a similar precept, "Do not to another that which is hateful to yourself." Seneca, Ep. 94, says, "Expect from another the same that you do to him." Each of these, and indeed all of them combined fail to come up to the precept of Jesus. At best, they cover only the negative and least important side of the great rule of disinterested and active beneficence which he has laid down. But independently of the precise meaning of the precept standing by itself, he has infused into it a religious power which takes it up out of the region of moral precepts and endows it with his own spiritual life. The warm religious atmosphere which is thrown around his instructions gives them a new vitality. Take, e. g. the first of the beatitudes, "Blessed are the poor in spirit; for theirs is the kingdom of Heaven." Here is a precept relating to a disposition or habit of mind, and, as far as the ethical rule is concerned, it might be translated, Cultivate a lowly, unambitious spirit. Who does not see that the words of religious benediction and joy in which it is here imbedded lift it up out of the sphere of prudential or ethical rules, animate it with a religious life, and press it upon us with the holy and beneficent sanctions of a divine authority? It is so with all our Saviour's moral instructions. They are never presented as naked precepts. The spiritual life which enters into them, and the religious sanctions which are thrown around them, and which mould them into conformity with the will of God, bring them to us, not as formal rules, but as spirit and life. They do not stand outside as stern monitors to remind us of our duties and enforce obedience; they enter our hearts as vitalizing influences. They quicken our affections, subdue us to themselves, and lead to obedience as the spontaneous act of souls thus prepared. In this way, the Golden Rule, urged from a religious motive on hearts already touched by a sense of God's infinite condescension and kindness, is filled out with a divine life, which gives it inspiration and power.

But it is no easy work to which the followers of Jesus are called. They are to strive, Luke xiii. 24, — ἀγωνίζεσθε, *struggle*, as in a crowd and a contest, — on account of the multitudes that are pressing into the broad way that leads to destruction, and the narrow, afflictive way that leads to life. Especially they must beware of the false teachers, who would come as prophets to deceive them, and who could be known only by their works. Here he warns his followers against the danger of ostentatious and heartless professions.

"Not every one that saith unto me, Lord, Lord, shall enter into the kingdom of the heavens, but he that doeth the will of my Father who is in the heavens." In that kingdom, and in the great day of its consummation to each individual soul, when the secret thoughts and acts of men are revealed, to the astonishment of themselves most of all, then shall they who have lived in outward formalities and professions cling still to their old protestations, and endeavor by them to shut out the new and dreadful revelations that are breaking in upon them. "Then will I confess unto them, I never knew you; depart from me, ye that work unlawfulness" ἀνομίαν, i. e. 'ye violators of the law.' We should note the force of this word which in this connection shows what he means by the violation of the law which he came to fulfil. They who, instead of doing the will of God, trust to their professions of honor and respect for him, are the violators of the law whom he drives away from his presence.

How grand and awful these words, in which Jesus as the representative of the divine justice announces the rejection of those who, honoring him with their lips, had yet refused to submit themselves to the will and the law of God.

But these words of terrible warning to one class of offenders are not sufficient. Referring back to his whole discourse, in which all that is significant and vital in the law has been condensed and set forth, by images borrowed from that land of mountain-torrents, and sudden, violent, and destructive floods, he tells them that he who hears and does these words of his, is like a wise man who built his house upon a rock, and rain and floods and winds fell upon it in vain, for it was founded on a rock. But he who hears and does them not, is like a foolish man who built his house on the sand, and rain and floods and winds beat violently against it, and it fell in a ruin great and terrible in proportion to the expectations and hopes which he had been building on that precarious and deceitful foundation.

Here is the solemn and appalling close of the greatest, the most comprehensive and most important discourse ever spoken to man. The multitudes were filled with astonishment at his instructions. The extraordinary ascendency of Jesus over them is shown by the fact, that, though he had so utterly disappointed them in all their most deeply cherished expectations, they nevertheless recognized his authority, and were astonished at the power with which he spoke.

It has been questioned by critics whether the words here brought together were actually spoken at one time. It has been suggested that Matthew may have put together as one discourse words spoken on different occasions. But those who have carefully followed us in our analysis will, we think, come to a different conclusion. The intimate connection of the parts; the orderly whole which they make; the touching and beautiful introduction; the body of the sermon freighted with profound and various instructions, yet all bearing upon the same subject, viz. the fulfilment of the law in its highest and most comprehensive sense; — the solemn and almost overpowering close; are to us an unanswerable proof that the whole was spoken on one occasion and as one discourse, though there may have been a pause here and there to mark the succession of topics.

---

## NOTES.

2 JUDGE not, that ye be not judged. For with what judgment ye judge ye shall be judged; and with what measure ye
3 mete it shall be measured to you again. And why beholdest thou the mote that is in thy brother's eye, but considerest not

---

1, 2. A general law of retribution is here announced. As we give, so shall we receive. "Justice," says Tholuck, "is elastic; the unjust blow I inflict upon another recoils upon myself." He who is kind, merciful, and gentle to others, will disarm them of their severity, and make them kind, merciful, and gentle to him. Especially are we to remember this in the judgments we pass on those who differ from us in their religious views, where we sometimes indulge our personal or sectarian animosities under the pretence of allegiance to the truth. "It has been made known to me," says Swedenborg, "by much experience, that persons of every religion are saved, if so be, by a life of charity, they have received the remains of good and of apparent truth. The life of charity consists in man's thinking well of others, and desiring good to others, and receiving joy in himself at the salvation of others; whereas they have not the life of charity who are not willing that any should be saved but such as believe as they themselves do, and

the beam that is in thine own eye? or how wilt thou say to thy 4
brother, Let me pull out the mote out of thine eye; and, behold, a beam is in thine own eye? Thou hypocrite, first cast 5
out the beam out of thine own eye; and then shalt thou see
clearly to cast out the mote out of thy brother's eye. ——
Give not that which is holy unto the dogs, neither cast ye your 6

---

especially if they are indignant that it should be otherwise." 3, 4. Only the eye that is single can see clearly. The faults which offend us most in others are often those of which we are guilty ourselves. The proud man is most annoyed by the pride of others, and the quickest to see it. The offences which we suspect in others are often only faults of character or of temper projected from our own minds, and having no substantial existence except in ourselves. **the mote . . . . . the beam**] From quotations given by Lightfoot, this would appear to have been a proverbial form of expression among the Jews.

5. **to cast out the mote out of thy brother's eye**] Before, 3, it was only looking, or staring at the mote in the brother's eye; but now, with clear sight, and a charitable intent, we help him to put it away. The lesson taught in these five verses is a rebuke to the fault-finding, satirical spirit, in which the pharisees and hypocrites of all times delight to indulge. One of the few legends respecting Jesus, which are not utterly worthless, is to the same effect, and, as told by Mrs. Jameson, is nearly as follows: "Jesus arrived one evening at the gates of a certain city, and he sent his disciples forward to prepare supper, while he himself, intent on doing good, walked through the streets into the market-place. And he saw at the corner of the market some people gathered together looking at an object on the ground; and he drew near to see what it might be. It was a dead dog with a halter round its neck, by which it appeared to have been dragged through the dirt; and a viler, a more abject, a more unclean thing never met the eye of man. And those who stood by looked on with abhorrence, and gave vent to strong expressions of disgust. And Jesus heard them, and, looking down compassionately on the dead creature, he said, 'Pearls are not equal to the whiteness of his teeth.' Then the people turned towards him with amazement, and said among themselves, 'Who is this? This must be Jesus of Nazareth, for only he could find something to pity and approve even in a dead dog;' and, being ashamed, they bowed their heads before him and went each on his way."

6. **dogs**] Dogs (Phil. iii. 2; Rev. xxii. 15) stand as a type of the shameless, passionate, and profane, while swine were abhorred as impure, sensual, and obscene. This passage, Dr. Barnes says, "gives a beautiful instance of the introverted parallelism." In Hebrew poetry, one member of a sentence generally answers to another, expressing the same thing with some slight modification:

" The heavens declare the glory of God;
 And the firmament showeth his handy work." — Ps. xix. 1.
" Create in me a clean heart, O God;
 And renew a right spirit within me."
 — Ps. li 10.

In these examples, as is usually the case, the parallelism is between the first clause and the second. Sometimes, where there are four clauses, it is between the first and third, and the second and fourth, as in the following:

" On her house-tops,
 And to the open streets,
 Every one howleth,
 Descendeth with weeping."
 Isa. xv. 3.

Sometimes, but rarely, the first and fourth, and the second and third correspond. In Matt. xii. 22,

pearls before swine; lest they trample them under their feet, 7 and turn again and rend you. —— Ask, and it shall be given you; seek, and ye shall find; knock, and it shall be opened unto 8 you. For every one that asketh receiveth; and he that seek- 9 eth findeth; and to him that knocketh it shall be opened. Or what man is there of you, whom if his son ask bread, will he 10 give him a stone? or if he ask a fish, will he give him a ser- 11 pent? If ye then, being evil, know how to give good gifts unto your children, how much more shall your Father which is in 12 heaven give good things to them that ask him? Therefore all things whatsoever ye would that men should do to you, do ye even so to them; for this is the law and the prophets. —— 13 Enter ye in at the strait gate; for wide is the gate, and broad is the way, that leadeth to destruction; and many there be 14 which go in thereat. Because strait is the gate, and narrow is

the forms of expression correspond in this way. He healed him, insomuch that

"The blind
And dumb
Both spake
And saw."

So in the passage before us:

"Give not that which is holy unto dogs,
Neither cast ye your pearls before swine,
Lest they [the swine] trample them under their feet,
And [the dogs] turn again and rend you."

**7, 8. Ask, seek, knock**] Usually supposed to refer to different degrees of earnestness in prayer. The following, from Clowes's notes on this passage, may possibly suggest a better interpretation: "To *ask* has relation to the desire of heavenly good in the will, to *seek* has relation to the desire of heavenly truth in the understanding, and to *knock* has relation to the joint effect of such desire in opening communication with the Lord and his kingdom. In like manner, in the succeeding verse, 8, to *receive* has relation to the appropriation and possession of heavenly good, to *find* has relation to the appropriation and possession of heavenly truth, and to *have it opened* has relation to the communication thereby effected with the Lord's kingdom and the Lord himself." The limitation to the promise is in James iv. 3.

**11. If ye then, being evil**] "i. e. in comparison with God." Alford.

13. The gate is put before the way, and refers to that decisive exercise of will by which we enter on a Christian course, and the narrow way indicates the perseverance which is also needed in order that we may enter into life.

**14. Because strait**] *Strait* means narrow, and the word translated *narrow* has a more intense signification. It is from the same root — to *squeeze, bruise, crush* — as the word rendered "*tribulation*" (Acts xiv. 22), "We must through much tribulation enter into the kingdom of God," and without doubt has here something of the same meaning. It was a way so narrow as to be afflictive. There is almost always a contrast between the narrowness, the straits, the tribulation, through which the Christian must pass in the eyes of the world, and the spiritual freedom and joy in which he walks. **life**] In the New Testament death is often regarded as the offspring of sin (James i. 15), and life as the effect or consequence of holiness. The term death, therefore, often stands for sin and its sorrowful consequences, as *life* is made to stand for holiness and its blissful results.

the way, which leadeth unto life; and few there be that find it.

—— Beware of false prophets, which come to you in sheep's 15 clothing, but inwardly they are ravening wolves. Ye shall 16 know them by their fruits. Do men gather grapes of thorns, or figs of thistles? Even so every good tree bringeth forth 17 good fruit; but a corrupt tree bringeth forth evil fruit. A 18 good tree cannot bring forth evil fruit, neither can a corrupt tree bring forth good fruit. Every tree, that bringeth not forth 19 good fruit, is hewn down and cast into the fire. Wherefore 20 by their fruits ye shall know them. Not every one that saith 21 unto me, Lord, Lord, shall enter into the kingdom of Heaven; but he that doeth the will of my Father which is in heaven. Many will say to me in that day, Lord, Lord, have we not 22

---

Absolute life is absolute holiness and blessedness. This is the common, though not the only use of the word ζωή, which is here translated *life*. It refers to the life of the soul, a principle of divine life with its attendant blessedness and peace, and hardly more than two or three times, as Luke xvi. 25 and James iv. 14, to the life of the body. See Trench's Synonymes of the New Testament.

**16. by their fruits**] Solemnly repeated at v. 20. "The fruit is that which a man, like a tree, puts forth, from the good or evil disposition which pervades the whole of his inward being. Learning, compiled from every quarter, and combined with language, does not constitute fruit; which consists of all that which the teacher puts forth from his heart, in his language and conduct, as something flowing from his inner being." Bengel.

**of thorns**] "Although their berries resemble grapes, as the heads of thistles do figs." Bengel.

**17. Every good** (ἀγαθόν) **tree bringeth forth good** (καλούς) **fruit.**] There is a peculiar fitness of adaption in the use of these two epithets, which is lost in our version. The tree is *good*, the fruit which it bears is not only good, but *beautiful*. A good and faithful life brings forth its good and beautiful fruits, not only in good deeds, but in the knowledge to which it leads of what is true and fair. **22. Many**

**will say to me in that day**] Here is one of those indefinite expressions, which, like *life, death, kingdom of Heaven, outer darkness*, &c., have a more powerful effect on the imagination and the heart than any precise terms could ever have, even if it were possible to apply them to this class of subjects. They draw us into the realm of infinite being. Its vast background of light or darkness is thrown around them. They cannot be defined because they are employed in relation to matters which have no bounds, and which in our present state of existence, we can but imperfectly comprehend. In "that day," when the Son of Man shall come (John xiv. 20); in "that day" when the crown of righteousness shall be given to him who has fought a good fight and finished his course (2 Tim. iv. 8); in "the day when God shall judge the secrets of men by Jesus Christ" (Rom. ii. 16); in "the day of judgment" (Matt. xi. 24), when "it shall be more tolerable for the land of Sodom than for thee," — in "that day" only those who do the will of God shall be allowed to enter into the kingdom of Heaven. *When* "that day" shall be, or what precisely shall be the sign of its coming, is wisely hidden from us. But it has been fully revealed to us by what means we shall best prepare to meet it. "Blessed is that servant whom his Lord, when he cometh, shall find so doing." See

prophesied in thy name, and in thy name have cast out devils,
23 and in thy name done many wonderful works? And then
will I profess unto them, I never knew you; depart from me,
24 ye that work iniquity. —— Therefore whosoever heareth these
sayings of mine, and doeth them, I will liken him unto a wise
25 man, which built his house upon a rock; and the rain descended, and the floods came, and the winds blew, and beat
upon that house; and it fell not, for it was founded upon a
26 rock. And every one that heareth these sayings of mine, and
doeth them not, shall be likened unto a foolish man, which
27 built his house upon the sand; and the rain descended, and
the floods came, and the winds blew, and beat upon that house;
and it fell; and great was the fall of it.
28 And it came to pass, when Jesus had ended these sayings,
29 the people were astonished at his doctrine. For he taught
them as one having authority, and not as the scribes.

---

xxv. 31 – 46. **23. I never knew you**] Never recognized them as his disciples. For all their loud professions and words of honor and reverence to him, he knows them not. Only those who receive his truth into their hearts and show it forth in righteous living are recognized as his. With what sublime and majestic authority are these words uttered! No king or prophet could ever have used such language without an almost insane presumption. **24. whosoever heareth these sayings of mine**] To *hear* the words of Jesus implies something more than to perceive them with the outward ear. When on the mountain of Transfiguration, the words, "This is my beloved Son, in whom I am well pleased, *hear ye him*," were spoken, the command implied that the disciples should hear with loving and believing hearts, that they should bring themselves so into sympathy with him, or rather into such an attitude of loving submission before him, that his words should find a welcome in their minds. When Mary, sitting at his feet, *heard* his word (Luke x. 39), it was with reverential affection that she received his instructions. And this loving reverence for Christ is still needed in order that we may truly hear his words.

**upon a rock**] The living rock. Is there not here an allusion to Christ himself as the foundation? The expression was one familiar to the Jews in relation to the Messiah: " Behold, I lay in Zion for a foundation a stone, a tried stone, a precious corner-stone, a sure foundation " (Isa. xxviii. 16). " He founds his house on a rock," says Alford, " who, hearing the words of Christ, brings his heart and life into accordance with his expressed will, and is thus by faith in union with him founded on him. Whereas he who merely hears his words, but does them not, has never dug down to the rock, nor become united with it, nor has any stability in the hour of trial." **25, 27. and beat upon that house**] In verse 25, the Greek word προσέπεσαν means to *fall upon;* in 27, προσέκοψαν means to *strike* or *dash against.* The two words are wisely chosen to describe the different effects produced by the same temptations on different persons; *falling* upon the good to purify and confirm them, but *dashing violently* on others so as entirely to overthrow in them every principle of faith and love.

## CHAPTER VIII.

### Gospel View of Miracles.

In this and the next four chapters we have detailed accounts of our Saviour's actions, and particularly of his miracles. There lie in some minds objections so strong against miracles, and the assaults on the credibility of the Gospel narratives have rested so much on these objections, that it may be well here to look carefully into the subject.

What is a miracle? Not a violation or suspension of the laws of nature. "If," says Olshausen, Vol. I. p. 236, "we start from the Scriptural view of the abiding presence of God in the world, the laws of nature do not admit of being conceived of as mechanical arrangements, which would have to be altered by interpositions from without; but they have the character of being based, as a whole, in God's nature. All phenomena, therefore, which are not explicable from the known or unknown laws of the development of earthly life ought not for that reason to be looked upon as violations of law and suspensions of the laws of nature; rather, they are themselves comprehended under a higher general law, for what is Divine is truly according to law. That which is not Divine is against nature; the real miracle is natural, but in a higher sense. It is true, the cause of the miracle must not be sought within the sphere of created things; the cause of it exists rather in the immediate act of God."

A miracle, then, is not a violation of the laws of nature.

It is not an effect without an adequate cause, but in a miraculous act the usual course of physical events is changed, the usual succession of physical causes and effects is stayed, by the intervention of a higher power. When a man raises his hand, the law of gravitation is not suspended in its action upon the hand; but its influence is resisted and overcome by the higher power which intervenes through an act of the will. If, as may be the fact in some cases of animal magnetism, a man is able, by a simple act of the will, to raise not only his own arm but the arms of another, in opposition to the law of gravitation, there would be no violation or suspension of that law. He would merely overcome its resistance in this particular case by the intervention of another and superior power. So if, by a yet more effective exercise of the will, he could stay the progress of disease, quicken again the stagnant current of life in the veins, or bring back to the physical organs the functions of a suspended vitality, it might all be, so far as we can know, in harmony with the laws of nature, and in conformity with what is everywhere recognized as an established fact or law; viz. that where two influences or forces come into collision, the weaker must yield to the stronger. Now, according to the Gospel narratives, Christ was endowed with powers through which he was able to cleanse the leper of his foul disease, quench the fever in its fiery progress, calm the winds, restore the maniac to his right mind, and expel demons, by an exercise of the will to him as easy and as natural as that by which we raise an arm, or with a word silence the noise of playful children. There are no thaumaturgical displays, such as we always find with professed wonder-workers. There are no marks of violent effort. He never, in performing a miracle seems to go out from his usual and normal condition. So far as his methods of action are concerned, there is nothing to separate these from his other works.

In conformity with this supposition, there is a peculiar fitness in the term which Jesus usually applied to his miraculous acts. In the Gospels there are four different words applied to miracles, 1. *prodigies* or *wonders*, τέρατα; 2. *powers* or *mighty works*, δύναμεις; 3. *signs*, σημεῖα; and, 4. *works*, ἔργα. The only instance in which the word τέρατα, corresponding to our word miracles, is applied to miraculous acts by Jesus is where he speaks of them (Matthew xxiv. 24; Mark xiii. 22) as performed by false prophets, with whom they must indeed have been prodigies or wonders, and (John iv. 48, "Except ye see signs and wonders, ye will not believe,") where he speaks of them as they appear to those who, not believing in him, could regard them only as prodigies. The similar word, wonderful things, θαυμάσια, occurs but once (Matthew xxi. 15), and there when mention is made of the acts of Jesus as they appeared to the chief priests and scribes who did not believe in him. Jesus himself never used either of these words as properly describing what he had done. It is to be regretted that the distinction which is so carefully observed in the original should not have been retained in the translation, and especially that the word miracle, in which the idea of something wonderful etymologically predominates, should not have been confined, as it is in the original Gospels, to the few cases where such a meaning was specially applicable. This would have cut off at once the whole class of objections which arise from the habit of viewing these acts as something monstrous and unnatural. "The very word Miracle," says Mr. Emerson, in his Divinity College Address, p. 12, "as pronounced by Christian churches, gives a false impression; it is Monster. It is not one with the blowing clover and the falling rain." But this "false impression" is not authorized by any language of Christ, or any name or view of miracle which has been used by the Evangelists.

Usually, Jesus places his miracles among his other acts

without any word to distinguish them from the rest, as in his message to John the Baptist (Matthew xi. 5), or where he alludes to them by a single word, he calls them simply his deeds or works ἔργα. To him, if we may judge from his language, they were neither wonders nor acts requiring an extraordinary exertion of power, nor signs, but simply actions performed in the natural exercise of his faculties. He seldom refers to them at all. And when he does refer to them, except on two or three occasions when the state of mind in those to whom or of whom he was speaking required him to hold them up in the light in which they appeared to others, he speaks of them merely as *his works*. He never calls them *signs*, except that twice (Matthew xii. 39, xvi. 4; Luke xi. 29) he alludes to his death and resurrection as a sign like that of the prophet Jonah, and once (John vi. 26) he says that the multitudes seek him not because they saw the signs, σημεῖα, but because they ate of the loaves and were filled. Nor does he speak of them as powers or mighty acts, except Matthew xi. 21, 23, and Luke x. 13, when upbraiding the faithless cities in which most of them had been wrought. Ten times in the Gospel of John (v. 20, 36; vii. 21; x. 25, 37, 38; xiv. 10, 11, 12; xv. 24) he speaks of them, but always with the single exception already noticed (vi. 26) the same term, *works*, is used.

This use of language is significant in many ways. 1. It gives an indication of the construction which our Saviour himself put upon these extraordinary acts. They were such as man had never done before (John xv. 24), but still they were only his works, not wonders, monsters, or prodigies, which by the very name would indicate a violation of the laws of nature. 2. If Jesus had been an impostor, seeking to impose on men by the display of such marvellous powers, he would have been inclined to make the most of them as signs and wonders, and to refer to them constantly as such. 3. If, on the other hand, as Strauss and others suppose, Jesus, a pure and gifted teacher of sublime moral and religious truths, never performed such miraculous acts as are ascribed to him in the Gospel, but they gradually, as myths or legends, grew up round his life in the minds of those who came after him, and thus became at length a part of his personal history, then they who put the Gospels into their present shape, whether they invented these stories themselves, or honestly received them as traditions from an earlier age, must always have viewed them as wonders and prodigies, and spoken of them as such, whether referring to them in their own assumed character as evangelists or in the person of Jesus. From their point of view they could not have regarded them, nor could they have conceived of Jesus as regarding them, in the easy, natural, and subordinate relation which they now hold to him. No one but him who had himself lived within the sphere of powers adequate to such works, and to whom they were only his fitting and appropriate acts, could teach men to regard them in such a light, or stand as the original model for such a conception. And writers who had not been conversant with such a being, or known these to be the real facts of the case, could never so represent him and them, and preserve throughout on such a scale the grand but harmonious proportions of his divine thought, life, and acts. Especially would this have been impossible on the mythical hypothesis, which implies that the writers must have wrought their accounts of miraculous events into the life of Jesus from a conviction, on their part, of the superior dignity and importance of those events, and from a desire through them to make the strongest possible impression on the minds of others.

Δύναμεις, *powers*, is applied to miracles seven times in Matthew, four times in Mark, twice in Luke, and not at all in John; σημεῖον, *sign*, twice in Matthew (xii. 39; xvi. 4), twice in Mark (xvi. 17, 20), twice in Luke (xi. 29; xxiii. 8), and fourteen times in John; ἔργον, twelve times in John, but not at all in any other Gospel, and in John, in every instance but one, it is used by Jesus himself. The dramatic propriety in the use of these words by Jesus is remarkable. The name *wonders* is given to miracles from their effect; *powers*, from their cause; *signs*, from their purpose. *Works*, the only word literally describing them as they are, is the one used by Jesus.

To *him*, living in the bosom of the Father, by whom all power had been given to him, there was nothing wonderful or extraordinary in the fact that he should still the tempest or raise the dead. From the deeper spiritual insight which he possessed, and the higher spiritual powers which he had come into the world to exercise and to impart, he regarded the power of working miracles as among the inferior gifts, not only of himself, but of his disciples (Luke x. 20), and declared that they who believed in him (John xiv. 12) should [in the exercise of their spiritual endowments] perform even greater works than those which he had done. And if he had actually lived in the conscious exercise of such powers, looking out on the world of matter and of spirit, as with the eye of God, from the central point of life and thought, and so impressing himself on the minds of his followers, he would stand before them as the great reality which they were to describe. The ascendency which he would have over them would bring their minds into harmony with his. His modes of thought would become theirs. The miracles which at first awakened their astonishment, and seemed to stand out as prodigies, would at length, through his higher influences and instructions, gradually subside into a subordinate place, and there, in concert with his diviner words and acts, give their modest testimony to his authority.

Here we are enabled to show the peculiar office of the miracles of Jesus in testifying to the truth of his religion. 1. They served then, as they have in all ages since, to attract the attention of those whose spiritual natures were not yet sufficiently unfolded to see the moral beauty of his life or to feel the spiritual power of his instructions. 2. He referred to them (John v. 36; x. 25; xiv. 11) as a proof of the divine authority with which he spoke. Standing by themselves, they could furnish no such proof. They might excite our wonder, but they could not gain our confidence. We should painfully feel the want of a moral basis for their support, and therefore would find it hard to free ourselves from a suspicion of fraud. But the spotless purity which marked the conduct of Jesus, the moral grandeur of his instructions, and the whole tendency and bearing of his ministry, give a perfect assurance that he could not have meant to deceive when he appealed as he did to his miracles. And the fact that they were actually performed would take away all suspicion of his having been imposed upon himself. When he announced the doctrine of man's immortality, for example, as if it were a fact known to him through spiritual powers of vision more than human, we should feel that, however lofty his genius and puré his life, he might be deceived. The habit of dwelling so earnestly and exclusively on subjects of this kind might lead him into a state of ecstasy, in which the conceptions of his own mind would be mistaken for objective realities, or facts. But when he who announces such a doctrine stands by the grave of one who has been dead three days, and at his voice the dead man comes forth alive, this work, the effect of more than human powers of action, prepares us to receive the doctrine which professes to come from more than human powers of spiritual perception. He cannot be mistaken as to the miraculous fact which he places before us; and this takes away all reasonable suspicion of self-delusion or mistake in regard to the doctrine. The more than human powers of action which the miracle has put beyond question must, when taken in connection with the purity of his life, oblige us to recognize the more than human powers of spiritual perception which he claims to possess, and to receive on his authority the doctrines which he announces as revealed to him in the exercise of those powers. Restoring a dead man to life by an effort of the will is in itself no evidence of our immortality; but it is evidence of superhuman powers of action on the part of him who has performed it, and, as such, taken in connection with a life of perfect purity, constrains us to admit his claims to superhuman powers in other directions. Man could not have done such deeds without assistance from some power or agency mightier than his own. Jesus says (Luke xi. 20) it was by the finger of God that he cast out devils, and (John xiv. 10) that it was the Father dwelling in him who did the works. The nature of the doctrines to be confirmed and of the kingdom to be established by them shows, as he justly reasoned (Luke xi. 17) that they could not have been wrought by any Satanic agency. They must then have been wrought by a power (Matthew xi. 27, xxviii. 18) specially derived from God, and in attestation of his authority as a teacher from God. In this way the miracles confirm, beyond all possibility of doubt or suspicion, the divine authority with which he spoke, — an authority which without them could not have been so firmly established on any just principles of reasoning, or by any other agencies that were likely to act so powerfully on the human mind or heart.

3. There is a sense of harmony and completeness which the miracles are needed to fill out and sustain, in our conception of Christ. Without the superhuman endowments implied by them, words such as we find on almost every page of the Gospels would seem to us almost like blasphemy. When he says (John vi. 41), "I am the bread which came down from heaven," or (John xi. 25), "I am the resurrection and the life," or (Matthew xi. 28), "Come unto me, all ye that labor and are heavy laden, and I will give you rest," the words seem to proceed from the depths of a profound humility. They are the natural utterance

of a being divinely endowed, and condescending with inexpressible dignity and tenderness to our weaknesses and sorrows. If they had been spoken by a man of the most exalted piety and genius, by Milton or Fénelon, or by the greatest among the prophets or apostles, by Moses or Elijah, by Peter, John, or Paul, they would fall harshly upon us. As spoken by Jesus, they awaken a sense of harmony and repose. They are in character with all that he did and was. But if the divine endowments through which his miracles were wrought should be taken from him, and he should be to us in this respect like other men, the words to which we turn now for comfort and support, and which draw us so affectingly and reverently to him, would be emptied of their indwelling life and power. They would no longer come to us as the pledges of God's mercy and his presence among men, but would mock our dearest affections and our hopes.

When, after announcing on the Mount truths such as man had never uttered, speaking with an authority which awed and subdued those who heard him, though by those very words he was breaking up and disappointing all the ideas and expectations of the Messiah which had been cherished for centuries in the heart of the nation, — when from the utterance of divine truths such as these he came down and commanded the leper to be cleansed or the centurion's son to be healed, he was only exercising in another direction the same divine power that he had already manifested in words which stand a perpetual sign and proof of his more than mortal endowments. The whole bearing of Christ, as he appears in the Gospels, is simple and consistent with itself. It everywhere testifies to his identity. Whosoever recognizes the miracles, and enters into their meaning, is prepared to receive his instructions. He who understands his words most thoroughly, and who enters most deeply into his spirit, will find himself admitted there within "the hidings of a power" wholly adequate to the performance of any deeds which are recorded as his. For he who with a divine authority uttered truths kept secret from the foundation of the world, and who in his life so far transcended the loftiest ideals of virtue and holiness that ever dawned upon the soul, was only acting in perfect consistency with himself when he did works "which none other man" had ever done.

1 – 4. — HEALING THE LEPER.

When Jesus came down from the mountain — it probably was not till the morning after the sermon — he was still followed by vast numbers of people. Among others a leper, *one full of leprosy* (Luke v. 12), cut off by his unclean disease from familiar intercourse with others, hanging upon the skirts of the crowd, and having perhaps heard the kind words of Jesus to them that are afflicted, watched his opportunity, and, as soon as he could reach him without coming into immediate contact with the crowd, approached him, and, with the mark of respect usually paid by an inferior to a superior, throwing himself before him, said, "Sir, if thou wilt, thou canst make me clean." And Jesus, stretching out his hand, touched him, and said, "I will; be thou clean." And immediately his leprosy was cleansed. There is nothing, it will be observed, in the manner of the narrative to distinguish this from any other act of Jesus, or to indicate any unusual exertion or exercise of power on his part. He charged the man to say nothing about it to any one, but to go show himself to the priest, and offer the gift which Moses had commanded for a testimony to them. The reason for enjoining silence may have been to secure from the priest a certificate of the cure before his jealousy was excited by a knowledge of the manner in which it had been effected. The certificate once obtained would be a testimony unto them — whether "*them*" refers to the priests or the people, or, as it well may, to both — that the miraculous cure had actually been wrought. The caution may have been given because Jesus foresaw the danger either to the man's person or character to which he would be exposed by the notoriety that must follow such a disclosure, or, as would seem from Mark i. 45, Jesus wished himself to avoid the notoriety and the increasing crowds which were likely to be caused by the report of such a miracle, and which, according to Mark, were such as to oblige him to withdraw into unfrequented and desert places. One or all of these reasons may have influenced Jesus, and he may also, as Ambrose has said, have wished to set to his disciples an example of the unostentatious way in which they were to exercise their miraculous powers.

It has been supposed that leprosy was set apart by the Jewish law from all other diseases as in a peculiar sense the emblem of sin. All diseases in some way and degree immediately or remotely come from sin or a violation of God's law. But this, as the most fearful and revolting form of disease, was selected from all the rest, and held up as a proof of the Divine displeasure, and to excite the religious horror of men against all sin and uncleanness. The cases of Miriam (Numbers xii. 10–15), Gehazi (2 Kings v. 27), and Uzziah (2 Chronicles xxvi. 16–21) served to connect it in a forcible manner with the direct inflictions of Divine justice. "The Jews themselves," says Trench on Miracles, p. 177, "termed it 'the finger of God,' and emphatically, 'the stroke.' They said that it attacked first a man's house, and, if he did not turn, his clothing; and then, if he persisted in sin, himself: a fine symbol, whether the fact was so or not, of the manner in which God's judgments, if men refuse to listen to them, reach ever nearer to the centre of their life." Even the Persians, according to Herodotus, Lib. I. cap. 138, cut off the leper from intercourse with other men as if he were suffering for some peculiar offence against their divinity.

The disease assumed different forms, and the marks by

which the different kinds are distinguished are pointed out with great minuteness in the thirteenth and fourteenth chapters of Leviticus. Sometimes it covered the whole body as with shining scales of snow, and when these flakes were rubbed off the flesh appeared raw and inflamed underneath. Sometimes it did not seriously affect the general health, and sometimes the whole system wasted away, toes and feet, fingers and arms falling off joint by joint. "The best authors of the present day, who have had an opportunity of observing the disease," says Dr. Kitto, "do not consider it to be contagious." But when the Crusades threw hundreds of thousands of Europeans into Asia, the seat of this plague, it spread like an epidemic over all Europe, and in France alone there were no less than two thousand leper-houses set apart for its victims, who were viewed with a sort of religious horror, "looked upon," says Calvin, "as already dead," and clothed in shrouds while the masses for the dead were said for them.

In Palestine these miserable beings are now confined to a spot near Jerusalem, and to Nablous which occupies the site of the ancient Shechem. A little south of Jerusalem, "and hard by the city gate," says Williams, Holy City, Vol. I. Sup. p. 24, "are the *Lepers' Huts*. They are allowed to intermarry, and thus propagate this loathsome malady which is hereditary. And a most pitiable sight it is to see the poor wretches, laid at the entrance of the gates of the city, asking alms of the passengers, with outstretched hands or stumps, in various stages of decay, under the influence of this devouring disease, for which, I believe, no effectual remedy is known. I saw no case of that whiteness, which is mentioned in Scripture as the symptom of this disorder; but I own that my eyes shrunk with horror from the contemplation of such misery, and I avoided contact with them as I would with one plague-stricken." "The children," says Dr. Robinson, Vol. I. p. 359, "are said to be healthy until puberty or later; when the disease makes its appearance in a finger, on the nose, or in some like part of the body, and gradually increases so long as the victim survives. They are said often to live to the age of forty or fifty years."

These probably are afflicted by that variety of the disease which is called Elephantiasis. But in whatever form we regard it, and whether it was contagious or not, we see enough in it that was terrible and revolting to justify Moses in setting it apart by itself, and in making it, if any disease were to be used for that purpose, an emblem of the unclean, revolting, and deadly nature of sin, creeping in from the extremities to the centre of life. The leper, says Trench, "was himself a dreadful parable of death. It is evident that Moses intended that he should be so contemplated by all the ordinances which he gave concerning him. The leper was to bear about the emblems of death (Lev. xiii. 45), the rent garments, that is, mourning garments, he mourning for himself as for one dead; the head bare, as they were wont to have it who were in communion with the dead (Num. vi. 9; Ezek. xxiv. 17), and the lip covered (Ezek. xxiv. 17). In the restoration, too, of a leper, exactly the same instruments of cleansing were in use — the cedar-wood, the hyssop, and the scarlet — as were used for the cleansing of one defiled through a dead body, or aught pertaining to death, and which were never in use upon any other occasion. (Compare Num. xix. 6, 13, 18 with Lev. xiv. 4-7). "The leper was as one dead, and as such was to be put out of the camp (Lev. xiii. 46; Num. v. 2-4; 2 Kings vii. 3), or afterwards out of the city; and we find this law to have been so strictly enforced, that even the sister of Moses might not be exempted from it (Num. xii. 14, 15), and kings themselves, Uzziah (2 Chron. xxvi. 21) and Azariah (2 Kings xv. 5), must submit to it."

The eminent Jewish writer, Philo Judæus, whose Platonizing habits of thought, however, allow little weight to his authority in matters of this kind, whenever he refers to the

Mosaic accounts of leprosy speaks of them (Unchangeableness of God, xxvii., xxviii.) as describing the taint of sin in the soul; and there is little doubt that the disease was regarded by the Jews as in a peculiar manner caused by the Divine displeasure in punishment for sin, and to be healed, not by the skill of man, but by the immediate act of God. When Jesus, therefore, healed the leper, he, in their eyes, not merely cured him of his disease, but cleansed him from his sin. Evidently this idea of cleansing him in the sight of the law is that which is uppermost in the mind of Matthew, who is writing for Jewish readers; while Mark and Luke, writing for those who might not understand the full force of the Jewish expression to cleanse, add that "the leprosy departed from him."

This view of the disorder, and of the light in which it was regarded by the Jews, will enable us to understand something of the feeling with which the wretched man who believed himself smitten of God, and cut off by a moral taint as well as by a most loathsome and terrible disease from the companionship of man, threw himself before Jesus, and looked up to him with that supplicating expression of confidence, "Lord, if thou wilt, thou canst make me clean." It may enable us to see how Jesus, when he touched him, and said, "I will; be thou clean," must have appeared to the Jews as standing in the place of God, and as by the finger of God removing, not only a foul disease, but at the same time and by the same act the moral taint which was connected with it as cause with effect. And it may also enable us to see in this what is characteristic of all his miracles, that the moral influences are inseparably connected with the physical power which he put forth, so that when "himself took," v. 17, "our infirmities and bare our sicknesses," he also, in a deeper sense, as our version of the passage in Isaiah has it (Isa. liii. 4), "hath borne our griefs and carried our sorrows," or even, according to the Septuagint version, "bears our sins, and is afflicted in our behalf."

In its primary meaning, the expression, "be thou clean," or "his leprosy was cleansed," refers to the law. He was clean who was pronounced to be so by the priest. There was therefore a special propriety in using the word *cleanse* in connection with the command to go to a priest. But in its secondary meaning, which was undoubtedly uppermost in the mind both of Jesus and of the sufferer, it referred to the removal, not of a legal restraint, but of the disease itself. Whether Jesus at the same time had reference to the moral cleansing from sin, the renovation of soul as well as of body, cannot with certainty be inferred from anything that is related by either of the Evangelists, though, if the view above given of leprosy being set apart in the Mosaic law as a visible type and expression of sin and its consequences be true, it is probable that this idea was also included in the words of Jesus.

This passing from things sensible to things spiritual and the reverse, without changing the language, or changing the language without a corresponding change in the thought, is very common with Jesus, and is often the occasion of perplexity to those commentators who would determine in each case precisely what was his meaning. Familiar instances will occur to every diligent student of the Gospels. Indeed it is characteristic of all figurative language, especially when that language, suggested by immediate objects or events, is charged with a new meaning, and made to contain and perpetuate thoughts of wide application and extent. "The light of the body is the eye." "Whosoever shall smite thee on thy right cheek, turn to him the other also." "Destroy this temple, and in three days I will raise it up." "Lift up your eyes and look on the fields; for they are white already to harvest." Here are examples in which familiar images stand before us as representatives of an outward and material, or of an inward and spiritual fact.

5 - 13. — HEALING THE CENTURION'S SERVANT.

Jesus had now come into Capernaum, which might be regarded as his home, though, as he says, v. 20, he had no home of his own. He only accepted the hospitality that was offered him. The centurion who met him as he entered the city was not (Luke vii. 1 – 10) a Jew, though from his kindness in helping the Jews to build a synagogue he probably was a believer in their religion. From his acquaintance with heathen forms of worship and of faith, in which he had doubtless been educated, and which could hardly have been effaced from his mind, the idea of spiritual beings occupying different subordinate positions, and ready, as the inferior heathen gods were supposed to be, to do the bidding of their superiors, must have been familiar to him. It is difficult to determine precisely what idea he, from his peculiar religious associations and habits of thought, may have had of Jesus. He evidently regarded him as one endowed with more than human attributes, whom he felt himself unworthy to have under his roof, but who might command his agents, as inferior spirits, to remove the disease from his servant. All that he asks is that Jesus will only say the word, for then he is sure that his servant will be healed. Since even he, in his subordinate position as a man *under* authority, had soldiers under him who would go and come and do as he commanded them, it must be that Jesus could by a word send his unseen agents to do whatever he might command. It was this perfect confidence, connected as it was with his sense of personal unworthiness, that called out from Jesus the strong language of commendation which he used. Such faith, — such a readiness to believe and trust in him, — he had not found, no, not in all Israel.

And in this humble-minded believer, who is not of the seed of Abraham, he sees a type of the thousands, from the Gentile nations, who shall crowd into his kingdom, and be accepted as his friends. From the east and the west, from the north and the south (Luke xiii. 29), they shall come to the feast, and recline at the table with Abraham and Isaac and Jacob, in the kingdom of Heaven, while the sons of the kingdom who reject his offers will be cast out into the outer darkness.

The allusion is to a great feast held in the evening, where the worthy guests are admitted to partake of its joys, while they who come without the fitting qualifications are turned out from the pleasant light and festivity within the banqueting-hall, into the darkness of night, which prevails without.

The image, viewed in the light of Oriental usage, is an exceedingly striking one, and is often repeated by our Saviour under different forms. They who believed themselves the exclusive sons of the kingdom, entitled above all others to its honors and its joys, in the day of its festal triumph and rejoicing, when their king, the long-expected Messiah, should be seated on his throne and invite the faithful to partake of his feast, should see him whom they had rejected exalted over all, and those whom they had despised as outcasts called in to take their honored places with Abraham and Isaac and Jacob, while they themselves should be thrust out from the light and splendor and festivity of the banquet-hall to the outside darkness that was pressing upon them, and the shame, sorrow, indignation, and contempt which awaited them there. No image could be more full of meaning or of terror to the Jews, than to be not only excluded from the great company of illustrious men, — patriarchs and prophets and kings, — whom they professed to reverence; but to be cast out into darkness and despair at the very hour when those whom they had despised as outcasts from the kingdom should be brought in to the royal banquet.

Jesus then spoke the word, and the centurion's servant,

whom he had never seen, was healed at that very hour. Here, again, we see how intimately the exercise of his miraculous power was connected with the high religious purposes of his mission. Not merely was that power put forth to relieve the sufferings of a painful disease and to reward the kind-hearted master by restoring to him the dying servant to whom he was fondly attached, but it was so put forth as to confirm his religious faith, and give the weight of his authority to the sublime instructions by which it was accompanied, and which reached through temporal disease and death to the festive light of spiritual joy and the outer darkness, which lie in realms beyond.

### 14 – 17. — BEARING OUR INFIRMITIES.

After healing the leper and the centurion's servant, Jesus healed Peter's mother-in-law, at the house (Mark i. 29) which was owned by Simon [Peter] and Andrew. Jesus evidently (Mark i. 33, 35) spent the night there, and it may have been his usual place of abode while in Capernaum. He probably arrived there in the morning, and according to the custom of the place had remained unoccupied through the hottest part of the day. Towards night, when the heat had so far abated that the sick could be taken abroad without exposure to its severity, many feeble and suffering persons, especially those who were called demoniacs, were brought to him, and the whole city was gathered together in the court by the door, to witness the cures that he wrought. As the evening shadows began to fall, and those afflicted with various fevers and violent madness were borne to him, he took away their diseases, and thus, in the view of the writer, fulfilled in himself the remarkable words of the prophet (Isaiah liii. 4). Matthew translates the words literally from the Hebrew, " Himself took our infirmities, and bare our sicknesses." But in our translation of Isaiah liii. 4, it reads, "Surely he hath borne our griefs and carried our sorrows." In the Septuagint it is rendered, "He bears our sins and is pained in our behalf," from which undoubtedly is borrowed (Heb. ix. 28), "Christ was once offered to bear the sins of many," and (1 Pet. ii. 24), "Who his own self bare our sins in his own body on the tree."

But which of these meanings is the true one, or may we accept them all? Throughout the Scriptures, as indeed in all the writings (particularly those of an imaginative character) which affect us most deeply, words primarily expressing ideas connected with matter and our physical condition or sensations, extend their influence into the region of mental or moral and religious ideas. The different shades of meaning melt insensibly into one another, or the words are placed in such relations that we may with almost equal propriety regard them as standing for ideas belonging to any one, or to all, of these classes. The passage just quoted is an instance of this. In its primary and literal signification (Lowth, Noyes, Barnes, &c.) it undoubtedly applies to bodily sufferings (infirmities and sicknesses), and therefore furnishes Matthew from the Messianic prophecies with a striking illustration of the cures which he had just described as performed by Jesus. But these same words (infirmities and sicknesses), in their secondary meaning, pass over into the region of mental affections, and, as expressing the disorders and sufferings of the mind, are properly translated, as in our common version, *griefs* and *sorrows*. Again, the same words may with equal propriety be taken in their relation to the moral nature, and then, as expressing moral disorders and the sufferings consequent upon them, they may be rendered, as in the Septuagint, by words which mean sins and sorrows: "He bears our sins, and endures sorrows in our behalf."

The interpretation given by Matthew, which is unquestionably the true, as it is the literal one, in its application to the scene before him, is important as showing in what sense the Apostle, writing after the resurrection of Jesus, understood him to have taken upon himself our infirmities and our sicknesses. When he healed the sick and took away from them their diseases, then, so far as bodily infirmities and sicknesses were concerned, the words of the prophet were fulfilled. If therefore the infirmities and sicknesses which the prophet speaks of should have a deeper meaning and refer also to diseases which afflict the soul, i. e. to our sins and the sorrows which proceed from them, we are authorized by the Apostle's example to infer that Jesus takes them upon himself in the same way in which he takes our bodily diseases, and that, as in healing our bodily infirmities and removing our sicknesses from us, "himself bare" them, so in healing the diseases of the soul and removing our sins from us, he in like manner bears them in his own body and takes them upon himself. In this last expression, however, from Peter, as also in Hebrews ix. 28, the view which impressed Matthew so strongly is intensified by the great and additional thought of the crucifixion.

But while the passage admits of these three different meanings without doing violence to its language, can we suppose that such language was used by the prophet in order that we might deduce from it any one or all of these different meanings? There is nothing in the context to decide this question, and, in the absence of any such aid, the literal interpretation is the most natural, and therefore the one to be preferred in a translation. But is there, considered by itself, any absurdity or any violent improbability, in the supposition that language may intentionally be so used as to express a fact, which, according to our state of mind and the light in which we view it, may be taken either in its physical, its mental, or its spiritual bearings and relations, especially in writings so intensely imaginative as those of the Hebrew prophets, or in words made to bear such unaccustomed and hitherto unknown burdens of thought and life as those which Jesus was obliged to employ?

From the beginning to the end of his mission Christ was obliged to impose upon words meanings which they had never borne before, and which, however familiar they may be to us, were perpetually misunderstood and stumbled over, not only by the Jews, but by his own immediate disciples. The expression *kingdom of Heaven* was used by him in a sense entirely different from that in which they understood it. And yet there must have been some common point of intelligence, or the expression could not have been used as a medium of communication between his mind and theirs; it could only have misled them, or been to them as a strange tongue. That common point was the Messiah's kingdom. Both he and they used the words kingdom of Heaven to express that idea. But while he meant that they should understand it in that sense till they were capable of something better, and used the expression, knowing that they would so apply it, how infinitely above their conceptions was the thought which to his mind radiated from those words and threw its divine glories around them, and which by and by should open on their minds to enlarge and spiritualize their gross, earthly conceptions. There is then in this case, understood and intended by Christ, a double meaning, — one, the primary meaning, adapted to their present condition, making a lodgement in their minds ; and the other, a higher spiritual meaning which should unfold itself from the germ lodged there with the higher spiritual development of their natures. In this way may not material images, borrowed from an earthly kingdom, have been employed by the ancient prophets to familiarize the minds of the people with conceptions as pure as they could understand, and thus keep alive the heart and expectation of the nation through the long and desolate days of their preparation, till at last, in a higher spiritual light, and with a purer type of character, they see in those words a meaning which they had never dreamed of before? The subject is mentioned here only to call the reader's attention to it, but will be recurred to hereafter more than once.

## 18 – 22. — LET THE DEAD BURY THEIR DEAD.

A somewhat similar use of language occurs almost immediately in the narrative before us. Jesus, oppressed by the multitudes, had commanded his disciples to prepare to pass over the lake, when a scribe, i. e. a teacher of the law, and therefore a man of some consequence, offered to follow him whithersoever he might go. Jesus, perhaps seeing that motives of worldly ambition may have influenced him, announced to him his own homeless condition. Then another person came and asked to be excused from following him till he had gone and buried his father. Jesus replied, "Follow me, and leave the dead to bury their own dead." The first *dead* is used in a spiritual sense, of those who, having no interest in Christ, are spiritually dead. The second part of the sentence takes up the word in the literal and bodily sense in which it has just been used. Thus there is a passing from one meaning to another, and a commingling of different meanings of the same word within the limits of a very short, and, in its grammatical construction, a very simple, sentence. The probability is, that the disciple, wishing to make his filial duty an excuse for not immediately following Christ, of whose success or divine mission he may have had doubts, and therefore asking to be permitted to tarry at home till he had buried his father, i. e. till his father had died, found his secret motives laid bare and his temporizing policy rebuked, by Christ's suddenly turning upon him in its higher and more awful application, the very word which he had used. "Suffer me first to *bury* my father." No, "Leave the dead to bury their own dead," "but go thou (Luke ix. 60) and preach the kingdom of God." It is impossible to bring out the whole force that is compressed into these few words. It was as if he had said: "If you are really my disciple, you have received a higher life, and it is your part to go forth with the words of eternal life, causing the dead to live, and not linger here by your earthly home, waiting till your father dies, in order that you may perform the rites of sepulture for him. It is a higher duty to save the living than to bury the dead." The condensed force and pungency of the command, which rings with such power even in the ears of those who cannot analyze it, is lost in every attempt to explain it by amplification. The force consists very much in the sudden retort of the word *bury*, the rapid change from a literal to a figurative meaning, and the blending of both in one with such a compressed energy of utterance.

It is not probable that the father was already dead; for the burial usually took place in the evening after the decease. But if he were dead, the words of Jesus will express all the more earnestly the uncompromising urgency of the call.

### 23 – 27. — STILLING THE TEMPEST.

The Lake or Sea of Galilee, of Tiberias, or of Genesareth, is about fourteen statute miles long, and in its widest part about seven miles wide. Except on the northwestern side, about Capernaum and northward, where the ascent is a gradual one, and reaches to a height of from 300 to 500 feet, the hills on its borders rise steep, but seldom precipitous, till they attain to an elevation of 800 or 1,000 feet above the lake. Beyond the hills on the north, the snowy summit of Mount Hermon rises 10,000 feet or more above the level of the sea. The impression made by the lake and the surrounding scenery is differently described by different writers. Dr. Robinson says that the attraction lies more in the associations than in the scenery. "The hills," he says, Vol. III. p. 253, "are rounded and tame, with little of the picturesque in their form; they are decked by no shrubs or forests. . . . . . Whoever looks here for the magnificence of the Swiss lakes, or the softer beauty of those of England and the United States, will be disappointed." Again, at p. 312, he says, "The form of its basin is not unlike an oval; but the regular and almost unbroken heights which enclose it bear no comparison, as to vivid and powerful effect, with the wild and stern magnificence around the caldron of the Dead Sea." Prof. Hackett, on the other hand, says, p. 318, "For myself, I cannot hesitate to say that the appearance of the lake, reposing so quietly in its deep bed, the framework of hills which encase it on almost every side, the steep precipices coming down in some cases so boldly to the shore, the cloudless sky above, having its every hue and variation reflected back from the watery mirror beneath, formed in my eye a combination of landscape beauty equal, to say the least, to any other which it has been my privilege to see in any land."

It was one of the sudden gusts which sweep down through mountain gorges that threatened to destroy the little vessel in which Jesus and his disciples, with a few others, were crossing the lake from the northwestern towards the southeastern shore. It was in the evening (Mark iv. 35, 36), after he had sent the multitude away, and probably at a later period in the ministry of Jesus than its place in the narrative of Matthew would indicate. Jesus entered the boat *just* "*as he was*," without any preparation for the journey; and being doubtless fatigued by the exhausting labors of the day, he had fallen asleep at the stern, lying on a pillow (Mark v. 38), or rather a "seat cover," which was probably (Smith's Dis. on the Gospels, p. 287) "a sheep-skin with the fleece, which when rolled up served as a pillow." A sudden "squall of wind," λαῖλαψ ἀνέμου, (Luke viii. 23,) came down upon the lake. There was a violent commotion in the sea, 24, "the waves beating into the vessel," (Mark iv. 37,) so that it was hidden by them, and filling with water. The danger was imminent and instant. The disciples came, one of them crying out, "Lord, save us, we perish;" another, "Rabbi, carest thou not that we perish?" (Mark iv. 38;) and another, with yet more emphatic urgency, "Master, master, we perish." (Luke viii. 24.) He, though suddenly awakened, mildly expostulated with his disciples, "Why are ye fearful, O ye of little faith?" Then he arose, and, rebuking the winds and the sea, — "the wind and the raging of the water," (Luke viii. 24,) — he said, "Peace, be still," and immediately there was a great calm.

Some modern writers have endeavored to throw discredit upon the narrative by denying that these storms on the lake are dangerous, and even Dr. Robinson has said, that in our day they are neither frequent nor severe. But Mr. Bartlett, in his "Footsteps of our Lord and his Apostles," thus describes a storm which he witnessed there on one occasion after sunset: "As it grew darker, the breeze increased to a gale, the lake became a sheet of foam, and the white-headed breakers dashed proudly on the rugged beach." If such storms were unusual, they would on that account be all the more terrific when they did come, and this circumstance would account for the extreme terror of the disciples.

We cannot help quoting here, slightly transposed, a few sentences from a discourse by a friend whose pure mind and spiritual insight, united with earnest and untiring habits of study, would have done much for Biblical learning if his life had been spared. "This incident in the Saviour's life," says Rev. George F. Simmons in his Sermon on Christ in the Storm, "lies, like the mirror of the lake on which it transpired, amidst the solemnities and eventfulness of the Gospel history. It lies by itself, forming a little picture of bounded outline. Though a mere glimpse, — as it were a stream of sunlight upon distant water, that comes out for a moment, and is over, — yet it impressed itself upon all the reporters; for each of the Gospels has given it, with but slight circumstances of difference. The imperturbable calmness of the great leader's mind makes the scene itself as placid as a summer's day. It raises in us a momentary commotion, and then quiets us with the stillness of his heaven-fast mind. The fear of the disciples was by no means unreasonable, so far as the circumstances were concerned. But in the midst of it all, we see the man Jesus, whose name is to become a heavenly name to all the world, and who first is to go through such a cruel martyrdom, sunk in the unconsciousness of natural slumber. Neither responsibility nor the unquiet lake disturbed him. While the water was still, much might have occurred to him as to the danger of losing an opportunity of exhortation and teaching. But he knew that Divine Providence needed not that means should be pressed beyond their natural measure. A lesson for all whose care allows them no rest. The bed is hard; the wind is bleak; the waves dash over the little craft. But Jesus sleeps on. We see there the child of innocence and nature. We see there the child of labor and simplicity. Heaven is to him what the sky and air are to the natural man. His sleep therefore has this double side. It is the sleep of nature and the repose of holiness. All sweet affections, all good desires, the deep calm of prayer, the prophetic vision of piety, both natural and heavenly graces, — are garnered up in that heart which now lives only in holy dreams, — that steadfast will taking rest from the watchful guidance of the magnificent powers intrusted to it.

Too soon that sleep will be disturbed. Too soon they who now call to him will not be able to watch with him one little hour. Rest, holy child! Saviour and Guide of the innocent, rest! It is well for us to covet that capacity for sweet and perfect sleep. We should aim at that tranquillity which care shall not disturb; at that sweetness of a trustful disposition which anxiety shall not embitter."


32-38. — ANGELIC EXISTENCES AND AGENCIES.

The subject here introduced brings us into one of the most obscure departments of theological and metaphysical discussion. The region of pure intelligence, and the province of physical laws and forces, have been explored with great care, and many mature and satisfactory results have been reached. In both these departments we have well-established facts as a scientific basis for further investigations, even if we have not arrived at any thoroughly digested and perfected system of philosophy. But the border region, in which mind and matter are connected and acting on one another, is particularly difficult of exploration, as is the whole realm of being between man and God. How the mind is here united with a physical organization, how it acts upon the nerves and brain, or is acted upon by them, so as to gain through them a knowledge of material things, are questions of great interest, but involved in much obscurity. Whether, under abnormal conditions, particularly when the finer parts of our physical organization are unusually excited by disease or powerful mental emotions, the sensibilities may be so quickened as to lay open to the mind new avenues of information, or new senses may be awakened, are questions which belong to a still more delicate and difficult province of inquiry. Allowing these preternatural sensibilities, or, as they seem to us, these new senses, to exist in some extraordinary instances, and that through them knowledge may be gained of what is passing in the minds of others or what is going on in distant places, have we any reason to suppose that here is anything more than an extraordinary quickening of the perceptive faculties, and through that the recognition and employment of some new physical agent? Or are we to suppose that, as our spirits act through our physical organizations, and in ways heretofore unknown make impressions on other minds, or under certain conditions are admitted to a knowledge of what they think or believe, so also we may be brought into connection with spirits divested of their material forms, and receive communications or impressions from them? Can we, especially in certain extremely delicate or disordered states of the nerves, lay ourselves open to these spirits, or put ourselves under their influence, so that we, as passive instruments or mediums, may be swayed and moved by them, consciously or unconsciously uttering their words, thrilled by their emotions, imparting their thoughts?

These questions, which in all ages have more or less exercised the minds of men, have been pressed upon us under new names and forms by the still unsatisfactory experience and experiments of the last quarter of a century.

There are two ways of looking at the universe.

1. According to one, we recognize the existence of God and men, and the world of material laws and forces. Knowing them, we know all that it is worth our while to know. We have only to worship God, to be just and true to our fellow-men, to study and obey the laws of nature. All beyond this we reject as fanciful and unreal, and therefore unworthy the attention of a strong, enlightened, and philosophical mind.

2. On the other hand, while admitting these facts as containing what it is most essential for us to know, we may believe in the existence and agency of intervening spirits between man and God. We know that the earth

is intimately connected with all the heavenly bodies, seen or unseen, bound by the same laws, acted upon by influences from them, and that it would be left in utter darkness and desolation if they should be withdrawn. These bodies, reaching through the infinite realms of space, are but parts of one vast and orderly system of worlds, mutually dependent one upon another, as all depend on Him who is the Creator and Governor of all. Now, as the earth is thus united in fellowship with all the heavenly constellations, and is affected by every motion in their distant spheres, may it not be that we also, as spiritual and intelligent beings, are in like manner connected with a vast community of spirits, rising in well-ordered ranks one above another, all bound together by the same laws, sympathizing with one another, worshipping the same Father, and seeking to accomplish his ends? As in all that we know of his works here we see his designs carried on by his ministers and agents,— the sun diffusing his light, the earth bringing forth his plants, the lightnings his messengers, and man employed to accomplish his ends,— so, beyond what our eyes can see, may not his higher purposes still be carried on by intervening agents, by the ministry of angels, and the watchfulness and care of attendant spirits? As the severest rules of mathematical reasoning lead to the conclusion that the most distant star is affected by every motion on the earth, might we not, from the analogies of the physical universe, be led to infer that there is a living sympathy between the highest order of spiritual beings and their brethren of kindred nature who are passing through the infancy of their being upon the earth? When Jesus speaks (Matthew xviii. 10) of the intimate relation between his Father in heaven and the angels of little children, and when he speaks (Luke xv. 10) of the joy there is in the presence of the angels of God over one sinner that repenteth, he implies nothing inconsistent with reason, but by those few words lights up the realms of spiritual being, and reveals to us relations which the analogies of nature might suggest as existing between us and God's unseen ministering spirits. The fact that they are invisible furnishes no presumption against their existence; for some of the most important agents in nature, as electricity or magnetism, were, in their constant and essential operation, so hidden from the cognizance of man, that for thousands of years he had no knowledge of their existence.

The doctrine then of the existence of intelligent beings, intermediate between man and God, employed by their Creator and ours in carrying out his purposes, and sustaining important relations to us, is one not unreasonable in itself, though it belongs to a class of facts which lie beyond the cognizance of our perceptive faculties.

Which of the views given above is most in accordance with the language of the New Testament? The question is one of interpretation. In the first chapter of Matthew we twice meet the expression *angel of the Lord*, and the word *angel* occurs three times (once, v. 9, with a peculiar explanation) in the last chapter of the Apocalypse. Throughout the Gospels the existence of angels is constantly recognized, and it evidently enters into the religious consciousness of nearly every writer in the New Testament. An angel (Luke i. 13, 31) foretold the coming of John the Baptist and of the Messiah; an angel (Luke ii. 9, 13) announced the birth of Jesus, and a multitude of the heavenly host joined in the song of gladness which welcomed that event. After the Temptation in the Wilderness angels came and ministered to Jesus. In the mountain of transfiguration (Luke ix. 30, 31) Moses and Elijah appeared in glory talking to him of his departure which he was about to accomplish at Jerusalem. In the agony of the garden (Luke xxii. 43) there appeared unto him an angel from heaven, strengthening him. According to Matthew and John, angels at the sepulchre announced his resurrection, while, evidently referring to the same thing, Mark speaks of a young man at the sepulchre clothed in a long white robe, and Luke, of two men in shining garments. At the ascension, while the disciples were looking steadfastly towards heaven, two men stood near them, in white raiment (Acts i. 10), and as beings from another world spoke to them.

In accordance with these accounts were the teachings of Jesus. "We learn from our Lord's discourses," says Archbishop Newcome, in his Observations on our Lord, Chap. I. Sec. 6, "that the heavenly angels are a numerous host (Matthew xxvi. 53), that they are raised above the imperfect condition of humanity (Matthew xxii. 30), and are holy (Matthew xxv. 31; Mark viii. 38), glorious (Luke ix. 26), and immortal (Luke xx. 36) beings; that they are acquainted (Matthew xxiv. 36; Mark xiii. 32) with many of God's counsels, though not with all, that they are occasionally ministering spirits to mankind, both in this life (Matthew xviii. 10) and the next (Luke xvi. 22); that at the last day our Lord will come to judgment, and all the holy angels with him (Matthew xxv. 31), and that in their presence he will confess those (Luke xii. 8, 9) who boldly confess him before men, and deny those who timidly deny him."

It is impossible to explain these expressions away as figurative on any just grounds of interpretation. The language both of Jesus and of the Evangelists is often specific and minute; it is used, not merely in passages of an imaginative and poetical character, but in the plainest historical details, and is applied under circumstances which admit of no other construction. Where there is no specific and formal reference to them, their existence is sometimes implied by undesigned and spontaneous allusions which show how the thought of them entered into the religious conceptions, and made a part of what is called the religious consciousness of Jesus and the Evangelists.

## 28 – 34. — EVIL AND DISORDERLY SPIRITS.

But what shall we say of the existence and agency of other spirits than those of an angelic character? The subject has already been opened in the chapter on the Temptation in the Wilderness. To deny the existence of evil spirits is not to destroy the kingdom of evil. So long as sin actually exists in the world, and evil spirits are allowed to dwell as wicked men in human bodies, and under the limitations and restraints of our nature, the moral objection to the existence of evil or disorderly spirits under other forms is wholly without force. The objection lies against sin itself and its fatal influences. But as sin does exist and prevail, why may it not show itself in other modes of being as well as in that with which we are familiar? By denying the existence of the devil, we, as Goethe says, "get rid of the wicked one, but the wicked ones remain." Besides, what becomes of all the wicked men who are constantly going from this present mode of life to another? We cannot suppose the bare act of dying, or changing the form of life, to work an essential change of character, and transform them from sin to holiness. If they exist at all, they exist, at least for a time, as evil spirits. Are they then permitted to go at large for a season? As in this world good and bad grow up together, and are open to influences whether of good or of evil from one another, as a bad man often is permitted to have access to innocent minds and to corrupt their virtue, may it not also be, as Swedenborg has supposed, in those modes of being which lie next beyond us, that the good and the bad are for a season allowed to live, to be employed in their different spheres, and, within the rules and limits established by the all-wise Creator and Ruler of all, to labor for the establishment of their kingdom, and to hold out its influences to those who are still upon the earth, that they may receive or reject them? May there not be a

kingdom of evil as well as a kingdom of righteousness
having its seat beyond us, but, within the conditions and
limitations assigned by God, reaching down its poisonous
influences into the sphere of our human interests and relations?

The great and terrible fact that sin with its baleful
influences does exist cannot be denied. Its enticements
and seductions, its pestilence that walketh in darkness,
and its destruction that wasteth at noonday, meet us at
every turn. The world groans under a sense of the degradation and misery and sorrows which it inflicts. Where
is its source? In the soul of man or in the world beyond?
Is there a kingdom of darkness, — the devil and his angels,
as there is a kingdom of light, — the Son of Man and the
holy angels with him? When Christ came to save the
world from sin, did he have to contend only with wicked
men, their passions and crimes, and to infuse into men's
minds the elements of a diviner life? Or did he have
to contend with and overthrow a kingdom of darkness,
lying beyond this world, and yet intimately associated with
it, sending out its emissaries of wrong with every form of
temptation to take advantage of the weaknesses of our
nature and lead us into sin? Did the Prince of Darkness with his agents, recognizing Jesus as one who had
come to destroy their kingdom, meet him in the wilderness, follow him through his ministry, incite Judas to betray
him, and throw every obstruction that they could in his
path? By the reference which Jesus so often makes to
Satan, his kingdom, and his messengers; in the terrible
depth of his anguish at Gethsemane and his cry of desolation upon the cross; are we to recognize merely the existence of sin in its impersonal influence and authority,
seated deeply in the heart of the race, and incorporated
into all its institutions and habits; or are we also to recognize a Prince of Darkness with his attendant and obedient subjects constituting a kingdom of iniquity, and per-

mitted for a season, in the wise providence of God, to range at large through the world?

In this supposition we are always to remember that wicked ones are not omnipotent because they are spiritual, and that, as wicked men here, so wicked spirits there, must be limited by the laws of God, and by the very conditions of their being, in the sphere and mode of their operations. The moral freedom of man, which God himself respects in all his dealings with him for his salvation, he will unquestionably constrain wicked spirits to respect and leave untouched in all their efforts to injure and destroy him. Whatever Jesus may have taught in regard to the agency of evil spirits, the whole force of his instructions goes to show, that, if we only are on our guard, they can have no influence over us for evil.

The question of the existence and agency of evil spirits, like that of good spirits, is not one embarrassed by any physical impossibility or moral improbability. It is simply a question of fact, which lies open to evidence, and is to be treated by commentators on the New Testament as a question of interpretation. What then is taught by Jesus on this subject? In the account of the Temptation, which must have been derived from him, he speaks of Satan as a personal being. The wicked one (Matthew xiii. 19), Satan (Mark iv. 15), and the devil (Luke viii. 12), are used as equivalent terms. Jesus (John viii. 44) tells the Jews that they are of their father the devil, and (Matthew xii. 26) he speaks of Satan as establishing a kingdom in opposition to the kingdom of God. He speaks (John xiv. 30) of the prince of this world, who hath nothing in him, who (John xvi. 11) is judged, and (John xii. 31) shall be cast out. He says (Luke x. 17, 18), "I beheld Satan as lightning fall from heaven," and (Matthew xxv. 41) he speaks of the "everlasting fire, prepared for the devil and his angels."

It is possible that this may be figurative language, used

to express in vivid terms the power of evil. But in reading the Gospels, and the whole of the New Testament with care, seeking, without any prepossessions on our part, to enter into the conception of Christ and his disciples on this subject, we should hardly fail to infer that, to *their minds*, Satan and his angels were personal beings, acting in opposition to them, and exercising a dominion which it was Christ's office to overthrow. The language of the New Testament, its direct expressions and indirect allusions, harmonize more readily with this than with any other hypothesis. For further considerations, see chapter xiii. 39.

There is still another class of beings referred to in language which is to be taken either literally or figuratively. As there are the Son of Man and the holy angels with him, and the devil and his angels, so there are demons, δαιμόνια or δαίμονες, and demoniacs, or persons supposed to be possessed by demons. The word Devil, see Whately on "Good and Evil Spirits," pp. 57, 80, is a proper name, always in the singular number. Wherever the word *devils* occurs in the New Testament it should read *demons*, that being the word in the original. It is unfortunate that in our version these beings are called devils. They were considered by the Jews to be disorderly, mischievous, and, as they are sometimes called (Matthew x. 1, xii. 43, Mark iii. 11, 30, &c.), unclean spirits. The idea seems to have been, that they were wandering about the earth, seeking, as the language of Jesus (Matthew xii. 43–45) suggests, a dwelling-place in some human being, whose will they might control, and whose mental and physical organs they might succeed in subordinating to their own uses.

Two different views of this subject have been taken.

On the one side, it has been maintained, that demoniacs were persons affected by nervous diseases of different kinds, especially when those diseases were so severe as to unsettle the powers of reason and of self-control. In short, they were either subject to fits, or belonged to that large class of sufferers who now find a home, and often, from physical and moral treatment combined, a cure, in our hospitals for the insane.

The other view is, that while the demoniacs were unquestionably diseased, suffering particularly from those nervous affections which are induced by sensual indulgence, and through which the whole system, physical, mental, and moral, is disordered and deranged, they were actually besieged and taken possession of by these mischievous spirits, who were wandering about in quest of a dwellingplace. The spirits, taking advantage of the utter disharmony in their natures, enter through the rents that have been made, usurp the place which their own wills have held so unsteadily, and exercise over them in body and mind a control more or less entire according to the degree of disorder and incapacity that they find. These unhappy victims of demoniacal influence are not represented as adepts in sin. They are not wholly given over to what is evil. They are rather imbecile, or without self-control, given over perhaps to habits of sensual indulgence, and the disorders growing out of it, with a perception, as the Gadarene had, of their unhappiness, but waging a feeble war against temptation, and making a feeble and therefore ineffectual resistance to the tyrannous power which has taken possession of them, and which substitutes his will and at times his consciousness in the place of theirs. He inflames their passions, arms them, as paroxysms of insanity sometimes arm men now, with an almost preternatural strength, drives them into unfrequented and desolate places, weans them from the companionship of man, fills them with delusions and evil thoughts, or forces them to isolate themselves in the midst of their friends by refusing to see or to speak.

In support of the opinion that these cases as described

in the New Testament are only cases of insanity and other severe diseases, particularly nervous affections, it is said,— 1. That language similar to that which is applied to these cases in the New Testament was applied by classical writers of Greece (Xenophon, Mem. I. 9; Aristoph. Plut. II. 3, 38) to sick persons who were to be cured by medical prescriptions. 2. That the symptoms, as they are brought out in the narratives, are such as truly describe those classes of diseases. 3. That the Evangelists apply the same language to sick, melancholy, and insane persons; e. g. (John x. 20), "He hath a demon, and is mad." 4. That as the Jews were accustomed to attribute all effects proceeding from unknown causes to invisible personal agents, they attributed these mysterious diseases particularly to demons, and Jesus and his disciples, in speaking of them as they did, only used the popular language by which those diseases were generally designated, just as we use the words lunatic (moonstruck), sunrise, and sunset, without any regard to their literal and erroneous meaning. 5. The demoniacs are the only insane persons whom Jesus is said in the Gospels to have cured, which is very remarkable, if the two words, demoniacs and insane, do not describe the same class of sufferers. 6. If these were really cases of demoniacal possession, how happens it that they were so numerous then, and so entirely unknown now?

On the other side it is said,— 1. That as these cases were usually attended by disease, the medical prescriptions were not out of place; and, 2. Of course the symptoms would, for the most part, be such as would characterize the disease, whatever it might be. 3. That in the expression (John x. 20), "He has a demon, and is mad," there is no more reason to consider the second clause an explanation of the first than in the expression, "He has a fever, and is delirious." Considering how general and unqualified the belief in demoniacal influences was among the Jews, there can be no doubt that they in their anger against Jesus did intend to describe him as one possessed by an evil spirit, and therefore raving, when he spoke to them in language so utterly beyond their comprehension. 4. Though Jesus often used the popular language without stopping to explain the errors involved in it, yet he applies this language to demoniacs in ways and under circumstances hardly consistent with his perfect veracity, if he knew that they were only cases of insanity. Let any one read carefully the whole passage (Luke xi. 14 – 26), and ask whether on such a supposition this language is quite consistent with our ideas of perfect truthfulness. Even if the first part of the passage should be regarded as an *argumentum ad hominem*, reasoning with the Jews on their own ground, as it might be, it is impossible so to understand the last three verses, where he describes the unclean spirit, after he is gone out of a man, as wandering through deserts, in search of a resting-place, and finding none. Not only in public, but in private conversations with his disciples, Jesus uses similar language. In private directions to them, he says (Matthew x. 8), not "heal demoniacs," but "cast out demons," and (xvii. 21) when they come to him confidentially for instructions in regard to a case of this kind over which they had no power, he says, "This kind goeth not out but by prayer and fasting," — language which must have confirmed them in the belief that it was a case of demoniacal possession, and which it is very difficult to reconcile with his veracity unless he so regarded it. 5. To the question why demoniacs were so common then, and so unknown now, the reply is, that, in the moral as in the physical world, particular periods are marked by the prevalence of particular forms of evil. Why was the plague of Athens, of Florence, or of London a disease so fatal once, and so unknown now? "In looking over the past history of the world, with reference to this kind of phenomena," says an able Swedenborgian writer, Hayden on Spiritualism, p. 43, "we shall find that they have been exceedingly active in periods preceding great changes in the religious state of the world, and have been the forerunners of events that have powerfully affected the minds of men on a variety of subjects, especially in regard to their religious sentiments." If such beings do exist around us, we should expect them to show their power most of all in a time of moral disorder and chaos like that which preceded our Saviour's coming, and be excited by the fiercest desire to extend their power over men at the time when he was about to put down these disorderly agents, and establish the kingdom of Heaven. "If," says Trench, on The Miracles, p. 134, "there was anything that marked the period of our Lord's coming in the flesh, and that immediately succeeding, it was the wreck and confusion of men's spiritual life which was then, the sense of utter disharmony, . . . . . with the tendency to rush with a frantic eagerness into sensual enjoyments as the refuge from despairing thoughts. . . . . . It was exactly the crisis for such soul maladies as these, in which the spiritual and the bodily should be thus strangely interlinked, and it is nothing wonderful that they should have abounded at that time; for the predominance of certain spiritual maladies at certain epochs of the world's history which were specially fitted for their generation, with their gradual decline and disappearance in others less congenial to them, is a fact itself admitting no manner of question." "We must not," says Neander, "Life of Jesus," p. 146, "take the spirit of an age of materialism or rationalism as a rule for judging of all phenomena of the ψυχή [soul] which veils within itself the *Infinite*, which is capable of such manifold excitement, and whose various powers are alternately dormant and active, — now one prevailing, and now another." If it was one important part of the mission of Christ to overthrow here the dominion of evil spirits, and to break up their dangerous intercourse with man, this alone will account for the fact that such moral disorders as demoniacal possessions should no longer be found. 6. Such expressions as (Mark i. 34) are hardly consistent with any other conception on the part of the writer than that of an actual possession by demons; Jesus "did not suffer the *demons* to speak, *because they knew him.*"

The argument is not decisive on either side. Each person will be likely to adopt that view which accords best with his opinions in regard to the existence and influence of spirits. If we believe in the ministry of angels, — that the spirits of the departed may still linger for a season near their accustomed abodes and friends, — if we believe that "this world of ours stands not isolated, not rounded and complete in itself, but in living relation with two worlds," a higher and a lower, — that we are not only to welcome every impression from the world above, but to keep the gate of the soul closed against influences from the world below, — we shall find no difficulty in admitting, that at that momentous crisis when the moral faculties of the race were so dislocated and disordered, evil and unruly spirits may have had an extraordinary sway, and that just at the time when their kingdom was about to receive a blow which must prove fatal in the end, they may have been excited to put forth unusual efforts in order to fortify and extend their authority.

This view of the case seems to us upon the whole best to harmonize the different terms used in the New Testament, both those directly connected with demoniacal possessions, and those which refer in different relations to the connection between this and other worlds. We have very little doubt that this was the belief of the Evangelists themselves. Whether it was entertained by Jesus is not so certain. The whole subject is an obscure one. It can be known to us only through a divine revelation. From its very nature, and our acknowledged ignorance of such matters, we must expect to find in it things which we cannot fully comprehend.

We shall endeavor to explain the narrative before us, 28 – 34, in accordance with each of these views. On the first supposition we may say that the symptoms, as they are minutely described in Luke viii. 26 – 37, and more vividly still in Mark v. 1 – 17, are those of extreme insanity. The fierce and habitual violence, the almost preternatural strength, the shrinking from the society of men, living naked among the sepulchres and in the mountains, the savage outcries, and fierce tearing of his flesh with stones, are symptoms of the most violent insanity. So is his double consciousness, speaking now in his own person, as when he came and threw himself down before Jesus, and then, in the violence of the struggle which ensued when Jesus commanded the unclean spirit to come out of him, speaking in the person of the spirit, and afterwards in his still more violent ravings identifying himself with an army of demons by whom he supposes himself to be possessed. These are the wild, rapid, inconsistent starts of a madman. The whole narrative, so natural and life-like, bears indisputable marks of truth. Even the transfer of the disease to the swine is as easily accounted for on this supposition as on any. Perhaps there is no one feature of the case which may not be thus explained, except his recognition of Jesus as the Son of the Most High God, and his falling down in reverence before him. It is possible, but very improbable, that in his fierce and isolated condition he should have heard reports to produce such an impression on his mind.

We will now explain it on the other theory. We will suppose that, in addition to the insanity which had been brought upon himself and aggravated in all its symptoms by habits of sensual indulgence and the attendant disorders of his inward life, he was actually possessed by a demon whom he, having once admitted, has no longer the power to expel. This evil spirit has taken possession of his faculties, fills out his consciousness, excites in him the fiercest enmities and passions, drives him away from the abodes of men, and subordinates his nature to his own mischievous and disorderly will. There may be moments of awakening consciousness, when the despotic tyranny is relaxed, and the poor man returns to himself and feels his misery. Such a moment may have come, when the spirit, recognizing with awe the presence of Jesus, was thrown off his guard, and the man, thus made aware of the character of Christ and seizing at once on the hope of deliverance, ran and threw himself at his feet. But immediately the spirit regained his control, the frenzy returned upon his victim, and believing himself now to be the demon by whom he was possessed, the act of homage by which he had thrown himself down in the hope of relief was turned into a fierce cry of rage and despair. "What hast thou to do with me, Jesus, thou Son of the Most High God. Hast thou come hither to torment me before the time? I adjure thee by God, torment me not." For Jesus had commanded the unclean spirit to come out of the man. Then, as if to call him to himself, Jesus asked him his name. But the power that had dominion over him was not then relaxed, and, as if he were a whole army of demons, he said, "Legion is my name." And still, under the same control, in the person of the demons whom he supposes himself to be and whose words he speaks, he besought Jesus that he would not (Mark v. 10) send them away out of the place, or command them (Luke viii. 31) to go out into the abyss, but allow them to enter a vast herd of swine that was feeding in the distance (Matthew viii. 30) there on the mountain near the sea (Mark v. 11). The request is not refused. The swine, seized with a sudden fury, rush headlong down the precipice into the sea, and perish in the waters.

The whole account, on this supposition, is perfectly natural and consistent. It places before us in terrible colors the features of that disjointed and discordant life which must belong to a human being subjected to such a foreign control before his whole nature is consciously and voluntarily surrendered to what is evil.

There are one or two remarkable expressions here which, on this supposition, may throw a little light on a dark and difficult subject. "What hast thou to do with us (Matthew viii. 29), Jesus, thou Son of God?" indicates their knowledge of Christ as of a superior being who has authority over them. But how could the maniac have known him by this title? The second clause of the same sentence, "Hast thou come to torment us before the time?" would seem to indicate that they knew that they could be allowed to range at liberty only for a season. The same fact is also indicated yet more strongly by their beseeching Jesus (Luke viii. 31) that he would not command them to go out into the deep, the abyss, which word, wherever it is used in the New Testament, refers to the abode of the dead (Romans x. 7) or the abode of wicked spirits (Rev. ix. 1, 2, 11; xi. 7; xvii. 8; xx. 1, 3). The same idea is probably implied in the request of the demons (Mark v. 10), that Jesus would not send them out of the place. The inference is that these spirits, who were perhaps, as Swedenborg asserts, the souls of departed men, were allowed to linger for a time about the earth before they entered the abyss.

It ought to be added that this is the strongest case to be found in the Gospels, on the side of actual demoniacal possession.

## NOTES.

When he was come down from the mountain, great multi-
2 tudes followed him. And, behold, there came a leper and
worshipped him, saying, Lord, if thou wilt, thou canst make
3 me clean. And Jesus put forth his hand, and touched him,
saying, I will; be thou clean. And immediately his leprosy
4 was cleansed. And Jesus saith unto him, See thou tell no
man; but go thy way, show thyself to the priest, and offer the
gift that Moses commanded, for a testimony unto them.
5 And when Jesus was entered into Capernaum, there came
6 unto him a centurion, beseeching him, and saying, Lord, my
servant lieth at home sick of the palsy, grievously torment-
7 ed. And Jesus saith unto him, I will come and heal him.
8 The centurion answered and said: Lord, I am not worthy that
thou shouldest come under my roof; but speak the word only,
9 and my servant shall be healed. For I am a man under authority, having soldiers under me; and I say to this man, Go, and
he goeth; and to another, Come, and he cometh; and to my
10 servant, Do this, and he doeth it. When Jesus heard it, he
marvelled, and said to them that followed, Verily I say unto
11 you, I have not found so great faith, no, not in Israel. And I
say unto you, that many shall come from the east and west,
and shall sit down with Abraham, and Isaac, and Jacob, in

---

5. **there came unto him a centurion**] In the Roman army for a long time each legion contained sixty centuriæ, and each centuria, as the name implies, was supposed to consist of a hundred men. The commander of one of these companies was called a centurion, and according to Polybius (VI. 24), he was usually remarkable less for his daring valor than for his calmness and sagacity. He sat as a judge in minor offences, and was, of course, in a province like Galilee, a man of considerable distinction and importance. According to Luke (vii. 1 – 10), the centurion sent elders of the Jews to Jesus, and did not himself meet him, till Jesus had come near his house, when he spoke to him substantially as here in verses 8 and 9. It is not unusual to represent a man as doing himself what he does through others. 6. **Lord**] A term by which, according to Grotius and Kuinoel, the Jews were accustomed to address even strangers. It was also a term which, like our *Sir*, might be used in the most respectful salutations.

8. **my servant**] Literally, "*my boy*," or "*my son*;" but in Luke it is explained as *servant*, δοῦλον.

10. **faith**] The first use of this word in the Gospels, though the corresponding adjective is found (vi. 30). The noun here, as is suggested by the adjective there, and viii. 26, means *trust*, *confidence*, and implies a believing, trusting heart.

11. **and shall sit down with**] *shall recline with*. At their

the kingdom of Heaven. But the children of the kingdom shall 12 be cast out into outer darkness; there shall be weeping and gnashing of teeth. And Jesus said unto the centurion, Go 13 thy way, and as thou hast believed, so be it done unto thee. And his servant was healed in the selfsame hour.

And when Jesus was come into Peter's house, he saw his 14 wife's mother laid, and sick of a fever. And he touched her 15 hand, and the fever left her; and she arose and ministered unto them. —— When the even was come, they brought unto 16 him many that were possessed with devils; and he cast out the spirits with his word, and healed all that were sick; that it 17 might be fulfilled which was spoken by Esaias the prophet, saying, "Himself took our infirmities, and bare our sicknesses."

Now when Jesus saw great multitudes about him, he gave 18 commandment to depart unto the other side. And a certain 19 scribe came, and said unto him, Master, I will follow thee whithersoever thou goest. And Jesus saith unto him, The 20 foxes have holes, and the birds of the air have nests; but the Son of Man hath not where to lay his head. And another of 21

---

meals the Jews, in common with other Oriental people, reclined on couches. 12. **there shall be weeping**] *There* shall be *the* weeping; "a remarkable article used emphatically," "as though that were the true ideal of sorrow, the normal standard of suffering, the archetypal reality of agony." "In this life, grief is not yet really grief." Bengel. 12. **gnashing of teeth**] " from impatience and bitterest remorse. Self-love indulged on earth will then be transformed into self-hate; nor will the sufferer be ever able to depart from himself." "Another exposition is, the soft will weep, the stern will rage." Bengel. This whole imagery is from the marriage feast, — a favorite similitude with our Lord, — lamps and torches within, the darkness of night without.

16. **the even**] The Jews reckoned two evenings, the first evening beginning with the declining sun, or about three o'clock, P. M.; the second evening beginning with the setting sun. The hour of evening sacrifice and prayer was the ninth hour, or about three o'clock. See Robinson's Lexicon. 19. **a certain scribe**] *one scribe*. Few of that class came to Jesus with a disposition to receive and follow him. He probably saw the mistaken motive, or the infirmity of purpose with which this scribe had come; and knowing that such followers could only weaken his cause, gave him such an answer as would reveal him to himself, and lead him voluntarily to go away, though he may, like the young man (xix. 22), have gone away disappointed and sorrowful. 20. **the Son of Man**] Dr. Palfrey supposes that Jesus used this phrase "as containing a reference to a form of conception and of speech derived from (or at least according with) a passage in the Book of Daniel (vii. 13, 14), where it is said, 'I saw in the night visions, and behold, one

his disciples said unto him, Lord, suffer me first to go and
22 bury my father. But Jesus said unto him, Follow me, and
let the dead bury their dead.

23 And when he was entered into a ship, his disciples followed
24 him. And, behold, there arose a great tempest in the sea, insomuch that the ship was covered with the waves; but he was
25 asleep. And his disciples came to him, and awoke him, say-
26 ing, Lord, save us, we perish. And he saith unto them, Why
are ye fearful, O ye of little faith? Then he arose, and rebuked the winds and the sea; and there was a great calm.
27 But the men marvelled, saying, What manner of man is this,
that even the winds and the sea obey him?

28 And when he was come on the other side, into the country
of the Gergesenes, there met him two possessed with devils,

---

like a [or *the*] son of man came with the clouds of heaven,' &c. In these words, the subject in the writer's contemplation was the coming of the Messiah to establish the kingdom of Heaven. Occurring in a passage of such brilliancy, the phrase *Son of Man*, though by no means sufficiently specific in its meaning to be restricted into a designation of the Messiah, yet was likely to take a place among those titles which might properly be applied to him." — Relation between Judaism and Christianity, pp. 66, 67.   **22. let the dead bury their dead**] It may be, as Bengel suggests, that this is meant to imply that even the most imperative offices of life — such as the burying of the dead — should be left to be performed by others, since the command to follow him was too immediately urgent and imperative to be put aside on any such grounds. "But go, thou, and preach the kingdom of God; that is, arouse those who are dead; being called to this, leave burying to others, who, alas! do it naturally enough, as long as they themselves are as dead as *their* dead."  "Ye are called, as the living, to diffuse life; leave everything else as burying-work to the dead." Stier.   **23. into a ship**] The size of the ship or boat may be inferred from the size of the lake. There is great weight in a remark of Bengel, which might be carried out more fully than in his words: "Jesus had a moving school (*scholam ambulantem*); and in that school his disciples were instructed much more solidly than if they had dwelt under the roof of a single college, without any anxiety or temptation."   **26. and rebuked the winds**] *hushed them*, or commanded them to be silent. The word rebuke, ἐπιτιμάω, is not used to express displeasure or anger, but as a command to cease from what one is already doing or saying. "And he charged [rebuked, ἐπιτίμησεν] them not to make him known." (xii. 16.)
**28. the Gergesenes**] In Tischendorf, *Gadarenes*. In Luke it is *Gadarenes*, but according to Tischendorf, *Gerasenes*. It is difficult to decide among these different readings. If Um Keis occupies the same spot as the ancient Gadara — and of that there seems to be little doubt — Gadara could not have been the scene of this miracle; for it is, according to Thomson, "about three hours," i. e. about seven or eight miles, "to the south of the extreme shore of the lake in that direction." But Gersa or Chersa, says Thomson, Vol. II. pp. 35, 36, " is within

coming out of the tombs, exceeding fierce, so that no man might pass by that way. And, behold, they cried out, saying, 29 What have we to do with thee, Jesus, thou Son of God? Art thou come hither to torment us before the time? And there 30 was a good way off from them an herd of many swine feeding.

---

a few rods of the shore, and an immense mountain rises directly above it, in which are ancient tombs, out of some of which the two men possessed of the devils may have issued to meet Jesus. The lake is so near the base of the mountain that the swine, rushing madly down it, could not stop, but would be hurried on into the water and drowned. The place is one which our Lord would be likely to visit, having Capernaum in full view to the north, and Galilee 'over against it,' as Luke says it was (Luke viii. 26). The name, however, pronounced by the Bedawin Arabs, is so similar to Gergesa, that to all my inquiries for this place they invariably said it was at Chersa, and they insisted that they were identical, and I agree with them in this opinion."

**two possessed with devils**] Mark and Luke speak of only one, and represent him as so wild and ungovernable, that he dwelt without clothing among the tombs, driven by the demon into desert places, (Luke viii. 29), continuing day and night among the sepulchres and on the mountains, crying out and cutting himself with stones (Mark v. 5), so fierce that chains and fetters had been broken by him, and no man was able to subdue him. Yet when he saw Jesus coming, while he was yet afar off (Mark v. 6), he ran and prostrated himself before him, and shrieked out the words, "What hast thou to do with me, Jesus, thou Son of the Most High God? Art thou come hither to torment us before the time? I adjure thee by God, torment me not." Matthew (xx. 30) speaks of two blind men, where Mark and Luke mention but one. In each case their attention may have been confined to the more conspicuous of the two as the one on whom our Saviour's power was most decisively exercised. Matthew, from his office as a publican or tax-gatherer, would be likely to be more precise in the use of numbers, and therefore to mention both, even though the particulars of the account which the other Evangelists have preserved actually applied only to one.

30. **a good way off**] μακρὰν, *far from* them. Mark and Luke say, ἐκεῖ, "*There*, on the mountain." There is no inconsistency. They were *there, in the distance, on the mountain*. This miracle, which has more the air of a legend than any other in the Gospels except the taking of money from the mouth of a fish (xvii. 27), is nevertheless remarkably lifelike and natural in its details, especially as they are given by Mark and Luke. With the exception of his destruction of the fig-tree (xxi. 19), it is the only miracle of Jesus that was not wholly beneficent in its effects. But the very destruction of property, as in a similar case (Acts xvi. 16–19), may have been to show how much more valuable and sacred is a human soul than any amount of gain. It may have been intended as a rebuke to those who, if Jews, were keeping swine in violation of the law. It may, in some way unknown to us, have been necessary, in order to effect the cure and make it permanent. Or still more probably, it may have been intended, by the very considerable magnitude of the loss, to attract the attention of the community, as the cure of the maniac alone could not do, and prepare them to receive the Gospel at some future day. For such a loss would produce a lasting impression on their sordid minds; and evidently the people in the vicinity were moved with awe and dread by this more than by any other of his mir-

31 So the devils besought him, saying, If thou cast us out, suffer
32 us to go away into the herd of swine. And he said unto them,
Go. And when they were come out, they went into the herd
of swine. And, behold, the whole herd of swine ran violently
down a steep place into the sea, and perished in the waters.
33 And they that kept them fled, and went their ways into the
city, and told everything, and what was befallen to the pos-
34 sessed of the devils. And, behold, the whole city came out to
meet Jesus; and when they saw him, they besought him that
he would depart out of their coasts.

---

acles. As to any injustice to the owners, it was "God who inflicted this loss; and, viewed in this light, all inquiry respecting the particular cause why it was inflicted, and all discussion of its reason or justice in reference to the owner, are as much out of place as they would be concerning a fire, or a shipwreck, or an earthquake." Norton's "Internal Evidences of the Genuineness of the Gospels," p. 282. That the miracle was intended to produce a very strong impression is a suggestion countenanced by the fact that Jesus directed the man (Luke viii. 39) to go home and declare what great things God had done for him. The leper, v. 4, had been commanded to tell no one. But this was on the opposite side of the lake, where Jesus had not the same need of privacy as on the western side. As he was immediately to leave the place, and seldom if ever to visit it again, he may have been desirous of doing what he might to extend the knowledge of his mission in that region.

## CHAPTER IX.

### 18-26. — Christ's Way of viewing Death.

The explanation of these miracles will belong more properly to Mark v. 22-43. A single expression will here be noticed (24), "The maiden is not dead, but sleeping." Olshausen supposes that Jesus intended by these words to say that she really was not dead, but only "in a deep trance." We think the expression is rather to be regarded as indicating the view which Jesus took of death. To him who looked through the shadowy envelopments of mortality, and saw in its higher experience the ongoings of the life here begun, death could not appear as it did to others; and, except when he was specially obliged, as in John xi. 14, and Matthew xvi. 28, to adapt himself to their understanding, he would naturally apply to it forms of speech different from those which were then in use. Here is one of those forms, borrowed possibly from the Old Testament (Deut. xxxi. 16; 2 Kings xx. 21). But the limited expression there, "He slept *with his fathers,*" is taken without any such qualification, and the act of sleep is held up as the peaceful and fitting emblem of death. "Our friend Lazarus has fallen asleep." The expression fixed itself among his followers. "Many bodies of saints who had fallen asleep arose." (Matthew xxvii. 52.) "And having said this, he fell asleep." (Acts vii. 60.) "Of whom the greater part remain to this day, but some have fallen asleep." (1 Cor. xv. 6.) "They who have fallen asleep in Christ." (1 Cor. xv. 18.) This softened mode of expression, entering the Christian consciousness, has changed the whole aspect of the grave. The pall of death is but a veil of slumber thrown over the mortal form of those who, having lived in Christ, have now fallen asleep in him. How in harmony is all this with the character of Jesus! He to whom the issues out of this life into a higher realm were as real and visible as its ordinary transactions here, could hardly accept as truthful accounts of death the terms which were employed by men on whom the shadows of the tomb fell with their deep and hopeless mystery. Sometimes he is obliged to adapt himself to the comprehension of others. But usually he speaks of death in other ways. It is a sleep. It is rendering back a gift (Matthew x. 39; Luke xvii. 33; John xii. 25), that it may be safely preserved, or the laying down of a possession (John x. 17), that it may be taken again. It is the coming of the Son of Man. (Matthew xxv. 13, 31.) It is the harvest at the end of the world (Matthew xiii. 39), where the reapers are the angels. "The beggar died (Luke xvi. 22), and was carried by the angels into Abraham's bosom." "Father, into thy hands I commend my spirit." (Luke xxiii. 46.) There is nothing constrained in his language. The whole subject is transfigured by it; but it flows so easily from his own higher point of view, that we hardly see what power there is in his words, unless our attention is particularly called to them. He does not formally announce the continuance of our being beyond this world, but rather takes it for granted. The doctrine enters into all his conceptions of life, makes up a part of his daily consciousness, and shows itself spontaneously in his words and acts. "God is not the God of the dead, but of the living." So, not Moses and Elias alone, but Abraham and Isaac and Jacob, the maiden here, and his friend Lazarus at Bethany, together with the faithful of all times, were still among the living inhabitants of a living world. Death, in his view, belonged to the soul as a consequence of sin, and not to the body. As life with him means spiritual life, so death (a word he seldom uses) means spiritual death.

## NOTES.

And he entered into a ship, and passed over, and came into his own city. And, behold, they brought to him a man sick of 2 the palsy, lying on a bed. And Jesus, seeing their faith, said unto the sick of the palsy, Son, be of good cheer; thy sins be forgiven thee. And, behold certain of the scribes said 3

1. This verse belongs properly to the preceding narrative, and should be placed at the end of the eighth chapter. **his own city]** Capernaum. **2 Jesus seeing their faith]** Matthew speaks of their faith. Mark (ii. 2 – 4) and Luke (v. 18 – 19) explain how they showed their faith by the extraordinary exertions they made to bring the sick man through the roof. The crowd was such that they could not enter the door. They carried him up, therefore, by an outside stairway to the roof, and "unroofing the roof [over] where he was," they "having broken it up, let him down." "The horizontal aperture in the flat roof had necessarily a secondary roof or porch over it, to keep out the rain. The aperture may be compared to the cabin hatchway of a ship, and the porch to the companion. The main roof is covered with cement, but, if my memory serves me right, the secondary roof is not unfrequently sloping, and covered with tiles. It is fitted to allow persons in an upright position to enter; but we can easily conceive that it might not be fitted to admit of a person recumbent on a couch without removing the porch." Smith's Diss. on Gospels, p. 272. **thy sins be forgiven thee]** Jesus, seeing their faith, and probably seeing at the same time the anxiety and excitement of the young man, in order to remove his agitation and prepare the way for his cure, addressed himself first to his mental condition, and with great tenderness said to him, "Son, be of good cheer; thy sins are forgiven." There was in the Jewish mind an intimate connection between sin and disease, as between cause and effect. "Who forgiveth all thine iniquities: who healeth all thy diseases." (Ps. ciii. 3.) "Who did sin, this man or his parents, that he was born blind?" (John ix. 2.) In the case before us, it is most likely that the disease, or prostration of the nervous system, had been brought on by vicious irregularities and excesses, and that, from a consciousness of this, the young man in approaching a being of such reputed holiness as Jesus, may have been so disturbed and overcome with a sense of guilt as to need the comforting assurance of sins forgiven even more than of bodily health restored.

3. **certain of the Scribes said]** The form of expression gave offence to the Scribes of the neighborhood who were present. "Who," they ask among themselves (Luke v. 21), "can forgive sins but God alone?" Jesus does not assent to the truth of what they say, that God, who acts by his agents so often in the moral administration of the universe, may not have bestowed on some other being than himself the authority to forgive sins, and remit the penalty which they bring; but in a word, $\dot{\epsilon}\nu\theta\nu\mu\epsilon\tilde{\iota}\sigma\theta\epsilon$, which applies both to the thought and the emotions occasioned by it, asked, why they were cherishing evil thoughts and emotions in their hearts? "For which," he continues, pressing the point home to them, "is the easier to say (not to do), 'Thy sins have been forgiven thee,' or 'Arise and walk'?" But, that they may know, that (not God alone,

4 within themselves, This man blasphemeth. And Jesus, knowing their thoughts, said, Wherefore think ye evil in your
5 hearts? For whether is easier, to say, Thy sins be forgiv-
6 en thee? or to say, Arise, and walk? But that ye may know
that the Son of Man hath power on earth to forgive sins (then
saith he to the sick of the palsy), Arise, take up thy bed, and
7 go unto thine house. And he arose, and departed to his house.
8 But when the multitude saw it, they marvelled, and glorified
God, which had given such power unto men.
9 And as Jesus passed forth from thence, he saw a man, named
Matthew, sitting at the receipt of custom; and he saith unto
10 him, Follow me. And he arose, and followed him. And it

---

but) "the Son of Man on earth hath authority to forgive sins," he commands the young man to take up his bed and go home. The outward miracle of healing which they had thus seen, and which therefore he plainly had the power to do, was to be to them an evidence of his authority to forgive sins; though the forgiveness of sins was something which they could not see. "By these visible tides of God's grace, I will give you to know in what direction the great under-currents of His love are setting, and that both are obedient to my word." Trench. It may be that the two expressions, "*Thy sins are forgiven,*" and "*Thy disease is healed,*" were synonymous in the mind of Him who saw in the disease the effect and punishment of sin; and in its removal the withdrawal of the penalty, and consequently the forgiveness of the sin. This passage has been forced into a controversial position which it will not sustain. The reasoning of the Scribes, that God alone can forgive sins, has been taken on *their* assertion, notwithstanding the pointed rebuke which they received from Jesus. Whatever may be meant by the authority to forgive sins which Christ here claims for himself, it was not confined to himself. He ascribes the same authority to his disciples in the same words (in the Greek) that are here used to express the forgiveness of sins, with the addition of a still stronger clause, " Whosoever sins ye forgive, they are forgiven to them, and whosoever ye retain they are retained." (John xx. 23.) Whether, in either case, the act implies anything more than the authority to *declare* that forgiveness is granted is not shown by anything connected with either of the passages before us. 9. **at the receipt of custom**] The place for collecting taxes. **And he arose and followed him**] The readiness with which the call of Jesus is obeyed by Matthew intimates, if it does not positively imply, a previous acquaintance, as it did in the calling of Peter and Andrew, John and James (iv. 18. 22). In the conciseness of the Gospel narratives the facts actually recorded are not always sufficient to explain the causes and motives which led to them, or the relation in which they stand to one another. Often something must be understood beyond what is told. The reader will also observe here the modesty with which the writer speaks of himself, especially in regard to the feast (v. 10). "A great feast" (Luke v. 29) which Matthew gave to Jesus in his own house. His associates, many tax-gatherers, and sinners as the Pharisees considered them, were present. The Pharisees probably were not there personally to partake of the feast. They would not pollute themselves by eating in so promiscuous a com-

came to pass, as Jesus sat at meat in the house, behold, many publicans and sinners came and sat down with him and his disciples. And when the Pharisees saw it, they said unto his 11 disciples, Why eateth your Master with publicans and sinners? But when Jesus heard that, he said unto them, They 12 that be whole need not a physician, but they that are sick. But go ye and learn what that meaneth, "I will have mercy, 13 and not sacrifice." For I am not come to call the righteous, but sinners, to repentance.

---

pany. Their censorious remarks must have been made after the feast. "Why," they ask (v 11), "does your master eat with publicans and sinners?" "Because," Jesus in substance replies (12, 13), "these are the very men to whom I have been sent. As the physician is needed, not by the healthy, but the sick, so am I come to save, not the righteous, but the sinful." No language can be plainer than this. He does not say that these persons are sinful above others, or that the Pharisees are truly righteous. He answers the Pharisees on their own supposition, taking the subject as it lies in their minds. It is as if he had said: "Suppose things are as you think; suppose that these persons are the sinners, and you the righteous ones; that is the very reason why I, as the physician of souls, should go to them rather than to you." It is one of the cases in which the language of Jesus applies in many ways. 1. It announces the general truth that those who are already righteous do not need a Saviour. This, as a general proposition, is equally true, whether there are any such persons actually living or not. 2. As directed to the Pharisees, it takes them on their own ground, and gives them from their own point of view a reason, the validity of which they must admit, why he should seek out the sinful and abandoned. 3. But beyond this, with a keener edge and a more pungent personal application, he turns the same words against them, and lays bare the emptiness of their pretensions to righteousness, by pressing upon them the language of a prophet (Hosea vi. 6) whose authority they could not reject, and who, by the words, "I will have mercy, and not sacrifice," unmasks them to themselves, and rebukes their unforgiving and uncharitable judgments. At the same time that Hosea is made to expose and condemn the Pharisees, he also shows the character and office of Jesus, who mercifully came, not to call the righteous, but sinners. 13. **I will have mercy, and not sacrifice**] The Hebrew form of comparison, instead of " I will have mercy rather than sacrifice," — the spirit indicated by sacrifice, which was only a form, rather than the form without the spirit. **the righteous**] This word, $\delta\iota\kappa\alpha\iota\text{os}$, it has been said, is used to express an outside, formal, or self-righteousness. We can find no such use of it. It is an epithet for what is right in the sight of God. "Prophets and righteous men desired to see my day." (Matt. xiii. 17.) "Then shall the righteous shine forth as the sun." (xiii. 43.) "Then shall the righteous answer him." (xxv. 37.) "The *just* [righteous] shall live by faith." (Rom. i. 17.) "For scarcely for a righteous man will one die: though for a good man perhaps one even dares to die. But God commended his love towards us, in that while we were yet sinners Christ died for us," (Rom. v. 7, 8.) Here righteous and good, as synonymous terms on the one hand, are contrasted with sinners on the other **to repentance**] is omitted by Tischen-

14 Then came to him the disciples of John, saying, Why do
15 we and the Pharisees fast oft, but thy disciples fast not? And
Jesus said unto them, Can the children of the bride-chamber
mourn, as long as the bridegroom is with them? But the days
will come, when the bridegroom shall be taken from them, and
16 then shall they fast. No man putteth a piece of new cloth
unto an old garment; for that which is put in to fill it up tak-
17 eth from the garment, and the rent is made worse. Neither do
men put new wine into old bottles; else the bottles break, and

---

dorf, and the sense is greatly improved by the omission.
**14. Then**] Not necessarily at that very time (though it may have been so), but about that time, the disciples of John, who had not then risen far enough above the old dispensation to comprehend the new, in its true character, came to ask why he did not fast as they and the Pharisees did? 15. **children of the bride-chamber**] Not ordinary guests, but the particular friends of the bridegroom, who go to fetch the bride from her father's house to the bride-chamber, or who go with the bridegroom to the house where the festival is prepared and the bride is to be found. John the Baptist had already publicly spoken of Jesus (John iii. 29) as the "bridegroom." This gives peculiar force to the illustration here used by Jesus in his reply to John's disciples. "How," he asks, "shall the very sons of the bride-chamber, during the days of the marriage festivities, while the bridegroom is with them, fast?" It would be a forced, unnatural, and unseemly act. But the days will come when the bridegroom shall be taken from them, and then, in their loneliness and sorrow, they will have no heart for feasting, but will fast. The meaning is, that fasting is not to be a forced, external observance at stated times, whatever the condition of a man's soul, but that when he feels his desolation and sinfulness, then he will mourn, and, in the true sense of the word, fast. "Fasting should be the genuine offspring of inward and spiritual sorrow, of the sense of the absence of the bridegroom in the soul, — not the forced and stated fasts of the "old covenant now passed away." "It is remarkable how uniformly a strict attention to artificial and prescribed fasts accompanies a hankering after the hybrid ceremonial system of Rome." Alford. 16. Then, following out the same thought with illustrations, — the garments and the wine, — borrowed still from the wedding feast, he asks John's disciples, how it is possible to patch up an old, worn-out, ceremonial system with something new and stronger, but still of the same sort, of the same outside, superficial, ceremonial character? By patching this piece of strong, unfulled, badly-matched cloth on the old and rotten garment you do not remedy the defect, but, on account of the strain that is put upon it, you enlarge the rent, and by the contrast make the poverty of the old garment appear even worse than it did before. 17. **new wine into old bottles**] And not only can you not preserve the old ceremonial observances by patching new rites and ceremonies upon them, but you cannot preserve them by infusing new life into them. The old bottles, made of skin, smeared perhaps on the inside with pitch, growing stiff and weak and brittle as they grow old, are not fit to hold the new wine in its state of vehement fermentation. No more is the new religion, with its restless and boundless activities, coming as a new life into the world, to be compressed within the old and now de-

the wine runneth out, and the bottles perish; but they put new wine into new bottles, and both are preserved.

While he spake these things unto them, behold, there came 18 a certain ruler and worshipped him, saying, My daughter is even now dead; but come and lay thy hand upon her, and she shall live. And Jesus arose and followed him, and so did his 19 disciples. —— And, behold, a woman, which was diseased with 20 an issue of blood, twelve years, came behind him, and touched the hem of his garment. For she said within herself, If I may 21 but touch his garment, I shall be whole. But Jesus turned him 22 about, and when he saw her, he said, Daughter, be of good comfort; thy faith hath made thee whole. And the woman was made whole from that hour. —— And when Jesus came 23 into the ruler's house, and saw the minstrels, and the people making a noise, he said unto them, Give place; for the maid 24

---

bilitated forms; for so it would burst them asunder. The forms would perish, and with them the religion which had sought shelter, expression, and the means of activity and influence in them. The new faith must assume the new and elastic forms adapted to the living energies with which it is endowed; and then both will be preserved. 18. **My daughter is even now dead**] Not, as some commentators say, *is just dying;* but she *is just dead;* ἄρτι ἐτελεύτησεν, by this time she is dead. 23. **the minstrels and the people making a noise**] "During my stay in Jerusalem," says Professor Hackett, "Ill. of Scrip.," p. 113, "I frequently heard a singular cry issuing from the houses in the neighborhood of the place where I lodged, or from those on the streets through which I passed. . . . . . I ascertained, at length, that this peculiar cry was, no doubt, in most instances, the signal of the death of some person in the house from which it was heard. It is customary, when a member of the family is about to die, for the friends to assemble around him, and watch the ebbing away of life, so as to remark the precise moment when he breathes his last; upon which they set up instantly a united outcry, attended with weeping, and often with beating upon the breast, and tearing out the hair of the head. How exactly, at the moment of the Saviour's arrival, did the house of Jairus correspond with the condition of one, at the present time, in which a death has just taken place! It resounded with the same boisterous expression of grief for which the natives of the East are still noted. The lamentation must have commenced, also, at the instant of the child's decease; for when Jesus arrived he found the mourners already present and singing the death-like dirge. (See Mark v. 22, &c.) The account discloses another mark of accuracy which may be worth pointing out. Matthew speaks of 'minstrels' as taking part in the tumult. The use of instruments of music at such times is not universal, but depends on the circumstances of the family. It involves some expense, which cannot always be afforded. Mr. Lane mentions that it is chiefly at the funerals of the rich, among the Egyptians, that musicians are employed to contribute their part to the mournful celebration. The 'minstrels,' therefore, appear very properly in this particular history. Jairus, the father of the damsel

is not dead, but sleepeth. And they laughed him to scorn.
25 But when the people were put forth, he went in, and took her
26 by the hand; and the maid arose. And the fame hereof
went abroad into all that land.

27 And when Jesus departed thence, two blind men followed
him, crying, and saying, Thou son of David, have mercy on
28 us. And when he was come into the house, the blind men
came to him, and Jesus saith unto them, Believe ye that I am
29 able to do this? They said unto him, Yea, Lord. Then
touched he their eyes, saying, According to your faith be it
30 unto you. And their eyes were opened. And Jesus straitly
31 charged them, saying, See that no man know it. But they,
when they were departed, spread abroad his fame in all that
country.

32 As they went out, behold, they brought to him a dumb man,
33 possessed with a devil. And when the devil was cast out, the
dumb spake. And the multitudes marvelled, saying, It was
34 never so seen in Israel. But the Pharisees said, he casteth out
devils through the prince of the devils.

35 And Jesus went about all the cities and villages, teaching

---

whom Christ restored to life, since he was a ruler of the synagogue, must have been a person of some rank among his countrymen."

24. **And they laughed him to scorn**] A most vivid contrast, — these hired mourners scornfully laughing at him who had interrupted their noisy demonstrations of grief; and Jesus, with serene benignity, going in, taken the little maiden by the hand, and calling to her to arise from the sleep of death.

27. **Thou son of David**] It is a little remarkable that this expression should be used in each of the three cases of healing the blind which are mentioned by Matthew (xii. 23; xx. 30). **have mercy on us**] A confession of misery and a cry for mercy, which has become a part of the solemn and affecting litany for all suffering and penitent souls. Ἐλέησον, *eleeison*, has been transplanted by music and poetry into the devotions of all languages. (See Longfellow's

Blind Bartimeus. 30. Jesus charged them on pain of his displeasure, saying, "See that no man know it." Why the prohibition here, when he had already commanded the Gadarene demoniac (Mark v. 19) to go home to his friends and tell them how great things the Lord had done for them? That was on the east side, near the farther end of the lake, in a remote place which Jesus never probably visited except at that time. The report there of what he had done could therefore cause him no inconvenience. Besides the different characters of the men may have been such that the Gadarene would advance his cause, and the others bring discredit upon it, by being its advocates. The conduct of the two men, who when they had received their sight did the opposite of what he had strictly commanded them, shows that they were not men to be depended upon. 34. **prince of the devils**] (See xii.

in their synagogues, and preaching the gospel of the kingdom, and healing every sickness and every disease among the people. But when he saw the multitudes, he was moved with 36 compassion on them, because they fainted, and were scattered abroad, as sheep having no shepherd. Then saith he unto his 37 disciples, The harvest truly is plenteous, but the laborers are few. Pray ye therefore the Lord of the harvest, that he will 38 send forth laborers into his harvest.

---

24). **35. and healing every sickness**] Every kind of sickness and disease.
**36. fainted**] Tischendorf substitutes for this word another which is still more significant, ἐσκυλμένοι, *worried, harassed, torn in pieces, distracted*, for want of true and competent guides. How touching a picture do these verses (35 – 38) give of the extent of our Saviour's labors and the intensity of his sympathy for the multitudes whom he saw worried and scattered abroad like sheep without a shepherd! The harvest truly is plenteous, but the laborers are few, &c. No one takes these words in a literal sense; and no one can fail to recognize something of their exquisite beauty in our English version, which admirably preserves, not only the meaning, but almost exactly the musical rhythm of the Greek. With such a command from Him, how can we help praying the Lord of the harvest that he will send forth laborers into his harvest?

## CHAPTER X.

### 5 – 22. — DIRECTIONS TO THE APOSTLES.

JESUS here gives his disciples specific directions for their conduct during the present journey; though even these directions are marked by a wisdom which belongs to all times.

5 – 15. He directs them to confine their ministry to the lost sheep of the house of Israel. This was not owing to a Jewish prejudice on the part of Jesus. The disciples were now entirely inexperienced. They were not yet educated and prepared to go forth to evangelize the world. They must not yet go out beyond the reach of their Master. The object now, as Chrysostom suggests, was not so much to make converts, though that also was a part of his plan, as to train and exercise and educate the disciples within the narrow limits of Palestine, as in a school, that, when the time should come, they might be prepared for the larger work that was before them. Besides, it was important to have a nucleus somewhere. And where could it be so well as among the people, who, during so many centuries under Moses and the prophets, and more recently from the preaching of John the Baptist, had been in training for the dispensation which was now at hand? The disciples were to go forth not to proclaim Jesus as the Messiah. The time for that had not yet come. They were to complete the work which John had begun, of preparing the popular mind for his advent, by proclaiming as his heralds or preachers that the kingdom of the heavens was at hand. And they were to give weight to their message by the miracles which they wrought in the name of their Master.

They are to receive nothing for the cures they may effect. As the gift, 8, is one freely bestowed on them, so are they to exercise it without reward. But as they go forth thus endowed with power from on high, so, 9, 10, they are not to burden themselves with any provisions for their journey. No money, no wallet (scrip), no extra garments or shoes or staves are to be purchased so as to encumber them in their movements. Nor were they, on entering a village, to go about from house to house. Where, 10, they found one worthy and willing to receive them, with him they were to stay till their ministry in that village was ended. They, 12, 13, were not to be unmindful of the courtesies due to those who should receive them. If the house were worthy, their peaceful salutation would rest upon it; and if the house were not worthy, no harm would be done; the blessing which they had bestowed upon it would return in peace to their own bosom. They were not to waste their time and gifts on those, 14, who would not receive them; but by the symbolic act of shaking the very dust from their feet were to show that they regarded them as heathen and aliens. But a heavy retribution would fall on the city which should reject them. Not even Sodom and Gomorrah, which had refused to listen to Lot and Abraham, had been given over to so terrible a destruction in their day of retribution, as at length, in its day of judgment and condemnation, would fall on that city.

16–20. In the 16th verse, it has been thought, Jesus rises from specific directions for the present journey to considerations which apply to them and those who shall come after them in future ministrations. "Behold *I* send you,"—the *I* emphatic, as if to inspire and strengthen them by the thought who it is that sends them forth as lambs in the midst of wolves. He dwells upon the dangers that lie before them, and points out distinctly what they are, partly to put them on their guard and make them feel how circumspect and unoffending they must be, and partly, that, when the trials should come, they, remembering how he had foretold them, should not be cast down and disheartened by them. "Beware of men," he says, "for they will deliver you up, or betray you to councils, or Jewish courts of justice in provincial towns, and they will scourge you in their synagogues, and ye shall be brought before governors (the Roman pro-consuls, like Pilate) and kings (tetrarchs or viceroys, ruling as kings under the Roman government, like Philip and Herod) for a testimony or witness ($μαρτύριον$) to (not against) them and the nations or Gentiles," as they were in their time, and as Christian martyrs in all subsequent times have been.

But here, lest from these warnings they should carry their prudence and precautions too far, he, v. 19, reminds them of the opposite dangers, and tells them to make no anxious preparation as to how or what they should say when arraigned. It is as if he had said, "Be wise and unoffending. Go forth in thoughtful simplicity and faith, as my disciples, as the agents and messengers of God. And then, when perils come, better than any labored forethought or preparation of yours, it shall be given you in that very hour what ye shall speak." "A new spirit," says Mr. Norton, "was to be breathed into them. God would elevate their souls, and would inform their minds with religious truth. . . . . . With this confidence, this knowledge of the truth, and this moral elevation, what they should speak would always be given them; the spirit of their Father would speak in them." "It is to be observed," says Alford, "that, in the great work of God in the world, human individuality sinks down and vanishes, and God alone, his Christ, his Spirit, is the great worker." Does not the promise apply to all times, and does it not rebuke the unbelief and hesitating fidelity of those who, in seeking to advance the highest interests of man, trust only to their own wisdom and strength? And does not this vanishing away of the human individuality in Christ, by his entire surrender of himself to the Divine will, show in·what sense he and his Father were one?

21, 22. Having thus confirmed their faith, Jesus places before them a yet darker picture of impending dangers. Members of the same household shall be divided in deadly hostility against one another. And not only in your own homes, he goes on to say, but everywhere, ye shall be hated of all men on my account. But he who endureth to the end shall be saved. He who endureth as the early martyrs Stephen and James did, to the end of life, shall be saved. In this sense it applies to the faithful of all times and places. But as in the previous verses especial notice is given of the domestic feuds which should precede the destruction of Jerusalem, dividing the inmates of the same household in mortal enmity against one another, and turning the common hatred of the Jews with peculiar fierceness against the Christians, "the end" here in its primary application probably denotes the end of the Jewish polity, which may be said to have terminated with the destruction of Jerusalem by Titus, the Roman general, A. D. 70. For at that time the political existence of the Jews was blotted out, and their national religious observances, "the sacrifice and the oblation" (Daniel ix. 27) ceased. In this sense the deliverance here announced, v. 22, refers to the freedom which the Christians should then enjoy from the persecutions to which they had been so cruelly subjected by the Jews, and of which some instances are given in the Book of Acts.

### 23. — THE COMING OF THE SON OF MAN.

"Till the Son of Man come." This expression probably means the same here as "the end" in the previous verse. "Till his religion is established and fully confirmed," says

Mr. Norton. The words are used by Jesus and the Evangelists with entirely different meanings at different times. Matthew (xi. 19, "The Son of Man came eating and drinking,") speaks of him in the ministry in which he was then engaged. So (xviii. 11), "For the Son of Man is come to save that which was lost." On the other hand, in xvi. 27, xxiv. 30, xxv. 31, When the Son of Man shall come "in the glory of his Father with his angels," "in the clouds of heaven with power and great glory," "in his glory, and all the holy angels with him," the expression evidently reaches on to some future, and, in one case (xvi. 27, 28), not far distant event. For it is there distinctly and emphatically asserted by Jesus, that there were those then standing by him who should not taste of death till they had seen him coming in his kingdom. What is meant by this coming which was then so near at hand? Primarily it meant the establishment of Christ's religion consequent upon the removal of the Jewish polity at the destruction of Jerusalem. But may it not also be, that he used language which, while foreshadowing the establishment of his religion on earth, should also, under the most solemn figures of speech, set forth the more thorough and decisive establishment of its principles in their retributive application to every soul that goes out from its mortality to meet him in his glory? "Throughout this discourse," says Alford, "and the great prophecy in chap. xxiv., we find the first Apostolic period used as a type of the whole ages of the Church,— and the vengeance on Jerusalem,— which historically put an end to the old dispensation, and was in its place with reference to that order of things, the coming of the Son of Man, as a type of the final coming of the Lord. These two subjects accompany and interpenetrate one another in a manner wholly inexplicable to those who are unaccustomed to the wide import of Scripture prophecy, which speaks very generally, not so much of *events them-*

*selves, points of time,* — as *processions* of events, all ranging under one great description. Thus in the present case there is certainly direct reference to the destruction of Jerusalem; the "end" directly spoken of is that event, and the "shall be saved" the preservation provided by the warning afterwards given in chap. xxiv. 15 – 18. And the next verse directly refers to the journeys of the Apostles over the actual cities of Israel, territorial, or where Jews were located. But as certainly do all these expressions look onwards to the great final coming of the Lord, the "end" of all prophecy; as certainly the "shall be saved" here bears its full Scripture meaning, of *everlasting salvation;* and the endurance to the end is the *finished course of the Christian,* and the precept in the next verse is to apply to the conduct of Christians of all ages with reference to persecution, and the announcement that hardly will the Gospel have been fully preached to all nations (or, to all the *Jewish nation,* i. e. *effectually*) when the Son of Man shall come. It is most important to keep in mind the great prophetic parallels, which run through our Lord's discourses, and are sometimes separately, sometimes simultaneously, presented to us by him."

24 – 38. — FURTHER DIRECTIONS TO THE APOSTLES.

If the most contemptuous of names, v. 25, is given to the lord of the house, how much more will it be given to those who, as his inferiors, belong to his house. The scholar must be satisfied if he is treated as well as his teacher; the servant, if he is treated as well as his master; But fear them not, v. 26. The time of darkness cannot last. The real condition of things, and with it the nature of your mission and of the truths you teach, will be brought to light. "Why," says Chrysostom in his paraphrase, "do ye grieve? Because they call you impostors and deceivers? Wait a little, and all men will declare you saviours and benefactors of the world." Proclaim, then, in the light and from the house-tops what I have told you in our obscurity and in secret. Fear not them who can kill only the body, and have no power over the soul, but rather fear him who is able to destroy both soul and body in Gehenna. We can see no reason to believe, with some modern critics, as Olshausen and Stier, that Satan or Beelzebub is the one whom the disciples are directed to fear. It is not Satan, but God alone, who has the power which is here held up as the cause of dread. Yet not alone by images like this of his power to destroy body and soul alike is their reverence for him to be strengthened. Calling their attention to the little birds around them, of which two were sold for an assarion, or half a cent, Jesus tells them that not even one of these should fall upon the ground unnoticed by their Father. [The sparrows, according to a recent traveller, Hackett, p. 86, are still numerous in Palestine, and are sometimes sold for food.] Why then shall they who are of so much more value than many sparrows, and the hairs of whose head are all numbered, — why shall they distrust the Providential care of God, or fear what man can do to them? In v. 32, by a connection so natural that it is hardly noticed, Jesus rises from actions here to their consequences in higher worlds; and, in order to confirm his disciples in their fidelity to him, he emphatically declares that they who confess or deny him before men, will be confessed or denied by him before his Father in the heavens.

Still he wishes them (34 – 39) to understand fully what their trials and their sacrifices here must be. "I come, not to send peace, but a sword." Here, as in other passages of Scripture, the consequences of an action are mentioned as if they were the intended results. In Exodus iv. 21 God says of Pharaoh, "I will harden his heart, that he shall not let the people go," i. e. the effect of all these fearful exhibitions of the Divine power will be only to harden his heart and confirm him in his wicked purposes. In 1 Kings xxii. 19 – 23, God is represented as putting a lying spirit into the mouth of the king's prophets; i. e. as they were all wicked and deceitful men, he allowed them to be deceived and misled by the lying spirit which they sought. So in the passage before us, one of the consequences of Christ's coming is put as if it were a part at least of his design in coming into the world to effect it. The connection is this. Notwithstanding that God suffers not a sparrow to fall unnoticed, and every one of you who confess me on earth shall be recognized and accepted by me in heaven, still, you are not to expect that I shall quiet at once the warring elements of the world. On the contrary, I shall introduce a new cause of hostility, and thus send, not peace, but a sword, setting a man at variance against his father, and the daughter against her mother. This is the inevitable result. The bitterest hostility of their friends will be roused against the disciples because of their allegiance to him. And here, 37, is to be a new test of their fidelity. In the contests which are to come up they must decide which they will choose, him or their friends; and he that loveth father or mother, son or daughter, more than him, and who, besides that, is not willing even to take up his cross and follow him, giving up friends and life for his sake, is not worthy of him. That is, they must be ready to give up and to endure everything in his service.

This was the primary idea, and probably the only one that impressed the disciples at the time. But the cross was not a Jewish instrument of punishment, and therefore would not naturally suggest to the Jewish mind the imagery by which it would describe the extreme degradation and sufferings of a cruel and infamous death. It is probable that Jesus employed this then unusual form of expression, not only to convey the idea of the personal sacrifices which his followers must make for his sake, but also to familiarize their minds beforehand with the terrible images of torture and death which he was to meet. Here, as in other places (Matthew xvi. 24, John iii. 14, viii. 28, xii. 32), though they did not fully understand him at the time, the cross threw its darkening shadow before them, and he was thus preparing their minds, unconsciously to themselves, that when he had been crucified, and had risen from the dead, these words, which at first had awakened only vague and unintelligible forebodings, should stand out in their prophetic character, as pointing all to the same result.

### 39. — LIFE OR SOUL.

He who findeth, i. e. who seeketh to find, his life, shall lose it; and he who loseth, i. e. who is willing to lose it, shall find it. Here is another instance, in which Jesus, whose soul was full of thoughts which the earthly language that he spoke had no terms to express, used the same word to express very different meanings. At least the Evangelists so represent him. The word ψυχή, which is here rendered *life*, like πνεῦμα, and the Latin words *anima* and *spiritus*, as well as the corresponding Hebrew words נֶפֶשׁ and רוּחַ, means primarily *breath* or *air*. It is used in the New Testament: 1. For the animal life, common to beasts and men (Matthew ii. 20, vi. 25, xx. 28). 2. It stands for the rational as well as sensitive, animating principle, — a something, it has been thought, between the animal and spiritual principle of life. "The first man Adam was made a living soul," *psychē*, in contradistinction to the second Adam, who was a life-making *spirit, pneuma*. 3. It is used as nearly synonymous with our word *soul*. "Thou wilt not leave my soul in Hades." (Acts ii. 27.) "I saw under the altar the souls of them that were slain for the word of God." (Rev. vi. 9; see also Rev. xx. 4; 1 Peter iv. 19; Matt. x. 29.) It naturally bears all these meanings;

for strictly speaking, the word ψυχή stands for the vital, sentient principle in which our consciousness resides, and with it our sense of personal identity. It is that which constitutes a man's *self*, and might better be translated by the word *self* than by any other single word in our language. It is the sentient, conscious principle which pervades our whole being, animal, intellectual, and spiritual, and which may be considered in its relation to either one, or to all, of these departments of our nature. It may, therefore, refer to our physical, our intellectual, or our spiritual life. In v. 29 of this chapter Jesus uses it as we do the word *soul*, as something distinct from our physical life. In v. 39, he passes from one meaning to the other; and the better translation would be: He who findeth, or (John xii. 25) loveth himself, shall be lost, and he who loseth himself shall be saved. That is: He who is bound up in himself shall perish; but he who, in his devotion to me, is willingly exposing himself to death, as if (John xii. 25) he hated himself, shall live. The expression goes deeper than is intimated in our common version. There may be a selfish regard to our souls and spiritual interests, as well as to our earthly life and bodily interests. The Saviour's words are directed against every form of selfishness and self-seeking, whether in relation to body or soul, to this world or the world to come. Whosoever seeketh first himself, though it be his own soul, shall perish; and he who is willing to cast away everything, even his care for his own soul, in his devotion to me, shall be saved. He who is saving his soul in this selfish way shall lose it; and he who is losing his soul, in this unselfish devotedness to me, shall save it. At the same time the connection with the cross of v. 38 implies that there is a reference here to the loss of life, in our sense of the word life; and so there is a passing from the lower to the higher meaning of the word, from the mortal to the immortal life, and the verse may be thus paraphrased, "Whosoever seeks first of all his life (an earthly one), shall lose it (as an immortal inheritance); and he who (in his supreme devotion to higher things) is ready to cast his life (his earthly life) away, shall find it (as an immortal inheritance).

This practice of so using language that it shall reach from its primary and narrow meaning, spiritually up into higher realms of life, or prophetically on to more distant scenes and events, is one of the greatest difficulties in the way of the commentator, who would give a precise and definite meaning, and only one, to every expression that he meets. The charm, as well as much of the power that lies in the words of Jesus, consists in the fact that they open before us worlds of thought and being into which we may enter, but which are too full to be emptied of all their treasures, and too vast to be bounded by any exact definitions of ours.

### 40–42.—Different Degrees of Reward.

And while men may thus save or lose their souls, there are different degrees of recompense, and not the smallest act shall be permitted to go unrewarded. To receive the Apostles is, of course, not merely to give them a hospitable reception, kindly supplying them with food and shelter; it is to receive them with their instructions into the heart and life. In so doing men receive Christ, who is represented by them, and whose life-giving doctrines they teach; nay, they receive God himself. The reward would depend on the kind of reception that was given. He who is far enough advanced in the Jewish religion to recognize and welcome a prophet or righteous man *as such, because* he is a prophet or a righteous man, shall receive the reward of a prophet or righteous man. In receiving him as a prophet, he is made partaker of the prophet's thought and life, and of course will share the prophet's reward. But he who has enough of the spirit of Christ to receive a little child as his disciple or representative, shall in no wise lose a disciple's reward, for in so doing he is receiving the spirit and the life of Jesus into himself. Perhaps there were children present. The term "little ones" is applied by Jesus to children (xviii. 2 – 6). Or it may be, as Mr. Norton and others suppose, that by "little ones" Jesus means his own inexperienced disciples; as if he had said, "whosoever shall give a cup of cold water to one of these, my children," &c. In either case the fundamental meaning is the same. There is a climax from the prophet, who, though a special messenger of God, was sometimes meagre in spiritual attainments, through the just man in his legal righteousness to the disciple in whom, as coming from Christ, is the fulness of a diviner life and through it of a larger reward. "Many a benevolent, pious Jew," says Olshausen, "might receive the Apostles as prophets or righteous men, because, from his point of view, he could not recognize anything higher in them; but he who was able to recognize in the messengers of Christ that specifically new thing which they brought, and who, from love to it, would receive them, received the full blessing from Him." The prominent idea in these sentences relates to the different kinds and degrees of reward which men shall receive according to their different attainments in the Jewish or the Christian life.

## NOTES.

AND when he had called unto him his twelve disciples, he gave them power against unclean spirits, to cast them out, and to heal all manner of sickness, and all manner of disease.

1 – 4. We have four different catalogues of the Apostles, viz.: Matt. x. 9 – 4; Mark iii. 16 – 19; Luke vi. 14 – 16; Acts i. 13. That the different accounts may be easily compared, we subjoin the following table: —

2 Now the names of the twelve apostles are these: the first, Simon, who is called Peter, and Andrew his brother; James 3 the son of Zebedee, and John his brother; Philip and Bartholomew; Thomas, and Matthew the publican; James the son of Alpheus, and Lebbeus, whose surname was Thaddeus; 4 Simon the Canaanite, and Judas Iscariot, who also betrayed

| MATTHEW. | MARK. | LUKE. | ACTS. |
|---|---|---|---|
| Simon | Peter | Simon | Peter |
| Andrew | James | Andrew | James |
| James | John | James | John |
| John | Andrew | John | Andrew |
| | | | |
| Philip | Philip | Philip | Philip |
| Bartholomew | Bartholomew | Bartholomew | Thomas |
| Thomas | Matthew | Matthew | Bartholomew |
| Matthew | Thomas | Thomas | Matthew |
| | | | |
| James of Alpheus | James of Alpheus | James of Alpheus | James of Alpheus |
| Lebbeus | Thaddeus | Simon Zelotes | Simon Zelotes |
| Simon Cananaios | Simon Cananaios | Judas of James | Judas of James |
| Judas Iscariot | Judas Iscariot | Judas Iscariot | |

In all these catalogues the names may naturally be divided into three classes. In the first two classes the names in the different accounts are the same; and in the third class there is no difference of statement in regard to the first name and the last. Simon Cananaios is only the Hebrew name corresponding to Simon Zelotes, in Greek. Probably before being called by Jesus, he was a member of the sect called Zealots, who, according to Josephus (B. J. 4. 3. 9; *ib.* 4. 5. 1 – 4; *ib.* 4. 6. 3; and 7. 8. 1), were guilty of the greatest excesses and crimes a short time before the destruction of Jerusalem. The only name about which there is any difficulty is that of Lebbeus, or Thaddeus, or Judas [the son or brother] of James. "Thaddeus," says Lightfoot, "is a warping of the name 'Judas,' that this apostle might be the better distinguished from Iscariot." Like Elijah and Elias, they were only different forms of the same name. In John xiv. 22 we find a "Judas," not "Iscariot," among the Apostles. Lebbeus and Thaddeus have been supposed to mean the same thing; but, according to De Wette and Alford, this view is not sustained by the etymology of the words. The probability is that Lebbeus was a surname, borrowed possibly, as Lightfoot conjectures, from his place of residence, and given to him, as the name Iscariot was given to the other Judas, from *his* place of residence, to distinguish them from one another. "Whose surname was Thaddeus," the reading of our common version is marked as doubtful by Griesbach, and omitted by Tischendorf. If we knew nothing about Simon's name, beyond what we find here, we should think there was a contradiction in the accounts, Mark, and the author of the Acts saying Peter, where Matthew and Luke say Simon. Simon Peter, and Andrew his brother, sons of Jonas, and John the son of Zebedee, with James his brother, were (Luke v. 10) partners in the fishing-trade, and, together with Philip (John i. 44) belonged to Bethsaida. This James is the one put to death by Herod (Acts xii. 2). Bartholomew is, with reason, supposed to be the same as Nathaniel, who is mentioned by John twice (i. 46; xxi. 2) among the Apostles. He was from Cana of Galilee. Without any good reason, it has been conjectured that Philip and Bartholomew were brothers ; and that Thomas and Matthew were twin-brothers. The humility of Matthew has been inferred from his applying to himself

him. —— These twelve Jesus sent forth, and commanded them, 5 saying, Go not into the way of the Gentiles, and into any city of the Samaritans enter ye not. But go rather to the lost 6 sheep of the house of Israel. And, as ye go, preach, saying, 7 The kingdom of Heaven is at hand. Heal the sick, cleanse the 8 lepers, raise the dead, cast out devils; freely ye have received, freely give. Provide neither gold, nor silver, nor brass, in 9 your purses; nor scrip for your journey, neither two coats, 10 neither shoes, nor yet staves. For the workman is worthy of his meat. And into whatsoever city or town ye shall enter, in- 11 quire who in it is worthy; and there abide till ye go thence. And 12

---

here the reproachful epithet "publican." James, the son of Alphæus (Alphæus and Cléopas or Clopas, being only different ways of turning the same Hebrew word into Greek), presided over the church at Jerusalem, and "from the austere sanctity of his character was commonly called, both by Jews and Christians, "James the Just." Mention is made (Matt. xiii. 55, and Gal. i. 19) of James, a brother or kinsman of Jesus. (See note to xiii. 55.) If Judas of James is Judas the brother of James, this supposition agrees with xiii. 55, where we read of James and Judas as among the brethren of Jesus; and with Jude 1, where we read of "Judas, the servant of Jesus Christ, and the brother of James." 3. **Matthew, the publican**] a collector of taxes. Matthew's humility is seen in his applying to himself in his catalogue of the apostles the odious name, which no other Evangelist applies to him in this connection. "On no point," says Milman, Hist. Christ. B. I. c. IV., " were all orders among the Jews so unanimous as in their contempt and detestation of the publicans. Strictly speaking, the persons named in the Evangelists were not publicans. These were men of property, not below the equestrian order, who farmed the public revenues. Those in question [those mentioned in the Gospels] were the agents of these contractors, men, often freed slaves, or of low birth and station, and throughout the Roman world proverbial for their extortions; and in Judæa still more hateful, as among the manifest signs of subjugation to a foreign dominion. The Jew who exercised the function of a publican was, as it were, a traitor to the national independence." 5. **Gentiles**] The nations, — those who are not Jews. **Samaritans**] Samaria lay between Galilee and Judæa, and was inhabited by the Samaritans, who were descended from the ten tribes, and from people of heathen nations who at different times had been sent as colonists with them. Their religion was drawn partly from the law of Moses, and partly from pagan superstitions. 9. **Provide neither gold**] *Provide* is the emphatic word. Take no pains to provide or purchase anything for your journey; but go as you are, trusting in God. *Purses* were girdles worn about the waist, in which money was carried. 10. **scrip**] a wallet usually of leather, in which shepherds and travellers carried provisions. **neither shoes**] " but be shod with sandals" (Mark vi. 9). Lightfoot says that there was a marked distinction between shoes and sandals, the former being more like an article of luxury than the latter. **nor yet staves**] Do not take pains to *provide* them. Mark says Jesus commanded them to take nothing for their journey, except a staff.
11. **and there abide**] With him

13 when ye come into an house, salute it. And if the house be worthy, let your peace come upon it; but if it be not wor-
14 thy, let your peace return to you. And whosoever shall not receive you, nor hear your words, when ye depart out of that
15 house or city, shake off the dust of your feet. Verily I say unto you, it shall be more tolerable for the land of Sodom and Gomorrah in the day of judgment, than for that city.——
16 Behold, I send you forth as sheep in the midst of wolves. Be
17 ye therefore wise as serpents, and harmless as doves. But beware of men. For they will deliver you up to the councils,
18 and they will scourge you in their synagogues; and ye shall be brought before governors and kings for my sake, for a testi-
19 mony against them and the Gentiles. But when they deliver you up, take no thought how or what ye shall speak; for it
20 shall be given you in that same hour what ye shall speak. For it is not ye that speak, but the spirit of your Father which
21 speaketh in you. And the brother shall deliver up the brother to death, and the father the child; and the children shall rise up against their parents, and cause them to be put to death;
22 and ye shall be hated of all men for my name's sake. But he

---

who is worthy, and when ye come into *the* house (not *an* house, as in our translation), i. e. with him into his house, salute it. Be courteous. Observe the customary forms of salutation. "A servant of the Lord is truly courteous, for he has learned to be so in the high court of his king." 13. **if the house be worthy**] Here *house*, passing from its meaning in the previous verse, is used as comprehending the family who lived in it.

**let your peace rest upon it**] pray for its good, and if it be unworthy the blessing that you ask for, it will return into your own bosom. Thus, if those for whom we pray do not allow our prayers for their good to be answered as it regards them, still we shall not pray in vain. The peace we ask for them will come to us.

**14. shake off the dust of your feet**] The dust of heathen land defiled. By shaking off the dust of a city, the disciples were to show that they esteemed it heathenish, profane, and impure. 16. **harmless as doves**] Not *harmless*, but *pure*. The dove, an emblem of the Holy Spirit, stands for Christian gentleness and purity of soul. Let your wisdom, of which you will have abundant need, never degenerate into a selfish prudence or cunning; but let it be united with the purity of soul which includes within itself singleness of purpose and the love "which seeketh not her own," and "which thinketh no evil." 9. **take no thought**] give yourself no anxiety about what you shall say. (See vi. 25.) 22. **for my name's sake**] By the *name* of Jesus is meant the spirit, the qualities, and attributes belonging to him. To come together in his name, is to come together in his spirit; to ask anything in his name, is to ask it as in his stead or in his spirit; and to be hated for his name's sake, is to be hated on ac-

that endureth to the end shall be saved. But when they per- 23
secute you in this city, flee ye into another. For verily I say
unto you, ye shall not have gone over the cities of Israel till
the Son of Man be come. The disciple is not above his mas- 24
ter, nor the servant above his lord. It is enough for the disci- 25
ple that he be as his master, and the servant as his lord. If
they have called the master of the house Beelzebub, how much
more shall they call them of his household? Fear them not 26
therefore. For there is nothing covered, that shall not be
revealed; and hid, that shall not be known. What I tell you 27
in darkness, that speak ye in light; and what ye hear in the
ear, that preach ye upon the house-tops. And fear not them 28
which kill the body, but are not able to kill the soul; but rather fear Him which is able to destroy both soul and body in hell.
Are not two sparrows sold for a farthing? and one of them 29
shall not fall on the ground without your Father. But the 30
very hairs of your head are all numbered. Fear ye not there- 31
fore; ye are of more value than many sparrows. Whosoever 32
therefore shall confess me before men, him will I confess also
before my Father, which is in heaven. But whosoever shall 33
deny me before men, him will I also deny before my Father,
which is in heaven. Think not that I am come to send peace 34

---

count of the qualities which belonged to him. "It is to be observed," says Swedenborg, "that the ancients, by the name of a thing, understood nothing but its essence; and by seeing and calling by name, they meant the knowledge of its nature and quality." 23. **flee ye into another**] not only, as Mr. Norton suggests, that they may escape persecution, but that they may carry on their work more effectually. 24, 25. The different relations of Christ to the Apostles, viz. the teacher to his pupils, the master [lord] to his servants, and the lord or head of the house to his dependents; literally, *his domestics.* 27. **What ye hear in the ear**] "Allusion is here made to the manner of the schools, where the doctor whispered out of the chair into the ear of the interpreter, and he with a loud voice repeated to the whole school that which was spoken in the ear." Lightfoot. **the house-tops**] the flat roofs of the houses, where trumpets were sounded to attract attention, and proclamations were made. 32. **him will I confess also**] The emphatic I. What personal dignity and authority must lie under it, to sustain it in such a connection! Who is this that promises to recognize and acknowledge us before the throne of God, in the presence of his Father who is in the heavens? Could any prophet or righteous man, — Gideon or Barak, Abraham or Samuel, — promise thus to confess before God those who had confessed him before men? Only the "ONE mediator between God and man, the man Christ Jesus," (1 Tim. ii. 5) can stand in this relation between us and God. 34. **not to send peace, but a sword**] Not my wish, but the inevitable result.

35 on earth; I came not to send peace, but a sword. For I am come to set a man at variance against his father, and the daughter against her mother, and the daughter-in-law against her 36 mother-in-law: and a man's foes shall be they of his own 37 household. He that loveth father or mother more than me is not worthy of me; and he that loveth son or daughter more 38 than me is not worthy of me; and he that taketh not his cross, 39 and followeth after me, is not worthy of me. He that findeth his life shall lose it; and he that loseth his life for my sake 40 shall find it. He that receiveth you receiveth me; and he that

---

Think not that you can escape the trial. The throne of peace is to be established in the midst of discord and war. Love enters with its divine message, its rebuke against sin, its offers of mercy, but men turn against it, and strife and wars ensue. "What now follows," says Stier, "down to ver. 39, form 'a circle of ideas which,' as Winzenmann says, 'never came from the mind of mortal, before Jesus.' It is the subliming of all the prophetic expectations concerning the kingdom of God into the transcendent and future and heavenly; in perfect correspondence with the true sense of all prophecy, which never could, however, till now be so clearly apprehended and expressed. This is a testimony which is effectually thrown in the way of all who would build up the kingdom of peace on this side. . . . . . But, although everything in his kingdom looks forward to the beyond and the future, to the finding of life, in respect to all who shall be found worthy of him, this heavenly kingdom does not give up the earth. Upon it, and in hot conflict, must the heirs of everlasting peace secure and prepare for their inheritance." This is an effectual answer to those timid sentimentalists and prudent conservatives, who think more of peace and present security than of righteousness and truth, which, however mildly urged, awaken the anger and deadly opposition of those whose interests they would compromise, and whose lives they rebuke.

38. **that taketh not his cross**] This is the first mention that is made of the cross, that great symbol of Christian self-denial and self-sacrifice and death, and through death of victory. The word must have fallen with a strange chill on the hearts of the disciples. All that they could then understand by it savored of humiliation and pain and infamy. It was not till after the resurrection of Christ that the hallowed and triumphant associations, now connected with it, could have power over them, or any meaning for them. 39. **He that findeth his life**] "We have once more ψυχή in that deeper sense in which we found it at v. 28, pointing from the life of the body to a yet higher life. This striking declaration contains, if both sayings are taken literally, a perfect contradiction; consequently the *finding* and *losing* must obviously, in the first place, be understood in different senses. In the second place, ψυχή also must be used in two opposite senses. The ψυχή which is to be killed, which must be crucified, is the sinful self-life of the old man, which is truly death; and this dead life must be mortified and lost by an internal, continual crucifixion and self-denial (of which the taking up of the external cross is only an external expression), in order that we may find the living life, — our sanctified, glorified, and eternal life. . . . . . He who gives up, in the fellowship of the cross of Christ,

receiveth me receiveth him that sent me. He that receiveth 41
a prophet in the name of a prophet, shall receive a prophet's
reward; and he that receiveth a righteous man, in the name
of a righteous man, shall receive a righteous man's reward.
And whosoever shall give to drink unto one of these little ones 42
a cup of cold water only, in the name of a disciple, verily I say
unto you, he shall in no wise lose his reward.

---

all that which must die and pass away, has by such loss obtained the gain of eternal blessedness." Stier.

42. **verily I say unto you**] This impressive form of affirmation comes in at the close of each separate train of thought in this discourse, viz. at verses 15, 23, and 42. In the Sermon on the Mount, the peroration goes up and finds its solemn climax in the greatest and most terrible consequences of unfaithfulness and sin; here it comes down and finds its affecting anti-climax in the certain reward of the smallest act of kindness performed in the spirit of a disciple to any one of Christ's little ones.

## CHAPTER XI.

#### JOHN THE BAPTIST AND HIS MESSAGE.

JESUS continued in Galilee. John the Baptist had been for some time imprisoned by Herod. This was Herod Antipas, the son of Herod the Great, who is mentioned in the second chapter of Matthew. His father had once by will named him as his successor in Judæa; but he afterwards changed his mind, and leaving his son Archelaus, king of Judæa, appointed Herod to the inferior dignity of tetrarch or viceroy of Galilee to the north, and of Perea which lies on the east side of the Jordan. Herod Antipas was a cunning, unscrupulous man. His usual place of residence was at Tiberias, a name which, in honor of the Roman Emperor Tiberius, he had given to a town on the southwestern border of the Lake of Galilee, probably somewhere from eight to eleven miles south from Capernaum. In the other extremity of his kingdom, only a few miles eastwardly from the place where the Jordan empties into the Dead Sea, he had a castle called Machærus, which had been enlarged and fortified by his father, and in which, as appears, Herod Antipas sometimes resided. In this castle, according to Josephus (Ant. XVIII. 5. 2), John was imprisoned. He had never quite comprehended the nature of the kingdom of Heaven which he had announced as near at hand, nor could he fully understand either the character or the office of Jesus, to whom he pointed his disciples (John i. 29) as "the Lamb of God that taketh away the sins of the world," and of whom he had afterwards said (John iii. 30), "he must increase, but I must decrease." In this respect he was like other prophets chosen for a specific purpose, who sometimes

(Dan. xii. 8) had but an imperfect understanding of the symbolical images which they saw, and the words they used. Even to the seers themselves "the words were closed up and sealed" for the time.

We sometimes attribute a sort of omniscience to men raised up by God, and inspired only for a particular purpose. And when a man has once been set apart in this way, we are too apt to suppose that he must be entirely unlike other men, and free from human infirmities and passions. But even Moses, who was favored with a nearer and more frequent access to God than any other of the prophets, had his seasons of distrust (Ex. iii. iv.), of unrestrained passion (Ex. xxxii. 19), and unbelief (Num. xx. 12). Elijah, the greatest of the prophets who came after him, showed himself to be of like passions with other men, and (1 Kings xix. 4 – 10) had his time of almost angry impatience, despondency, and doubt. In this they were only subject as men to the laws of our physical and mental constitution. The more they were raised above themselves in their moments of religious exaltation, the more severe would the reaction be likely to be, and the greater the depression that followed.

John the Baptist, who in his public ministry had been followed by thousands to whom he had been devoting himself with all the zeal and energy of his earnest and powerful nature, proclaiming the near approach of the long-expected kingdom of Heaven, and having the head of that kingdom pointed out to him by a voice from heaven, was now cut off from his public labors, and shut up in a prison far away from the scene of Christ's ministry. He had been urging the necessity of immediate repentance as a preparation for the immediate coming of the kingdom of God. He waits in awe and expectation, but the silence is not broken by the sound of its coming. What can be the meaning of this delay? The energies of his active and powerful nature are thrown in upon themselves. He is moved by strong and violent emotions. He broods over the unpromising condition of things, and is disturbed by the tardy development of the Divine plans. He becomes impatient and distrustful. "Can it be," he may have asked himself amid the many thoughts that rushed upon his mind, "that there is any mistake in this matter?" The slightest doubt is too painful to be borne, when the whole thing can so easily be set at rest by one word from Jesus himself. The impatient doubt could hardly have gone further than this. His faith in Jesus could not have been seriously disturbed, or he would not have sent his followers to ask *him* the question which he put. He would have sent them rather to see for themselves, and to inquire of others. But tired of the delay, brooding over the possibilities of mistake, with apprehensions and forebodings which bear some proportion to the grandeur of his previous anticipations, in his forced inactivity and confinement, he sends two of his disciples across the whole length of the province, to ask Jesus whether he is really the one who was to come, or whether they were to look for another? In these few words, John intimated his impatience of delay, his secret misgivings, and his desire that Jesus would adopt some more decided and effective course. The whole proceeding on the part of John is perfectly natural, and in no way inconsistent with the assurance which had been miraculously given to him in regard to the office and person of the Messiah. Such alternations of feeling, and such convulsive movements of the mind, leading them for the moment to question the reality of their most cherished convictions, and even of what their eyes have seen, belong to men of his temperament, even where, as in the case of Martin Luther, there is the strongest faith and the most courageous and determined energy of will.

How admirable the course which Jesus took to satisfy John, and how in its calmness does it show his infinite superiority, and the easy, majestic ascendency which he had over men! Merely to declare in words that he was the Messiah would not have satisfied the prisoner in his present state of mind. "Why then," he might have asked, "if he is the Messiah, does he so long delay?" Nor had the time yet come for Jesus publicly to announce himself as the Messiah. He knew that whenever that announcement was made, his earthly ministry must be brought speedily to an end, and, therefore, in the presence of John's disciples, in that same hour (Luke vii. 21) he performed many and various kinds of miracles; and, having thus impressed them with a conviction of more than earthly authority and power, he directed them to go back and tell their master what they had seen and heard, — how the blind see, the lame walk, the lepers are cleansed, the deaf hear, the dead are raised up, and the poor have the good tidings proclaimed to them, — in this message using just enough of the old prophetic language (Isaiah xxxv. 5, 6, xlii. 7, lxi. 1) to give, in the mind of John, additional significance and solemnity to his message. Then he added, in words of mild rebuke and encouragement, coupling a benediction with his reproof, "And blessed is he who shall not be offended in me," — who does not allow himself to be disturbed, or to lose his faith in me, because, in my divinely appointed work, I am not pursuing precisely the course which he had expected. No reply could have been better fitted to the state of John's mind, which was impatient because it was so earnest, — disappointed and doubting because it had believed and expected so much.

Then, 7 – 14, turning to the multitude, Jesus made this an occasion of admonition and instruction to them. At the same time he would renew their respect for John, which might have been lessened by the doubts into which he would appear, from his questions, to have been betrayed. There is nothing which the multitudes bear with less patience than any seeming vacillation, or want of steadfastness in their great men. "What went ye out into the wilderness to see?" Did ye go out expecting to find one who would bend to your changing wishes, as a reed to the wind; or one who would gratify your voluptuous tastes, like courtiers who are in kings' houses, with their soft, effeminate garments? Or did you go into that solitary place to find a prophet? Yea, I say unto you, and more than a prophet. He is one who has been foretold by prophets as the herald who should be raised up to announce the new dispensation, and to prepare the way for its coming. Among those born of women no greater man than he has ever been raised up. And yet, he adds, with solemn emphasis, calling their attention to the higher kingdom which is now to be established, the least in the kingdom of Heaven is greater than he. That higher kingdom is of such transcendent dignity and power, that its lowest subject shall be greater than he who stood foremost in the old dispensation. Possibly Jesus may have had in his mind the Roman empire, whose *citizens* were greater, and bore with them the ensigns of a mightier power, than *kings* of other nations. But what does he mean in saying that the least of his own disciples is greater than John the Baptist? He means that the humblest of those who really belong to his kingdom are made the partakers of a diviner life, and better understand the nature of his kingdom, and the elements of a true spiritual greatness, than even the greatest of those who had gone before. "They are greater," says Lightfoot, "in respect of clear and distinct knowledge in judging of the nature and quality of the kingdom of Heaven." The knowledge of a divine life unfolded in the Sermon on the Mount, and set before the humblest of his followers in the words, the life, death, and resurrection of Jesus, is beyond all that the prophets and righteous men of old were able to attain to. They indeed, 13, — i. e. the law and the prophets until John, — only predicted the coming of the heavenly kingdom, — only pointed on to it in the remote and distant future. John, in this respect greater and more favored than they, proclaimed it as already at hand, and from his time (the idea is drawn from a besieged city) men are forcing their way into it, and taking it as by violence. In these words Jesus alludes to the crowds who, first attracted by John's preaching, were now, from their misapprehension of his kingdom, pressing round him, and seeking as it were to force their way in. "And this," he adds, 14, "if ye will only receive it," i. e. not take the language literally, but understand it as it should be understood, is Elijah, whose coming (see note xvii. 10) before the Messiah was generally looked for among the Jews.

15 – 19. The comparison here in our common version is rendered obscure. The children who say to their companions, "We have piped to you, and ye have not danced; mourned to you, and ye have not lamented," are sometimes thought to represent John and Jesus, while the others, who were so unreasonable as to respond to them neither in their merriment nor their mourning, represent those who condemned both the Saviour and his forerunner. The objection to this is, that it is precisely the opposite of what Jesus says: It — this generation — "is like children sitting in the market-places, and saying," &c., &c. On the other hand, it is difficult to see how the unbelieving Jews were represented by the children, who complained that their companions would sympathize with them neither in their make-believe mirth nor their lamentation. Luke (vii. 32) says, "They were saying to one another," &c., &c. And Tischendorf adopts a similar expression as the correct reading in Matthew. The true interpretation is thus made easy. To what shall I compare this generation? It is like a crowd of children in some public place, seeking amusement, and able to agree upon nothing, but chiding one another as hard to please, and by their mutual reproaches only adding to the general confusion and discontent. Such a capricious, dissatisfied, complaining race is this generation, who complain of John as a half-crazed demoniac because of his austere and ascetic life; and yet when Jesus came eating and drinking as others did, reject and stigmatize him as self-indulgent and intemperate, the companion of the low and the abandoned. But, he

continues, 19, whatever these may say or do, wisdom is justified, i. e. is recognized and honored, by those who in spirit are really her children. Whatever the outward form under which she may come, however she may be despised and rejected among men, they who are her children, whose hearts are open to her influence, will hear her voice, and hold her in honor. To them she needs no word of commendation or defence, whether she come under the severe guise of John, the preacher in the wilderness, or in the more divinely attractive life and teachings of the Son of man.

## 20 – 24. — Great Privileges Unimproved Visited by a Heavier Condemnation.

These words were probably spoken after a pause. The word "then" with which they are introduced rather intimates that some time, minutes or days, had intervened. The idea is the same as in Matthew x. 15. In proportion to our privileges are our responsibilities; and the greater the opportunities that we cast aside or neglect, the heavier the condemnation that must fall upon us "in the day of judgment," i. e. as Mr. Norton translates it, "when sentence is passed." As to the cities Tyre and Sidon, they had, many centuries before our Saviour, been among the most opulent and enterprising cities in the world. At the present time, and for centuries past, they have been places of no importance, and remain in a comparatively desolate and ruinous condition. But in the time of Jesus they were populous and flourishing cities, and continued so for generations afterwards. Why then are they mentioned, in connection with Sodom, as examples of a Divine retribution? They were noted, even among heathen nations, for the profligacy, licentiousness, and degrading superstitions to which they were given over. The force of the comparison lies in this. It is as if Jesus had said,

"You know how utterly degraded and abandoned these cities are, to what lewd, debasing superstitions they have bound themselves, and how hopeless their moral and religious condition is. And yet, notwithstanding all this, I declare unto you, that if the mighty works which have been done here had been done long ago in Tyre and Sidon, they would have repented in dust and ashes, and even Sodom, if it had witnessed such works of divine goodness and power, would have remained to this day. And thou Capernaum, which art exalted to heaven, which art above all others in privileges, shalt be brought down to hell, — to Hades, i. e. to the abode of the dead, to utter destruction. It was the strongest language that could be framed to express the privileges which Christ was offering, and the heavy condemnation and sorrow which must fall on those who reject them. As a matter of fact, the words of Jesus have been fulfilled in regard to the places themselves. Tyre and Sidon, though in a ruinous and degraded condition at the end of the last century and the beginning of this, are now more prosperous, and have never been so utterly blotted out from the knowledge and memory of man as Chorazin and Bethsaida, of which no trace can be found by the most careful researches. Nor have modern travellers been able to fix with any degree of certainty on the site of Capernaum, which was favored above all other cities during our Saviour's ministry as the place of his residence.

### 25 – 30. — Christ's Thankfulness, and his Call to the Heavy Laden.

According to Luke (x. 17 – 21), who in this case marks the time more particularly than Matthew, these words were spoken after the return of the seventy disciples. They had come back with joy on account of the miracles which they had performed. In this their first success Jesus sees the token of the ultimate triumph over the powers of darkness. "And he said unto them, I beheld Satan as lightning fall from heaven." Yet he warns them not to rejoice in their miraculous powers, but rather that their names are written in heaven. Then, at the thought of the way in which these simple, unlearned men, these babes in knowledge, have received and proclaimed his truth, he breaks out into the sublime exclamation of thanksgiving which is here recorded by Matthew. Though his instructions were hidden from men whose wisdom is only the blinding prudence of this world, and though he may have been pained to find his offers rejected by them, and to foresee the sorrows which they who would not hear him bring upon themselves, he nevertheless bows in thankfulness: "Even so, Father, for so it seemed good in thy sight." He turns with a perfect trust to the infinite and holy Father, and rests in his will with gratitude and joy. He stops in no lower sphere. He asks not and he explains not how the hiding of these things from the wise and prudent, to their overthrow and destruction, though they were revealed unto babes, should be a reason for rejoicing; but he goes to the good pleasure of his Father in heaven as the centre of all that he could wish. The benignant will of God was so entirely his will, — that central Fountain of life and joy so filled to overflowing his own soul, that whatever might come was to him a source of thankfulness, *because* it came from Him. "Even so, Father, for so it seemed good in thy sight." And, as an additional cause for gratitude, he goes on to say, "All things are delivered or taught unto me by the Father. "Everything has been given to me by the Father." Though man cannot understand me, the Father does; and so, though men do not understand the Father, yet I and they to whom I shall reveal Him, do understand him. Then, in the fulness of the Divine wisdom, power, and love which had been given to him, he uttered, 28 – 30, the words of invitation, and the promise of relief and rest, which, from that day to this, have fallen with such infinite tenderness on laboring and burdened souls. No commentary can add to or bring out their meaning. They pour out their sweetness, with ever-increasing freshness and power, into the souls of those who accept his offer, and who, giving themselves up entirely to him, take his yoke upon them, and learn of him in meekness and lowliness of heart.

## NOTES.

AND it came to pass, when Jesus had made an end of commanding his twelve disciples, he departed thence, to teach and to preach in their cities.

Now when John had heard in the prison the works of Christ, he sent two of his disciples, and said unto him, Art thou he that should come, or do we look for another? Jesus answered and said unto them, Go and show John again those things which ye do hear and see; the blind receive their sight, and the lame walk, the lepers are cleansed, and the deaf hear, the dead are raised up, and the poor have the gospel preached to them; and blessed is he, whosoever shall not be offended in me.——

---

2. **the works of Christ**] *of the Christ* or *Messiah*. This is the only instance, except in the first verse of the first chapter, where Matthew in his own narrative applies this name to Jesus. It probably is used here as particularly appropriate, in consequence of John's state of mind in regard to Jesus as the Messiah. In that case it harmonizes with the view we have taken of John, and the object of his message. 5. **the dead are raised up**] Matthew has specified only one case (ix. 24, 25) of raising a person from the dead. The expression here implies more, and should remind us of the multitude of his extraordinary acts which are not recorded. The Gospels can hardly be regarded as containing more than samples of the different sorts of *works* which he performed. We must not, therefore, be surprised that single acts, such as raising the widow's son at Nain (Luke vii. 11 – 15), and the raising of Lazarus (John xi. 1 - 46), should be mentioned only by one writer. 6. **offended**] The root from which this expression comes in Greek means a trap or snare, and thence a stumbling-block. Whatever might trip one up or cause him to stumble. Blessed is he who is not offended in me, i. e. who finds nothing in my course which may serve as a stumbling-block or impediment in the way of

MATTHEW XI. 211

7 And, as they departed, Jesus began to say unto the multitudes
concerning John: What went ye out into the wilderness to
8 see? a reed shaken with the wind? But what went ye out for
to see? a man clothed in soft raiment? Behold, they that wear
9 soft clothing are in kings' houses. But what went ye out for to
see? a prophet? Yea, I say unto you, and more than a prophet.
10 For this is he of whom it is written, "Behold, I send my messenger before thy face, which shall prepare thy way before
11 thee." Verily I say unto you, among them that are born of
women there hath not risen a greater than John the Baptist;
notwithstanding, he that is least in the kingdom of Heaven is
12 greater than he. And from the days of John the Baptist until
now, the kingdom of Heaven suffereth violence, and the violent

---

his faith in me. "When persecution and tribulation arise because
of the word, immediately he is
offended (Matt. xiii. 21), i. e. he
finds an impediment or stumbling-
block in the way of his fidelity to
Christ. So xiii. 57, xv. 12, xvii. 27.
Lest we should offend them, i. e.
put a stumbling-block in their way.

10. **Behold, I send
my messenger before thy face**]
This is taken, with a slight alteration, from Malachi iii. 1: "Behold I
will send my messenger, and he shall
prepare the way before me; and the
Lord [not Jehovah], whom ye seek,
shall suddenly come to his temple."
John, therefore, is represented as
the forerunner of the Lord, or the
Messiah. The word here translated
"the Lord," says Dr. Noyes, "when
used without the article, is everywhere applied to human beings in
the Old Testament. And though
with the article, which it has here,
it denotes the Supreme Being as
the Lord of all the earth, when no
other use of the article can be assigned except to denote the Supreme
Being; yet in this verse the article
may be used merely to denote that
particular lord who was an object
of expectation and desire."

11. **Among them that are
born of women**] Possibly this
expression is used, as Oldshausen
asserts, by way of contrast to those
who are born of God in the higher
and Christian sense. 12.
**the kingdom of Heaven suf-
fereth violence**] This is one of
the obscure and difficult passages, on
which very different constructions
have been put. We have given one
in our general remarks above, p. 205;
but are by no means sure that the
following is not a more satisfactory
explanation. The verb may be considered in the passive voice, and
translated *is forced*, or *suffereth
violence;* or it may be taken as in
the middle voice, and translated,
*forces itself*, or *makes its own way
by force.* Mr. Norton renders it,
"until now the kingdom of Heaven
is forcing its way." Stier adopts the
same interpretation. "The kingdom of Heaven," he says, "pro-
claims itself loudly and openly,
breaking in with violence; the poor
are compelled (Luke xiv. 23) to
enter in ; those who oppose it are
constrained to take offence. In
short, all things proceed urgently
with it; it goes with 'mighty movement and impulse' (as Dräseke
preaches), it works effectually upon
all spirits in both directions, and on
all sides. The first [clause of the
sentence] speaks of that mighty
excitement which the breaking in
of the kingdom of Heaven in itself
occasions ; the second points out
inferentially the result. Its con-
straining power does violence to
all; but it excites at the same time,

take it by force. For all the prophets and the law prophesied, 13 until John. And if ye will receive it, this is Elias, which 14 was for to come. He that hath ears to hear, let him hear. 15 But whereunto shall I liken this generation? It is like unto 16 children sitting in the markets, and calling unto their fellows, and saying, We have piped unto you, and ye have not 17 danced; we have mourned unto you, and ye have not lamented. For John came neither eating nor drinking; and they 18 say, He hath a devil. The Son of Man came eating and 19

in the case of many, obstinate opposition. He who will not submit to it must be offended and resist, and he who yields to it must press and struggle through this offence. Thus the kingdom of Heaven *does* and *suffers* violence, *both* in its twofold influence: it exerts a mighty power itself, and a mighty power must be put forth towards it, whether it be of faith or of unbelief."

**15. He that hath ears]** A solemn call of attention to what has been said. **16. It is like unto children]** According to Tischendorf's reading, this should be translated, "It is like children sitting in the markets, who, calling *to one another*, say," &c.

**17. We have piped]** Hired musicians were employed at weddings and at funerals (ix. 23). The children are represented as imitating in their sports these hired minstrels; and in their vehement recriminations crying out against one another, they only add to the general confusion and inconsistency. This generation reject at one time the Baptist, because of his ascetic habits; and at another time the Son of Man, because of his free and liberal course of life, and add to the general confusion and to their own inconsistency by their divisions among themselves, accusing one another; one party exclaiming, "You refuse to have this," and the other retorting, "You refuse to have that," like noisy, unreasonable children, who are crying out against each other; one party exclaiming, "We have given you merry music, and you have not danced," and the other party replying in anger, "We have given you funeral music, and you have not lamented;" so that in the disturbance both strains alike — the merry and the mournful — are rejected. The picture is given to the life; and the comparison is a most interesting one, showing as it does how our Saviour, with the weight of his great mission upon him, entered into the amusements of boys, as he did with a deeper sympathy into the disposition and temper of babes. **18. He hath a devil]** a demon. The Jews believed insanity to be caused by evil spirits, or demons. To say that a man has a demon might with them mean either that he was a wicked man, given over to an evil spirit, or that he was a maniac, or not improbably, as in this case, a union of the two. "Thou hast a devil, and art crazy" (John x. 20); — the first expression representing the cause, and the second the effect.

**19. is justified]** This word occurs in the Gospels six times, and always with the same meaning, viz. in the active voice, to cause to be recognized as just or approved. "By thy words thou shalt be justified," i. e. approved, or recognized as just. (xii. 37.) "The people ..... justified God," i. e. approved of what he had done, or declared him to be just. (Luke vii. 29.) "He, wishing to justify himself," i. e. to cause himself to be recognized as just. (Luke x. 29.) "Ye are they who justify yourselves before men," i. e. would cause men to recognize you as just. (Luke xvi. 15.) "This man went down to

drinking, and they say, Behold, a man gluttonous and a wine-
bibber, a friend of publicans and sinners. But Wisdom is jus-
20 tified of her children. —— Then began he to upbraid the cities
wherein most of his mighty works were done, because they
21 repented not: Woe unto thee, Chorazin! woe unto thee, Bethsaida! for if the mighty works which were done in you had
been done in Tyre and Sidon, they would have repented long

---

his house justified," i. e. approved by God, recognized by him as right. (Luke xviii. 14.)

21. **Tyre and Sidon**] It has been usual with travellers to point out the literal fulfilment of ancient prophecies (Isa. xxiii. 1 – 15; Ezek. xxvi. xxviii.) in regard to these places. We quote a few passages on this subject from Stanley's "Sinai and Palestine": "There is one point of view in which this whole coast is specially remarkable. 'A mournful and solitary silence now prevails along the shore which once resounded with the world's debate.' This sentence, with which Gibbon solemnly closes his chapter on the Crusades, well sums up the general impression still left by the six days' ride from Beyroot to Ascalon; and it is no matter of surprise that in this impression travellers have felt a response to the strains in which Isaiah and Ezekiel foretold the desolation of Tyre and Sidon. In one sense, and that the highest, this feeling is just. The Phœnician power which the prophets denounced has entirely perished; even whilst 'the world's debate' of the middle ages gave a new animation to these shores, the brilliant Tyre of Alexander and Barbarossa had no real connection with the Tyre of Hiram; and perhaps no greater stretch of imagination in ancient history is required than to conceive how the two small towns of Tyre and Sidon, as they now exist, could have been the parent cities of Carthage and Cadiz, the traders with Spain and Britain, the wonders of the East for luxury and magnificence. So total a destruction, for all political purposes, of the two great commercial states of the ancient world has been frequently held up to commercial states in the modern world, as showing the precarious tenure by which purely mercantile greatness is held; and in this respect the prophecies of the Hebrew seers were a real revelation of the coming fortunes of the world, the more remarkable because experience had not yet justified such a result. But to narrow the scope of these sublime visions to the actual buildings and sites of the cities is as unwarranted by facts as it is mistaken in idea. Sidon has probably never ceased to be a populous, and, on the whole, a flourishing town; small, indeed, as compared with its ancient grandeur, but never desolate, or without some portion of its old traffic; and still encompassed round and round with the lines of its red silk manufacture. Tyre may perhaps have been in a state of ruin shortly after the Chaldæan, and subsequently after the Greek conquest of Syria. But it has always been speedily rebuilt. . . . . . The period during which it sunk to the lowest ebb was during the last years of the past and the first years of the present century; and the comparative desolation which it then exhibited no doubt presented some of the imagery on which so much stress has been laid, in order to convey the impression of its being a desolate rock, only used for the drying of fishermen's nets. But as this was not the case before that period, and is certainly not the case now, it is idle to seek for the fulfilment of the ancient prediction within those limits; and the ruin of the empire of Tyre, combined with the revival and continuance of the town of Tyre, is thus a striking instance of

ago in sackcloth and ashes. But I say unto you, it shall be 22
more tolerable for Tyre and Sidon, at the day of judgment,
than for you. And thou, Capernaum, which art exalted unto 23
heaven, shalt be brought down to hell; for if the mighty works
which have been done in thee had been done in Sodom, it
would have remained until this day. But I say unto you, that 24
it shall be more tolerable for the land of Sodom, in the day of
Judgment, than for thee. —— At that time Jesus answered and 25
said, I thank thee, O Father, Lord of heaven and earth, because thou hast hid these things from the wise and prudent,
and hast revealed them unto babes. Even so, Father, for so 26

---

the moral and poetical, as distinct from the literal and prosaic, accomplishment of the Prophetical Scriptures." pp. 266, 267. 23.
**And thou, Capernaum**] "It would almost seem," says Stanley, pp. 376, 377, "as if the woe pronounced against Capernaum had been literally fulfilled, as if the doom of the cities of the southern sea had been visited upon those of the north, as if it had been more tolerable for the land of Sodom, in the day of its earthly judgment, than for Capernaum. It has indeed been more tolerable in one sense; for the name, and perhaps even the remains, of Sodom are still to be found on the shores of the Dead Sea, whilst that of Capernaum has, on the Lake of Genesareth, been utterly lost. . . . . . Still, it would be contrary to the general spirit of prophecy, whether in the Old or New Testament, to press this argument too far. The woe, here as elsewhere, was doubtless spoken, not against the walls and houses of those villages, but against those who dwelt within them; and, as a matter of fact, it would appear that they [the walls and houses] did survive the terrible curse for many generations." 23. **to hell**] to Hades. The abode of the dead, — not like Gehenna, — a place of torture for the wicked alone. The expression, *shalt be brought down to hell*, means, *shall be utterly destroyed.*

25. **and hast revealed them unto babes**] Pure and childlike persons, — those who in singleness of heart, without prejudices or prepossessions of their own, receive the words of Jesus. The worldly prudence of the wise blinds them to truths which require the entire surrender of themselves to Christ. The philosophical wise men have their minds too much circumscribed by their speculations to take in spiritual truths like those taught by Jesus, which transcend the bounds of their reasoning, and take them into higher and broader worlds of intelligence. Distinct from these are the babes; to whom the kingdom of God is revealed, and to whom in all ages of the world the Saviour's words apply. But in his exclamation of thanksgiving, he probably had more immediately in his mind at the time the seventy who had just returned rejoicing from their first evangelizing mission. "These unlearned, sincere, and childlike men, who," to use the language of a friend, "had no previously cherished system to support, — no abundant treasury of words, which they were liable, consciously or unconsciously, to substitute for the very words of Jesus; no habits of abstract reasoning which might lead them to state the results of reasoning for the facts of observation, — had been present at the giving of sight to the blind and hearing to the deaf. They had seen the lame freed from their infirmity, the sick healed, the dead raised, and those possessed of evil spirits restored to sanity and self-control

27 it seemed good in thy sight. All things are delivered unto me
of my Father; and no man knoweth the Son but the Father;
neither knoweth any man the Father, save the Son, and he to
28 whomsoever the Son will reveal him. Come unto me all ye
29 that labor and are heavy laden, and I will give you rest. Take
my yoke upon you, and learn of me; for I am meek and lowly
30 in heart; and ye shall find rest unto your souls. For my yoke
is easy, and my burden is light.

---

by His word. They continually had wondered at the 'gracious' words which proceeded out of his mouth. They were full of expectation and reverence and admiration and of love. And they had gone out telling just what they had seen and heard, just as, at the time, it had impressed their receptive minds and moved their hearts. The name of their Master was continually upon their tongues, and, by the power of the Spirit of Jesus, their whole being became, for the time, merged in his; they were one with him, and, in his name, they had performed his works. Now they were full of joy, and said, 'Lord, even the devils are subject to us, through thy name.' And Jesus himself rejoiced in spirit, thankfully acknowledging the wisdom which had led, not the lettered and logical, not pre-occupied and trained minds, not the Pharisee or Sadducee, but the fishermen of Galilee, — the Seventy, and such as they, — to be at first his followers and witnesses to receive the true impression of Him, and to give it unchanged to others, — that the world might have transmitted to it, not a plan, a philosophy and abstract system, but a whole, concrete Gospel of salvation." 27. **All things are delivered unto me of my Father**] "I have been instructed in all by my Father." Norton. "My Father hath imparted everything to me." Campbell. "All things appertaining to my office are delivered to me of my Father." Whitby. Of these translations Campbell's is the most exact, the word "imparted" bearing the double meaning, *delivered* and *taught*, which belongs to the original παρεδόθη. **and no man knoweth the Son but the Father**] The blindness of most commentators to the explicit assertion of Jesus here is very remarkable. There is no more distinct, unequivocal, and unqualified assertion in the New Testament. And yet, in direct opposition to it, creeds have been formed, defining the metaphysical nature of Christ, and enforcing their distinctions on a subject which Jesus expressly declares that no man understands, as the only condition of church-membership in this world or of salvation in the world to come. It would be difficult to find a more audacious and presumptuous violation of the words of Jesus than the Athanasian Creed, with its thrice repeated curses against those who do not receive its doctrines. Jesus here declares, that, while the Son reveals the Father, his own nature is not known except by the Father. He reflects the image of God, as the perfect mirror reflects the sky so entirely that it remains itself unseen. 29. **lowly in heart**] " This expression describes the humility of the Redeemer, as in entire accordance with the bent of his holy will, and originating in the very depth of his heart; hence humility appears in Him as the cheerful result of free choice." Olshausen. Poverty of spirit comes from a sense of want; lowliness of heart arises from a cheerful, unquestioning, and almost unconscious submission to the will of God; or rather it comes from so living in the presence of God, that his love reaches into the soul, and calls out its powers in harmony with his will.

# CHAPTER XII.

### 1–14. — Christ's View of the Sabbath.

It is exceedingly difficult to get from the Gospels a clear idea of the order of events, or the length of time that elapsed between different events. The expression, "then," or "at that time," which recurs frequently in Matthew, does not, as in our language, indicate that what is now to be related belongs to the same occasion with that which has gone immediately before, but rather, that it belongs to a different time and occasion. It is merely a transition clause, nearly equivalent to the phrase, "and it came to pass," or "about that time." "It came to pass in those days" (Matthew iii. 1) applies to an event which took place after an interval of thirty years.

1–8. According to a humane provision of the Mosaic law (Deut. xxiii. 25), those who were passing through a neighbor's field were allowed to pluck the ears of grain with their hand, though not to use a sickle. Dr. Robinson says, that when near Hebron, passing by the fields of ripening wheat, "We had here a beautiful illustration of Scripture. Our Arabs 'were an hungered,' and going into the fields, they 'plucked the ears of corn, and did eat, rubbing them in their hands.' On being questioned, they said this was an old custom, and no one would speak against it." The offence of the disciples consisted, not in taking the grain, but in doing it on the Sabbath. "He that reaps on the Sabbath," says a Jewish authority quoted by Lightfoot, "though never so little, is guilty. And to pluck the ears of corn is a kind of reaping; and whosoever plucks anything from the springing of his own fruit is guilty, under the name of a reaper." It was to sweep away all sophistries of this kind, and to re-establish the substance and spirit of the law in the place of the trifling and superstitious observances which had grown out of it, that Jesus, in this instance, replies to the fault-finders by facts, which they as Jews must admit to be right, and then (verse 8, Mark ii. 27) lays down the true principle by which all ceremonial rites and institutions are to be interpreted. 1. Necessity knows no laws of this kind, and cannot be bound by their authority. Have ye not read, he asks, how David (1 Sam. xxi. 6) and those who were with him, when driven by hunger, took bread, which by the law (Ex. xxix. 33) only the priests were allowed to eat? 2. Where the worship of God requires the violation of the Sabbath, the lesser should yield to the greater. The form must give way, that the substance may be retained. "Have ye not read in the law," (Num. xxviii. 9, 10,) he says, addressing them still as Jews, "that on the Sabbath days the priests in the temple profane the temple, and are guiltless? And I say unto you, that something greater than the temple is here." He then (Mark ii. 27) lays down the great principle by which all these rites are to be determined. "The Sabbath was made for man, and not man for the Sabbath. Wherever, therefore, it interferes with man's highest good, its severity must be relaxed. "If," he adds, "ye had recognized the meaning and the authority of the divine precept," (Hosea vi. 6,) 'Mercy is more to me than sacrifice,' ye would not, as you are now doing, condemn the innocent." The Son of Man has power to regulate the observance even of the Sabbath-day.

9 – 14. On another occasion (another Sabbath, Luke vi. 9) he, under the general principle already quoted from Mark, brought up a third case, not wholly distinct perhaps from the first, in which the letter of the law is to be relaxed, and its spirit observed by works of charity

and mercy. There was present in the synagogue a man whose right hand was withered. The Pharisees were eagerly watching, with the hope that they might catch him violating the law. They ask him, therefore, whether it is allowable to perform cures on the Sabbath! Jesus, knowing their thoughts (Luke vi. 8), asked the man to rise up and stand in the midst, which he did. Then, in reply to their question, he asked, which of the two is allowable on the Sabbath, to do good or to do evil, to save life or to kill? If any one among you have one sheep, and it fall into a pit on the Sabbath, will he not lay hold on it and lift it out? But is not a man of far more consequence than a sheep? So that it is lawful to do well on the Sabbath. They, unable to answer him, were silent. And Jesus, having looked round on them with anger, being grieved at the hardness of their hearts (Mark iii. 5), directed the man to stretch forth his hand. And he stretched it forth; and it was restored whole as the other. The principle on which Jesus here reasoned is, that it is a sin to neglect the opportunity to do a good deed, and therefore works of mercy must not be neglected even on the Sabbath. He has thus clearly taught, 1. that a man's own necessities, 2. that the offices of public worship, and 3. that works of charity, may justify what would otherwise be a violation of the Sabbath.

Jesus is recorded to have performed cures on the Sabbath at seven different times;— the cure of the demoniac (Mark i. 21); of Peter's wife's mother (Mark i. 29); of the impotent man (John v. 9); of the man born blind (John ix. 14); of the woman with a spirit of infirmity (Luke xiii. 10-17); of the man who had a dropsy (Luke xiv. 1); besides the one related above. Unquestionably one object which he had in performing so many miracles on the Sabbath, was to do away the narrow superstitious formalities in which that merciful institution had become incrusted, and by which its beneficent design was perverted or impaired and destroyed.

14 – 37. — HATRED OF THE PHARISEES AGAINST JESUS.

14 – 21. Here is the first allusion to any conspiracy against his life by the enemies of Jesus. It was evident that he was producing a decided and powerful impression on the minds of the people, and that he carefully abstained from any violation of the law, yet his principles of interpretation, and the feelings with which he regarded its observances, were diametrically opposite to theirs. In this case, feeling the pungency of his rebuke, and unable to say a word in reply to his reasoning, the Scribes and Pharisees were (Luke vi. 11) inflamed with rage, and took counsel (Mark iii. 6) with the Herodians, who were probably the adherents of Herod, and rather political than religious partisans, how they might destroy him. Jesus, knowing their designs, withdrew to the Sea of Galilee, where immense multitudes gathered round him from all the neighboring country, — from Jerusalem, from Idumea and beyond the Jordan on the east, and from Tyre and Sidon on the west. This would only increase the apprehensions and malice of his enemies. Jesus did all that he could consistently with the great purpose of his ministry to avoid notoriety. He severely charged those on whom his healing miracles were wrought not to make him known.

22 – 37. — CASTING OUT SATAN BY SATAN.

About this time, when the popular mind was wrought up to a high pitch of expectation and excitement, there was brought to Jesus a demoniac, blind and dumb, whom he healed, so that the blind and dumb both spake and saw. There is nothing mentioned that would indicate insanity, nor is it possible to discover what the symptoms were that marked the case as one of demoniacal possession. It seems, however, to have been regarded as an extraordinary case, and the cure caused an unusual sensation of astonishment among the multitudes, who ask if this is not the Son of David, i. e. the Messiah? Such a suggestion could not be endured by the Pharisees. In the extremity of their malignant jealousy and scorn, hardening themselves against the holiness of his life and the merciful character of his acts, they contemptuously reply, that he does not cast out demons except by Beelzebub, the prince of demons. He, knowing all that was passing in their minds, overthrew their taunt by reasoning which they from their point of view could not answer, and then, 31, 32, exposed their unpardonable wickedness in the severest sentence that ever fell from his lips.

The 21st verse is one of some difficulty. "If I by Beelzebub cast out demons, by whom do your children, i. e. your disciples, cast them out? wherefore they shall be your judges." There is no doubt that there were at that time men who practised among the Jews the pretended art of expelling demons. Josephus, Antiq., VIII. 2. 5, appeals to an extraordinary proof of this fact which one of these exorcists had given before Vespasian in the presence of a part of the Roman army. There was a belief among the Jews that these men actually expelled demons by their art, and it was from this their point of view that Jesus addressed his argument to the Pharisees. If I, in my cures, which shake to its very centre the dominion of Satan, am in league with him, by whom do your disciples perform *their* cures? Let them answer the question, and be your judges. Jesus was doing nothing more than they were pretending to do. Why then should he be adjudged as guilty of a greater crime?

But does not he, in using such language, countenance the belief that they had the power to cast out demons? This brings up a very interesting and important subject of inquiry. How far could a being with the more than human endowments and knowledge which Jesus possessed, looking through men's thoughts, and the shadows around them, be among the Jews, and converse freely with them, without suffering their false ideas and conceptions to pass uncorrected? Parents are every day pursuing this course with their children, knowing that it would be a vain thing to try to correct them in regard to many false ideas which they are not yet able to understand, but which they will outgrow in the natural progress of their minds. It is not by specific corrections now, but by the gradual unfolding and enlightenment of their minds, that they are to be set free from these mistaken notions. So Christ came, not to correct specific errors, one by one, but to bring into the world those great elements of moral and religious life and thought, which, as they are received and applied, may lift men up above their errors, and set them free from their mistaken ideas. In order to gain access to them, he must meet them as they are, and reason with them from premises which *they* believe to be true. By seeking to correct their established convictions and habits of thought in regard to common and comparatively unimportant matters, he would rouse their prejudices, and close their minds against him in his more important influences and instructions. Their errors, therefore, he sometimes uses as illustrations or arguments by which to introduce into their minds truths which, once lodged there, and acting through their lives, shall at length set them free, and drive out the very errors by which they gained admittance. It is evident that this must essentially modify the form of any revelation from God to men, in its adaptation to the existing wants and limitations of their nature.

The reasoning of this whole discourse proceeds in this way. It meets the Pharisees on their own ground, without one word to show whether that ground be tenable or not. In this way, he brings before them the momentous truth which it is his purpose to declare. If the very centre of Satan's kingdom is shaken by these works of mine, and if, as I have shown from your own point of view, I have done these works, not by the aid of Beelzebub, but, 28, by the spirit, and Luke xi. 20, the finger of God, then in this overthrow of the powers of darkness you may be sure that the kingdom of God has come upon you unawares. For how can the house of the strong man, thoroughly armed and on his guard (Luke xi. 21), be entered, unless a stronger than he overcome, and disarm, and bind him? But, in this warfare, he continues, he who is not with me is against me. "Wherefore," he says, 31, 32, referring to the whole course of reasoning by which he has proved that these are the works of God against which they have set themselves, — " wherefore, though every sin and blasphemy shall be forgiven to men, yet blasphemy against the Holy Spirit shall not be forgiven to men, . . . . . either in this world [αἰῶνι, — *æon*] or the world to come."

### 31, 32. — THE UNPARDONABLE SIN.

What is the sin thus fearfully and hopelessly condemned? All enlightened modern commentators, we believe, agree that "it is not one particular act of sin which is here condemned, but a state of sin, and that a wilful, determined opposition" to what is highest and holiest. He who speaks against the Son of Man may do it ignorantly, or through traditional prejudices, or from a sudden impulse, and may repent and be forgiven. "But he," to use the words of the Greek father Euthymius, "who, seeing my Divine works which God alone can perform, ascribes them to Beelzebub as you now do, and so blasphemes against the Holy Spirit, or the Divinity itself (for he now calls it the Holy Spirit), — he, plainly determined and fixed on what is evil, and knowingly insulting God, sins without excuse, and shall not be forgiven." His sin is not one of impulse, ignorance, or weakness. But he has gone on knowingly sinning and hardening himself against the Holy Spirit, maligning its influences, and attributing them to a diabolical agency, till he has reached such a degree of hardihood in wickedness that he is beyond all hope of repentance or amendment, and therefore beyond all hope of forgiveness. The settled frame of his mind is so wilfully and knowingly turned against God in his plainest and holiest influences and teachings, that he has made repentance, and through it reformation, an impossibility to him, whether in this world [*æon*] or the world to come.

Jesus then turns again to their blasphemous charge against the Holy Spirit, in ascribing actions such as they had witnessed to the Prince of demons. Do at least, he says, be consistent with yourselves. Allow either that the tree and fruit are both good, or that they are both bad together. The tree is known by its fruit. But, 34, how, on this principle, can we expect anything good from you, since, as is the heart, so must the words be. So true is this law of our nature, so is even the careless, idle word imbued with the spirit, and so does it indicate the disposition, from which it comes, that, "I say unto you, for every idle word that men shall speak, they shall give account in the day of judgment." The careless, idle words which men utter are perhaps the truest index to their character.

### 38 – 50. — FURTHER REMARKS OF JESUS.

38 – 40. On another occasion the Scribes and Pharisees, in a captious, unbelieving spirit, asked of him a sign. He knew their motives, and declared to them that no sign should be given except that of the prophet Jonah, as foreshadowing his own death. It is remarkable, as Dr. Furness has said, that whenever a sign was asked of Jesus, he invariably referred to his death, "as the greatest sign that he could possibly give of his truth." (John vi. 30, 51.) The reference to the book of Jonah proves nothing conclusively respecting the view that Jesus

might have of it, whether as an historical narrative, or an instructive allegory, framed like some of his own parables, to set forth important lessons of truth and duty.

He then, 41 – 45, as he had done twice before in different connections, spoke of the way in which the generation must be condemned by those who had gone before, if they should slight the greater privileges which were granted to them. And finally he likens them to a demoniac who is for a time apparently cured, but with a relapse of his malady is in a far worse condition than before. The picture, which is in accordance with the prevalent ideas of the Jews, is full of life and interest. The unclean spirit, cast out of its comfortable abode, wanders, 43, into dry, i. e. desert, uncultivated, and desolate places, seeking rest, and finding none. And at last, tired of this he joins to himself seven other spirits worse than himself, and finding his old abode empty, swept, and furnished, they enter in and dwell there. So with this generation. However the Jews may have been freed for a time by their afflictions from their old idolatries, yet the old spirit and others far worse had returned, and now their last end (xxiii. 45) is worse than all that had gone before. The same remarks apply to an individual, reformed for a season, and then relapsing into his old sins, with others still worse added to them.

### 46 – 50. — JESUS AND HIS MOTHER.

Any impression that we might get here of apparent harshness in the conduct of Jesus towards his mother will be removed by attending to all the circumstances. Not only was the house where he sat full of people, but probably, as in another case (Mark ii. 2) the way of approach to the door was crowded, so that those who were out could not get at him (Luke viii. 19) on account of the multitude. While he was in the midst of his weighty and impressive discourse, word was passed in to him (Luke viii. 20) that his mother and brethren were without desiring to speak to him. Immediately he turned this incident into an occasion of teaching the higher spiritual relationships which he had come to establish, and asked, " Who is my mother, and who are my brethren? " Then looking round about on those who were sitting around him (Mark iii. 34) he stretched forth his hand towards his disciples, and said, " Behold my mother and my brethren. For whosoever shall do the will of my Father who is in heaven, he is my brother, and sister, and mother."

We learn from John vii. 5, that his brethren did not believe in him, and Mark, iii. 21, tells us that when his friends or relatives heard how he was situated and what he was doing, they went out to lay hold on him; for they said, "He is beside himself." They evidently at that time did not at all understand him. It is more difficult to enter into the feelings of his mother. His past history and his character, as it showed itself to her in the intimate relations of life, must, we infer from the few glimpses that are given to us (Luke ii. 41 – 52, John ii. 1 – 12) have been such as to fill her with wonder and expectation. She pondered these things in her heart. But, as a human being, she doubtless had her alternations of feeling. She knew not how his work should be accomplished or what it was. When her relatives and possibly even her own sons declared that he was beside himself, her maternal feelings must have been touched, and, without sympathizing with them in their unbelief, she may have been painfully moved by vague apprehensions of impending danger, and hopes of coming greatness, so that she went with them to ease her anxieties by seeing him, and perhaps to persuade him to withdraw himself for a season from the perils that were gathering round him. If such were her feelings, nothing could do more to assuage her fears, awaken her reverence, and re-establish her faith, than the words here uttered, which in their calm dignity lifted him above all earthly interests and relationships.

---

## NOTES.

At that time Jesus went on the sabbath day through the corn; and his disciples were an hungered, and began to pluck the ears of corn, and to eat. But when the Pharisees saw it, 2 they said unto him, Behold thy disciples do that which is not lawful to do upon the sabbath-day. But he said unto them, 3 Have ye not read what David did, when he was an hungered, and they that were with him? how he entered into the house 4 of God, and did eat the shew-bread, which was not lawful for him to eat, neither for them which were with him, but only for the priests? Or have ye not read in the law, how that on the 5 sabbath-days the priests in the temple profane the sabbath, and are blameless? But I say unto you, that in this place is one 6 greater than the temple. But if ye had known what this mean- 7 eth, "I will have mercy and not sacrifice," ye would not have condemned the guiltless. For the Son of man is Lord 8 even of the sabbath-day.

---

2. **when the Pharisees saw it**] They must have been following him through the fields in that hypocritical spirit of ceremonial observance that would be ready to measure his steps after him, and find it out, if he should walk one yard beyond the prescribed length of a sabbath-day's journey. This whole chapter, down to the 46th verse, is taken up in showing this trait of the Pharisees, and the terrible severity with which it was rebuked by Jesus. 3. **Have ye not read**] "At that very time of year Leviticus was being read on sabbaths, the book in which there occur so many precepts as to sacrifices which were required to be performed, even on the sabbath." Bengel. 4. **house of God**] Strictly speaking, there was no house of God at that time, but only a tent in which the Ark of the Covenant was kept. But, as in Ex. xxiii. 19, the tent was sometimes called the house of God.
**which is not lawful for him to eat**] Ex. xxix. 33. For the *shew-bread*, see Leviticus xxiv. 5-8. From this reference and verse 8, as well as from a Jewish authority cited by Lightfoot, it is rendered probable that David went there either on the sabbath, or just as the sabbath was going out, which would make his example still more pertinent in this case. 8. **for the Son of man**] "Why is Christ called the Son of man, but just because he represents humanity as a whole,—because, as a second

9 And when he was departed thence, he went into their syna-
10 gogue. And, behold, there was a man which had his hand
withered. And they asked him saying, Is it lawful to heal on
11 the sabbath-days? that they might accuse him. And he said
unto them, What man shall there be among you that shall
have one sheep, and if it fall into a pit on the sabbath-day,
12 will he not lay hold on it, and lift it out? How much then is
a man better than a sheep! Wherefore it is lawful to do well
13 on the sabbath-days. Then saith he to the man, Stretch forth
thine hand. And he stretched it forth; and it was restored
14 whole, like as the other. Then the Pharisees went out, and
held a council against him, how they might destroy him. ——
15 But when Jesus knew it, he withdrew himself from thence;
and great multitudes followed him; and he healed them all,
16 and charged them that they should not make him known;
17 that it might be fulfilled which was spoken by Esaias the
18 prophet, saying: "Behold my servant, whom I have chosen,
my beloved, in whom my soul is well pleased; I will put my
spirit upon him, and he shall show judgment to the Gentiles.

---

Adam, he bears in himself and sets up a new humanity? This is the key to the whole statement, according to which, in the first place, Mark ii. 27, as the words stand, contain a truth as profound as it is simple. So, in the Talmud, R. Jonathan says, literally, 'The sabbath is in your own hands, not you in its hands, for it is said: The sabbath is for you.' (Ex. xvi. 29; Ezek. xx. 12.) It is, according to God's design, an ordinance and institution of mercy for the good of man, appointed, in the first instance, for rest and refreshment (Deut. v. 14; Ex. xxiii. 12); and then further for blessing and sanctification." Stier.

11. **and lift it out**] "Our Lord evidently asks this as a thing allowed and done at the time when he spoke; but subsequently (perhaps, suggests Stier, on account of these words of Christ) it was forbidden in the Gemara; and only permitted *to lay planks for the beast to come out*." Alford. 15. **and great multitudes**], The populousness of Galilee at that time, compared with what it is at present, was very great. According to Josephus, it had more than 200 cities, the least of which contained 15,000 inhabitants; and the whole province contained more than 3,000,000 of people. According to Strabo, Galilee was full of Egyptians, Arabians, and Phœnicians. (Lib. XVI.) See Milman's Hist. Christianity, I. 4.

18-20. "This quotation," says Dr. Palfrey, "from the prophecy of Isaiah (xlii. 1-4) accords precisely with neither the Hebrew nor the Septuagint." The Hebrew is thus translated by Dr. Noyes:

"Behold my servant, whom I uphold,
My chosen, in whom my soul delighteth;
I have put my spirit upon him;
He shall give laws to the nations.
He shall not cry aloud, nor raise a clamor,
Nor cause his voice to be heard in the street.
The bruised reed he shall not break,
And the glimmering flax he shall not quench;
He shall give laws according to truth.
He shall not fail, nor become weary,
Until he shall have established laws in the earth,
And distant nations shall wait for his instruction."

He shall not strive, nor cry, neither shall any man hear his 19
voice in the streets; a bruised reed shall he not break, and 20
smoking flax shall he not quench; till he send forth judgment
unto victory. And in his name shall the Gentiles trust." 21

Then was brought unto him one possessed with a devil, blind 22
and dumb; and he healed him, insomuch that the blind and
dumb both spake and saw. And all the people were amazed, 23
and said, Is not this the son of David? But when the Phari- 24
sees heard it, they said, This fellow doth not cast out devils,
but by Beelzebub, the prince of the devils. And Jesus knew 25
their thoughts, and said unto them, Every kingdom divided
against itself is brought to desolation; and every city or house
divided against itself shall not stand. And if Satan cast out 26
Satan, he is divided against himself; how shall then his kingdom stand? And if I by Beelzebub cast out devils, by whom 27
do your children cast them out? Therefore they shall be your
judges. But if I cast out devils by the spirit of God, then the 28
kingdom of God is come unto you. Or else, how can one enter 29
into a strong man's house, and spoil his goods, except he first
bind the strong man; and then he will spoil his house. He 30
that is not with me is against me; and he that gathereth not
with me, scattereth abroad. Wherefore I say unto you, all 31
manner of sin and blasphemy shall be forgiven unto men; but
the blasphemy against the Holy Ghost shall not be forgiven

---

20. **a bruised reed . . . . . smoking flax**] introduced here to show the merciful and compassionate nature of Jesus in his dealing with the broken-hearted and the contrite. Lightfoot, however, says: "He shall not make so great a noise as is made from the breaking of a reed now already bruised and half broken, or from the hissing of smoking flax only, when water is thrown upon it." 23. **Is not this the son of David?**] A name which evidently among the Jews was applied to the Messiah (ix. 27; xv. 22; xxi. 9; and especially xxii. 42). 24. **Beelzebul**] (for such is the established reading here, as well as x. 25) means Lord of mire, or Lord of place, as Beelzebub does Lord of flies. It was the name of a God worshipped, at Ekron, by the Philistines (2 Kings i. 2). The Jews applied it to the prince of devils, as the most contemptuous of all names. 25. **their thoughts**] their thoughts, imaginations, and feelings; i. e. he knew the secret motives from which they spoke, when they charged him with doing his beneficent and divine works with a diabolical design, and by the aid of the prince of devils. The Greek word, $\dot{\epsilon}\nu\theta\nu\mu\dot{\eta}\sigma\epsilon\iota\varsigma$, is much stronger and more comprehensive than the English word *thoughts*, including as it does the emotions and purposes connected with the thoughts. 28. **is come unto you**] Wesley, who avowedly copied from Bengel, explains the passage: "The kingdom of God is come upon you — unawares, before you expected: so the

32 unto men. And whosoever speaketh a word against the Son of man, it shall be forgiven him; but whosoever speaketh against the Holy Ghost, it shall not be forgiven him, neither in 33 this world, neither in the world to come. Either make the tree good, and his fruit good; or else make the tree corrupt, 34 and his fruit corrupt; for the tree is known by his fruit. O generation of vipers, how can ye, being evil, speak good

---

word implies." 32. **speaketh against the Holy Ghost**] "This probably refers to the *Divine nature* of Christ, — the power by which he wrought his miracles. There is no evidence that it refers to the third person of the Trinity." Barnes. "It was blasphemy against the Spirit of God to ascribe acts which bore the manifest impress of the Divine Goodness in their essentially beneficent character to any other source but the Father of Mercies." Milman. "Against the Holy Ghost means against the most direct and conclusive testimony by which the person . . . . . is entirely convinced, and consequently sins with the most complete knowledge and will ; and this is the idea most essentially belonging to the unpardonable sin. . . . . . It is committed when the man knows, with entire conviction, what he is doing. . . . . . It is distinguished from every other pardonable sin of man by this, that in it there is not even a minimum of satanic deceit practised upon the understanding, or compulsion of any nature, or by any creature upon the will; but the purely evil is willed, spoken, and done instead of the known and rejected good, the lie as such instead of the blasphemed truth." Stier.

**in this world, neither in the world to come**] The word αἰών (*æon*), which is here translated *world*, can be rendered by no corresponding word in our language. It means a period of time, an age, or a dispensation. In 2 Tim. i. 9 we read, " before the world began," more exactly, " before the worlds began," and still more literally, "before the times of the worlds," ages, *æons*. In 1 Cor. ii. 7 we read of the wisdom "which God ordained to our glory *before the worlds*," i. e. the æons, ages, or dispensations. These passages imply in the past a succession of æons, ages, or dispensations. Jesus speaks more than once (xiii. 39, 40, 49) of "the end of the world ; " more exactly, the winding up or consummation of the æon, the age, or dispensation then existing. In Heb. ix. 26 we read, " in the end of the world," literally, at "the completion," or " consummation of the ages." As the word æon, in its application to the past and present condition of things implies only a limited duration of time, the natural inference is that in its application to the future condition of things, it does not necessarily involve the idea of endless duration. As the word is applied to the past in the plural number, and thus denotes a succession of æons in the past, so when applied to the future in the plural number (Eph. ii. 7, "in the æons, or ages which are to come,") it in like manner denotes a succession of æons. These æons thus extend from the past into the future, each one at its completion giving way to that which is to succeed, and each, whether in the past or the future, being only one in the succession of ages. When, therefore, we read in the passage before us of a sin which shall be forgiven neither in this world (æon) nor the world (æon) to come, we find in the language nothing that necessarily involves the idea of eternity, since the age to come may, like each of those which have gone before, at length fulfil its purpose, and give place to a yet higher dispensation beyond. See xxv. 46.

things? for out of the abundance of the heart the mouth speaketh. A good man, out of the good treasure of the heart, 35 bringeth forth good things; and an evil man, out of the evil treasure, bringeth forth evil things. But I say unto you, that 36 every idle word that men shall speak, they shall give account thereof in the day of judgment. For by thy words thou shalt 37 be justified, and by thy words thou shalt be condemned.

Then certain of the Scribes and of the Pharisees answered 38 saying, Master, we would see a sign from thee. But he an- 39 swered and said unto them, An evil and adulterous generation seeketh after a sign; and there shall no sign be given to it, but the sign of the prophet Jonas. For as Jonas was three 40 days and three nights in the whale's belly, so shall the Son of man be three days and three nights in the heart of the earth. The men of Nineveh shall rise in judgment with this genera- 41 tion, and shall condemn it; because they repented at the preaching of Jonas; and, behold, a greater than Jonas is here. The queen of the south shall rise up in the judgment with this 42 generation, and shall condemn it; for she came from the uttermost parts of the earth to hear the wisdom of Solomon; and, behold, a greater than Solomon is here. —— When the un- 43 clean spirit is gone out of a man, he walketh through dry

---

36. **every idle word**] There is no authority for giving any worse meaning to the adjective. The idle word may be a wicked, or it may be a good, word. To *give account* does not necessarily imply condemnation. The meaning is, that for everything we say, down even to our idle words, we are to be held responsible, when in the day of reckoning the account of our lives shall be rendered up.

40. **three days and three nights**] By the Hebrew reckoning, the day when the account begins, and that when it ends, are included in the number of days. "A day and a night," says a Jewish tradition, "make an onah, and a part of an onah is as the whole." 41. **with this generation**] Here is an indication of the cumulative nature of sin in a community, and of the judgments visited upon it from generation to generation, till at last the measure of iniquity is full, and hopeless ruin ensues. For the same thought more fully carried out, see xxiii. 35.

43. **When the unclean spirit is gone out of a man**] Man, the individual, stands here for the Jewish nation, who are represented as being then sevenfold worse than ever before. The connection with the previous sentences is unbroken. You wicked men seeking a sign, shall find none except the sign of the prophet Jonah ; and even that, while it foreshadows my death, shall likewise testify to your condemnation, as will also the Queen of the South. But what better could be expected? When the unclean spirit is gone out of a man, and the man fails to fortify himself by religious thoughts and faithful deeds, and remains empty, and thus prepared for the return of what is evil, then that spirit, with seven others worse than

44 places, seeking rest, and findeth none. Then he saith, I will return into my house, from whence I came out. And when he 45 is come, he findeth it empty, swept, and garnished. Then goeth he, and taketh with himself seven other spirits, more wicked than himself, and they enter in and dwell there; and the last state of that man is worse than the first. Even so shall it be also unto this wicked generation.

46 While he yet talked to the people, behold, his mother and 47 his brethren stood without, desiring to speak with him. Then one said unto him, Behold, thy mother and thy brethren stand 48 without, desiring to speak with thee. But he answered and said unto him that told him, Who is my mother? and who are 49 my brethren? And he stretched forth his hand toward his dis- 50 ciples, and said, Behold, my mother, and my brethren. For whosoever shall do the will of my Father, which is in heaven, the same is my brother, and sister, and mother.

---

itself, shall enter in and dwell there. So shall it be with this evil generation, as compared with the generations which have gone before.

**47. thy brethren**] The word brother is still used in the East, as it was in the days of Abraham (Gen. xiv. 16, compared with xi. 31), to denote a near relative, as, e. g. a nephew or cousin, and even to denote a friend. It has been supposed that the word is so used here; but its connection with the word mother would imply that it is used in its stricter sense. See xiii. 55.

## CHAPTER XIII.

### Parables.

The fountain of life within flows forth into outward acts, and those outward acts are an emblem of the mind from which they come. So in nature, whatever we see proceeds from a fountain of life within, and is an emblem and token of the divine source from which it proceeds. Everything in nature, therefore, is an expression of the Divine Mind, and has its message or its influence from Him for us. The lightest forms of nature associate themselves with our deepest feelings or our highest thoughts, and the more entirely we are born into the realm of spiritual things, that is, the more alive our spiritual perceptions are, the more shall we be able to see the tokens and to feel the influences of the Divine Mind in our intercourse with nature. To him who looks through the visible forms to the great spiritual realities which they would express, every object around us, every change in nature, as an expression of the Divine Mind, is the outshadowing or the foreshadowing of something higher than itself. This great fact finds its way more or less into our common speech. The morning or evening of the day leads us spontaneously to think of the morning and evening of life. When we see the sun go down, and as it departs light up the western heavens with a richness and glory which the day has never known, we can hardly help thinking of the good man's life, which when withdrawn from our sight throws around the whole place where he dwelt, in gracious and touching remembrances, affections, virtues, and prayers more beautiful and holy than when he was bodily present with us. So the flower, the fruit, the leaf is each suggestive to us of thoughts and emotions which lie in a higher plane of life. Thus it was that Jesus saw all outward objects and events in their higher relations, and made use of them to express the higher facts which they bodied forth to his mind. No one can understand his language who receives it merely in its literal acceptation; "for the letter killeth, but the spirit giveth life" (2 Cor. iii. 6). We have only to open the Gospels to see how in his use of speech material things are made to lift us up into the realm of spiritual being. When he says, "Ye are the salt of the earth," he speaks in no literal sense. When he speaks of light and darkness, it is the light and darkness of the soul. When he speaks of hell fire, he speaks of it, not in its material, but its spiritual sense, as an emblem of the anguish into which the souls of the wicked shall be cast, unless they repent and are converted. So when he says, "Whoso eateth my flesh and drinketh my blood hath eternal life," it is in the higher and spiritual sense that these expressions are used. The devout heart catches this inner meaning of the Saviour's words, and finds them, as he has said, becoming to him "spirit and life." He that would read the Gospels in any other way loses all that is most holy and divine. It is as if we should confine our eye to the glass of the telescope, instead of looking through it to the worlds of light which it reveals beyond.

These remarks are especially applicable to the chapter before us, which has been called the chapter of parables. The parables, like all figurative language and most of our reasoning from analogy, derive their power from the fact that material things, not only have certain established relations among themselves, but also certain relations to spiritual things, which they may help to illustrate, explain, and enforce. The connection is not one arbitrarily assumed by man, but has its foundation in the constitution of the universe and of the human mind. The analogies which reach from one department of thought to another, from things material to things intellectual or spiritual, have impressed themselves on all languages, and perhaps most decidedly on those which have been used to express the highest spiritual ideas. The simplest mind catches these resemblances, and delights in the higher meanings which are bodied forth in the most common forms of speech. The image borrowed from some familiar object of sense, and standing as the representative of some higher truth, fixes itself in the mind, and acts upon it through the imagination with a power which more literal terms could not have. The greatest poets, the profoundest reasoners, and the common language of mankind alike abound in examples of this kind. Shakespeare, for instance, may be taken to show how, in the highest poetry, images drawn from material things or common life shadow forth to the heart a deeper, higher, or more affecting meaning.

"The immortal part needs a physician."— *Henry IV.*

"The benediction of these covering heavens
Fall on your heads like dew."— *Cymbeline.*

"Death lies on her, like an untimely frost
Upon the sweetest flower of all the field."— *Romeo and Juliet.*

No literal terms of description could convey to the mind the ideas here suggested with such exquisite beauty and tenderness. The Scriptures abound in expressions of this sort, which introduce into the mind some image easily comprehended, that fills the whole soul with sentiments and emotions suggested by it. Take expressions like these: "The harvest is past, the summer is ended, and we are not saved." (Jer. viii. 20.) "The night is far spent, the day is at hand." (Rom. xiii. 12.) "Abide with us; for it is toward evening, and the day is far spent." (Luke xxiv. 29.) "I am the good Shepherd, and know my sheep, and am known of mine: and I lay down my life for the sheep." (John x. 14, 15.) "Take my yoke upon you, and learn of me . . . . .

and ye shall find rest unto your souls. For my yoke is easy, and my burden is light." (Matt. xi. 29, 30.) We see at once how the simple facts, which are presented in the words, spontaneously awaken other ideas; and the images, so familiar to us in nature, carry us on to thoughts which lie wholly beyond them. And not merely are other thoughts suggested, but sentiments and emotions, which we can hardly define, are awakened by the words, and lift us up into a higher sphere.

"It is not merely," says Trench in the introduction to his Notes on the Parables, "that these analogies assist to make the truth intelligible, or, if intelligible before, present it more vividly to the mind, which is all that some will allow them. Their power lies deeper than this, in the harmony unconsciously felt by all men, and by deeper minds continually recognized and plainly perceived, between the natural and spiritual worlds, so that analogies from the first are felt to be something more than illustrations, happily but yet arbitrarily chosen. They are arguments, and may be alleged as witnesses; the world of nature being throughout a witness for the world of spirit, proceeding from the same head, growing out of the same root, and being constituted for that very end. All lovers of truth readily acknowledge these mysterious harmonies, and the force of arguments derived from them."

All just reasoning from analogy depends on the recognition of a unity of purpose running through all the works of God, and making them all, as parts of one great plan, point upward to the same results. The outward system of things stands forth to the mind as the representative of higher powers than address themselves to the senses. "The heavens declare the glory of God." (Ps. xix.) "The invisible things of Him, even his eternal power and godhead, are clearly seen from the creation of the world being understood by the things that are made." (Rom. i. 20.) "All things here," says Tertullian, "are witnesses of a resurrection; all things in nature are prophetic outlines of Divine operations, God not merely speaking parables, but doing them." Not only in processes of reasoning, but in the finer and more important processes by which the imagination is quickened and the affections reached, we are constantly drawn up from what is material and temporal to what is spiritual and eternal. Works like those of Dante and Milton borrow their marvellous power from this fact. Bunyan's "Pilgrim's Progress," and Baxter's "Saint's Rest," delight the heart, and feed the religious sentiments of generation after generation through the mysterious but vital connections which bind what is seen to what is unseen. This alone makes it possible to weave, from scenes and incidents addressed to the eye, a narrative which shall bring us into connection with a higher order of beings and events. The language which has most deeply moved the heart of the world, and especially that which acts most powerfully on the masses, and at the same time on the purest religious minds, partakes largely of this character. The world is, not only a school-room, in which visible objects serve as diagrams by which to prove the reality of spiritual things; but on every side are pictures addressing themselves to the eye, through the eye to the imagination, and through the imagination to the heart, awakening our spiritual sensibilities, and educating our whole natures to a higher life. We can hardly overestimate the influence in the religious training of the world, which has been exercised in this way by the pictures from nature, or from common life, which have been used by Jesus to represent spiritual ideas, excite religious emotions, or help us on in our religious experience.

The parables belong to this department of religious instruction. The value of a parable is not to be estimated by the single truth which it is employed to set forth, however great that truth may be. Its accompaniments, its indirect and subtle influences, through the imagination, the new meaning which it thus gives to nature or to life, the atmosphere of spiritual beauty, joy, or reverence, in which it enfolds the mind of the child, and by which it ministers to its spiritual and immortal life, are to be taken into account as adjuncts, apart from which the truth would be left comparatively without interest and without power. The parable of The Sower who went forth to sow, of the Wheat and the Tares, of the Ten Virgins, the Rich Man and Lazarus, The Good Samaritan, and the Prodigal Son, are among the most impressive and influential agencies in our religious education.

As to the rules of interpretation, too much stress must not be laid on the details in judging of their relation to the main truth. Their office is rather, by completing the picture, to act on the imagination, to touch the feelings, and subdue the mind to the tone which is needed in order that it may receive the truth. This is a most important office. In the Prodigal Son, for instance, the little details which go to fill out the picture of want and wretchedness are what give its affecting pathos to the story. And the fact that they perform this essential office should put us on our guard against trying to force all the minute particulars into our interpretation. A parable is not an allegory.

### 1 – 9, 18 – 23. THE PARABLE OF THE SOWER.

IT is not improbable that as Jesus, from the boat in which he sat, looked up along the sweep of the hills that converged downward to the lake, he may have seen a sower actually going forth to sow, and pointing to him, or directing the eyes of the multitude towards him for a moment, he may have drawn his instruction from what was actually passing before them. It is also possible that the opening words, "Behold, a sower went forth to sow," were made more touchingly impressive to the devout Jews by calling to mind the affecting language of Psalm cxxvi.: "They that sow in tears shall reap in joy. He that goeth forth and weepeth, bearing precious seed, shall, doubtless, come again with rejoicing, bringing his sheaves with him." It may also, there by the waters of the lake, have connected itself with the promise in Isaiah xxxii. 20: "Blessed are ye that sow beside all waters." Stanley, in his Sinai and Palestine, pp. 42–48, speaks of a field in the plain of Genesareth, where all the conditions involved in this parable were fulfilled;— the cornfield running down to the lake, the trodden pathway through it, the rich soil, the rocky ground protruding into it here and there, large bushes of thorns springing up in it, and countless birds of all kinds.

The object of the parable is to show the different states of mind, on account of which different persons hear the same truth with such widely different results. There is the hardened mind, which, hearing the word but not understanding it, does not take it in at all, but leaves it on the surface to be carried away at once by the slightest temptation, the first suggestion of the wicked one. There is the shallow mind, quick and transient in its emotions, receiving it with a momentary warmth of joy which causes it quickly to spring up, but the plant having no depth of character in which to take root, in the first heats of opposition or persecution wilts away. There is the rich, strong mind, already preoccupied by other things, which receives it with them. But they, the cares of the world, the deceitful allurements of riches, the pleasures of life, and, as Mark says, the passionate desires for other things, strangle it, and though it struggles along with them, it brings no fruit to perfection. Then there are the good and honest minds which, in proportion to their strength, bring forth fruit, a hundred, sixty, or thirty fold.

### 10–23.—Teaching in Parables.

This conversation, see Mark iv. 10, took place privately afterwards, and is introduced here parenthetically by the writer as in the proper place for the explanations which it gives. After Jesus had withdrawn from the multitudes, and the disciples seeing that he had not been understood, asked him why he spoke to the multitudes in parables? "Because," he replied, "while to you [whose spiritual perceptions are awakened] the hitherto undeclared mysteries of the kingdom of heaven are revealed, yet (Mark iv. 11) to them who are without," i. e. who are not my disciples, "all things are in parables," i. e. are not plain, but veiled and hidden. It made no difference, therefore, to them whether he spoke in parables or not. They would not in any case understand him. But if, in the plainest terms, he should declare the truths which were embodied in these parables, they would misapprehend entirely the nature of his kingdom, and some of them would violently oppose him, while others with equal violence, as in John vi. 15, would endeavor to force him to become their king. In order to avoid this, and at the same time to impart encouragement and instruction to those who in lowliness and simplicity of heart were waiting for his kingdom, he adopted a method of teaching, which, while it taught nothing to those whose views and characters were all wrong, gave the needed help to those who were ready to receive it. Under this kind of instruction, it was peculiarly true, 12, that to him who had, i. e. who had the teachable spirit, it was given, i. e. was given to understand the words of Christ, and from him who had not this spirit was taken away even that which he had, viz. the sort of understanding which he might have had, if plain instructions had been given. Thus it was strictly true that Jesus spoke to them in parables, "*because* they did not," or, as in Mark iv. 12, and Luke viii. 10, "*in order* that they might not," understand, while they saw and heard him. If they had caught the only meaning respecting his kingdom which they were capable of receiving from the plainest instructions, it would probably have led to violence and the premature close of his ministry. The parables were as letters in cipher, intelligible to his friends, but without meaning to those who did not belong to him.

### 24 – 30. — THE TARES AND THE WHEAT.

The parable of the sower speaks of the different results produced by the same seed according to the different states of mind in those who receive it. This parable of the tares and wheat is to illustrate the different effects produced by different sorts of seed. If we interpret the parable and its explanation, 38, 39, literally, we find that good men proceed from seed sown by the Son of Man, and bad men from seed sown by the Devil. But the words are not to be construed so strictly. As, in the parable of the sower, the seed was identified with the man in whom it grew up, so here the man is identified with the seed which essentially modified his whole nature. The tares are a bastard sort of wheat, or a mischievous plant, not easily distinguished from good wheat in the early stages of its growth. Both therefore for a time must be permitted to grow up together, since the bad cannot be rooted up without injury to the good. But when they have reached their maturity, and their entirely different characters are manifest, a separation is made. The good wheat is preserved, the bad consumed.

The doctrine of the existence of moral evil and the delay in its punishment is here compressed into a single sentence. The most labored and profound investigations of philosophy have not been able to go farther, or to throw even a clouded ray of additional light on this dark and terrible problem. Those who are interested to know how far this problem may be solved without the aid of Christianity by a very able, thoughtful, and devout man, would do well to read, in Plutarch's Morals, his fine essay "Concerning those whom God is slow to punish." Among other less weighty considerations which he illustrates with pertinent examples, he says that punishment may be delayed in order to give those who commit great crimes an opportunity to do what good they will. The man who gains a kingdom by crime may then seek to make up for his crime by using his power for good ends, and the world would be the loser if he were cut off at once. Or the offender's life may be spared, because his own conscience, in the apprehensions and terrors which it holds over him, may inflict a more dreadful punishment than immediate death. Or if the punishment is deferred in this world, it is only that it may hereafter be inflicted with the greater severity, before its purpose is accomplished, and the man's sin and guilt purged away. Or it may be in order to allow an opportunity for amendment, which is shown by the example of a young man who, after a dissolute, dishonest, and cruel course of life, being stunned by a fall and while in a swoon seeing as in another world how crimes are exposed, the souls of the guilty turned inside out, and vengeance wreaked upon them, he determined to reform his character, and lived afterwards purely and uprightly. Jesus goes far deeper than this into the very constitution and nature of things. Without exposure and temptation to evil, we conclude from his teachings, there can be no virtue. Bad deeds and men cannot be extirpated now except by destroying the good with them. Evil does exist. It cannot be rooted out without rooting out also the virtues that are growing with it, and which often in the early period of their growth can hardly be distinguished from it. Nor can bad men be destroyed at once without a fatal influence on the good. But by and by, when their deeds and characters have fully developed themselves, in the consummation to them of this earthly dispensation, that is, in the end of the world to each of them, a separation shall be made in accordance with the principles of a righteous retribution. In these parables Jesus "gathers up ages into one season of seed-time and of harvest." So the end of the world, or the day of judgment to each individual when his earthly course is ended, is set forth by one majestic figure in which all the generations of men are brought together to be separated according to what they have done, 41, 42, and been, 48 – 50.

There are nowhere more sublime images of moral grandeur than are placed before us here. Earthly scenes that impress themselves most powerfully on the imagination, earthly thrones and kingdoms and the mightiest displays of human authority shrink away. "The field is the world. The harvest is the end of the world. The reapers are the angels. . . . . . The Son of man shall send forth his angels and he shall gather out of his kingdom all those who cause others to sin, and all who work iniquity, and shall cast them into a furnace of fire; there shall be the wailing and gnashing of teeth. Then shall the righteous shine forth as the sun, in the kingdom of their Father." The last sentence would probably come with still greater force to the Jews from its bringing to their minds a most impressive passage in one of their sublimest prophets. "And they that be wise shall shine as the brightness of the firmament; and they that turn many to righteousness, as the stars for ever and ever." (Daniel xii. 3.) To them at least, language like this used by the sacred writers of old, and for generations educating the hearts of the people to a deeper solemnity, became, when intermingled with the speech of Jesus, more impressive than words wholly unfamiliar to them could have been.

We do not like to discuss the duration of future punishment in the presence of images such as are thrown around the condition of the wicked hereafter. Jesus undoubtedly intended to represent them as full of misery. But he says nothing in this place, if he does anywhere, in regard to the period of its continuance; not one word to show whether, like tares, the wicked themselves shall be utterly burned up, or whether the penal fires (taken of course in a figurative sense) shall only consume and purge away their sins, so that at last (as is intimated in 1 Cor. xv. 24 – 28), after we know not how many years or ages, they may be restored to life and peace, or whether they are left there in endless sin and pain. He places before us in the most impressive and terrible language the dreadful character and consequences of sin, that we may be warned against it; and it is much wiser in us, — it shows a deeper reverence for him, to use these expressions as undefined but awful warnings for ourselves and others, than by attempting to lessen or to aggravate their horrors by any speculations of ours in regard to the precise method of inflicting punishment, or the term of its duration. Why can we not learn to respect the reserve of Jesus in regard to such themes?

The field is the world according to our use of the word. The harvest is the end of the world, the consummation of the *æon*, age, or dispensation, as applied to the Jewish nation and to each individual soul. See Note. In this great field of the world we are sowing seed, and at the same time are ourselves growing up and ripening for the harvest. Whatsoever we sow, that shall we also reap. "For he that soweth to his flesh, shall of the flesh reap corruption; but he that soweth to the Spirit, shall of the Spirit reap everlasting life." (Gal. vi. 8.) As in the ripened fruit, every shower that fell upon it, every hour of sunshine, every night that folded it round with darkness, every ingredient in the soil beneath, entered into its texture, and helped to make it what it is in the time of harvest, so with us, every incident in life, the passions we indulge, the actions we perform, the hopes we cherish or reject, the privileges we improve or leave unimproved, are entering into the texture of our souls, and preparing us, or leaving us unprepared, for the harvest. Nothing that has entered into our life's experience shall be lost. Our riches and honors, our pleasant homes and comfortable situations, except in their influence on the soul, shall pass from us. But every kind deed that we have done, every pang of contrition, every earnest effort in behalf of what is good, every prayer that we have uttered from the heart, every longing after holiness, every unselfish affection that we have cherished and obeyed, every sorrow that has helped to wean us from the world or draw us towards God, every pain or disappointment patiently or meekly borne,— every one of these, in the influences which it is having upon us, shall be gathered in, the only treasures we can carry with us, when our harvest, which is the end of the world to each one of us, shall come. And the harvest must be whenever the Son of man shall send forth his reapers, the angels, to gather us in. The little child that without one questioning thought or fear resigns itself into their hands, though but an opening bud, is gathered into the harvest of its Lord. The young girl who, through some mysterious sympathy with them or some strange monition to the soul, seems to hear the sound of their coming from afar, and without apprehension or surprise composes herself for the solemn change, and with encouraging farewells and a perfect trust leaves all that she loves on earth, goes already ripe for the harvest. The aged servant of Christ who has long been waiting for his Master's call, departs from us at last as one prepared and ripened for the kingdom of Heaven. He has finished his labors; he has had his trials. He has been opposed and maligned, he has been praised and honored by man; but he has done justly, loved mercy, and walked humbly with his God. Nothing that he has once gained in his religious progress is lost. His principles confirmed by a life of scrupulous fidelity; his mind expanded and enriched by a conscientious search after truth; his affections chastened and mellowed by disappointments and sorrows; his faith strengthened by every varying experience of life and carried into every department of activity and thought; — all growing up and ripening here under the clouds or sunshine of God's love, are gathered in when the revolving years have completed their circuit, and to him the end of the world, — the fulfilment and consummation of the age, — has come. And the wicked too! — There is no more sublime or beautiful or awful picture than this of the world as a field, and the end of the world as the harvest, in which for joy or sorrow we all of us shall be gathered in.

### THE WICKED ONE.

But how are we here to interpret "the wicked one," "the enemy," "the devil" and "the angels"? As already stated, we are not to press the adjuncts of a parable too literally. They are to be considered as the surrounding scenery fitted to make an impression on the mind through the imagination, and thus prepare it to receive the truth which is taught. When Jesus speaks of a merchantman finding one pearl of great price, and selling all that he has in order to purchase that, we do not suppose that he asserts this as a fact which had actually taken place. He holds it up as a picture to illustrate an important truth; and this it does equally well, whether he regarded it as a veritable fact or as an imaginary incident. Some of the parables may have been suggested by passing events; but the particulars he undoubtedly supplied and arranged in such a way as might most effectually accomplish his purpose, as a teacher of divine truth. And this is the case, whether he draws his illustrations from familiar and well-known objects here, as the Sower and his Seed, the Good Samaritan, and the Prodigal Son, or from objects which lie beyond our personal cognizance, as the devil, the angels, &c. For example, in the parable of the Rich Man and Lazarus (Luke xvi. 19 – 31), as in the details belonging to this world, the crumbs, the dogs, the sores, we do not suppose that Jesus speaks of facts which actually took place in precisely the manner there represented; so in the details belonging to another world, the being carried by the angels into Abraham's bosom, the conversation between the rich man and Lazarus, the gulf and the flames, we do not suppose that Jesus intended to set before us a representation of literal facts which actually took place. Are we to give a more strict and literal interpretation to the terms which are used here?

It is impossible to draw a line which shall distinguish precisely between what is literal and what is figurative, what is a matter of fact and what is imaginative. The two provinces are constantly interpenetrating one another, in such a way as to set forth the central truth with the greatest distinctness and power. A few considerations, however, may help us to a just interpretation.

In borrowing images from the outward world Jesus never, so far as we know, draws them from fabulous orders of being. The particular man, tares, wheat, pearl, leaven, which he refers to, may be imagined or assumed for the occasion; but they all belong to species which have an actual existence, and he never attributes to them properties which they do not really possess. There is everywhere this rigid conformity to the great essential facts of nature. Have we not a right to infer that in going beyond this world there will be the same adherence to the great essential facts of existence? As he never *here* draws his illustrations from any species of plant, animal, or other being, which does not really exist, will he speak to us of orders of beings *there* who have only a fabulous existence? In going beyond this material world, and placing before us agents of whom we cannot judge from our personal knowledge, but whom he with his spiritual powers of vision could recognize, would he be likely to speak of beings wholly fabulous and imaginary as if they really existed, or assign to them in their relation to us very important offices which they do not hold? We may doubt whether the angels carried Lazarus and placed him in Abraham's bosom. These are only incidental illustrations which answer the same purpose, whether they are literally true or not. But, in the face of what Jesus says there and here, can we doubt that there are such beings as angels, and that they, as God's ministers, hold important relations to us? So, when he speaks of the evil one, the enemy, the devil, Satan, we may doubt as to the special agency assigned to such a being in any particular case; but are we at liberty to say that the very idea of such a personage is drawn from a wholly fabulous and imaginary order of beings? When Jesus speaks, 42, of casting the wicked into a furnace of fire, we are not obliged to take it as a literal fact. It may be, and probably is, only a terrific image borrowed from what is most dreadful in this world to describe the intolerable anguish of the guilty in the world to come. The illustration, however, is drawn, not from a fabulous source, but from something which has a substantial basis of reality. Nor can it be shown that in a single instance Jesus has in any of his instructions assumed the existence of anything which belonged to a fabulous class of beings. What right, then, have we to suppose that the moment he goes beyond the reach of our faculties and the limits of this world, he violates the proprieties of truth which he always observes where we have the power to judge, and sets before us orders of beings which have no existence, as if they really existed, and sustained some important relations to us?

Another consideration is entitled to some weight; though it ought not to be pressed so far as it is by some of our ablest modern commentators. The language here, 19, 39, 41, is taken, not from the parables, but from the explanation which Jesus gave of two of his parables. When, therefore, he says, "He who sows the good seed is the Son of man," and "he who sows the tares is the devil," by what principle of interpretation are we justified in accepting one clause of the sentence as true, and rejecting the other as merely an accommodation to the false ideas and prejudices of the Jews? His language asserts, as distinctly as language can, the existence and agency of an evil spirit. It does this while explaining the meaning of a parable, in a private and confidential conversation with his disciples.

We must not, however, insist on a literal application of his words in all their particulars even here. In verses 19 and 20, we see in a similar explanation how figurative and literal expressions are blended together. The insufficiency of a language unused to the expression of abstract ideas required a liberal and constant use of figurative terms. Truths relating to the unseen spiritual world must be set forth by such images as can be received by those who are addressed. The most exact terms that can be used even now to give an idea of spiritual beings and agencies are doubtless only such clouded images of divine truth as we are able to receive, seeing them, according to St. Paul (1 Cor. xiii. 12), not face to face, but "darkly, as by the reflection of a mirror." When Jesus says, that he will send forth his angels to gather together those who have been stumbling-blocks in the way of others and those who work iniquity, and cast them into a furnace of fire where there shall be wailing and gnashing of teeth, we are to consider these as terms which set before us, in language as exact and intelligible as any that could be used, the momentous fact of a future retribution. The images must, from the nature of the case, be borrowed from what is known and experienced in this world. Earthly facts and conceptions are made to set forth "darkly" the higher facts belonging to our spiritual natures when they shall be transferred to a spiritual world. Still, if the angels and the devil have no personal existence, or no personal agency in bringing about the results here placed before us, is it easy to suppose that Jesus would have used such language merely by way of accommodating himself to the prejudices and false conceptions of the Jews? In meeting the Greeks who are spoken of in John xii. 20, could he have taught them, by conceptions drawn from their mythology, and going necessarily to confirm them in their erroneous habits of belief? Could he have spoken to them of Centaurs, of Rhadamanthus, of Jupiter and Pan, as he does to the Jews, of Satan and the angels?

It is said that the idea of Satan, or, as Dr. Palfrey calls it, "the mythology of an evil spirit (answering to the Oriental *Ahriman*)," Lectures on the Jewish Scriptures, Vol. IV. p. 21, was learned by the Jews from the Chaldæans during their seventy years captivity in Babylon. This is possible. The word Satan with this signification occurs but two or three times in the Old Testament, viz. 1 Chron. xxi. 1, Zech. iii. 1, 2, and perhaps in the first and second chapters of Job. Before the time of Christ, the doctrine (of which hardly a trace is to be found in the Old Testament) pervaded the philosophy and religious conceptions of the Jews. But may it not be, that, in the providential training of the Jews for the reception of higher religious ideas, the notions of diabolical as well as of angelic agencies, which grew up round the sublime Theism that became more and more the established faith of the nation, may have performed an important work in preparing them for the idea of a great Christian commonwealth, the kingdom of God, or of the heavens? To them, at the time of our Saviour's coming, the invisible realms were peopled with living beings, acting as God's agents, or in opposition to his will. The contest between good and evil was not confined to this visible world of theirs. Through their long and varied experience, these ideas were added to the Theism taught by Moses, and had become incorporated among their established religious conceptions and convictions. They held no small or unimportant place in their religious culture. If they were false, Jesus might have left them, as he did most of the prevailing sins and errors without specific notice, to vanish away and perish, before the higher conceptions of truth and duty which he came to reveal. But if they were false, and as false pernicious also, could he, not merely in his reasoning with the Jews, but in his private instructions to his disciples, from the temptation in the wilderness to his last solemn conversation with them the evening before his crucifixion (Luke xxii. 31, John xiv. 30, xvi. 11), have used language which must have confirmed them in the belief that those false ideas and conceptions were true? He has left no word which condemns or calls them in question. On the other hand, they harmonize with all that he has taught us respecting the unseen world, and God's methods of action there as here through intervening agents.

It is sometimes suggested, that Jesus may have shared the opinions of his age in regard to this subject, and so have been mistaken in his views. We know that he emphatically disclaimed for himself (Mark xiii. 32) the gift of omniscience. But in regard to any doctrine which he has taught, we have no disposition to go behind or to question his authority. To us his word, clearly announced and understood, is evidence and authority enough. Those who are interested in this subject are particularly requested to read the note to verse 39 of this chapter, and to remember that, even though such a being or such beings as a devil or devils exist, our popular or even our philosophical notions respecting them are not therefore to be assumed as true or as reasonable.

## NOTES.

The same day went Jesus out of the house, and sat by the
2 sea-side; and great multitudes were gathered together unto
him, so that he went into a ship, and sat; and the whole multi-
3 tude stood on the shore. And he spake many things unto them
4 in parables, saying: Behold, a sower went forth to sow. And
when he sowed, some seeds fell by the way-side; and the fowls
5 came and devoured them up. Some fell upon stony places,
where they had not much earth; and forthwith they sprung
6 up, because they had no deepness of earth; and when the
sun was up, they were scorched; and because they had no
7 root, they withered away. And some fell among thorns; and
8 the thorns sprung up, and choked them. But other fell into
good ground; and brought forth fruit, some an hundred-fold,
9 some sixty-fold, some thirty-fold. Who hath ears to hear, let
10 him hear. —— And the disciples came, and said unto him,
11 Why speakest thou unto them in parables? He answered and
said unto them: Because it is given unto you to know the
mysteries of the kingdom of Heaven; but to them it is not
12 given. For whosoever hath, to him shall be given, and he

---

2. **a ship**] or rather a boat adapted in its form and dimensions to the size of the lake, and the purposes for which it was used.
**and sat**] while the multitude stood. "So was the manner of the nation, that the masters, when they read their lectures, sat, and the scholars stood." Lightfoot.   3. **Behold, a sower went forth to sow**] The literal translation is more picturesque, and brings the whole scene more vividly before us, "*Behold, the sower went forth to sow.*" There is a profound truth conveyed under this image of sowing seed. The truths which Jesus taught were not dead and unproductive; but seeds endowed with an inward vitality, and to be understood and appreciated only in the living plants and luxuriant harvests into which they should grow up when received into good and honest hearts. It is in the soul ripened for the kingdom of Heaven, in the church abounding in Christian virtues and graces, in the community where Christian ideas and affections are bringing forth their pure and peaceable and beautiful fruits, that the truths of our religion are to be seen. Their whole character and influence can be recognized only in that world where all the harvest matured and perfected is gathered in.
11. **mysteries of the kingdom of Heaven**] the system of Divine counsels, doctrines, and ordinances, which, as above man's powers of discovery, was revealed through Jesus Christ. The word mystery, "when used in the New Testament respecting any doctrine or truth, means one which has been secret or unknown, but is now revealed. It never denotes one which is obscure or mysterious, because partially incomprehensible." Norton.
12. **whosoever hath**] In propor-

shall have more abundance; but whosoever hath not, from him shall be taken away even that he hath. Therefore speak I to 13 them in parables, because they seeing see not, and hearing they hear not, neither do they understand. And in them is 14 fulfilled the prophecy of Esaias, which saith: "By hearing ye shall hear, and shall not understand; and seeing ye shall see, and shall not perceive. For this people's heart is waxed gross, 15 and their ears are dull of hearing, and their eyes they have closed, lest at any time they should see with their eyes, and hear with their ears, and should understand with their heart, and should be converted, and I should heal them." But blessed 16 are your eyes, for they see; and your ears, for they hear. For verily I say unto you, that many prophets and righteous 17 men have desired to see those things which ye see, and have not seen them; and to hear those things which ye hear, and have not heard them.—— Hear ye therefore the parable of the 18 sower. When any one heareth the word of the kingdom, and 19 understandeth it not, then cometh the wicked one, and catcheth away that which was sown in his heart; this is he which received seed by the way-side. But he that received the seed 20 into stony places, the same is he that heareth the word, and anon with joy receiveth it; yet hath he not root in himself, 21 but dureth for a while; for when tribulation or persecution

---

tion to a man's spiritual susceptibility and his fidelity will be what he gains from the teachings and life of Jesus. **14. in them is fulfilled**] "In them is filled up," or re-fulfilled, "the prophecy of Isaiah," i. e. what the prophet said (Isa. vi. 9, 10) of the blinding effect, in his day, of disobedience and practical infidelity, finds its fulfilment, and is equally true now. John, xii. 38-40, applies the same words on another occasion, and many years afterwards, Paul (Acts xxviii. 25-27) applied them with great emphasis to the unbelieving Jews in Rome. In these different applications of the same prophetic words as being fulfilled in different people, at different times, and under different circumstances, we have an intimation of one of the ways in which the ancient prophecies were applied by Jesus and the Apostles. A great spiritual fact, like that which is here announced in the blinding and hardening effect of sin, reaches forward with its prophetic warning to all times, and is fulfilled in the religious experience of all who belong to the class which it points out. In verses 14 and 15, is ascribed to the perverse and unbelieving Jews, in the language of the prophet, the effect of such wickedness as theirs, which was to dull their religious sensibilities, "This people's heart is waxed gross,"— to cloud their spiritual perceptions,— "their ears are dull of hearing, and their eyes they have closed,"— so that they could not at any time — "lest at any time they should " — see and understand their true condition, and turn in penitence — "be converted" — to God, and be healed by him. **20. stony places**] Rather, rocky ground,— a little

MATTHEW XIII.       253

22 ariseth because of the word, by and by he is offended. He
also that received seed among the thorns is he that heareth the
word, and the care of this world, and the deceitfulness of riches,
23 choke the word, and he becometh unfruitful. But he that received seed into the good ground is he that heareth the word,
and understandeth it; which also beareth fruit, and bringeth
forth, some an hundred-fold, some sixty, some thirty. ——
24 Another parable put he forth unto them, saying: The kingdom
of heaven is likened unto a man which sowed good seed in his
25 field. But while men slept, his enemy came, and sowed tares
26 among the wheat; and went his way. But when the blade
was sprung up, and brought forth fruit, then appeared the
27 tares also. So the servants of the householder came and said
unto him, Sir, didst not thou sow good seed in thy field? from
28 whence then hath it tares? He said unto them, An enemy
hath done this. The servants said unto him, Wilt thou then
29 that we go and gather them up? But he said, Nay; lest
while ye gather up the tares, ye root up also the wheat with
30 them. Let both grow together until the harvest; and in the
time of harvest I will say to the reapers, Gather ye together
first the tares, and bind them in bundles, to burn them; but

---

earth scattered on the large rocks which lie beneath.   **23. he that heareth the word, and understandeth it**] contrasted with him, v. 19, who heareth and understandeth not.   **24. The kingdom of Heaven**] Literally, the kingdom of the heavens, as if to denote different spheres of life, one beyond another, and all pervaded by the spirit of God. The widely different applications of the term in this chapter show how comprehensive and how various was the thought which Jesus set forth, and how rich and full of meaning his language was. Having ascertained precisely what his words mean in one case, we are not therefore at liberty to fix on that as their only interpretation whenever we may meet them. The kingdom of Heaven is here first represented, 24 – 29, 38 – 43, as a kingdom embracing, not those alone who continue good, but also those who are corrupted by evil influences. It is represented, 31, 32, as a plant, spreading out its branches, and furnishing shelter to those who seek it. Next it is represented, 33, as an influence, reaching through the man, or the world, subduing and assimilating all things to itself. Then it appears, 44, as a hidden treasure, to set forth its exceeding preciousness, as a pearl of great price, to indicate at once its costliness and its beauty; and finally, 47, 48, as a net drawing good and bad alike into its folds, out of the sea of time to the shores of eternity, that they may there be separated according to what they are.   25 – 40. **tares**] a species of darnel or bastard wheat, which, according to St. Jerome, who lived in Palestine, was, till the ear was formed, so much like the good wheat that it could not, without much difficulty, be distinguished from it. His enemy " sowed [the field] *over again* " [ἐπέσπειρεν] with tares. The force of the origi-

gather the wheat into my barn. —— Another parable put he 31 forth unto them saying: The kingdom of Heaven is like to a grain of mustard seed, which a man took and sowed in his field. Which indeed is the least of all seeds; but when it is grown, 32 it is the greatest among herbs, and becometh a tree, so that the birds of the air come and lodge in the branches thereof.

—— Another parable spake he unto them: The kingdom of 33 Heaven is like unto leaven, which a woman took, and hid in three measures of meal, till the whole was leavened. —— All 34 these things spake Jesus unto the multitude in parables, and without a parable spake he not unto them; that it might be 35 fulfilled which was spoken by the prophet, saying: "I will open my mouth in parables; I will utter things which have been kept secret from the foundation of the world."

Then Jesus sent the multitude away, and went into the 36 house. And his disciples came unto him, saying, Declare unto us the parable of the tares of the field. He answered and said 37 unto them, He that soweth the good seed is the Son of man; the field is the world; the good seed are the children of 38 the kingdom; but the tares are the children of the wicked

---

nal word is impaired in our version. The man, v. 24, sowed; his enemy sowed over again, or upon what had already been sown.

32. **so that the birds of the air come and lodge in its branches**] Hackett, "Illustrations of Scripture," p. 124, speaks of this plant, which he found in blossom, full grown, in some cases six, seven, and nine feet high. "But still," he says, "the branches or stems of the branches were not very large, or, apparently, very strong. 'Can the birds,' I said to myself, 'rest upon them?' . . . . . At that very instant . . . . . one of the fowls of heaven stopped in its flight through the air, alighted down on one of the branches, which hardly moved beneath the shock, and then began, perched there before my eyes, to warble forth a strain of the richest music." The mustard-seed and the plant growing from it illustrate the self-developing power by which the religion of Jesus, from the smallest beginnings, spreads out its branches for those who might seek a shelter within them.

33. **leaven**] The leaven shows its power of imparting its own properties to those who receive it, and assimilating them till they partake of its own nature. "Another striking point of comparison," says Alford, "is the fact that leaven, as used ordinarily, is a piece of the leavened loaf put amongst the dough, just as the kingdom of heaven is the renewal of humanity by the righteous Man Christ Jesus."

38. **the field is the world**] κόσμος, *the world*, this outward universe or world, according to our use of the word. But in the next verse, in the clause **the harvest is the end of the world**] entirely a different word is used. There it is *αἰών* or *æon*, — an age or dispensation, — referring, not to the outward universe, but in this case including our earthly discipline and experience. The harvest is the

39 One; the enemy that sowed them is the devil; the harvest is
40 the end of the world; and the reapers are the angels. As,

consummation of the *æon*, the age, or dispensation in which we now live, and our consequent entrance on another, and (with the faithful) higher age or dispensation. Αἰών, as applied to the Jews, includes everything relating to their condition and experience under the Mosaic dispensation, and the consummation of the *æon*, — the end of the world, — to them was the overthrow of the Jewish polity at the destruction of Jerusalem in the year 70, and the consequent advent of a new *æon*, — the coming of the Son of man, — in the establishment of the Christian religion, which was the fulfilment or consummation of the Jewish dispensation. But in its wider application, as in the passage before us, *æon* refers to our whole earthly dispensation and experience, and includes everything that may act upon us in this life. The consummation of the *æon*, or end of the world, means the consummation of our earthly life, whether for good or for evil. But on leaving this *æon*, we enter into another, and the adjective, αἰώνιος, or *æonian*, which is translated *eternal* and *everlasting* (Matt. xxv. 46), is borrowed from this next *æon*, and is applied to qualities and conditions, which, whether for weal or woe, shall belong to us in that more advanced stage of our existence. "*Eternal life*" is the blessedness which belongs to that condition of our being, and which, in its elementary principles, as Jesus has said (John vi. 47), may begin within us now; and *eternal* (not everlasting, for the idea of time is not included in the word), — "*eternal punishment*" is the sorrow and anguish which shall belong to those who enter unprepared into that more advanced *æon* or stage of existence, and which, in its elementary principles, may begin within us now. See p. 229. 39. **the enemy that sowed them is the devil**] We must be careful not to press this matter too far. The existence of evil spirits, and especially of one pre-eminent among them as *the* wicked one, the devil, or Satan, is not to be held to by us as among the facts which Jesus has unquestionably taught. Our view of the subject has been stated in Chapters IV. and VIII. We have no doubt that the Evangelists believed in such existences and agencies. From a careful study of the language of Jesus, we incline to think that he also believed in them. But a close and critical examination of all that he has said on the subject has satisfied us, 1. That he did not *directly* teach the existence and agency of such beings; and, 2. That in almost every case where he speaks of the devil or Satan, his words are certainly to be taken in a figurative sense. The word Satan is used sixteen times in the Gospels; but, except in the passages given below, viz. 1, 4, and 7, where it is used as synonymous with devil, it occurs only on five different occasions. 1. Matt. xii. 26: "If Satan cast out Satan," where Jesus is arguing with the Jews from their own point of view. 2. Matt. xvi. 23: "Get thee behind me, Satan," words addressed to Peter. 3. Luke x. 18: "I beheld Satan as lightning fall from heaven," language evidently figurative. 4. Luke xiii. 16: "Whom Satan hath bound, lo! these eighteen years," language personifying the cause of disease as Satan. 5. Luke xxii. 31: "Behold, Satan hath sought for you, that he may sift you as wheat." The principles of spiritual evil may be personified here as that of physical evil in the previous passage. In every one of these cases the expression may be construed as a striking and natural figure of speech without necessarily implying the personal existence of an evil spirit. The word devil, διάβολος, not demon, occurs in the Gospels on seven different occasions: 1. In the account of the Temptation. 2. Matt. xiii. 39: "The ene-

therefore, the tares are gathered and burned in the fire, so shall it be in the end of this world. The Son of man shall 41

my that sowed them is the devil." 3. Matt. xxv. 41: "Into everlasting fire, prepared for the devil and his angels." 4. Luke viii. 12: "Then cometh the devil and taketh away the word out of their hearts," parallel to Matt. xiii. 19, where the expression "the wicked one" is used, and to Mark iv. 15, where the word "Satan" is used. 5. John vi. 70: "Have not I chosen you twelve, and one of you is a devil?" 6. John viii. 44: "Ye are of your father, the devil." 7. John xiii. 2: "The devil having put it into the heart of Judas Iscariot to betray him." In verse 27 of the same chapter, it reads, "And after the sop, Satan entered into him."

The first and seventh of these instances may be set aside as the language of the Evangelists, and not of Jesus. The seventh may be interpreted figuratively; and as to the first, we refer to our comments on the account of the Temptation in Chapter IV.

The fifth case, "Have I not chosen you twelve, and one of you is a devil?" is certainly figurative, and gives a decisive intimation of the way in which the word may have been used by Jesus. It is probable that this expression referring to Judas may have led to the use of the same term by St. John, when speaking of Judas in the seventh instance.

The sixth case is as follows: "Ye are of your father, the devil, and the lusts of your father ye wish to do. He was a murderer from the beginning, and stood not in the truth; because there is no truth in him. When he speaketh a lie, he speaketh of his own; for he is a liar, and the father of it." The natural and obvious interpretation, at first sight, of this rather extended description of the devil, would be a literal one applying to a personal being actually existing and answering to this character; but on a closer inspection of the passage, we see that the word *father* cannot be used in a literal, but only in a spiritual sense; and does not this almost require, in order to the harmony and completeness of the meaning, that the rest of the passage should likewise be taken, not in its literal, but in its spiritual sense? Is not the extended description given to show in what sense Jesus used the word, devil, viz. as the impersonation of wickedness? — Ye are of your father the devil, that spirit of wickedness, which prompted to the first murder, which is the very essence and parent of what is false; and on account of your affinity with it, ye believe me not, because I tell you the truth. As he had a little while before referred to Judas as a devil (John vi. 70), because of his wickedness, so he may here call the Jews the children of the devil, because of their affinity with what is evil. As in the one case, the word devil as the personification of wickedness is applied to a bad man, why may it not in the other case be used in the same way as the personification of evil, especially of murder and falsehood, to describe the spirit and temper of the Jews who were seeking his life and refusing to receive the truth? Does not this better adapt itself to the inward and profound thought of Jesus, than the interpretation which requires him here to speak literally of a personal devil in his direct and personal relation to them? Even if Jesus had believed in such a being, would not this figurative and spiritual application of the term be more natural and more in accordance with his usual mode of speech?

In the fourth case, "Then cometh the devil, and taketh the word out of their hearts," or, as it is in Matt. xiii. 19: "Then cometh the wicked one and catcheth away that which is sown in his heart," the whole sentence is figurative, and this word is plainly used to personify the evil influences which remove from shallow minds the truths which they gladly receive in a moment of re-

send forth his angels, and they shall gather out of his kingdom
42 all things that offend, and them which do iniquity, and shall
cast them into a furnace of fire; there shall be wailing and
43 gnashing of teeth. Then shall the righteous shine forth, as
the sun, in the kingdom of their Father. Who hath ears to
44 hear, let him hear. —— Again the kingdom of Heaven is like
unto treasure hid in a field, the which, when a man hath found,
he hideth, and for joy thereof goeth and selleth all that he
45 hath, and buyeth that field. —— Again the kingdom of Heav-
46 en is like unto a merchant-man, seeking goodly pearls; who,

---

ligious excitement, but which they do not understand.

There remain now only two passages to be considered. One is the awful declaration, "Depart from me, ye cursed, into everlasting fire, prepared for the devil and his angels." The other is the passage before us, "The enemy that sowed them is the devil." It may be, that Jesus meant nothing more in either case than the impersonation of evil. The accompanying language in both instances is intensely figurative. It is difficult to distinguish between the main point of his instructions and the images under which it was conveyed. But the presumption to our mind is, that in using language such as this, he does imply the actual, personal existence of such beings as are suggested by the words, "the devil and his angels." He has never directly taught the existence of such beings. Every passage in which they are spoken of may be interpreted figuratively, without any violent wrench to the language. Still, the impression left upon us is that Jesus did believe in a vast background of evil beyond what we can see, — an empire of darkness where evil spirits live, from which evil influences have been permitted to enter, even into this world, and whose power he came to overthrow. The result of this whole investigation, which we have carefully gone through many times, as a matter of Scriptural interpretation, has been to leave us very decidedly with the impression that Jesus did believe in evil spirits, and the disastrous influence which they might exercise over men who allowed themselves to be acted upon by them. But we find very little evidence that he believed in Satan or the devil as a real, personal being, who ruled over the realm of evil spirits, as a king over his subjects. It does not seem entirely certain to us; but we think the most natural and satisfactory explanation of his language, on the principles of a just and exact interpretation, is to be found in the supposition that he alluded to Satan or the devil as the personification of wickedness, and in that sense called him the Prince of Devils, and spoke of *him and his angels*, as he called him the father of the murderous and lying Jews, and spoke of him as the prince of this world. (John xii. 31, xiv. 30, xvi. 11.) Evil spirits were his angels and subjects, just as wicked men were his children, in a figurative, and not a literal sense. 44. **treasure hid in a field**] The kingdom of Heaven, i. e. the religion of Jesus, is like a hidden treasure, which a man, while employed on other things, discovers, and with joy secures for himself. His hiding it, while he went to purchase the field, is one of the adjuncts, which, though indicating the great value of what had been found, is not to be construed as having any direct bearing on the main object of the parable. 45, 46. As a contrast to the man who happened to find the treasure is the merchant-man who, while seeking for beauti-

when he had found one pearl of great price, went and sold all
that he had, and bought it.—— Again the kingdom of Heaven 47
is like unto a net, that was cast into the sea, and gathered of
every kind; which, when it was full, they drew to shore, and 48
sat down and gathered the good into vessels, but cast the bad
away. So shall it be at the end of the world. The angels 49
shall come forth, and sever the wicked from among the just,
and shall cast them into the furnace of fire; there shall be 50
wailing and gnashing of teeth.—— Jesus saith unto them, 51
Have ye understood all these things? They say unto him,
Yea, Lord. Then said he unto them, Therefore every scribe, 52
which is instructed unto the kingdom of Heaven, is like unto a
man that is an householder, which bringeth forth out of his
treasure things new and old.—— And it came to pass, that, 53
when Jesus had finished these parables, he departed thence.

And when he was come into his own country, he taught 54
them in their synagogue, insomuch that they were astonished,
and said, Whence hath this man this wisdom, and these mighty
works? Is not this the carpenter's son? Is not his mother 55
called Mary? and his brethren, James, and Joses, and Simon,

---

ful pearls, found one very costly, and went and sold all that he had in order to purchase it.

52. **Therefore**] For this reason, i. e. taking into account the new truths and hopes and life which have been here set forth, every Scribe, who is instructed in my religion, being already learned in the law, is like a householder who brings out from his treasury things both new and old. It was customary in the East to preserve in houses costly garments and other articles for many generations; and this perhaps is what more particularly suggested the comparison.

53 – 58. He went into his own country, i. e. to Nazareth. For a fuller account of what occurred there, see Luke iv. 16 – 24. Though Jesus had astonished them by his wisdom and his mighty works, still they found a stumbling-block to their belief in the fact, that his father, the carpenter, and his brethren or kinsmen, were known to them as ordinary men. Jesus, seeing that they were not in a state of mind to be benefited by it, refused to perform (Luke iv. 24 – 27) many miracles among them. Their unbelief, 58, does not refer so much to the fact that they did not, as that they would not, believe. It indicates a spirit of unbelief which set itself against him, and would not be convinced by anything that he might do. "Is not this," they asked contemptuously, "the carpenter's son? Is not his mother called Mary? and his brethren, James, and Joses, and Simon, and Judas? And his sisters, are they not all with us?"

55. **and his brethren**] Who were the brethren of Jesus? This has been, among commentators, one of the difficult questions, and the ablest among them have given different answers. The brethren of Jesus are spoken of on six different occasions, viz. Matt. xii. 46, and parallel passages in Mark and Luke; the present passage and its parallel, Mark vi. 3; John ii. 12; vii. 3, 5, 10; Acts i. 14; 1 Cor. ix. 5.

## MATTHEW XIII.

56 and Judas? and his sisters, are they not all with us? whence
57 then hath this man all these things? And they were offended
in him. But Jesus said unto them, A prophet is not without
58 honor, save in his own country, and in his own house. And he
did not many mighty works there, because of their unbelief.

---

Mr. Norton, in his note on this passage, supposes that "the brethren" or "kinsmen" of Jesus, — for the original allows either interpretation, — were the sons of Alpheus (the same name in Hebrew as Clopas or Cleopas), whose wife Mary is said (John xix. 25) to be the sister or kinswoman of Mary the Mother of Jesus. In Matt. xxvii. 56, Mark xv. 40, she is said to be the mother of James and Joses, i. e. Joseph. Luke, in his catalogue of the Apostles (Luke vi. 16; Acts i. 13), mentions Judas of James, i. e. the son or brother of James. Thus we have applied to the sons either of Alpheus, or of his wife Mary, three of the names, which are here applied to the brethren of Jesus, viz. James and Joses and Judas. Would these three names be likely to be repeated in two different branches of the same family? Is it not more reasonable to suppose that these brethren of Jesus, as they are called, were the sons of Alpheus (Cleopas) and Mary, of whom at least two, James and Judas, and possibly, as Mr. Norton supposes, a third, Simon, were among the Apostles? The reply is: 1. That the names were among the most common Jewish names, and might be repeated in two different branches of the same family. We are acquainted with three different branches of a family in each of which may be found the names William, James, and John. 2. The brethren of Jesus spoken of in John vii. 5, following John ii. 12; vii. 3, did not at that time believe on him, and therefore they could not have been among the Apostles. 3. Wherever they are mentioned in the New Testament, except in the seventh chapter of John, and 1 Cor. ix. 5, they are mentioned in connection with Mary, the Mother of Jesus. For these reasons, we suppose that the brethren of Jesus were the sons of Joseph, though they may not have been the sons of Mary. James, the son of Alpheus, was probably the James whom St. Paul speaks of (Gal. i. 19) as "the brother of the Lord." Nor is it improbable that James and Judas, sons of Alpheus, are "the brethren of the Lord," whom he refers to, 1 Cor. ix. 5, as among the Apostles.

## CHAPTER XIV.

#### HEROD ANTIPAS.

1–12. OF Herod Antipas some account has already been given in chap. xi. Contemporary records, to those who care to enter into such horrible details, furnish examples enough to show that the beheading of John, with the revolting circumstances attending it, was no extraordinary instance of cruelty in those times. Lardner, Part I. Bk. I. Chap. I. Herod seems to have been a weak and crafty,—for the two qualities often go together,—rather than an able and cruel man, as his father, Herod the Great, whom we find in the second chapter of Matthew, had been. When he was on a visit to his half-brother, Philip, a private citizen, and not to be confounded with Philip, the Tetrach of Ituræa and Trachonitis, mentioned in Luke iii. 1, he became enamored of his brother's wife, Herodias, whom he persuaded to leave her husband, and to marry him. This act was a violation of the Jewish law, and called down on Herod a severe rebuke from the stern preacher in the wilderness, who thus incurred her lasting displeasure. She was a bold, bad, unscrupulous woman. "Josephus," says Dr. Lardner, "has represented Herodias as a woman full of ambition and envy, as having a mighty influence on Herod, and able to persuade him to things he was not of himself at all inclined to." It is therefore entirely in character with all that we know of her, that in her anger against John, she should, as we read (Mark vi. 19), seek to destroy him, and that she should have recourse to indirect means for revenging herself, when she had failed in other ways to accomplish her purpose. It was undoubtedly by her direction, that her daughter Salome, at a feast on the birthday of Herod, when he was probably heated with wine, won his favor by dancing before him, and gained from him a promise, given with an oath, that he would grant any favor that she might ask of him, even (Mark vi. 23) to the half of his kingdom. She went to her mother, and being instructed by her, came back immediately with earnest haste, and said, "I desire that thou give me forthwith on a dish the head of John the Baptist." This extreme haste probably arose from a fear lest the king, after the excitement of the hour was over, should relent, or refuse to grant her request. See Robinson's Calmet, art. Antipas. The evident reluctance of Herod, even then, to comply with her demand confirms this view of the case. An executioner was sent immediately, and the head of John was brought to the girl, who carried it to her mother. John, as we have seen in chapter xi. was imprisoned near the Dead Sea. The narrative of the Evangelists, particularly that of Mark, indicates that he was not far off from the festive party, who must therefore have been in that part of Herod's dominions which was most distant from Galilee.

Herod had thus beheaded John from a false sentiment of honor, and grievously against his will, for he feared him, (Mark vi. 20,) "knowing that he was a righteous and holy man;" and, though he desired to put him to death, he feared the people, for they accounted John as a prophet. The circumstances attendant on the life of John, his uncompromising attitude as a prophet of God, the reverence in which he was held, and the strange ascendency which such men sometimes gain over the imagination of the worldly minded and corrupt, may have wrought with peculiar force on Herod, and roused his superstitious apprehensions. So that when he heard of Jesus and his extraordinary acts, and the sensation that he was producing in his dominions, he may have been (Luke ix. 7) sorely perplexed, and have broken out in the words which were spoken, half in rage and half in fear, "John have I beheaded; but who is this?" And in order to allay his apprehensions, to satisfy himself whether the reports that he heard were true, and also, as we might infer from the words and conduct of Jesus (Luke xiii. 31, 32), to get him into his power, he sought to see him. At another time his words, as in the passage before us, took a different turn; and, as Mr. Norton in his note on Matt. xiv. 1 – 12, suggests, may be regarded as the excited, figurative language of an angry man; as if he had said: "John have I beheaded. But what have I gained by it? Here we have him, the same thing over again, raised from the dead, and therefore showing forth these powerful works."

Herod, it has been said, was a Sadducee, and as such (Matt. xxii. 23, Acts xxiii. 8) believed in "no resurrection, neither angel nor spirit." We find no evidence that he was a Sadducee. But even if he were so, it would not have secured him from all dread of the supernatural, under the circumstances in which he was placed. The annals of superstition are marked by no greater absurdities than those which are drawn from the most unbelieving times. Nor have any men, when under the pressure of extraordinary circumstances of emotion, shown themselves more the victims of an unreasonable credulity than those who have prided themselves most on their philosophical unbelief. Herod, more than half a Jew, with the superstitious ideas of his nation hanging over his mind, driven by the more powerful will of a woman into crimes at which his own nature revolted, on hearing from all quarters accounts of sick men healed, demoniacs exorcised, and the dead raised to life, may, in spite of his hardness and unbelief, have been so disturbed and conscience-smitten as in amazement and terror, to utter the language attributed to him in the Gospels. In Shakespeare's Macbeth we have, drawn by a master's hand, the inconsistencies, absurdities, and horrors which mark the speech and conduct of a man, betrayed like Herod into crimes which he could never have committed unless impelled by the overpowering ambition of an artful, merciless, unscrupulous woman. The perplexities which oppressed the mind of Herod, and drew from him the exclamation, "It is John whom I beheaded; he has been raised from the dead, and by him these mighty works are wrought," may have been not unlike those which wrenched from the terrified Macbeth at the appearance of Banquo whom he had murdered: — the words, —

> "The times have been,
> That, when the brains were out, the man would die,
> And there an end: but now, they rise again,
> With twenty mortal murders on their crowns,
> And push us from our stools."

The great misdeeds and consequent misfortunes of Herod's life, his repudiating of his wife, the daughter of Aretas, king of Petræa, and his disastrous defeat by that monarch, his murder of John the Baptist, his attempt to supplant the influence of his wife's brother Herod Agrippa with the Roman emperor, Caligula, and to secure for himself the title of king, and his consequent banishment, first to Gaul, A. D. 39, and thence to Spain where he died, were caused by the instigations of the jealous, unprincipled, ambitious woman, with whom he was united by an adulterous and incestuous marriage.

Herod is referred to again on two occasions. The Pharisees (Luke xiii. 31, 32) tell Jesus to depart; for Herod is seeking his life. The reply of Jesus, "Go ye and tell that fox," &c. shows how well he understood his crafty character. He appears again in the trial of Jesus. He was (Luke xxiii. 8) exceedingly glad to see him, for he had long desired it on account of the reports which he had heard of him, and, besides, he now hoped to see him perform some miracle. But when Jesus not only refused to do anything to gratify his curiosity, but would not even reply to his wordy questions, he gave way to the natural and cruel levity of his character, and, by the most extravagant marks of homage, subjected him to the heartless mockery and scoffs of the soldiers. The Herod who appears in the thirteenth chapter of Acts is Herod Agrippa I., grandson of Herod the Great, and brother of Herodias.

### 13 – 21. — FEEDING THE FIVE THOUSAND.

After Jesus knew that Herod was making inquiries concerning him, 13, as connected with 1 and 2, he crossed over the lake with his disciples to an uninhabited place, near the city of Bethsaida, which was at the northeastern corner of the lake, not far from the entrance of the Jordan. They sought rest; "for there were many coming and going, and they had not leisure even to eat." (Mark vi. 31.) Jesus probably desired also to have a season of undisturbed intercourse with his disciples. For this purpose he went up into a mountain with them. But the people soon saw which way he had gone. They ran together round the lake, and some of them reached the spot even before Jesus had come to the shore. He could not therefore long be left with his disciples. They were flocking towards him from all the neighboring villages. And when, on the mountain where he was sitting with his disciples, he lifted up his eyes, he saw an immense multitude coming towards him. He came out to meet them, and, being moved with compassion for them, he healed their sick, and taught them many things. But seeing that in their haste they had come without their customary supply of food, he asks Philip (John vi. 5) how they are to be fed. Philip probably conferred with the other disciples, and they advise Jesus to send the multitude away, that they may purchase bread in the neighboring fields and villages. "They need not go away," said Jesus. "Give ye them to eat." "But we have nothing here," say they, "except five loaves and two small fishes." And these, according to John vi. 9, belonged to a lad who was with them. Jesus directed the multitudes to be seated on the green grass of which there was much there, in companies, by hundreds and fifties. They sat down as it were in garden plots, each company making a square by itself. Jesus, having lifted up his eyes to heaven and blessed the food, caused it to be distributed among the people, and they all, five thousand men, besides women and children, ate as much as they desired, and twelve baskets of fragments remained.

In the different accounts here, we have the characteristics of the different Evangelists. In Matthew there is the plain statement of facts, with his peculiar exactness as to numbers, he being the only one who adds to the 5,000, " besides women and children." Luke's is a clear historical account. He mentions the name of the place, Bethsaida. There were two cities of this name, one on the west side, and the other where they now were, near the northeastern corner of the lake. Mark, on the other hand, throws in those graphic details, which indicate an eyewitness. " For there were many coming and going, and they had not leisure even to eat." He speaks of many finding out whither Jesus had gone, and "running together on foot," so that they reached the place before him. He speaks of the green grass, and of the appearance — like garden plots — of the separate groups, as the multitude reclined at their meal. John's account also has the marks of an eyewitness. He alone speaks of Jesus as going up into a mountain and sitting there with his disciples, of his lifting up his eyes and seeing the great multitude coming towards him, of the conversation with Philip, of the lad with his five *barley* loaves, and two little fishes." These graphic details and the parenthetical clause — " now there was much grass in the place " — are characteristic of one who was personally present. 22, 23. After the miracle Jesus constrained his disciples to enter a vessel, and go back to the other side before him. The language indicates a reluctance to go on their part. Probably they had become aware of the disposition in the multitude

(John vi. 14, 15) to take him by force and make him a king, and, sympathizing with the movement, were unwilling to go away. For this very reason, in order to prevent their becoming implicated in any such movement, Jesus may have obliged them to enter the vessel. Then, having dismissed the multitudes, he went up into the mountain alone to pray. When the night came on he was there, apart from the confused excitement of the crowds and their ambitious schemes in his behalf, the silent heavens bending over him, and the mountain solitudes around. These retired seasons of meditation and prayer were peculiarly grateful to him. "It seems to me that no one can remember how the Holy One found strength and peace in prayer, and ever again doubt that we need it. Judas did not pray. Herod did not feel the need of it. Pilate felt no need of it. The worldly and the cruel did not pray. But the Holy One, alone on the mountain, by the grave of Lazarus, at his own last hour, felt the need of prayer; and so long as the record of that example remains, we have an unanswerable evidence of the necessity of prayer." — E. Peabody, D. D.

## JESUS WALKING ON THE WATER.

21 – 34. While Jesus was alone on the mountain, in the gray twilight of the dawn, as it broke faintly into the darkness of the night, Jesus saw the disciples tossed about by the waves, and struggling with their oars to make some headway against the opposing wind. At about the fourth watch of the night, which extended from three to six o'clock, he went towards them, walking on the water. As they saw him approaching, they screamed aloud with fear, thinking it a spirit, or an apparition. A word from him calmed their apprehensions. Peter with the vehemence and the sudden revulsion of feeling which he showed on other occasions more than once, asked that he might

walk to him on the waters, and then, in the violence of the wind his courage failing him, and he beginning to sink, he cried to Jesus for help. When they had come into the vessel, the wind ceased. This miracle evidently produced on those who were there (Mark vi. 51, 52) a stronger impression of amazement and wonder, than that which they had witnessed the day before with unmoved and hardened hearts. Their sense of personal danger from the storm, the terrors of the night heightened by what they feared at the time as a phantasm or apparition from another world, had prepared them to recognize with gratitude and wonder the power which interposed to save them. They immediately came to the land of Gennesaret, a rich and beautiful plain on the west side of the lake, lying four or five miles north from Tiberias, and probably a little to the south from Capernaum.

## NOTES.

AT that time Herod the tetrarch heard of the fame of Jesus, 2 and said unto his servants, This is John the Baptist; he is risen from the dead, and therefore mighty works do show forth 3 themselves in him.—— For Herod had laid hold on John, and bound him, and put him in prison, for Herodias' sake, his 4 brother Philip's wife. For John said unto him, It is not law-5 ful for thee to have her. And when he would have put him to death, he feared the multitude, because they counted him as a 6 prophet. But when Herod's birthday was kept, the daughter of 7 Herodias danced before them, and pleased Herod; whereupon he promised with an oath to give her whatsoever she would 8 ask. And she, being before instructed of her mother, said, 9 Give me here John Baptist's head in a charger. And the king was sorry; nevertheless, for the oath's sake, and them which 10 sat with him at meat, he commanded it to be given her. And 11 he sent and beheaded John in the prison. And his head

---

10. **and beheaded John in prison** ] Josephus, who is less likely to be correct in this matter than Matthew, assigns a different

was brought in a charger, and given to the damsel; and she brought it to her mother. And his disciples came and took up 12 the body, and buried it; and went and told Jesus. —— When 13 Jesus heard of it, he departed thence by ship into a desert place

---

reason for the death of John from that which is here given. His account of John is as follows (Ant. XVIII. 5. 2): "Now some of the Jews thought that the destruction of Herod's army came from God; and that very justly, as a punishment of what he did against John, who was called the Baptist. For Herod slew him, who was a good man, and commanded the Jews to exercise virtue, both as to righteousness towards one another, and piety towards God, and so to come to baptism. For that the washing with water would be acceptable to him, if they made use of it, not in order to putting away, or the remission of some sins only, but for the purification of the body: supposing still that the soul was thoroughly purified beforehand by righteousness. Now when many others came in crowds about him—-for they were greatly moved or pleased by hearing his words—Herod, who feared lest the great influence John had over the people might put it into his power and inclination to raise a rebellion (for they seemed ready to do anything he should advise), thought it best, by putting him to death, to prevent any mischief he might cause, and not bring himself into difficulties by sparing a man who might make him repent of it when it should be too late. Accordingly he was sent a prisoner, out of Herod's suspicious temper, to Machærus, the castle I before mentioned, and was there put to death."

13. **When Jesus heard of it, he departed thence by ship into a desert place**] "The news of John's execution," says Mr. Norton, "probably produced a sudden excitement among the people, and a feeling of strong resentment,—for 'all believed John to be a prophet,'—and might powerfully tend to turn their attention on Jesus, and direct their hopes to him as their expected king. John's disciples came to tell him of it, his own Apostles collected about him, and the multitude flocked to him. From this excited multitude, eager to force on him an office so foreign from that which he was appointed to sustain, our Lord was desirous of withdrawing himself, till their passions should subside, and he should, in consequence, be able with less difficulty to repress their misdirected zeal. He probably wished also to withdraw his disciples, who were very likely to share in the popular ferment. He therefore passed over from Galilee to the other side of the lake, into the dominions of Philip, a part of the country where he appears to have spent but little time during his ministry. Here, however, a great number of persons soon collected, whom he fed miraculously. The performance of this miracle, with its effect on the multitude, which our Lord must have foreseen, may seem inconsistent with the reasons that have just been assigned for his leaving Galilee. But it is to be observed, that, while he repressed those feelings of the multitude which arose from false expectations concerning the Messiah, it was necessary for him, at the same time, to give the most decisive proofs of his Divine authority. As he but seldom visited this part of the country, we may suppose that it was his purpose to perform a miracle so astonishing and so public that it would make a deep impression, and that the knowledge of it would be spread everywhere round about. Under this aspect the miracle resembles that of the cure of the demoniacs, related in the eighth chapter of Matthew, which was so remarkable in its circumstances, and which was likewise performed on the eastern

apart; and when the people had heard thereof, they followed him on foot out of the cities.

14 And Jesus went forth, and saw a great multitude; and was moved with compassion toward them, and he healed their sick.

15 —— And when it was evening, his disciples came to him, say-

---

shore of the lake." In the work of educating the disciples as Apostles and Evangelists, while it was important that they should at times be sent out by themselves, and at times be brought into connection with large and excited multitudes of men, it was also important that they should sometimes be alone with Jesus to receive his private and confidential admonitions and instructions, as well as to have the spirit and habit of devotion established in them. We must still regard them as a peripatetic school, going about with their master, and preparing under him for the great and responsible office which is soon to devolve on them. 14.
**And Jesus went forth**] He had probably been with his disciples in some retired part of the mountain from which he now came out. This may not have been the same day as that on which he crossed the lake. Mr. Norton supposes that one or more days had intervened. The narrative in Mark vi. 33, 34, at first sight would indicate that the multitudes were fed on the same day that Jesus arrived there. His account is as follows : " And the people saw them departing, and many knew him, and ran afoot thither out of all cities, and outwent them and came together unto him. And Jesus when he came out, saw much people." According to the text in Tischendorf's edition, we must read : " And many saw them departing and knew them ; and on foot from all the cities they ran together thither, and came before them. And when Jesus came out," &c. This may mean, that when Jesus came out from the boat he saw the multitudes, and then fed them. But considering the circumstances of the case, and the rapid, sketchy manner in which the

Evangelists group events that were separated in point of time, it is more probable that Jesus had spent some time there, perhaps a day or more, healing and instructing them, but seeking also for himself and his disciples seasons of retirement; and that once, when he came out from his retirement, and saw the people who had been there so long, weary, scattered, and hungry, — like sheep without a shepherd, — his compassion for them was excited, and he fed them. There has been a difference of opinion in regard to the place where the five thousand were miraculously fed, and which Jesus left to walk upon the lake. We think, however, there can be no longer any doubt that it was, as we have placed it, at the northeast corner of the lake, near Bethsaida, afterwards called Julias, where Philip, the tetrarch, resided at least a portion of the time, and where he died and was buried in a costly tomb. (See Robinson's Researches, III. p. 308.) John vi. 23 speaks of other vessels coming that night from Tiberias to the place where they had eaten bread. "The contrary wind," says Stanley in his Geography, p. 374, "which, blowing up the lake from the southwest, would prevent the boat from returning to Capernaum, would also bring 'other boats' from Tiberias, the chief city on the south, to Julias, the chief city on the north, and so enable the multitudes, when the storm had subsided, to cross at once, without the long journey on foot which they had made the day before." This accords with the account given by John vi. 22 – 24. 15. **And when it was evening**] 23. **and when the evening was come**] From these two verses it would seem as if there were two evenings

ing, This is a desert place, and the time is now past; send the multitude away, that they may go into the villages, and buy themselves victuals. But Jesus said unto them, They need 16 not depart; give ye them to eat. And they say unto him, We 17 have here but five loaves and two fishes. He said, Bring 18 them hither to me. And he commanded the multitude to sit 19 down on the grass, and took the five loaves and the two fishes, and, looking up to heaven; he blessed, and brake, and gave the loaves to his disciples, and the disciples to the multitude. And they did all eat, and were filled; and they took up of 20 the fragments that remained twelve baskets full. And they 21 that had eaten were about five thousand men, beside women and children.

And straightway Jesus constrained his disciples to get into a 22 ship, and to go before him unto the other side, while he sent the multitudes away. And when he had sent the multitudes 23 away, he went up into a mountain apart to pray. And when the evening was come, he was there alone. But the ship was 24 now in the midst of the sea, tossed with waves; for the wind was contrary. And in the fourth watch of the night, Jesus 25 went unto them, walking on the sea. And when the disciples 26 saw him walking on the sea, they were troubled, saying, It is a spirit; and they cried out for fear. But straightway Jesus 27 spake unto them saying, Be of good cheer, it is I; be not afraid. And Peter answered him and said, Lord, if it be 28 thou, bid me come unto thee on the water. And he said,

---

that day. "This," says Trench on the Miracles, p. 224, "was an ordinary way of speaking among the Jews, the first evening being very much our afternoon (compare Luke ix. 12, where the evening of Matthew and Mark is described as the day beginning to decline); the second evening being the twilight, or from six o'clock to twilight." Lightfoot, on the other hand, a great authority in such matters, comparing 15 with 23, says: "That denotes the lateness of the day; this, the lateness of the night. So, 'evening' in the Talmudists, signifies not only the declining part of the day, but [of] the night also." Either explanation meets the case before us; but the first seems to us the most satisfactory. The words rendered "evening" or "even" (Exod. xii. 6, xxx. 8; Levit. xxiii. 5) mean "between the evenings," or "between the twilights."

20. **twelve baskets full**] Not improbably these were the baskets in which the disciples carried their provisions. "The Jews," says Mr. Norton, "seem to have been, in some degree, distinguished by the use of such baskets." Juvenal, Sat. VI. 542, speaks of Jews at Rome, whose "whole furniture is a basket and some hay." 28. **bid me come unto thee**] "In the questionable little word 'me,' always questionable when it too hastily re-

29 Come. And when Peter was come down out of the ship, he
30 walked on the water, to go to Jesus. But when he saw the
wind boisterous, he was afraid; and beginning to sink, he
31 cried, saying, Lord, save me! And immediately Jesus
stretched forth his hand, and caught him, and said unto him,
32 O thou of little faith, wherefore didst thou doubt? And when
33 they were come into the ship, the wind ceased. Then they
that were in the ship came and worshipped him, saying, Of a
truth thou art the Son of God.

34 And when they were gone over, they came into the land of

---

plies to Christ's powerful *I*, ere it has been specially asked and called, lurks the secret flaw in the great faith, on account of which it must soon again become very little. Had Christ of himself called out: 'And thou, Peter, come out to me,' he certainly would not have sunk. But, because he will outrun the others in showing his faith, the real Peter must show himself just as, alas! he still is, and give a warning of the future denial of his Lord; falling back again as suddenly as he had raised himself." Stier.
29. **And he said, Come**] But why did he allow him to come? Because the presuming and presumptuous disciple needed the lesson, which he could not learn from any words of Jesus so well as from his own precipitate and humiliating experience. And so it is that God deals with us in his providence, often allowing us to adventure on our own rash and foolish schemes, because only by failure and disaster, through our own humiliating experience and exposure, can we come to ourselves, and learn the true and humble gauge of our own powers. This is a great thing in the training of children and the education of the young, as well as in the discipline of maturer life. Not that system which is for the present the safest for the child is most to be desired, but that which will best call out all his powers, and by his own experience teach him the truest measure of himself. In this way only will he attain a true Christian modesty, which is always connected with a nice adjustment of a man's consciousness to all his faculties, so that he will not presume on what lies wholly beyond him, nor shrink from what lies within his compass. The fitting measure of our faith in ourselves, and, as with Peter, of our faith in God, can be gained only in this way by exposures which sometimes end in defeat and humiliation. 30. **to sink**] καταποντίζεσθαι, a stronger word than to sink, — beginning to be *buried in the sea*. 31. **And Jesus stretched forth his hand, and caught him**] The calmness of Jesus, and the ease and naturalness of the movement by which the affrighted disciple was rescued, are worthy of notice. There is nowhere in our Saviour's life any indication of surprise. He is never, even for a moment, thrown off his guard. He does not seek an occasion for the exercise of his wonderful gifts, but accepts them when they come. One woman, of a despised race, at the well of Jacob in Samaria (John iv. 1-43), called forth a discourse full of his richest and sublimest instructions; and here, the violence of the storm and the terror of his disciples, excite him to no unusual effort. "He reached out his hand, and laid hold of him, and said unto him, 'O, thou of little faith, wherefore didst thou doubt?'" 32. **and worshipped him**] did homage to him, saying, "Truly thou art God's Son."

Gennesaret. And when the men of that place had knowledge 35
of him, they sent out into all that country round about; and
brought unto him all that were diseased, and besought him that 36
they might only touch the hem of his garment; and as many
as touched were made perfectly whole.

## CHAPTER XV.

1–20. — JESUS AND THE JEWISH TRADITIONS.

1–6. THE SCRIBES AND MOSES. The Scribes and Pharisees, who had come down from Jerusalem in order to find some serious charge against Jesus, ask him why it is that his disciples transgress the traditions of the elders as they do by eating with unwashed hands. Jesus replies to them in language of great severity, "Why do *ye* transgress the commandment of God by your tradition? For God hath commanded, (Ex. xx. 12,) saying, Honor thy father and thy mother; and (Ex. xxi. 17) He that curseth father or mother shall be put to death. But ye teach, If a man say to his father or mother, Whatever I have which might benefit you is a gift to God, [and cannot therefore be used for your benefit], he shall not honor his father or mother, i. e. he shall even be exempt from the obligation to honor and provide for them. And ye thus annul or render of none effect the commandment of GOD by *your* tradition."

Lightfoot has shown that the Jewish Talmudists attached greater weight to the Rabbinical traditions than to the law. "The words of the scribes," say they, "are lovely, above the words of the law; for the words of the law are weighty and light; but the words of the scribes are all weighty." Alford says, "The Jews attached more importance to the traditionary exposition than to the Scripture text itself. They compared the written word to water; the traditionary exposition to the wine which must be mingled with it. The duty of washing before meat is not inculcated in the law, but only in the traditions of the Scribes. So rigidly did the Jews observe it, that Rabba Akiba, being imprisoned, and having water scarcely sufficient to sustain life given him, preferred dying of thirst to eating without washing his hands."

It is customary among the Jews to cut themselves off from the obligation of certain acts by consecrating their property to God as a gift so far as those specific acts were concerned. Their property might be used for anything else, but not for those particular acts. For example, if a man wished to free himself from the obligation to support his parents, he might set aside his whole property as a gift to God, so far as any advantage might accrue to them from it, and, according to the traditions of the elders, he would then have no right to use any part of it for the benefit of his parents, though he might use it for any other purpose. Thus they set at naught the law of God by their quibbling traditions, and justified by their traditions those who did not honor their father or their mother.

### 7, 8. — FULFILMENT OF PROPHECY.

Jesus has confronted the Scribes by the authority of Moses, their great lawgiver. He here shows how the condemnation of one of their prophets falls on them: "Well did Isaiah prophesy of you, when he said, This people honor me with their lips, but their hearts are far from me. But in vain do they worship me teaching for doctrine the commandments of men." Dr. Noyes's translation of this passage (Isa. xxix. 13, 14) is as follows: —

"Since this people draweth near to me with their mouth,
And honoreth me with their lips,
While their heart is far from me,
And their worship of me is according to the commandments of men,
Therefore, behold, I will proceed to deal marvellously with this people;
Marvellously and wonderfully.
For the wisdom of their wise men shall perish,
And the prudence of the prudent shall be hid."

These words were undoubtedly applied by the prophet to the men of his own day; and we have no reason to suppose that he had in his mind the thought of any further application. How then could Jesus say, "Well did Isaiah prophesy concerning you when he said, 'This people," &c. They not only contain a direct message to the Jews, who lived in the time of Isaiah; but that message is so put as to contain in itself a general truth which is prophetic of the condition of all men, whenever and wherever they may live, who seek to propitiate the favor of God by their distant, outside, hypocritical worship. See above, xiii. 14.

But does not this involve a double sense? Is it right to use the authority of the prophet in applying his words to persons whom he could not have had in his mind at the time he spoke? This is what Jesus has done in the passage before us. And, notwithstanding the dread many persons have of attributing a double or rather a twofold meaning of this kind to the language of Scripture, it is what is constantly done with other language. Every expression which, originally spoken solely with reference to a specific case, is so put as to involve a general truth, may be used in this way. If the Scriptures more than all other writings have been so applied, it is only because, under the simplest forms of speech, and often with direct reference to specific cases, they more than all other writings express the most profound and universal truth.

The Supreme Court of the United States may give a decision which is of little consequence in its application to the case immediately in hand. And that case is the only one which is before the Court, and to which they specifically apply their decision. But that decision may involve considerations of momentous importance in cases to which the principles there established by the authority of the highest judicial tribunal of the land may hereafter be applied. The language which is at first applied specifically only to a single case, nevertheless embraces within its scope and within the intention of the Court, all cases of the same character that may arise afterwards. What is said of one is said of all, — that one case is a type of all the rest, and the authority which decides it applies with equal force to all the rest. So in the decisions of the great Judge of all, as announced by his prophets, the principles involved in the case to which they are specifically applied and the consequences flowing from those principles, reach on with the weight of their divine authority, and find their fulfilment in every analogous case that may afterwards arise. Whatever may be said of the doctrine of types, and the absurd extent to which it has been carried, or of the interpretation sometimes put on the prediction of specific events, many of the ancient prophecies stand forth as types or outshadowings and foreshadowings of divine truths, which shall be perpetually fulfilling themselves in the experience of all times. The passage quoted here from Isaiah is one of this kind. The predicted destruction of Sodom and Gomorrah, immediately fulfilled in the fatal retribution which fell on those wicked cities, became, through that fulfilment, a type or sign of the retribution which is in store for every corrupt and ungodly people. The principle of retributive justice, which is involved and announced in that case, holds true always, and applies with more or less force to every new case that may arise.

Of this character are the instructions here given to the Pharisees. The question immediately at issue between them and Jesus relates to a matter which is in itself of no sort of interest or importance now. But this specific case of washing before meat is made to stand out as the type or representative of all similar cases, and brings out the great essential principles in such a way as to elucidate the whole subject of a spiritual or formal worship, and to furnish instruction in this matter for all times. Where a sincere and vital religion is dying out, there is always a disposition, with a numerous class of men, to seek refuge in forms, and to put their consciences to sleep by multiplying religious forms at the expense of the essential principles of devout and holy living. This fatal tendency, belonging alike to unenlightened and to the most luxurious times, making void the law of God by human traditions and observances, is here exposed and condemned. The heart as the centre of the life is the one thing to be kept pure. The thoughts which proceed from that, and not the neglect of outside forms, are what defile the man. Mr. Norton has quoted from Philo Judæus a passage very similar to this. " Through the mouth, as Plato says, mortal things enter, and imperishable things pass out. For food and drink enter it, perishable nutriment of the perishable body; but words proceed from it, immortal laws of the immortal soul, by which the rational life is governed." — Philo, De Mundi Opificio, Opp. I. 29.

The fact that so plain a statement as that of Jesus, 11, should appear to the disciples, 15, a parable or dark saying which needed explanation, shows how dull their spiritual perceptions were at that time, and how slow they were to free themselves from the superstitious formalities of the Jews. The same attitude of mind towards Jewish teachers and observances is indicated by the vehemence with which they put the question, 12, " Dost thou know how the Pharisees were offended by thy words?" His reply is, "Every plant which my Father hath not planted shall be rooted up." As if he had said, The Pharisees are here the recognized and authoritative teachers of the law. Still, if they teach anything not in accordance with the truth, anything which my Father doth not approve and sustain, it cannot stand, but will be rooted up as a plant which he hath not planted. Give them up as your guides. They are only blind leaders of the blind; and no good, but mischief only, can come of their instructions. Here, 15, Peter asks an explanation of the parable, 11. It was not a parable in one sense of the word; but the disciples could not understand it. With an expression of sorrowful surprise that they even yet should be unable to understand words so simple, he explains his meaning in such a manner as to do away forever, one would think, at least among his followers, all superstitious regard for merely external observances in matters of religion.

### The Syro-Phœnician Woman.

21–28. In order to escape from the crowds, with the tumults and controversies connected with them, as well as to prevent any premature and mistaken movement in his behalf, he retired from the lake of Galilee towards the northwest, to the vicinity of Tyre and Sidon. It is a question among commentators whether he actually entered their territory or remained still within the limits of Galilee. He sought retirement. "He went (Mark vii. 24, 25) into a house, and would have no man know it; but he could not be hid; for a woman, whose daughter had an unclean spirit heard of him," and came crying after him. The desire to escape observation will account for the anxiety of the disciples to stop her cries. For in calling after them she must necessarily attract attention. She was a Grecian by descent, a Syro-Phœnician by birth, and from her birthplace called, as she is here, a woman of Canaan. At first Jesus paid no regard to her. His object probably was to call out and strengthen her faith, by subjecting it to trial. This is in accordance with the whole discipline of life. He therefore, said within her hearing, "I am sent only," i. e. his personal ministry was confined, "to the lost sheep of the house of Israel." But instead of being discouraged, she threw herself at his feet, and with affecting earnestness entreated him to assist her. He replied to her, "It is not right to take the children's bread and throw it to the little dogs." "Yes, Lord," she exclaimed, "it is; for even the little dogs eat of the crumbs which fall from their master's table." The humble, trusting character of this speech showed that nothing more was needed for her. "O woman, great is thy faith. Be it to thee as thou wishest." And her daughter was healed from that hour. What was this faith? Not knowledge; she had not that. Not a belief in certain theological doctrines. It is certain that she knew nothing of them. Her faith consisted in a readiness to believe, — an humble, trusting attitude of mind and heart, — "the tenderest susceptibility for what is heavenly." As to the apparent severity of Jesus towards her, "It is," as Olshausen has said, "Christian experience alone which opens our way to the right understanding of this. . . . . . The restraining of his grace, the manifestation of a treatment wholly different from what the woman may at first have expected, acted as a check usually does on power when it really exists, the whole inherent energy of her living faith broke forth, and the Saviour suffered himself to be overcome by her. . . . . . Where faith is weak, he anticipates and comes to meet it; where faith is strong, he holds himself far off in order that it may in itself be carried to perfection."

### Feeding the Four Thousand.

32 – 38. It has been supposed by some modern writers, as Schleiermacher, Neander, &c., that this account and that in xiv. 14 – 21, are but different accounts of the same transaction. The circumstances, it is said, the place, the multitude, the compassion of Jesus, the perplexity of the disciples as to what should be done, the sort of food at hand, are substantially the same in the two accounts. But these would be likely to be substantially the same if the miracle had been repeated anywhere in that vicinity. The only exception to what we should look for is in the perplexity of the disciples. How could they, after witnessing the

first miracle, be so much at a loss here? The reply is, that, though they had seen Jesus perform many miracles, they had never, except in a single instance, known him to use his miraculous power for such a purpose as that. Why, then, should they expect it now? Some of the circumstances are alike in the two cases, but others again are different. In the first, there were 5,000 persons; in the second only 4,000. In the first, there were five loaves and two fishes; in the second, seven loaves and a few fishes. In the first, it is not said how long the multitudes were with Jesus; in the second they were with him three days. In the first, specific mention is made of a storm on the lake and of Jesus walking on the water; in the second he is represented as crossing the lake in a vessel without any such occurrence. In so concise an account of two similar events we should hardly expect a greater variety in the details, which certainly point to two distinct transactions. Besides (xvi. 9, 10) Jesus explicitly refers to the two miracles. It may also be added, that in the first account the word translated baskets is κοφίνους, while here it is σπυρίδας, a long basket, which travellers sometimes used as a bed when they pass the night in the open air, and the same as that in which Saul was let down from the wall (Acts ix. 25). The same distinction is observed in our Saviour's reference to the two miracles, and in all these cases the distinction is found in the Curetonian Syriac Gospels. In the repetition of the miracle, there is nothing improbable. When we consider what multitudes thronged around the steps of Jesus, and that the east side of the lake was a desert place, at a distance from villages where food could be procured for such a concourse of people, we can hardly think it strange, if more than once towards the close of the day, he should have had compassion on the weary multitudes, and fed them by his miraculous power lest they should hunger and faint by the way.

MATTHEW XV. 281

39. Having dismissed the multitude, Jesus went into a vessel and passed to the vicinity of Magdala, or, as the best copies have it, Magadan. Magdala is near the southeast corner of the plain of Genesareth. For an interesting and graphic description of this fertile and populous region, see Stanley's Sinai and Palestine, pp. 366-375. After his account of what that country once was, he says, "Of all the numerous towns and villages in what must have been the most thickly peopled district of Palestine, one only remains. A collection of a few hovels stands at the southeastern corner of the plain, — its name hardly altered from the ancient Magdala or Migdol, — so called, probably, from a watch-tower, of which ruins appear to remain, that guarded the entrance of the plain; deriving its whole celebrity from its being the birthplace of her, through whom the name of 'Magdalen' has been incorporated into the languages of the world. A large solitary thorn-tree stands beside it. Its situation, otherwise unmarked, is dignified by the high limestone rock which overhangs it on the southwest, perforated with caves, recalling, by a curious, though doubtless unintentional coincidence, the scene of Correggio's celebrated picture."

NOTES.

THEN came to Jesus scribes and Pharisees, which were of 2 Jerusalem, saying, Why do thy disciples transgress the tradition of the elders? for they wash not their hands, when they 3 eat bread. But he answered and said unto them, Why do ye

1. **which were of Jerusalem**] The fact that Scribes and Pharisees had come from Jerusalem to watch and oppose Jesus, shows incidentally what an impression he had been making, and what an ascendency he has now gained. 2. **for they wash not their hands when they eat bread**] Not that they did not have *clean* hands, but that they did not wash them. It was a superstitious duty to wash

also transgress the commandment of God, by your tradition? For God commanded, saying, "Honor thy father and mother;" and, "He that curseth father or mother, let him die the death." But ye say, "Whosoever shall say to his father or his mother, It is a gift, by whatsoever thou mightest be profited by me; and honor not his father or his mother, he shall be free. Thus have ye made the commandment of God of none effect by your tradition. Ye hypocrites! well did Esaias prophesy

---

their hands before eating bread, whether they were clean or not,— particularly before eating *bread*.
**8.** Observe the solemn contrast between the commandment of God, and the tradition of men, even though the tradition was held to by the elders and teachers. **4. Honor thy father and mother**] The stress which Jesus lays on this great commandment is remarkable. Its observance is to an extraordinary extent a criterion of the morals of a people. There is a saying among the Chinese, "If a man show reverence for his father and mother in his house, why go farther to burn spices?" There is a place holy enough for sacrifice and worship. Where there is this reverence for parents, the simplicity of the character and the freshness of the heart are preserved. He who honors his father and mother will honor God.
**6. he shall be free**] These words, inserted by our translators, do not belong here. The second clause of the sentence is the *apodosis* to the first, which begins in verse 5: "Whosoever shall say to his father or mother, 'Anything I have which might be used for your benefit is, so far as you are concerned, set aside as a consecrated gift [and therefore not to be employed for you],' he shall not honor his father or his mother." Thus setting aside all his property, so far as relates to his parents, he has freed himself from all obligation to provide for them: and, therefore, rightly, so the Scribes taught, he shall not be obliged to honor them. "Whosoever shall say to his father or mother, 'Let it be a [devoted] gift in whatsoever thou mightest be helped by me'; then let him not honor his father and mother at all." Lightfoot. **7. Ye hypocrites**] This is the first time that Jesus directly addresses the Scribes and Pharisees by this term. Hitherto he has rather reproved them by holding up the principles of righteousness which opposed and overthrew all their superstitious conventionalisms. But now, when they put to him a question which directly involves the principles that separate him and them, he at first states strongly the inconsistency between their tradition and the commandments of God, and then directly charges them with the one crime which vitiated all their religion, and which from that day to this has been the characteristic of their successors. When men separate the forms of religion from its substance, and substitute man's traditions for the commandments of God, however specious the pretence, and however artfully disguised the processes by which their purpose is to be accomplished, they are led by a superstitious spirit through dishonest methods into hypocrisy,— that hideous crime against man and God, on which the heaviest denunciations of our Saviour fell. Every step away from the simplicity of the truth, as it stands revealed to us by God in Christ, is a step in this direction. It gives to human explanations, glosses, institutions the authority which belongs only to the commandments of God. It substitutes human formulas of faith, and forms of worship, with the idle ceremonies growing out of them, for the wor-

8 of you, saying, "This people draweth nigh unto me with their mouth, and honoreth me with their lips; but their heart is far 9 from me. But in vain do they worship me, teaching for doc- 10 trines the commandments of men." —— And he called the mul- 11 titude, and said unto them, Hear, and understand. Not that which goeth into the mouth defileth a man; but that which 12 cometh out of the mouth, this defileth a man. —— Then came his disciples, and said unto him, Knowest thou that the Phari- 13 sees were offended, after they heard this saying? But he an- swered and said, Every plant which my heavenly Father hath 14 not planted, shall be rooted up. Let them alone; they be blind leaders of the blind. And if the blind lead the blind, both shall 15 fall into the ditch. Then answered Peter, and said unto him, 16 Declare unto us this parable. And Jesus said: Are ye also yet 17 without understanding? Do not ye yet understand that what- soever entereth in at the mouth goeth into the belly, and is cast 18 out into the draught? But those things which proceed out of the mouth come forth from the heart, and they defile the man. 19 For out of the heart proceed evil thoughts; murders, adulte- 20 ries, fornications, thefts, false witness, blasphemies. These are the things which defile a man; but to eat with unwashen hands defileth not a man.

21 Then Jesus went thence, and departed into the coasts of

---

ship and the morality which Jesus has taught, and thus renders the law of God of none effect through its superstitious and hypocritical traditions. So true in regard to them is the language of Isaiah, that their heart is alienated from God, and their moral and spiritual per- ceptions blunted. If the pure and devout, who are led away by these subtle processes from the simplicity of the Gospel, could only give up the human hindrances which offer themselves to them as helps, and sit at the feet of Jesus to learn of him, and thus receive their religion directly from him, rather than from the perverse and impure channels through which it comes to them, how would the face of the world be changed! But there is always this tendency and weakness in our hu- man nature; this clinging to helps beyond what God has given; and the strong man, hardened into hy- pocrisy, knows how to avail him- self of the timid consciences of the weak, and how to turn to his own ends the pliant, trusting faith of the unsuspecting. 13. **Every plant**] Not that which has grown naturally, but that which is planted and fostered by man, — *the com- mandments of men*, which are taught for doctrines. 16. **yet without understanding**] What, *still* not able to understand so simple a truth, — ye who have been with me so long? This conversation with the disciples (12 – 20) was after he had entered into the house (Mark vii. 17), and when he was probably with them alone. 20. **which defile the man**] "In the very appellation of *man* is contained an argument: for the spiritual nature, which is the superior part in man, is not reached by outward filth."

Tyre and Sidon. And, behold, a woman of Canaan came out 22
of the same coasts, and cried unto him, saying, Have mercy on
me, O Lord, thou son of David; my daughter is grievously
vexed with a devil. But he answered her not a word. And 23
his disciples came and besought him, saying, Send her away,
for she crieth after us. But he answered and said, I am not 24
sent but unto the lost sheep of the house of Israel. Then 25

---

Bengel. **23. Send her away**] The disciples probably meant to ask of Jesus that he should grant her request, heal her child, and let her go. **for she crieth after us**] They wished to escape the attention and notoriety which her cries were likely to attract. "We may suppose," says Bengel, "that the disciples feared the judgment of men, and made their petition to our Lord, both for their own sake, lest her crying should produce annoyance, and for the sake of the woman herself."

**24. I am not sent but unto the lost sheep of the house of Israel**] "*After those flocks which have strayed away from,*" &c., seeking the scattered Israelites in the regions of Tyre and Sidon, Jesus confined his personal ministry almost entirely to the Jews. In his directions to the Apostles he commanded them (Matt. x. 5) not to go into the way of the Gentiles, or into any city of the Samaritans. Not, as some have supposed, that his personal sympathies were bound in by Jewish prejudices. His conversation with the woman of Samaria, and his remaining at Sychar two days, show the kindness of his feeling towards them, and his readiness to do them good. But the disciples, who were slow to rise above their Jewish prejudices, were not yet prepared so as to be trusted with people or in places where their national antipathies were likely to be excited. "Jesus," says Dr. Nichols, "plainly intended to restrict his labors, and those of his Apostles also, during his own life, within the limits of the Jewish nation. We may not know his reasons, but one naturally occurs. The Judaic element was important to his church at that period, in several respects. Before Christianity had gained an establishment in the world, it had special occasion for those aids which this element might afford it. One aid was the remarkable attachment of the Jew to his own Scriptures; and to these Scriptures, especially the Prophecies, Christianity appealed as one of its principal supports. The Old Testament was the classic, the rubric, the oracle, the glory of the Hebrew. He counted its very letters. It was to him the word of God; and let him embrace a religion as being based upon this foundation, and no superstition or philosophy would occasion any peril to his faith. We cannot overlook this reason, why, in that system of moral harmonies which always characterizes the Divine administration, the Christian seed should have been sown in a Jewish soil. The Gospel was not left to stand alone on its own simple moral claims, which the world was so little prepared to appreciate, — no, nor even on its own miraculous testimonials. But there was a religious culture in the Jewish mind adapted to yield it a powerful support, such as it could derive from no other human source. God was pleased to connect the two systems of Judaism and Christianity; and while the one was a schoolmaster to bring men to Christ, the other was a completion and confirmation of its predecessor. . . . . . The Jewish convert to Christianity felt an intensity of interest in his new belief such as a Jew only could feel. Accustomed to look upon his own nation as the chosen subject of a Divine administration, familiar with special manifestations in its

26 came she and worshipped him, saying, Lord, help me! But
he answered and said, It is not meet to take the children's
27 bread, and to cast it to dogs. And she said, Truth, Lord;
yet the dogs eat of the crumbs which fall from their master's

---

favor through all his ancestral history, he took up his adopted religion with a trust and a zeal of which no Gentile belief was capable, and which were so necessary to bear it triumphantly over the sea of prejudice and persecution upon which it was then launched. Blessings which ask no assistance from circumstances are of rare occurrence in our world." Hours with the Evangelists, Vol. I. pp. 390 – 393.     26. **to dogs**] *little dogs*, a diminutive, which may have been used somewhat as a term of endearment, and which therefore may have taken away something from the apparent harshness of our Saviour's language in speaking thus to a distressed mother respecting her suffering child.

27. **And she said, Truth, Lord; yet the dogs eat of the crumbs**] Our English version fails, we think, to give the true meaning of this passage. The exact translation is as follows : " Yea, Lord ; for the little dogs eat," &c. In conformity with the Greek idiom, we are to suppose an ellipsis or omission before the word γαρ, *for*, which must be supplied in English, in order to make the passage intelligible, and may be given as follows: " Yea, Lord [but do not deny me] ; for even the little dogs," &c. Bengel, whom even Winer regards as a great authority in such matters, says : "The particle ναι [yea] partly assents ; partly, as it were, places on our Lord's tongue the assent to her prayers, i. e. prays." She puts such a construction on his words, that while by the expression, 'Yea, Lord,' she assents to them, she, at the same time, turns aside the apparent edge of their denial, and draws from them encouragement to continue her petition, which she does in the most delicate way, by a turn of expression (" Yea, Lord ; for even the little dogs," &c.) which implies a further entreaty on her part, though it does not state it in words. It is impossible to supply the ellipsis in English without marring the exceeding fineness and delicacy of the sentiment. The modesty and reverence towards Christ which are here implied, — her humility in regard to any claims which she might have upon him, — her ready assent to the apparently disparaging terms in which he had alluded to her and hers, — her perfect faith in him, and the devoted love for her child which, while it could not accept any refusal, yet pressed its claims with such a delicate and reverential reserve towards him from whom she knew that relief might come, — give a peculiar and affecting moral beauty to these words, which evidently touched our Saviour as indicating to him the finest qualities of character. In Dr. Cureton's Syriac Gospels, a word is added, which is found both in the Peshito and the Jerusalem Syriac, and which heightens the interest and pathos of the passage : " She saith to him, Yea, my Lord ; for even the dogs eat of the crumbs which fall from their masters' tables, *and live*." The expression, *and live*, in allusion to the sick child for whose life she is pleading, is one of those fine touches of nature which can hardly be counterfeited, and which bear in themselves decisive marks of genuineness. The whole narrative is worthy of study; this refined and delicate woman, as her language shows her to have been, in her distress on account of her daughter, and her efforts for her relief, forgetting herself and everything around her so entirely as to follow after Jesus and his company of men, with cries which were bringing on them an unpleasant amount of attention; her following

table. Then Jesus answered and said unto her, O woman, 28 great is thy faith; be it unto thee even as thou wilt. And her daughter was made whole from that very hour.

And Jesus departed from thence, and came nigh unto the 29 Sea of Galilee; and went up into a mountain, and sat down there. And great multitudes came unto him, having with 30 them those that were lame, blind, dumb, maimed, and many others; and cast them down at Jesus's feet, and he healed them; insomuch that the multitude wondered, when they saw 31 the dumb to speak, the maimed to be whole, the lame to walk, and the blind to see; and they glorified the God of Israel.——
Then Jesus called his disciples unto him, and said, I have 32 compassion on the multitude, because they continue with me now three days, and have nothing to eat; and I will not send them away fasting, lest they faint in the way. And his disci- 33 ples say unto him, Whence should we have so much bread in the wilderness, as to fill so great a multitude? And Jesus 34 saith unto them, How many loaves have ye? And they said, Seven, and a few little fishes. And he commanded the multi- 35 tude to sit down on the ground. And he took the seven loaves 36

---

after him still, and beseeching him to help her, though he answered her not a word; the entreaty of the disciples that he would send her away, and his reply to them "that he is not sent except to the lost sheep of the house of Israel;"—all these things, instead of discouraging her, only leading her to prostrate herself before him, and calling out from her a more affecting appeal to him for help;—every one of the particulars is worthy of attention, and may furnish an instructive lesson. Such persistency in asking, and yet such submissiveness; such earnestness, and yet such reverence and delicacy, are rarely combined, and they furnish a beautiful type of Christian character. We see here as elsewhere how the miracle is subordinated to its higher influences and teachings. 30.
**And great multitudes]** Jesus returns to Galilee, and is encompassed again by multitudes of people. To those who travel in that region now, it is a matter of wonder where such crowds could have come from. But according to Josephus (See Milman's Hist. of Christianity, Bk. I. Chap. IV.) the whole province of Galilee was at that time crowded with flourishing towns and cities, beyond almost any other region of the world. According to his statements, "the number of towns, and the population of Galilee, in a district of between fifty and sixty miles in length, and between sixty and seventy in breadth, was no less than 204 cities and villages, the least of which contained 15,000 souls." This would make, for the whole province, a population of more than three millions. There is some reason, we think, to question the exactness of the large numerical statements which are found in ancient writers; but after all reasonable deductions have been made from this account, there will still remain a population sufficiently dense to confirm the Gospel narratives in regard to the ease with which large multitudes were col-

and the fishes, and gave thanks, and brake them, and gave to
his disciples, and the disciples to the multitude. And they did
all eat, and were filled; and they took up of the broken meat
that was left seven baskets full. And they that did eat were
four thousand men, beside women and children. And he sent
away the multitude, and took ship, and came into the coasts of
Magdala.

---

lected in that region.
**Magdala**] In Tischendorf's edition, this is Magadan. "As Herodotus (II. 159) turns Megiddo into 39. Magdalum, so some MSS., in Matt. xv. 39, turn Magdala into Magadan." Stanley. In the Curetonian Syriac Gospels it is Magadun.

## CHAPTER XVI.

### 1–4.— A Sign from Heaven.

1–4. THE Pharisees and Sadducees demand a sign from *heaven*. They had witnessed his miracles, but wished for something more. "In the Jewish superstition," says Alford, "it was held that demons and false gods could give signs *on earth*, but only the true God, signs *from heaven*." "And thus we find that, immediately after the first miraculous feeding, the same demand was made, (John vi. 30,) and answered by the declaration of our Lord, that He was the true bread from heaven." Reference to the same habit of the Jewish mind is found in 1 Cor. i. 22, "The Jews demand signs, and the Greeks seek for wisdom." It probably was at the close of the day when the demand for a sign from heaven was made of Jesus, and the sunset glow of the heavens suggested his answer. For the Jews, according to Lightfoot, were curious in observing the seasons, and in foretelling the state of the weather. They asked of him a sign from heaven. He replies, looking probably to the western sky, "It being now evening, ye say, It will be fair, for the sky is red; and, in the morning, ye say, there will be a storm, for the sky is red and lowering. Ye know how to distinguish the aspects of the sky, and can ye not also understand the signs of the times." As if he had said: "It is your business to understand things spiritual and divine. You profess to be the moral and religious teachers of this people. And here you are asking a sign from heaven. But how is it that ye do not understand the signs which are actually given? You know how to foretell the state of the weather from the aspect of the sky, and can ye not, in the miracles which I have wrought, and the truths which I have been teaching, and the new life that I am awakening, see the signs of the times? Can ye not see in them the signs of a new era, of a purer and higher kingdom to be established on earth? If your minds were open to spiritual, as your eyes are to material things, you would see all around you manifest indications of the changes that I am to introduce."

5 – 13. The noticeable fact here is the extreme slowness of spiritual apprehension which is manifested by the disciples, especially when their perplexity here about bread is compared with the specific instructions on that point which had just been given to them, (xv. 11,) and repeated with an explanation, (xv. 17 – 20,) which could not be misunderstood.

### 13 – 18. — ON THIS ROCK I BUILD MY CHURCH.

The above conversation took place on the vessel as they were crossing the lake. They arrived at Bethsaida on the northeast corner of the lake, and in passing from that city to Cæsarea Philippi, which lies far to the north, near Mount Hermon, the remaining incidents recorded in this chapter took place.

Who do men say that I the Son of man am? They reply, some say John the Baptist, some Elijah, and some Jeremiah, or one of the prophets. These different views prevailing at that time show the vague, but at the same time the active and wide-spread expectations of the time. The reply of Peter, "Thou art the Christ, the Son of the living God," is the first distinct declaration of faith on the part of the disciples. Jesus excepts this one article of faith as containing the true idea of his office, and the foundation of his Church. " Blessed art thou, Simon, son of Jonah, because flesh and blood hath not revealed this unto thee, but my Father who is in the heavens. And I say unto thee that thou art a rock (Peter means rock), and on this rock will I build my Church, and the gates of death (Hades, not Gehenna) shall not prevail against it."

There are two explanations of this passage. According to one, Peter is identified with the declaration which he has just made, as the person hearing the word is identified with what he hears (xiii. 20.) When Jesus therefore says, "Thou art a rock, and on this rock will I build my Church," he means that this confession of faith in him as the Messiah, the Son of the living God, is the foundation on which his Church is to be built. According to the other explanation, Peter himself, as the foremost of the disciples, and the first to recognize from the teachings of Jesus this essential truth, is the stone or pillar on which his Church is to be built. "He was," says Alford, "the first of those *foundation-stones* (Eph. ii. 20, Rev. xxi. 14,) on which the living temple of God was built: this building itself beginning on the day of Pentecost by the laying of three thousand living stones on this very foundation." For this sort of reference to the pillars and stones of the spiritual building see 1 Peter ii. 4 – 6, 1 Tim. iii. 15, Gal. ii. 9, Eph. ii. 20, Rev. iii. 12.

### 19. — The Keys of the Kingdom of Heaven.

In verse 19 the figure is changed. "I give to thee the keys of the kingdom of Heaven, and whatsoever thou shalt bind on earth shall be bound in heaven, and whatsoever thou shalt loose on earth shall be loosed in heaven." The kingdom of Heaven is, 1. The religion of Jesus, with its Divine influences, entering the individual soul, and establishing its dominion over it. 2. When it has entered different souls and united them under its authority into a community, it becomes an outward institution or kingdom, receiving or rejecting men according to its influence over them individually. 3. But the kingdom of Heaven does not fulfil and complete its work here on the earth. When those who have submitted to its influence and authority here lay down the burden of the flesh, the kingdom of Heaven is the name applied to the more perfect and glorious condition of being into which they then enter. Jesus uses the expression in these three different ways. When therefore he says to Peter, "I will give to thee the keys of the kingdom of Heaven," he means, I will give to thee the truths by which my religion shall be unlocked and laid open to the souls of men, so that it may act upon them as a spiritual power, and receive them into itself as an outward institution, or a divinely organized community of souls. And more than this. So far, its work is on the earth. But it is not confined to the earth. What is done here, in this lower sphere of the kingdom of Heaven in accordance with its laws, applies with equal force in its higher sphere, in the heavens, where those same laws prevail. Whatever is done in accordance with those laws here is recognized as in accordance with them there above, wherever that kingdom extends. Whatever is bound or loosed in accordance with them here, has the sanction of Heaven, and is bound or loosed there. They who, accepting the offers of salvation, become members of the kingdom of Heaven on earth, become by that act members of the kingdom of Heaven above; and they who by rejecting its offers exclude themselves from it here, at the same time close its doors against them in the heavens. In this sense, what is bound or loosed on earth is bound or loosed in heaven.

But how is it that Jesus uses this language in his address to Peter alone? It is addressed to him as the spokesman or representative of the Apostles. As Olshausen has said, "That which at verse 19 is spoken to St. Peter is at Matt. xviii. 18, John xx. 23, addressed to all the Apostles. One cannot therefore find in these words anything that is peculiar to St. Peter; he merely answers as the organ of the college of Apostles, and Christ, acknowledging him as such, replies to him, and speaks through him to them *all*." "That which is through St. Peter bestowed on the Apostles, was again through the Apostles conferred on the whole Church." " That the Apostles then, and their true successors in the Spirit, turned with the word of truth towards one place, and away from another, that they followed up their labors on one man and not on another, in this consisted the binding and loosing. The whole new spiritual community which the Saviour seems to found took its rise from the Apostles and their labors. No one became a Christian save *through them*, and thus the Church through all time is built up in living union with its origin. Christianity is no bare summary of truths and reflections to which a man even in a state of isolation might attain; it is a life-stream which flows through the human race, and its fountains must reach every separate individual who is to be drawn within this circle of life. The Gospel is identified and grown into union with the persons. The explanation, therefore, of the passage which the Protestant Church usually opposes to the view of the Catholics, according to which the *faith of Peter, and the confession of that faith,* is the rock, is entirely the correct one, — only the faith itself and his confession of it must not be regarded as apart from Peter himself personally."

## 21 – 28. — THE HUMILIATION AND SUFFERINGS OF THE MESSIAH.

21. Here commences a new era in the ministry of Jesus. He now for the first time openly and plainly (Mark viii. 32) announced to his disciples the sufferings and death and resurrection from the dead through which he was soon to pass. They could not take in the idea. They remembered his words, but it was not till after his resurrection that they understood what was meant by them. The words were indeed so fearfully distinct, that at first they could not be misinterpreted. Peter, adhering still to his mistaken ideas of the Messiah and his kingdom, and unable to admit the possibil-

ity of such degradation and sufferings as have just been foretold, in the ardent impetuosity which so often showed itself in his conduct, laid hold on Jesus, and remonstrated with him as one does with a friend in despondency. (See Whately, Good and Evil Spirits, p. 135.) "God be gracious to thee, Lord; this thing shall not be to thee." As if he had said, "There is no ground for such gloomy apprehensions. This cannot be." It was an act of ignorant presumption for him to address Jesus in this way. The suggestion evidently touched him most keenly. Turning to Peter, and looking at the disciples (Mark viii. 33), he rebuked Peter, and said to him, "Get thee behind me, Satan; thou art a stumbling-block to me, because thou regardest not the things of God, but the things of men."

Why does Jesus show such extreme sensitiveness? He had used the same expression once before (Matt. iv. 10), in his last reply to the tempter in the wilderness. It has been supposed that it is not applied to Peter so much as to the evil spirit from whom the suggestion came. But the language is *very* explicit. "Turning, he said *to Peter*, Get thee behind me, Satan," thou tempter. Here, as in the other case (iv. 10, see note there), where the same expression is used, there is something which indicates a peculiar sensitiveness, as if Jesus entered enough into the feeling of the disciple to be himself not wholly insensible to the temptation which came here under its most insidious form. "Unquestionably," says Olshausen, "the Saviour must be conceived of as having maintained one *continuous* conflict with temptations. The great periods of such temptations at the commencement and termination of his ministry exhibit, merely in a concentrated form, what ran through his whole life. Here then, for the first time, there meets our view a moment in which temptation assails him by holding forth the possibility of escaping sufferings and death. It was all the more concealed and dangerous that it came to him through the lips of a dear disciple, who had just solemnly acknowledged his divine dignity. From the clear and pure fountain of Christ's life no unholy thought could flow; but inasmuch as he was to be a conqueror victorious over sin, it had to draw near, that in every form he might overthrow it; and upon his human nature, which only by degrees received within itself the whole fulness of the divine life, sin, when it drew near, did make an impression." Instantly, however, in this case, on feeling the power of the temptation, he recognized the source from which it came, and by the harsh word which he used in his reply to Peter, he laid open to him the wicked agency or wrong principle and motive by which the suggestion had been prompted.

Nor does he stop with the disclosure of what is wrong in the disciple. He lays down, 24-28, more strongly, and with words of more fearful and solemn interest, the utter self-renunciation which would be required of his followers. We have no language which comes up to the full force of the idea here set forth. Utterly to deny and renounce themselves, — to take up the cross, that appalling instrument of degradation and torture and death, and follow Him — is what he sets before them as their duty now. But he rises into a region of thought which makes even these sacrifices seem small. "For what," he asks, "shall a man be profited, if he shall gain the whole world and lose his own soul? Or what shall a man give in exchange for his soul? For the Son of man shall come in the glory of his Father with his angels; and then shall he reward every man according to his doing." Here we are lifted up amid the retributions of another world. The sacrifices made here, the obedience, in self-renunciation and holy living, of those who follow him in his conflicts and humiliation, will be rewarded by him, when in that higher world he shall meet them with the ensigns of his greatness, in the glory of his Father, and attended by his angels.

Then, v. 28, by one of those sudden transitions which are so common with him, he comes down from the thought of his kingdom, in its glorious consummation with ransomed souls above, to the time of its establishment and ascendency on earth, i. e. to the time when, with the destruction of Jerusalem, the dispersion of the Jews, and the overthrow of the whole Jewish polity, the sacrifice and the oblation should cease, the old religion no longer be recognized in the region where it had so long prevailed, and the religion of Christ, the Son of man coming in his kingdom, should take its place as the only true worship among men.

## NOTES.

The Pharisees also, with the Sadducees, came, and, tempting, desired him that he would show them a sign from heaven.
2 He answered and said unto them, When it is evening, ye say,
3 It will be fair weather; for the sky is red. And in the morning, It will be foul weather to-day; for the sky is red and lowering. O ye hypocrites! ye can discern the face of the
4 sky, but can ye not discern the signs of the times? A wicked and adulterous generation seeketh after a sign; and there shall no sign be given unto it, but the sign of the prophet Jonas. And he left them and departed.

**1. The Pharisees also, with the Sadducees**] The Pharisees overlaid the Law with their traditions, and thus made it of none effect through their superstitious and hypocritical observances. (See xv. 1-20.) The Sadducees by their unbelief, retaining the letter of the law, but explaining it away in a captious and sceptical spirit, rendered it of none effect. These hostile sects, however, could forget their differences long enough to attack one whose simple, energetic, and life-giving truths laid open the emptiness of their pretensions, and overthrew alike the religious reasonings of both. 2.
**He answered**] Mark (viii. 12) shows how grieved our Saviour was. "Groaning in his spirit, i. e. with a deep sigh, he says, 'Why is this generation seeking for a sign?'" It was not anger, but grief, that tempered his indignation. 3.
**O ye hypocrites**] These words, or rather the one word *hypocrites*, is omitted by Tischendorf. The term *hypocrites* is one which Jesus never in any other case applied to the Sadducees; and it is not probable that it was so applied here. They were rather an unbelieving than a self-righteous and hypocritical sect. He applies the word to the Scribes and Pharisees, but not to them.
4. **the sign of the prophet Jonas**] (See note to xii.

And when his disciples were come to the other side, they had 5
forgotten to take bread. Then Jesus said unto them, Take 6
heed, and beware of the leaven of the Pharisees and of the
Sadducees. And they reasoned among themselves, saying, 7
It is because we have taken no bread. Which when Jesus 8
perceived, he said unto them, O ye of little faith, why reason
ye among yourselves, because ye have brought no bread? Do 9
ye not yet understand, neither remember the five loaves of the
five thousand, and how many baskets ye took up? neither the 10
seven loaves of the four thousand, and how many baskets ye
took up? How is it that ye do not understand that I spake it 11
not to you concerning bread, that ye should beware of the
leaven of the Pharisees and of the Sadducees? Then under- 12
stood they how that he bade them not beware of the leaven
of bread, but of the doctrine of the Pharisees and of the Sadducees.

When Jesus came into the coasts of Cæsarea Philippi, he 13
asked his disciples, saying, Whom do men say that I, the Son
of man, am? And they said, Some say that thou art John 14
the Baptist; some, Elias; and others, Jeremias, or one of the
prophets. He saith unto them, But whom say ye that I am? 15

---

39.) If the account of the prophet Jonah were, like the parable of the Good Samaritan or of the Prodigal Son, not a historical narrative, but a story invented for the purpose of teaching the impossibility of fleeing from the requirements of God; it would none the less serve as a *sign* of the Saviour's death and resurrection from the dead. Some holy man may have been inspired of God to teach this great truth, in the way in which it is there taught, as by a poem or a parable. The lesson is none the less true or important because it is thus taught; nor does Jesus, in alluding to it in the manner he does, express any opinion as to whether it is historical or not.

**7. It is because we have taken no bread**] How could they have forgotten so soon what Jesus had told them? (xv. 16 – 20.) Their dulness in this case shows how they needed line upon line and precept upon precept. We are not then to wonder that he repeated often the same thought in nearly the same words. If, therefore, we find in the different Evangelists nearly the same instructions given under different circumstances, we are not to suppose that one or the other of the writers has made a mistake, but that Jesus, in conformity with the wants of his hearers, repeated his instructions again and again.

9, 10. **baskets**] In the ninth verse it is *cophini*, and in the tenth *spurides*, entirely different words. The same distinction is found in Mark. In Dr. Cureton's Syriac Gospels, the first word is translated *baskets*, the second *panniers*. The distinction is important, as indicating two different miracles.

13. **that I, the Son of man**] Observe how often Jesus uses this expression, as if to indicate his intimate relationship to our humanity. The Son of man, who stood with the Jews for the Mes-

16 And Simon Peter answered and said, Thou art the Christ, the
17 Son of the living God. And Jesus answered and said unto him,
Blessed art thou, Simon Bar-jona; for flesh and blood hath not
18 revealed it unto thee, but my Father, which is in heaven. And

siah, though it was not a term exclusively applied to him. 16. **Thou art the Christ, the Son of the living God**] Here is the counterpart to our Saviour's own expression. He was the Son of God as he was the Son of man, and thus the mediator between God and man. Here is the first and only Gospel creed respecting Jesus, and it gained his earnest and emphatic approval. Perhaps it is in reference to this that St. John more than once in his first Epistle uses this expression : "Whosoever shall confess that Jesus is the Son of God, God dwelleth in him, and he in God." "He that believeth in the Son of God, hath the witness in himself." "These things have I written unto you that believe in the name of the Son of God; that ye may know that ye have eternal life, and that ye may believe in the name of the Son of God." "Who is he that overcometh the world, but he that believeth that Jesus is the Son of God?" It had been well for the peace and unity of the Church, if the successors of the Apostles had been as modest and as truthful as they were in what they required as articles of faith on this great subject. There never can be unity in the Church of Christ till his professed followers consent to come back to the simplicity and power of his instructions as we find them set forth and expounded in the Gospels, and in the other writings of the New Testament. We accept the words of Peter as indorsed and approved by his Master. They were heard from heaven ("This is my beloved Son," Matt. iii. 17) as Jesus came up from the baptismal waters of the Jordan, and the heavens were opened to him. They were repeated again from heaven on the Mountain of Transfiguration. (Matthew xvii. 5.) They are dwelt upon with affecting earnestness by St. John, both in his Gospel and his Epistles. At what was perhaps originally the close of his Gospel (John xx. 31) he says : "But these are written, that ye might believe that Jesus is the Christ, the Son of God; and that believing ye might have life through his name." Why can we not be content with this? Why must we go beneath it with any poor metaphysical analysis of ours to determine precisely what is meant by these great words, and impose our definition on others as an article of faith, without assent to which they cannot be admitted into the Church of Christ, but must, in the blasphemous words of the Athanasian creed, "without doubt perish everlastingly." It is a presumptuous and awful thing for men to impose conditions which Christ never imposed, and to erect barriers which were never authorized by him in the way of admission to his Church.

17. **Simon Bar-jona**] *Simon, son of Jonas.* "It is exceedingly probable that this is intended to form a contrast to the foregoing *Jesus, Son of God. Simon* denotes here, as does *Jesus,* the human personality of the individual ; *son of Jonas* is probably used here in a figurative sense. Primarily it is indeed a genealogical designation (John i. 42, xxi. 16, 17 ); but as Hebrew names generally are descriptive, Christ here looks to the import of the name. Perhaps he referred it to *Jona, a dove ;* and in that case this meaning would arise, 'Thou, Simon, art a child of the Spirit (alluding to the Holy Spirit under the symbol of a dove) : God, the Father of Spirits (Heb. xii. 9), hath revealed himself to thee.' Where God reveals himself there is formed a spiritual man." Olshausen. **flesh and blood**] No man, no merely human faculties, have revealed this to you; " only

I say also unto thee, That thou art Peter; and upon this rock I will build my church, and the gates of hell shall not prevail against it. And I will give unto thee the keys of the kingdom 19 of Heaven; and whatsoever thou shalt bind on earth shall be bound in heaven; and whatsoever thou shalt loose on earth shall be loosed in heaven. Then charged he his disciples, that they 20

the divine can teach us to know the divine." 18. **Thou art Peter** [a rock]; **and upon this rock I will build my church**] From the earliest days of our religion, the Christian Church or community of believers has been represented as a building. The Greek word *ecclesia*, like its English synonyme the church, means either the community of worshippers, or the place in which they meet for worship. The word synagogue, in its Greek form, is applied either to the congregation or to the building in which they assemble. The Greek word ἐκκλησία, or *church*, is seldom used in the New Testament to denote a building set apart for religious purposes. The Christians at that time had no such buildings. But in one case at least the place of worship is called the church (1 Tim. iii. 15): "in the house of God, which is the *church* of the living God." The Church itself, the community of believers, is constantly represented as a building, and its members are represented as living stones of which it is built, or as foundations or pillars on which it rests. "Ye are God's building." (1 Cor. iii. 9.) "Ye are the temple of the living God." (2 Cor. vi 16.) "Ye also, as living stones, are built up a spiritual house." (1 Peter ii. 5.) "And are built upon the foundation of the Apostles and prophets, Jesus Christ himself being the chief corner-stone, in whom all the building, fitly framed together, groweth unto a holy temple in the Lord." (Eph. ii. 20, 21.) "And the wall of the city had twelve foundations, and in them the names of the twelve Apostles of the Lamb." (Rev. xxi. 14.) If we familiarize ourselves with these forms of speech, the words of Jesus in the passage before us will be found to harmonize with them easily, and to express, though by a more pointed and individual application, no more than Paul meant when he spoke of being "built on the foundation of the Apostles and prophets," or than the author of the Apocalypse meant when he spoke of the Twelve Apostles as the twelve foundations of the wall of the new Jerusalem. **the gates of hell**] gates of death, — the power of the kingdom of death. An Oriental form of speech still used when we speak of the Turkish power as "the Ottoman Porte." 19. **And I will give unto thee the keys of the kingdom of Heaven**] "The Jews familiarly used the terms 'to bind' and 'to loose' metaphorically, in the sense of 'to forbid' and 'to permit.' They used them concerning the teachers of their Law, who were supposed capable of explaining its requirements, — what it forbade and what it permitted. When Jesus says, 'I will give you the keys of the kingdom of Heaven,' his meaning is, I will appoint you a minister of my religion, to make known to men the terms on which they may enter the kingdom of Heaven. What follows is an amplification of this idea: — I appoint you a teacher and expositor of my religion, to declare to men its requirements, what it forbids and permits; and, be assured that what is thus forbidden and permitted by you is forbidden and permitted by God. It is of the authority of Peter as a minister of his religion that Jesus speaks, and not of any power to be exercised according to his discretion as an individual." Norton.

21 should tell no man that he was Jesus, the Christ. —— From that time forth began Jesus to show unto his disciples, how that he must go unto Jerusalem, and suffer many things of the elders, and chief priests, and scribes, and be killed, and be 22 raised again the third day. Then Peter took him, and began

---

**20. that they should tell no man that he is the Christ**] The disciples now received him as the Messiah; but the time had not yet come when he was publicly to be declared and recognized as such. When that time should come, his death would be near at hand.

**21. From that time forth**] The altered tone of our Saviour's communications to his disciples, "from that time forth," is very observable. The confession of faith in him as the Messiah, which had been made by Peter, seems to have quickened his sympathy for them, and to have increased his confidence in them. A new era in his intercourse with them had arrived. Hitherto he has alluded mysteriously to his death. But now, as in the strong language of Peter, they have expressed their belief in him as the Christ, the Son of the living God, he sees that the time has come when he must teach them as plainly as possible in regard to the true nature of his mission. Thus he speaks of his humiliation and death here, and shows these things in connection with his exaltation in the next chapter. He wished them to understand what lay before him, and so to understand it in its relation to a true spiritual greatness that they might not be permanently depressed and discouraged by it. They receive his communications at first like men who have been stunned by some dreadful, and, therefore, incredible disclosure. That he, the Son of God, the long-expected Messiah, who was to overcome and rule the world, should die a violent and shameful death, was something too astounding to be believed, or even understood. And that further communication, **and be raised again on the third day**] which to us now throws such a halo over the cross and the tomb, was even more unintelligible to them. After the Transfiguration, it is said (Mark ix. 10), "And they kept that saying with themselves, questioning with one another what the rising from the dead should mean." Again, in reference to the same subject, it is said (Mark ix. 32), "But they understood not that saying, and were afraid to ask him." No plainer language than his could be used; but the idea itself, in its relation to him, was one which they could not take in; and it was not till after his resurrection that his plainest instructions respecting his death could be understood. The thought was too strange and repulsive to be accepted by them. Their first feeling, therefore, when the words were urged and pressed upon them, was one of astonishment and incredulity. It seemed to them that their Master, in a moment of depression and discouragement, had given way to unreasonable apprehensions and forebodings. This supposition alone explains the conduct and the language of Peter. **22. And Peter took him, and began to rebuke him**] For the moment, Peter assumed the attitude of a superior. Not in anger, but with a condescension of sympathy, such as a loving child may exercise towards a suffering parent, or a faithful servant towards an unfortunate and discouraged master, he laid his hand [soothingly] upon him, and said, in opposition to the disheartening words which Jesus had just spoken, "God be gracious to you, Lord: this shall not happen to you." The word ἐπιτιμῶν, which is translated *rebuke*, does not involve the idea of personal anger or of moral disapprobation. Thus, Jesus "rebuked the wind and the sea" (Matt. viii. 26); i. e. he said to them,

to rebuke him, saying, Be it far from thee, Lord; this shall not be unto thee. But he turned and said unto Peter, Get 23 thee behind me, Satan; thou art an offence unto me; for thou savorest not the things that be of God, but those that be of men. —— Then said Jesus unto his disciples, If any man will 24 come after me, let him deny himself, and take up his cross, and

"Peace, be still." (Mark iv. 39.) The word is used to express an earnest remonstrance against what one is doing, or what he might be inclined to do. "And Jesus *charged* (it is the same word) them not to make him known" (Matt. xii. 16); i. e. he remonstrated with them against what he saw was their wish and purpose to make him known. So Peter here remonstrated with Jesus against (what seemed to him) the desponding and humiliating view which he had just given of his ministry. **But he turned and said unto Peter**] The language in Mark (viii. 33) is more graphic: "When he had turned about, and looked on his disciples, he rebuked Peter." He first looked at his disciples. He saw how they were affected by this act of patronizing familiarity and remonstrance on the part of Peter, and that they probably were all moved by the same unworthy view of his words which Peter had taken. He may also himself have sympathized with them, so far as to feel a momentary shudder at the thought of that which afterwards, at its near approach, brought upon him such an agony of grief. And, therefore, to regain instantly his ascendency over them, and on the same instant to shake off the thought which had come to him as the last and sharpest temptation in the wilderness, he uttered the strong words, **Get thee behind me, Satan**] The word *satan* means *adversary* or *seducer*, and is undoubtedly applied here to Peter, who for the moment had put himself in opposition to his Master, and would seduce and draw him away from the path of humiliation and sorrow which he had chosen. **for thou savorest not the things that be of God, but the things that be of men**] *savorest*, to *have the mind and heart fixed upon*. Your mind is fixed on things earthly and human, not on those which are heavenly and divine. Therefore, you cannot take in the true meaning of my words. We must remember, that all this while the disciples are as a school, exercised and disciplined under the various training of their Master. After this private remonstrance with Peter, and through him with his companions, in order to make a still deeper impression upon them, he called the people to him (Mark viii. 34), and in their presence laid down still more strongly the doctrine of self-denial and self-sacrifice, which he has already taught (Matt. x. 37 - 39) with such distinctness and force.

24, 25. These two verses are but carrying out, in its application to all his followers, the great idea which he was to exemplify in his life and death, and which he has just now severely remonstrated with Peter for refusing to accept. It is impossible for us to understand how appalling to the Jews this image of the cross must have been. It was not *their* mode of punishment. It was introduced by the Romans as an instrument of cruelty and oppression, too shameful and too dreadful to be used among their own citizens, and to be inflicted on the lowest criminals and strangers. "We can hardly feel," says Mr. Norton, "the impression which it must have made upon those to whom the horrible torture of crucifixion, as inflicted upon the most wretched outcasts of society, was not an uncommon spectacle." It was connected in their mind with all that was hateful and unjust in a foreign domination; and nothing

MATTHEW XVI. 301

25 follow me. For whosoever will save his life shall lose it; and
26 whosoever will lose his life, for my sake, shall find it. For
what is a man profited, if he shall gain the whole world, and

---

could be more abhorrent to all their most cherished convictions than that their Messiah, who was to break every yoke and free them from foreign rule, should himself be subjected to this vilest and most painful of deaths, and that he should hold up this to his followers as what they also must be ready to endure in their devotion to him. Nothing shows more powerfully the personal and moral ascendency of Jesus over those around him, than the fact that, with such images of reward as this, he could still bind them to him. 25. **Whosoever will save his life**] We have already (Matt. x. 39) commented on this passage. The words are repeated here with a slight alteration, and bearing with a mighty pressure on what he has already foretold respecting his own fate. The meaning of the word ψυχή, which is translated *life* here, and *soul* in the next verse, is to be borne in mind. There is in the Greek, as also in the Syriac, a nice distinction which is lost in our English version. "Whosoever may wish [ἐὰν θέλῃ] to save his life [soul] shall lose it; and whosoever will lose his life [soul] for my sake shall find it." It is not, *he who may wish to lose his life* for his sake : he does not require that of us. He only requires that we shall not wish to save it at the expense of what is better than life. He has spoken of the cross. He now speaks of the *life* which may be lost upon it; but in the same sentence uses the same word to designate the *life* which makes that earthly, mortal life of no account. 26. **For what is a man profited**] Literally, "What *shall* a man be profited," &c. There are those who translate *psychē* here by the word *life*, because it is the same word that is so rendered in the previous verse. But this does not convey the true meaning so well as our common version. We must think of him who spoke, and who by his spiritual perceptions reaching into higher worlds, saw the *soul* saved by that which seemed to destroy it, and lost by that which to mortal eyes seemed to save it. And when the soul is lost everything is lost ; for "what shall a man be profited if he gain the whole world and lose his own soul? or what shall a man give in exchange for his soul?" There is no more impressive and awful passage in the sacred writings, and few which are more perfectly rendered in our English version. Verbal comments upon it are poor and small. They who would force it into a proof-text for the doctrine of everlasting damnation, and they who would explain it away as referring to nothing beyond this world, show themselves alike insensible to its power. Its solemn and dreadful appeal should come home to every soul that is in danger of wasting its immortal energies on the things of time, or of giving to them more of its affections than is consistent with its highest good. A very striking illustration of the manner in which a man may ruin his soul in this world, and have no suspicion of the work of death which is going on within the fair and prosperous exterior of his life, is given by Archbishop Whately in his Annotations on Lord Bacon's Essays. "Most persons," he says, "know that every *butterfly* (the Greek name for which, it is remarkable, signifies the same also as the *soul,—psychē*) comes from a grub, or caterpillar ; in the language of naturalists, called a *larva.* The last name (which signifies literally a *mask*) was introduced by Linnæus, because the caterpillar is a kind of outer covering, or disguise of the future butterfly within. For it has been ascertained by

lose his own soul? or what shall a man give in exchange for his soul? For the Son of man shall come in the glory of his 27

curious microscopic examination, that a distinct butterfly, only undeveloped and not full grown, is contained within the body of the caterpillar; that this latter has its own organs of digestion, respiration, &c., suitable to its *larva* life, quite distinct from, and independent of, the future butterfly which it encloses. When the proper period arrives, and the life of the insect, in this its first stage, is to close, it becomes what is called a *pupa*, enclosed in a crysalis or cocoon (often composed of silk, as is that of the silk-worm which supplies us that important article), and lies torpid for a time within its natural coffin, from which it issues, at the proper period, as a perfect butterfly. But sometimes this process is marred. There is a numerous tribe of insects, well known to naturalists, called ichneumon-flies, which in their larva state are *parasitical;* that is, inhabit and feed on other larvæ. The ichneumon-fly, being provided with a long, sharp sting, which is in fact an *ovipositor* (egg-layer), pierces with this the body of a caterpillar in several places, and deposits her eggs, which are there hatched, and feed as grubs (larvæ) on the inward parts of their victim. A most wonderful circumstance connected with this process is, that a caterpillar that has been thus attacked goes on feeding, and apparently thriving quite as well, during the whole of its larva-life, as those that have escaped. For, by a wonderful provision of instinct, the ichneumon-grubs within do not injure any of the organs of the larva, but feed only on the future butterfly enclosed within it. And consequently, it is hardly possible to distinguish a caterpillar which has these enemies within it from those that are untouched. But when the period arrives for the close of the larva-life, the difference appears. You may often observe the common cabbage caterpillars retiring, to undergo their change, to some •sheltered spot, — such as the walls of a summer-house ; and some of them — those that have escaped the parasites (the other grubs which are injured sometimes do the same) — assuming the pupa-state, from which they emerge, butterflies. Of the unfortunate caterpillar that has been preyed upon, nothing remains but an empty skin. The hidden butterfly has been secretly consumed. Now is there not something analogous to this wonderful phenomenon in the condition of some of our race? May not a man have a kind of secret enemy within his own bosom, destroying his soul, *psyche,* — though without interfering with his well-being during the present stage of his existence ; and whose presence may never be detected till the time arrives when the *last great change* should take place?" 27. **For the Son of man shall come**] For this world is not all. This mortal life is nothing compared with that which rises over it. It is worthy of notice how every sentence here, in verses 25, 26, 27, is introduced by a *for*, each one taking us up yet farther into the height of its sublime argument. " If any one wishes to come after me, let him deny himself, and take up his cross and follow me;" "for he who wishes to save his life shall lose it ;" and then everything is gone, "*for* what shall a man be profited, if he gain the whole world, and lose his own soul?" "*For* the Son of man shall come in the glory of his Father, with his angels, and then shall he reward every man according to his works." What a contrast this closing picture of the Son of man coming in the glory of his Father, with that in verse 21, of his suffering and dying at the hands of wicked men! How are we lifted up by his words above all earthly considerations of gain or loss, as we see him rising through the same path of humiliation and suffering and death, which he assigns to his followers, and coming with his angels to reward every man accord-

Father, with his angels; and then he shall reward every man
28 according to his works. Verily I say unto you, there be some

---

ing to his works! **according to his works**] Literally, *according to his doing.* Works, perhaps, give us too superficial an idea of the *doing* or *working* which begins in the soul of a man, — his inmost life, — and reaches out through all his deeds. 28. **there be some standing here which shall not taste of death, till**] Thus far every sentence in this discourse has been closely and logically connected with that which went before. We have been taken through the scene of our probation here, to that of our retribution hereafter. But in this sentence there is a sudden, and apparently abrupt change from one great subject to another. These apparently violent transitions are not uncommon in our Saviour's discourses. But if we could place ourselves at his point of vision, we should see how natural and easy the transition is. The central principles of a great thought connect together topics which, to a superficial eye, seem to have no relation to one another. In order to understand the transition, we must not only learn, but make ourselves familiar with, the different applications of the expression, *the kingdom of Heaven,* and of the similar expression, *the coming of the Son of man.* The kingdom of Heaven is the religion of Jesus in the individual soul, or in the community of believers called the Church, — first on earth, and then in the heavens. When the kingdom of Heaven, or the religion of Jesus, with its divine truths and agencies, comes to any one, and is received by him, it is to him the coming of the Son of man in his kingdom. When the religion of Jesus, or the kingdom of God, finds its more perfect consummation in him on his leaving this world and entering into a higher condition of being, it is to him the coming of the Son of man in the glory of his Father with his angels, who are then first revealed to his spiritual perceptions. So the kingdom of Heaven, or the religion of Jesus, may be viewed, on a larger scale, in its relation to the human family. When it took the place of the old Mosaic dispensation, as it did at the destruction of Jerusalem and the dispersion of the Jews, and was left free to unfold its powers and establish itself in the earth, that was, in a peculiar sense, the coming of the Son of man in his kingdom, to the earth. And when, through successive ages, the whole work of redemption is accomplished, and the whole family of man are grouped together in thought, and placed before the eye as finishing their earthly course, and entering on a further stage of existence, then, in reference to them, the Son of man is said to come in the glory of his Father, and all the holy angels with him. Whether by *his coming* we are to understand his personal presence in these different ways, or only that he should be present in his religion, his spirit, and his teachings, which should be, like his disciples, his representatives among men, is not distinctly taught. We believe that he meant to intimate his actual and personal presence in his religion and his Church with his followers on earth and in Heaven. We know too little of the power which a spiritual being like Christ may have of diffusing and extending his personal and conscious presence, to oppose these views by objections of this sort, which carry no reasonable weight with them. Now, if it be not presumptuous in us so to speak, drawing our inferences not from any data of ours, but from the forms of expression which he has used, we may suppose that the mind of Jesus, equally at home in all these developments of his religion, or different forms of his coming, connects them all together as parts of one great plan, and passes easily from one to another. In asking what a man could

standing here which shall not taste of death, till they see the Son of man coming in his kingdom.

---

give in exchange for his soul, he follows him beyond this mortal life, and speaks of meeting him there to reward him according to his works. Then pausing a little, and thinking of the time when the Jewish nation shall be dispersed, their city and altars overthrown, and his own religion take the place of the ancient worship; and seeing around him some who shall outlive the bloody changes by which his kingdom is thus to be established on the earth, he, in verse 28, gives utterance to this other thought, "Verily I say unto you, There be some standing here who shall not taste of death, till they see the Son of man coming [not in the glory of his Father with his angels, but] in his kingdom." This is the same coming of the Son of man as that referred to in Matt. x. 23. In these sudden transitions from one theme to another, we must remember that the Evangelists do not give all the words that Jesus spoke, but only the salient points, often leaving the connecting and explanatory clauses and events wholly out of sight. The events related in this chapter may have extended through several weeks, and must have occupied a number of days.

## CHAPTER XVII.

### 1–9. — THE TRANSFIGURATION.

THERE has been much discussion in regard to the place where this remarkable event occurred. Traditions reaching back nearly to the middle of the fourth century have fixed on Mount Tabor as the spot. It is thus referred to before the end of the fourth century by Cyril of Jerusalem, and by St. Jerome who resided in Palestine. A little more than two hundred years later, mention is made of it by Antoninus. Martyr speaks of three churches erected on Mount Tabor, corresponding to the three tabernacles which Peter proposed to erect. But, as Dr. Robinson in his Biblical Researches, Vol. III. pp. 220, 221, has shown, from an early date, and down to the time of Josephus, the summit of Mount Tabor was occupied by a fortified city. It could not therefore have been the "high mountain" here mentioned by the Evangelists. Dr. Robinson supposes that the "Mount of Transfiguration is rather to be sought somewhere around the northern part of the lake, not very far from Cæsarea Philippi, where there are certainly mountains enough."

The last locality that has been mentioned in the Gospel narrative, xvi. 13, is Cæsarea Philippi. Jesus had gone up from Bethsaida at the northeast corner of the lake to the village of Cæsarea, which was at the eastern source of the Jordan, and near the foot of Mount Hermon. Six days after the conversation recorded as having taken place in that locality, occurred the scene of the Transfiguration. Those few days may have been spent by Jesus partly in the villages instructing the people and healing their sick, and partly in private and confidential intercourse with his disciples amid the solitudes of the mountains. This was the extreme northern limit of his ministry. At length, the time having now come when he must set his face for the last time towards Jerusalem, wishing to make on the minds of the leading disciples an impression which could never be effaced, and seeking also, as he often did before his heaviest trials, for the inward supports which came from retirement and prayer, he took Peter and James and John, and went up into a high mountain to pray. May not this mountain have been Mount Hermon? Stanley, in his Sinai and Palestine, pp. 391, 392, says: "It is impossible to look up from the plain to the towering peaks of Hermon, almost the only mountain which deserves the name in Palestine, and one of whose ancient titles was derived from this circumstance, and not be struck with its appropriateness to the scene. That magnificent height — mingling with all the views of Northern Palestine from Shechem upwards — though often alluded to as the northern barrier of the Holy Land, is connected with no historical event in the Old or New Testament. Yet this fact of its rising high above all the other hills of Palestine, and of its setting the last limit to the wanderings of Him who was sent only to the lost sheep of the house of Israel, falls in with the supposition which the words inevitably force upon us. High up on its southern slopes there must be many a point where the disciples could be taken 'apart by themselves.' Even the transient comparison of the celestial splendor with the snow, where alone it could be seen in Palestine, should not, perhaps, be wholly overlooked. At any rate, the remote heights above the sources of the Jordan witnessed the moment, when, his work in his own peculiar sphere being ended, he set his face for the last time 'to go up to Jerusalem.'"

But how are we to interpret the account of the Transfiguration itself? Dr. Furness entitles it, "The Dream of Peter." In his History of Jesus, p. 155, he supposes that Peter, after a time of great mental excitement, falling asleep, "began to dream; and in the visions of his sleep, his eyes having closed, perhaps, while fixed on the venerated form of his Master, and his mind being filled with the idea of the Messiah's glory, he still saw Jesus; but now all arrayed in robes of dazzling whiteness, in all that external glory associated with the person of the Messiah. And there appeared also to Peter, in his dream, two others, who, he thought, were Moses and Elias; and they conversed with Jesus about what was to take place, — that mysterious decease at Jerusalem. While he was thus dreaming, a cloud came up, and it thundered; and the sound, startling the dreamer from his sleep, was instantly connected, as is not uncommon in dreams, with an articulate voice," &c., &c.

Dr. Palfrey regards it rather as a visionary representation given for the encouragement of the disciples. In his relation between Judaism and Christianity, pp. 92, 93, he says: "It was fit that they should be instructed and reawakened by a glorious vision, presenting to them their Master, not with the environments of regal pomp, but as the equal associate of the venerated ancient teachers of their faith. And such being the case, I understand further, that the presence of Moses and Elijah was visionary, and not real; that it was not Moses and Elijah actually conversing with Jesus that the Apostles saw, but that a vision of such a scene was presented to their view."

Neander, in his Life of Jesus, though he rather inclines to regard the whole as an objective historical event, makes a supposition which embraces the substance of these two views. The disciples, he supposes, were deeply impressed by the prayer of Jesus. "His countenance beamed with radiance, and he appeared to them glorified and transfigured with celestial light. At last, worn out with fatigue, they fell asleep; and the impressions of the Saviour's prayer and of their conversation with him were reflected in a vision thus: Beside him, who was the end of the Law and the Prophets, appeared Moses and Elias in celestial splendor; for the glory that streamed forth from him was reflected back upon the Law, and the Prophets foretold the fate that awaited him at Jerusalem. In the mean time they awoke, and, in a half-waking condition, saw and heard what followed." "Still," he adds, "the difficulty remains, that the phenomena, if simply psychological, should have appeared to all the three Apostles precisely in the same form. It is, perhaps, not improbable, that the account came from the lips of Peter, who is the prominent figure in the narrative."

The more carefully we examine the narratives of the different Evangelists, the greater does the difficulty in the way of these views appear. In the first place, the account is given by each of the three Evangelists with no word to indicate that it is not a narrative of real events. Jesus, with his three most intimate disciples, went up into a high mountain by themselves to pray. And while praying he was transfigured before them. His countenance was changed, shining as the sun, and his garments were white as the light, or, as Mark says, "exceeding white, like snow, so as no fuller on earth could whiten them." And Luke speaks of their overpowering brightness as of lightning flashes. And behold there were two men talking with him, Moses and Elijah, who appeared to them in glory, and who spake of his departure which he was to accomplish at Jerusalem. Peter and those who were with him *had been* — not *were*, as in our translation — weighed down with sleep. But when they were fully awake (Luke ix. 32) they saw his glory, and the two men that were standing with him. And as they — the two men — were departing from him, Peter, in his fear not knowing what to say, said, "Lord, it is good for us to be here; let us make here three tabernacles, one for thee, one for Moses, and one for Elijah." While he was yet speaking, a shining cloud; or, according to Griesbach's reading, a cloud of light overshadowed them. They were filled with awe as they entered it. And there came from it a voice, saying, "This is my beloved Son, in whom I am well pleased; hear ye him." And when the disciples heard it, they fell upon their faces and were exceedingly afraid. Then Jesus came and touched them, and said, " Rise, be not afraid," when they raised their eyes, and saw Jesus alone. And as they were going down from the mountain, Jesus charged them saying, "Tell what you have seen to no one, till the Son of man has risen from the dead." "And they kept it to themselves (Mark ix. 10), reasoning together what the rising from the dead was."

The particulars of the transaction are given with minuteness and precision. It could not have appeared to one only, for "Peter and they who were with him" (Luke ix. 32) saw his glory and the two men that were standing with him." "And when the disciples" (not *one* of them) " heard," &c. they fell on *their* face. Nor could it have been a dream; for, apart from the improbability of the same dream occurring to them all, Luke says expressly, that, though they had been heavy with sleep, they now *when fully awake* saw his glory, &c. Neither could it have been merely a vision; for they not only saw Moses and Elijah, but also heard what they said, and the subject of their conversation is reported to us: "They spake of his departure," &c. What the disciples heard from the cloud is also precisely reported. Besides, if the whole matter had been only a dream, or a scene only subjectively present to their minds, if "the presence of Moses and Elias was visionary and not real," why should it occupy the conspicuous and significant place it does in three of the Gospels? Still more, if " only a vision of such a scene was presented to their view, how was it possible that Jesus could attach so much importance to it as he did in charging the disciples to tell no one of it till after he had risen from the dead? Among the incidental indications of truthfulness in the narratives themselves, are the words in Mark, — "they reasoned among themselves what the rising from the dead should mean." How natural that they should thus reason together, and yet who, writing long after the event, and when the resurrection from the dead had become a common idea, could have thought to mention it unless it were a fact?

The only objection to receiving these accounts as faithful historical narratives arises from the character of the facts themselves. They do not fall within the sphere of our common thought and experience. But one great object of Christ's coming into the world was to enlarge the sphere of our conceptions, to free us from the narrow, blinding, and despotic dominion of the senses, and open to us a glimpse at least of the great and spiritual realities by which we are environed. The disciples could not be reconciled to the idea of a suffering and crucified Messiah. They were perplexed and filled with grief by what Jesus had told them of his approaching death. Here for a moment the chosen three were allowed, with their quickened perceptions, to look through the veil, to see the glorified forms of two persons who had passed from the earth centuries before, and to hear them talk with Jesus of his departure which he was about to accomplish at Jerusalem. And although in their troubled and bewildered apprehension they did not then understand fully the import of what they saw and heard, yet afterwards they remembered it with a new perception of its significance, and recorded it for the instruction of those who should come after them. (See John i. 14, 2 Peter i. 16-18.) For once, as an emblem to all times, of the Divine glory in which he lived, the spirit of Jesus shone through and irradiated its mortal covering, lighting up his countenance till it was like the sun, and his very garments were, like the lightning, of a dazzling brightness, so as no fuller on earth could whiten them. In associating with him Moses and Elijah in their glorified forms, the Transfiguration furnishes a connecting link between two worlds. By these visible images of the departed it helps us in our conceptions of a spiritual and immortal condition, and enables us in our thought to people with bright and living forms the otherwise void and shadowy regions of the dead. Not only is Christ transfigured, and Moses and Elijah made visible, but a whole world of spiritual thought and life is revealed as filled, not merely with the one infinite intelligence, but with the tender sympathies and affections which drew those ancient benefactors of mankind to talk with Jesus when the time of his heaviest sorrows was at hand.

The place which this event holds in the Gospel narrative is not without its significance. Jesus had been speaking of his approaching death and of the entire self-renunciation which he required of his followers. They could not understand him. He led them away therefore by themselves. Leaving the populous places about Cæsarea Philippi, he probably took them into the mountain solitudes, and during a period of six days was imparting to them there instructions, of which no record has come down to us. Then, as a teacher sometimes does with the most advanced of his class, he chose out three of his disciples to impress on them a lesson which they alone were at all prepared to receive. He leads them up into a high mountain, and, while he is praying, his countenance glows with a celestial radiance, spirits of just men made perfect stand by him, and a voice is heard speaking to them from heaven. They did not fully understand it then, but after his death and resurrection from the dead had laid open to them its meaning, they publish their account of it to enrich forever the minds of Christian believers.

"The design of this miracle," says Mr. Norton, "appears to have been, — 1. By a scene which should make the most powerful impression on the senses and the imagination, — a 'sign from heaven' such as the Pharisees had demanded, — to produce in the minds of the three leading Apostles who were present with Jesus the strongest conviction of his Divine mission, and to prepare them, as far as possible, for the overwhelming disappointment of their cherished hopes in his approaching death; 2. To show them that a close relation existed between himself and those earlier messengers of God whom they held in peculiar reverence, Moses, the founder, and Elijah, the restorer of their ancient religion, who had prepared the way for him who 'came not to annul the law and the prophets, but to perfect;' 3. To give the disciples direct and palpable evidence of the reality of a future life."

### 10 – 13. — The Coming of Elijah.

"It would," says Lightfoot in his note on this passage, "be an infinite task to produce all the passages out of the Jewish writings, which one might, concerning the expected coming of Elias." The following, given here in a condensed form, is among the passages quoted by Lightfoot from the Jewish writers. "God shall restore the soul of Elias, which ascended of old into heaven, into a created body like to his former body, and shall send him to Israel before the day of judgment, and he shall admonish both the fathers and the children together, to turn to God." It was the expectation of the Jews that at the coming of the Messiah there should be a resurrection from the dead, and that Elias was to come before the resurrection. When Jesus, therefore, tells the disciples to say nothing about what they had seen till he had risen from the dead, they immediately in their minds connect this rising from the dead with the expected resurrection, and ask, If this appearance of Elias is all, and we are not permitted to speak of it till after the resurrection, how is it that the Scribes say that Elias must come first, i. e. before the resurrection? Jesus replies, nearly in the words of Mal. iv. 6, "Elias is coming, and will restore all things," or put all things in order. He merely repeats this passage which the Jewish teachers were accustomed to use, to show, in reply to the disciples' question, why Elijah was expected first. Then he goes on in his own language to give his own view, which is, that the prophecy is already accomplished, that Elias has already come, and that the Jewish teachers who had made such account of his coming did not recognize him while he was with them, but did to him what they chose, and that in like manner the Messiah, the Son of man, would also suffer from them. "Then understood they that he spake of John the Baptist." Luke (i. 17) shows in what sense Elias was to come: "And he (John) shall go before him in the spirit and power of Elias."

### 24 – 27. — THE TRIBUTE-MONEY AND THE FISH.

The tribute-money was not paid to the Roman government, but for the Jewish and temple worship. (See Ex. xxx. 13, 2 Kings xii. 4, 2 Chron. xxiv. 6, 9.) Jesus in his conversation with Peter refers to his peculiar position as the Son of God, so as to impress it on the minds of his disciples. "It was necessary for him," says Mr. Norton, "to direct their thoughts to the fact of his and their extraordinary relation to God, and the peculiarity in his manner of doing it upon this occasion would tend to make a deeper impression on their minds than a simple declaration of the truth might have done."

We agree with Olshausen in considering this the most difficult miracle in the Gospels. It, more than any other, has an air of marvellousness about it such as we find in later and apocryphal writings. But there is no reason to question the genuineness of the passage. There is nothing derogatory to the Saviour's character in the performance of such an act. The Gospels are intended to meet the wants of all classes of minds, from the most ignorant to those most advanced in intellectual and moral culture. That which is needed to impress the ignorant may seem to others trivial and unworthy of a Divine author, while that which is the most striking evidence of a Divine authority to him who has made the greatest advances in spiritual improvement may be wholly without meaning to his ignorant neighbor. This, under the circumstances of the case, may have been the most effectual way of impressing important truths on the mind of Peter. Peter had made an inconsiderate promise. May it not be also that Jesus took that opportunity to show that even a hasty promise, if it involved no act of injustice to others, was in his sight so sacred that a miracle was to be performed, rather than that a disciple of his should fail to keep it? Bengel significantly says, "Men who are occupied in worldly affairs most easily take offence at the saints when money is in question."

## NOTES.

And after six days Jesus taketh Peter, James, and John his brother, and bringeth them up into a high mountain apart, and was transfigured before them; and his face did shine as 2 the sun, and his raiment was white as the light. And, behold, 3 there appeared unto them Moses and Elias, talking with him. Then answered Peter, and said unto Jesus, Lord, it is good 4 for us to be here; if thou wilt, let us make here three tabernacles; one for thee, and one for Moses, and one for Elias. While he yet spake, behold, a bright cloud overshadowed 5 them; and, behold, a voice out of the cloud, which said, This

---

5. **a voice out of the cloud**] "A voice came from heaven, first, chap. iii. 17; secondly, at this central period; thirdly, and lastly,

MATTHEW XVII. 315

is my beloved Son, in whom I am well pleased; hear ye him.
6 And when the disciples heard it, they fell on their face, and
7 were sore afraid. And Jesus came and touched them, and
8 said, Arise, and be not afraid. And when they had lifted up
9 their eyes, they saw no man, save Jesus only. And as they
came down from the mountain, Jesus charged them, saying,
Tell the vision to no man, until the Son of man be risen again
10 from the dead. —— And his disciples asked him saying, Why
11 then say the scribes that Elias must first come? And Jesus
answered and said unto them, Elias truly shall first come, and
12 restore all things; but I say unto you, that Elias is come
already, and they knew him not, but have done unto him what-

---

a little before our Lord's Passion, John xii. 28. After each of these voices from heaven, fresh virtue shone forth in Jesus, fresh ardor and fresh sweetness in his discourses and actions, fresh progress." Bengel. 9. **the vision**] "What things they had seen." Mark ix. 9. 11. **Elias truly shall first come, and restore all things**] But how did John the Baptist *restore all things?* "Seminaliter," says Bengel, i. e. "he will sow the seed of these things: he will initiate them, as the preparation for what is to follow." 12. **but I say unto you, that Elias is come already**] "With the preaching of John the Baptist, as described by the Jewish and Gospel writers, and the history of the eventful era announced by him, is associated the memorable prophecy in Malachi: 'Behold, I will send my messenger, and he shall prepare the way before me: and the Lord, whom ye seek, shall suddenly come to his temple, and the messenger of the covenant, whom ye delight in [or wish for]: behold, he shall come, saith the Lord of Hosts. But who may abide the day of his coming? And who shall stand when he appeareth? For he is like a refiner's fire, and like fuller's soap; and he shall sit as a refiner and purifier of silver: and he shall purify the sons of Levi, and purge them as gold and silver, that they may offer unto the Lord an offering in righteousness.' In

his denunciations of divine retribution, the prophet sets forth the prominent sins of the times referred to in his prediction, and it will be perceived that they are principally those which Christ especially noticed in his reprobation of the degenerate people of his day: 'I will be a swift witness against the sorcerers, and against the adulterers, and against false swearers, and against those that oppress the hireling in his wages, the widow, and the fatherless, and that turn aside the stranger from his right, and fear not me, saith the Lord of Hosts.' These words find a correspondence in those bold and cutting rebukes in which our Lord exposed the profligacy of his own times, and which he so pointedly directed against adulterers, and those who betrayed others into adultery by their false doctrines of divorcement, — against false swearers and those who encouraged false swearing by their absurd distinctions between oaths, — against those who wronged the fatherless and the widow, and who were the signal objects of his most solemn denunciations.

"But perhaps no portion of the prophecy exhibits more striking coincidences with the events of the Gospel age than the conclusion: 'Behold, the day cometh that shall burn as an oven; and all the proud, yea, and all that do wickedly, shall be stubble: and the day that cometh shall burn

soever they listed. Likewise shall also the Son of man suffer of them. Then the disciples understood that he spake unto ¹³ them of John the Baptist.

And when they were come to the multitude, there came to ¹⁴ him a certain man, kneeling down to him, and saying, Lord, ¹⁵ have mercy on my son; for he is lunatic and sore vexed; for ofttimes he falleth into the fire, and oft into the water. And I ¹⁶ brought him to thy disciples, and they could not cure him. Then Jesus answered and said, O faithless and perverse gen- ¹⁷

---

them up, saith the Lord of Hosts, that it shall leave them neither root nor branch. But unto you that fear my name shall the Sun of Righteousness arise with healing in his wings. . . . . . Behold, I will send you Elijah the prophet, before the coming of the great and dreadful day of the Lord; and he shall turn the heart of the fathers to the children, and the heart of the children to their fathers, lest I come and smite the earth with a curse;'— or, in other words, so as to prevent, if possible, or take the appropriate means to prevent, the infliction of punishment on the *land*,— not *earth*, as the original, not only here, but often elsewhere also, is inappropriately rendered in the common version of the Scriptures.

"When this prophecy was uttered, the Jews had returned from that long captivity in Babylon to which the predictions of national judgments in the Old Testament so frequently refer. But the spirit of prophecy foresaw in the distant future a still heavier judgment awaiting them for their sins. Such a calamity actually befell them in the Gospel age, — a calamity far exceeding any they had ever before experienced. Moreover, not many years anterior to this catastrophe, a remarkable person, styling himself a messenger from God, and who authenticated his commission by miracles, made his appearance in Judæa, preaching everywhere a sublime system of piety and virtue, severely reproving the people for their immoralities, and denouncing the corruption of the priesthood. Thus was it foretold. As his immediate precursor, came also one who might be termed another Elijah, from the strong resemblance he bore to that stern and minatory prophet, assailing the vices of the day with remarkable zeal and boldness, and endeavoring to persuade the Jews to a general reformation as the only means of averting an impending destruction which would prove, he observed, as 'an axe laid to the roots of the trees.' A personage every way resembling him had been announced by the Messianic prophets, and our Saviour declared that John was the individual foretold.

"Does any one say that all this is certainly quite remarkable, but that still it is possible that John, notwithstanding he was a just man, and held in the highest reverence, might have been misled by an ardent imagination in supposing himself the Forerunner predicted? One thing is plain. The destruction of Jerusalem shortly after his day was no illusion of the imagination. The catastrophe really took place, whatever may be thought of its being a fulfilment of the judgment denounced by Malachi. It followed the preaching of John, precisely as it had been predicted that a tremendous calamity to Judæa would follow the preaching of a prophet whose description strikingly answers to that of the Baptist. And as that terrible event which overthrew and scattered the Jewish nation, soon after the time of the Forerunner, was no matter of fancy, neither could any imagination have foreseen it." Nichols's Hours with

eration! how long shall I be with you? how long shall I suffer
18 you? Bring him hither to me. And Jesus rebuked the devil,
and he departed out of him; and the child was cured from
19 that very hour.—— Then came the disciples to Jesus apart,
20 and said, Why could not we cast him out? And Jesus said
unto them, Because of your unbelief; for verily I say unto
you, if ye have faith as a grain of mustard seed, ye shall say
unto this mountain, Remove hence to yonder place, and it
shall remove; and nothing shall be impossible unto you.
21 Howbeit this kind goeth not out, but by prayer and fasting.
22 And while they abode in Galilee, Jesus said unto them, The
23 Son of man shall be betrayed into the hands of men; and they
shall kill him, and the third day he shall be raised again. And
they were exceeding sorry.
24 And when they were come to Capernaum, they that received

the Evangelists. Vol. I. pp. 270 – 274. 14 – 21. The critical notice of this miracle belongs more properly to Mark ix. 14 – 29, where the particulars are given more fully.

**17. how long shall I be with you?**] The following remark of Bengel here may be true, though it belongs to a province in which we should be slow to speculate. "He was in haste to return to the Father; yet he knew that he could not effect his departure until he had conducted his disciples into a state of faith. Their slowness was painful to him." Something of the same feeling is shown in John xiv. 9: "Have I been so long time with you, and yet hast thou not known me, Philip?" **how long shall I suffer you?**] how long shall I put up, or bear, with you? The change from the Mountain of Transfiguration to this scene of misery and unbelief was very great, and evidently a most trying one to our Saviour. The very susceptibilities by which he was capable of being lifted up into such a height of joy and glory would make him feel more painfully the contrast here. How natural is this outburst of holy impatience, and yet how different from the passionless level in which a writer of fiction would be likely to cause so exalted a being as Jesus to move! This sudden expression of feeling gives a most valuable insight into the life of Jesus; and while it shows how strong his emotions were, it also shows that his struggle against temptation was not confined to the wilderness. "Only he can speak thus," says Stier, "who, as the Holy One among sinners, bore the burden of all, and whose whole life was in the innermost sense, from the very first, a profound *suffering* through the feeling and enduring of sin. Thus, according to the Father's counsel, it was necessary in this word, which was drawn from the usually closed depths of his heart, immediately after the revelation of his glory, to manifest the glory also of his human endurance, the pain of divine love in his human nature, which was alike strongly susceptible of this on account of meekness and purity. If we had not this word, and that other in Luke xii. 50, we should want the true, entire insight into the self-denying, atoning nature even of his whole earthly course in our flesh and blood. What complainings, known only to the Father, does this single expression, which he neither can nor will restrain, presuppose?" 21. **but by prayer and fasting**] by entire devotion to God, and self-

tribute-money came to Peter, and said, Doth not your Master
25 pay tribute? He saith, Yes. And when he was come into
the house, Jesus prevented him, saying, What thinkest thou,

---

renunciation. 24. **tribute-money**] τὰ δίδραχμα, the *two-drachma*, a sum paid annually by the Jews of twenty years old and upwards towards the Temple in Jerusalem, Exod. xxx. 11–16; 2 Kings xii. 4; 2 Chron. xxiv. 6–9. The original sum was half a shekel, which was not a coin, but a certain weight of silver. "In the time of the Maccabees (1 Macc. xv. 6) the Jews received the privilege, or won the right, from the kings of Syria of coining their own money, and the shekels, half-shekels, and quarter-shekels, now found in the cabinets of collectors, are to be referred to this period. These growing scarce, and not being coined any more, it became the custom to estimate the temple dues as two-drachms, a sum actually somewhat larger than the half-shekel, as those who have compared together the weights of the existing specimens have found." As the produce of the miracle was to pay for two persons, the sum required was four drachmas, or a whole shekel; and the *stater*, which is translated *piece of money*, in verse 27, is just that sum. Josephus (Ant. XVIII. 9. 1) speaks of this as an annual payment in his time; and Philo, also, "who tells us how conscientiously and ungrudgingly it was paid by the Jews of the Dispersion, as well as by the Jews of Palestine, so that in almost every city there was a sacred treasury for the collection of these dues, some of which came from cities beyond the limits of the Roman empire." **Doth not your Master pay tribute?** "We may presume," says Trench, "that our Lord and Peter, with others also, it is most probable, of his disciples, were now returning to Capernaum, which was 'his city,' after one of his usual absences. The Lord passed forward without question, but the collectors detained Peter, who, having lingered a little behind, was now following his Lord. Chrysostom suggests that this question [that of the collectors to Peter] may be a rude and ill-mannered one: 'Does your Master count himself exempt from the payment of the ordinary dues? We know his freedom: does he mean to exercise it here?' Yet, on the other hand, it may have been, as I suppose it was, the exact contrary. Having seen or heard of the wonderful works which Christ did, they may really have been uncertain in what light to regard him, whether to claim from him the money or not; and in this doubting and inquiring spirit, they may have put the question to Peter. This Theophylact suggests. But, after all, we want that which the history has not given, the *tone* in which the question was put, to know whether it was a rude one or the contrary. To their demand Peter, overhasty, as was so often the case, at once replied that his Master would pay the money. No doubt zeal for his Master's honor made him so quick to pledge his Lord; he was confident that his piety would make him prompt to every payment sanctioned and sanctified by God's Law. Yet at the same time there was here, on the part of the apostle, a failing to recognize the higher dignity of his Lord: it was not in this spirit that he had said a little while before, 'Thou art the Christ, the Son of the living God.' He understood not, or at least for the time had lost sight of, his Lord's true position and dignity, that he was a Son over his own house, not a servant in another's house. . . . . . . It was not for Him who was 'greater than the temple,' and himself the true temple (John ii. 21), identical with it according to its spiritual significance, and in whom the Shekinah glory dwelt, to pay dues for the support of that other temple built with hands, which was now fast losing its significance, since the true taber-

Simon? Of whom do the kings of the earth take custom or tribute? of their own children, or of strangers? Peter saith
26 unto him, Of strangers. Jesus saith unto him, Then are the
27 children free. Notwithstanding, lest we should offend them, go thou to the sea, and cast a hook, and take up the fish that first cometh up; and when thou hast opened his mouth, thou shalt find a piece of money; that take, and give unto them, for me and thee.

---

nacle was set up, which the Lord had pitched, and not man. It is then for the purpose of bringing back Peter, and with him the other disciples, to the true recognition of himself, from which they had in part fallen, that the Lord puts to him the question which follows; and being engaged, through Peter's hasty imprudence, to the rendering of the didrachm, which now he could hardly recede from, yet did it in the remarkable way of this miracle. . . . . . Here, as so often in the life of our Lord, the depth of his poverty and humiliation is lightened up by a gleam of his glory. And thus, by the manner of the payment, did he reassert the true dignity of his person, which else by the payment itself might have been obscured and compromised in the eyes of some, but which it was of all importance for the disciples that they should not lose sight of, or forget. The miracle, then, was to supply a real need,— slight indeed as an outward need, for the money could assuredly have been in some other and more ordinary way procured; but as an inner need, most real; in this, then, differing in its essence from the apocryphal miracles, which are continually mere sports and freaks of power, having no ethical motive or meaning whatever." Notes on the Miracles.    25. **custom or tribute**] *a property-tax, or a poll-tax*.    26. **Then are the children free**] Referring to himself, according to Peter's confession, as the Son of God, and therefore not liable to pay money for the support of worship in his Father's temple. It is important to bear in mind that this money was not paid to the Roman government, but for the temple service.    27. **for me and thee**] As the tribute here paid was for those twenty years old and upwards, and as it was paid only for Jesus and Peter, Bengel infers that the other disciples had not then passed their twentieth year. They were, probably, most of them very young men; but notwithstanding Bengel's sagacity and learning in such matters, we do not think there is any sufficient reason to suppose that at that time any of them, with perhaps the exception of John, were less than twenty years of age.

# CHAPTER XVIII.

### The Primitive Church of Christ.

We look upon this chapter as indicating, 1. (1-4.) The terms of admission into the kingdom of Heaven, or the Church of Christ; 2. (5-10.) The thoughtful tenderness and solicitude with which his followers, or the members of his Church, are to watch over the weak and inexperienced among them; 3. (11-14.) The earnestness with which they are to seek out and save the lost; 4. (15-17.) The manner in which, as members of his Church, we are to deal with those of our brethren who injure us; 5. (18-20.) The power which is given to us as united together in him and he in us; and 5. (21-35.) The forgiving and forbearing spirit which we are to exercise towards our brethren, however often they may sin against us. The meaning of each passage is perhaps in itself plain enough; but it requires close attention and a careful analysis to see how intimately the different clauses are connected, and how they all bear on the same subject.

1-10. First, there are the disciples with their minds so blinded by schemes of personal ambition and their obstinate Jewish prejudices, that they are hardly able to understand the plainest teachings of their Master. Their jealousy and pride had perhaps been excited by the particular favor which had been shown (xvii. 1) to Peter, James, and John, and they were disputing by the way as to which of them should hold the highest offices in his kingdom. Jesus (Luke ix. 47), knowing the feeling by which they were moved, asked them (Mark ix. 33), after coming into the house, what they had been disputing about by the way. They, obviously abashed by his question, at first made no reply. But afterwards, concealing the invidiousness of their personal dispute under the general form of their question, they asked Jesus who is greatest in the kingdom of Heaven, i. e. in the community or kingdom which he is about to establish on the earth? He replied in such a way as not only to meet the specific question, but the feeling out of which their dispute and all similar disputes have arisen.

He called to him a child, and with this impressive emblem before them, said, "Unless ye be converted and become as little children"—far from being the greatest —"ye shall not enter into the kingdom of Heaven,"—shall not belong to my kingdom, or my church, at all. These proud, ambitious thoughts and prejudices of yours must be put aside. For he who like this little child makes himself of no account, and has his mind and heart open with childlike docility to every pure influence and teaching,—he is greatest in the kingdom of Heaven. Then, rising from the literal to the figurative meaning of the word child, and carrying the idea of self-renunciation or humility out into deeds of active beneficence, he adds, whosoever shall receive one such child, i. e. one weak and inexperienced disciple of mine in *my name*, i. e. in my spirit, receiveth me, and, Luke ix. 48, not only me, but Him who hath sent me. As the rulers of a mighty empire throw their defences around the least of their obedient subjects, and identify themselves with him if his rights are violated, so Christ identifies himself with the most helpless and ignorant of his disciples, and makes their cause his. And not only will he who receives such an one in a spirit of childlike humility and love, receive Christ, but, 6, he who shall offend such an one, i. e. who shall be the means of causing a weak brother to sin, shall be exposed to the heaviest condemnation. He shall be cut off from the community of believers. Sad it is for the world, 7, that it should abound in temptations to sin; but that, alas for them! is no excuse for those who lead others astray. And as there is no way to avoid being the cause of temptation to others, except by cutting off whatever is wrong in our own lives and hearts, *therefore*, 8, 9, if thy hand or thine eye is causing thee to sin, cut it off, tear it out, and cast it from thee. Then, in a still stronger form, he repeats the admonition that they must not let their pride and want of charity injure the weak and inexperienced disciples, for, he adds, the angels who watch over them are highly honored by my Father who is in heaven, and, unworthy and lost though these feeble ones may seem to you, it is for that very reason that the Son of man has come to save them. And his coming to save them is a further reason why you should be the more careful and thoughtful for them. How does it seem to you? Then, 12, 13, follows the pertinent and beautiful parable of the shepherd on the mountains searching for the one foolish sheep that had wandered away, as they also — *his* disciples — must go out and search for the erring and the lost. For in so doing, they will only be acting in accordance with the will of God. Even so it is not the will of your Father who is in heaven, that one of these little ones — these frail and erring ones — should perish.

If then your brother sin against you, do what you can to "gain" or win him back, — 1. By going to him and setting the matter truthfully before him between you and him alone, that his pride may not be excited by the presence of others, and that he may be touched by your kindness; 2. If he does not hear you alone, then take two or three with you, that he may be moved by the weight of their authority, and think more carefully of what he has done; but, 3. If he disregard them, refer it to the church, and, if he refuse to listen to them, you have done all that you can do, and are henceforth to regard him as no longer a Christian brother. For an explanation of v. 18, which is closely connected with this, see note to xvi. 19. The authority there given to St. Peter is here assigned to all the Apostles, and also, we think, to the Church in all ages, which of course overthrows the papal claim of supremacy through St. Peter.

18 – 20. The condition of fulfilment for the promises in verses 18 and 19 is given in 20. "For where two or three are brought together *in my name*, i. e. in my spirit, there am I in the midst of them, and whatsoever they, thoroughly united in my spirit and in harmony with one another, shall in accordance with that spirit bind or loose on earth, it shall be bound or loosed in heaven, and whatever they shall ask, it shall be granted to them." The perfect harmony with the spirit of Christ, i. e. in his name, is the condition on which the action on earth shall be ratified in heaven, and on which the prayer of the disciples on earth will be answered by their Father in heaven. So in John xiv. 13, 14, and xvi. 25, 26, the same condition, "in my name," is annexed.

Have we not here (17 – 20) Christ's idea of a church? Where two or three are gathered together in his name, and he is in the midst of them, is not that, in its simplest form, a Christian Church? The church spoken of in this passage is, as Stier says, "the society, called together in unity of faith and love, of those who believe on him, who are united in his name; a society in which is carried out and exercised upon earth what is valid in heaven. This is the simple, fundamental idea here clearly expressed." The presence of Christ is, of course, a spiritual presence, and the form of speech here and elsewhere (e. g. John xiv. 23) would indicate that it is also a personal presence. Here then is a Christian Church — a community of believers, though only two or three — coming together in his name, united in his spirit, and he himself in the midst of them, the medium to them of a divine life, which flows in upon them, and by which they grow up in him, "the one Mediator between God and men." Here is the seminal idea of a Christian Church, and with this as a centre, in accordance with the directions given in this chapter, each separate community of believers, formed in direct communion with Christ, has life in itself through him, and is in itself through him a living organism, with all the elements of Christian growth and life. And wherever two or three of its members find themselves, in the Providence of God, cut off by change of place or other circumstances from the primitive community, they also meeting together in the name of Christ may be united with him as members of his body, and so long as they live in accordance with his precepts they are truly a church of Christ, owned, assisted, blessed by him, and growing up into him who is the head. What they shall bind or loose in his name, i. e. in accordance with his spirit, on earth, shall be bound or loosed in heaven, and what they shall agree on earth to ask in accordance with his spirit, it shall be done for them by their Father who is in heaven. This is the primitive idea of the Church, — and the only one which was given by Christ. Archbishop Whately says, that "the churches founded by the Apostles were all quite independent of each other, or of any one central body." Out of this simple community of Christian believers, united with one another in Christ, and having such officers, or servants rather and ministers, as might be required for the purposes of general convenience, order, and edification, have grown up the monstrous ecclesiastical assumptions and prerogatives, by which men, under different names, but always in the spirit of arrogance and presumption that is here rebuked, have lorded it over God's heritage. What can be more directly in violation of the teachings of Jesus than the prerogatives and despotic authority which have been assumed over his Church? His language is: "Whosoever, therefore, shall humble himself as this little child, the same is greatest in the kingdom of Heaven;" and the kingdom of Heaven in the question, verse 1, to which these words are a reply, is the kingdom of Christ on earth, his Church here on earth. In Luke xxii. 24 – 26 (with which compare Matthew xx. 25 – 27) he uses still stronger language. There was a strife among the disciples, which of them should be accounted the greatest. And he said unto them, "The kings of the Gentiles exercise lordship over them; and they that exercise authority upon them are called Benefactors. But ye shall not be so: but he that is greatest among you, let him be as the younger; and he that is chief as he that doth serve." The same idea is again urged upon the disciples by Jesus in language which looks as if it had been directly aimed at the distinctions which have sprung up to feed a low, earthly ambition in his Church. "Be not ye called Rabbi: for one is your Master [Schoolmaster], even Christ; and all ye are brethren. And call no man your father upon the earth: for one is your Father, who is in heaven. Neither be ye called masters: for one is your Master, even Christ. But he that is greatest among you shall be your servant." (Matthew xxiii. 7 – 11.) Of course these terms are not to be taken literally; but if they have any purpose or meaning whatever, it is to condemn the spiritual domination and pride which have been cherished and exercised within the Church, and under the pretence of sustaining its dignity and authority.

21 – 35. As to the question put by Peter, and the reply to it, it is not certain whether they made a part of this same conversation or not. Even if they did not, the Evangelist has evidently introduced them in this place as bearing upon the subject which has just been under consideration. The circumstances of the case, especially the manner in which the question is put, would seem to indicate that Peter was prompted to ask the question by what had just been said. After the directions which Jesus had given, 15 – 17, for dealing with an offending brother,

Peter asked for some specific rule. He wished to know precisely how many times he is to forgive, and in mentioning seven as the number, he undoubtedly thinks that he is carrying his forbearance to the farthest possible limit. The reply of Jesus, "I say not unto you, until seven times, but until seventy times seven," implies that there are to be no limits of the kind which Peter has suggested. And to illustrate and enforce the duty of forgiving others from our need of the Divine forgiveness, he added the parable of the unmerciful servant, which shows in the most forcible manner that we cannot expect God to forgive us unless we from our hearts forgive every one his brother. It is the same doctrine implied in the Lord's prayer (vi. 12), and more explicitly urged in the remarks which follow it (vi. 14, 15).

---

## NOTES.

At the same time came the disciples unto Jesus, saying, Who is the greatest in the kingdom of Heaven? And Jesus called a little child unto him, and set him in the midst of them, and said, Verily I say unto you, except ye be converted, and become as little children, ye shall not enter into the kingdom of Heaven. Whosoever therefore shall humble himself as this little child, the same is greatest in the kingdom of Heaven. And whoso shall receive one such little child in my name, receiveth me. But whoso shall offend one of these little ones which believe in me, it were better for him that a millstone were hanged about his neck, and that he were drowned in the

---

1. **At the same time**] Literally, *at that hour*, but not thus to be taken. It is nearly equivalent to *Then*, or *At that time*.

6. **a millstone**] The form of expression here is very strong. The millstone is of the heavy kind turned by animals, and the drowning is in the midst of the open sea, where there could be no possible hope of escape. This mode of punishment was not practised by the Jews, though it was in use among some other nations. It is better for a man to be drowned now in the sea, than to live till he has

7 depth of the sea. —— Woe unto the world because of offences! for it must needs be that offences come; but woe to that man 8 by whom the offence cometh! Wherefore, if thy hand or thy foot offend thee, cut them off, and cast them from thee; it is better for thee to enter into life halt or maimed, rather than, having two hands, or two feet, to be cast into everlasting fire. 9 And if thine eye offend thee, pluck it out, and cast it from thee; it is better for thee to enter into life with one eye, rather than, having two eyes, to be cast into hell-fire. —— 10 Take heed that ye despise not one of these little ones; for I say unto you, that in heaven their angels do always behold 11 the face of my Father which is in heaven. For the Son of 12 man is come to save that which was lost. How think ye? if a man have an hundred sheep, and one of them be gone astray, doth he not leave the ninety and nine, and goeth into 13 the mountains, and seeketh that which is gone astray? And if so be that he find it, verily I say unto you, he rejoiceth more of that sheep than of the ninety and nine which went not astray. 14 Even so, it is not the will of your Father which is in heaven

---

caused these little ones to sin, and then die. 8. **if thy hand or thy foot offend thee**] Whatever is to you a cause or occasion of sin, though it be a hand, or foot, or eye, cut it off, pluck it out, and cast it from you. "Hand, foot, eye," says Olshausen, "here appear to be used by the Saviour to denote mental powers and dispositions, and he counsels their restraint, their non-development, if a man find himself, by their cultivation, withdrawn from advancing the highest principle of life." "It is, however, a more elevated thing to succeed in learning how to cultivate even the lower faculties in harmony with the higher life." 10. **their angels**] *Behold the face, &c.* indicates a place of honor and peculiar favor. "This saying of our Lord," says Alford, "assures us that those angels whose honor is high before God are intrusted with the charge of the humble and meek, — the children in age and the children in grace." "We speak to our children," says Stier, "far too little about their angels, and we ourselves, as believers, do not think enough of ours. The angels are in heaven, and yet occupied at the same time in service and business on earth about their wards; for the heaven is not closed in space over the earth, but is ever open to us in everything which it sends. Where the angels of God go and stand, there also is heaven, and the face of God, which they at all times, without interruption from anything else, behold." 12. **he not leave the ninety and nine, and goeth into the mountains**] Luke xv. 4 says, "in the wilderness." "The combined description of the pastures in the wilderness, and on the mountains, can hardly find any position in Palestine precisely applicable, except 'the mountainous country' or 'wilderness,' so often called by these names, on the east of the Jordan. The shepherd of this touching parable thus becomes the successor of the wild herdsmen of the trans-Jordanic tribes who wandered far and wide

that one of these little ones should perish.——— Moreover, if 15 thy brother shall trespass against thee, go and tell him his fault between thee and him alone; if he shall hear thee, thou hast gained thy brother. But if he will not hear thee, then take with 16 thee one or two more, that in the mouth of two or three witnesses every word may be established. And if he shall neg- 17 lect to hear them, tell it unto the church; but if he neglect to hear the church, let him be unto thee as an heathen man and a

---

over those free and open hills, — the last relics of the patriarchal state of their ancestors." Stanley's Sinai and Palestine, p. 416.

**17. unto the church**] This word, ἐκκλησία, is found nowhere in the Gospels, except in this verse and Matt. xvi. 18: " On this rock I will build my church," — a remarkable fact, when we consider how much the Church has arrogated to itself, so that the history of the Church is considered synonymous with the history of Christianity. The gradual ascendency of the Church and its offices, — of an outward despotic authority over the inward life and precepts of our religion, — furnishes one of the saddest exhibitions of human ambition and depravity. The word, as used by Jesus, was undoubtedly intended to express what he meant by a community of believers united in him, and endowed by him with all the means of grace which are needed for their Christian life and advancement. In the passage before us he refers to one such community of believers as complete in itself and as having authority to deal with offenders. In Matt. xvi. 18 he uses the word *Church* to express in the abstract the whole system of means and powers and agencies by which his kingdom was to be established in the world, resting, as they all do, on faith in him as the Christ, the Son of the living God. The word itself, says Trench, Synonymes of the New Testament, pp. 17, 18, " is one of those words whose history it is peculiarly interesting to watch, as they obtain a deeper meaning, and receive a new consecration in the Christian Church, which, even while it did not invent, has yet assumed them into its service, and employed them in a far loftier sense than any to which the world had ever put them before. . . . . . ἐκκλησία, as all know, was the lawful assembly in a free Greek city of all those possessed of the rights of citizenship, for the transaction of public affairs. That they were summoned is expressed in the latter part of the word ; that they were summoned *out of* the whole population, a select portion of it, including neither the populace, nor yet strangers, nor those who had forfeited their civic rights, this is expressed in the first. Both the *calling*, and the *calling out*, are moments to be remembered, when the word is assumed into a higher Christian sense, for in them the chief part of its peculiar adaptation to its auguster uses lies. It is interesting to observe how, on one occasion in the New Testament, the word returns to its earlier significance." (Acts xix. 32, 39, 40.) The meaning of the word *ecclesia*, church, may derive some light from the use, by our Saviour, of the word ἐκλεκτοί, the *elect*, or the *chosen*, since the *ecclesia* was the body of the *eclectoi, the chosen*. " For many are called, but few are *chosen*," *eclectoi*. (Matt. xxii. 14.) " But for the sake of the elect [*eclectoi*] those days shall be shortened." (Matt. xxiv. 22.) " So as to deceive, if possible, even the *elect*." (Matt. xxiv. 24.) In verse 31 of the same chapter, " And they shall gather together the *elect* from the four winds." " And he shall avenge his *elect*." (Luke xviii. 7.) " Let him save himself, if he be the Christ, the *chosen* [the elect] of

18 publican.——Verily I say unto you, Whatsoever ye shall bind on earth shall be bound in heaven; and whatsoever ye shall 19 loose on earth shall be loosed in heaven. Again, I say unto you, that if two of you shall agree on earth as touching anything that they shall ask, it shall be done for them of my Father 20 which is in heaven. For where two or three are gathered together in my name, there am I in the midst of them.

---

God." (Luke xxiii. 35.) The Church of Christ is the body or community of *the elect*, of those who are not only called, but called *out*, i. e. *chosen* as true and faithful believers. It includes the weak, the inexperienced, and those who are easily led astray, and directs the strong to watch over them; to seek them out when they wander away; to deal kindly but honestly with them, when they do wrong; and to forgive them whenever they sincerely and penitently ask to be forgiven. Here is the Christian Church, calling in those who are without, and receiving those who, by accepting the call, cause themselves to be effectually called, and numbered among the elect. The word church, in the New Testament, is almost always applied to a single body of believers, united in one another and in Christ, and thus forming a community by themselves, with all the privileges, ordinances, and means of grace essential to salvation, so that if every other Church in the world should be cut off, in this one would be left the germ of all that would be needed to evangelize and convert the world. The word church, in Matt. xvi. 18, is used to express in the abstract that system of powers and agencies, human and divine, by which the kingdom of Heaven, the religion of Jesus, is to sustain, extend, and perpetuate itself in the world, so that the gates of death, the powers of evil, shall not prevail against it. It is also used, though very rarely, and never by our Saviour, or in the Gospels, to designate the great body of the faithful throughout the world, who live and believe in Christ, keeping the commandments of God and the Faith of Jesus. In this sense the word is used by St. Paul, e. g. Col. i. 18, "And he is the head of the body, the Church." 20. **in my name**] Name denotes the person, the being himself, or his spirit. To assemble in the name of Jesus, and pray in his name, presupposes the life and the spirit of Jesus to be already existing in those so meeting together. "It is no isolated act," "but requires rather as a necessary condition, that man should be under the power of living Christian principle." The influence of combined and associated prayer, through the sympathetic quickening of the religious nature is here implied.

**there am I in the midst of them**] He is present by his spirit, which they are thus cherishing in their own hearts, and in his religion which they are thus seeking to establish as the rule and law of their lives. He also, we suppose, promises to be himself *personally* present with them. Such a promise does not of itself prove him omnipresent. We are too apt to infer that powers more than human can belong only to God. It is said that because Jesus stilled the tempest, he must therefore have been omnipotent; that because he knew that Peter would catch a fish with the piece of money in his mouth, *therefore* he was omniscient; and that because he is personally present with all those who come together in his name, *therefore* he is omnipresent. Such reasoning is altogether unauthorized. Between the limitations of man's faculties and the omnipotence of God, there is room for the exercise of powers which lie beyond the reach of all that we can know and distinctly conceive. We cannot define the ranks of be-

Then came Peter to him, and said, Lord, how oft shall my 21
brother sin against me, and I forgive him? till seven times?
Jesus saith unto him, I say not unto thee, Until seven times, 22
but, Until seventy times seven. Therefore is the kingdom of 23
Heaven likened unto a certain king, which would take account
of his servants. And when he had begun to reckon, one was 24
brought unto him which owed him ten thousand talents. But 25
forasmuch as he had not to pay, his lord commanded him to be
sold, and his wife and children, and all that he had, and payment to be made. The servant therefore fell down and wor- 26
shipped him, saying, Lord, have patience with me, and I will
pay thee all. Then the Lord of that servant was moved with 27
compassion, and loosed him, and forgave him the debt. But 28
the same servant went out, and found one of his fellow-servants,
which owed him an hundred pence; and he laid hands on him,
and took him by the throat, saying, Pay me that thou owest.

---

ings and intelligences which may range through the boundless fields of existence between us and the Supreme Mind. We cannot set any precise limits to their powers. Between the limitations of man's presence, while he is in the body, and the ubiquity of the Infinite Spirit, the power of being personally present in places distant from one another at the same moment, may be possessed in entirely different degrees by different beings. A man may be present to ten thousand men at the same moment, acting by his voice and gestures on every one of the vast assembly. It may well be, that spiritual beings of a higher order, not bound by a material organization, may with their clearer perceptions and finer powers of action be present at the same moment to millions of beings widely separated from one another. It will not do then to accept the reasoning by which one class of Christians argue that the promise here made by Jesus to be personally present with his disciples is an impossibility; or that by which others argue, that because he is thus present he must therefore be omnipresent. Bad reasoning is as much out of place in a religious as in a scientific investigation, and is as dangerous in the interpretation of the words of Divine Truth as in the limitations which it would put on the works of the Divine Mind.

24. **ten thousand talents**] The largest sum that was spoken of, as we sometimes say a thousand millions of dollars. According to Olshausen, it could not be less than $13,000,000. "In the construction of the tabernacle, twenty-nine talents of gold were used. (Exod. xxxviii. 24.) David prepared for the temple three thousand talents of gold, and the princes five thousand." According to Plutarch, it was exactly this sum of 10,000 talents with which Darius sought to buy off Alexander; and the payment of the same sum was imposed by the Romans on Antiochus the Great, after his defeat by them.

26. **fell down and worshipped him**] A customary act of respect from an inferior to a superior. 28. **an hundred pence**] less than a millionth part of ten thousand talents, showing the smallness of our brother's obligation to us, compared with ours to God. **he laid hands on him,**

29 And his fellow-servant fell down at his feet, and besought him,
30 saying, Have patience with me, and I will pay thee all. And he would not; but went and cast him into prison, till he should
31 pay the debt. So when his fellow-servants saw what was done, they were very sorry; and came and told unto their lord all
32 that was done. Then his lord, after that he had called him, said unto him, O thou wicked servant, I forgave thee all that
33 debt, because thou desiredst me; shouldst not thou also have had compassion on thy fellow-servant, even as I had pity on
34 thee? And his lord was wroth, and delivered him to the tor-
35 mentors, till he should pay all that was due unto him. So likewise shall my Heavenly Father do also unto you, if ye from your hearts forgive not every one his brother their trespasses.

---

**and took him by the throat**] more exactly and literally, *he seized and choked him.* **Pay me that thou owest**] Observe here the haughty mode of expression which is so exactly in character with the reckless and cruel servant. He does not mention the trifling sum of one hundred pence, which would lessen his consequence and rebuke his pride, but shows his insolence while he conceals the smallness of his claims, as some do the poverty of their ideas, by a grand, imperious, and generalizing form of speech. If the sum due to him had been ten thousand talents, he could not have made a more lofty and sounding demand. 29. **fell down at his feet, and besought him**] Not as in verse 26, fell down and *worshipped* him. The different degrees of homage customary in the two cases, according to the dignity of the persons, is nicely indicated by the language.

32. **O thou wicked servant**] His cruelty to his fellow-servant was more severely regarded than his wasting *his lord's goods.*

34. **till he should pay all that was due unto him**] and as that can never be done, the condition, it has been said, amounts to a perpetual imprisonment, and therefore proves the doctrine of eternal punishment. The Roman Catholics, on the contrary, and some Protestant writers, e. g. Olshausen, infer from it, that as the word *until* implies that a limit is fixed, so there is such a thing after death as deliverance, in behalf of some. It seems to us, however, unreasonable to deduce any doctrine from one of the minor adjuncts of a parable.

## CHAPTER XIX.

### 1–12. — THE CHRISTIAN LAW OF DIVORCE.

1, 2. JESUS now left Galilee for the last time. As the Samaritans (Luke ix. 53) refused to receive him, he turned eastward from the direct route to Jerusalem, and crossing the Jordan entered the Peræa, a part of the kingdom of Herod Antipas. Strictly speaking, Judæa did not extend beyond the Jordan. But here, as Mr. Norton remarks, it is "to be understood in its more extended meaning, as equivalent to Palestine. The name Peræa is not used in the New Testament. The expression, *Judæa beyond the Jordan* is, as Reland remarks, used by Josephus in one instance to denote Peræa." Antiq. XII. 4, 11.

3–6. The Pharisees come to try and perplex him by their questions, and ask him if it is lawful for a man to put away his wife for *every cause*. This, as De Wette suggests, was a delicate subject to be discussed in the dominions of Herod Antipas. See xiv. There was a division of opinion among the Rabbins as to the construction to be put upon the Mosaic law of divorce in Deut. xxiv. 1. The School of Hillel maintained from it that when anything in his wife displeased a husband, "even if she had only oversalted his soup," it would be a sufficient reason for giving her up. Rabbi Schammai took the expression in a more limited sense, as referring only to what was scandalous and dishonorable. "In the words *for every cause*," says Olshausen, "there is expressed that exposition of the Mosaic law which agrees with the opinions of Hillel's followers, and the question accordingly is so put as to request his opinion on that view." Jesus, in his reply, pays no regard to these disputes. He goes not only behind them, but also behind the law of Moses, to the fundamental reason on which the law of marriage and divorce must rest. But he does this in a way not to offend their Jewish prejudices. From the constitution of the sexes as shown in the act of man's creation, Jesus declares, in words sacred to the Jews (Gen. ii. 24) the priority and sacredness of the marriage relation beyond all others. Not by the law of Moses, but long before that, in the constitution of the sexes, by the very act of creation, God ordained the law which is to be binding in this relation, and, "What God hath thus joined together, let not man put asunder."

7, 8. But if this be so, they ask, "Why did Moses command [*permit*, Mark x. 4] to give a writing of divorcement, and put her away." In reply to this question, Jesus again lays down one of those fundamental principles which so widely distinguish his views of law from all others. God in his dealings with man, he here intimates, must adapt his specific laws and regulations to the necessities of man's condition. Hence a succession of dispensations, each adapted to the existing state of things, and preparing the way for something better. Hence in many respects, because of the hardness of men's hearts, because they on account of their blunted moral sensibilities are able to bear only so much, God allows and even enjoins at one period of human progress that which is forbidden in a more advanced stage of moral and religious culture. Even Milton, in his Tetrachordon, allows the necessity of this adaptation, though it is opposed to his general course of argument. "For this hardness of heart," he says, "it was that God suffered, not divorce only, but all that which by civilians is termed the secondary law of nature and of nations. He suffered his own people to waste and spoil and slay by war, to lead captives, to be some masters, some servants . . . . . in his commonwealth; some to be undeservedly rich, others to be undeservingly poor. . . . . .

In the same manner, and for the same cause, he suffered divorce as well as marriage, our imperfect and degenerate condition of necessity requiring this law among the rest, as a remedy against intolerable wrong and servitude above the patience of man to bear." This graded principle of adaptation to man's condition and capabilities in the laws which are designed for his use even by the Divine wisdom, must always be borne in mind by those who would study the laws of Moses in the light of the highest philosophy. Law is always given, as St. Paul says of the Jewish law (Gal. iii. 19), because of transgressions; and not that which is perfect when judged by the rules of absolute rectitude, but that which is the best that men are able to bear at the time, is the law which is dictated by the highest wisdom.

Considering the character of the Jews in the time of Moses, the difficulty with which they were brought to recognize the highest sentiments of religion and morals, and especially the violence of their passions and their tendency continually to lapse into idolatry and a low sensualism, it is easy to see that some regard must have been had to these things in the laws of marriage. In many respects the Jews of that time were but a race of semi-barbarous, half-emancipated slaves. Lightfoot in his commentary on this passage has shown that, had it not been for the permission of divorce and the legal forms by which the rights of the wife were thus guarded, she might have been summarily dismissed, or exposed to the most harsh and cruel treatment, or even to death from the violence of her husband.

8. Jesus here returns again to the fundamental principle which existed before Moses, before Jacob or Abraham, and according to that the law of God was and is, as he has already declared (v. 32), that there shall be no divorce except for the one crime which destroys the sacredness, and is therefore in fact a dissolution, of the marriage re-

lation. The remarkable thing here again is the facility with which Jesus, even in discussing rules of legislation with the most bigoted adherents to the letter of the law, goes behind specific rules, and rests his doctrine on the substantial reality of things. "Christ taught, as the men of his day remarked, on an authority very different from that of the scribes. Not even on his own authority. He did not claim that his words should be recognized because he said them, but because they were true. 'If I say the truth, why do ye not believe me?'" — F. W. Robertson.

10 – 12. The conversation which follows took place (Mark x. 10) in the house, and was addressed particularly to the disciples. "If," say they, "the case of a man is so," i. e. if the law and his liability under it are such, "it is better for a man not to marry." To this remark of theirs Jesus assents with particular reference, we may suppose, to the hardships and persecutions which his followers must endure in those times. Still, he adds, this rule of celibacy is not one of universal application. None but those to whom the power has been given, 11, are able to bear it; and of those to whom it has been given, some, 12, are by nature free from the passions which make a life of continence without marriage difficult to them, some by hardships and privations are made so, while others from their own high motives and convictions rise above the control of the passions, and cheerfully put aside all thought of these domestic relations for the kingdom of Heaven's sake, i. e. that they may give themselves entirely to the advancement of that kingdom.

### CHRIST BLESSING THE CHILDREN.

13 – 15. The beautiful incident related here and Mark x. 13 – 16, of Jesus, when he took little children into his arms, and put his hands upon them, and blessed them, shows the relation which he looks on them as sustaining

towards himself. The disciples would have sent them away as too young for his adoption. But with a degree of displeasure which he seldom manifested, he commanded them not to forbid, but to let the little ones come to him; for, said he, of such is the kingdom of Heaven. In saying this, he used words which are not confined to those then present, but which reach forward, indicating his relation to all little children, and coming, a gracious invitation, to all parents and guardians who would consecrate their children to him by the waters of Christian baptism and the processes of Christian culture. "All gifts of God," says Roos, "do not enter by the *understanding* into the soul." "Not only," says Alford, in his notes on Mark x. 14, "is Infant Baptism *justified*, but it is ..... the NORMAL PATTERN OF ALL BAPTISM; none can enter God's kingdom except *as an infant*. In adult baptism ..... we strive to secure that state of simplicity and childlikeness, which in the infant we have ready and undoubted to our hands."

## THE YOUNG MAN WHO CAME TO JESUS.

16–22. The young man here, who was a ruler (Luke xviii. 18), and who in his eagerness to see Jesus (Mark x. 17) came running to him, and kneeled before him, was probably an amiable, well-meaning young man, susceptible of moral and religious impressions, who had carefully observed the rules of a conventional morality, and who, not finding in them the peace of mind which he sought, came to Jesus with the expectation, as Mr. Norton has said, that he "would enjoin, for instance, some unusual austerity, some long-continued exercise of fasting and prayer, or some peculiar vow, or some extraordinary almsgiving, or some large gift to the treasury of the temple, or some other definite act or course of conduct of a like character, by the performance of which he might assure himself of eternal life." He was probably sincere, and, as he supposed, very much in earnest. The fact of his using the expression *eternal life*, shows that he was not wholly superficial in his ideas. Jesus in reply to his question, by the words, " Why callest thou me good?" or rather, " Why askest thou me respecting what is good?" " No one is good, but God alone" (Mark x. 18), turns his attention first of all to the infinite Source of all goodness. Then, as a practical test of his fidelity to God, he says to him, If thou really desirest to enter into life, keep the commandments. Which? he asks in reply, and with surprise, as if he had expected something more, and doubted whether he had not misapprehended the answer. Jesus specifies the moral precepts of the Decalogue. The young man, as if wondering and amazed at the easiness of the terms, replies in a tone which shows how little he understood what it was to observe the commandments in their thorough and spiritual application, as Jesus had already expounded them in his Sermon on the Mount. These, he says, I have always kept. But is there not something more still wanting? he asks, not with self-complacency, but from a secret uneasiness, and a conviction that something is still wanting to secure his peace. Jesus, looking upon him (Mark x. 21) with an expression of love as he saw where his weakness lay, applied at once the test which should reveal to him the fatal defect in his character. Yes, one thing is wanting (Mark x. 21), and if thou wouldst be perfect, go and sell whatsoever thou hast, and give to the poor; and thou shalt have treasure in heaven, and come, take up the cross, and follow me. The sadness and grief caused by these words prove that the young man came to Jesus, as he believed, with an honest purpose; but they prove also that the one essential condition of discipleship, the readiness to give up everything at the call of duty and of God, was lacking, and that this one want was undermining all his virtues. The one thing which he lacked was not, that he did not sell all his goods and give them to the poor, but that there was something which he valued more than his allegiance to God. The outward test revealed the inward want, and this inward want, loving the things of God less than the things of the world, was the fatal defect which Jesus in thus bringing it to his knowledge would have him supply. "It is not here commanded," says Clement of Alexandria, "as some readily receive, to cast away our possessions and separate ourselves from them; but to drive out of the soul its idea of riches, its diseased passion and longing for them, the anxieties which are the thorns that choke the seed of life." While the words of Jesus revealed the young man to himself, they were also something more than a test. They show what was a necessary condition of discipleship in that day. What could a young man do with his riches then as a follower of Jesus? Must they not have been almost of necessity a fatal encumbrance? There is nothing to show that the condition was to be a general one. As Lord Bacon has said, "But sell not all thou hast, except thou come and follow me; that is, except thou have a vocation, wherein thou mayest do as much good, with little means, as with great." — Furness's Thoughts, &c., p. 167.

### Hard for the Rich to enter Christ's Kingdom.

23 – 26. The words here are suggested by the young man who went sorrowfully away from Jesus, because he had great possessions, and therefore apply primarily to those who are outwardly rich. Jesus looked on this young man as the representative of a class, and saw in him how difficult it was for those encumbered by wealth to give themselves up entirely to him. For in those days it was only by leaving all that they could become his followers, and thus enter the kingdom of Heaven. And at all

times, though not always perhaps to the same extent, there are peculiar temptations and perils connected with the enjoyment of great wealth, and however shining the examples of humble, self-forgetting, and self-sacrificing fidelity among the rich, the Saviour's words still apply, as a fearful and needed admonition, to those who in the midst of their earthly abundance are in danger of neglecting the higher wants and interests of the soul. But the words apply also with a more searching power to all, whether rich or poor, who (Mark x. 24) trust in riches, i. e. whose heart is in them. They are the opposite of the "poor" (Luke vi. 20) and "the poor in spirit" (Matthew v. 3). The words in their more extended meaning apply to a state of mind. In the kingdom of God, every individual, being merely a steward of God, and viewing himself as such, has renounced all his possessions, and having consecrated them to God holds them subject to his disposal. In this sense the beggar may be rich, cleaving to his bit of a possession, and striving for more, while the possessor of wealth, renouncing all, is poor. So in the dangerous meaning of the word, a man without money may be rich, when his heart is enamored of his own virtues, genius, artistic tastes, intellectual attainments and capabilities, or anything else which his self-love may appropriate as his own. In respect to all such it may be said, that it is easier for a camel to go through the eye of a needle than for them to enter the kingdom of God. The proverb, as verse 26 proves, indicates, not an impossibility, but a very great difficulty. The amazement and consternation of the disciples exhibited by the question, Who then shall be saved? show how unprepared they were for principles of conduct so severe. Jesus comforts them somewhat by the assurance, that, though this is impossible with men, still all things are possible with God.

27 – 29. — GAINING BY RENOUNCING.

27 – 30. Peter's state of mind may have been one of self-complacent confidence, when he recollects that he and his fellow-disciples had given up everything, and asks what is to be their reward; what shall be to us? Perhaps, after recovering a little from the astonishment occasioned by the severity of the doctrine just announced, which at first had seemed to leave no room for hope to any one, and recollecting what sacrifices he and his fellow-disciples had made, his mind recurs to the command in verse 21, and the promise there of treasure in heaven; and in a sudden burst of feeling, with too keen an eye to the reward, he exclaims, Lo! we have left all and followed thee; how then shall it be with us? or, what shall be our portion? In order to understand the reply of Jesus, we must transfer our thoughts into these Oriental forms of speech, or translate them into our more literal and prosaic dialect. *In the regeneration* may be joined with either branch of the sentence, but belongs, we think, rather to the second than the first. Verily I say unto you, that ye who have followed me, shall in the regeneration, when the Son of man sits upon his throne, also sit on twelve thrones judging the twelve tribes of Israel; i. e. in the new order of things which shall prevail when my religion is established, and I shall rule among men, then shall ye also who have followed me now rule with me as my representatives in the advancement of my kingdom, i. e. of my religion, through the world. He may possibly allude here, as in xvi. 28, to the destruction of Jerusalem, as the decisive moment when the old religion shall be overthrown, and the new established in its place, with a glance forward to yet higher scenes of kingly glory. In verse 29, the thought is carried into the future world with greater distinctness. All who have made sacrifices on my account shall (Mark x. 30) receive an hundred-

fold now in this time, houses, and brethren, and sisters, and mothers, and children, and lands with persecutions, and in the world to come, eternal life. But how can they receive in brothers, sisters, and mothers, an hundredfold? We must look for a deeper meaning than that which lies upon the surface. As a man abounding in wealth is in the *best and spiritual sense* of the word poor, if his heart is not bound up in his riches; as in the *bad* sense of the word he is rich who in the midst of his poverty clings with all his heart to the little which he has and lusts for more; so do we in a still different sense, really receive, not in proportion to what we outwardly possess, but in proportion to what we are able to appropriate and enjoy. They therefore whose souls are born into the higher life of the Gospel of Christ, shall, in their renovated affections, desires, and powers of thought and emotion, enjoy an hundred-fold more than before even here in their houses, fields, and friends. To them alone can it be said now in this present time, "All things are yours" (1 Cor. iii. 21), while in the world to come they shall inherit eternal life.

## NOTES.

AND it came to pass, that, when Jesus had finished these sayings, he departed from Galilee, and came into the coasts of 2 Judæa, beyond Jordan. And great multitudes followed him; and he healed them there.

1. **When Jesus had finished these sayings**] These words indicate a connection and completeness in what he had been saying in the previous chapter. **into the coasts of Judæa, beyond Jordan**] Mark (x. 1) says, "Into the coasts of Judæa, and beyond Jordan," which would allow though it does not oblige us to suppose that Jesus was employed at that time on both sides of the Jordan. **Jordan**] *the* Jordan. Our translators evidently did not understand the use of the definite article in Greek. Accord-

The Pharisees also came unto him, tempting him, and say- 3
ing unto him, Is it lawful for a man to put away his wife for
every cause? And he answered and said unto them, Have 4
ye not read, that he, which made them at the beginning, made
them male and female; and said, "For this cause shall a 5
man leave father and mother, and shall cleave to his wife; and
they twain shall be one flesh"? Wherefore they are no more 6
twain, but one flesh. What, therefore, God hath joined to-

---

ing to Bengel and Winer, the highest authorities on this subject, "there is scarcely an instance in the Scriptures where the article is redundant," and it is "utterly impossible that the article should be omitted where it is decidedly necessary, or employed where it is quite superfluous." "Ὄρος can never denote *the mountain*, nor τὸ ὄρος *a mountain*." Yet this distinction is constantly overlooked in our English version. Often, as in the case here, the omission of the article is of little consequence; but usually it implies something which adds to the lifelike character of the expression. In Matt. v. 1, it is quite a different thing to say, as it is in the Greek, "he went up into *the* mountain," from what it is to say, as in our version, "he went up into *a* mountain." "Ye call me *the* Master, and *the* Lord; and ye say well," (John xiii. 13,) is much more forcible and graphic than with the omission of the article as in our version. So in Matt. xviii. 17, "Let him be to thee as *the* (not *a*) heathen man and *the* publican;" in John iii. 10, "Art thou *the* (not *a*) Master of Israel, and knowest not these things;" Matt. xxvi. 26, "And as they were eating, Jesus took *the* bread," i. e. the bread which had been specially provided for the purpose, just as in the following verse he took "*the* cup;" John i. 21, "Art thou *the* Prophet?" i. e. the prophet predicted by Moses and expected as the Messiah, not as in our version, "*that* prophet;" Matt. i. 23, "Behold, *the* virgin shall conceive," not *a* virgin; Matt. xii. 35, "*The* (not *a*) good man, out of the good treasure of the heart, bringeth forth good things; and *the* (not *an*) evil man," &c.; Matt. xiii. 3, "*The* (not *a*) sower went forth to sow," i. e. *the* Son of man; John xiii. 5, "He poureth water into *the* (not *a*) basin," that usually stood there for use. These matters are not of great importance, but the use of the article in the New Testament well deserves the attention of the critical student.

3. **for every cause**] *upon every pretence.* Josephus gives this sense to the law, and owns that he divorced his wife, "not being pleased with her manners and behavior." Antiq. IV. 5. **And said**] And he said, i. e. Jesus said, using the words to be found in Gen. ii. 24. **and they twain shall be one flesh**] Here is described the peculiarity of the marriage relation, that which distinguishes it from all other relations of interest or friendship. "They are two," says Stier, "and yet no longer two: this is, in the shortest and profoundest expression, the mystery of marriage, the great mystery whose further typical significance the Apostle Paul opens to us in Eph. v. 31, 32. The bodily fellowship is not merely the basis of marriage, but also that which is alone essential to it, which may indeed, and in a certain sense, should be sweetened and glorified by friendship of soul, being superadded to it, but which subsists as marriage apart from that." "This bodily union," says Olshausen, "when it is founded on an antecedent combination of soul and spirit, is the very summit and flower of all union and communion, and

7 gether, let no man put asunder. —— They say unto him, Why did Moses, then, command to give a writing of divorcement
8 and to put her away? He saith unto them, Moses, because of the hardness of your hearts, suffered you to put away your
9 wives; but from the beginning it was not so. And I say unto you, whosoever shall put away his wife, except it be for fornication, and shall marry another, committeth adultery; and whoso
10 marrieth her which is put away doth commit adultery. —— His disciples say unto him, If the case of the man be so with his
11 wife, it is not good to marry. But he said unto them, All men
12 cannot receive this saying, save they to whom it is given. For there are some eunuchs, which were so born from their mother's womb; and there are some eunuchs, which were made eunuchs of men; and there be eunuchs, which have made themselves eunuchs for the kingdom of Heaven's sake. He that is able to receive it, let him receive it.
13 Then were there brought unto him little children, that he should put his hands on them, and pray; and the disciples re-

---

for this very reason forms the condition of the continuance of the whole human race. It is owing to the holy nature of this bodily union that it is to be considered indissoluble, as one which man cannot, and which only God can dissever."

9. **And whoso marrieth her which is put away doth commit adultery**] The point of this prohibition is brought out by the way in which Josephus expounds the Jewish law of divorce. "He that desires to be divorced," he says, "for any cause whatsoever, (and many such causes happen among men,) let him in writing give assurance that he will never use her as his wife any more; for by this means she may be at liberty to marry another husband." This temptation to be divorced in order to marry again Jesus cuts off by his severe prohibition. By every possible means he would make the marriage union inviolable and indissoluble. By the finer affections which he would cherish in human hearts, by the purer morals flowing out from righteous affections, by more delicate and generous acts, by the sanctities of heaven thrown over the marriage tie and all the domestic relations, he would make a Christian home more sacred and endearing in its relations than any other home had ever been. In this as in other things the world, even the Christian world, though slowly rising towards his idea, is still far below it. Lawgivers still and perhaps necessarily allow his precepts to be violated on account of the hardness of men's hearts and the low state of morals among them.

12. **He that is able to receive it, let him receive it**] Jesus makes allowance for differences of temperament and constitution. He does not ask the same things of all. Though he requires self-renunciation in all his followers, he does not require that all shall show it by the same acts.

13. **And the disciples rebuked them**] Rebuked not the children, but those who were bringing them.

**But the disciples**] "The greater part of whom," says Bengel, "appear to have been unmarried: and unmarried men, unless they are humble-minded, are not so kind to

buked them. But Jesus said, Suffer little children, and for- 14
bid them not, to come unto me; for of such is the kingdom
of Heaven. And he laid his hands on them, and departed 15
thence.

And, behold, one came and said unto him, Good Master, 16
what good thing shall I do, that I may have eternal life? And 17
he said unto him, Why callest thou me good? there is none
good but one, that is, God. But if thou wilt enter into life,
keep the commandments. He saith unto him, Which? Jesus 18
said, "Thou shalt do no murder; Thou shalt not commit
adultery; Thou shalt not steal; Thou shalt not bear false
witness; Honor thy father and thy mother;" and, "Thou 19
shalt love thy neighbor as thyself." The young man saith unto 20

---

infants." **14. Suffer little children**] *Suffer the little children, — the little ones to come to me.* Better as in the original with the article. Jesus has just been defending the law of marriage. Here, as a branch of the same subject, he is upholding the claims of children, by rebuking those who would keep them from him, and by taking them into his arms, laying his hands upon them, and blessing them.

**for of such is the kingdom of Heaven**] There is nothing more beautiful in the New Testament than the relation of Jesus to little children and his sympathy with them. What do words like these teach in regard to them? If his kingdom is made up of those who are like them, what shall we say of them, and of the doctrine of innate depravity? That doctrine is found in metaphysical systems of divinity, but nowhere is it taught or indicated by the words or the acts of Jesus. An hereditary liability to sin, coming out with the development of our natures, and showing itself in times of temptation, we all of us may feel, and should be constantly on our guard against. "Not," says Richter, "the children must become as you, but *vice versa*, you must become as the children." "If we have to do with men, then the rule is, Be *no* child; trust, look to — whom? But if we have to do with God, then it cannot often enough be repeated: Be only a child, — follow the call, trust to the promise, take the gift, obey the word, all as if thou didst let thyself be lifted, carried, comforted, blessed." Stier. **16. eternal life**] This expression occurs here and in the corresponding passages in Mark and Luke for the first time. It is used at v. 29 of this chapter, Luke xviii. 30, and only once again, xxv. 46, in the first three Gospels. It is difficult to ascertain the precise meaning in which it is used by the young man, though it undoubtedly is intended to denote a future state of blessedness. **17. Why callest thou me good?**] According to Tischendorf, the reading should be, *Why askest thou me respecting the good? One is good: but if thou wishest, &c.* This agrees with the reading in the Curetonian Syriac Gospels. One is good. One only is good in the absolute sense of the word, uniting in himself all perfections. The natural inference from this language of Jesus, is that by it he meant to disclaim for himself this absolute goodness, which excludes, not only all sin, but the possibility of being tempted. "For God cannot be tempted with evil." (James i. 13.) "Then was Jesus led up of the spirit into the wilderness to be tempted of the devil." (Matt. iv. 1.) "For in that he him-

him, All these things have I kept from my youth up; what
21 lack I yet? Jesus said unto him, If thou wilt be perfect, go
and sell that thou hast, and give to the poor; and thou shalt
22 have treasure in heaven; and come and follow me. But when
the young man heard that saying, he went away sorrowful;
23 for he had great possessions. —— Then said Jesus unto his
disciples, Verily I say unto you, that a rich man shall hardly
24 enter into the kingdom of Heaven. And again I say unto you,
It is easier for a camel to go through the eye of a needle, than
25 for a rich man to enter into the kingdom of God. When his
disciples heard it, they were exceedingly amazed, saying,
26 Who then can be saved? But Jesus beheld them, and said
unto them, With men this is impossible; but with God all
27 things are possible. —— Then answered Peter, and said unto
him, Behold, we have forsaken all and followed thee; what
28 shall we have therefore? And Jesus said unto them, Verily

---

self hath suffered being tempted, he is able to succor them that are tempted." (Heb. ii. 18.)
**20. from my youth up**] These words are omitted by Tischendorf as not contained in the best manuscripts. The omission is an improvement in the passage. It is a little harsh to write, The young man, ὁ νεανίσκος — the youth — said, All these have I kept from my youth up, ἐκ νεότητός μου.
**21. go and sell that thou hast**] "It is a command, not a counsel; necessary, not optional; but particular, not universal, accommodated to the idiosyncrasy of his soul, to whom it was addressed. For many followed Jesus to whom he did not give this command. He may be perfect, who still possesses wealth; he may give all to the poor, who is very far from perfection. Our Lord's words laid an obligation on the man who offered himself of his own accord, and that so unreservedly. If the Lord had said, Thou art rich, and art too fond of thy riches, the young man would have denied it; wherefore, instead of so doing, he demands immediately a direct proof." Bengel. **22. sorrowful**] because he could not keep his great possessions, and at the same time follow Christ. These divided affections are always a source of anxiety and sorrow. **23. hardly**] *with difficulty*. They are too much taken up with present comforts to think of better things; but if, as in this case they think of them and really desire to possess them, they are too much attached to their present comforts and possessions to make the needed sacrifice.

**24. easier for a camel**] The similar proverb of the elephant is said to be familiar in the Koran and the Talmud. "Perhaps thou art one of those who can make an elephant go through the eye of a needle." The substitution which is sometimes proposed of κάμιλον, meaning a cable, for κάμηλον, a camel, — camilon for camelon, — is entirely without authority.

**26. with God all things are possible**] So Mark ix. 23, All things are possible to him that believeth. **27. forsaken all**] "The all which the Apostles had left was not in all cases contemptible. The sons of Zebedee had hired servants (Mark i. 20), and Levi (Matthew) could give a great feast in

I say unto you, that ye which have followed me in the regeneration, when the Son of man shall sit in the throne of his glory, ye also shall sit upon twelve thrones, judging the twelve tribes of Israel. And every one that hath forsaken houses, or breth- 29

his house. But whatever it was, it *was their all.*" Alford. 28.

**in the regeneration**] As *the kingdom of Heaven* is used to express the condition of a Christian individual, of the Christian commonwealth, and of the redeemed above (xvi. 27, 28), so regeneration, being born again, refers to the act by which the individual soul, or the Christian community, are born into the kingdom of Heaven. Among the Stoics this word expressed the periodic renovation of the earth when in the spring it revived from its winter death. Josephus (Antiq. XI. 3. 9) speaks of the restoration of the Jews after the Captivity as "the regaining and regeneration of the country." The word is used only twice in the New Testament. In Titus iii. 5, it plainly refers to the new birth of the individual, when it is awakened to the higher thought and life of the Gospel. In the passage before us it refers to the same newness of life in its more extended influence among men, whether on earth or in heaven. "The first seat of the regeneration is the soul of man; but, beginning there, and establishing its centre there, it extends in ever widening circles." "Man is the present subject of the regeneration, and of the wondrous transformation which it implies; but in that day it will have included within its limits the whole world of which man is the central figure; and here is the reconciliation of the two passages, in one of which it is spoken of as pertaining to the single soul, in the other to the whole redeemed creation." Trench's Synonymes of the New Testament. *In the regeneration* is certainly to be joined with the second, and not, as in our Bibles, with the first, clause of the sentence.

**when the Son of man shall sit in the throne of his glory, ye also shall sit upon twelve thrones, judging the twelve tribes of Israel**] The religion of Jesus is *the kingdom of Heaven;* where it comes, the Son of man comes in his kingdom; where it prevails, as it does in the thorough regeneration of the soul or of the race, there he, as the head of the new dispensation, is said to come in his glory, to reign or to sit upon the throne of his glory, and there, he now declares, the Apostles shall be associated with him, sitting on twelve thrones, and thus under him sharing the regal influence and authority which he is exercising over the souls of men, whether in this world or the world to come. Dr. Palfrey, in his Relation between Judaism and Christianity, pp. 98, 99, has well explained this passage: "As, adopting the phraseology in Daniel (vii. 13, 14), Jesus calls his establishment in a moral dominion, a sitting upon 'the throne of his glory,' so he tells his Apostles, who were to be the agents and representatives of his spiritual administration, that they too shall sit on thrones. And the figure is still further carried out. There were as many Apostles as there had been Jewish tribes; and this coincidence is brought to view in the language in which they are told that they are to have spiritual rule over God's people. The word judge here, as often in Scripture (comp. 1 Sam. viii. 5, Isa. xl. 23), means simply to govern, to exercise sway; not to administer law, but to give, to promulgate it, which latter function belonged strictly to the Apostolic office. The twelve Apostles together were to give law to collective Israel. Nothing is said of any such distribution of power as that each Apostle should have a tribe for his separate jurisdiction. One name of Israel regarded collectively was *the twelve tribes,* or *the twelve-tribed nation.* (Comp. Acts xxvi. 7.)" *The twelve tribes of Israel* mean here the

ren, or sisters, or father, or mother, or wife, or children, or lands, for my name's sake, shall receive an hundred-fold, and 30 shall inherit everlasting life. —— But many that are first shall be last; and the last shall be first.

---

people of God. *When* the Son of man shall sit (active voice) on his throne (genitive case), ye shall sit (middle voice) on twelve thrones (accusative). Greek scholars who are curious about such things have supposed that they saw in these nice distinctions of language an intimation of the different kinds or degrees of power which Jesus and the Apostles were respectively to exercise. *When the Son of man shall sit*, the active form expressing the act absolutely, united with the genitive, *on his glorious throne*, as the case denoting source or cause, the whole expression may seem to represent him as sitting independently on his throne, while the middle voice with something of a passive signification and the accusative case, the case of direct limitation, give in respect to the Apostles the idea of a more limited and dependent authority. This distinction is indicated by Stier and Alford. But it will not do to lay any stress on these nice distinctions of language, for such delicate shadings of expression may be turned in almost any direction by a fanciful or ingenious mind. The distinction here suggested may have been in the writer's mind. But in Luke xxii. 30, *ye shall sit on thrones*, thrones is in the genitive, and in Rev. iv. 2, where God is represented as sitting on his throne, sitting is put in the middle voice, and *throne* in the accusative case. While the preposition remains the same, the genitive, dative, and accusative cases are used indiscriminately (Rev. iv. 9, 10; v. 13; vi. 19; vii. 10; xi. 16).

**ye shall sit on twelve thrones**] Figures of speech in the oriental languages are carried out more minutely than with us. Where we should say, "I am exposed to death among those who are like enraged lions," David in a far more picturesque and expressive way says: "My soul is among lions: and I lie even among them that are set on fire, even the sons of men, whose teeth are spear and arrows, and their tongue a sharp sword." (Ps. lvii. 44.) No one thinks of construing this literally. Where we might describe the great and terrible calamities impending over a nation as a dark and tempestuous night overwhelming the land and shutting out the light of heaven, our Saviour in accordance with modes of expression natural to the East, and perfectly well understood as figurative, says: "Immediately after the tribulation of those days shall the sun be darkened, and the moon shall not give her light, and the stars shall fall from heaven, and the powers of the heavens shall be shaken." (Matt. xxiv. 29.) So in the passage before us, where we might say, In the new order of things they shall be united with him in his reign over the saints in glory, Jesus, in language far more impressive and august, but not literal, says, "In the regeneration, when the Son of man shall sit in the throne of his glory, ye also shall sit upon twelve thrones, judging the twelve tribes of Israel." In this way he sets before them their future condition of honor and greatness connected with the thought of the more than regal influence which they, as his representatives and Apostles, are to exercise in advancing and establishing his kingdom among men, and thus ruling over them.

# CHAPTER XX.

### 1–16.—The Laborers in the Vineyard.

1–16. This has seemed to us the most difficult of all the parables. Its precise relation to what goes before it is obscure, and it is quite impossible to show the precise bearing of all the incidents, whatever explanation may be adopted. It is much easier to overthrow any one of the many interpretations which have been given, than to supply its place by another which is altogether satisfactory. Some, according to Trench, regarding the equal penny to all as the key to the parable, say that the lesson here taught is the equality of rewards in the kingdom of God. Others make, not the equal penny, but the successive hours at which the laborers are called, the prominent lesson of the parable. Some of these, as Origen and Hilary, suppose the different hours apply to Adam, Noah, Abraham, Moses, and lastly to the Apostles; others, that they apply first to the Jews and then to the Gentiles; while others suppose that they apply to the different periods of life at which the laborers enter on the work of the Lord. Luther, as quoted by Stier, says, "If we would interpret strictly, we must understand the penny of the temporal good, and the favor of the householder of the eternal good," and he sees quite clearly that the murmuring laborers trot away with their penny and are damned." Stier assents to this, and asserts that "the penny is certainly a temporal good, different from eternal life, only not of a mere outward and earthly nature," "the promise (1 Tim. iv. 8) of the life that now is." Alford thinks the salient point of the parable to be, that "the kingdom of God is of grace, and not of debt; that they who were called first and have labored longest have no more claim upon God than those who were called last." Its primary application, he thinks, is to the Apostles who had asked the question; and its secondary applications "to all those to whom such a comparison of first or last called, will apply," nationally to the Jews, individually to those whose call has been in early life, as well as to those who are first in point of talents, labor," &c. Mr. Livermore, in a few clear and truthful words, gives the immediate application of the parable. "Peter," he says, "had inquired respecting the rewards of discipleship. The Saviour replies, that the Apostles would attain the highest honors, next to himself, and that all other disciples would receive abundant rewards, both in this life, and in that which is to come. But, he adds, do not suppose that the earlier converts under the Gospel dispensation will on that account be any more meritorious, or better rewarded, than those, who, being called later, manifest an equal fidelity and zeal." "The first as to time and privileges, may become inferior to the last, and the last become first."

In order to understand the parable, we must consider carefully its surroundings and the relation in which it stands to them. The words (xix. 30, and xx. 16) with which it is introduced and ended are so closely connected with it, that it plainly must be interpreted so as to be an illustration of them. Peter (xix. 27) asks, "What shall *we* have?" Jesus in the two following verses answers the question, and then answers the state of mind which had prompted the question, and which he evidently intended to rebuke. "Ye, and all who have made such sacrifices for me, shall indeed be rewarded. But while you seem to yourselves thus worthy of honor and reward, it is well for you to remember that many who are first shall be last, if in looking too much to their reward they allow in themselves a wrong disposition and temper of mind." To illustrate this characteristic of his kingdom, by which the first are often made last, and the last first, he relates a story of a householder, who in the morning engaged laborers for a specific sum, and afterwards at different hours of the day engaged also other laborers to go into his vineyard without any agreement as to the exact sum which they were to receive. When the day was ended, the laborers were called together, and those who came last received each one a penny, which was all that had been promised to those who came first. The selfish feelings of those who had labored all the day were excited; they expected for themselves a larger reward than had been agreed upon; and began to murmur because it was not given to them. Because of the envious, complaining spirit which they thus showed, they were rebuked and sent away with their penny, while the master evidently looked with more favor on those who had modestly received his bounty. "So," Jesus adds, repeating emphatically under a different form the expression with which the parable had been introduced, — "so the last shall be first and the first last." The outward distinctions which come from time, birth, talent, or labors, and which are most apparent among men, must in the reckoning at the end give way to the higher distinctions which rest on the condition of the mind and character; so that often they who are first in time, office, gifts, accomplishments, or even the length and apparent usefulness of their labors, shall in the disclosures of that hour be found worthy only of a subordinate place, while others who were the least thought of here and who thought the least of their own merits, shall then be found among the first.

But what construction is to be put upon the equal penny which every one received? It will not do to insist upon pressing every minor circumstance of a parable into the interpretation. But in this case the equality of the wages is brought forward so prominently that it can hardly be overlooked. All who were sent into the vineyard, were, as faithful laborers, the representatives of those who, through the bounty of their Lord, shall alike receive the gift of eternal life. But while eternal life is equally bestowed on all, they who from their superior services had presumed on a superior reward, have thus been cherishing a spirit, which, though it may not exclude them from eternal life, will nevertheless place them below those who in shorter and less conspicuous services have been more meek and lowly in heart.

The substance of the parable is this. While all who obey the call of their Master and labor faithfully in his vineyard shall equally receive the reward of eternal life, yet if any by reason of their pre-eminent place or services here presume to look down on others, and selfishly or proudly to claim for themselves more than is given to others, they are indulging a disposition and temper of mind which must at length reverse the present order of precedency, and make many who are first last, and last first. The great law of our spiritual being, by which pride abases and humility exalts, is here held up by the Saviour, and applied to the Apostles as a warning against the self-seeking, self-complacent spirit indicated by the question which Peter has asked in their behalf. As Bengel has said, it is in respect to the Apostles, not a prophecy, but a warning.

While the parable was directly given for the admonition of the Apostles, who were evidently presuming too much on their place next to the Saviour, and their labors and sacrifices, it after the manner of Jesus lays open a grand principle of spiritual advancement and decline which shall stand forth a perpetual admonition to all who from their conspicuous position, endowments, or services are in danger of cherishing the spirit which is here condemned. It applies to the Jews, who as a people prided themselves on account of their superior privileges, and who by their pride cut themselves off from the high place which they once held. It applies as a warning to all who hold distinguished places in the Church, or distinguished posts of Christian usefulness and honor, to those whose reputation for learning, ability, or sanctity gives them a peculiar influence in the Christian community, and to all who from their early calling, the richness of their gifts, or the abundance and success of their labors are tempted to think too highly of themselves, or to despise others. "This parable," says Luther, "hits even excellent people, nay, it terrifies the greatest saints, and therefore Christ holds it up before the Apostles themselves." "How many shining stars," says Ramback as quoted by Stier, "have already been struck by the tail of the dragon, and cast down by pride to the earth." Stier also borrows from Herberger a story which, as he says, strikingly portrays in an extreme light what Christ here mildly represents in a softer light. A monk died, leaving a great name for sanctity; a robber who had heard him preach repented, ran to confess, but fell on the way and broke his neck. A devout man saw both, wept at the death of the saint, but rejoiced at that of the robber. Why so? 'When the monk died, the devil took him because of his pride; when the robber broke his neck, angels received his penitent soul.'"

A more pertinent illustration of the parable might be given. Aran was a follower of Jesus the Crucified, and a teacher of his truth in the early days of the Church. He labored unsparingly, and saw the work of the Lord prospering marvellously in his hands. Thousands of new converts honored him as their spiritual father; his name was pronounced with loving admiration in many and distant lands, and pilgrims came from the remotest parts of the earth, that they might profit by his counsels and the sanctity of his life. But, unawares to himself, his heart was beginning to be elated by the honor and success which followed him in his labors. He rejoiced, not so much that souls were redeemed from their sins, as that they were won to Christ through the eloquence of his speech. And so it happened, that while his labors and his zeal increased, and multitudes more than ever thronged around him, and throughout the whole of Christendom he was regarded with reverence and wonder, the lowliness and simplicity of his own heart were leaving him, and even while he exclaimed, *Non nobis, domine,* "Not unto us, O Lord, not unto us," pride and vainglory from underneath the very altar on which they had been laid in sacrifice whispered to him that the glory must indeed be given to God, but that few among men had been privileged to do so much for the advancement of his name and cause.

Near him was Garnan, a simple disciple who honored Aran as in the hands of God the instrument of his salvation from the worship of idols, and who labored among the menials of his household, — rejoicing if at any time he could lead the trembling pilgrim within the reach of his master's influence. His knowledge was the instinct of a loving and faithful soul. He was thankful if he could revive the drooping hopes of a fellow-servant or bestow a cup of water on the fainting traveller, to refresh him after the burden and the heat of his journey, — repeating while he did it some comforting words of Jesus, or uttering some prayer of faith as it came unbidden from his heart. Thus day and night, in season and out of season, unnoticed by the eye of man, he employs himself thinking only of his Master and his Master's work, — praying in his simple way, and thus keeping the well-spring of piety alive in his heart, but never dreaming that he is doing anything for others, and least of all that he is doing anything to help on that great movement which is already causing the earth to tremble at its coming, and by which the kingdoms of this world shall become the kingdoms of our Lord, and his Christ.

At length the day of persecution arrived. Aran welcomes its approach. Amid the admiration of thousands, who greet him almost with plaudits as they witness the alacrity with which he gives himself into the hands of his persecutors, he goes bravely to the flames, praising and thanking God for the strength which he has given *him*, that the honors of such a life may not be tarnished nor its influence weakened by a mean and cowardly death. Garnan also is seized and bidden to make ready. No sympathizing or admiring eyes are turned towards him. He thinks of the Saviour who died for all, — of the saintly man whom it has been his privilege to serve. He hardly remembers to pray even for the salvation of his own soul. But he prays for his friends, that they may serve God in their lives, and glorify him in their death. He prays for lonely and trembling ones, that their faith may be strengthened. He prays for the kingdom of God, that it may come throughout the world.

The flames encircle them, and at the same moment the souls of both escape from their fiery shroud.

One is canonized in the church, and numbered among the starry names which have power to stir men's souls through all coming generations. The other, no man except a few of his fellow-servants cared for or remembered, and soon his name had utterly perished from all human records. Beyond the veil, angels indeed received Aran as one of the "many" who have been "called" into the kingdom of God; but Garnan they surround with brighter gleams of joy as they bear him with songs of joy and place him among the few whom their Lord has "chosen" to lean upon his bosom. So the last shall be first, and the first last.

---

## NOTES.

For the kingdom of Heaven is like unto a man that is an householder, which went out early in the morning to hire la-

---

1. **For the kingdom of Heaven is like unto a man that is an householder**] The comparison is not with the householder

MATTHEW XX.   355

2 borers into his vineyard. And when he had agreed with the
laborers for a penny a day, he sent them into his vineyard.
3 And he went out about the third hour, and saw others standing
4 idle in the market-place, and said unto them, Go ye also into
the vineyard, and whatsoever is right I will give you. And
5 they went their way. Again he went out about the sixth and
6 ninth hour, and did likewise. And about the eleventh hour he
went out, and found others standing idle, and saith unto them,
7 Why stand ye here all the day idle? They say unto him, Because no man hath hired us. He saith unto them, Go ye also
into the vineyard; and whatsoever is right, that shall ye re-
8 ceive. So when even was come, the lord of the vineyard saith
unto his steward, Call the laborers, and give them their hire,

---

alone, but with the whole action of the householder as related in the parable. **went out early in the morning to hire laborers**] Morier, in his Second Journey through Persia, p. 265, mentions having noted in the market-place at Hamadan, a custom like that alluded to in the parable: "Here we observed every morning before the sun rose, that a numerous band of peasants were collected with spades in their hands, waiting to be hired for the day to work in the surrounding fields. This custom struck me as a most happy illustration of our Saviour's parable, particularly when, passing by the same place late in the day, we found others standing idle, and remembered his words, 'Why stand ye here all the day idle?'" Trench.
**his vineyard**] "Vineyard is, since Isa. v. the similitude kept up by Christ to denote God's institution upon earth, his people, his kingdom." Stier.   2.
**a penny a day**] The penny was equal to about sixteen cents of our coin. "He promises the due reward, the *denarius*, which also in Tacitus still appears as the usual ample day's wage for working soldiers. But if those who are called at the very first begin distrustfully to ask, How much am I certain to get?' then, indeed, it is not good, and they are to be warned of the unhappy end of such a course." Stier.   3. **about the third hour**] The third, sixth, ninth, and eleventh hours correspond to our 9 A.M., 12 M., 3 P.M., and 5 P.M. "These would not, except just at the equinoxes, be exactly the hours; for the Jews, as well as the Greeks and Romans, divided the natural day, that between sunrise and sunset, into twelve equal parts (John xi. 9), which parts must of course have been considerably longer in summer than in winter." "Probably the day was also divided into four larger parts here indicated, just as the Roman night into four watches, and indeed the Jewish no less." Trench.
7. **because no man hath hired us**] It appears that all went as soon as they were called. They, therefore, are not blamed by the question, Why stand ye here all the day idle?   8. **So when even was come**] In paying the laborers at the close of the day, a merciful provision of the Jewish law was followed: "At his day thou shalt give him his hire, neither shall the sun go down upon it, for he is poor, and setteth his heart upon it." (Deut. xxiv. 15.) "The wages of him that is hired shall not abide with thee all night until the morning." (Lev. xix. 13.) Job (vii. 2) implies a similar custom. The evening of each day resembles the evening of life, and the reckoning at the close of the day stands here

beginning from the last, unto the first. And when they came 9
that were hired about the eleventh hour, they received every
man a penny. But when the first came, they supposed that 10
they should have received more; and they likewise received
every man a penny. And when they had received it, they 11
murmured against the good man of the house, saying, These 12
last have wrought but one hour, and thou hast made them equal
unto us, which have borne the burden and heat of the day.
But he answered one of them, and said, Friend, I do thee no 13
wrong; didst not thou agree with me for a penny? Take that
thine is, and go thy way; I will give unto this last even as 14
unto thee. Is it not lawful for me to do what I will with mine 15
own? Is thine eye evil, because I am good? So the last 16
shall be first; and the first, last. For many be called, but few
chosen.

And Jesus going up to Jerusalem, took the twelve disciples 17
apart in the way, and said unto them, Behold, we go up to 18
Jerusalem; and the Son of man shall be betrayed unto the
chief priests and unto the scribes; and they shall condemn

---

as a symbol of the reckoning at the close of life. **12. and heat of the day**] τὸν καύσωνα. The word is used in the Septuagint, Hos. xiii. 15, for the dry, burning east wind, so fatal to all vegetable life. The word is found in the New Testament only here (Luke xii. 55), and in James i. 11, where it is appropriately rendered "*burning heat.*"
**13. Friend**] "At first sight a friendly word merely, assumes a more solemn aspect when we recollect that it is used in xxii. 12 to the guest who had not the wedding garment, and in chapter xxvi. 50 by our Lord to Judas." Alford. **17. And Jesus going up to Jerusalem**] The incidents and conversations which begin with chapter xix., and which probably took place on the east side of the Jordan, end with the sixteenth verse of this chapter. The expression *going up* to Jerusalem refers to the remarkable ascent from the valley of the Jordan. "There is no such second gash," it is said, "on the surface of the earth" as "the depression of the Jordan valley." In a distance of only about twenty miles from the Dead Sea, which is 1,312 feet below the Mediterranean, to Jerusalem, which is 2,200 feet above it, is a perpendicular ascent of more than 3,500 feet. How long Jesus had remained in the valley of the Jordan, on its eastern side, we have no means of ascertaining, but probably not more than a day or two. He had set out from Galilee, to go directly up to Jerusalem through Samaria; but when the Samaritans (Luke ix. 53) refused to receive him, he probably turned to the left, crossed the Jordan, and came by a less direct route through the Peræa.
**18. unto the chief priests and unto the scribes**] The appellation chief priests seems to have been a common one at that time. According to Bengel, it was the especial province of the Scribes to *know* the written law, as it was of the priests to *decide* and *give sentence* in accordance with it. " Scribis] quorum erat scientia; uti *pontificum*

19 him to death, and shall deliver him to the Gentiles, to mock, and to scourge, and to crucify him; and the third day he shall rise again.

20 Then came to him the mother of Zebedee's children, with her sons, worshipping him, and desiring a certain thing of him.
21 And he said unto her, What wilt thou? She saith unto him, Grant that these my two sons may sit, the one on thy right
22 hand, and the other on the left, in thy kingdom. But Jesus answered and said, Ye knew not what ye ask. Are ye able to

---

sententia." 19. **and shall deliver him to the Gentiles**] Observe in these two verses the minuteness and exactness of the prediction. "The Son of Man shall be delivered to the chief priests and scribes, and they shall condemn him to death," as they did; but having no authority to execute the sentence, "they shall deliver him to the Gentiles,"—to the Roman governor and soldiers,—"to mock and scourge and crucify him; and on the third day he shall be raised up." Luke, who records this prediction with some slight variations, and whose language, even more than that of Matthew, indicates the solemnity and emphasis with which our Lord spoke, and the amazement of the disciples, adds (xviii. 34) that they nevertheless did not understand one word of what he had said respecting his death and resurrection. They were so intently fixed upon the thought that he was now speedily to establish his kingdom on earth, that they were utterly blind to any other idea, and could not receive it. This state of mind, which is mentioned here only by Luke, who does not relate the following incident, will account for the otherwise improbable request which is afterwards made by two of the disciples (Mark x. 35), through their mother. 20. **the mother of Zebedee's children**] *the mother of Zebedee's sons with her sons.* Salome (Matt. xxvii. 56 compared with Mark xv. 40). "From the adoration and discourse of this woman, it is evident that she entertained a high idea of our Lord's majesty, but possessed very little knowledge." "The flesh," says Luther, in reference to this chapter, "is always for becoming glorious before it is crucified; exalted before it is humbled." **desiring a certain thing of him**] asking *something* which she does not specify at first, as if she were a little diffident about making the request, and half conscious that it ought not to be made, and that a refusal was not improbable or unjust. 21. **may sit, the one on thy right hand, and the other on the left**] that they may occupy the highest places in his kingdom, which she and they believed was speedily to appear. (Luke xix. 11.) 22. **Ye know not what ye ask**] Jesus replies to them, not to her, "Ye know not what it is that ye are asking." Some have supposed that in this reply Jesus refers to the position at his right hand and his left when he should be upon the cross. But he refers rather to the utter incompatibility of their request with the spirit and nature of his kingdom, and their entire ignorance of what, from the nature of his kingdom, must be involved in their request. **Are ye able**] They, still ignorant of the whole matter, and supposing that the questions of Jesus which involved so much self-renunciation and suffering were some easy conditions on which their request would be granted reply hastily that they are able. Yet even as Jews they ought to have taken the words of Jesus in a different and profounder sense. "The phrase that goes before this,

drink of the cup that I shall drink of, and to be baptized with the baptism that I am baptized with? They say unto him, We are able. And he saith unto them, Ye shall drink in-23 deed of my cup; and be baptized with the baptism that I am baptized with; but to sit on my right hand, and on my left, is not mine to give; but it shall be given to them for whom it is prepared of my Father.—— And when the ten heard it, they 24 were moved with indignation against the two brethren. But 25 Jesus called them unto him, and said, Ye know that the princes of the Gentiles exercise dominion over them, and they that are

---

concerning the cup, is taken from divers places of Scripture, where sad and grievous things are compared to draughts of a bitter cup." " So cruel a thing was the baptism of the Jews, . . . . . that not without cause, partly by reason of the *burying*, as I may call it, under water, and partly by reason of the cold, it used to signify the most cruel kind of death." Lightfoot. "To be overwhelmed with grief, to be immersed in affliction, will be found common in most languages." Campbell. "Afflictions and calamities in the sacred writings are often compared to waves and billows by which the suffering are overwhelmed." Ps. lxix. 1, 2; Isa. xliii. 2. Kuinoel. Being baptized into the death of Christ is, in its spiritual sense, a favorite figure with St. Paul. (Rom. vi. 3, 4 ; Col. ii. 12.) They say to him, " *We are able.*" " The one of these brethren was the first of the apostles to . . . . . be baptized with the baptism of blood (Acts xii. 1, 2); the other had the longest experience among them of a life of trouble and persecution." Alford. 23. **Ye shall drink indeed of my cup**] We may suppose that Jesus made this reply to them, that they should indeed share with him his sufferings even to the baptism of death with a solemnity of emphasis which showed how much more meaning he attached to the words than they had done. **but to sit on my right hand, and on my left, is not mine to give**] As the majesty of Jesus shines out from his humility, so here his humility shows itself in his majesty. Though by the words, *to sit on my right and on my left*, he admits that he holds a royal office in a more than earthly kingdom, still he acknowledges one loftier and greater than himself, without whose authority and consent it was not for him to appoint to the highest places of honor and of power in his kingdom. That "is not mine to give, but [it is for those] for whom it has been prepared by my Father."

**it is prepared**] the perfect tense is here used to describe a future event in its relation to another event still farther in the future. **but**] $\dot{\alpha}\lambda\lambda'$ $o\hat{\iota}s$. "The conjunction $\dot{\alpha}\lambda\lambda\dot{\alpha}$, when, as in this place, it is not followed by a verb, but by a noun or pronoun, is generally to be understood as of the same import with $\epsilon i$ $\mu\dot{\eta}$, *unless, except;* otherwise the verb must be supplied as is done here in the common version." Campbell. We doubt whether $\dot{\alpha}\lambda\lambda\dot{\alpha}$ is used in this way like our *but* to mean *unless* or *except*. The most natural translation of this passage, and that which retains most exactly the Greek idiom, is, "It is not mine to give, but [is] for whomsoever it has been prepared by my Father."

25. **the princes of the Gentiles exercise dominion over them**] " the rulers of the Gentiles [of the nations] lord it [rule] over them, and the great [the imperial] ones exercise authority over *them;*" i. e. over the rulers. Among the Gen-

26 great exercise authority upon them. But it shall not be so
among you; but whosoever will be great among you, let him
27 be your minister; and whosoever will be chief among you,
28 let him be your servant; even as the Son of man came not to
be ministered unto, but to minister, and to give his life a ransom for many.

29 And as they departed from Jericho, a great multitude fol-
30 lowed him. And, behold, two blind men, sitting by the way-

---

tiles there are different grades of authority, the inferior officers ruling over the people, and at the same time subject to the authority of those higher than themselves.

**26. But it shall not be so among you**] *Not so shall it be among you.* With the Gentiles are different grades of official power and authority. Not so shall it be among *you*. But whosoever may wish to be *great* among you, let him be your *servant;* and, verse 27, whosoever may wish to be *first* among you, let him be your *slave;* " i. e. the greater the distinction sought, so much the humbler let the office and the service be. The only test of greatness with Christ is the humility and fidelity which are ready to engage in the lowest offices, and without any thought of self to do what can be done for the good of others. This is the foundation of Christian duty and distinction. It is the great doctrine expressed in the first of the beatitudes, implied in almost every conversation of our Saviour, repeated again and again (x. 38, 39 ; xvi. 24-27), directly enforced (xviii. 4), illustrated by the parable at the beginning of this chapter, and confirmed by his own example at the last supper (John xiii. 4-16), and by his death. " Then it was, " says Dr. Furness, " that Jesus, perceiving their ambition, gives them, — gives *them!* — gives the world! — that immortal definition of true greatness, the depth of whose meaning is yet to be fathomed, and of which his life is the only adequate illustration which the world has yet seen." " Of this whole passage in which Jesus defines greatness, I think it

may be said, without exaggeration, that, if it were the only saying of his that had come down to us, and, even if it had been unaccompanied by the splendid illustration of his personal example, it would have been recorded among the deathless sayings of the world's best wisdom. Truly he was a world-teacher, and the world's wisest may sit at his feet, finding all their wisdom anticipated." **28. a ransom for many**] " As the synoptical Gospels (with the exception of Matt. xxvi. 28) do not contain any other similar declaration in Christ's own words, impartiality requires from us the confession, that this passage taken by itself cannot *prove* the doctrine of Christ's vicarious death, especially as the same expressions here used to describe it *may* denote any kind of death in way of sacrifice." Olshausen.

**29. And as they departed from Jericho**] **30. And, behold, two blind men**] Matthew mentions *two* blind men, Mark and Luke only *one*, probably the one who made himself prominent: " Bartimæus, a blind man, the son of Timæus " (Mark x. 46). So Matthew (viii. 28) speaks of two demoniacs; Mark (v. 2), and Luke (viii. 27) mention but one; probably the one who was most remarkable, and with whom the extraordinary conversation took place. In chapter xxi. 5-7, Matthew mentions both the ass and the colt ; Mark only the *colt* on which our Lord rode. Matthew, the tax-gatherer, is usually more minute and precise in regard to numbers. Where the other Evangelists speak of 4,000 or 5,000, Matthew adds to those num-

side, when they heard that Jesus passed by, cried out, saying, Have mercy on us, O Lord, thou Son of David! And the multitude rebuked them, because they should hold their peace. But they cried the more, saying, Have mercy on us, O Lord, thou Son of David! And Jesus stood still, and called them, and said, What will ye that I shall do unto you? They say unto him, Lord, that our eyes may be opened. So Jesus had compassion on them, and touched their eyes; and immediately their eyes received sight; and they followed him.

---

bers, "besides women and children." See Matt. xiv. 21 compared with Mark vi. 44, Luke ix. 14, and John vi. 10; and Matt. xv. 38 compared with Mark viii. 9. But Matthew and Mark speak of meeting the blind men [man] as they were going *out from* Jericho, Luke as they were *drawing nigh to* Jericho. Attempts have been made to reconcile the two accounts, by rendering Luke's expression, ἐν τῷ ἐγγίζειν αὐτὸν εἰς Ἱεριχώ, "when he was drawing nigh [Jerusalem] at Jericho," or "while he was nigh to Jericho" [in going out]. Both these interpretations are forced. The explanation given by Bengel is less unreasonable. He supposes that one of the blind men, Bartimæus, met Jesus on his way into Jericho, and that while Jesus was dining, or rather passing the night, with Zaccheus, this man joined himself with another blind man, and both sitting by the side of the way through which Jesus must pass, made their appeal to him and were healed by him, as he was leaving Jericho. It may have been so; but even then there is a discrepancy which is not removed; since Luke says that one was healed when Jesus was approaching Jericho, and Matthew says that both were healed when he was leaving Jericho. It is better to allow that in an unimportant particular either one or two of the Evangelists has made a mistake. It is such a mistake as detracts nothing from the authority of the writer, or the trustworthiness of the narrative. These positive contradictions in the different Evangelists, when thoroughly examined, are found to be very few, and relate to insignificant matters. If we knew all the details as they occurred, it is possible that even here the apparent discrepancy might be explained. We know the sympathy that often exists between persons suffering from the same infirmity. It is possible that the blind man whom Luke represents Jesus as healing on his approach to Jericho, may have gone in quest of two others whom he had known, and induced them to sit by the wayside where they could call on Jesus as he was leaving the city the next morning. There is nothing impossible or very improbable in such a supposition. But we think any explanation of very little consequence.

# CHAPTER XXI.

### Reckoning of Time.

There are few difficulties in this chapter except in the chronological succession of events. Matthew is evidently more careful to give the incidents and conversations than to arrange them in their exact order. Indeed he hurries through the transactions of the first four days, including that on which he left Jericho, that he may give in full the remarkable words uttered by Jesus on the last day that he spent in the temple.

Six days before the Passover (John xii. 1) Jesus came to Bethany. As the legal day of the Jews extended from sunset to sunset, the arrival of Jesus at Bethany was probably a little after sunset on Friday, i. e. just at the beginning of the last day of the week, which was the Jewish Sabbath. Carpenter, Harmony of the Gospels, p. 196, and Greswell, Diss. Vol. III. p. 19, suppose the triumphal entry into Jerusalem to have been on Monday. The common opinion they say, "rests on no better authority than that of prescription." We think that the probabilities are not on their side. We know that the crucifixion took place on Friday, and that the Passover was eaten by Jesus and his disciples the evening before, which was the beginning of Friday according to the Jewish mode of reckoning.

Jesus arrived at Bethany (John xii. 1) six days before the Passover. The Paschal lamb was to be killed the afternoon before it was eaten. "The festival of unleavened bread began strictly with the Passover-meal." But it was customary for the Jews "to cease from labor at or before midday; to put away all leaven out of their houses before noon." Hence, in popular usage, the day before the

Paschal supper came very naturally to be reckoned as the beginning or first day of the festival, which, including this day, continued eight days. See Robinson's Greek Harmony of the Gospels, pp. 211, 213. Thus the feast or festival of the Passover, or the feast of unleavened bread, which in its larger compass reached through more than a week, may have been accounted to begin either with the day when the lamb was killed, or the day following. In strictness of speech, the festival began with the Paschal supper. But Matthew (xxvi. 17) speaks of the day before that as "the first day of unleavened bread," and Josephus (Wars of the Jews, V. 3. 1 and Ant. XI. 4. 8) speaks of it in the same way. Now "the feast of unleavened bread" and "the feast of the Passover" were used as synonymous terms to denote the same festival, and that festival may have been regarded as beginning on either of the above-mentioned days. Too little is known of the usage of language in this respect by the Evangelists to enable us to determine with certainty which of the two days is meant by them as the day from which to reckon when mention is made of the Passover (or feast of the Passover) by John (xii. 1) and by Matthew (xxvi. 2), and of "the Passover and the unleavened bread" by Mark (xiv. 1). If their language is to be taken in its strictest sense, Jesus arrived at Bethany on Sunday, and "two days before the Passover" would be on Wednesday. If they followed what Dr. Robinson calls the "popular usage," and reckoned back from what Matthew calls "the first day of unleavened bread," then each of those events falls a day earlier. Carpenter and Robinson take the later date; Alford, in accordance with the traditions of the Roman Catholic and Episcopal church, assumes the earlier; and in this particular we accord with him, though, as it appears to us, there is no weight of reason or authority which decidedly preponderates either way.

Finding Jesus at Bethany on the eve of the Jewish

Sabbath, that is, on Friday evening, we suppose that he remained there through the Sabbath, and partook of the supper which had been prepared for him, and at which Mary anointed his feet with the pure and costly ointment. (Matt. xxvi. 6 – 13; Mark xiv. 3 – 9; John xii. 1 – 8.) The next day, which corresponds to our Sunday, he entered Jerusalem. (Mark xi. 1 – 10.) Such a procession, with its incidents and delays, must have taken up the greater part of the day. Mark says that when he had gone into the temple and looked round on everything there, it was now evening, and he returned to Bethany with the twelve. The next morning, Monday (Mark xi. 12 – 15), he came back to Jerusalem, destroying the barren fig-tree as he cáme, expelled the money-changers &c. in the temple, and in the evening went out of the city. "And as they passed by in the morning" (of course, the next morning, or Tuesday), seeing the withered fig-tree as they came, they entered Jerusalem again, and, after a day crowded with conversations and events, Jesus (Mark xiii. 1, 3) went from the temple to the Mount of Olives, where he uttered the remarkable warnings and predictions which are recorded in the twenty-fourth and twenty-fifth chapters of Matthew, and the corresponding chapters in Mark and Luke. After this conversation, which must have extended far into the evening (the beginning of Wednesday, or the fourth day of the week), it was now (Matt. xxvi. 2; Mark xiv. 1) "two days" to "the feast of the Passover, and of unleavened bread."

If this view is correct, we have no record of the manner in which Wednesday was spent by Jesus. Probably he was in the comparative retirement of Bethany or the Mount of Olives, gaining strength for the severer trials and sufferings before him.

## 1–17. TRIUMPHAL ENTRY INTO JERUSALEM.

1–17. We are here brought within the last week of the Saviour's life. Heretofore his usual practice has been to avoid all publicity. But now, knowing that his hour is at hand, he is evidently willing to make a more general and public impression. He has probably spent the Sabbath with Mary and Martha and Lazarus whom he loved at Bethany, which lies secluded at the foot of the Mount of Olives on the eastern side, and about fifteen furlongs (John xi. 18), or a little less than two miles from Jerusalem. While he was there, many of the Jews (John xii. 9, 11) came out from the city, not only to see Jesus, but also to see Lazarus whom he had raised from the dead. These men, many of them doubtless strangers who had come up to celebrate the great national festival, were probably very much excited by what they heard and saw at Bethany, and on their return to Jerusalem heightened the already impatient expectations of others, and prepared to welcome Jesus on his approach to the city the following day. Jesus on Sunday morning left the house of his friends, and on reaching that part of the Mount of Olives where Bethphage and Bethany meet, he paused and sent forward two of his disciples to procure an ass and her foal from the opposite village. There is no evidence that any arrangement had previously been made with the owner, nor is there anything to show decisively that such an arrangement had not been made. In either case it is most likely that the owner was one of the friends of Jesus, who knew the disciples, and therefore understood the reply which Jesus, 3, directed them to make to him. The ass, and the foal whereon never man sat, were brought, garments were placed upon them, and Jesus sat upon them, i. e. on the garments. These preparations must have caused a very considerable delay, during which the multitudes were gathering round him, rousing one another to a still higher pitch of enthusiasm, while some had spread their garments before him, others were cutting branches from trees and spreading them in the way. At the descent of the Mount of Olives (Luke xix. 37 – 40), the whole multitude of the disciples broke forth into acclamations of joy and praise. Some of the Pharisees who were present asked him to rebuke his disciples for using such language. But he replied, that if these were silent, the very stones would cry out, — by this hyperbolical expression intimating the sympathy which even inanimate things have with the highest spiritual and moral forces of the universe. Then, as he reached that point on the southwestern slope of the Mount of Olives, where the city with all the magnificence of its towers and palaces and temple glittering in the noonday sun broke upon his sight, his thoughts were turned on scenes and events wholly different from those which met the eyes and filled the wondering minds of his followers. Unmindful of the shouts of gladness and triumph which filled the air, he thought of the long catalogue of crimes, and the approaching day of doom, when her enemies should compass her about and keep her in on every side, and her walls and her children alike should be overthrown and destroyed. Beholding the city, "the mother and altar of saints," he wept over it, saying, "If thou, even thou, hadst only known, even yet in this thy day, the things which belong to thy peace! but now they are hid from thy eyes." The long succession of sins and crimes had blinded them, and destroyed in them the sense of their true condition, and prevented a knowledge of the sorrows which must inevitably fall upon them.

10, 15 – 17. The whole city was moved at his coming, and as he entered within the courts of the temple the children took up the words of ancient prophecy which had announced his approach, and sent up their welcoming cries of Hosanna to the son of David. Jesus refused to rebuke them at the request of the Chief Priests and

Scribes. Having thus finished his triumphal entry, and looked round on everything in the temple (Mark xi. 11), it being now eventide he went out unto Bethany with the twelve.

19 – 22. The withering of the fig-tree from its very roots is given much more fully and exactly in Mark xi. 12 – 14, 20 – 26. Matthew mentions the different parts of the transaction as if they had all occurred at the same time.

---

## NOTES.

AND when they drew nigh unto Jerusalem, and were come to Bethphage, unto the Mount of Olives, then sent Jesus two disciples, saying unto them, Go into the village over against you, 2 and straightway ye shall find an ass tied, and a colt with her; loose them, and bring them unto me. And if any man say aught 3 unto you, ye shall say, The Lord hath need of them; and straightway he will send them. All this was done, that it might 4 be fulfilled which was spoken by the prophet, saying, "Tell 5

---

1. **Bethphage**] the house of figs, as Bethany is the house of dates. Its precise geographical position has not heretofore been ascertained; but Barclay (City of the Great King, p. 65) thinks, for reasons which seem to us satisfactory, that he has identified the spot on the southern spur of the Mount of Olives, just before reaching the point from which Jerusalem is visible. Mark says, "When they were drawing nigh to Jerusalem, at Bethphage and Bethany by the Mount of Olives," i. e. at the dividing line between Bethphage and Bethany. 2. **Go into the village**] There may have been some previous understanding between Jesus and the owner of the animals; but there is no word here to intimate such an arrangement. A miraculous knowledge on the part of Jesus seems to be implied by the language of the Evangelists.
3. **ye shall say, The Lord hath need of them**] "If now the disciples should at first be almost suspected of the intention to steal the animals, a single word is to satisfy the owner. It is by all means implied in this, that these people belonged to the number of those who believed on him, that they at once understood who 'the Lord' was, and without hesitation willingly served him. . . . . . The need of the Lord who has not even an ass of his own for his festal procession, presents a significant contrast which the preachers on the advent from the earliest times do not fail to notice." Stier.
4. **All this was done, that it might be fulfilled**] This is Matthew's most common method of introducing passages from the Prophets. (See i. 22; ii. 15; iv. 14; xxi. 4; xxvii. 35.) See also, with a slight variation in the introductory word, ὅπως for ἵνα, ii. 23; viii. 17;

ye the daughter of Sion, Behold, thy King cometh unto thee, meek, and sitting upon an ass, and a colt the foal of an ass."

---

xii. 17; xiii. 35. In xxvi. 56 we read, "All this was done that the Scriptures (or writings) of the prophets might be fulfilled." The expression, *that, in order that*, is used not so much to indicate a purpose as a fact. Sometimes it is employed merely to introduce a passage from the sacred writings by way of accommodation, perhaps to remove a Jewish prejudice. "Out of Egypt have I called my Son" (ii. 15); "He shall be called a Nazarene" (ii. 23), are examples of this sort. The coincidence is verbal and incidental, and forms no part of the original meaning or purpose of the writer. *In order that it might be fulfilled* (see Notes, pp. 43, 44) does not then involve the necessity of certain specific acts in order to the fulfilment of certain prophecies. It may be used merely to point to an undesigned and apparently incidental coincidence, and never necessarily implies that the act was done with the express intention of fulfilling the letter of the ancient writing. But there is a deeper sense in which the word *fulfil* is applied in the New Testament to every part of the Jewish dispensation, to its law, its history, and its prophecies. They all pointed on to the more perfect dispensation for which they were preparing the way, and in which they were to find their fulfilment. The law was to be fulfilled, v. 17 (see Notes above, pp. 88 – 92, 94), not by the literal observance of all its precepts, but in the purer life and spirit by which it should be emancipated from its now burdensome forms and ritual observances. So the prophecies, foreshadowing, by such types and images as could be used the richer life and diviner glories which should belong to the Messiah's kingdom, are fulfilled, not so much by the precise reproduction of each one of those types and images in the outward acts and events of his life, as by the unfolding of its spirit and power and truth through him. The fifty-third chapter of Isaiah, e. g. foreshadowing the humiliation and sufferings and death of the Messiah, has its fulfilment in Christ, even though some of the terms used should not literally describe any specific action or event connected with him, or his kingdom. Still, in a few cases, our attention is called to the fulfilment of prophecy, not only in this higher sense, but in minute and apparently unimportant particulars. Isa. liii. 7, 9, 12: "As a sheep before her shearers is dumb, so he opened not his mouth. And he made his grave with . . . . . the rich in his death. And he was numbered with the transgressors." The passage before us is of this kind. The prophet Zechariah, in his anticipations of the Messiah's kingdom and the blessings which should attend it, breaks out, ix. 9, into language which, taken figuratively, would describe the character and office of Christ. "I suppose," says Dr. Noyes, "the mild, pacific disposition of the Messiah, rather than his humility, to be particularly denoted by the adjective, and by the circumstance of his riding upon an ass. It seems to have been appropriate to princes and magistrates to ride upon asses, especially white asses (see Judges v. 10 ; x. 4 ; xii. 14); but it was a sign of peace to ride upon an ass rather than a war-horse." But while the prophetic language here used has its fulfilment in the mild and pacific character as well as the kingly office of the Messiah, it is also literally fulfilled to a remarkable degree in its minute and apparently unimportant particulars. The very images which were employed to foreshadow his character and office are actually reproduced before the eyes of men, though, as St. John says (xii. 16), even the disciples did not understand or call to mind the prophetic words till after "Jesus was glorified." The language in its connection with the events is very extraordinary: —

And the disciples went, and did as Jesus commanded them, 6
and brought the ass, and the colt, and put on them their 7
clothes, and they set him thereon. And a very great multitude 8
spread their garments in the way; others cut down branches
from the trees, and strewed them in the way. And the multi- 9
tudes that went before, and that followed, cried, saying, Hosanna to the Son of David! blessed is he that cometh in the
name of the Lord! Hosanna in the highest!—— And when 10
he was come into Jerusalem, all the city was moved, saying,
Who is this? And the multitude said, This is Jesus, the 11
prophet of Nazareth of Galilee. And Jesus went into the 12
temple of God, and cast out all them that sold and bought in

---

"Rejoice greatly, O daughter of Zion,
Shout, O daughter of Jerusalem!
Behold thy King cometh to thee!
He is just, and having salvation;
Meek, and riding upon an ass,
Even upon a colt, the foal of an ass."

Were these particulars, thus circumstantially fulfilled, merely incidental coincidences, or were they foreseen and foretold as events which should actually and literally take place? We incline to the opinion that they were thus foreseen and foretold. But if this view is the correct one, here and in a few other cases we must remember that such a minute and literal specification of apparently unimportant facts which are to be, forms no essential part of the prophet's work. It belongs rather to the art of the conjuror than to the inspiration of the prophet *to insist* on such verbal coincidences. 8. **spread their garments in the way**] a token of extraordinary respect. An instance is mentioned by Dr. Robinson, in his Biblical Researches, II. p. 162. At a time when the inhabitants of Bethlehem were in deep distress on account of some oppressive act of the government in 1834 or 1835, "Mr. Farran, then English Consul at Damascus, was on a visit to Jerusalem, and had rode out with Mr. Nicolayson to Solomon's Pools. On their return, as they rose the ascent to enter Bethlehem, hundreds of the people, male and female, met them, imploring the consul to interfere in their behalf, and afford them his protection; and, all at once, by a sort of simultaneous movement, they spread their garments in the way before the horses. The consul was affected unto tears ; but had of course no power to interfere." The time is to be observed in the Greek. The very great multitude spread (aorist) their garments in the way, and others were cutting (imperfect) branches from the trees, and strewing them in the way. 9. **Hosanna to the Son of David**] Save now, salvation to the Son of David,—a term which seems to have been given to the Messiah. The rest of the sentence is from Ps. cxviii. 26. 12. **went into the temple**] not the temple proper, but within the sacred enclosure, where the mercenary spirit was cherished while furnishing doves for sacrifice, or exchanging at a profit the money with which the people might make their purchases for sacrifice. This took place in the outer court, or court of the Gentiles. "By the authoritative act of cleansing this part of the temple, our Lord not only testified his zeal for God's house, agreeably to the construction put on it by the disciples (John ii. 17), but his zeal for the Gentiles also: it being a way of teaching by action that the Gospel was open to them as well as the Jews." Archbishop Newcome. "Our blessed Saviour, who came to redeem, not the Jews only,

the temple, and overthrew the tables of the money-changers
13 and the seats of them that sold doves; and said unto them,
It is written, "My house shall be called the house of prayer;
14 but ye have made it a den of thieves." And the blind and the
15 lame came to him in the temple, and he healed them. And
when the chief priests and scribes saw the wonderful things
that he did, and the children crying in the temple, and saying,
Hosanna to the Son of David! they were sore displeased, and
16 said unto him, Hearest thou what these say? And Jesus
saith unto them, Yea; have ye never read, "Out of the
mouth of babes and sucklings thou hast perfected praise"?
17 And he left them, and went out of the city into Bethany, and
he lodged there.
18 Now in the morning, as he returned into the city, he hun-
19 gered. And when he saw a fig-tree in the way, he came to it,
and found nothing thereon, but leaves only; and said unto it,
Let no fruit grow on thee henceforward forever. And pres-

---

but the Gentiles also, and to make them a principal part of his fold, would not suffer them to be thus neglected; but in this act of his gave them a *præludium* of his further favor intended towards them; and he that was to vindicate their souls from death, and take away the partition wall between them and the Jews, first vindicates their *oratory* from profanation." Mede. According to Mark, this cleansing of the temple did not take place till the day after the triumphant entry. A similar cleansing of the sacred enclosure occurred near the commencement, as this was near the close, of our Saviour's ministry. (John ii. 18 – 17.) 13. Two passages from the prophets are here brought together. "My house shall be called a house of prayer for all people," or, as in Mark xi. 17, "for all nations." (Isa. lvi. 7.) "Is this house, which is called by my name, become a den of robbers in your eyes?" (Jer. vii. 11.) 19. **And when he saw a fig-tree]** Jesus had come from Bethany early in the morning, and apparently without having taken any food. Being hungry, and seeing a single fig-tree, i. e. a fig-tree either standing by itself or distinguished from others by its leaves, while *they* were still bare, he went to it and found nothing on it but leaves. Mark says that it was not yet time for figs, but Jesus, seeing from a distance this tree covered with leaves, may have supposed from the fact of its having leaves, that as one of the early kinds it might have fruit, since the fruit of the fig-tree is formed before the leaves come out. A great deal of learning has been spent on this passage with little profit. Early figs are now ripe at Jerusalem in May. Barclay's City of the Great King.
**Let no fruit grow on thee henceforward forever]** "And yet this *forever* has its merciful limitation, when we come to transfer the curse from the tree to that of which the tree was as a living parable; a limitation which the word itself favors and allows. . . . . . None shall eat fruit of that tree till the end of the present *æon*, not until these times of the Gentiles are fulfilled." Trench. The withering of the fig-tree from its very roots is described much more fully and exactly in Mark xi. 12 – 14, 20 – 26.

x

ently the fig-tree withered away. And when the disciples saw 20 it, they marvelled, saying, How soon is the fig-tree withered away! Jesus answered and said unto them, Verily I say 21 unto you, if ye have faith, and doubt not, ye shall not only do this which is done to the fig-tree, but also if ye shall say unto this mountain, Be thou removed, and be thou cast into the

---

Matthew mentions the different parts of the transaction, and the words connected with it, without any reference to time, as if all had happened at once. Mark mentions the visit to the fig-tree and the words of Jesus, "Let no one eat fruit of thee hereafter," as occurring on the morning (Monday) of the second visit to Jerusalem, while it was not till the morning of the third day, or Tuesday, that the disciples saw how it had withered away, and Jesus added his remarks on the power of faith. This shows how careful we must be about assigning to one specific date facts which are found related together without any notice of a change of time. The important words and events (all that can be essential for our instruction) are sometimes brought together under a single head, as if they had all occurred at once, when they may in fact have been separated from each other by considerable intervals of time. This withering of the fig-tree stands apart from all the rest of our Saviour's miracles, as a work of destruction. There is no mark of impatience or anger, such as some critics think they find indicated by it. Amid the impressive and solemn imagery which Jesus in those last days is throwing around the subject by his terrible words of warning, this blasted tree stands forth a perpetual type and symbol of the curse of death which rests on all unfruitful lives, whether of nations or of men. Especially did it then apply to the Jews, whose political history was drawing rapidly to a close. On passing the spot the next day (Mark xi. 20), the disciples being greatly impressed by what they saw, Jesus took occasion from it to repeat (see xviii. 19) what he had before taught respecting the power of faith and prayer. In Mark xi. 21, Peter says, "Master, behold the fig-tree which thou didst curse has withered away." We shrink from applying the word *curse* to any expression used by our Saviour. It has an air of harshness and almost of profaneness in our language which it has not in the Greek. In order to understand its meaning here, we have only to bear in mind the words which called out Peter's remark, "Let no man eat fruit from thee hereafter forever;" or, as in Matthew, "Let there be no fruit from thee forever." Neither of these expressions implies disappointment, vexation, or anger. It is only the calm and terrible sentence of death pronounced upon the unfruitful tree, as a symbol of the more terrible ruin which must fall on man's unfruitfulness. It was also, as the words following show, a proof of his power to strengthen the faith of the disciples. "In view of the dangers that surrounded them," says Davidson, Intr. to New Testament, I. p. 102, "this impressive act was fitted to call forth their highest faith in his ability to save from every foe, whether human or spiritual."

**21. if ye shall say unto this mountain, Be thou removed**] "The Jews used to set out those teachers among them that were more eminent for the profoundness of their learning, or the splendor of their virtues, by such expressions as this, 'He is a rooter up (or a remover) of mountains.' The same expression with which they sillily and flatteringly extolled the learning and virtue of their men, Christ deservedly useth to set forth the power of faith." Lightfoot.

22 sea; it shall be done. And all things whatsoever ye shall ask in prayer, believing, ye shall receive.

23 And when he was come into the temple, the chief priests and the elders of the people came unto him as he was teaching, and said, By what authority doest thou these things? and who 24 gave thee this authority? And Jesus answered and said unto them, I also will ask you one thing; which, if ye tell me, I in like wise will tell you by what authority I do these things. 25 The baptism of John, whence was it? from Heaven, or of men? And they reasoned with themselves, saying, If we shall say, From Heaven; he will say unto us, Why did ye not then be- 26 lieve him? But if we shall say, Of men; we fear the people; 27 for all hold John as a prophet. And they answered Jesus, and said, We cannot tell. And he said unto them, Neither tell I 28 you by what authority I do these things. —— But what think ye? A certain man had two sons; and he came to the first, 29 and said, Son, go work to-day in my vineyard. He answered and said, I will not; but afterward he repented, and went. 30 And he came to the second and said likewise. And he an- 31 swered and said, I go, sir; and went not. Whether of them

---

**22. And all things whatsoever ye shall ask in prayer, believing, ye shall receive**] "As respects the idea that believing prayer will be heard, St. John (xiv. 13; xv. 16; xvi. 24) has given it in its complete form, by adding the clause *in my name* (Comp. on Matt. xviii. 19); for in that clause the *pure* origin of such prayer is traced to the mind and spirit of Jesus, and in this very *origin* of the supplication there lies the necessity of its fulfilment." Olshausen. "Faith in God would place them [the disciples] in relation with the same power which he wielded, so that they might do mightier things even than this." Trench. 23–27. **And when he was come into the temple**] Jesus had now, Tuesday morning, entered the sacred enclosures of the temple (not the temple itself), probably for the last time. The chief priests and elders have come with artfully prepared questions to entrap him. "It was," says Alford, "an official message, sent with a view to make our Saviour declare himself to be a prophet sent from God,—in which case the Sanhedrim had power to take cognizance of his proceedings, as of a professed teacher." The question which he puts to them by way of reply confounds and baffles them in their attempt, and opens the way for the condemnation which he by the two ensuing parables leads them (31–41) indirectly to pronounce upon themselves.

28–32. **But what think ye?**] Here you are making your professions of fidelity to God; but how does it seem to you? A certain man had two sons, &c. Which of the two did the will of his father? They say unto him, The first. Even so, is the reply; the very publicans and harlots, who were at first disobedient to God, but afterwards believed in John and repented at his preaching, shall enter the kingdom of God sooner than you, who with all your professions neither believed in him at first, nor after-

twain did the will of his father? They say unto him, The
first. Jesus saith unto them, Verily I say unto you, that the
publicans and the harlots go into the kingdom of God before
you. For John came unto you in the way of righteousness, 32
and ye believed him not; but the publicans and the harlots
believed him; and ye, when ye had seen it, repented not afterward, that ye might believe him. —— Hear another parable: 33
There was a certain householder, which planted a vineyard,
and hedged it round about, and digged a wine-press in it, and
built a tower, and let it out to husbandmen, and went into a
far country. And when the time of the fruit drew near, he 34
sent his servants to the husbandmen that they might receive
the fruits of it. And the husbandmen took his servants, and 35
beat one, and killed another, and stoned another. Again, he 36
sent other servants, more than the first; and they did unto
them likewise. But last of all he sent unto them his son, say- 37
ing, They will reverence my son. But when the husband- 38
men saw the son, they said among themselves, This is the
heir; come, let us kill him, and let us seize on his inheritance.
And they caught him, and cast him out of the vineyard, and 39
slew him. When the lord, therefore, of the vineyard cometh, 40

---

wards repented that you might believe, when you had seen him in
the way of righteousness.

33. **a vineyard**] " The vinestock
often appears on the Macabæan
coins as the emblem of Palestine,
sometimes, too, the bunch of grapes
and the vine-leaf." "The image
of the kingdom of God as a vinestock, or as a vineyard, runs through
the whole Old Testament. (Deut.
xxxii. 32; Ps. lxxx. 8–16; Isa. v. 1
–7; xxvii. 1–7; Jer. ii. 21; Ezek.
xv. 1–6; xix. 10.)" Trench. We cannot lay much stress on such references.     **a tower**] i. e. a watch-
tower. These towers "first caught
my attention as I was approaching
Bethlehem from the southeast.
They appeared in almost every field
within sight from that direction;
they were circular in shape, fifteen
or twenty feet high, and, being built
of stone, looked, at a distance, like
a little forest of obelisks. . . . . .
Those which I examined had a small
door near the ground, and a level
space on the top, where a man could
sit and command a view of the plan-
tation." Hackett. According to
Professor Hackett, these towers are
sometimes forty or fifty feet high,
and so built as to serve for houses.

38. **come, let us kill
him**] In the original we have here
the very words that are used in the
Septuagint (Gen. xxxvii. 20) by
the brothers of Joseph. As then
against Joseph, so now against
Jesus, counsel had already been
taken (John xi. 53) to destroy him.

40. **When the lord,
therefore**] " We may observe that
our Lord here makes *When the lord
of the vineyard cometh* coincide with
the destruction of Jerusalem, which
is unquestionably the overthrow of
the wicked husbandmen. This passage forms, therefore, an important
key to our Lord's prophecies, and a
decisive justification for those who,
like myself, firmly hold that *the com-*

MATTHEW XXI. 373

41 what will he do unto those husbandmen? They say unto him, He will miserably destroy those wicked men; and will let out his vineyard unto other husbandmen, which shall render him
42 the fruits in their seasons. Jesus saith unto them, Did ye never read in the Scriptures, " The stone which the builders rejected, the same is become the head of the corner; this is
43 the Lord's doing, and it is marvellous in our eyes"? Therefore say I unto you, the kingdom of God shall be taken from

*ing of the Lord* is, in many cases, to be identified primarily with that overthrow." Alford. The Lord of the vineyard here is not the Son, but He who sent the Son. The minute adjuncts of a parable are not to be insisted upon in any interpretation we may put upon it. 41. **They say unto him**] The language here put into the mouth of those standing by is represented by Mark and Luke as spoken by Jesus. Luke (xx. 16) adds, that " when they heard it, they said, God forbid." De Costa in The Four Witnesses, pp. 32, 33, Edinburg Edition, says, " Who sees not that, in order to explain the difference between St. Mark, and still more between St. Luke and St. Matthew, we must look in the two former for the manner in which the thing actually happened; while from a higher point of view St. Matthew's narrative expresses that inward conviction felt by the enemies of Jesus and of his truth, which compels them involuntarily, in their own consciences, to justify the sentence he pronounces against them?" We have no right to infer any such purpose, or such insight into the secret thoughts of men, on the part of St. Matthew. We rather infer, from a comparison of the different narratives, that Matthew, with his characteristic exactness, here relates things as they actually took place, — that Mark and Luke give the sentiment of this verse, which was actually spoken by others, as coming from Jesus, since, in drawing it from others in the manner he did, he in fact adopted and confirmed it as his own. And though the bystanders may

have uttered the speech here attributed to them, they also, at the thought of the terrible example which was to be made of the unfaithful, as taught by Jesus from their own lips, may have added the words, $\mu\grave{\eta}\ \gamma\acute{\epsilon}\nu o \iota \tau o$, " may it not be," or, " heaven avert the necessity of such an infliction." The whole has been represented in a parable. They assent to the dreadful conclusion; but since it is all represented under the conditions assumed in the parable, they couple their assent with the hope or prayer that a state of things requiring such punishment may never be. It is not improbable that, after their reply in Matthew, Jesus, in words not recorded by either of the Evangelists, made the application of their sentence more directly to the Jewish nation, and that the deprecating words, *Not so*, or *God forbid*, were then called from them.

43. **Therefore I say unto you**] Therefore refers to the whole previous parable, and not to the quotation alone. Jesus, according to Luke xx. 9, directed this parable of the wicked husbandmen rather to the people than to the priests and scribes. The parable itself is too plain to need any explanation, being spoken directly against the Jewish people, and having its fulfilment in the destruction of Jerusalem. In its form there is perhaps a reference to Isa. v. 1-7, which would make it more impressive to the Jewish mind. The great law of retribution, however, which is illustrated by it, and applied to the Jewish nation, is so set forth as to be a warning to all those who live unfaithful to their

32

you, and given to a nation bringing forth the fruits thereof. And whosoever shall fall on this stone shall be broken; but on 44

---

religious privileges. For a moment, at verse 42, Jesus leaves the wicked husbandmen, who have slain the son and heir, and carries out the subject of his rejection by a figure of speech, which under the sanction of what the Jews regarded as a prophecy of the Messiah, Ps. cxviii. 22, 23, shows forth not only his rejection, but his subsequent promotion to the highest place, — the chief corner-stone. (See note to verse 44.) And whosoever falleth on this stone, to him it shall be a rock of stumbling and offence on which he shall be bruised and broken; but he on whom in his perverse and obstinate disobedience this stone shall fall, it shall grind him to powder. By the stone is meant Christ himself, the impersonation of his religion and his kingdom, which shall be a stumbling-block on which some shall fall to their hurt, and which shall fall on others with its grinding retributions. If we do not build upon it in faith, either we shall fall upon it in unbelief, or it will fall on us in judgment. "*For this reason*," Jesus adds, 43, referring back to the parable, i. e. *because* this religion with its righteous retributions bruises those who stumble upon it, and falls with crushing, grinding power on those who set themselves against it; *therefore* the kingdom of God shall be taken away from you, and given to a people, i. e. the true followers of Christ, who bring forth its fitting fruits. **44. And whosoever shall fall** ] This verse is omitted by Tischendorf, who thinks it has been interpolated from Luke xx. 18. Griesbach and Alford retain it. Its proper place is between the 42d and 43d verses. Verses 42 and 44 have been thought to refer, not only to Ps. cxviii. 22, 23, but to Isa. viii. 14, xxviii. 16, and especially to Daniel ii. 44, 45. The passage from the Psalms is the only one distinctly cited in this place. It is also cited in Acts iv. 11. The words used in the triumphal entry,

9, "Blessed is he who cometh in the name of the Lord," are from the same psalm. "Some of the ancient Jews," says Dr. Noyes, "perhaps those who lived in the time of Christ, regarded the psalm as prophetic of the Messiah; and some supposed that Christ and the Apostles regarded it as such. But the most common opinion of interpreters is, that those verses are quoted only by way of accommodation, or rhetorical illustration, or, at least, are applied to Jesus in a mystical, not a literal sense." In opposition to such interpreters, Stier says, "He who will acknowledge in the Old Testament no foreseeing sense of the Spirit transcending the human consciousness of the prophets, moving above the typical histories and relations in independent miraculous power, finds the just recompense of this false inspiration-theory. . . . . (especially in such passages as that now before us), in a most unworthy degradation of the words of Christ and his apostles to a mere play upon Old Testament phrases in moments of most exalted and holy earnestness." A favorable specimen of the mystical interpretation which prevailed particularly among the early fathers is to be found in Cyprian's Treatise on the Lord's Prayer, and is applied to this quotation in verse 42: "We ought to renew our prayers again at the setting of the sun, and the close of the day. For because Christ is the true sun, and the true day, when at the departure of the sun and day we pray that the light may at length come again, we pray for the coming of Christ who shall afford the grace of eternal light. But that Christ is called the day, the Holy Spirit declares in the Psalms." The stone, it says, which the builders rejected is become the head of the corner. By the Lord this was made, and is marvellous in our eyes. This [or he] is *the day* which the Lord hath made; let us walk and rejoice therein." This may serve

45 whomsoever it shall fall, it will grind him to powder. —— And
when the chief priests and Pharisees had heard his parables,
46 they perceived that he spake of them. But when they sought
to lay hands on him, they feared the multitude; because they
took him for a prophet.

---

as poetry to embellish a thought, or as rhetoric to commend an exhortation, but it can hardly be soberly accepted as sound reasoning, or as a truthful explanation of the passage above quoted from Psalm cxviii.

## CHAPTER XXII.

### 1–14. THE WEDDING FEAST.

1–14. A SIMILAR parable to this of the Wedding Feast is given in Luke xiv. 16–24, and has been thought by many critics to be the same. But the two are unlike in so many particulars that they may be considered as separate parables.

The parable here speaks of the calling of the Jews, their neglect, 3, *they would not come,* their contemptuous indifference, 5, *they made light of it,* and finally their insults and murderous cruelty, for which the king sent his armies and destroyed their city;—foretelling the coming of the Roman armies, instruments in the hands of God, whose eagles may possibly be alluded to in xxiv. 28, and by whom the great city of the Jews should be burned up. Jerusalem was destroyed by the Romans within a little less than forty years from the time of the prediction. From 9 to 13 mention is made of the Gospel invitation, which, since the Jews refuse it (Acts xiii. 46), goes to all, bad and good, with its offers of mercy, and would gather all in to the marriage feast. But it must be remembered, that though all, even the wicked, are called, yet there are conditions to be fulfilled, and that, without the wedding garment, "the internal adornment of the soul" in righteousness, the very guests at the table will be cast out from the lighted festal-room into the outer darkness of the night, where in shame and grief there shall be wailing and gnashing of teeth.

We would call attention here to the quiet manner in which the prophecy rises from the loss of national privileges, and an earthly retribution to the fulfilment of that same law of retribution in the judgments of another world. Intervals of time vanish away. The boundaries between this life and that which is to be are disregarded. The spiritual insight of our Lord, following the great laws of God's kingdom on to their results, whether in the conduct of individuals or nations, fixes itself on national ruin here, and exclusion from the society of the redeemed hereafter, as the condition of the unfaithful, without any broad line of distinction to separate them from each other, as if they belonged to two different orders of events. The sharp distinctions between this world and another, or this life and another, which enter into all our thoughts, do not seem to have had the same place in his mind. He looked through both alike, and saw in both alike the operation of the same divine principles and laws. His kingdom, having its seat in the soul of every follower here, receives and cherishes within itself all faithful souls, whether on earth or in heaven. So as his thought reaches alike through seen and unseen worlds, facts which in their outward surroundings seem to us to belong to entirely distinct orders of events, are in his mind and language intimately connected together, as brought about by the same laws. The shadows of time which imprison us within this material world, and make us look on all that lies beyond as of a character entirely different, never with him separate causes from their effects, or deeds done in the body from their legitimate results, whether in this world or that which shall succeed.

### 15 – 22. PAYING TRIBUTE TO CÆSAR.

15 – 22. The Pharisees, foiled in their previous attempt (xxi. 23) to entrap Jesus, hold a consultation, and in their extreme craftiness lay a snare for him which they believe it will be impossible for him to escape. The leading men keep in the background. But they have arranged their

measures with the Herodians, who, though usually their
enemies, are now brought to act together with them by
their common hatred against Jesus. The Pharisees did
not believe in paying tribute to the Romans; the Herodians
were the creatures of a dynasty established and sustained
by the Roman government. The disciples of the Pharisees, and the Herodians, "spies" Luke calls them, were
to come as if engaged in a dispute on this subject, and to
refer the question to him as to one of such impartiality,
truthfulness, and wisdom, that they are willing to abide by
his decision. "Is it right," they ask, "to pay tribute to
Cæsar or not?" If he should answer, No, then the Herodians are ready to charge him with rebellion against the
Roman government, and his destruction is sure. If he
should say, Yes, then the Pharisees will make use of his
reply to turn the popular prejudices of the Jews against him,
and destroy his authority with them. But he saw through
their artful disguise, and, with words which laid open their
hypocrisy, asked them to bring him the tribute money.
Pointing out to them the image and superscription of Cæsar,
he said, "Render unto Cæsar the things which are Cæsar's,
and unto God the things which are God's." He is not satisfied with simply baffling them in their inquiries, and sending
them away confounded and silenced, but in his reply he
lays down a broad and most important principle of conduct.
Give to the government the money and the allegiance which
are due to it, but let it be done in accordance with the
higher allegiance and the more unqualified obligations
by which you are bound to him in whose image you have
been created. By uniting the two, he shows that the lesser
obligation is to be limited and explained by the greater.

They who put the question had supposed that he must
join himself either to one side or the other. But, as has
been finely said, "the very peculiarity, the very proof of
the divinity of his doctrine, was that they could not square
it with any of their existing systems. It was with his

doctrine, as it was in the legendary tale which describes how the tree of the wood of the True Cross had been of old rejected, because it would not fit into the building of the ancient temple. It was too long for one corner, it was too short for another. . . . . . And so it was laid aside till it came forth at last to be the means and symbol of the world's redemption." "The true Creed of the Church, the true Gospel of Christ, is to be found, not in proportion as it coincides with the watchwords or the dilemmas of modern controversy, but rather in proportion as it rises above them and cuts across them. How often are we told that we must be either Pharisees or Herodians; that we must follow everything to its logical extreme. . . . . . But there is a 'right division of the word of truth,' — there is a middle way of religion, which, not from weakness, not from indolence, not from halting between two opinions, but from sincere love of Christ, and from desire to conform ourselves to his image, we may humbly desire to walk." — *Stanley's Canterbury Sermons*, pp. 112, 113.

23 – 33. THE RESURRECTION FROM THE DEAD.

23 – 31. The Pharisees, amazed and wondering, left Jesus. They believed in the resurrection of the dead. But the Sadducees, who say that there is no resurrection, "neither angel nor spirit" (Acts xxiii. 8), came with a question which they believed would be wholly unanswerable. A woman who has had seven husbands, — "in the resurrection, whose wife shall she be?" We may imagine the cunning, sharp, triumphant look with which these closing words were uttered. Jesus did not argue with them after their own fashion, but in one of the most instructive passages in the New Testament, in the calmness and depth of his spiritual insight, he pointed out to them how utterly they had been mistaken, not knowing either the Scriptures or the power of God. From that day to this a class of

keen, but shallow and conceited men, sometimes nominally as friends and sometimes as enemies of our religion, have founded their objections to Christian doctrines or to Christianity itself on this double mistake, attributing to the Scriptures what the Scriptures do not teach, and shutting up the power of the Almighty within the limits of their narrow, short-sighted conceptions. In no particular perhaps has this been more remarkable than with the two classes represented by the Pharisees and Sadducees; — the latter denying altogether the immortality of the soul, and the former believing, as Martha did (John xi. 24), in the resuscitation of the body at a general resurrection in the last day. The reply of Jesus, while directed against the Sadducees, is so framed as to meet both these classes. Though the great laws of spiritual life prevail in all worlds alike, it will not do, he says in substance, to carry into the world to come the limitations and connections which here grow out of our sensuous and material organization. "The sons of this world are given in marriage," but in the resurrection, "when (Mark xii. 25) they rise from the dead," "they (Luke xx. 35, 36) who shall be accounted worthy to obtain that world, and the resurrection from the dead, neither marry nor are given in marriage; neither can they die any more; for they are as angels, and are children of God, being children of the resurrection." The sublime view which is here opened to us of that world, and the spiritual relations which alone prevail there, ought to banish forever from our minds all thought of the resurrection of the present body, with its outward, material organization.

31 – 33. But lest the doctrine of the resurrection should still be misunderstood, Jesus quotes from the sacred writings which Pharisees and Sadducees alike reverence, a passage (Ex. iii. 6) which not only implies the fact of a resurrection of the dead, such as the Sadducees denied, but which also proves, in opposition to the belief of the Pharisees, that the dead are already risen. As touching

the resurrection of the dead" (Matthew), "concerning the dead that they *are* raised" (Mark), "that the dead *are raised*, even Moses showed at the bush" (Luke). For as the Lord is not the God of the dead, but of the living, so when he called himself the God of Abraham and Isaac and Jacob, he declared by this form of speech that they were *then* risen from the dead, "for all (Luke xx. 38) live unto him." It is worthy of remark, that when Martha said (John xi. 24), "I know that he shall rise again in the resurrection at the last day," Jesus immediately corrected this view of a distant resurrection by announcing the true doctrine of a spiritual, uninterrupted, eternal life. "I am the resurrection and the life." "And whosoever liveth and believeth in me shall never die."

### 34 – 40. THE TWO GREAT COMMANDMENTS.

34 – 40. The lawyer who put the question, Which is the great commandment in the law? may have supposed that Jesus would propose some precept of his own as more important than any commandment in the law, and thus lay himself open to the condemnation of the Jews. But in reply to their captious questioning, he brings out from the law itself (Deut. vi. 5; Levit. xix. 18) two precepts, which contain within themselves the substance of all our duties to God and man, — of all that has been taught by the law and the prophets.

Thus the enemies of Jesus could not question him in their craftiness and malice, without being astonished and overwhelmed by some principle of Divine truth. He did not answer them according to their folly, but took advantage of the occasions which they made to expound our relation to human governments and to God, to unfold the true doctrine of the eternal life, and to set vividly before us the sum and substance of our duties to God and man.

## 41–45. CHRIST THE SON OF DAVID.

41–45. There are those who believe that Jesus here intended nothing more than to silence and confound his enemies. "Alike from the terms of the conversation and from its context," says Dr. Palfrey in his Relation between Judaism and Christianity, p. 108, "I infer that the object of Jesus was not to prove or disprove anything, but simply to perplex the Pharisees, and show to the bystanders what incompetent teachers they were, and what shallow and unskilful interpreters of the Old Testament Scriptures." Hase says, "He (Jesus) proved to them his dialectical embarrassment by proposing a sophistical question on the Messianic signification of Psalm cx." But as Jesus, in reply to the captious questions which his enemies have put to him, has taken occasion to unfold or announce to them great and important principles of political duty and of moral and religious life, and to silence them, not by sophistical reasonings after their own fashion, but by the profound and majestic truths which he uttered, is it probable that now, when they are all silenced, he of his own accord would propose a question respecting a passage in their sacred writings with no higher purpose than to perplex them and show off their incompetency as religious teachers? Unless the language pretty decisively indicates this design on his part, we should be slow to believe it. It is not countenanced by his conduct on any other occasion.

What then is the true interpretation of this passage? Jesus has already been announced publicly as the Messiah, and the last day of his public ministry has now come. But all the Jews, his friends hardly less than his enemies, view the Messiah as an earthly king, exercising a wider and holier sway than any king who had gone before, but still an earthly dominion. Jesus would prepare the way for the overthrow of these erroneous ideas. But they will not receive plain instructions, or a direct contradiction of prejudices so deeply rooted in their minds. He can reach them only through their Jewish habits of thought. He therefore asks them, "What think ye of the Christ," i. e. the Messiah or the Anointed One?" "Whose son is he?" They say unto him, "The son of David." "How then," he asks, "doth David in spirit call him Lord, saying (Ps. cx. 1), Jehovah said unto my Lord?" &c. "If David then call him Lord, how is he his son?" These questions are put by Jesus in regard to the interpretation of a psalm which all around him regarded as a prediction of the Messiah, and they are put in such a way as to show that the construction which they put upon these words is wholly inconsistent with the fact certainly established by their prophetic writings that the Messiah was to be of the seed of David. As no one among the learned Pharisees and lawyers could explain the contradiction, would not his friends at least, and might not some even of his enemies, be led to reconsider the whole matter, and to admit different and higher views of the Messiah and his kingdom, when the spiritual claims and authority of Jesus should be more distinctly presented? "There is certainly," they would say to themselves, and perhaps among themselves, "a difficulty here. These two views of ours cannot be harmonized with one another. If the Messiah is really, and on this point there can be no question, the son of David, and David nevertheless looks up to him with reverence and calls him Lord, may it not be that he and his kingdom are of a more exalted and divine character than we have supposed? And these wonderful works which are attributed to Jesus, his resurrection from the dead, his ascension into heaven, and the everlasting kingdom which he professed to establish, — the kingdom of God or the kingdom of Heaven, — may it not be that these after all are the true fulfilment of the ancient prophecies?" Those who were disposed to follow Jesus, and some of the more thoughtful even among his enemies might be led into reflections of this kind. A doubt lodged in the mind by a pertinent and suggestive question will often do more in the end to remove a deeply rooted prejudice and to revolutionize all one's habits of thought than any specific instructions or reasonings on the subject. A doubt thus introduced into the mind is like the water which is sometimes poured into the clefts of a granite ledge, and which freezing there rends the whole mass asunder, when direct and violent efforts to split it would be wholly unavailing.

These views of the passage agree substantially with those of Campbell, Kuinoel, and Norton.

---

## NOTES.

AND Jesus answered and spake unto them again by parables, and said, The kingdom of Heaven is like unto a certain king, which made a marriage for his son, and sent forth his servants to call them that were bidden to the wedding; and they would not come. Again, he sent forth other servants, saying, Tell them which are bidden, Behold, I have prepared my dinner; my oxen and my fatlings are killed, and all things are ready; come unto the marriage. But they made light of it, and went their ways; one to his farm, another to his merchandise. And the remnant took his servants, and entreated them spitefully, and slew them. But when the king heard thereof, he was wroth;

---

1. **answered**] "Not only he who has been questioned, but he also to whom a reason for speaking has been given, may rightly be said to answer." 2. **a marriage**] Any great celebration or festival was so called. The accession of a prince to his throne was called the marriage of a king with his people. "Blessed are they who are called unto the marriage supper of the Lamb." (Rev. xix. 9.) How often does Jesus set forth this festive character of his religion, and what a rebuke in the expression itself to those who would shroud his religion in gloom! 3. **to call them that were bidden**] It seems to have been customary in the East (Esther v. 8; vi. 14) to send a second time to call those who had already been invited to a feast. In this case, as there might have been some mistake in the matter, the king sends, 4, the third time a still more pressing call. 7. **But when the king heard thereof, he was wroth**] "Among the

and he sent forth his armies, and destroyed those murderers,
8 and burned up their city. Then saith he to his servants, The
wedding is ready, but they which were bidden were not worthy.
9 Go ye therefore into the highways; and as many as ye shall
10 find, bid to the marriage. So those servants went out into the
highways, and gathered together all, as many as they found,
both bad and good; and the wedding was furnished with guests.
11 And when the king came in to see the guests, he saw there a
12 man which had not on a wedding garment; and he saith unto
him, Friend, how camest thou in hither, not having a wedding
13 garment? And he was speechless. Then said the king to

---

Mohammedans, refusal to come to a marriage feast, when invited, is considered a breach of the law of God. Hedaya, Vol. IV. p. 91. It was probably considered in this light among all the Oriental nations." Ad. Clarke. 9. **and as many as ye shall find**] Pococke says, "that an Arab prince will often dine before his door, and call to all that pass, even to beggars, in the name of God, and they come and sit down to table, and when they have done retire with the usual form of returning thanks. It is always customary among the Orientals to provide more meats and drinks than are necessary for the feast, and then the poor who pass by, or whom the rumor of the feast brings to the neighborhood, are called in to consume what remains. This they often do in an outer room to which the dishes are removed from the apartment in which the invited guests have feasted; or, otherwise, every invited guest, when he has done, withdraws from table, when his place is taken by another person of inferior rank, and so on, till the poorest come and consume the whole." J. Cobbin. 10. **bad and good**] are alike invited and brought in (xiii. 47), with the expectation, however, that all will become fitted for the companionship of those who are there. 11. **a wedding garment**] It is disputed among the critics whether the master of the feast usually had such garments distributed among the guests, to be worn as a badge or token of their right to a place at the festival. There is no sufficient evidence in the Old Testament of such a custom. The passages quoted by Stier (Gen. xlv. 22; Jud. xiv. 12; 2 Kings v. 22) are not to the point. It seems, however, to be implied in the passage before us, and the custom, we believe, still exists in the East. "We may and ought, when he calls, to come just as we are; but we may not, if we would see his face and enjoy his last feast, remain as we are." "As the king clothes his guests, the bridegroom his bride, so does God himself clothe us with the robe of righteousness and garment of salvation," if we only will receive it with humble and faithful hearts. The wedding garment is spoken of in Rev. xix. 7, 8 : "For the marriage of the Lamb is come, and his wife hath made herself ready. And to her was granted that she should be arrayed in fine linen, clean and white; for the fine linen is the righteousness of the saints."

12. **Friend**] Ἑταῖρε, *comrade.* A word of ambiguous meaning, which may be addressed to an intimate friend, and also to those with whom we are not on terms of intimacy. **And he was speechless**] He had no word of explanation or excuse to give for having put himself among the wedding guests without the wedding garment, — for having come without the fitting preparation.

the servants, Bind him hand and foot, and take him away, and cast him into outer darkness; there shall be weeping and gnashing of teeth. For many are called, but few are 14 chosen.

Then went the Pharisees, and took counsel how they might 15 entangle him in his talk. And they sent out unto him their dis- 16 ciples, with the Herodians, saying, Master, we know that thou art true, and teachest the way of God in truth, neither carest thou for any man; for thou regardest not the person of men. Tell us therefore, What thinkest thou? is it lawful to give 17 tribute unto Cæsar, or not? But Jesus perceived their wick- 18 edness, and said, Why tempt ye me, ye hypocrites? Shew me the tribute money. And they brought unto him a penny. 19

---

All, bad and good, were invited; but some preparation of heart was needed, before they could properly accept the call. **13. bind him hand and foot**] These minor particulars in the parable are not of course to be literally interpreted and applied. As the guest who had here numbered himself among the chosen ones had not the qualities which would fit him for a place at the marriage feast of the Lamb, he could find no freedom or pleasure or fellowship there, but by the very condition of his heart, and the affinities of his nature, helpless and dumb, like one speechless and bound hand and foot, he is shut out from their society, and left in the outer darkness and sorrow in which his soul must dwell. **outer darkness**] Those who left the lighted hall of the marriage feast, were sent out into the outer darkness of the night,—a figure of speech to describe the darkness of a soul shut out from the light and warmth of God's truth and love.

**14. For many are called, but few are chosen**] (See Note xx. 16.) Though all are invited, yet few so accept the call, and use the means of salvation, as to be numbered among the chosen ones. These words apply to the whole parable, and not merely to its closing sentence. The idea is the same as in Matthew vii. 14, and refers to the difficulties which lie in the way of those who would follow Christ.

**16. with the Herodians**] Little is known of the Herodians. They were a political rather than a religious sect. They were attached to the party of Herod, and of course supporters of the Roman government. Their usual position was one of hostility to the Pharisees. But wherever they are mentioned in the Gospels (Mark iii. 6; xii. 13), they are acting with the Pharisees against Jesus. Some little light, but not much, is thrown upon their history by Josephus, Antiq. XVII. 8. Their flattering address here savors of political cunning, and is in keeping with their position as courtiers. . . . . . How terrible to such men the reply of Jesus, seeing as he did through their wicked design. **19. the tribute money**] a Roman coin, *denarius*. There was also another coin (xvii. 24 – 27) which would seem to have been used for temple money. Some have supposed that the reply of Jesus related merely to these two kinds of coins, one of which was to be paid to Cæsar, and the other to God. But his reply goes deeper than this, even if it does not tacitly refer to man as bearing in his image and superscription the same relation to God which the penny bears to Cæsar. The tribute money,—"it has been often described; it may still be

20 And he saith unto them, Whose is this image and super-
21 scription? They say unto him, Cæsar's. Then saith he unto
them, Render therefore unto Cæsar the things which are
22 Cæsar's, and unto God the things that are God's. When
they had heard these words, they marvelled, and left him, and
went their way.

23 The same day came to him the Sadducees, which say that
24 there is no resurrection, and asked him, saying, Master,
Moses said, "If a man die, having no children, his brother
25 shall marry his wife, and raise up seed unto his brother." Now
there were with us seven brethren; and the first, when he had
married a wife, deceased; and, having no issue, left his wife
26 unto his brother. Likewise the second also, and the third,
27 unto the seventh. And last of all the woman died also.
28 Therefore, in the resurrection, whose wife shall she be of the
29 seven? for they all had her. Jesus answered and said unto
them, Ye do err, not knowing the Scriptures, nor the power
30 of God. For in the resurrection they neither marry, nor are
given in marriage, but are as the angels of God in heaven.
31 But as touching the resurrection of the dead, have ye not read
32 that which was spoken unto you by God, saying, "I am the
God of Abraham, and the God of Isaac, and the God of Jacob"? God is not the God of the dead, but of the living.
33 And when the multitude heard this, they were astonished at
his doctrine.

34 But when the Pharisees had heard that he had put the Sad-
35 ducees to silence, they were gathered together. Then one of
them, which was a lawyer, asked him a question, tempting
36 him, and saying, Master, which is the great commandment
37 in the law? Jesus said unto him, "Thou shalt love the Lord
thy God with all thy heart, and with all thy soul, and with

---

seen, — the little silver coin, bearing on its surface the head encircled with a wreath of laurel and bound round with the sacred fillet, — the well-known features, the most beautiful and the most wicked, even in outward expression, of all the Roman Emperors — with the superscription running round, in the stately language of Imperial Rome, '*Tiberius Cæsar, divi Augusti filius Augustus, Imperator,*' Tiberius Cæsar Augustus, son of the divine Augustus, Emperor." Stanley. 30. **are as the angels of God in heaven**] as angels of God in heaven, not as *the* angels. They are not like *the* angels, but are themselves as angels in heaven. 32. **is not the God of the dead, but of the living**] God is God, not of dead but of living persons; — without the article, and more emphatically denoting the present and continuous

all thy mind." This is the first and great commandment. 38 And the second is like unto it; " Thou shalt love thy neighbor 39 as thyself." On these two commandments hang all the law and 40 the prophets.

While the Pharisees were gathered together, Jesus asked 41 them, saying, What think ye of Christ? whose son is he? 42 They say unto him, The son of David. He saith unto them, 43 How then doth David in spirit call him Lord? saying, " The 44

---

life of those whose God he is.

**40. on these two commandments hang all the law and the prophets]** " Christ appears to us to point by the metaphorical expression to the symbolical tassels worn by the Pharisees on their garments, and enjoined by Moses, as a memorial of the commandments: two as the two tables, in each many threads, but bound together in one blue string, i. e. 'many commandments of one indivisible heavenly law of love.'" Stier. The simpler interpretation, " On these two principles depend all the rest," seems to us the more natural and correct.

**43. in spirit]** " Vates, propheta," i. e. Seer, prophet. Kuinoel. " Speaking by inspiration." Campbell. " Under a Divine impulse." Norton. " In spiritual contemplation." Palfrey. The expression " in spirit" does not necessarily imply a special Divine influence, — " shall worship the Father in spirit and in truth" (John iv. 23), " in the spirit, and not in the letter" (Rom. ii. 29). " Walk in the spirit, and ye shall not fulfil the lust of the flesh" (Gal. v. 16). But when it is used to express the impelling cause, it does, we think, imply being moved by the Spirit of God, — divinely moved or inspired, — or, as Mr. Norton explains it, "under a Divine influence." " And he came *in* the spirit into the temple." (Luke ii. 27.) " And he was led in the spirit into the wilderness." (Luke iv. 1.) " As it is now revealed unto his holy apostles and prophets *in* the spirit." (Eph. iii. 5.) " I was in the spirit on the Lord's day." (Rev. i. 10.) Unless the phrase *in spirit* is here used to express a state of peculiar spiritual exaltation or sensibility to spiritual influences, the spiritual faculties peculiarly open to spiritual impressions, or peculiarly moved by the spirit of God, it is difficult to assign to it any meaning adapted to the place which it holds. This, we think, must have been the meaning intended by the writers. So in the passage before us, " *David in spirit*," or, as Mark has it (xii. 36), " *David in the holy spirit*," there is implied a state of mind more or less produced and guided by the special influences of the Divine Spirit. There can hardly be a question that Jesus was and meant to be, so understood at the time. It may be said that he was only accommodating himself to the views of others in order to confute them. But we cannot think that this would be quite in accordance with the perfect sincerity and truthfulness of his character. He plainly assumes, first, That David is speaking here of the Messiah; and, secondly, That he does this under a divine impulse, in the spirit. But because David was thus, in the spiritual exaltation of his faculties, enabled to foretell the kingdom of the Messiah, and its ultimate triumph, it does not follow that he had a perfectly clear and adequate conception of the Saviour's character and office. Divine illumination does not imply perfect infallibility. The prophet may not always understand entirely the vision that comes before him. Daniel (xii. 8, 9) says, " I heard, but I understood not," and when he asked for an explanation, the reply was, " the words are closed up and sealed till the time of the end." We should

Lord said unto my Lord, Sit thou on my right hand, till I 45 make thine enemies thy footstool." If David then call him

always bear this in mind in our attempts to explain the prophetical writings of the Old Testament. Visions of a future and holier kingdom than the world had known, — foregleams of one greater than any monarch or conqueror, who should put down all his enemies, and rule the nations in righteousness, were granted to prophets and holy men of old who spake as they were moved by the spirit of God. But they were obliged to employ such terms as were used among men; and the whole prophetic vision, as it stood revealed in the words of the prophet, must be marked by the imperfections necessarily inherent in our limited human conceptions, habits of thought, and forms of speech. As a single illustration of our meaning, we subjoin the whole of Psalm cx. as it stands in Dr. Noyes's version : —

1. Jehovah said to my lord,
"Sit thou at my right hand,
Until I make thy foes thy footstool."
2. Jehovah will extend the sceptre of thy power from Zion ;
Thou shalt rule in the midst of thine enemies.
3. Thy people shall be ready, when thou musterest thy forces, in holy splendor [in the beauty of holiness] ;
Thy youth shall come forth like dew from the womb of the morning.
4. Jehovah hath sworn, and he will not repent :
"Thou art a priest forever.
After the order of Melchisedek ! "
5. The Lord is at thy right hand,
He shall crush kings in the day of his wrath.
6. He shall execute justice among the nations ;
He shall fill them with dead bodies ;
He shall crush the heads of his enemies over many lands.
7. He shall drink of the brook in the way ;
Therefore shall he lift up his head.

We will suppose this psalm to be, as our Saviour himself assumes in speaking of it, composed by David. Could the opening words be applied by him to any one of his successors? The question of Jesus still comes in with all its original force: "If David call him Lord, how is he his son? Must there not then be a different and higher sense in which the language is used than in its application to a king of Israel? Besides, what Jewish monarch was there who united in the manner here indicated, 4, the priestly with the kingly character and office ? There is no suitable correspondence between the words and the subject. But if, on the other hand, David in spirit had a glimpse of the higher and holier kingdom of the Messiah with its attendant conflicts and victories and glories, are not the images here such as a warlike king like David might fittingly employ to body forth the essential facts of the case ? — 1. The exalted condition of the Messiah whom the prophet king looks up to as his Lord; 2. The sceptre of his power going forth from Zion, the seat of the Jewish religion, gaining its ascendency even in the midst of his enemies ; 3. His people in the beauty of holiness, and his followers coming forth in the freshness of their youthful zeal like dew from the womb of the morning; 4. His joining the priestly to the kingly office; Jehovah, 5, 6, putting down and destroying his enemies when kings and rulers rise against him, and executing justice among the nations, while he, 7, like one in a desert land suddenly refreshed by a running brook, lifts up his head in joy and triumph. Is there not here under these various images, 1 - 4, a picture of the Messiah in his exaltation and holiness, while the warlike images that follow show how amid violent opposition and bloody conflicts, where kings and people are overwhelmed and destroyed, his kingdom shall be established, and he, notwithstanding these wearisome wars, shall, like one refreshed by a stream in the sultry day, lift up his victorious head. The cruelties spoken of in the psalm are objected to. " The least," says Dr. Palfrey,

Lord, how is he his son? And no man was able to answer 46
him a word; neither durst any man, from that day forth, ask
him any more questions.

---

"that such a supernatural inspiration, had David possessed it, might have been expected to do, would be to keep him from describing the future Messiah, the meek and peaceful Jesus of Nazareth, as a furious soldier who should 'strike through kings,' and pile up heaps of bloody and helpless corpses, and slay till he should be exhausted with weariness and thirst." But is not this a caricature? The images in the psalm, of war and cruelty and desolation, do they not truthfully describe the condition of things through which the religion of Jesus, "extending the sceptre of its power from Zion," passed in its victorious progress? And do they not accord with the wars and rumors of wars, nation rising against nation, and kingdom against kingdom, which Jesus himself has spoken of as among the signs of his coming? We wish to state the matter precisely. Here is a psalm which the Jews received as written by David, and as referring to the Messiah. Jesus in quoting from it, speaks of David as saying these things in spirit, and with reference to the Messiah. The presumption from all this is that Jesus believed in David as the author of the psalm, and that the psalm was, or at least contained, a prediction of the Messiah and his kingdom. The psalm itself, in the first four verses, is altogether in harmony with this view of its Messianic character, and can hardly be explained naturally and intelligibly, on any other supposition. Is there in the last three verses anything inconsistent with this view? We leave it for the careful reader to judge whether the latter clause is not also perfectly in accordance with the dark and destructive conflicts which marked the early progress of Christianity, and whether its language may not without any violence be interpreted as a highly impassioned and condensed figurative description of the struggles and slaughters and conquests by which God in his providence was preparing for the establishment of the Messiah's kingdom. 44. **till I make thine enemies thy footstool**] We would refer to the striking coincidence between Ps. cx. 1, and 1 Cor. xv. 25, to the use made of the same verse in Acts ii. 34; Heb. i. 13, and x. 13: "The eternity of the session," says Bengel, "is not denied; but it is denied that the assault of the enemies will interfere with it. The warlike kingdom will come to an end; the peaceful kingdom, however, will have no end. Compare 1 Cor. xv. 25, &c. Even before that the Son was subordinate to the Father, but did not then appear so, on account of the glory of his kingdom: even after that he will reign, but as the Son, subordinate to the Father."

# CHAPTER XXIII.

### Christ's Denunciation of the Pharisees.

According to Matthew, the Sermon on the Mount was the first public discourse of Jesus to the Jews, and this the last. There is, in some respects, a remarkable resemblance or contrast between the two. As that opened with seven beatitudes, so this closes with seven woes. Verse 14 is omitted by Tischendorf. The beatitudes offer themselves in sounds of perpetual gladness and welcome to those who will come; the woes stand out as sad and awful warnings to those who will not hear. It is remarkable that in enumerating the crimes which made a national existence no longer possible for the Jews, Jesus did not dwell on the vices of the people, but on the spiritual wickedness, — the vainglory, hypocrisy, and religious insensibility of their spiritual teachers and guides.

3 – 12. As teachers of the law, holding the place and reading the precepts of Moses, the Scribes and Pharisees are to be respected; but beyond this, their example and their teachings are to be shunned. They, 4, profess much and do little, and what they do, 5 – 7, is in order to be seen of men. But do not ye, 8 – 11, seek these human distinctions, — these titles of honor, Rabbi, Teacher, Father. By Father is not meant the relation of parent to child, but some official title of respect which Jesus would not have his followers assume or apply, — as, e. g. the term Pope, Papa, Father, in the sense in which it is now assumed by the head of the Roman Catholic Church. The expression, "for one is your teacher, and all ye are brethren," strikes directly at the pretended supremacy of any one over the other disciples.

13 – 34. Some have thought the translation *Woe unto you* too severe, and have substituted for it, *Alas for you.* But the former expression comes more nearly to the meaning of the original in its union of severity and pity, and is more in accordance with the whole tone of our Saviour's discourse. Woe unto you, 13, because ye shut up the kingdom of Heaven, i. e. will not yourselves receive my religion, and as religious teachers and guides use your authority to prevent others from receiving it. Woe unto you, 14, because under the pretence of religious services and duties, ye contrive to appropriate the possessions of widows and devour as it were their houses. This verse is omitted by Tischendorf. Woe unto you, because without the vital religious faith through which alone a true convert can be gained, ye compass sea and land to bring one man over a proselyte to your hypocritical and wicked purposes. "A disciple," says Alford, "of hypocrisy merely, — neither a sincere heathen nor a sincere Jew, — doubly the child of hell, — condemned by the religion which he had left, — condemned again by that which he had taken," — not a sincere convert, but an apostate from the old religion, a hypocrite in regard to the new. Mr. Norton supposes that this may refer to Judas, whom the Pharisees had won over to their dark and murderous purposes. Woe unto you, 16 – 31 (see also v. 33 – 36), because ye evade and profane the most sacred religious obligations by your unfounded and bewildering distinctions. Woe unto you, 23, 24, because while punctiliously scrupulous about the slightest observances — the tithing of unimportant herbs — ye omit the weightier matters of the law, viz. righteousness, mercy, and love. Allusion is probably made here to Micah vi. 8: "He hath showed thee, O man, what is good; and what doth the Lord require of thee, but to do justly, and to love mercy, and to walk humbly with thy God?" Woe unto you, 25, 26, because ye regard only the outside of the cup and the platter, both in the literal and figurative sense of

the expression, while within they are full of rapine and
excess; yea, woe unto you, 27, because, being thus mindful
of the outside alone, ye are like whited sepulchres, fair
without, but within full of dead men's bones and all uncleanness. — Finally, woe unto you, 29 – 33, because, as
the last consummate act of hypocrisy and crime, at the
very time that ye are building and adorning the tombs of
the prophets, and saying, " if we had lived in the days
of our fathers, we would not have been partakers with
them in the blood of the prophets," ye by your very words,
and by actions which speak more powerfully than words,
testify to yourselves that ye are the sons of them who
slew the prophets. Go on then, if you will. Since there
is no hope of amendment for you, and no room for the
establishment of my kingdom except on the ruins of yours,
Fill up speedily the measure of your fathers. Complete
the work of cruelty and crime which they began, that, in
the national overthrow and destruction which must ensue,
the time of redemption to my followers from all your cruelties and oppressions may come. O ye serpents, ye generation of vipers, [no longer, as with John the Baptist, iii. 7,
" Who hath warned ye to flee from the wrath to come?
but] how can ye escape the damnation [or judgment] of
hell? *Wherefore,* or, *for this reason,* 34, refers to this
clause as well as to what goes before. It is as if Jesus
had said, If there were any hope of your amendment and
co-operation with me, — any hope that you would cease to
stand in the way of God's kingdom, and to persecute and
oppress my disciples, I might even yet bear with you.
But since there is no such hope, and no way in which my
religion can be established on earth except by the consummation, on your part, of crimes which must soon end in
the overthrow of your power and the destruction of your
city and nation, *therefore,* as the only way of shortening
those evil days, and hastening the coming of the Son of
man, behold, I send unto you prophets and wise men

and scribes, whom ye shall persecute and scourge and murder, so that your measure of iniquity may soon be full, and on you may come every kind of blood-guiltiness that the world has known, — all the righteous blood that has been shed from the blood of righteous Abel, unto the blood of the last righteous man, whom ye slew within the very precincts of the temple. Verily I say unto you, All these things shall come upon this generation.

### The cumulative Guilt of a Nation.

We have here stated by Jesus, in its terrible results the slow but constantly progressive power of sin among a people who give themselves up to what is evil. The catalogue becomes constantly darker from generation to generation. Children grow up into the crimes of their parents, and add to them yet other crimes of their own. Partial judgments fall upon them from time to time, and check somewhat the progress of corruption. Prophets and holy men are raised up and sent among them that all who will may yet repent and be saved. But these messengers of God's mercy only aggravate the guilt of those who will not hear. So they, hardened alike by the judgments and mercies of heaven, add to the murderous spirit of their fathers a deeper hypocrisy of their own, and fill up whatever has been left wanting in the measure of crime by those who went before, till they have reached such a point of obduracy and wickedness, that national dissolution and death must ensue, and in that crisis, that day of national retribution, all the crimes which have been accumulating through so many ages, unfolding new depths of iniquity in each successive generation, as they are now consummated in their lives, so also are they fulfilled in the judgments which fall upon them. "The mills of the gods grind late, but they grind clean." Mercy not less than justice requires that their reign of iniquity should be ended. When a people, through the slowly accumulating results of ages of infidelity and sin, are at length ripe for judgment, when the last terrible crisis, so long preparing, has come, and neither the warnings nor the promises of God will move them to turn from their iniquities and live, then mercy and justice alike require that the sorrowful retributions which have been gathering through the whole period of their history, from their earliest to their latest crime, shall fall in ruin on their sinful and devoted heads. The Jews were now reaching this period. They had had their opportunities. But now to them the end of the world, the end of their *æon* or dispensation, was at hand. All that can be done has been done. One thing only waits, — the cross of Christ. But except with the few who will hear, that will only deepen their guilt, and hasten the day of vengeance. All efforts in their behalf are in vain. It only remains to pronounce their sentence, though it be with tears and with the yearning of an infinite tenderness towards them. "O Jerusalem, Jerusalem, thou that killest the prophets and stonest them who are sent unto thee, how often would I have gathered thy children together, even as a bird gathereth her young under her wings, and ye would not! Behold, your house is left unto you desolate. For I say unto you, Ye shall not see me henceforth, till ye shall say, Blessed is he that cometh in the name of the Lord." These were the words of Jesus as he went out of the temple for the last time. And when he departed its glory also departed, and it was left indeed naked and desolate to them. Then was the beginning of that desertion which Josephus in his Wars of the Jews, VI. 5. speaks of as among the omens which preceded the destruction of the temple. "Moreover," he says, "at that feast which we call Pentecost, as the priests were going by night into the inner court of the temple, as their custom was, to perform their sacred ministrations, they said, that in the first place they felt a quaking, and heard a great noise; and after that, they heard a sound as of a multitude saying, Let us depart hence."

## NOTES.

THEN spake Jesus to the multitude, and to his disciples, saying, The scribes and the Pharisees sit in Moses' seat. All, therefore, whatsoever they bid you observe, that observe and do; but do ye not after their works; for they say, and do not. For they bind heavy burdens, and grievous to be borne, and lay them on men's shoulders; but they themselves will not move them with one of their fingers. But all their works they do for to be seen of men. They make broad their phylacteries, and enlarge the borders of their garments, and love the uppermost rooms at feasts, and the chief seats in the synagogues, and greetings in the markets, and to be called of men, Rabbi, Rabbi. But be not ye called Rabbi; for one is your

---

2. **sit in Moses' seat**] The Sanhedrim, which was composed mainly of the scribes and Pharisees, was the highest religious authority recognized among the Jews. 3. **therefore**] This word limits the command which it introduces. *Therefore, inasmuch* as they occupy the seat of Moses, and *so far* as they occupy it, and are the expounders of his law, observe their directions, but do not imitate them in their conduct. **for they say, and do not**] There is always this danger with those whose business it is to expound the duties of moral and religious obligation. They are so taken up with thinking about them, and enforcing them on others, that they are in danger of failing to receive them into their own hearts, and carry them out in their lives. There is no soul so impervious to the vital and vitalizing powers of divine truth as one encased in its own religious speculations and studies. Its intellectual processes on these great themes absorb into themselves the life which should enter into it and quicken alike its sensibilities, its affections, and its active powers. 4. **For they bind**] The allusion here is to beasts of burden, which when men have loaded with a heavy weight, they apply their hand to it to keep it steady, and prevent it from falling." Kenrick. "In what an entirely different light does the Saviour appear, who himself sought to bear the heaviest burdens, and by his love to make everything easy for his people." Stein. 5. **their phylacteries**] Strips of parchment with certain passages of Scripture, viz. Exod. xiii. 11-17, and 1-11; Deut. xi. 13-22; vi. 4-10, written on them, and worn on the forehead between the eyes, on the left side next the heart, and on the left arm. **and enlarge the borders of their garments**] The fringes were commanded to be worn for a memorial. (Num. xv. 38.) 6. **the uppermost rooms**] the highest place for reclining at the feasts. **the chief seats**] The uppermost seats in the Synagogue, i. e. those which were nearest the Chapel, where the sacred books were kept, were esteemed peculiarly honorable." Jahn. 8. **Be not ye called Rabbi**] Rabbi, my Master. The negative particle is sometimes used in Hebrew instead of the comparative " For thou desirest not sacrifice, else would I give it, and the sacrifices of God are a broken spirit."

9 Master, even Christ, and all ye are brethren. And call no man
your father upon the earth; for one is your Father, which is in
10 heaven. Neither be ye called masters; for one is your Mas-
11 ter, even Christ. But he that is greatest among you shall be
12 your servant. And whosoever shall exalt himself shall be
abased; and he that shall humble himself shall be exalted.
13 —— But woe unto you, scribes and Pharisees, hypocrites! for
ye shut up the kingdom of Heaven against men; for ye neither
go in yourselves, neither suffer ye them that are entering to go
14 in. Woe unto you, scribes and Pharisees, hypocrites! for ye
devour widows' houses, and for a pretence make long prayer;
15 therefore ye shall receive the greater damnation. Woe unto
you, scribes and Pharisees, hypocrites! for ye compass sea
and land to make one proselyte; and when he is made, ye
make him twofold more the child of hell than yourselves.
16 Woe unto you, ye blind guides, which say, Whosoever shall
swear by the temple, it is nothing; but whosoever shall swear
17 by the gold of the temple, he is a debtor. Ye fools, and
blind! for whether is greater? the gold, or the temple that

---

(Ps. li. 16, 17.) That is, outward sacrifice is less required than a broken spirit. So it may be here, that Jesus commands his disciples not to receive or bestow these titles of respect, for they are nothing when thus received and accepted, compared with what they are when applied to Christ their only master, and to God who alone in the highest import of the word is their Father. The meaning of the passage is the same, whether we adopt this or the common interpretation. In either case, Jesus forbids his disciples to seek or to use among themselves those titles of distinction which may interfere with their brotherly equality, or put any one on earth as a master between them and him.

16 – 22. Bishop Jebb (Thirty Years' Correspondence, Vol. II. pp. 56, 57) has pointed out in these passages a construction which corresponds very closely to the parallelism of Hebrew poetry, and which may interest those who are curious in some of the lighter matters pertaining to the form of our Saviour's teachings. The characteristic construction is less marked in English than in Greek, but may be represented as follows: —

Woe unto you, blind leaders, who say,
Whosoever shall swear by the temple,
   it is nothing, —
But he who shall swear by the gold of
   the temple, is bound thereby;
Ye fools and blind ones!
For which is the greater, the gold,
Or the temple that sanctifieth the
   gold?

And woe unto you, blind leaders, who
   say,
Whosoever shall swear by the altar, it
   is nothing;
But he who shall swear by the gift
   that is on it, is bound thereby:
Ye fools and blind ones!
For which is the greater, the gift,
Or the altar that sanctifieth the gift?

Whoso, therefore, shall swear by the
   altar,
Sweareth by it, and by all things
   thereon;
And whoso shall swear by the temple,
Sweareth by that, and by him who
   dwelleth therein;
And he who shall swear by heaven,
Swears by the throne of God, and by
   him that sitteth thereon.

sanctifieth the gold? And, Whosoever shall swear by the altar, it is nothing; but whosoever sweareth by the gift that is upon it, he is guilty. Ye fools, and blind! for whether is greater? the gift, or the altar that sanctifieth the gift? Whoso therefore shall swear by the altar sweareth by it, and by all things thereon; and whoso shall swear by the temple sweareth by it, and by him that dwelleth therein; and he that shall swear by heaven sweareth by the throne of God, and by him that sitteth thereon. Woe unto you, scribes and Pharisees, hypocrites! for ye pay tithe of mint, and anise, and cumin; and have omitted the weightier matters of the law, judgment, mercy, and faith. These ought ye to have done, and not to leave the other undone. Ye blind guides! which strain at a gnat, and swallow a camel. Woe unto you, scribes and Pharisees, hypocrites! for ye make clean the outside of the cup and of the platter, but within they are full of extortion and excess. Thou blind Pharisee! cleanse first that which is within the cup and platter, that the outside of them may be clean also. Woe unto you, scribes and Pharisees, hypocrites! for ye are like unto whited sepulchres, which indeed appear beautiful outward, but are within full of dead men's bones, and of all uncleanness. Even so ye also outwardly appear righteous unto men, but within ye are full of hypocrisy and iniquity.

---

23. **tithe of mint, and anise, and cumin**] These were unimportant herbs, and the scribes and Pharisees are represented as hypocritically magnifying the importance of paying their tenths on them, that they might cover up their short-comings in weightier matters. Jesus tells them that they should not omit the least, but above all they should observe the weightier matters of the law. "The tithe was a provision made by the law of Moses for the support of the Levites, the stranger, the fatherless, and the widow, Deut. xxvi. 12; and was therefore intended to proceed from the produce of the field, and not from garden herbs. The Pharisees, however, were so scrupulously exact in observing the injunctions of the law, that they tithed all small herbs." Kenrick.

24. **which strain at a gnat, and swallow a camel**] The Jews carefully strained their wine, that they might not drink any unclean insect in it. The camel was also an unclean animal. The meaning of the comparison is obvious. The translation should be who strain *out* a gnat, &c.

27. **Ye are like unto whited sepulchres**] "In order that those who were forbidden to approach unclean places might not be polluted, the Jews were accustomed to whitewash the sepulchres." Schleusner. "The Jews used once a year (on the 15th of the month Adar) to whitewash the spots where graves were, that persons might not be liable to uncleanness by passing over them. (See Num xix. 16.) This goes to the root of the mischief at once: your heart is not a temple of

## MATTHEW XXIII.

29 Woe unto you, scribes and Pharisees, hypocrites! because ye build the tombs of the prophets, and garnish the sepulchres of
30 the righteous, and say, If we had been in the days of our fathers, we would not have been partakers with them in the
31 blood of the prophets. Wherefore ye be witnesses unto yourselves that ye are the children of them which killed the
32 prophets. Fill ye up then the measure of your fathers.
33 Ye serpents, ye generation of vipers! how can ye escape the
34 damnation of hell? Wherefore, behold, I send unto you prophets, and wise men, and scribes; and some of them ye shall kill and crucify, and some of them shall ye scourge in
35 your synagogues, and persecute them from city to city; that upon you may come all the righteous blood shed upon the earth, from the blood of righteous Abel unto the blood of Zacharias, son of Barachias, whom ye slew between the tem-
36 ple and the altar. Verily I say unto you, all these things shall come upon this generation.

37 O Jerusalem, Jerusalem, thou that killest the prophets, and stonest them which are sent unto thee, how often would I have gathered thy children together, even as a hen gathereth her
38 chickens under her wings! and ye would not. Behold, your
39 house is left unto you desolate. For I say unto you, Ye shall

---

the living God, but a grave of pestilent corruption." Alford.

35. **Zacharias, son of Barachias**] It is not known with certainty who is meant here. There is a tradition mentioned by Origen that Zacharias, the father of John the Baptist, was slain by them in the temple. It may have been some other person of that name whom the Jews had recently murdered, or it may be that Jesus alluded to Zacharias the son of Jehoiada, who was killed there (2 Chron. xxiv. 21), and of whose blood the Jews had a saying, that it was never washed away till the temple was burnt at the captivity.

**Son of Barachiah**] "does not occur in Luke xi. 51, and perhaps was not uttered by the Lord himself, but may have been inserted by mistake, as Zecharias the prophet was son of Barachiah, see Zech. i. 1." Alford. **between the tem-ple and the altar**] between the ναός, temple proper and the altar, which was in the court, ἱερόν, just in front of the temple. The altar built by Solomon, was, according to Josephus, about 30 feet square and 15 feet high. According to the same writer the altar in the enclosure of Herod's temple was about 75 feet (50 cubits) square, and 22½ feet high. 39. **Ye shall not see me henceforth, till**] Many commentators find here a prediction of the future conversion and restoration of the Jews. "Until that day the subject of all prophecy," says Alford, "when your repentant people shall turn with true and royal hosannas and blessings to greet Him whom they have pierced." "Christ takes leave of them," says Stier, "not merely with the feeling that he can return to the temple only as Messiah or never (accord-

not see me henceforth, till ye shall say, Blessed is he that cometh in the name of the Lord!

---

ing to Hase), but with the clear-discerning prophecy that at one time the people of God shall honor him. The still future restoration of Israel according to the flesh is announced throughout all the Old Testament, from Deut. iv. 30, on to Zechariah; . . . . . he who has not read this is not yet able rightly to read the prophets." — "I depart from you: after this ye shall not see me in this temple till ye recognize me as the Messiah; i. e. ye shall never see me in this temple again." Kuinoel. But is there not another interpretation which is more in harmony with our Saviour's habits of speech? We have seen how often and almost insensibly he rises from the literal to the figurative and spiritual meaning of words. "He who saveth his life," i. e. his bodily life, "shall lose it," i. e. his spiritual life. In this very chapter, 25, 26 is an instance of the same transition from the literal to the spiritual, from the cups and platters which the Pharisees used, to themselves in their outside conduct and inward life. So here, after announcing the destruction which is soon to fall upon the Jews as a nation, may it not be that he turns from the outward ruin of the city and nation as a whole to the inward spiritual manifestation of himself which he will make to those among them who shall heartily receive and acknowledge him as the Messiah? Your house is left unto you desolate. My visible ministry among you is ended. Hereafter, none of you shall see me till, converted, and born into a higher life, ye joyfully behold and recognize me as the Son of God. This is substantially in accordance with Mr. Norton's view.

## CHAPTER XXIV.

### Our Saviour's Gift of Prophecy.

THE question of prophecy is intimately connected with the Scriptures, and any attempt to explain the Gospels must be incomplete unless it should treat this subject fully and fairly.

1. A prophecy may be merely a message or a simple communication in relation to some future event, as, e. g. (1 Kings xxi. 17 – 19) : " And the word of the Lord came to Elijah the Tishbite, saying, Arise, go down to meet Ahab, king of Israel, . . . . . saying, Thus saith the Lord, Hast thou killed, and also taken possession? And thou shalt speak unto him, saying, Thus saith the Lord, In the place where dogs licked the blood of Naboth shall dogs lick thy blood, even thine." The interpretation of dreams (Gen. xl. 8 – 23 ; Dan. ii. 31 – 45), the message to Cornelius (Acts x. 1 – 8), and the message to Peter in the same chapter are instances of this.

2. An impression in regard to the future may be made upon the mind, so as to act upon it with a mysterious power. Some insects are endowed with a prophetic instinct, by which they provide for the preservation and support of their offspring which are to be born after their death. We find this sort of blind but prophetic instinct having a marked influence in forming the minds and shaping the destiny of extraordinary men, such as Julius Cæsar, Lord Bacon, Oliver Cromwell, and Napoleon. As in the heart of the plant and insect, so in the heart of man, it would seem as if there had been sometimes implanted from his earliest years a propelling power urging him on, he hardly knows how or why, to the

work for which Providence has designed him. Do we not see something of this kind working in the heart of a nation? In Rome, e. g., did not this prophetic conviction of the great national destiny which lay before them nerve the people with a sterner fortitude under defeat, and prompt them to more daring enterprises, and thus help them to accomplish the designs of Providence? Or is this an idea attributed to them by later writers in describing the deeds of their ancestors, after the imperial grandeur of the nation had become an historical fact? The history of the Jewish nation furnishes a remarkable instance of the same kind. From the time of Abraham onward through all their individual and national reverses, they were led on by an indefinite but certain assurance of future greatness and glory. This impression, repeatedly renewed, was continued from Abraham to Moses, from Moses to David, from David on his throne, through a succession of prophets, to Daniel an exile and captive. Whatever may be thought of specific prophecies, this expectation of a destiny beyond what had fallen to the lot of any other people has followed them from the earliest times recorded in their history down to the present hour. However indistinct their expectations may have been, however mistaken the interpretation which they have put upon it, and however misguided their conduct under it, that such an expectation has existed among them for thousands of years is a fact which can hardly be called in question by any intelligent and careful student of history. As we examine their records, we find notices of great men rising up from age to age, who, professing to be moved by a divine inspiration, foreshadowed sometimes more and sometimes less distinctly the coming of a most extraordinary person, whose influence should be felt throughout the whole world. Abraham is told (Gen. xviii. 18) that "all the nations of the earth shall be blessed in him." Moses (Deut. xviii. 18) says, "The Lord thy God will raise up unto thee a Prophet from the midst of thee, of thy brethren, like unto me; unto him ye shall hearken."

Sometimes he is described as a conqueror (Ps. cx.), sometimes as the Prince of peace (Isa. ix. 6), under whose mild and powerful reign (Isa. ii. 4) "nation shall not lift up sword against nation, neither shall they learn war any more." He shall be endowed with a divine wisdom, authority, and strength (Isa. xi. 2−10) to uphold the poor and meek. "By him the eyes of the blind (Isa. xxxv. 5, 6) shall be opened, and the tongue of the dumb shall sing," and yet he is to be (Isa. liii.) a man of sorrows, and acquainted with grief, pouring out his soul unto death. These and other visions of future greatness and power, many of them conflicting with the prevailing notions of the times when they appeared, were given from generation to generation, especially when times of great national corruption were about to be followed by their just retribution. Through the darkness of the impending evils announced as the judgments of God there comes always this light of promise from beyond. This is a most remarkable feature running through all the prophetic writings. However severe the calamities which are announced, whatever desolation of fire and sword may fall upon the land, though the whole remnant of the people should be carried away into captivity, there is still a great and glorious future. We think no one can read even the minor prophets without recognizing this extraordinary feature in their predictions. Whether we call them seers or poets, whether we regard them as moral teachers or inspired prophets, this feature still remains in their writings, and it marked the conduct of their greatest men in the most hopeless periods of their history. The writers, even though they were divinely inspired prophets, may not themselves have comprehended in full the character of the deliverer or of the era whose coming they foretold. John the Baptist, whom Jesus declared (xi. 11) not inferior to the greatest of them all, evidently did not fully understand the Saviour, or the nature of his kingdom. Daniel, after one of his sublime prophecies, says (Dan. xii. 8, 9), "And I heard, but I understood not; then said I, O my Lord, what shall be the end of these things'. And he said, Go thy way, Daniel; for the words are closed up and sealed till the time of the end." This sort of impression in regard to future events, made upon the mind and bodied forth in words or images through a divine influence, is a mode of prophecy which we can easily conceive of as possible.

3. There may be another and still higher form of prophecy. Future events are folded up in the present as in a seed. The oak is already in the acorn, the bird in the egg, the man in the child. From the seed the naturalist to a certain extent foretells what will be the progress of the plant, through each successive period of its growth. So to some extent in human affairs, from our knowledge of men and the influences which act upon them, i. e. from our knowledge of causes and the habit of following those causes on in their workings, till we begin to understand the laws of succession or of progress, we may learn to anticipate events, and to catch some glimpses of the future in the present. In proportion to the completeness of our insight into causes, and the laws of their progress in any particular sphere of activity, will be our ability to foresee and foretell future events,

> "Till old experience do attain
> To something like prophetic strain."

If we suppose a mind divinely quickened in this respect so as to look at a glance through causes to their immediate or remote results, and determine with certainty the course of events in the complicated web of human affairs, we should have an instance of this third and highest form of prophecy. It is the way in which all future events lie open to the Omniscient Mind.

Now this is the form under which our Saviour's prophetic endowments manifested themselves in perfect harmony with all the other manifestations of his greatness. We have seen above (pp. 128 – 135) that his miracles were "his works," as natural and easy to him as our ordinary actions are to us. In his views of death (see above, pp. 174, 175) we have seen him, in the plane of his ordinary thought, recognizing the existence of a higher world, which lay as much open to his spiritual insight as the material world does to our bodily senses. So from time to time he foretells future events, not as something specially communicated to him, but as lying within the plane of his ordinary thought. As, from his knowledge of the laws of nature, to use his own illustrations, he foresaw that a cloud from the west would bring rain, that a south wind would be followed by heat, and that when the fig-tree put forth her leaves the summer would be nigh, so also from "the signs of the times" he foresaw future events. From his knowledge of the laws of the moral universe, and his insight into the condition of society and the souls of men, he saw in the world of human passions and interests, and the influences which encompassed them, unerring indications of events which must ensue. In the souls of Peter and Judas he foresaw the denial and repentance of one, and the treachery of the other. In the character of priests and rulers, as contrasted with his own pure doctrine and life, he foresaw the antagonism which could result only in his death. So at this time he saw the utter and irremediable corruption of the nation, — justice poisoned at the fountain, wickedness sustained and honored under the forms of law, falsehood, murder, impiety and all uncleanness disguised and reverenced under the forms of religion, the people rapidly ripening for judgment in the accumulated guilt of ages. The crimes enumerated in the twenty-third chapter are the premises from which the judgments afterwards announced follow as necessary and logical conclusions.

Those judgments consist in the destruction of Jerusalem and the retributions which lie beyond the sphere of the senses. The rapidity with which Jesus passes from one to the other class of judgments is what makes the difficulty in the interpretation of this prophetic discourse.

As was natural to one who looked with equal ease and clearness through the physical and the spiritual world, his thought and his language go easily from one to the other, and often without any word to mark the point of transition. The destruction of Jerusalem, which is so distinctly foretold as the judgment of God on a wicked people, is to him an emblem, or rather the foreground, of the judgments which reach on from their early indications and partial fulfilment here to their perfect consummation hereafter. It is difficult for us who are shut up so closely within the senses to understand the true perspective in the views of one who with equal ease comprises both worlds within the sphere of his vision. The present glances on to the future, and the future throws back its light or its shadows into the present. The two worlds are united and blended by almost insensible gradations into one comprehensive plan. The sharp distinctions by which they are separated to us are hardly recognized by him. This mortal life, with its germ of immortality unfolding itself here, is only the beginning of the eternal life which reaches through the everlasting ages. The horizon of his thought lies always in that higher life and world; and unless we constantly recognize this fact, we can hardly understand aright any word that he uttered. Least of all can we understand the prophetic imagery by which he lays before us the future judgments of God, which display them partially here and perfectly hereafter. From the foreground of visible circumstances and events he is constantly following his principles on to the vast and mysterious background beyond. There is no dark line of separation between the two, and we may not always be able to determine when the scenery is shifted from one to the other.

1-35. The Coming of the Son of Man in Judgment to the Jews.

Bearing these remarks in mind, we shall endeavor to explain the extraordinary predictions before us. In the previous chapter we are told that Jesus pointed out the causes of the national ruin, and foretold the destruction of Jerusalem. On leaving the temple, the disciples, as if incredulous, and supposing that they must have misunderstood what he had said, came to call his attention to the buildings within the sacred enclosure, and the immense stones of which they were composed. In this way they probably meant to indicate to him that it was impossible that the destruction of the city and temple which he had foretold should take place. Titus himself, after he had taken the city, when examining the strength of its fortifications, is represented by Josephus (Wars of the Jews, VI. 9. 1) as expressing a similar thought. "We have certainly," he said, "had God for our assistant in this war; and it was no other than God who ejected the Jews out of these fortifications. For what could the hands of men, or any machines, do towards overthrowing these towers?" Jesus knew the thought of his disciples. He also knew that walls and towers and the most desperate courage furnish no adequate security for a hopelessly corrupt and wicked people. He therefore replied to his disciples only by repeating more explicitly what he had already said. "See ye not all these things; verily I say unto you, There shall not be left here a stone upon a stone which shall not be thrown down." In less than forty years from the time when these words were spoken, i. e. in September, A. D. 70, Jerusalem was taken, and the temple was utterly destroyed, in spite of the earnest efforts of Titus, the Roman general, to save it. Dr. Robinson (Researches, &c., I. p. 436) says of Matt. xxiv. 1, 2: "This language was spoken of the buildings of the temple, the splendid fane itself, and its magnificent porticos; and in this sense the prophecy has been terribly fulfilled, even to the utmost letter. Or, if we give to the words a wider sense, and include the outer works of the temple, and even the whole city, still the spirit of prophecy has received its full and fearful accomplishment; for the few substructions which remain serve only to show where once the temple and the city stood."

After Jesus had uttered this prediction, he went out to the Mount of Olives. While he was sitting there, four of his disciples, Peter, James, John, and Andrew (Mark xiii. 3), came to him privately, and asked when these things should be. "And what shall be the sign of thy coming and of the end of the world?" These last two events, however imperfectly understood by the disciples, were grouped together, and evidently regarded by them as belonging to the same grand manifestation of the Messiah's kingdom. From 4 to 35 is the reply to their question. The principal subject is the destruction of Jerusalem, and the signs which should precede and accompany it, interspersed with such cautions and warnings as might be useful to his followers. First, he warns them, 5, against the false Christs, whose pretensions and influence in leading men astray would be a natural consequence of the feverish and mistaken expectations of the Messiah on the part of the Jews. Then, 6, 7, shall be wars and rumors of wars, nation rising against nation, and kingdom against kingdom, famines, pestilences, and earthquakes. Yet all these, 8, are only the beginning of sorrows, — the beginning of the death-agony in which the old order of things should perish, and of the birth-throes by which the world should be born into a higher life. Then shall succeed, 9, persecutions and martyrdoms; many, 10, shall be offended, and they shall betray and hate one another. False prophets, 11, who usually abound amid the superstitious fears which mark the great epochs of national corruption, shall rise and lead many astray, and, 12, because of iniquity many will be discouraged, and their love shall grow cold. But, he says, 13, rising in thought from these earthly calamities to the higher life into which the faithful shall enter, "He that shall endure unto the end, the same shall be saved." (See Rev. ii. 10.) The Gospel, 14, must first be preached in all the world, i. e. through all the known world, or the Roman empire.

Here were the signs which should precede the great event, and bring on the end. How far were they fulfilled? Any one who will read from the latter part of the second to the fifth Book of the Jewish Wars, by Josephus, may see how exactly, in its general features, the condition of the Jews, and of the Roman empire, as it appeared to the Jews during the few years previous to the destruction of Jerusalem, corresponded to the picture here given. The Jews were engaged in wars against one another, and in fatal outbreaks against the Romans. "War in the immediate neighborhood," says Stier, "ever growing alarms in the distance, terrifying rumors of war, commotions and tumults of the people against each other, this is in reality, on the small scale, the picture of the time as described by Josephus, which, with every year, became more exactly applicable. The wars were certainly, at that time, more of the nature of insurrections, tumults here and there (Luke xxi. 9), manifold commotions and massacres, for example, between the Syrian and Jewish inhabitants in the cities (nation against nation), such as are to be read of in Josephus, Jewish Wars, II. 17, 10, 18, 1 – 8: according to his expression, 'every city was divided into two opposing hosts.'" Confidence between man and man was lost. Governments were overthrown. The ties by which society is kept together were dissolved, and the wretched superstitions and fanatical pretensions which mark the absence of a living faith abounded and prevailed.

As to the literal fulfilment of the prophecy, point by point, in its minute specifications, history furnishes no sufficient materials for the decision. Christian writers, by whom alone any account could be given of the false Christs, 5, have left no records of the events belonging to that period, beyond what we gather from the later writings of St. Paul (2 Tim. iii. 1–13) and St. John. Commentators adduce from different historians of that period accounts of famines, pestilences, and earthquakes, enough to give a coloring of plausibility to the doctrine of a literal fulfilment of ver. 7; but we have not the historical details which are needed in order to put ourselves into the position of those who lived at that time, and to determine how they were affected by these events. For this reason, in accordance with the view which we have taken of our Saviour's gift of prophecy, and also in accordance with the poetical and prophetic use of language, we incline to regard the latter part of ver. 7 as carrying out in a figurative form the idea begun in the first clause of the sentence: "nation shall rise against nation, and kingdom against kingdom; and there shall be famines [Tischendorf omits "pestilences"] and earthquakes," i. e. great privations, sufferings, and commotions in divers places. As to the persecutions, 9, Peter, and Paul, and James the brother of John, and probably many others, were put to death before the destruction of Jerusalem. The manner in which some of the early Christians were led to betray and hate one another may be inferred from Tacitus (Ann. XV. 44), where, in giving an account of the destruction of the Christians at Rome by Nero A. D. 64, he says, that "some of them were taken who confessed, and through them *as informers* a great multitude were seized," and exposed to cruel tortures and death. Eusebius, referring to Vespasian as emperor, says (H. E. III. 8), "At that very time the sound of the sacred Apostles had gone out to all the earth, and their words to the uttermost parts of the world," the word used by him for *world* being the same that is used in the passage before us, ver. 14. St. Paul (Col. i. 23) speaks of the Gospel, which then, about A. D. 63, "was preached to every creature which is under heaven."

The preliminary signs are now finished. "Then shall the end come." The last and fatal series of events is at hand.

When, therefore, 15, ye see the abomination of desolation spoken of by Daniel the prophet stand in a (not *the*) holy place ("standing where it ought not," Mark xiii. 14), let them who are in Judæa flee *to*, or, as Alford translates it, *over, along, across* the mountains. *Whoso readeth, let him understand,* is a word of warning put in by the Evangelist, as it also is by Mark, to direct the attention of those who might be living at the time of its fulfilment to the sign here given. It is impossible now to determine precisely what the sign was. The passage referred to may be found in Dan. ix. 27, or xii. 11. Josephus says (Ant. X. 11. 7), " Daniel wrote concerning the Roman government, and that our country should be made desolate by them." But what was this "abomination of desolation," or " desolating abomination "? Whatever it may have been, as used by Jesus, it undoubtedly was meant to apply to some event which the Christians would understand as connected with the terrible calamities that should immediately precede the destruction of Jerusalem. Luke in the parallel passage says (xxi. 20), " But when ye shall see Jerusalem compassed by armies." This may have been the explanatory clause inserted by Jesus immediately after the words recorded by Matthew and Mark, so that the whole passage would read as follows: " When, therefore, ye shall see the desolating abomination spoken of by the prophet Daniel standing, where it ought not, in a holy place, — when ye shall see Jerusalem compassed by armies, then know that its desolation draweth near. Let them who are in Judæa flee over the mountains." This appears to us, upon the whole, to be the most probable reading of the passage. If so, we are to see its fulfilment in the Roman armies with their eagles, which, as objects of idolatrous worship on the part of the legions, were an abomination to the Jews ; and certainly in the miseries and slaughter which came with them they were a *desolating* abomination. Whenever, therefore, the Christians should see Jerusalem thus invested by armies, they were to seek for refuge among or beyond the mountains. This event took place when the Romans under Cestius Gallus encamped around Jerusalem, A. D. 66, or about four years before the final siege of the city by Titus, A. D. 70. Josephus, in his Wars of the Jews (II. 19. 6), says that when Cestius made his attack on Jerusalem, a horrible fear seized upon the seditious, and many of them ran out of the city as if it were to be taken immediately, and that after Cestius had left the city (II. 20. 1), "many of the eminent Jews *swam* away from the city, as from a ship when it was going to sink." The Christians must at that time have been numerous in Jerusalem. May not the precipitate flight urged by our Saviour when the sign should be given be that which is mentioned in these passages by Josephus? Eusebius (H. E. III. 5) says: "The people of the church in Jerusalem being commanded by a divine revelation, which had been given to their leaders before the war, to leave the city, and to dwell in a city of Peræa, which they call Pella, those who believed in Christ, removing from Jerusalem, dwelt there, while holy men utterly deserted the royal metropolis of the Jews, and the whole country of Judæa, and thus the judgment of God followed those who had acted unjustly towards Christ and his Apostles, and caused that race of ungodly ones utterly to disappear from among men." This account, which harmonizes with what Josephus has said of the flight from Jerusalem, shows that the warning given by Jesus was not in vain. Eusebius, however, does not mention what the warning was. As the sign was given for the Christians, it would be likely to be understood only by them, and as they have handed down no particular account of the events connected with the siege of Jerusalem, we must be content to remain in ignorance on this point. The fact that the sign, whatever it may have been, was understood by those for whom it was intended, and that they were saved by it, is the only fact that is clearly established here by the tradition which Eusebius has transmitted to us. The passage in the three Evangelists may be harmonized as follows: "When ye shall see Jerusalem compassed with armies, and the abomination of desolation spoken of by Daniel the prophet standing, where it ought not, in a holy place, then," &c. This rendering would seem to refer to some sign in or near Jerusalem, and immediately connected with the Roman armies; but, notwithstanding what has been said on the matter by Hug (see Livermore) and Alford, we are wholly unable to determine what specific event is pointed out. This harmony of the different expressions used by the Evangelist would accord perfectly with the passages which we have quoted above from Josephus and Eusebius.

When the sign, whatever it might be, should appear, then the Christians in Judæa were to flee, 16 – 20, with the utmost haste. But why this haste, if the sign were given four years previous to the final and fatal siege of Jerusalem? In our ignorance of the precise position which they held and the dangers which threatened them, it is impossible to give a specific answer to this question. The four years which followed were years of dismal and overwhelming calamities among the Jews. Their miseries were caused even more by the cruelty of opposing factions, and the wickedness and tyranny of their own leaders, than by the sword of the Romans. By separating themselves immediately and utterly from the Jews at this early period, the Christians were freed from the wretchedness among their countrymen, which excited the compassion even of their enemies. Unless they had taken this early opportunity to escape, while the Jews were wholly intent on driving away the Roman army, they might have turned the eyes of hostile factions upon themselves as a common enemy, and, thus being cut off from the possibility of escape, they might have been involved as innocent victims in the slaughter which the Jews were inflicting on one another with such merciless and indiscriminate vengeance. In the winter, 20, or rather stormy weather, fleeing as they must with their wives and little ones, their sufferings would have been greatly aggravated; and if they should flee upon the Sabbath, though they might not feel bound by the strictness of the Jewish observance, they would excite the suspicion and bring down upon themselves the hostility of the Jews.

For then, 21, during the four years ending with the siege of Jerusalem, shall be great tribulations, "such as was not since the beginning of the world, to this time, no, nor ever shall be." We have not room to copy from Josephus the details which go to prove the fulfilment of this prophecy. There were sieges, murders, famines, in Galilee, not less than in Judæa, hundreds of thousands slain, mutual and general hatred and distrust, with all the miseries attendant on this condition of things, before the final siege of Jerusalem; and then, according to the historian's estimates, more than two millions and a half of people who had come up to the feast of the Passover were crowded together within the walls of the doomed and devoted city. There were no cruelties and no extremities of suffering to which they were not subjected. "No other city," says Josephus (Jewish Wars, V. 10. 5), "ever suffered such miseries, nor did any age, from the beginning of the world, ever breed a generation more fruitful in wickedness than this was." Again, he says, in his Preface to the Jewish Wars, that "if the miseries of all mankind from the creation were compared with those which the Jews then suffered, they would appear inferior."

And except those days should be shortened, 22, no flesh would be saved, i. e. the whole race or nation would be utterly cut off; but on account of the elect or chosen ones, i. e. on account of their influence and prayers, those days shall be shortened. "And they," Luke (xxi. 24) adds in this place, "shall fall by the edge of the sword, and shall be led away captive into all nations, and Jerusalem will be trodden down of the Gentiles until the times of the Gentiles be fulfilled." Eleven hundred thousand Jews were slain in the siege of Jerusalem, thousands were destroyed by the sword or by wild beasts for the entertainment of the Romans at their national festivals, and of the ninety-seven thousand taken captive in the war, those above seventeen years of age were sent to the works in Egypt or distributed through the Roman provinces, and those under seventeen were sold as slaves. At Cæsarea, Titus murdered twenty-five hundred Jews in honor of his brother's birthday. "Some he caused to kill each other: some were thrown to the wild beasts, and others burnt alive."

If they, 23, 24, "shall say unto you, Lo, here is Christ, or there; believe it not. For there shall arise false Christs, and false prophets," &c. St. Paul, in what is probably the last Epistle that he ever wrote (2 Tim. iii. 1, 13), speaks of "the perilous times" that shall come, and of the "evil men and seducers," who "shall wax worse and worse, deceiving, and being deceived." This was probably written A. D. 68, or about two years before the fatal siege of Jerusalem. St. John, in his first Epistle (ii. 18), says, "Little children, it is the last hour; and as ye have heard that antichrist shall come, even now are there many antichrists." Again (iv. 1) he says, "But try the spirits whether they are of God; because many false prophets are gone out into the world." This Epistle was written either just before the siege of Jerusalem, or afterwards. In either case its words go with those of St. Paul to indicate the state of things which our Saviour had foretold as connected with the overthrow of the Jewish polity, when "the end," or, as St. John calls it, the "last hour," should come. Josephus also, in his Jewish Wars (VI. 5), says: "There was then a great number of false prophets suborned by the tyrants to impose upon the people. . . . . . Now a man that is in adversity does easily comply with such promises. . . . . . Thus were the miserable people persuaded by these deceivers, and such as belied God himself." Jesus, 26, warns his followers not to be led astray by any such pretensions. "For," 27, "as the lightning cometh out of the east and shineth even unto the west; so shall also the coming of the Son of man be." That is, he comes not with a limited, bodily presence, in the wilderness or the secret chambers, but in the power of his religion overspreading the whole land, like the lightning, which, confined to no one spot, fills the whole sky. With the downfall of the Jews, the new religion will rise as the fulfilment of the old, and in its advancement Christ will manifest his presence to the world, as he did in the judgments which fell at that time upon the Jews. "For," 28, "wheresoever the carcass is, there will the eagles," more properly the vultures, "be gathered together." Where moral death and corruption are, there the judgments of God, like vultures, shall come to clear away the pollutions of the land, — a retribution for the past, a preparation for the future.

Immediately after, 29, or rather in connection with, the tribulation of those days, shall the sun be darkened, and the moon shall not give her light, and the stars shall fall from heaven, and the powers of the heavens shall be shaken. Josephus speaks of "a star resembling a sword, which stood over the city; and a comet that continued a whole year." But the language is rather to be taken figuratively. "That is," says Lightfoot, "the Jewish heaven shall perish, and the sun and moon of its glory and happiness shall be darkened and brought to nothing. The sun is the religion of the church; the moon is the government of the state; and the stars are the judges and doctors of both." We doubt whether the language was intended for so specific an application. We speak of a dark and dreadful day, or a dark and troubled night, to describe a period of great public or private misery. Oriental writers carry their figures of speech more into details than is allowed by the usages of language among us, and give the particulars which go to fill out the idea of gloom and sorrow. It is not merely a dark day, but "the sun is darkened;" — not merely a dark and dismal night of grief and pain, but its darkness, the moon refusing to give her light, should be rendered more frightful by the portentous glare of falling stars, and in the universal consternation and distress, men's hearts failing them for fear, the very powers of the heavens should be shaken. Every source of light or hope to which men had been accustomed to look up should be withdrawn, amid troubles and terrific commotions in what had seemed to them most elevated and stable among the powers by which the order and government of the world had been sustained.

The same powerfully figurative language is continued. "And then shall appear the sign of the Son of man in heaven," 30; not the sign shall appear in heaven, but, "Then shall appear the sign of the Son of man that he is in heaven." Then, when the rites of their own religion shall no longer be observed, when (Josephus, Jewish Wars, VI. 2. 1) the daily sacrifice (Dan. xii. 11) shall be taken away, and the city overthrown with such sufferings and slaughters as never had been known before, — when such unspeakable calamities have fallen upon them, then shall all the tribes of the land smite their breasts, then shall appear the sign which I have now made known to you of the Son of man in heaven, and they who refused to recognize him before shall in these events see him coming in power and great glory to establish his kingdom on the earth. "The Jews," says Kuinoel, "will recognize the majesty and power of the Messiah as their Judge, when, as a punishment for their perversity and madness, he shall mournfully exhibit them in the overthrow of their temple and city. The Hebrew prophets use the same image which occurs here. When they would describe God as declaring his majesty, they speak of him as about to come sitting upon the clouds, whether it be to bring assistance or to pass judgment (Deut. xxxiii. 26; Isa. xix. 1)."

"And," 31, "he shall send his angels," &c. "When Jerusalem shall be reduced to ashes, and that wicked nation cut off and rejected, then shall the Son of man send his ministers with the trumpet of the Gospel, and they shall gather together his elect of the several nations, from the four corners of heaven." Lightfoot. He shall send forth his angels, the messengers of salvation, and as with the sound of a trumpet, which was used to call religious assemblies together, he shall gather his chosen ones, i. e. those who hear and obey the call, into his Church throughout the whole earth. As a matter of fact, the religion of Jesus prevailed wonderfully after its most influential and violent opponents and persecutors had been cut off in the wars which ended with the destruction of Jerusalem. "It was after this period," as Adam Clarke has said, "that the kingdom of Christ began, and his reign was established in almost every part of the earth." That there might be no mistake as to the time included in this prophecy, and as to what was there meant by his coming and the end of the world, — *æon* or *dispensation*, — he distinctly declares, 34, that the generation then before him should not pass away till all these things were fulfilled.

### 36 – 51. THE COMING OF THE SON OF MAN IN JUDGMENT TO ALL.

At the thirty-sixth verse is the point of transition from God's judgment, as shown in the destruction of a wicked city and nation, to his judgment in its wider application to the whole family of man. All that has been predicted thus far applies primarily to the destruction of Jerusalem, and would be accomplished before that generation should pass away. In the foreground of the prophetic picture lie the events which should precede, and the circumstances of dread and horror which should accompany, that great national catastrophe. These events are distinctly portrayed and their limits fixed. But beyond them, in a background reaching onward into eternity, is another and kindred class of events, which are also denoted by the coming of the

Son of man, and of which the precise limits are not to be distinguished or defined. The time when the holy city should be overthrown had been fixed, and the signs of its approach pointed out. But of *that* day and hour, when this more extended series of events included in the general judgment of our race should be completed, no man could know, not the angels in heaven, nor the Son, but the Father only (Mark xiii. 32). Only He whose omniscient mind takes in all causes, and sees in them all future results as already present, can determine that.

The idea which fills out the whole picture or succession of pictures, and harmonizes all their parts, is the idea of a divine retribution. This shows itself in the foreground; then, 37 – 39, it goes back to the times of Noah and of Lot, and from the past goes on again to the future, dwelling at first on single examples, and finally gathering up all separate incidents and souls and ages into one overpowering scene of divine majesty and justice.

At first we seem to be lingering still around Jerusalem in those days of impending ruin, as if, after its destruction had been foretold and language pointing on to a wider range of judgments had been used, he at first, in his reference to the flood and to Sodom (Luke xvii. 28), employed images equally applicable to both classes of events. From this point, however, there is nothing which can be construed as applying, like what has gone before, distinctly and exclusively to the destruction of Jerusalem. The coming of the Son of man carries us into a wider field, until at length we see the whole human family standing before him in judgment.

A great deal is said about types. May it not be that all the language relating to the destruction of Jerusalem was meant to be a type of the general judgment? Is there not this double meaning running through it? In the sense in which the expressions *type* and *double meaning* are commonly used by theologians, we answer, No.

Nothing has added so much to the perplexity and confusion of ideas in the study of this discourse, as the notion of a double meaning running through it. But, in another sense, it is typical, as every fact in nature is, of something beyond itself. A falling globule of water, as an expression of the law of gravitation, is typical of the form and motion of the stars, and thus a type of the whole frame and structure of the material universe. Almost every incident or fact mentioned by our Saviour is so put by him, that it stands forth as the expression of a general law, and the type of whatever may be brought about in accordance with that law. The clothing of the lilies, and the feeding of the ravens, as an expression of the paternal benignity and providence of God, is made a type of the still greater kindness which he always exercises towards us. The corn of wheat (John xii. 24), which, except it fall into the ground and die, abideth alone, but if it die it bringeth forth much fruit, as an expression of the great law of self-sacrifice in order to the attainment of the highest results, is typical of every fact included under that law, and especially of the death of Christ and the unmeasured benefits resulting from it. So the destruction of Jerusalem, as an expression of the Divine justice, or of the judgments of God, is typical of every fact included under that law, and especially of the righteous retribution which awaits every soul, when at the close of its probation here it is called to judgment. The coming of the Son of man in the destruction which fell on a city and people hopelessly corrupt, as an expression of a great law, is typical of Christ's advent to judgment, with regard to every soul that appears before him. The difficulty usually is in detecting the deep and hidden law which serves as a bond of union between one class of facts and another. As, in natural science, superficial resemblances are disregarded, and, by a law of association which it is difficult for the uninitiated to recognize, the strawberry, the mountain-ash, the blackberry, and the apple are placed side by side in the same family, so in our Saviour's words facts are sometimes grouped together which have little or no superficial resemblance, though they are vitally connected as representatives of the same law. In this way language is employed in describing one class of facts, which applies with equal force to other and kindred, though apparently dissimilar, classes of facts. Almost all the language on which we have been commenting in this chapter, and which describes with such terrific power the events connected with the overthrow of the Jewish ritual and nation, designates with great force the general law of retribution in its application to our race; and with most readers this last is the only lesson which it teaches. On the other hand, when the subject is really changed, as it is in verse 36, from one to another kindred class of facts, those two classes of facts are in the mind and the language of Jesus bound together so closely, by the same uniting law, that only a slight and indefinite notice is given of the transition, and it is only by the closest attention that we can discover precisely where the change has taken place.

Jesus has just spoken, 36, of the uncertainty of "that day and hour," and would make this uncertainty a reason for watchfulness to all. As, in the time of Noah, the flood came unexpectedly upon a world absorbed in other cares, so shall the coming of the Son of man be. No man can tell when his "day" shall come. "Then two men shall be in the field; one is taken, one is left. Two women grinding at the mill, turning with their hands the same stone; one is taken, one is left. Watch, therefore, for ye know not what day your Lord doth come." How could this language apply to the destruction of Jerusalem? Jesus has already, 15, 16, pointed out the sign by which his followers are to be saved from that catastrophe. In the 34th verse he has limited the time within which that series of events is to take place. But the same idea of a divine retribution, which is there characterized as the coming of the Son of man, is here carried out in the divine retribution which awaits every man at the close of this mortal life, and which is to him the coming of the Son of man in judgment, when, as St. Paul describes it, "we must all appear before the judgment-seat of Christ." We are not all called at once. Even with those most intimately connected, "one is taken, one is left." No man knoweth when the call shall be made to him. How perfectly and with what a powerful warning does this language hold up before us the uncertainty of life, and the certainty of judgment! No philosophical precision of speech could address itself to the heart with such truth and power. The same idea is dwelt upon and enforced with still greater distinctness in the ensuing parables. The parable which closes this chapter, and which applies to "that" unknown "hour" which comes to all, is too direct and explicit in its appeal to each soul to allow of any labored comment. It applies to our conduct here as a preparation for that solemn moment when the Son of man shall come to each one of us at the close of our mortal labors, and the interests of this world shall be lost in the retributions of the world to come. He comes, first, to every soul in the offers of mercy and salvation which he makes. He comes to all, when they receive him, and strive to obey him, with loving and believing hearts. His final coming to each one is when he shall call us to account for the use that we have made of his gifts.

### Conclusion.

We have endeavored to explain this remarkable prediction of our Saviour. We have shown how the part of it which applied to "that generation" was fulfilled, not literally perhaps in all its parts, but exactly in accordance with its spirit. And this is the way in which we are to interpret and apply, not only the highest prophecy, but the highest poetry, the profoundest inductions of philosophy, and the grandest generalizations of transcendental mathematics. The literal, precise interpretation of a single expression is often false, and false in proportion to the magnitude of the truth which soars up in its majestic proportions through such words and images as our human forms of speech and thought may furnish. Any one may see that a literal, prosaic interpretation of King Lear, or Paradise Lost, sentence by sentence, in order to show precisely what facts are proved by them, would do no sort of justice to the grander movements of soul which fill out with their inspiration every part of those wonderful works. Far more in the prophetic words of our Saviour, which so far surpass all the other words that have ever been spoken, it is the letter that killeth. No one, whether as the advocate or the enemy of our faith, can understand them, unless he enter beneath the letter into the spirit, and thus catch as he may something of the inspiration, the largeness of thought and affluence of life, which they are fitted to awaken and impart. The humble inquirer, entering thus into the heart of our Saviour's words that he may cherish their spirit and obey their commands, will come nearer to the essential truth which they are designed to teach, than the ablest scholar, who, without religious sympathies, or with a superstitious regard to the letter, seeks to analyze them by applying critically, sentence by sentence, the rules of the grammar and lexicon.

---

## NOTES.

AND Jesus went out, and departed from the temple; and his disciples came to him, for to show him the buildings of the

---

1. **to show him the buildings**] They were amazed at his words, and, wondering whether they could have understood him aright, instead of asking directly whether what he had said of the destruction of the temple could apply to an event so utterly improbable as that, they point out to him the massive structures within the sacred enclosure, and say, "Master, see what manner of stones and

temple. And Jesus said unto them, See ye not all these 2 things? verily, I say unto you, there shall not be left here one stone upon another, that shall not be thrown down. —— And 3 as he sat upon the Mount of Olives, the disciples came unto him privately, saying, Tell us, when shall these things be? and what shall be the sign of thy coming, and of the end of the

---

what manner of buildings." (Mark xiii. 1.) The temple had been built by Herod the Great, who employed 18,000 men on the work for nine years before the building could be used at all. Additions were continually making afterwards till A. D. 64. It was first occupied about eight years before the birth of Jesus; but as the work was still going on, it might be said to Jesus by the Jews, as in John ii. 20, that it had then been forty and six years in building. Sixteen years added to thirty — the age of Jesus at that time — would make the forty-six. Some of the stones employed in the building are represented by Josephus as more than 70 feet long, 10 wide, and 8 high. Even Tacitus, accustomed as he was to the imperial wealth and grandeur of Roman architecture, speaks of the temple as of unmeasured opulence, "immensæ opulentiæ templum."

**2. there shall not be left here one stone upon another]** According to Josephus (Jewish Wars, VII. 1. 1), the Roman general gave orders to demolish the entire city and temple, except three towers, which were left to show posterity what kind of a city it had been. "But for all the rest of the wall," he says, "it was so completely levelled with the ground by those that dug it up to the foundation, that there was nothing left to make those who came thither believe it had ever been inhabited."

**3. And as he sat upon the Mount of Olives]** Opposite to Jerusalem, and probably in full view of the temple, on which the light of the moon, then nearly full, would shine.   **when shall these things be?]** The question was put privately by four of the disciples (Mark xiii. 3).

**and what shall be the sign of thy coming, and of the end of the world?]** The fulfilment of the prediction, the coming of the Son of man, and the end of the world, i. e. the consummation of the *æon,* are here put together as belonging to the same family of events. In this instance they primarily and distinctly refer to the destruction of Jerusalem, the dispersion of the Jewish people, and the passing away of the Mosaic dispensation as the authorized religion of the land. The disciples who put the question to Jesus undoubtedly supposed that his great but earthly kingdom was then to be established in Judæa, and that when he came to close the old dispensation, (in the end of the world, — the consummation of the *æon,*) he would commence his kingly reign upon the earth, clothed with authority and power like other kings, only with a greater majesty and a more universal dominion. In his reply he uses the terms, *coming of the Son of man, the end,* first in reference to the destruction of Jerusalem, but also, according to his usual manner, in such a way as to show forth other and grander truths. The retribution which was at length to fall upon the Jews, the end of their dispensation, and the coming of the Son of man in judgment to them, were also terms equally applicable to every human being. The images here used to describe a particular case so set forth a universal principle of divine retribution, that in almost every instance they may be applied now to men in their individual experiences. The way in which the specific language of Jesus is made to embody principles of universal application is more marvellous than any miracle which he wrought. But because his lan-

4 world? And Jesus answered and said unto them, Take heed
5 that no man deceive you. For many shall come in my name,
6 saying, I am Christ; and shall deceive many. And ye shall
hear of wars, and rumors of wars: see that ye be not troubled;
for all these things must come to pass, but the end is not yet.
7 For nation shall rise against nation, and kingdom against
kingdom; and there shall be famines, and pestilences, and
8 earthquakes, in divers places. All these are the beginning of
9 sorrows. Then shall they deliver you up to be afflicted, and
shall kill you; and ye shall be hated of all nations for my
10 name's sake. And then shall many be offended; and shall
11 betray one another, and shall hate one another. And many
12 false prophets shall rise, and shall deceive many. And because
13 iniquity shall abound, the love of many shall wax cold. But
he that shall endure unto the end, the same shall be saved.
14 And this gospel of the kingdom shall be preached in all the
world, for a witness unto all nations; and then shall the end
15 come. —— When ye, therefore, shall see the abomination of
desolation, spoken of by Daniel the prophet, stand in the holy
16 place, (whoso readeth, let him understand,) then let them which

---

guage is so overcharged with meaning, reaching out in every direction, it is exceedingly difficult in any single instance to do justice to its fulness by any one specific interpretation. We must bear this in mind, especially in our attempts to understand a vast, sublime, and comprehensive discourse like this, which takes up almost as much space in the Gospels as the Sermon on the Mount, and which, if the whole of it were confined to the destruction of Jerusalem, would occupy a place wholly out of proportion to its importance in the records of a divine and universal religion.
4. **Take heed that no man deceive you**] Calamities may come, many and fearful, — impostors, rumors of wars, famines and earthquakes, — but these are only the preliminary symptoms, — the beginning of those birth-pangs by which the regeneration, the birth of the new world or dispensation, is to be accomplished. 13. **he that shall endure unto the end**] This may refer to the escape from impending death of the Christians, who remembered these warnings, and held out to the end in their fidelity to Christ. But the language applies with equal force to the reward of fidelity which shall crown with salvation every one who continues faithfully to the end.
14. **in all the world**] throughout the Roman empire, or the known and habitable world. In consequence of the unsettled state of Palestine, and the persecutions there, the ministers of Christ went abroad, more than they otherwise might have done, among all nations, — into Asia Minor, and the remote East, into Africa, and through Europe to the western boundaries of Spain.
15. **stand in the holy place**] in *a* holy place. There is no article. *The* holy place would denote the enclosures of the temple. But *a* holy place might be outside of the city; e. g. on the Mount of Olives, which was occupied by Roman troops previously to the destruction

be in Judæa flee into the mountains; let him which is on the house-top not come down to take anything out of his house; neither let him which is in the field return back to take his clothes. And woe unto them that are with child, and to them that give suck, in those days! But pray ye that your flight be not in the winter, neither on the sabbath-day. For then shall be great tribulation, such as was not since the beginning of the world to this time, no, nor ever shall be. And except those days should be shortened, there should no flesh be saved; but for the elect's sake those days shall be shortened. Then if any man shall say unto you, Lo, here is Christ, or there; believe it not. For there shall arise false Christs, and false prophets, and shall show great signs and wonders, insomuch

---

of the city. **whoso readeth, let him understand**] Matthew probably wrote his Gospel on the eve of the events here foretold; and it is supposed that he inserted these words to call the attention of his readers to the sign here indicated, and thus warn them of the approaching dangers. Mark inserts the same caution. 17. **on the house-top**] The roofs being flat, those who were on them in the city could pass from house to house, and thus escape over the walls. The expression, however, is designed merely to indicate the necessity of great haste.

19. **And woe unto them**] Here is an instance of our Saviour's tender, thoughtful, and compassionate sympathy for women. The expression, *woe unto them*, uttered here with such a depth of commiseration, may also have been spoken more in sorrow than in anger, even when it occurs in his most terrible denunciations, as, for example, in the twenty-third chapter.

22. **for the elect's sake**] *On their account.* God does interfere to change the direction of human affairs and shorten the season of terrible calamities on account of his elect, — of those who endear themselves to him by their fidelity.

24. **there shall arise false Christs**] "The nearer the Jews were to destruction, the more did these impostors multiply, and the more easy credit did they find with those who were willing to have their miseries softened by hope. Even during the conflagration of the temple, a false prophet encouraged the people with pretended miraculous signs of deliverance. The Jewish Christians themselves were very unwilling to give up all hope of deliverance from their subjection to the Romans: this accounts for the language of Christ, when he speaks of the danger which the *elect* were in of being deceived by these impostors; and shows his wisdom and goodness in forewarning them against trusting to the fallacious promises of persons who affirmed confidently that they were divinely raised up, to accomplish such a deliverance." Kenrick.

**great signs and wonders**] *signs*, to convince and mislead them; *wonders*, or portents and prodigies, to perplex and terrify them. In times of great public commotion and alarm, men's hearts failing them for fear because of the universal insecurity and distress, they feel that desperate measures are rendered necessary by the desperate condition of affairs. When not only governments are losing their authority, and laws and rulers are hated and rebelled against, but the whole social fabric is breaking up; when a universal distrust succeeds

25 that, if it were possible, they shall deceive the very elect. Be-
26 hold, I have told you before. Wherefore, if they shall say
unto you, Behold, he is in the desert; go not forth: Behold,
27 he is in the secret chambers; believe it not. For as the lightning cometh out of the east, and shineth even unto the west,
28 so shall also the coming of the Son of man be. For whereso-

---

to confidence in the family relations, and faith is dying out, — then, in the convulsive throes and agitations of society, bold, bad men are in the ascendant; impostors and deceivers reign amid the general wreck of earthly interests and heavenly hopes; with an insane and frantic desperation men rush into any extravagant delusions that are impudent enough to promise relief. The most reckless credulity, at such times, succeeds to an utter want of faith, in sudden and frenzied alternations. The dissolution of society, the disintegration of all the elements of social, moral, and religious influence, the universal breaking up, which comes as "the end of the world" ($\sigma \upsilon \nu \tau \epsilon \lambda \epsilon \iota \alpha$ $\tau o \hat{\upsilon}$ $\alpha \iota \hat{\omega} \nu o s$) to the old and long established order of things, are marked by these wild and terrific changes and exaggerations. It was so in the breaking up of the Jewish polity. It was so in Rome, where at about the same time, amid similar commotions and catastrophes in the moral and social condition of the people, the dissolution of the old civilization was preparing a way for the introduction of higher ideas in the coming of the Son of man. But there never was a period in the Roman history when such extravagances of superstitious credulity, accompanied by all the worst sorts of religious imposture, prevailed, as in that unbelieving and godless age. Against such times and dangers, though they had not begun to show themselves when he spoke, Jesus uttered these distinct and solemn warnings. With his profound and prophetic insight into the human soul, and into the moral relations of cause and effect, he saw then the seeds of impiety and superstition, credulity and unbelief, which must bring forth such a harvest of deception and crime, and thus, in the overthrow of the past, prepare the way for the introduction of the new dispensation. Compare with this the prophecies (before quoted) in the last two chapters of Malachi; and the destructive and warlike processes by which the kingdom spoken of in the one hundred and tenth Psalm was to be established. See note, xxiii. 39.

26. **Wherefore, if they shall say unto you**] "Christ here mentions the very places where these deceivers would appear, and Josephus tells us, that impostors, under pretence of a divine inspiration, endeavored to introduce novelty and change, and raised the common people to such a degree of madness, that they drew them forth into the desert, pretending that God would there make them see the tokens of liberty, i. e. of their being rescued from the Roman yoke. He also mentions some who appeared in secret chambers, or places of security in the city." Kenrick.

27. **so shall also the coming of the Son of man be**] He was to come in judgment to the Jews, — the end of the world to them, for their *world*, *age*, or *dispensation* was now to end, — but at the same time he was to come in his religion, with a new world, age, or dispensation, to those who would receive him. Herein his coming then was an emblem of his final coming to all, — in judgment and with the loss of all that they most valued to the unfaithful and unbelieving, to those who have lived only for this world; — with a *new world* of life and joy to the penitent and the faithful who believe in him.

ever the carcass is, there will the eagles be gathered together.

—— Immediately after the tribulation of those days shall the 29 sun be darkened, and the moon shall not give her light, and the stars shall fall from heaven, and the powers of the heavens shall be shaken. And then shall appear the sign of the Son 30 of man in heaven; and then shall all the tribes of the earth mourn, and they shall see the Son of man coming in the clouds of heaven, with power and great glory. And he shall send his 31 angels with a great sound of a trumpet; and they shall gather

29. **Immediately after the tribulation of those days shall the sun be darkened**] "'A day of darkness' is an obvious figure for 'a day of distress.' Hence, in the Oriental style, a time of utter calamity, the destruction of a nation, is described by the extinction of the sun, and the other lights of heaven. Thus Isaiah (xiii. 9, 10), in speaking of the destruction of Babylon, says: 'Behold, the day of Jehovah is coming, cruel with wrath and fierce anger, to lay the land desolate and to destroy its sinners out of it. For the stars of heaven and its constellations shall not give their light, and the sun shall be darkened in his going forth, and the moon shall not cause her light to shine.' So also Ezekiel, describing the fall of Egypt (xxxii. 7, 8)." Norton's Translation of the Gospels, II. 528.

30. **And then shall appear the sign of the Son of man in heaven**] The fulfilment of the events here predicted would be a sign of the Son of man in heaven; and while all the tribes of *the land* — not of the earth — should smite their breasts and mourn, they would recognize in these calamities, which he had foretold as the downfall of their polity and their nation, the evidence of his truth, and in them would see him coming as on the clouds of heaven, and with power and great glory, to establish the kingdom of heaven on earth. **in the clouds of heaven**] This was an image familiar to the Jews, and was perhaps derived, in the first instance, from the pillar of cloud which went before them in the wilderness as an emblem of God's providential care and presence. "The glory of the Lord appeared in the cloud." (Ex. xvi. 10.) God "called unto Moses out of the midst of the cloud." (Ex. xxiv. 16.) From these and similar expressions often repeated in the Pentateuch, the idea of any special act of Divine interference with human affairs would naturally clothe itself in imagery of this sort. Thus when Isaiah (xix. 1) would represent God as about to punish the Egyptians, he says, "Behold, the Lord rideth upon a swift cloud, and shall come into Egypt." The language of course was figurative. God was not represented as visibly or actually riding on a cloud. So in the passage before us, this image of impressive grandeur is employed to describe the majesty of the Son of man when he shall come in judgment to the Jews, i. e. in the power of those divine principles of justice, which, as embodied in his religion, were then to be enforced, and by which the way was to be prepared for the wide and speedy establishment of the kingdom of heaven, i. e. of his religion on the earth.

31. **And he shall send his angels**] Literally, *his messengers.* In the Gospels the word *angel* is almost always used to denote heavenly beings. But there are exceptions. "And when the messengers [*angels*] of John had departed." (Luke vii. 24.) "This is he of whom it is written, Behold, I send my messenger [*angel*] before thy face." (Luke vii. 27.) When Jesus was going up to Jerusalem, he "sent messengers [*angels*] before

together his elect from the four winds, from one end of heaven
32 to the other. —— Now learn a parable of the fig-tree; when
his branch is yet tender and putteth forth leaves, ye know that
33 summer is nigh. So likewise ye, when ye shall see all these
34 things, know that it is near, even at the doors. Verily I say
unto you, this generation shall not pass till all these things be
35 fulfilled. Heaven and earth shall pass away; but my words
36 shall not pass away. —— But of that day and hour knoweth no

---

his face." (Luke ix. 52.) These passages are all from Luke. In the other Gospels there is, we believe, no instance of a similar use of the word, unless in the case before us. In the Apocalypse (ii. 1, 8, 18; iii. 1) the expression "*angel* of the church" is evidently applied to the minister or bishop of the church. And this, we suppose, is the meaning of the word in the passage before us. When the hitherto powerful elements of Jewish hostility should be overthrown and destroyed, and the way open everywhere for the more rapid diffusion of the Gospel, the Son of man would send forth his messengers with a great sound of a trumpet — the trumpet was used by the Jews to call religious assemblies together — as heralds of salvation, to gather together his chosen ones, i. e. those who would hear and obey the call, from every quarter under heaven. They who were ready to hear and obey would thus be gathered into his church. 32. **Now learn a parable of the fig-tree**] "On my first arrival in the southern part of Syria, near the end of March, most of the fruit-trees were clothed with foliage, and in blossom. The fig-tree, on the contrary, was much behind them in this respect, for the leaves of this tree do not make their appearance till comparatively late in the season. As the spring is so far advanced before the leaves of the fig-tree begin to appear, (the early fruit, indeed, comes first,) a person may be sure, when he beholds this sign, that summer is at hand." Hackett. 33. **know that it is near**] When ye shall see all these signs fulfilled, then know that it — the coming of the Son of man in the destruction of Jerusalem — is near, nay, is at your very doors.
34. **This generation shall not pass**] In order to impress it upon his disciples' minds that he was not speaking of some event in the remote and indefinite future, he fixes the time, as in Matt. xvi. 28, within the lifetime of some of those who belonged to that generation. This definite limitation of time confines the signs thus far mentioned to a period harmonizing with their consummation in the destruction of Jerusalem and the events immediately preceding and following it. At the same time, we must admit that much of the language, which was unquestionably spoken with a specific reference to that class of events, may be read now with something of a personal application to ourselves. 36. **But of that day and hour**] The obvious interpretation of this passage is, that though all these things shall take place before the present generation shall pass away, yet no one knows the precise day and hour of their fulfilment. But there is another interpretation which seems to us more in accordance with our Saviour's usual method of instruction, mingling together as he often does things temporal and things eternal, and passing almost insensibly from the one order of facts and events to the other. The language which heretofore, in pointing to a single event, overflows with thoughts and images that reach beyond it, here ceases to dwell on the single instance of divine retribution as the principal topic, and, touching only incidentally on circumstances con-

man, no, not the angels of heaven, but my Father only. But as the days of Noe were, so shall also the coming of the Son of man be. For as in the days that were before the flood they were eating and drinking, marrying and giving in marriage, until the day that Noe entered into the ark, and knew not until the flood came and took them all away; so shall also the coming of the Son of man be. Then shall two be in the field; the one shall be taken, and the other left. Two women shall be grinding at the mill; the one shall be taken, and the other left. Watch, therefore, for ye know not what hour your Lord

nected with it, holds up, in the background, the termination of our human and mortal life, and the retributions which shall then succeed. The transition from the specific to the universal is indicated, if not distinctly announced, by the words employed. "The Lord," says Bengel, "shows the time of the temple and of the city in ver. 32-34; he denies in this verse that the day and hour of the world [to each soul] are known. The particle δέ, *but*, implies a contrast: the pronouns ταῦτα, *these*, αὕτη, *this*, refer to events close at hand; the pronoun ἐκείνης, *that*, to that which is distant." *These* things of which I have been speaking shall *all* take place in the present generation; but of *that* day and hour [when the Son of man in a still higher sense shall come] no one knoweth. *That day* is several times used in this sense. "In that day many shall say to me, Lord, Lord, did we not prophesy in thy name, &c. And then will I confess to them, I never knew you; depart from me, ye workers of iniquity." (Matt. vii. 22, 23.) "Henceforth there is laid up for me a crown of righteousness, which the Lord, the righteous judge, shall give me at that day." (2 Tim. iv. 8.) Some commentators suppose that there is no such transition as we have here suggested, but that the whole discourse of our Saviour down to the end of the twenty-fifth chapter relates to the destruction of Jerusalem. It requires much ingenuity to apply all his words to that subject, and the majestic images which he employs seem to us degraded by such a limitation of their meaning. But why, if he passed from one subject to the other, did he not more distinctly indicate the point of transition? We can only say, 1. that there is what seems to us an indication of such a transition; and 2. that it was not his habit to mark, like a modern logician, the different topics of his discourse, especially when, as in this case, they were, to his mind, only different phases of the same thought or illustrations of the same principle. To his wonderful intuitive perceptions, the particular included the universal. Particular facts were held up as illustrations of general principles, and facts which we from our superficial habits of thought regard as wholly distinct were grouped together by him, because the same underlying principle reaches through them all and makes them parts of the same series. It is only by going down to this underlying thought that we can learn the close logical connection by which the different parts of his discourses are bound together. 42. **Watch, therefore**] "You may ask why those who were so far distant from the last day were exhorted to watchfulness on that ground. I answer, — 1. The remoteness of the event had not been indicated to them. 2. Those who are alive at any particular time represent those who will be alive at the end of the world. 3. The principle of the divine judgments, and of the uncertainty of the hour

43 doth come. But know this, that, if the goodman of the house had known in what watch the thief would come, he would have watched, and would not have suffered his house to be broken
44 up. Therefore be ye also ready; for in such an hour as ye
45 think not, the Son of man cometh. Who then is a faithful and wise servant, whom his lord hath made ruler over his
46 household, to give them meat in due season? Blessed is that servant whom his lord, when he cometh, shall find so doing.
47 Verily, I say unto you, that he shall make him ruler over all
48 his goods. But and if that evil servant shall say in his heart,
49 My lord delayeth his coming; and shall begin to smite his
50 fellow-servants, and to eat and drink with the drunken; the lord of that servant shall come in a day when he looketh not
51 for him, and in an hour that he is not aware of; and shall cut him asunder, and appoint him his portion with the hypocrites; there shall be weeping, and gnashing of teeth.

---

of death, resembles in every age that of the last day; and the hour of death is equivalent to the hour of resurrection and judgment, as though no time had been interposed. 4. The feeling of the godly, which stretches forward to meet the Lord, is the same, whether with the longest or the shortest expectation." Bengel. To us who believe that the day of each one's death is the day also of his resurrection and judgment, these remarks come with greater force than to Bengel, who believed as Martha did (John xi. 24) before Jesus had taught her better, that we "shall rise again in the resurrection at the last day." 43. **his house to be broken up**] διορυγῆναι, *to be dug through*. The houses, being built of stones and clay, might be entered with little difficulty by digging through the walls. See note, vi. 19. 45. **Who then is a faithful**] *the faithful and wise servant.* 51. **and shall cut him asunder**] *cut him in pieces,* "a cruel kind of punishment practised among the Hebrews and other ancient nations." Here it is used figuratively, to denote a severe punishment. It may mean *to cut off* or *separate.* "He will cut him off [from his present associates] and assign him his portion with the hypocrites."

**the hypocrites**] This word is used by Jesus to denote those who have incurred the greatest possible guilt, making virtue and religion a cloak for their hideous crimes against God and man.

# CHAPTER XXV.

### Purpose of these Parables.

The conclusions at which we arrived in the last chapter make the interpretation of the present chapter easy. From the judgments of God which are represented by the coming of the Son of man in the retributions which fell on the Jewish city and people, the transition (xxiv. 36) is natural to the judgments of God which are represented by the coming of the Son of man in the retributions which await each individual soul when its period of earthly probation is ended. The twenty-fourth and twenty-fifth chapters are continuous parts of the same discourse, which treats of the coming of the Son of man in the retributions of God on a wicked city and people, on each individual soul at the close of its earthly life, and on all the nations of men. The momentous thought which presents itself to any one who carefully reads the parables here given, is unquestionably that which they were intended to teach. The impression which they make as a whole is the true one, and it ought not to be weakened or disturbed by any minute analysis of the parts. One after another, by images the most awful that can be presented to the soul, they would set before us, in their most personal and practical form, the principles of a divine retribution, and thus keep alive in us a sense of solemn accountability to God, and the need of constant diligence and watchfulness in our calling.

### Parable of the Virgins.

1–13. In xxiv. 37–51 we are exhorted to watch, because we know not how soon our Lord will come; and here, by the example of the wise and foolish virgins, we are taught not only to be ready now, but to make provision also for the future; for we know not how long we may have to wait for his coming. They who are represented by the wise virgins "foresee," says Trench, "that they may have a long life to live of toil and self-denial, before they are called to cease from their labors, before the kingdom shall come unto them;—and consequently feel that it is not a few excited feelings which will carry them successfully through all this. They feel that principles as well as feelings must be engaged in the work,—that their first good impulses and desires will carry them but a very little way, unless they be revived, strengthened, and purified by a continual supply of the Spirit of God. If the bridegroom were to come at once, perhaps it might be another thing, but their wisdom is, that, since it may possibly be otherwise, they see their need of making provision against the contingency." Another distinction between this and the previous parable is, that in that acts of wickedness are reproved; here, a lack of the Christian virtues,—not bad oil, but no oil. There is little reserved power for the unknown contingencies that may arise. "By the lighted lamps," says Gerhard, "may be understood the external profession and outward form of piety," as well as the sudden emotions connected with it; " by the oil in the vessels, the inward righteousness of the heart, true faith, sincere love, watchfulness, and prudence, which, though unnoticed by man, are God's alone." With what a solemn emphasis do the words, "and the door was shut," fall upon the heart! The privilege, whatever it may be, which we have neglected to prepare ourselves to improve, is closed against us. Thus day after day the door is shut; and if at its close the whole of life has failed of its great purpose in regard to us, its privileges are all withdrawn, the door is shut, and we are left outside in darkness and sorrow.

### Parable of the Talents.

14–30. This parable goes a step further. Not merely must we abstain from cruel and wicked acts; not merely must we have a reserved fund of religious principle for future emergencies; but we must increase that fund by constant fidelity in the use of it. Not only are we accountable for what has been given to us, but also for the gain which we might secure by using it with diligence and care. God provides us with opportunities according to our several abilities. These opportunities are really ours only as we avail ourselves of them. He who neglected to use the one talent had not even that. The great law of our nature and of retributive justice here laid down is, — 1. that we cannot really continue to possess any one of God's gifts, except so far as we faithfully exercise, appropriate, and improve it; and, 2. that we are accountable, not for the amount that we have gained, but for our diligence and fidelity in the use of what has been entrusted to us. It is not, Well done, good and successful, but good and faithful servant. He who had gained five, and he who had gained two talents, are in the same terms welcomed to the joy of their Lord. And he who came with his one talent was condemned, not because he had been unfortunate, but because, harboring evil thoughts towards his lord, he had shown himself a wicked and slothful servant in the use he had made of the talent intrusted to him. Verses 25–28 show how an evil disposition of mind and heart lies at the bottom of a sluggish and unfaithful life. The want of opportunity is oftener the fault than the misfortune of those who resort to it as an excuse for their evil conduct; and therefore it can only aggravate their condemnation.

### Parable of the Sheep and the Goats.

31–46. Thus far this world has been in the foreground, its characters and acts visibly ripening for the judgments

which are represented as taking place at the coming of the
Son of man. Here the higher world is brought forward,
and the actions of this mortal life, the deeds done in the
body, lie in the background, and appear only in their results.
Not the scenes and events of this life, hastening to judgment, but the judgments which await them in another world,
are foremost in the picture. Heretofore the mind has dwelt
on individual cases, — the wicked city and people, the cruel
servant, the ten virgins, the three servants to whom the
different talents were intrusted; but now, by one majestic
sweep of thought, all individual cases from all ages and
nations are brought together, and the view is the most awful
and sublime that has ever been presented in human language. "But when the Son of man shall come in his
glory, and all the angels with him, then shall he sit on the
throne of his glory, and before him shall be gathered all the
nations." So, 2 Cor. v. 10 : " For we must all appear
before the judgment-seat of Christ, that every one may
receive according to what he hath done in the body, whether
it be good or bad." So again, Rev. xx. 12 : " And I saw
the dead, small and great, stand before God; and the books
were opened." The great fact that every soul shall hereafter meet a retribution in accordance with its life here, is
thus set before us in language the most solemn and emphatic.
And the grounds on which the sentence rests, as in Matt.
vii. 22, 23, are not outward professions or forms of belief,
but the principles of holiness and love manifested on earth,
though in ways and acts obscure and unrecognized by
man. He who sits upon the throne of judgment identifies
himself with every one of his suffering brethren, and in the
great day of account will acknowledge any act of kindness
done to the least of them as if it had been done to him.
Both righteous and wicked are filled with amazement and
surprise; but not the less, therefore, shall the words of
Christ stand; and the inward life of all, as revealed to him
in their conduct, shall go on working out for each one the

awards of eternal justice. Now that the true character of that life is fully manifested in the light of divine truth, or the all-enlightening presence of Christ, it fixes its stamp on every soul, and divides them even as a shepherd separates his sheep from the goats. No longer united by ties of kindred, the bonds of neighborhood, or the necessities of our mortal condition, they are separated from one another, and drawn by the very affinities of their nature, these into eternal punishment, but the righteous into life eternal. *Eternal*, — an epithet applying to the new era, the more advanced condition of being on which they have entered, and applying also to the elements or principles of spiritual life, which are unfolded and exercised here on earth, and which then will be all in all.

The great facts of the Divine retribution — the eternal bliss into which the righteous are drawn up, and the eternal woe into which the wicked are cast down — are too plainly set forth to be the subject of criticism. These central and indisputable facts stand unaffected by any just principles of criticism. The images of uplifting or appalling grandeur in which they are enveloped cannot act too powerfully on the imagination and the heart of man. The obscurity in which the particulars of our future being are left, was undoubtedly intentional on the part of our Saviour. For though the whole matter in its blissful or terrible details may have been disclosed to him, he knew that we, in our present stage of existence, could not comprehend them, and would only be confounded or misled by any language in which they might be described. We cannot understand, except in a general way, that which in all its particulars must lie so far beyond all our experience here.

For this reason, we attempt no minute definition or analysis of the precise images or language employed in this grand and awful picture of the retributions of eternity. We take no notice of the doctrine of a first and a second resurrection, which some commentators think they find intimated here. And we should gladly avoid all other disputed doctrines involved in the criticism, were it not for the disastrous hold which some of them have taken on the popular mind.

## THE GENERAL RESURRECTION AND DAY OF JUDGMENT.

Does Jesus here, 31 – 46, teach that some specific day, separate from that of each man's death, is to be set apart for the general and simultaneous resurrection and judgment of all the tribes and generations of men? His language does not, we think, require any such interpretation. In the previous parables he has been singling out individual cases of sudden judgment. But lest they should leave upon the mind an idea of a partial and imperfect retribution, which some men might escape, he here in one awful picture represents all men of all nations and times as standing before him to undergo the searching ordeal which in the previous parables has been applied to individual souls. Nothing is said or intimated in regard to a resurrection of the body, or the simultaneous resurrection of the whole race. The meaning of the language is: Not one, or a few, like those already specified, shall meet the Son of man and be judged by him at his coming, but all the nations and generations of men shall be gathered before him in his glory, to receive from him — in the words which come from him as the great essential law of God's kingdom — the sentence of joy or woe which awaits them as they enter on their eternal state of being.

It will not do to bind down to a literal exactness language like this, intensified with emotion and abounding in the sublimest figures of speech. But even when construed in its stricter sense, the language here does not imply what is usually understood by *the day of judgment*. Suppose that every soul, when its earthly course is ended and its earthly garments laid aside, goes directly into the presence of Christ and his angels, to be judged according to the principles of life or death which it has cherished here, and which are there to work out their solemn retributions. In this individual manifestation, or coming of Christ to each individual soul, is it not strictly true that "all the nations shall be gathered before him"? As, in a vast military review, the armies of an empire pass, company by company, day after day, before the monarch, each battalion as it comes from its neighboring barracks or distant campaign, till all at length have been gathered before him, so in this grander procession and review of human beings, moment by moment, hour by hour, year after year, and generation after generation, each individual soul by itself, in the solemn depths of its own consciousness, and yet all in one ceaseless succession of companies, pass on, till at last all the nations shall be gathered before him, and separated one from another, as a shepherd divideth his sheep from the goats.

When we say, the hour will come when all who are on the earth must die, we do not mean that all shall die at the same hour. So when it is said, "We must all stand before the judgment-seat of Christ," or, "When the Son of man shall come in his glory, . . . . . all the nations shall be gathered before him," it is not implied that we shall all stand before him, or be gathered before him at one and the same moment. As the coming of the Son of man in mercy now to each soul is whenever that soul is ready to receive him, so the coming of Christ in judgment to each one of us is when we go from this to the next stage of our existence.

## NOTES.

THEN shall the kingdom of heaven be likened unto ten virgins, which took their lamps, and went forth to meet the bride-
2 groom. And five of them were wise, and five were foolish.
3 They that were foolish took their lamps, and took no oil with
4 them. But the wise took oil in their vessels with their lamps.
5 While the bridegroom tarried, they all slumbered and slept.
6 And at midnight there was a cry made, Behold, the bride-
7 groom cometh; go ye out to meet him. Then all those virgins
8 arose, and trimmed their lamps. And the foolish said unto the
9 wise, Give us of your oil, for our lamps are gone out. But
the wise answered, saying, Not so, lest there be not enough
for us and you; but go ye rather to them that sell, and buy for
10 yourselves. And while they went to buy, the bridegroom
came, and they that were ready went in with him to the mar-
11 riage; and the door was shut. Afterward came also the other
12 virgins, saying, Lord, Lord, open to us. But he answered
13 and said, Verily I say unto you, I know you not. Watch,
therefore, for ye know neither the day nor the hour wherein
14 the Son of man cometh. —— For the kingdom of heaven is as a

---

6. **And at midnight**] An Ar-
menian wedding is thus described
by a traveller quoted in Livermore's
Commentary. "The large number
of young females who were present
naturally reminded me of the wise
and foolish virgins in our Saviour's
parable. These being friends of the
bride, *the virgins, her companions*,
(Ps. xlv. 14,) had come *to meet the
bridegroom*. It is usual for the
bridegroom to come at midnight;
so that literally *at midnight the cry
is made, Behold, the bridegroom cometh; go ye out to meet him*. But on
this occasion *the bridegroom tarried;*
it was two o'clock before he arrived." 8. **are gone out**]
rather, *are going out*. 10.
**And the door was shut**] The
following account of a Hindoo wedding by Mr. Ward is also copied
from Mr. Livermore. "After waiting two or three hours, at length,
near midnight, it was announced,
as if in the very words of Scripture, Behold, the bridegroom cometh; go ye out to meet him! All
the persons employed now lighted
their lamps, and ran with them in
their hands to fill up their stations
in the procession; some of them
had lost their lights and were unprepared; but it was then too late to
seek them, and the cavalcade moved
forward to the house of the bride.
The bridegroom was carried in the
arms of a friend, and placed on a
superb seat in the midst of the
company, where he sat a short
time, and then went into the house,
the door of which was immediately
shut and guarded by Sepoys. I
and others expostulated with the
door-keepers, but in vain."

14. **the kingdom of heav-
en**] These words are inserted by
our translators without reason. Jesus has been speaking all along of
the coming of the Son of man, and

man travelling into a far country, who called his own servants, and delivered unto them his goods. And unto one he gave five 15 talents, to another two, and to another one; to every man according to his several ability; and straightway took his journey. Then he that had received the five talents went and 16 traded with the same, and made them other five talents. And 17 likewise he that had received two, he also gained other two. But he that had received one went and digged in the earth, 18 and hid his lord's money. After a long time, the lord of those 19 servants cometh and reckoneth with them. And so he that had 20 received five talents came and brought other five talents, saying, Lord, thou deliveredst unto me five talents; behold, I have gained beside them five talents more. His lord said unto 21 him, Well done, thou good and faithful servant; thou hast been faithful over a few things, I will make thee ruler over many things; enter thou into the joy of thy lord. He also 22 that had received two talents came and said, Lord, thou deliveredst unto me two talents; behold, I have gained two other talents beside them. His lord said unto him, Well done, 23 good and faithful servant; thou hast been faithful over a few things, I will make thee ruler over many things; enter thou into the joy of thy lord. Then he which had received the one 24 talent came and said, Lord, I knew thee that thou art an hard man, reaping where thou hast not sown, and gathering where thou hast not strawed; and I was afraid, and went and 25 hid thy talent in the earth: lo, there thou hast that is thine.

---

that fact is the one still to be illustrated. "Watch, therefore, because ye know not the day nor the hour: for it is as a man travelling into a far country," &c. 15. **to every man according to his several ability**] = not oppressing the servant of small powers with opportunities and responsibilities beyond his strength. And is it not so with us all? We may complain of the narrow sphere, the small opportunities, granted to us; but if we have the ability to use greater, shall we not find them? Our fidelity and skill in the use of what we have to-day will prepare us for greater opportunities, and them for us, to-morrow. It is not merely at the end of life, but all along, that this reckoning is made, and its terms enforced, — the diligent and faithful furnished with larger opportunities, the sluggish and unfaithful deprived of what they once had. But in the final summing up, we shall be called to account only for the use of what we have had. The much or little, if only faithfully used, will be all the same to us then. 24. **I knew thee that thou art an hard man**] Here the real character of the slothful servant comes out. And how true is the picture! They who neglect the means of success, who give way to indolence and refuse to make the required exertions, are

26 His lord answered and said unto him, Thou wicked and slothful servant, thou knewest that I reap where I sowed not, and
27 gather where I have not strawed; thou oughtest therefore to have put my money to the exchangers, and then at my coming
28 I should have received mine own with usury. Take therefore the talent from him, and give it unto him which hath ten talents.
29 For unto every one that hath shall be given, and he shall have abundance; but from him that hath not shall be taken away
30 even that which he hath. And cast ye the unprofitable servant into outer darkness: there shall be weeping and gnashing of teeth.

31 When the Son of man shall come in his glory, and all the holy angels with him, then shall he sit upon the throne of his
32 glory, and before him shall be gathered all nations; and he shall separate them one from another, as a shepherd divideth
33 his sheep from the goats; and he shall set the sheep on his
34 right hand, but the goats on the left. Then shall the King say unto them on his right hand, Come, ye blessed of my Father, inherit the kingdom prepared for you from the foundation of
35 the world. For I was an hungered, and ye gave me meat; I was thirsty, and ye gave me drink; I was a stranger, and ye
36 took me in; naked, and ye clothed me; I was sick, and ye
37 visited me; I was in prison, and ye came unto me. Then

---

the ones who complain most of the hardness of their lot and of the conduct of God towards them.
26. **thou knewest that I reap where I sowed not**] The slothful servant is answered on his own ground. This is made a little more explicit in Luke xix. 22: "Out of thine own mouth will I judge thee." 29. **unto every one that hath shall be given**] A great law of our nature, filling out as its complement the other law announced (v. 3, 6; Luke vi. 20, 21), that in proportion as we feel our want, will be the supply that is granted. To him that hath the disposition and the ability to use will be given, that he may have the more abundantly; and at the same time they who feel their wants, and in lowliness of spirit are hungering and thirsting after righteousness, will be filled, and theirs will be the kingdom of heaven.
**but from him that hath not**] He had had it; but yet, as he had made no use of it, it was as if he had it not. 30. **into outer darkness**] *the* outer darkness. A reference again to the feast and joy within, the darkness and sorrow without. 33.
**Come, ye blessed of my Father, inherit the kingdom prepared for you**] But not, 41, ye *cursed of my Father;* the curse they had brought upon themselves. Neither is it, 41, depart into eternal fire prepared *for you,* but prepared for the devil and his angels, i. e. prepared, in the very nature of things, for what is evil as its natural fruit. Not a punishment purposely and arbitrarily prepared by God, but growing as a necessary consequence out of the life which they had lived, and the characters they

shall the righteous answer him, saying, Lord when saw we thee an hungered, and fed thee? or thirsty, and gave thee drink? when saw we thee a stranger, and took thee in? or 38 naked, and clothed thee? or when saw we thee sick, or in 39 prison, and came unto thee? And the King shall answer and 40 say unto them, Verily I say unto you, Inasmuch as ye have done it unto one of the least of these my brethren, ye have done it unto me. Then shall he say also unto them on the left 41 hand, Depart from me, ye cursed, into everlasting fire, prepared for the devil and his angels. For I was an hungered, 42 and ye gave me no meat; I was thirsty, and ye gave me no drink; I was a stranger, and ye took me not in; naked, and 43 ye clothed me not; sick, and in prison, and ye visited me not. Then shall they also answer him, saying, Lord, when saw we 44 thee an hungered, or athirst, or a stranger, or naked, or sick, or in prison, and did not minister unto thee? Then shall he 45

---

had formed. **41. for the devil and his angels**] We have already given quite as much space to the subject of demonology as its importance demands, and would refer the reader interested in such things to the remarks which may be found in chapters iv., viii., and xiii. The expression here may denote a personal being and his agents, or it may be used only as a personification of evil, — sin, and those who are employed as its messengers to disseminate it. Go ye into the sorrows which have been prepared — not for you — but for sin and its agents, as its natural and necessary results. In partaking of sin you must partake also of the bitter fruits which it bears. The necessary and awful connection between sin and sorrow, so that those who engage in the former must also be involved in the latter, unless they repent and leave their wickedness behind, is the terrible fact which is here announced as a part of the great system of things. The doctrine of demons, or of a personal devil, is not found in the old Hebrew Scriptures; though the word Satan, an *adversary* or *enemy*, is sometimes used, as in Numbers xxii. 22; 1 Sam. xxix. 4; 1 Kings xi. 14. In 1 Chron. xxi. 1 and Zech. iii. 1, 2, is the first appearance in the Old Testament of Satan as *the evil one*, and both these writings belong probably to a period not antecedent to the Babylonian captivity. During the period of more than five centuries which intervened between that captivity and the birth of Christ, the minds of the Jews became imbued with the idea of demons and a prince of demons, such as we find in the New Testament. Traces of these notions may be found in some of the apocryphal writings, but the fullest development of the doctrine is seen in the *Apocalypse of Enoch*, a work which belonged to that period, which was known and quoted from by some of the New Testament writers (2 Peter, and Jude 14), but which was unknown in the Christian Church for nearly a thousand years. In 1773 Bruce the traveller brought three copies of it from Abyssinia, and in 1821 a translation of it into English was made by Richard Laurence, afterwards Archbishop of Cashel. See Christian Examiner for May, 1859, Art. The History and Doctrine of

answer them, saying, Verily, I say unto you, inasmuch as ye
46 did it not to one of the least of these, ye did it not to me. And
these shall go away into everlasting punishment; but the
righteous into life eternal.

---

the Devil. 46. **And these shall go away into everlasting punishment; but the righteous into life eternal**] *Everlasting* and *eternal*, in this verse and verse 41, are in Greek the same word αἰώνιον (*aionion*). For its meaning, see note, xii. 32. It relates to the condition, for good or for evil, in which we are when we pass from this to the next stage of our existence. As our *earthly* or *mortal* life relates to our external mode of being here, so our *eternal* life or *eternal* punishment relates to the spiritual qualities which, beginning here, shall abide with us hereafter, and bear in us the fruits of righteousness or sin, which belong to our condition there, i. e. to our *eternal* (*aionion*) condition. It relates rather to the nature than the duration of the condition in which we may be placed. The eternal life here begun shall enfold the righteous in the splendors of its bliss, and the eternal death or punishment shall envelop the ungodly in its ghastly shadows of sin and shame. "The same word, αἰώνιον, *eternal*, is applied to the punishment of the bad and the happiness of the good, and it refers not at all to duration in months and years. It means, rather, those opposite states of mind from which the idea of time and all its contingencies has been completely eliminated; one lifted up into the eternal glories, the other depressed into the shadows of eternal gloom. It is a happiness or disorder, transfused not from this world, but from another, and which, therefore, survives temporal duration and mortal dissolution, and exists in sharper contrasts than ever, after the fashions of this world have passed away." Foregleams of Immortality, pp. 129, 130. Bengel in his note on this passage says, "*Eternal* signifies that which reaches and passes the limits of earthly *time*." So in his note on Rom. xvi. 25, "*since the world began*, χρόνοις αἰωνίοις, [during the eternal ages,] from the time when not only men, but even angels, were created. The *times* are denoted, which with their first commencement as it were touch upon the previous eternity, and are, so to speak, mixed with it; not eternity itself, of which times are only the streams; for the phrase, Before *eternal* ages (English version, *Before the world began*) is used at 2 Tim. 1, 9; Ps. lxxvii. 5 (lxxvi. 6.)"

**punishment**] κόλασις, punishment, not τιμωρία, vengeance; "for *punishment* is inflicted for the sake of him who suffers; *vengeance*, for the satisfaction of him who inflicts it." Bengel.

## CHAPTER XXVI.

### 1–17. THE SUPPER AT BETHANY.—JUDAS.

1–2. It was now (see introduction to chap. xxi.) late on Tuesday evening, which, according to the Jewish method of reckoning, was the beginning of Wednesday. The expression "after two days is the Passover" would place that event on Thursday. 3–5. Here the scene changes, and the writer recurs to deliberations previously held by the chief priests and elders in regard to the best way of getting Jesus into their hands by subtlety or deceit, and putting him to death. They had concluded that it would not be expedient to do this during the festival. 6–13. The writer then, without explicitly stating his object, proceeds to show how their purpose came to be altered by the proposal of Judas to put Jesus into their hands. And in order to give what stood in his own mind as the immediate occasion of the traitor's proposal, he goes back four days (John xii. 1), and gives an account of a supper at Bethany, where an event had occurred which, with the comment of Jesus upon it, exasperated Judas, and hastened him on in his work of treachery. The passage is worthy of remark, as showing how, in the narrative of an unpractised writer like Matthew, the true order of events is departed from without notice being given, and how the object which is foremost in the mind of the writer may be left so obscurely indicated by his words, that we can discover what it is only by comparing his narrative with that which has come to us from another source. No mention is made of Judas in the account of the supper by Matthew, but at the close of the account he says, 14–16, "Then one of the twelve, called Judas Iscariot, went unto the chief priests," as if his going were in some way dependent on what had just been described. John, on the other hand, in his more precise and circumstantial detail of events (xii. 1 – 8), singles out Judas as the one most prominent in complaining of the waste. Judas, therefore, must have been the one who was most excited by the indignation which Matthew mentions, and who would feel most keenly the rebuke implied in the language of Jesus. Indignant, therefore, and exasperated, he sought an interview with the chief priests. The same avaricious spirit which had caused his indignation at the supper manifests itself in the offer which he made to the priests. "This might have been sold for two hundred pence," were his words when he saw the precious ointment poured upon the head and feet of Jesus; and now his question is, "What will you give me if I will give him up to you?" There is no formal connection between these two expressions in Matthew. He does not even tell us that the questions were both put by the same man. It is only by the help of John's Gospel that we discover this, and by his aid we see, not only how perfectly the two narratives, apparently different, harmonize with each other, but how important in its place the apparently irrelevant account of the supper at Bethany is in the Gospel before us. Where a man's mind is full of a subject, and he sees as an actual witness the relation of all its parts to one another, he is very apt to state facts as they lie in his mind in their true relation to one another, but without the explanatory clauses which a reader not conversant with the facts needs in order to understand their connection, and which a writer not personally familiar with the facts would hardly fail to put in.

## 17 – 29. THE LAST SUPPER.

17 – 19. The writer now returns to Jesus. It was the first day of unleavened bread when the disciples asked Jesus where they should prepare the Passover. There is nothing

miraculous implied in the narrative. All the houses in Jerusalem were open at that time for guests. Jesus may previously have spoken to some one in the city who was friendly to him, and engaged a chamber in his house. And now he tells two of his disciples (Mark xiv. 13), viz. Peter and John (Luke xxii. 8), go to such a one, probably mentioning his name, and say to him, " The teacher " — the title by which Jesus was best known to his followers — " saith, My time is near for me to keep the Passover with my disciples at thy house." Jesus probably sent Peter and John privately, so that the other disciples did not know the place until they had assembled there to eat the Passover. A reason for this may have been, that Judas might not know beforehand whither to bring those to whom he intended to betray him, and that Jesus might have a few last hours with his disciples entirely undisturbed.

21 – 29. Nothing could be more simple or more touchingly beautiful than the account which the Evangelists have given of the Last Supper. The chamber had been prepared. Jesus and his twelve disciples were there, reclining at the table. While they were eating, Jesus was troubled in spirit, and said, " Verily I say unto you, that one of you shall betray me." And they were exceeding sorrowful, and looked at one another, not knowing who it might be. But each one, being more ready to suspect himself than either of his associates, began separately and perhaps privately to ask, " Lord, is it I?" And he replied, but in such a way that Judas could not hear him, " He that dippeth his hand with me in the dish, the same shall betray me. The Son of man goeth, as it is written of him; but woe to that man by whom the Son of man is betrayed! It had been good for that man if he had not been born." Judas, recovering somewhat from the confusion occasioned by the announcement of Jesus that one of them should betray him, and supposing that he might be suspected by his associates unless he should put the question which they had put, now the last

of them all, asked, "Rabbi, is it I?" His guilty heart caused his tongue to stumble in its words, and instead of the hearty, loving reverence implied in the address, Lord, is it I? his treacherous purpose half revealed itself in the term which he used, — *Rabbi*, which is not, like Rabboni, expressive of the highest honor and reverence. The very word that Judas uttered so fixed itself in the minds of the disciples, that in Matthew, though his Gospel comes to us in another language, the Hebrew word is retained. "Rabbi," he asked, "is it I?" Jesus answered, "Thou hast said," i. e. It is even as thou hast said. Soon after this, when the others had received from Jesus the sign who it was that should betray him, Judas (John xiii. 30, 31) probably withdrew, and Jesus, relieved from the pressure caused by his presence, exclaimed, "Now is the Son of man glorified."

Then followed the institution of the Lord's Supper. The Passover had been eaten. But while they were yet at the table, Jesus took bread, and having blessed and broken it, he gave it to his disciples, saying, "Take, eat, this is my body, given [Luke xxii. 19] for you; this do in remembrance of me." "It was a round cake of unleavened bread which the Lord broke and divided; signifying thereby both the breaking of his body on the cross, and the participation in the benefits of his death by all his." Alford. What could be the meaning of the clause, *this do in remembrance of me*, unless it was intended that the Supper should be observed as a lasting memorial of himself? The bread thus broken is to us an emblem of the broken body of Christ, and his body expresses to us the truth, — the bread from heaven which he came to impart to man, — the words of his which are spirit and life (John vi. 63), loaded down as they are with the divine fulness of meaning and of redemptive power which is given to them by his whole "manifestation in the flesh." In this sense, our spiritual being is upheld "by the inward and spiritual process of feeding upon him by faith: of making that body our own, causing it to pass into and nourish our souls, even as the substance of the bread passes into and nourishes our bodies. Of this feeding upon Christ in the spirit by faith is the sacramental bread the symbol to us." " The commemoration is of him, in so far as he has come down into time, and enacted the great acts of redemption on this our world, — and shown himself to us as living and speaking *man*, an object of our personal love and affectionate remembrance; — but the other and higher parts of the sacrament have regard to the *results* of these same acts of redemption, as they are *eternized* in the counsels of the Father." Alford.

And he took the cup, and gave thanks, and gave it to them, saying, "Drink ye all of it; for this is my blood of the new testament, which is shed for many for the remission of sins." As the bread is an emblem of the body of Christ, and that an emblem of the divine truth which came through him into the world to feed and sustain the souls of men, so is the wine an emblem of his blood shed for many for the remission of sins, and his blood thus shed for sinful men is an emblem of the divine love manifested in him for the redemption of the world. As in partaking of the wine we rise through the symbol into that which it symbolizes, we receive into our souls the love of Christ, and are thus made partakers of his spirit. This it is in its highest spiritual sense to partake of the blood of Christ. The cup of blessing thus received in faith, " is it not the communion of the blood of Christ?" "Let us recur to the paschal rite. The lamb being killed, the blood (Ex. xxiv. 8) is sprinkled on the door-posts, and is a sign to the destroying angel to spare the house. The blood of the covenant is the blood of the lamb. So also in the new covenant. The blood of the Lamb of God, slain for us, being not only sprinkled on, but actually partaken spiritually and assimilated by the faithful soul, is the blood of the new covenant, and the sacramental cup is, signifies, sets forth, this covenant in his blood, i. e. consisting in a participation in his blood." Alford.

29. "But I say unto you, that I shall not drink henceforth of this fruit of the vine, until that day when I drink it new with you in my Father's kingdom." Here the fruit of the vine (see note) is used in its higher and spiritual signification. "The Lord's Supper points not only to the past, but to the future also. It has not only a commemorative, but also a prophetic meaning. In it we have not only to show forth the Lord's death till he come, but we have also to think of the time when he shall come to celebrate his holy supper with his own, new, in his kingdom of glory. Every celebration of the Lord's Supper is a foretaste and prophetic anticipation of the great Marriage Supper which is prepared for the Church at the second appearing of Christ." Thiersch.

### 31–35. WARNING PETER.

31–35. Probably the discourses and prayer recorded by John (xiv.–xvii.) were spoken after the paschal psalm or hymn, and before they left the city. They were certainly spoken (John xviii. 1) before the party had crossed the Kedron. From Luke xxii. 31–34, and John xiii. 36–38, it would seem as if some warning, 31, had been previously given, perhaps more than once, and with a more direct and exclusive application to Peter. It may be that they are only different accounts of the same conversation, each writer retaining or omitting the parts which made the strongest impression on his mind, and using the words as they remained in his memory. The different topics, however, which are introduced, especially in Luke as compared with Matthew and Mark, seem to us to indicate different occasions. And if Peter had been thus warned once or twice before, it will account for the eagerness with which he here repels from himself, 33, the charge which is made, 31, equally against all the eleven.

## 36–46.—The Agony of Gethsemane.

The external facts here narrated are easily understood. After the supper, late in the evening, Jesus with the eleven went out of Jerusalem across the brook Kedron to Gethsemane, a place which lay a little way up on the Mount of Olives, in sight of the eastern wall of Jerusalem. It is supposed that there may have been a house there, in which the eight disciples remained (for the night was cold), while Jesus, with Peter and James and John, went to a more retired part of the grounds. There, as the "agony," the struggle, as St. Luke calls it, came upon him, he said to them, "My soul is exceedingly sorrowful, even unto death; tarry ye here and watch with me." He yearned for their sympathy. He loved to have them near, though in the depth of his agony he wished also to be apart from them. He went, therefore, about a stone's throw from them (Luke xxii. 41), and, kneeling, fell on his face, and prayed, saying, "O my Father, if it be possible, let this cup pass from me! nevertheless, not as I will, but as thou wilt." After remaining thus for a season, he came back to the three disciples, and finding them asleep, he said, "What! could ye not watch with me one hour? Watch and pray, that ye enter not into temptation: the spirit indeed is willing, but the flesh is weak." He went away a second time, and prayed, saying, "O my Father, if this cup may not pass away from me, except I drink it, thy will be done." The altered form of the prayer shows that the sharpness of the struggle was over. He came to his disciples again, and finding them asleep, he went away the third time, and prayed, using the same words. Several hours may thus have been passed by him in Gethsemane. When he returned the third time to his disciples, he found them asleep. Grief (Luke xxii. 45) had overcome them. "Sleep on now, and take your rest," he said. A short interval of time now probably elapsed, while the disciples continued sleeping, when Jesus saw, as he might from that spot in the moonlight, Judas, and the crowd who were with him, coming through one of the eastern gates of the city. Then he roused his disciples, and said, "Behold, the hour is near, and the Son of man is betrayed into the hands of sinners. Rise, let us go: behold, he is near who doth betray me."

The narrative here is a plain one. It is a condensed statement of the prominent facts, which probably took up several hours, viz. from nine or ten in the evening till somewhere from twelve to two in the morning. It is objected that the disciples, being asleep, could not have heard what Jesus said in his prayer. But they were awake each time when he left them, and may each time have heard the first piercing words of his prayer, and then have fallen asleep while he still lay upon his face in agony. The distance, a stone's throw, would not prevent their hearing the words which were forced from him in his anguish.

But how shall we account for the intensity of his sufferings? Luther supposes that the physical pangs, and consequently the dread of death, were greatly aggravated in his case. "We men," he says, "conceived and born in sin, have an impure, hard flesh, which does not soon feel. The fresher and sounder the man is, the finer the skin, and the purer the blood, so much the more does he feel, and is susceptible of what befalls him. Now, since Christ's body was pure and sinless, whilst ours is impure, we therefore scarcely feel the terrors of death in one fifth of the degree in which Christ felt them. Since he was to be the greatest martyr, he therefore had to suffer death's extremest terrors." This may be true of the susceptibility to merely physical suffering. The exquisite physical organization of a perfect man may have the most acute sensibility to pain, as well as to enjoyment. But beyond its physical sufferings, we cannot conceive of death as having any terrors for Jesus. We have seen how he looked through it, and regarded it only as a sleep, an incident or change in the mode of living, — an entrance, through momentary pangs perhaps, into the heavenly and immortal life. The dread of death, therefore, could not of itself have been that which so weighed down and oppressed his soul in Gethsemane.

How, then, can we account for the agony which the Evangelists have described in language so remarkable? First, there may have been the exquisitely sensitive physical organization mentioned by Luther. All its natural susceptibilities would be increased, and its powers of endurance weakened, by the exciting and exhausting scenes through which he had been passing. After the excitement of some extraordinary effort is gone by, in the physical and mental prostration that succeeds, when the nerves are as it were unsheathed and laid open to every painful sensation, the soul itself is more than at any other time exposed to depressing and disheartening thoughts. Painful and discouraging views throng before it, and shut out the light which might come from other quarters. It was so with Jesus at Gethsemane. In the extreme physical exhaustion and the consequent nervous sensibility and depression of those hours of agony, his mind was in a state to look only on the dark side of his mission. Not the glorious line of apostles, martyrs, saints, the ransomed of the Lord, an innumerable company who shall owe their salvation to him, rose in vision before him; but the unthankfulness and hatred of those for whom he was about to die, the scorn and bitterness with which they would reject his offers, the cruelties to be endured by his followers, the long centuries through which they would be struggling with the world and its powers of evil. The treachery, desertion, and denial which he was to experience among his chosen friends, the cross, the bodily anguish, the howls of anger and derision with which his sufferings would be mocked and insulted by those for whom his keenest agonies were borne, the overshadowing darkness, the ensuing ages of sin and misery, which might be removed if men only would come to him, — all these lay with their intolerable weight upon his soul, making it exceeding sorrowful, even unto death. And this intolerable anguish, this bitterness and darkness, worse than of death, which was then pressing upon him and shutting out all light and hope, this was the cup which he could not think of without agony, and concerning which he prayed that, if it were possible, it might pass from him.

How strong his yearning for human sympathy was is indicated by his touching appeal to his disciples, ver. 38, "My soul is exceeding sorrowful, even unto death; *stay here and watch with me.*" And how keenly he felt the want of sympathy is shown by the exclamation when he returned and found them sleeping: "Were ye so entirely unable to watch with me for a single hour!" They who have gone through some terrible grief know how, for the time, all their painful susceptibilities were aggravated and inflamed, so that every little act of apparent neglect or thoughtlessness on the part of their friends was like vitriol poured into a deep and angry wound. Now if we consider that the sensibilities and sympathetic emotions of our Saviour, in delicacy, intensity, and extent, went as far as his other faculties beyond all that men have ever known, and that not only the unworthiness of those who were near, but the sins and cruelties, the infidelity and indifference of coming generations, were brought before his prophetic vision, to smite upon the soul that was pouring itself out in agony for a deliverance which they would not accept, we may have some inadequate idea of the causes of the unutterable anguish which oppressed and overpowered him beneath the shadows of Gethsemane. A mother may be made to suffer an agony worse than death, through her love and sympathy for an unworthy child. Every sin of his, every act of ingratitude, every new sign of increasing depravity in him, smites on her heart; and the more intense her love and sympathy for him, the more terrible the suffering which it is in his power to inflict.

What she feels for her child, Christ felt still more intensely for each one of the thousands who, in rejecting him, were sinning against God and their own souls. What she with limited powers endures for one, he, with his finer sensibilities, his deeper love, his enlarged sympathies and comprehensive insight, may have suffered an hundred-fold from every one of those whose salvation he was longing and struggling to secure. As she in the intensity of her love and sympathy bears in her own breast the sins and sorrows of her ruined child, so he in Gethsemane, and on the cross, bore in his own body the sins and sorrows of a lost world. And thus the words of the prophet were fulfilled in him: " He hath borne our griefs and carried our sorrows, and we esteemed him stricken from above, smitten of God, and afflicted. But he was wounded for our transgressions, he was bruised for our iniquities, the chastisement of our peace was upon him; and with his stripes are we healed. All we like sheep have gone astray; we have turned every one to his own way; and the Lord hath laid on him the iniquity of us all." (Isa. liii. 4 – 6.) When, through his love and sympathy for man, this dreadful weight of sin and pain was laid upon him, and only the dark and awful side of his ministry to a sinful world was open to him, for a little while he sunk beneath the burden, and in agony of soul cried out, "O Father," — not, O *my* Father, — "if it be possible, let this cup pass from me." When he prayed again, the intensity of the struggle had abated: "O *my* Father, if this cup may not pass away from me, except I drink it, thy will be done." A third time he prayed: it was in the same words; the darkness had gone; he "was heard in that he feared." (Heb. v. 7.) He had prayed to be delivered from the intolerable anguish that overpowered him, and while he prayed it was removed. In submitting himself to drink the cup, it had passed from him. And how often, when in an agony of prayer we strive to bring ourselves into the fitting frame to endure, by this very act of submission the cup is emptied of its bitterness, and the anguish which had seemed to us so dreadful in its approach has already passed away!

The intensity of our Saviour's sufferings in consequence of the greatness of his endowments is a subject which cannot be comprehended by us in all its length and breadth, and depth and height, any more than we can comprehend the full extent of his thought or emotion in any other direction. But what we learn here is in harmony with all that we know of him. Every part of his nature is on the same grand scale. The miracles which he wrought no more decisively indicate the possession of powers over material nature beyond what other men possess, than the truths which his words open to us, and the life which he lived, show the possession of powers of thought, spiritual perceptions, and moral energies beyond what has ever been revealed to us in the history of man. And here we find him exhibiting a sensibility to suffering on the same vast scale; and the agony of Gethsemane, in its mysterious and terrible severity, has awed and subdued the world, as a deeper and more affecting expression of the same greatness which reveals itself in his other acts and words.

But is there not a deeper meaning than this in his sufferings? May not these sufferings have been aggravated by the assaults of evil spirits? As, in the Transfiguration, the splendors which shone around him were from a world beyond the reach of our mortal senses, so may it not be now, in his humiliation and agony, that the cause of his severest agony lay beyond the limits of this mortal life?

Since the consequences of his victory over death and sin reach on into unseen worlds, and have their fullest consummation there, may it not be that the conflict, as, e. g., in the wilderness and Gethsemane, may have been aggravated by the action of invisible and spiritual agencies? Apprehending the influence of his victorious death in overthrowing and subduing their kingdom, may they not have rallied their forces for a last terrible conflict with him? We know so little in regard to the whole realm of unseen spiritual agencies, especially on the side of what is evil, that it becomes us to approach the subject with diffidence. So far as relates to the passage before us, there is no expression used by Jesus which implies the presence of any such influence. What we have said of his sensibility to suffering, through the exquisite texture of his physical and emotional organization, and his unbounded love and sympathy for man, *may* be sufficient to account for all his sufferings there and on the cross. Still there may have been these other agencies. His words immediately after, " This is your hour, and the power of darkness," (Luke xxii. 53,) will bear, and naturally suggest, such a construction. "His struggle," says Olshausen, " was an invisible agony of the soul; .... a contest against the power of darkness; for as in the beginning of his ministry the Saviour was tempted by the enemy through the medium of *desire*, so now at its end was he assailed through the medium of *fear*." This is the view taken by Mr. Parsons in his fine essay on "The Ministry of Sorrow." " All the hells," he says, " were admitted to assault, to *tempt*, that humanity...... All evil influences attacked him. There were no tendencies to sin in human nature which they who had lived in the indulgence of those sins, and had so gone down into darkness, and then and there become the embodiment of those sins, did not find in the humanity he assumed, and endeavor to rouse into activity. They were all resisted, all conquered...... No spot or stain from hell could cleave to him. And all the enemies of good yielded to his perfect goodness, and found themselves, all and forever, defeated and subdued...... He reduced them to order, and subjected them forever to the force of those laws which permit them to excite in man so much only of their own evils as shall leave man in full and perfect ability to resist them and reject what they would give to him." This, we suppose, is Swedenborg's view of the subject, and it is substantially the same as that taken by

Trench in his Notes on the Demoniacs in the country of the Gadarenes. "That whole period," he says, "was the hour and power of darkness. . . . . . We cannot doubt that the might of hell has been greatly broken by the coming of the Son of God in the flesh; and with this the grosser manifestations of his power."

We leave this whole branch of the subject, in connection with what we have already said of evil spirits, as lying in a region which can be only darkly and imperfectly explained or explored by us.

There is another view of the cause of our Saviour's sufferings which has entered deeply into the theology of Christendom. It is expressed by Olshausen in its mildest form, when he says that Jesus in Gethsemane, "as representative of mankind, sustains the wrath of God." We cannot accept this view of the subject, — 1. Because it is inconsistent with all the moral instructions of Jesus, and gives a shock to all the moral sensibilities and convictions which he came into the world to revive and sustain. We must throw aside the Sermon on the Mount, the Parable of the Prodigal Son, and everything else in the Gospels which relates to our duties and the character of God, before we can accept such a doctrine. 2. We cannot accept it, because we find nothing in the Scriptures to countenance it. In the different accounts of the agony of Gethsemane there is no indication of such a relation between God and his Son. Nor is the doctrine to be found in the Old Testament. Allowing the fifty-third chapter of Isaiah to refer, as we think it does, at least in its secondary sense, to the Messiah, the interpretation that we have given above seems to us much more in accordance with its language and its spirit than the horrible idea that the sinless One was under the wrath and curse of God. "We must not for a moment," says Alford, "think of the Father's wrath abiding on him as the cause of his sufferings. Here is no fear of wrath, but, in the depth of his human anguish, the very tenderness of filial love."

For a fuller view of this subject, see *Introduction* to "Theological Essays," edited by Dr. Noyes, and the *Notes* at the close of that volume.

### 47–56.— THE APPREHENSION OF JESUS.

The different narratives of this event are marked by the differences which we should expect from independent witnesses of actions which most of them took place in the night, which must have been hurried and confused, and which could not have been seen entire in all their relations by any one of those who were present. We must call to mind the disciples just waking out of their sleep at Gethsemane, the overshadowing trees, the glimmering of the moonlight through them, the crowd with weapons and staves or clubs, with lanterns and torches, hastening eagerly towards them, hardly knowing what to expect, and without the thorough understanding and concert among themselves that would be found if they had been only a military detachment or band. The *great multitude* which Matthew speaks of were,— 1st, a detachment of Roman soldiers (ἡ σπεῖρα, *a band*, the word used to express a cohort, John xviii. 3, 12); 2d, the officers or captains of the temple, who were Jews (Luke xxii. 52); 3d, servants and others deputed by the priests; and, 4th, some of the high-priests and elders (Luke xxii. 52). Among these was Judas. He had given some of them a sign by which they might know Jesus. Confused and disconcerted, we may suppose, by the consciousness of his treacherous purpose, he rushed forward and kissed his Master, who may still have been among the trees, and in such a position that the preconcerted signal would hardly be seen by the associates whom the traitor had left behind. The mild rebuke of our Saviour would increase the agitation and mental embarrassment of Judas, so that he may have fallen back, hardly knowing what he did, and therefore leaving his companions still in doubt as to which person was Jesus. The subsequent conduct of Judas, as inferred from his repentance and death, shows how keen his sensibilities were, and that he might now have been wholly confused and disconcerted. At this moment Jesus came forward, as represented by John (xviii. 4-9), and, giving himself up, by the extraordinary impression which his calm and majestic presence produced, gained for his disciples an opportunity of going away. But at that time another party of his assailants, perhaps, coming up and laying hands upon him, one of his followers asked, "Lord, shall we smite with the sword ($\mu\alpha\chi\alpha i\rho\alpha$)?" (Luke xxii. 49); and Peter, without waiting for a reply (John xviii. 10), drew his weapon (see note to verse 51) and cut off the right ear of one of the high-priest's servants. This would, of course, cause some commotion and delay. Jesus immediately commanded Peter to sheathe the weapon, and then healing the wound he thus allayed the anger of his enemies, which otherwise might have been dangerous to Peter. At the same time he rebuked the rashness of his disciple, by reminding him of the fatal consequences of such conduct, and, 53, the needlessness of any human interference; since even then he had only to ask for deliverance from his enemies, and it would be granted. It was still in his own power to live or die, as he had said (John x. 18), " No man taketh it (my life) from me, but I lay it down of myself. I have power to lay it down, and I have power to take it again." But how then could the purposes of Divine mercy, as revealed in the Scriptures, be fulfilled? In this same calm and self-collected spirit he appealed to the multitudes, — the high-priests, the officers of the temple, and the elders (Luke xxii. 52), — asking why they had come against him as against a robber, with weapons. But this also, he added, 56, was a part of the same divine plan as declared in the Scriptures. "All this was done in such a manner that the Scriptures of the prophets were fulfilled." Mark (xiv. 27), at an earlier period of the narrative, had quoted the passage (Zech. xiii. 7), " I will smite the shepherd, and the sheep shall be scattered." Matthew, after the general reference to the prophets, adds, as Mark also does (xiv. 50), " Then all the disciples forsook him and fled." But Mark goes on to say, "And there followed him a certain young man, having a linen cloth cast about his naked body; and the young men laid hold on him: and he left the linen cloth, and fled from them naked." All the Evangelists write that Peter followed Jesus afar off, and John adds (xviii. 15), undoubtedly speaking of himself, " and so did another disciple: that disciple was known unto the high-priest, and went in with Jesus into the hall [not the palace] of the high-priest."

### 57–68.—JESUS TAKEN BEFORE THE HIGH-PRIEST.

The distance from Gethsemane to the nearest gate of the city is less than a thousand feet. The house, or rather palace, of the high-priest was probably on the northeastern slope of Mount Zion, very near the temple, and perhaps a third of a mile from the fortress of Antonia, where the Roman Procurator or governor had his quarters. Jesus was taken first to Annas, who had been high-priest, and was father-in-law to Caiaphas (John xviii. 13). Annas, who may have been in the same palace with his son-in-law, sent Jesus bound to Caiaphas (John xviii. 24). His being sent to Annas is omitted by the first three Evangelists as a circumstance of little importance. This examination before Caiaphas was only an informal preliminary investigation; " for it was not lawful to try causes of a capital nature in the night." (Jahn's Bib. Arch. 246.) The object of the examination was, not to discover what crimes the prisoner had committed, but what charges could be brought against him with the best prospect of causing him to be put to death. As a trial, the whole proceedings were irregular and illegal.

He was taken to the high-priest, with whom (Mark xiv.

53) all the high-priests, elders, and scribes had assembled. The whole Sanhedrim (Council) sought false testimony against him in order to put him to death. After many unsuccessful efforts, 60, 61, they at last succeeded in getting two witnesses, who, by perverting both the words and the application of an expression which he had used a long time before (John ii. 19), gave some color of excuse for the charge of blasphemy. Whereupon the high-priest asked Jesus what explanation he could make in regard to the accusation. Jesus, knowing that they were only seeking to compass his death, made no reply. Then the high-priest said, "I adjure thee by the living God to tell me whether thou art the Christ, the Son of God." Jesus replied, "Thou hast said" ("I am," Mark xiv. 62.) Then addressing himself to the assembled representatives of the Jewish people, in language more impressive to them from its resemblance to a remarkable passage in one of their prophets (Dan. vii. 13, 14), he continued, "Hereafter shall ye see the Son of man sitting on the right hand of power, and coming upon the clouds of heaven." This was enough. The high-priest, as an expression of his horror at such blasphemy, rent his garments; when, catching his spirit, the attendants who held Jesus (Luke xxii. 63, 64) spit in his face, and, having blindfolded him, smote him with the palms of their hands and with sticks, saying in derision, "Prophesy to us now, thou Christ, who it is that is striking thee."

## 69 – 75. — PETER'S DENIAL.

While these things were taking place, another series of incidents was occurring, which is recorded, though with slight differences, by all the Evangelists. In order to understand the narratives, it is necessary to understand something of the architecture of a Jewish palace. It was "usually built round a quadrangular interior court; into which there is a passage (sometimes arched) through the front part of the house, closed next to the street by a heavy folding gate, with a small wicket for single persons, kept by a porter." (Robinson's Harmony, 225.) This interior court is sometimes called αὐλή, or the hall, and the passage from the street to it, προαύλιον or πυλών, the porch or gateway. When Jesus was first brought to the high-priest, Peter followed him at a distance as far as to the hall, 58, (not palace, but hall, or open court), into which he was brought by a disciple (John) who was known to the high-priest. There in the hall he sat by a fire which had been made (John xviii. 16, 18), to see what was passing in the room in which Jesus was, and which would be open on the side next to the court. While he was sitting *out* here, 69, i. e. outside of the room where Jesus was, he was recognized by a damsel as one of those who had been with Jesus, and charged with having been with him. But he denied the charge. In order to withdraw himself from observation, he then went out into the passage-way or porch, 71, and there being recognized very soon, he denied his Master the second time. After about an hour, during which time he had probably returned to the court, he was recognized a third time, when with vehement imprecations he denied all knowledge of the man. At that moment the cock crew, and Jesus, who was in a room that was open on the side towards the court, turned and looked upon him, and he, remembering the prediction, rushed out through the passage-way and wept bitterly. It is possible that the third denial took place just as they had bound Jesus and were leading him away to Pilate. For "the morning," spoken of Matt. xxvii. 1, began with the cock-crowing, or at three o'clock.

## NOTES.

AND it came to pass, when Jesus had finished all these say-
2 ings, he said unto his disciples, Ye know that after two days is
the feast of the passover; and the Son of man is betrayed to
be crucified.

3 Then assembled together the chief priests, and the scribes,
and the elders of the people, unto the palace of the high-priest,
4 who was called Caiaphas; and consulted that they might take
5 Jesus by subtilty and kill him. But they said, Not on the
feast-day, lest there be an uproar among the people.

6 Now when Jesus was in Bethany, in the house of Simon the
7 leper, there came unto him a woman having an alabaster box
of very precious ointment, and poured it on his head as he sat
8 at meat. But when his disciples saw it, they had indignation,
9 saying, To what purpose is this waste? For this ointment
10 might have been sold for much, and given to the poor. When
Jesus understood it, he said unto them, Why trouble ye the
11 woman? for she hath wrought a good work upon me. For ye
have the poor always with you; but me ye have not always.
12 For in that she hath poured this ointment on my body, she did
13 it for my burial. Verily I say unto you, wheresoever this
gospel shall be preached in the whole world, there shall also
this, that this woman hath done, be told for a memorial of her.

14 Then one of the twelve, called Judas Iscariot, went unto the
15 chief priests, and said unto them, What will ye give me, and I

---

2. **after two days is the feast of the Passover**] i. e. on the next day. 3. **the chief priests**] or *high-priests.* This office was originally for life, and was received by right of inheritance. But Herod the Great changed the high-priest at his pleasure, and the Roman Procurators or governors followed his example in this respect. Valerius Gratus, who appointed Caiaphas to the office, had, according to Josephus (Ant. XVIII. 2. 2), appointed and displaced five or six high-priests within a few years.

**who was called**] *surnamed,* i. e. being called in addition to his real name. Josephus calls him "Joseph Caiaphas." 5. **Not on the feast day**] Our translators have inserted the word *day* without authority. It should be, *Not during the festival.* The expression refers to the whole period of the feast or festival, which continued eight Jewish, or seven of our days.

12. **she did it for my burial**] rather, she did it to prepare me for burial. Sometimes a long period intervened between the preparation of a body for burial and the burial itself. The preparing of Jacob's body for burial (Gen. l. 2) took place in Egypt, his sepulture in

will deliver him unto you? And they covenanted with him for thirty pieces of silver. And from that time he sought opportunity to betray him.

Now the first day of the feast of unleavened bread the disciples came to Jesus, saying unto him, Where wilt thou that we prepare for thee to eat the passover? And he said, Go into

---

Canaan. 15. **And they covenanted with him for**] or *paid to him thirty pieces of silver, — thirty silverlings* it has been translated, or shekels of silver, — about fifteen or twenty dollars. As the thirty shekels were the estimated value of a slave's life (Ex. xxi. 32), that sum may have been fixed upon as a mark of contempt towards Jesus.

**17. the passover**] was instituted for the purpose of preserving among the Hebrews the memory of their liberation from Egyptian servitude, and of the safety of their first-born on that night when the first-born of the Egyptians perished. (Exod. xii.) It was celebrated for seven days (Lev. xxiii. 4–8), during the whole of which time the people ate unleavened bread. On the eve of the 14th day of the month Abib the leaven was removed. On the 10th of the month the master of a family separated a ram or a goat of a year old. It was taken to the appointed court of the temple, and there slain and prepared in the presence of a priest, that he might see that it was free from defect or disease, and sprinkle its blood on the altar. It was slain on the 14th day of the month, between the two evenings. "The Pharisees and Rabbinists, according to the Mishna (Pesach 5. 3) held the first evening to commence with the declining sun; and the second evening with the setting sun. This latter view was the prevailing one in the time of our Lord; the hour of evening sacrifice and prayer being then the *ninth* hour, or 3 P. M. (Acts iii. 1); and the paschal lamb being regularly killed between the ninth and eleventh hours. (Josephus, Jewish Wars, VI. 9. 3.)" Robinson's Lexicon. It was roasted whole, with two spits thrust through it, the one lengthwise, the other transversely, so that the animal was in a manner crucified. Its flesh was divided, and served to those who partook, with a salad of wild and bitter herbs. Not fewer than ten nor more than twenty persons assembled in one place to observe the feast. At first the Passover was eaten by them standing, with the loins girt about, and with shoes on the feet. But this was not the case at the time of our Saviour, when the Greek and Roman custom of reclining at the table prevailed. "It is the custom of slaves," says the Jerusalem Talmud, "to eat standing; but now Israelites eat reclining, to denote that they passed from servitude into freedom." Jahn's Archæology. "The paschal supper, 1. began with the first cup of wine, before drinking which the master of the household offered a prayer of thanksgiving to God for the gift of wine. Then was put on the table, 2. a supply of bitter herbs, commemorative of the bitter life led in Egypt: of these, dipped in an acid and salt liquid, each partook amid songs of praise. Then followed, 3. the serving of the unleavened bread, of the highly-seasoned *kharoset*, or broth of the paschal lamb, and the peace-offerings (Lev. iii. 3; x. 14). Thereupon, 4. the master, after blessing Him who made heaven and earth, dipped a portion of the bitter herbs, about the size of an olive, into the *kharoset*, and ate the sop. In this act he was imitated by all at the table. 5. The second cup was made ready; and this was the point at which the father of the family, asked or unasked by his son, explained the import of the feast in all its parts." After singing, 6. the first part of the series of Psalms

the city to such a man, and say unto him, The Master saith, My time is at hand; I will keep the passover at thy house with
19 my disciples. And the disciples did as Jesus had appointed
20 them; and they made ready the passover. Now when the
21 even was come, he sat down with the twelve.—— And as they did eat, he said, Verily, I say unto you, that one of you shall
22 betray me. And they were exceeding sorrowful, and began
23 every one of them to say unto him, Lord, is it I? And he answered and said, He that dippeth his hand with me in the
24 dish, the same shall betray me. The Son of man goeth, as it is written of him; but woe unto that man by whom the Son of man is betrayed! it had been good for that man if he had not
25 been born. Then Judas, which betrayed him, answered and said, Master, is it I? He said unto him, Thou hast said.
26 —— And as they were eating, Jesus took bread, and blessed it, and brake it, and gave it to the disciples, and said, Take,
27 eat; this is my body. And he took the cup, and gave thanks,
28 and gave it to them, saying, Drink ye all of it; for this is my blood of the new testament, which is shed for many for the re-
29 mission of sins. But I say unto you, I will not drink hence-

---

termed the Hallel (Ps. cxiii., cxiv.), the master, 7. washed his hands, and, breaking a loaf, pronounced a thanksgiving, and then, the ceremonial preparation being finished, the meal, 8. properly was eaten. It was at this period probably that Jesus, troubled in spirit, said, 21, "Verily I say unto you, that one of you shall betray me." See Beard's Biblical Reading-Book, p. 254.

**24. it had been good for that man if he had not been born**] "This phrase does not necessarily imply the interminable eternity of perdition: for it is a proverbial expression. Cf. Luke xxiii. 29, Ecclesiasticus xxiii. 14. Judas obtains a situation of exclusively pre-eminent misery amongst the souls of the damned. For so long a time he accompanied our Lord, not without sharing the sorrows connected therewith; a little before the joyful pentecost he died."

**that man]** " The words, *that man*, might seem a predicate. *That* is the designation of one who is considered already far off." Bengel. We find in the Gospel narratives no ground for sympathy with those who would excuse or palliate the conduct of Judas. He who could be so long a time with Jesus, and yet gain nothing of his moral and spiritual power, must have closed his heart against all that was high or holy. The very terms of his proposal to the rulers, 15, "*What will ye give me if I will deliver him to you?*" show how base and shameless his motives were, and are entirely inconsistent with the view sometimes entertained, that Judas took this step only that he might urge Jesus on to announce his real purpose and to assume the royal authority which belonged to him as the Messiah. His subsequent remorse, ending in death, shows indeed strong sensibilities, but this only aggravates his guilt. For it indicates what he had to struggle against in his own heart before he could bring himself to betray his Lord for the price at which a

forth of this fruit of the vine, until that day when I drink it new with you in my Father's kingdom.

And when they had sung an hymn, they went out into the 30

---

slave's life was valued, and thus proves him to have been, in spite of his better nature, guilty of the two most detestable crimes, avarice and treachery, if not also of murder. No good can come from the attempt to extenuate the guilt of such a character. 29. **when I drink it new with you in my Father's kingdom**] The word *new*, καινόν, used here, is not the same as that which is used, ix. 17, νέον, to describe the newly-made wine which was not to be put into old bottles. It is the same word which is applied to the *new covenant*, or Christian dispensation, to distinguish it from the *old covenant*, or *Mosaic dispensation.* It means, not something newly made of the same sort, but something of a different sort. As the religion of Jesus is the spiritual fulfilment of that which was shadowed forth in the Mosaic dispensation, so "*the wine*" which he will drink "*new*" with his disciples in the kingdom of his Father, is the spiritual refreshment and life which shall be the perfect fulfilment of that which is now only symbolized by the eucharistic wine, or, in its spiritual sense, the blood of Christ. "The Jewish Passover was superseded by the Lord's Supper; this will be again succeeded by further things of a heavenly nature." Bengel. Another instance this of the way in which Jesus rises from the natural to the spiritual signification of language, without a single explanatory word to show where the transition takes place. We have only the connection in which the words are found to guide us in the interpretation. "Emblem," says Lord Bacon, "reduceth conceits [conceptions] intellectual to images sensible, which strike the memory more." "The scope or purpose of the Spirit of God is not to express matters of nature in the Scriptures otherwise than in passage, and for application to man's capacity, and to matters moral or divine." 30. **sung an hymn**] The word thus translated may mean that the hymn was either sung or recited.

**into the Mount of Olives**] One of the most affecting incidents in the Bible is related in connection with the Mount of Olives, and forms no unsuitable introduction to the agony of Gethsemane. When Absalom had rebelled against his father, David, leaving the ark of God in Jerusalem, "went up by the ascent of Mount Olivet, and wept as he went up, and had his head covered, and he went barefoot: and all the people that was with him covered every man his head, and went up, weeping as they went up." (2 Sam. xv. 30.) The western base of the Mount of Olives is bounded by the brook Kedron, and is one or two hundred yards distant from the eastern wall of the temple. The summit is about 2750 feet above the Mediterranean, and 4060 feet above the Dead Sea, and 137 feet above the highest part of Jerusalem. (See Barclay's Jerusalem, pp. 104, 105.) The mean distance of that part of the summit which lies opposite to the city, from the eastern wall of Jerusalem, is about half a mile by the nearest pathway, and of course, in a straight line, much less. "When about half the way up the ascent," says Prof. Hackett, "I found myself, apparently, off against the level of Jerusalem." "Three paths, deeply worn," he says, "lead over the mount. . . . . We gaze at those paths the more intently because we have no doubt that the feet of the Saviour trod them again and again as he approached the city or left it. That reflection came over me with such power, as my eyes fell upon them for the first time, that I could not refrain from weeping." Olivet "must have been adorned, anciently, with fields of grain, groves, and

31 Mount of Olives. Then saith Jesus unto them, All ye shall be offended because of me this night; for it is written, "I will smite the Shepherd, and the sheep of the flock shall be 32 scattered abroad." But after I am risen again, I will go be-33 fore you into Galilee. Peter answered and said unto him,

---

orchards. At present it exhibits, on the whole, a desolate appearance. Rocky ledges crop out here and there above the surface, and give to the hill a broken, sterile aspect. The loose soil, which might cover them in part, is left to be washed away. Yet the mount is not wholly destitute of verdure even now. A few spots are planted with grain; and fruit-trees, as almonds, figs, pomegranates, olives, are scattered up and down its sides. The olives take the lead decidedly, and thus vindicate the propriety of the ancient name." Barclay, in his "City of the Great King," p. 60, says that "there is not in all the world a prospect so delightful to behold as the panorama to be enjoyed by ascending the minaret alongside the Church of the Ascension, that now crowns the elevation nearest the city." From this point towards the east are to be seen the Dead Sea, the valley of the Jordan, where a green streak"— "a blue strip" it appeared to Dr. Hackett — "on a whitish ground marks the course of the river," and beyond the plain of the Jordan, from north to south, appears a continuous chain of mountains, as far as the steep cliffs of the Dead Sea, above which rises, deeper in the country, Jebel Shihan, with its compressed and gently rising summit, which in the winter time is frequently covered with snow." 31. **for it is written, I will smite the Shepherd**] These words (Zech. xiii. 7) are from a prophecy which, we think, in several places glances on through the shadows of intervening events to the Messiah. "My servant, the Branch" (Zech. iii. 8), and again (vi. 12, 13), "the man whose name is the Branch," who "shall build the temple of the Lord," who "shall bear the glory," and "be a priest upon his throne," refers, according to Dr. Noyes, to the Messiah. So does (ix. 9) "Rejoice greatly, O daughter of Zion," "behold thy king cometh unto thee," "lowly, and riding upon an ass, even a colt, the foal of an ass." See Matt. xxi. 5. The words (xii. 10), "they shall look on me whom they have pierced," (see John xix. 37,) may have looked forward to the same period for their fulfilment. The passage here quoted by the Saviour is more obscure in the connection from which it is taken in Zechariah, but in the obscured gleams of coming conflicts and glory which passed before the prophet's mind, the vision may have been designed by the Omniscient Spirit to foreshadow the specific event to which the words are here applied by Jesus. With our views of prophecy, there is no serious difficulty in this interpretation. 32. **But after I am risen again, I will go before you into Galilee**] This passage has troubled the commentators. "It is something extremely improbable," says Schleiermacher, "that Jesus, if he foresaw so exactly the days of his resurrection, and therefore could not but know that he should see his disciples again more than once in Jerusalem, should here have said that he would lead them into Galilee." At this distance of time, and with our ignorance of the circumstances, it is impossible for us to say why such a promise should or should not be made at that particular time. The meeting of the disciples with the Lord in Galilee after the resurrection holds a prominent place in the Gospel of Matthew (xxviii. 7, 10, 16,) and makes the impressive close of the Gospel of John. And there may

Though all men shall be offended because of thee, yet will I never be offended. Jesus said unto him, Verily, I say unto thee, that this night, before the cock crow, thou shalt deny me thrice. Peter said unto him, Though I should die with thee, yet will I not deny thee. Likewise also said all the disciples.

Then cometh Jesus with them unto a place called Gethsemane, and saith unto the disciples, Sit ye here, while I go and

---

have been special reasons for fixing in the minds of the disciples the fact that they, and perhaps the larger company, "above five hundred brethren at once," mentioned by St. Paul (1 Cor. xv. 6), were to meet him in Galilee. The ardent and confiding impetuosity of Peter's character, 33, shows itself here. Probably the precise reply of Jesus is given by Mark (xiv. 30) as he received it from St. Peter himself: "Verily I say unto thee, that thou to-day, this very night, before the cock has crowed twice, shalt deny me thrice." But Peter could not believe that the warning was needed, and replied, "Though it should be necessary to die with thee, I will not deny thee;" and likewise all the rest of the disciples asserted the same, in their vain self-confidence.

**34. this night, before the cock crow, thou shalt deny me thrice**] How is this to be reconciled with Mark xiv. 30, "Before the cock has crowed *twice*, thou shalt deny me thrice"? The difference is so slight that it may be allowed to stand without impairing our confidence at all in the writers. But the passages may perhaps be reconciled. "The *first* cock-crowing is at midnight; but inasmuch as *few hear it*, when the word is used *generally*, we mean the *second* crowing, early in the morning, before dawn. If this view be taken," the two expressions, *before the cock-crow*, and *before the cock crow twice*, "amount to the same, — only the latter is the more accurate expression. It is most likely that Peter understood this expression as only a mark of time, and therefore received it, as when it was spoken before, as merely an expression of distrust on the Lord's part; it was this solemn and circumstantial repetition of it which afterwards struck upon his mind when the sign itself was literally fulfilled." Alford. We do not think this explanation perfectly satisfactory. We know too little about it to speak with confidence. It has been questioned whether cocks were kept in Jerusalem. But even if they were not kept by the Jews, which is by no means certain, they may have been kept by the Romans who resided in the city. The different night watches among the Roman soldiers were announced by the sound of the trumpet. (Livy, XXVI. 15.) Cicero, Pro Murena, 9, in contrasting the civil with the military life, says, "You [the civilian] are roused by the crowing of the cock, he [the soldier] by the sound of the trumpet." In Jerusalem the night watches may have been indicated to the citizens generally by the sound of the trumpet in the tower of Antonia, which was the headquarters of the military, and from which the blast of the trumpet might easily be heard in the hall of the high-priest's palace. "*The cock crew*" may have been the customary form of expression for the sounding of the trumpet which announced the completion of that period of the night which was called "*the cock-crowing.*" The watches were reckoned backward; midnight beginning at nine, and cock-crowing at twelve (Mark xiii. 35), and were announced, not at the beginning, but at the close.

**Gethsemane**] To some persons the fact that Kedron, the name of

37 pray yonder. And he took with him Peter and the two sons
38 of Zebedee, and began to be sorrowful and very heavy. Then
saith he unto them, My soul is exceeding sorrowful, even unto
39 death: tarry ye here, and watch with me. And he went a
little farther, and fell on his face, and prayed, saying, O my
Father, if it be possible, let this cup pass from me! never-
40 theless, not as I will, but as thou wilt. And he cometh unto

---

the brook over which Jesus passed on his way to Gethsemane, means, *to be black*, and Gethsemane, *an olive-press*, may suggest thoughts in accordance with the associations of the place and hour. Gethsemane is but a very short distance from the city, the north end of the garden being about 145 feet beyond the bridge over the Kedron, and 985 feet from the nearest gate of the city. "It is the spot," says Professor Hackett, "above every other which the visitor must be anxious to see. It is the one which I sought out before any other, and the one of which I took my last formal view on the morning of my departure. The tradition which places the agony and betrayal of the Saviour here has a great amount of evidence in its support. . . . . The space enclosed as Gethsemane contains about one third of an acre, and is surrounded by a low wall covered with white stucco. It is entered by a gate, kept under lock and key, under the control of one of the convents at Jerusalem. The eight olive-trees here are evidently very aged, . . . . and it is not impossible that those now here may have sprung from the roots of those which grew there in the days of Christ. . . . . As I sat beneath the olives, and observed how very near the city was, with what perfect ease a person there could survey at a glance the entire length of the eastern wall, and the slope of the hill towards the valley, I could not divest myself of the impression that this local peculiarity should be allowed to explain a passage in the account of the Saviour's apprehension. Every one must have noticed something abrupt in his summons to the disciples,—'Arise, let us be going; see, he is at hand that doth betray me.' (Matt. xxvi. 46.) It is not improbable that his watchful eye, at that moment, caught sight of Judas and his accomplices, as they issued from one of the eastern gates, or turned round the northern or southern corner of the walls, in order to descend into the valley."

37. **to be sorrowful and very heavy**] "To be in great distress, and almost beside one's self for trouble." Bengel.   38. **My soul is exceeding sorrowful, even unto death**] A Hebrew form of speech indicating sorrow in the greatest possible degree. *Soul*, the sentient principle of animal and spiritual life. This is the only instance, we believe, in which Jesus uses the word *death* to express bodily dissolution, unless when obliged to do so in order to prevent misapprehension. *Death* with him applies to the soul. (John v. 24; viii. 51, 52; xi. 26.) Can it be that he uses the word in this sense here, to intimate that in the extremity of his anguish it was as if he were subjected, for the time, to the pangs of spiritual death, and brought so into contact with the sins and consequent sufferings of the world, that he felt their dreadful weight of woe and death, as if they had been laid upon his own soul?   39. **this cup**] "We may be sure that the cup which he prayed might pass from him could not have been merely the bodily pain and death, which so many men have endured with unshrinking fortitude." Whately. It was the shuddering sense of horror and grief that was overwhelming him, respecting which he prayed that it might pass from him, and in regard to which his prayer was heard.

the disciples, and findeth them asleep, and saith unto Peter, What! could ye not watch with me one hour? Watch, and 41 pray, that ye enter not into temptation; the spirit indeed is willing, but the flesh is weak. He went away again the sec- 42 ond time, and prayed, saying, O my Father, if this cup may not pass away from me, except I drink it, thy will be done. And he came and found them asleep again: for their eyes were 43 heavy. And he left them, and went away again, and prayed 44 the third time, saying the same words. Then cometh he to his 45 disciples, and saith unto them, Sleep on now, and take your rest; behold, the hour is at hand, and the Son of man is betrayed into the hands of sinners. Rise, let us be going; behold, 46 he is at hand that doth betray me.

And while he yet spake, lo, Judas, one of the twelve, came, 47 and with him a great multitude with swords and staves, from the chief priests and elders of the people. Now he that be- 48 trayed him gave them a sign, saying, Whomsoever I shall kiss, that same is he: hold him fast. And forthwith he came 49 to Jesus, and said, Hail, Master; and kissed him. And 50 Jesus said unto him, Friend, wherefore art thou come? Then

---

40. **asleep**] *sleeping for sorrow.* (Luke xxii. 45.) "There is another symptom of grief, which is not often noticed, and that is profound sleep. I have often witnessed it even in mothers, immediately after the death of a child. Criminals, we are told by Mr. Akerman, the keeper of Newgate, in London, often sleep soundly the night before their execution. The son of Gen. Custine slept nine hours the night before he was led to the guillotine in Paris." Dr. Rush. 41. **but the flesh is weak**] "We ought to take this, not as an excuse for torpor, but as an incentive to watchfulness." Bengel. "An abandonment to sorrow and its sequent emotions, diminishes the dominant energy of the spirit, and thus facilitates the victory of indwelling sin; whilst to struggle against the besetting disposition, and to give ourselves to prayer, which supplies man with fresh energy from the spiritual world, secure us against temptation." Olshausen.

45. **Sleep on now**] The agony is now over. Jesus no longer requires their sympathy. He therefore lets them sleep on, though the hour and the man of treachery are at hand. After this, the disciples may have taken their rest for a considerable time, before he saw the company with their torches and lanterns coming to seize him, when, verse 46, he roused his disciples that they might have a few moments in which to awake and recover themselves before they were assailed.

49. **and kissed him**] "It was not unusual for a master to kiss his disciple; but for a disciple to kiss his master was more rare. Whether, therefore, Judas did this under pretence of respect, or out of open contempt and derision, let it be inquired." Lightfoot.

50. **Friend**] *companion.* See xx. 13, "Friend, I do thee no wrong." The word must have come home sharply to the heart of Judas. "Friend, wherefore art thou come?" "Betrayest thou the Son of man

51 came they and laid hands on Jesus, and took him. —— And, behold, one of them which were with Jesus stretched out his hand, and drew his sword; and struck a servant of the high-

---

with a kiss?" The latter half of the appeal is from Luke. We suppose that both the expressions were used by Jesus, and not, with Alford, that the meaning of the words reported by Luke is involved in the expression recorded by Matthew. It may have been thus: When Jesus saw Judas coming near, he may have said, "Friend, why art thou coming?" and then after the kiss was given, he may in a different tone have added, "Judas, betrayest thou the Son of man with a kiss?" 51. **and drew his sword**] What was the weapon or instrument here denoted? The word used by all the Evangelists is μάχαιρα, *machaira*, of which the primary meaning is *a knife, a large knife, a slaughter-knife*. Among the Greeks in the heroic ages it was worn suspended in a sheath by the sword on the left side of the body, and was used on all occasions as a knife. (See Smith's Greek and Roman Antiquities; Homer's Iliad, III. 271–273; Herod. II. 61.) It was used either as a weapon or a knife. In the Septuagint version of the Old Testament the word is used to designate just such an instrument, and whether it is to be rendered *knife* or *sword* must be determined by the accompanying circumstances. For example, in Ezekiel xxvi. 15, "Thus saith the Lord God to Tyre, Shall not the islands be shaken at the sound of thy fall, when the wounded groan, when the *machaira* is drawn in the midst of thee?" In our English version this last clause is rendered, "When the *slaughter* is made in the midst of thee," and the word *machaira*, an instrument employed not only in war, but primarily in slaughtering cattle, may have been used in this its primary sense, to describe the butchery of an effeminate and helpless people at the hands of their enemies. In Genesis xxvii. 40, "And by thy *machaira* shalt thou live, and shalt serve thy brother," the word may be rendered as a *knife* to be used by the hunter, rather than as a sword to be used only in war. In Ex. xv. 9, "The enemy said, I will pursue, I will overtake, I will divide the spoil, I will fill my soul, I will destroy with the *machaira*, my hand shall prevail," the word is used to designate a weapon of war; as it also is in Gen. xxxi. 26, "and carried away my daughters as captives taken with the *machaira*." On the other hand, in Gen. xxii. 6, 10, *machaira* is the instrument (properly translated *knife*) which Abraham took with him: "And he took the fire in his hand, and a knife." "And Abraham stretched forth his hand, and took the knife to slay his son." And in 1 Kings xviii. 28, the *machairai* were the *knives* with which and with lancets the priests of Baal cut themselves, "till the blood gushed out upon them." Now the language of the Septuagint was evidently as familiar to the Evangelists as that of the Hebrew Scriptures. Their quotations are often made from it, and its use of Greek words would have great influence with them. As far as that influence was concerned, they may have used the word *machaira* in either sense; but its primary meaning was that of knife, and they had at least one other word, ρομφαία (Luke ii. 35; Rev. i. 16; ii. 12, 16; vi. 8; xix. 15, 21) by which to denote a *sword* without ambiguity. We must then be guided by the circumstances of the case in the construction that we put upon the word in any particular instance in which it is used by them. There is no doubt that *machaira* would properly designate the knives used by the Jews in killing, dressing, and dividing sacrifices, in preparing animal food before it was cooked, and in carving it afterwards. When carried, they were, for safety and convenience, secured in a

priest, and smote off his ear. Then said Jesus unto him, 52
Put up again thy sword into his place; for all they that take

---

sheath. Except in the passage before us, and those connected with it, the word is found in the Gospels only twice. "I came not to send peace, but a *machaira;* for I am come to divide a man from (or against) his father, and a daughter against her mother." (Matt. x. 34, 35.) Here, as opposed to peace, the warlike use of the weapon is first suggested; but in the explanation which follows, dividing one against another, or separating one from another, the other use of the instrument may possibly be indicated. "And they shall fall by the edge of the *machaira*, and shall be led away captive into all nations." (Luke xxi. 24.) In this case it is spoken of as a weapon of war. In the Acts it occurs twice: "And he killed James the brother of John with the sword" (xii. 2), the executioner's sword. "And the keeper of the prison, awaking out of his sleep, and seeing the prison doors open, he drew out his *machaira* and would have killed himself." (xvi. 27.) In both these cases the word is rightly translated *sword*, though the instrument spoken of may have been used both as a knife and a sword. In the Epistles of Paul the word occurs twice. "Who shall separate us from the love of Christ? Shall tribulation or distress, . . . . . or peril, or *machaira?*" (Rom. viii. 35.) "For he [the ruler] beareth not the *machaira* in vain." (Rom. xiii. 4.) In both these cases the warlike use of the instrument is what is first suggested by the connection. In the Epistle to the Hebrews (xi. 34, 37), "escaped the edge of the *machaira*," "were slain with the *machaira*," the same idea evidently lies uppermost. But Heb. iv. 12 appears to describe the other and peaceful uses of the instrument. "For the word of God is living and effective, sharper than any two-edged *machaira*, penetrating even to the dividing asunder of soul and spirit, both of joints and marrow, and a discerner of the thoughts and imaginations of the heart." The *machaira*, as a knife, was used to separate the joints, to take out the marrow, and to divide and open the animal offered for sacrifice, so that the priest could inspect all its inward parts. Thus it might be said to be a discerner (the idea of division lying at the root of the expression) of the thoughts and imaginations of the heart. In the Apocalypse the word occurs three times. (Rev. vi. 4, xiii. 10, 14), and in each case as a destructive weapon. The result of this examination goes to show that the word *machaira*, primarily signifying an instrument which was used both as a weapon of war and as a knife, was employed by the writers in the New Testament to denote an instrument which might be used for either of these purposes, but which was most frequently named in reference to its warlike uses. In which capacity is the instrument spoken of in the connection before us? We give the reply nearly in the words of a very intelligent and painstaking student of the Scriptures, who has kindly favored us with his views:—

"About sunset Peter and John, in obedience to the command, 'Go and prepare for us the Passover,' (Luke xxii. 8,) had killed and prepared the paschal lamb. In doing this, and in dividing the roasted lamb for those who partook, they must have had knives. Those now used by the Jews for such purposes vary from six to eighteen inches in length, and when carried are secured in a belt, girdle, or sheath. *Machaira* is unquestionably a word which might well be used to denote such an instrument. Between the Paschal feast and the institution of the Lord's Supper, soon after Judas had left the chamber, while warning his disciples of the inhospitality for which they must now be prepared (Luke xxii. 35 – 38), Jesus inquired of them if, when he had sent them without any provision for their physical wants, 'without

53 the sword shall perish with the sword. Thinkest thou that I cannot now pray to my Father, and he shall presently give me

purse and scrip and shoes,' they had lacked anything; and they answered, 'Nothing.' '*But now*,' he said, as if circumstances had changed, and they must do something to provide for themselves, — 'But now he that hath a purse let him take it, likewise also a bag; and he who has not [one], let him sell his cloak and buy a *machaira*. For I say unto you that this which is written, "And he was reckoned among the transgressors," must now be accomplished [τελεσθῆναι] in me. And indeed the things [written] concerning me are having their accomplishment [τέλος].' And they said, 'Lord, behold, here are two *machairai*.' And he said to them, 'It is enough.' Were not these the *machairai* which had been used late in the afternoon by Peter and John in killing and dressing the paschal lamb, and later still at the table in dividing the lamb among those who partook? Chrysostom, commenting on Matt. xxvi. 51, says: 'But whence were these *machairai*? They [the disciples] had come from supper and from the table. Wherefore it is probable that the *machairai* were there on account of the lamb, and that they [the disciples] hearing that an attack would be made upon their Master, took them for aid against those who should assail him.' In Matt. Hom. lxxxiv. al. lxxxv. Opp. VII. 797, 798, ed. Montfaucon. Theophylact, on the same passage of Matthew, says: 'He [Peter] had a *machaira* because he had just slain the lamb which they ate.' Opp. (Venet. 1754, fol.) I. 151. Cornelius a Lapide, in his note on Matt. xxvi. says: 'That this *sword* of St. Peter was a knife which the Apostles had used in slaying and eating the lamb, is maintained by Toletus on John xviii. 10. This view is favored also by Chrysostom, Theophylact, Joannes Maior, Jansenius on Matt. xxvi.' Comm. in Matt. p. 494. Neander says: 'The word (*machairai*) may be translated

*knives*, and these were in common use among travellers in those regions.' Life of Jesus, Am. Version (New York, 1848), p. 393.

"Later in that night, Judas came, and with him a great multitude, with *machairai* and staves, — not spears, the more appropriate weapon of warriors, but staves or clubs, and such other weapons, most likely knives, as were at hand, to be hastily seized by the multitude. Alexander, in his Comm. on Mark xiv. 43 – 48, suggests the rendering '*knives and sticks*.' Some of the multitude laid hands on Jesus. 'And when his followers saw what was about to take place, they said to him, Lord, shall we smite with the *machaira*?' And one of them smote the servant of the high-priest, and struck off his right ear.' (Luke xxii. 49, 50.) Then Jesus saith unto him, 'Put up again thy *machaira* into its place; for all they who take the sword shall perish by the sword.' (Matt. xxvi. 52.) In his rebuke to Peter, Jesus evidently implied that the disciple, in making the use of the *machaira* which he did as a weapon of war and violence, had misunderstood and perverted his meaning in the conversation respecting it at the paschal table. But were *they* who put the question, 'Lord, shall *we* smite with the sword?' Peter and John, or one of them for both? There were but two *machairai* among the disciples, the same, we suppose, which had been used by Peter and John in killing, preparing, and dividing the paschal lamb. One of these disciples who had a *machaira* was Peter, a fact which we learn only from John (xviii. 10). He was warned by his Master not to use it in that way, and probably escaped unknown while Jesus was healing the wound which had been inflicted. Was John heard to ask the question, 'Shall we smite with the *machaira*?' Or was he seen to draw, or to have such a weapon, and was he *there-*

40*

more than twelve legions of angels? But how then shall the 54
scriptures be fulfilled, that thus it must be? —— In that same 55

---

*fore* 'laid hold of' so that he could escape only with the loss of his garment? It was like John to inquire and wait for his Lord's reply (Luke ix. 51 - 56), and it was like Peter to rush into action without waiting for advice. If such were the facts, then the narrative relating to 'a certain young man' (Mark xiv. 51, 52), given after the general statement, 'they all forsook him and fled,' is a recurrence back, such as is 'natural and common in all narrative style,' to state what had happened to one of their number before they fled."

Thus a careful review of the occasion and related facts does not, we think, authorize a departure from the primary meaning of the word *machaira* in these passages, by translating it *sword*. We have no reason to suppose that the disciples, in procuring the two which they possessed, had reference to anything further than the peaceful uses to which they might be applied. We may not be able to show why it was that Jesus should think it so important for his disciples to have a knife of that sort after the supper. But that he did not mean to command them to arm themselves with it as a weapon of war, is a supposition consistent with the use of the word *machaira*, and with the uses to which the instrument itself was put; while the other supposition, that he did mean to command them thus to arm themselves with it as a sword, is at variance with the general spirit of his life and his religion, and is directly contradicted by his words to Peter after he had so used it. 52, 53. Here Jesus contrasts the aid which comes from man's violence with that which may come from God. *Thinkest thou that I cannot now pray to my Father, and he shall presently give me more than twelve legions of angels?* A legion consisted of about 6,000. The language may be figurative; but it seems to us much more reasonable to suppose that it was intended to give us a glimpse into the vast economy of God's kingdom and the multitudes of the heavenly hosts who act as his spiritual agents. But always in our prayers for help, "*Not as I will, but as thou wilt,*" must underlie our petitions. We must not ask for the intervention even of God's angels, except as it may be in accordance with his higher purposes. "The cup which my Father hath given me, shall I not drink it?" is given (John xviii. 11) as the qualifying clause here, where Peter is forbidden to use the weapon. In Matthew, however, 54, the same idea is conveyed by the words, "*But how then shall the Scriptures be fulfilled, that thus it must be?*" which are thus explained by Mr. Norton: "Your prophets and you have anticipated a great messenger from God; what they and you have anticipated, I am; but what is now taking place is necessary in order that I may fully sustain the character and perform the offices of such a messenger." In ver. 53 Jesus distinctly implies his own free agency. It lies within his choice to live or die. And knowing this, he cheerfully bows to the higher purposes for which he had come into the world. The same idea is repeated in ver. 56, and brought out still more forcibly in John xii. 27. Jesus asserts man's freedom, but he quite as distinctly recognizes the overruling Providence and all-pervading designs of the Divine mind. He asserts them both as facts, and shows how we practically are to act in regard to them, though he does not show on metaphysical grounds how the two are to be reconciled; especially when the purposes of God have been revealed in prophecies which are to be fulfilled by men. Good men will choose to work for their fulfilment, and whatever bad men in their freedom may choose, their actions in the orderings of the Almighty and Omniscient mind will help on to the fulfilment of his purposes, as contrary winds, while they

hour said Jesus to the multitudes, Are ye come out as against a thief, with swords and staves, for to take me? I sat daily with you teaching in the temple, and ye laid no hold on me; 56 but all this was done, that the scriptures of the prophets might be fulfilled. Then all the disciples forsook him, and fled. 57 And they that had laid hold on Jesus led him away to Caiaphas the high-priest, where the scribes and the elders were 58 assembled. But Peter followed him afar off, unto the high-priest's palace; and went in, and sat with the servants to see 59 the end. Now the chief priests and elders, and all the council, 60 sought false witness against Jesus, to put him to death. But found none; yea, though many false witnesses came, yet found 61 they none. At the last came two false witnesses, and said, This fellow said, I am able to destroy the temple of God, and 62 to build it in three days. And the high-priest arose, and said unto him, Answerest thou nothing? what is it which these 63 witness against thee? But Jesus held his peace. And the high-priest answered and said unto him, I adjure thee, by the living God, that thou tell us whether thou be the Christ, 64 the Son of God. Jesus saith unto him, Thou hast said: nevertheless, I say unto you, hereafter shall ye see the Son of man sitting on the right hand of power, and coming in the 65 clouds of heaven. Then the high-priest rent his clothes, saying, He hath spoken blasphemy; what further need have we of witnesses? behold, now ye have heard his blasphemy.

---

are left to blow where they list, are by the art of man made to propel the ship on against their current.

**57. to Caiaphas**] "The palace of the high-priest . . . . . was situated between Millo and the Armory, on the northeastern slope of Mount Zion. As thus situated on the declivity, a story below the chief suite of rooms was very natural, and indeed almost unavoidable: and this circumstance enables us the better to understand the expression (Mark xiv. 66), Peter was *beneath* in the $αὐλῇ$," i. e. the court or hall. Barclay, p. 171. Without regard to this declivity, the court would be a few steps below the floor of the surrounding rooms, so that it would be a natural mode of expression to say, that while Jesus was in the room with the high-priest, Peter was down ($κάτω$) in the court. **64. sitting on the right hand of power, and coming in the clouds of heaven**] These remarkable words are intended to describe the power and majesty of Christ as it shall at length appear, even to those who now reject him. The words "Christ 'coming,' 'coming in the clouds,' &c., not only indicate his advent at a far distant period, but also his spiritual world-historical manifestation." Neander. 65. **Then the high-priest rent his clothes**] "They that judge a blasphemer first ask the witness and bid him speak plainly what he

What think ye? They answered and said, He is guilty of 66
death. Then did they spit in his face, and buffeted him; and 67
others smote him with the palms of their hands, saying, Proph- 68
esy unto us, thou Christ, who is he that smote thee?

Now Peter sat without in the palace. And a damsel came 69
unto him, saying, Thou also wast with Jesus of Galilee. But 70
he denied before them all, saying, I know not what thou sayest.
And when he was gone out into the porch, another maid saw 71
him, and said unto them that were there, This fellow was also
with Jesus of Nazareth. And again he denied with an oath, I 72
do not know the man. And after a while came unto him they 73
that stood by, and said to Peter, Surely thou art also one of
them, for thy speech bewrayeth thee. Then began he to curse 74

---

hath heard; and when he speaks it, the judges, standing on their feet, rend their garments and do not sew them up again." Lightfoot. Josephus, Jewish Wars, II. 15. 4.

70. **But he denied**] We place the different accounts of Peter's denials side by side, that our readers may compare them:—

### FIRST DENIAL.

| MATTHEW. | MARK XIV. | LUKE XXII. | JOHN XVIII. |
| --- | --- | --- | --- |
| And Peter sat without in the hall, and a maid came to him, saying, "Thou also wast with Jesus of Galilee." But he denied before them all, saying, "I know not what thou sayest." And when he had gone out into the porch, | And as Peter was down in the hall, there cometh one of the maids of the high-priest; and when she saw Peter warming himself, she looked upon him and said, "Thou also wast with Jesus the Nazarene." But he denied, saying, "I know not, neither understand I what thou sayest." And he went out into the porch, and the cock crew. | And when they had kindled a fire in the midst of the hall, and were set down together, Peter sat down among them. But a certain maid beheld him as he sat by the fire, and earnestly looked upon him, and said, "This man was also with him." And he denied, saying, "Woman, I know him not." | John, who was known to the high-priest, came into the hall, leaving Peter at the gate without. John spoke to the maid who kept the gate, and she brought Peter in, i. e. to the hall. And she saith to Peter, "Art not thou also one of this man's disciples?" He saith, "I am not." And the servants and officers, having made a fire of coals because it was cold, stood there warming themselves, and Peter was with them, standing, and warming himself. |

### SECOND DENIAL.

| | | | |
| --- | --- | --- | --- |
| another damsel saw him, and saith to those who were there, "This one also was with Jesus the Nazarene." And again he denied with an oath, "I do not know the man." | And a maid saw him, and began to say to those standing by, "This is one of them." But he again denied it. | And after a short time another [masculine gender] saw him and said, "Thou art also of them." And Peter said, "Man, I am not." | They said, therefore to him, "Art not thou also one of his disciples?" He denied it, and said, "I am not." |

and to swear, saying, I know not the man. And immediately
75 the cock crew. And Peter remembered the word of Jesus,

---

### THIRD DENIAL.

| MATTHEW. | MARK. | LUKE. | JOHN. |
|---|---|---|---|
| And after a while came unto him they that stood by, and said to Peter, "Surely thou also art one of them; for thy speech makes thee manifest." Then began he to curse and to swear, saying, "I know not the man." And immediately the cock crew. And Peter remembered the word of Jesus which said unto him, "Before the cock crow, thou shalt deny me thrice." And he went out and wept bitterly. | And a little while after, they that stood by said again to Peter, "Surely thou art one of them; for thou art a Galilæan". [*and thy speech agreeth thereto*, is not in Tischendorf]. And he began to curse and to swear, saying, "I know not this man of whom ye speak." And the second time a cock crew. And Peter called to mind the word that Jesus said unto him, "Before the cock crow twice, thou shalt deny me thrice." And rushing out, he wept. | And about the space of one hour after, another [ἄλλος, masculine] confidently affirmed, saying, "Of a truth, this man also was with him; for he is a Galilean." And Peter said. "Man, I know not what thou sayest." And immediately, while he was yet speaking, the cock crew. And the Lord turned and looked at Peter, and Peter remembered the word of the Lord, how he had said unto him, "Before the cock crow, thou shalt deny me thrice." And Peter went out and wept bitterly. | One of the servants of the high-priest (being his kinsman whose ear Peter cut off), saith to him, "Did not I see thee in the garden with him?" Again, therefore, Peter denied; and immediately a cock crew. |

At the first recognition and denial of Peter, all the Evangelists agree in stating that he was in the hall, and that he was accosted by a maid. Her manner of speaking, though differing slightly in the words used, is substantially the same. The variations are only such as we should expect to find in the honest report of the same transaction by different witnesses. All the different expressions here assigned by the different writers to her and to him may have been used. She may have asked, as in John, "Art not thou also one of this man's disciples?" and when he answered, "I am not," she may have added, as in Matthew, "Surely thou wast with Jesus of Galilee." When Peter denied, saying, "I know not what thou sayest," she may have repeated her assertion, with the slight variation in Mark, "Thou surely wast with Jesus the Nazarene;" and he would naturally meet the charge, thus repeated, with the still stronger denial, "I know not, neither understand I what thou sayest." Then the woman, looking earnestly at him, so as to satisfy herself that it was he, may have said, as in Luke, to those around her, "This man certainly was with him;" and Peter in reply might say, "Woman, I know him not." All the expressions would thus belong to one act of recognition and denial. Such repeated assertions and denials are in themselves more probable than a single one, under the circumstances. Luke says that Peter was *sitting* by the fire; John says that he was *standing*. Both the accounts may have been true, as nothing is more probable than that the parties should have changed their place and posture during the altercation. At the second recognition and denial Matthew and Mark both speak of Peter as being in the porch or passage-way. Matt., πυλῶνα, a gateway. Mark, προαύλιον, which exactly describes the passage leading from the street to the hall. Luke and John say nothing of Peter's having left the hall. According to Matthew and Mark, it was

which said unto him, Before the cock crow, thou shalt deny me thrice. And he went out, and wept bitterly.

---

a *woman* who recognized and spoke to him ("another maid," Matthew); according to Luke, it was a different person from the one who at first spoke to him, and a *man*. John, in using the plural number, "*they said*," intimates that the charge against Peter was made by more than one person, and thus authorizes us to suppose that both the other accounts are true, and that he was addressed both by a woman and a man. In the account of the third denial, no one of the writers tells where Peter was; but it is not improbable that, after he was discovered in the passage-way, he returned to the hall, and remained there during the considerable time (Luke says "about an hour") that intervened. Then those who were standing by (Matthew and Mark) recognized him by his Galilæan dialect. Luke says, that a different person from the one who spoke to him before, *a man*, charged him with being one of the party who had been with Jesus; and John says, that a servant of the high-priest, the kinsman of him whose ear Peter cut off, said to him, "Did not I see thee in the garden with him?" There is no reason to suppose that this servant of the high-priest is the same person mentioned by Luke, especially as the plural number used by Matthew and Mark intimates that several persons were engaged in making the charge. Peter replied to them, one after another, growing more excited as the charge was repeated, till at length his loud and earnest imprecations attracted the attention of Jesus, who was in a room that was open towards the hall or court, and just after the cock crew turned and looked on Peter, who, thus reminded of the Lord's words, rushed out and wept bitterly. In this way the different accounts are perfectly harmonized, except for those who are "slavishly bound to the inspiration of the letter." We do not usually make sufficient allowance for what is left out in each of the Gospel narratives. We unjustly charge the Evangelists with contradicting one another, when in fact they are only giving different incidents connected with one common event. In this instance we think of three distinct charges, each made by one person in a single short sentence, and each replied to by Peter in one single expression of denial. But it is far more likely that each case of recognition would lead to a considerable altercation, in which the original charge would be repeated, as it would also be denied, in different words, and that different persons as they recognized Peter would add their testimony to that already given. Each of the writings, which are drawn from independent sources, and none of them giving an account of all the particulars, would be likely to bring out different persons and expressions. Each one, therefore, may be regarded as supplying what is wanting in the others. By bringing together the different accounts in this way, we are able, at least in the case before us, to give a much more life-like and probable narrative of events than in the way which is usually adopted either by the friends or the enemies of the Gospels. The variations in the accounts show that the writers draw their statements from independent sources, and with such writers it must often happen that, in our ignorance of the details familiar to them, we may find it impossible to reconcile, as we can in this case, incidents which did nevertheless truly occur. These apparent differences, says Alford, to whom we are indebted for important suggestions here, we value "as testimonies to independence: and are sure, that if for one moment we could be put in complete possession of all the details as they happened, each account would find its justification, and the reasons of all the variations would appear."

## CHAPTER XXVII.

PRELIMINARY TRIAL OF JESUS BEFORE THE SANHEDRIM.

IT is impossible even for the ablest scholars, with the scanty means of information which are now within their reach, to speak with any confidence concerning the precise forms of judicial proceeding which were held to be necessary among the Jews in a case like this. "From the time when Archelaus was deposed," A. D. 6 or 7, says Alford, " and Judæa became a Roman province, it would follow by the Roman law that the Jews lost the power of life and death." From Josephus (Ant. XX. 9. 1) it would appear that the high-priest had no right to assemble the Sanhedrim in a capital case without permission from the Roman governor or Procurator. In John xviii. 31, the Jewish elders and high-priests say to Pilate, that they have no legal right to put any one to death. Still, in order to accomplish their designs against Jesus, it was important that the Sanhedrim should go through the customary forms of judicial investigation, and secure his condemnation before the highest Jewish tribunal, with such a weight of authority on their side that they might be able to extort from the Roman ruler the assent, without which their own judicial decisions could not be carried into effect. The examination at the house of the high-priest was only for the purpose of seeing what charges and witnesses could be used against him most effectively at his trial.

When, therefore, the morning ($\pi\rho\omega\iota\alpha s$ — Mark xiii. 35 — the watch of three hours which ended at six o'clock in the morning) had come, and the elders of the people, the high-priests, and scribes were gathered together, so as to form a legal Sanhedrim at their room in the vicinity of the temple, Jesus was taken up (Luke xxii. 66) from the house of Caiaphas to the council-chamber. It is not improbable that they had been in session for a considerable time, and had already determined on the course which they were to pursue, when Jesus was brought before them. Luke (xxii. 66 – 71) is the only one of the Evangelists who gives any account of the proceedings here, which were little more than a repetition of what had already taken place, and resulted in a more formal act of condemnation. Being thus by the highest judicial tribunal of his own nation condemned to death, Jesus was bound and taken before Pilate.

3–10. — REPENTANCE AND DEATH OF JUDAS.

This account is found only in Matthew. When Judas saw Jesus condemned to death, and delivered over to the Roman power, he was smitten with sudden remorse, and brought back to the Jewish rulers the thirty pieces of money, with an acknowledgment of his guilt in his fatal treachery against innocent blood. But driven to desperation by their cold and contemptuous reply, he threw down the money in the midst of the temple, and went off and hanged himself, or was choked to death (strangled) by the intensity of his anguish. Many attempts have been made to reconcile this account of the death of Judas with that which is given in Acts i. 18. Matthew says, he "strangled himself," the natural meaning of which is, that he "hanged himself," though the words may possibly be construed as implying that he died of suffocation from the intensity of his emotions. In the Acts (i. 18) it is said, "falling headlong, he burst asunder in the midst, and all his bowels gushed out." In the notes may be found some of the explanations by which commentators have tried to harmonize these two passages. No one of them seems to us perfectly satisfactory. We know too little of the circumstances and of the language used, to assert with confidence that the two accounts directly contradict one another, or that any explanation given is certainly the true one. The consultation among the priests, and the purchase of the potter's field, probably took place at a later period, and not on the day of the crucifixion.

## 11 – 31. — JESUS BEFORE PILATE.

It is necessary to compare the Evangelists carefully with one another to get a clear and full account of these transactions. Matthew alone, 19, speaks of the message sent to Pilate by his wife, and of his washing his hands, 24, in token of his innocency. Luke alone (xxiii. 7 – 12) mentions the fact that Jesus was sent away to Herod. John (xix. 1 – 13) enters more fully into the state of Pilate's mind, his conversations with Jesus, and his repeated efforts to induce the Jews to set him free.

While it was yet early in the morning (John xviii. 28) Jesus was taken to the Prætorium, or hall of judgment, in the tower of Antonia, a little north of the temple, where he stood before the governor. This Prætorium is the same as the hall (Mark xv. 16) or open court in the centre of the building, while in front of the palace was apparently a wide open space with a tessellated pavement, where Pilate on that day placed his judgment-seat (John xix. 13). The Jews on account of their religious scruples could not enter the court, lest it should make them unclean, and unfit for the feast. Pilate, therefore, several times during the trial passed back and forth between the Jews in front of the palace and Jesus, who, with the Roman soldiers, was in the Prætorium. Two or three times Jesus was taken out into the presence of the Jews. Bearing these things in mind, we may get a clear view of the transactions of the morning. Jesus is brought into the Prætorium (John xviii. 28 – 32). Pilate comes out and asks the chief priests and rulers what their accusation against him is? They reply, "If he were

not a malefactor, we should not have delivered him up
unto thee." This vague form of accusation did not suit the
Roman governor's ideas of a judicial trial, and he told them
that they had better take him and condemn him according
to their law. They said, in reply, what he undoubtedly
knew perfectly all the time, that they had no legal authority
to put any man to death. Then they began (Luke xxiii. 2)
to accuse him of perverting the nation, of forbidding to give
tribute to Cæsar, and of making himself to be Christ a king,
or an anointed king. Then Pilate went back into the
Prætorium, and had with Jesus the conversation which is
most fully recorded in John xviii. 33 – 38, — a conversation
which evidently produced a very strong impression upon his
mind. He then went out to the Jews, probably taking Jesus
with him, to declare that he found no fault in him. And
when they, growing more urgent, spoke of Jesus as beginning
his work of insurrection in Galilee (Luke xxiii. 5 – 12),
Pilate sent him to Herod, who probably occupied the magnificent
palace built by Herod the Great, in the western part
of the city, near the Tower of Hippicus. More than an
hour probably intervened before Jesus was brought back
to the Prætorium. Pilate then called the Jewish rulers
together again, and after asserting that neither he nor Herod
found any fault in Jesus, he proposed to set him free, since
it had been his custom always to set some prisoner free at
this festival. Just at this time, while he was sitting on the
judgment-seat outside the palace, he received a message
from his wife, warning him to have nothing to do "with that
righteous man;" "for," she said, "I have suffered many
things this day in a dream, because of him." Her language
shows that she must have known the reputation which Jesus
had for purity and sanctity. Her message must have added
to the perplexity and awe of Pilate. For dreams were regarded
by many of the Greeks and Romans as sent from
the gods. The classical reader will call to mind the expression
of Homer, "for dreams are from Jupiter," and the

warning dream by which Cæsar's wife endeavored to keep him at home on the day when he was assassinated in the Capitol. Pilate redoubled his efforts to release Jesus. But the multitude had been already persuaded by the chief priests and elders, and only became the more clamorous for the blood of their victim. He then, to express in the strongest and most solemn terms his sense of the prisoner's innocence, took water and washed his hands before the multitude, saying, "I am innocent of the blood of this righteous man; see ye to it." And all the people answered, "His blood be on us, and on our children;" — an imprecation fearfully and terribly fulfilled in the manifold sufferings and slaughters which attended the destruction of Jerusalem before that generation had passed away. Pilate now gave him up to his soldiers to scourge and mock him; but even then (John xix. 4 – 12) he tried again and again to awaken their compassion. The majestic and mysterious bearing of his prisoner, the message from his wife, and the character of the charges against the prisoner created in him a sentiment of awe, and perhaps of superstitious fear. Whether any, however distant, perception of the truth touched him, is not shown by either of the narratives. We have no right to judge him by the Christian standard, and condemn him because he did not receive Christ as the Son of God. But we have a right to judge him by his own law, and to condemn him, because, in spite of the warnings and misgivings which he had, he weakly and wickedly, against his own convictions, consented to condemn the prisoner, in violation of the law by which he was to be judged.

## 32 – 61. — THE CRUCIFIXION.

We come now to the most solemn, the most affecting, the most significant and majestic event in the history of our race. Here is the deepest and most touching expression of God's love, stooping with infinite compassion to save man from sin and the misery consequent upon it. We shrink from interrupting the account by any critical remarks, and give the narrative as we find it in the four Evangelists, reserving our comments for the notes at the end of the chapter.

Jesus, being worn down by the sorrows and watchings of the night, and the indignities and sufferings to which he was subjected after his apprehension, especially the scourging which had just been administered, the cross was bound upon his shoulders, and a little before the third hour, or nine o'clock in the morning, he went bearing his own cross with pain, as the expression (John xix. 17) seems to intimate, towards a place called Golgotha. A man named Simon, a Cyrenian, who had come in from the country, having shown probably some marks of pity for the sufferer, was compelled to lift up the end of the cross, and, perhaps without materially lightening the Saviour's burden, was made to share the insults and mockery that were heaped upon him. This Cyrenian, however, was not the only one who sympathized with him in his sorrows. In the midst of that scoffing multitude who were howling after him, and making him the butt of their impious jests, was a great number of people, especially of women, who were lamenting and bewailing him. Jesus turned towards them, and, thinking of the terrible calamities which were to fall on them and their children (Luke xxiii. 28), he said, "Daughters of Jerusalem! weep not for me; but weep for yourselves and for your children."

In a short time their mournful journey was finished, and they reached the spot whose name must always be sacred in the thoughts and affections of the Christian world. There they crucified him, having previously stripped him of his garments and offered him a stupefying potion, which, when he had tasted it, he refused to drink. Either at the moment when they were driving the nails through his hands and his feet, or at the moment of excruciating anguish when the cross, with his body nailed to it, reaching an upright position, sunk down with a shock into the hole prepared for it in the earth, the sharp and sudden agony wrenched from him, as in a shriek, the cry, his first utterance on the cross, "Father! forgive them; for they know not what they are doing." Now the cruel and blasphemous acts of mockery and scorn were renewed, Jewish priests and Roman soldiers, rulers and people alike, wagging their heads as they passed by, and scoffing at him and his sufferings. Even one of the two malefactors who were crucified with him, one on either side, joined in the revilings, and said scoffing (Luke xxiii. 39), "If thou art the Christ, save thyself and us." But the other, subdued by what he had seen of divine benignity in Jesus, after rebuking his companion, said to Jesus, "Remember me, when thou comest in thy kingdom." Jesus, moved with compassion towards him, said, and this was his second utterance on the cross, "Verily I say unto thee, To-day shalt thou be with me in paradise."

The long hours of torture passed. Near the cross where he hung helpless and submissive in his agony stood (John xix. 25) Mary, the mother of Jesus, and her sister, and Mary the *wife* of Clopas, and Mary Magdalene. When Jesus, therefore, saw his mother and the disciple whom he loved standing by her, he said to his mother (this was his third utterance on the cross), "Woman, behold thy son," and to the disciple, "Behold thy mother." "Everything which she had experienced in the happiest part of her life had now become darkened to her; doubts agitated her," and unable to bear longer a sight so full of anguish, which, turning her hopes into despair, pierced as a sword through her soul, she allowed herself to be taken away, "and from that hour the disciple took her to his own home."

It was noonday, when darkness overspread all the land, and continued for three hours. The sufferings on the cross now reached their sharpest and most dreadful extremity. There is no record of any word that was spoken, or of any act or sound to break the terrible stillness of the scene. For three hours forward from that awful moment when at noonday the unearthly darkness began, so far as we can learn, "not a word of derision is heard all around the cross. All is hushed into absolute silence." The angry passions of men subside. They gaze through the darkness in fear and wonder. "Jesus is silent: the sufferings he endured at the hands of men now give place to more painful inward sufferings. The darkening of the heavens accompanies and expresses the dreadful darkness that prevails in the soul itself of the suffering Saviour," when those around are suddenly startled by the agonizing cry, "My God, my God, why hast thou forsaken me?" But why this cry as of utter desolation and despair? How could God leave his beloved Son so unsustained in the moment of his keenest anguish? It is not for us to comprehend all the wonders and mysteries of the Divine mercy in the great work of our redemption. The sufferings of the righteous at all times, but most of all the sufferings of the Son of God, in their relation to the sins of the world, are, so far as we are concerned, among the secret things of the Most High. They have indeed a most affecting significance. They show the personal sympathy of Jesus with the keenest pangs of conflict, or of pain and despair, that can ever rend our hearts, and indicate to us how we, through the victory which he has gained, may triumph over them. But we cannot tell how far his sufferings were essential to our salvation in their influence on the counsels of God. The mighty train of causes and effects in God's spiritual kingdom, reaching up through the highest heavens and down through all the depths of sin and its attendant sorrows, must be involved in mystery to us. We cannot comprehend in all the fulness of their meaning these highest moments in God's dealings with man, when in the hidings of his power he is bringing to a crisis those vast designs, which, in working out the redemption of our race, reach, we know not how far, into the infinite realms of being. Such a moment it was that heard from the cross the cry of anguish and desolation which has pierced the heart of the world, "My God, my God, why hast thou forsaken me?"

These words of Jesus, his fourth utterance upon the cross, were misunderstood by those around him. But there were no marks of levity or contempt. It would seem as if even those who came to scoff at his sufferings had been subdued, or at least silenced, by the solemnity of the scene. Immediately afterwards Jesus, moved by what is said to be the severest physical suffering of those who die by that painful death, said, "I thirst." A sponge filled with vinegar was raised to his mouth, and when he had received it, he said, "It is finished." The great work which he came into the world to accomplish was now done. He had drained to its dregs the cup which his Father had given him to drink. The agony was over. And with his seventh and last utterance, "Father, into thy hands I commend my spirit," he bowed his head and gave up the ghost. "And, behold, the veil of the temple was rent in twain from the top to the bottom; and the earth did quake, and the rocks rent; and the graves were opened, and many bodies of the saints which slept arose, and came out of the graves after his resurrection." And "when the centurion, and they that were with him, watching Jesus, saw the earthquake and those things that were done, they feared greatly, and said, 'Truly this was a son of God'" (literally, 'a God's son'). "Certainly, this was a righteous man." And all the multitudes who had come out with angry and revengeful feelings, demanding his life, and making a mock of his sufferings, when they saw the things which had come to pass (Luke xxiii. 48), smote their breasts and turned sorrowfully away from what their own malice or excited passions had helped to accomplish. Joseph of Arimathea, a rich man, went hastily to Pilate, and begged the body of Jesus. He then, with the assistance of Nicodemus, who brought about a hundred pounds of a mixture of myrrh and aloes (John xix. 39), prepared the body for burial, and interred it in his own new sepulchre, which he had hewn out in a garden adjoining the spot where Jesus had been crucified. And the women who had come from

Galilee, Mary Magdalene and the other Mary, were there, over against the sepulchre, seeing the tomb and how the body was laid. "And now in the tomb lay the holiest being the earth had ever seen — dead, — a terrible symbol of the universal death of man, — an image of utter, remediless despair, — a scene to darken the earth. Then the powers of darkness seemed to have triumphed. Selfish ambition, cruelty, rage, hate, still remained on the earth; but the Holy One was gone from it. Then might the powers of darkness have looked out from the clouds, and proclaimed, 'It is the hour of our triumph; henceforth the earth is ours.'" E. Peabody.

## 62–66. — Precautions against his Resurrection.

There is a little difficulty in this passage. If the Apostles so utterly failed to understand the words of Jesus that they had no expectation of his resurrection, how could his enemies have had any such idea in their minds? The words announcing his resurrection after three days, had been spoken by him, and repeated by his disciples. The greatness of the fact foretold prevented their understanding the plain and literal meaning of the words they had heard and reported. But when the priests and rulers saw that the body of Jesus was in the hands of his friends, they recalled to mind these words, and seeing what their obvious and literal meaning was, they, with the keenness of religious bigots, suspected some trick on the part of the disciples, and therefore applied to the governor to allow them to take the precautions which would render any such imposition as they feared impracticable. The stone, therefore, was sealed, and a guard was set. But the very precautions which they had taken turned against them. The very measures which they had adopted to expose the cheat which they suspected, served only to confirm the truth, against which they had set themselves.

## NOTES.

WHEN the morning was come, all the chief priests and elders of the people took counsel against Jesus, to put him to death. 2 And when they had bound him, they led him away and delivered him to Pontius Pilate the governor.

3 Then Judas, which had betrayed him, when he saw that he was condemned, repented himself, and brought again the thirty 4 pieces of silver to the chief priests and elders, saying, I have sinned in that I have betrayed the innocent blood. And they 5 said, What is that to us? see thou to that. And he cast down the pieces of silver in the temple, and departed, and went and 6 hanged himself. —— And the chief priests took the silver

---

**2. and delivered him to Pontius Pilate the governor**] Very little is known of Pilate beyond what we find in the Gospels. He was not properly governor of Judæa, but only the Procurator or deputy-governor, and was subject to the Proconsul of Syria, who resided at Cæsarea. In the thirteenth year of Tiberius, A. D. 26, he came to Judæa as the successor of Valerius Gratus. Josephus, Ant. XVIII. 2. 2. He is barely mentioned by Tacitus as Procurator when Christ was punished. (Ann. XV. 44.) Josephus speaks of him, Ant. XVIII. 3. 1, in a way that shows the weakness of his character, and afterwards, in that and the following chapters, he speaks of him as engaged in transactions which indicate the timidity and rashness, the sensibility and cruelty, which are not unfrequently combined in the same person. After having been in Judæa ten years he was sent to Rome by Vitellius, governor of Syria, to answer for his conduct to the Emperor Tiberius, but that crafty and malignant tyrant was dead before he reached Rome. According to Eusebius (Hist. Eccl. II. 7), the tradition was that in the reign of Caligula Pilate fell into such misfortunes that he "from necessity destroyed himself, and with his own hand became the avenger, as it seemed, of the divine justice which at no distant interval followed after him."

**4. have betrayed the innocent blood**] This means, not merely that he had betrayed an innocent man, but that he had betrayed him *to death*. **What is that to us? see thou to that.**] Nothing could be more cool and contemptuous. They had used the traitor, and now had nothing more to do with him. His guilt and anguish were *his* concern, not theirs. The fewness of the words that they were willing to spend upon him added to the fatal poignancy of their sting. 5. **And he cast down the pieces of silver in the temple**] ἐν τῷ ναῷ. This word does not apply to the temple enclosures, but to the holy temple itself, into which none but the priests were permitted to enter. It is then an indication of the utter confusion and desperation into which the mind of Judas was thrown, that he should rush in there to throw down from his guilty hands the price of blood. **and went and hanged himself**] Alford, in his commentary on Acts i. 18, says: "It is obvious that, while the general term used by Matthew points mainly at *self-murder*, the account given here [in Acts] does not preclude the catas-

pieces, and said, It is not lawful for to put them into the
treasury, because it is the price of blood. And they took 7
counsel, and bought with them the potter's field, to bury

trophe related having happened, in some way, as a Divine judgment, *during the suicidal attempt.* Further than this, with our present knowledge, we cannot go. *An accurate acquaintance with the actual circumstances* would account for the discrepancy, but nothing else." Olshausen, after speaking with severity of the forced interpretations by which the two passages have been reconciled, adds: "Yet we must confess that the accounts may be so connected as to permit the conjecture that Judas hanged himself, and, falling down, was so injured that his bowels gushed out." Prof. Hackett, whose learning and candor cannot easily be called in question, adopts this conjecture as not unreasonable. In his "Illustrations of Scripture," pp. 266, 267, he says: "We have no certain knowledge as to the mode in which we are to combine the two statements, so as to connect the act of suicide with what happened to the body. Interpreters have suggested that Judas may have hung himself on a tree near a precipice over the valley of Hinnom, and that, the limb or rope breaking, he fell to the bottom, and was dashed to pieces by the fall. For myself, I felt, as I stood in the valley, and looked up to the rocky terraces which hang over it, that the proposed explanation was a perfectly natural one. . . . . I measured the precipitous, almost perpendicular walls, in different places, and found the height to be, variously, forty, thirty-six, thirty-three, thirty, and twenty-five feet. Olive-trees still grow quite near the edge of these rocks, and, no doubt, in former times they were still more numerous in the same place. A rocky pavement exists also at the bottom of the precipices; and hence, on that account, too, a person who should fall from above would be liable to be crushed and mangled, as well as killed. The traitor may have struck, in his fall, upon some pointed rock, which entered the body, and caused his bowels to gush out." Lightfoot's summary method of dealing with the matter may interest rather than instruct the reader. "Interpreters," says he, "take a great deal of pains to make these words agree with his hanging himself; but, indeed, all will not do. I know the word ἀπήγξατο is commonly applied to a man's hanging himself, but not to exclude some other way of strangling. And I cannot but take the story (with good leave of antiquity) in this sense: After Judas had thrown down the money, the price of his treason, in the temple, and was now returning again to his mates, the devil, who dwelt in him, caught him up on high, strangled him, and threw him down headlong, so that, dashing upon the ground, he burst in the midst. . . . . This agrees very well with the deserts of the wicked wretch, and with the title of Iscariot [i. e. one who perished by strangling]. The wickedness he had committed was above all example; and the punishment he suffered was beyond all precedent."
6. **into the treasury**] " κορβανᾶς is the sacred treasure of the temple, which was kept in seven chests, called trumpets. Comp. Mark vii. 11." Olshausen.
7. **to bury strangers in**] Not foreigners, but Jews who were strangers there.

**the potter's field**] "The Aceldama, or field of blood, which was purchased with his money, tradition has placed on the Hill of Evil Council. It may have been in that quarter, at least, for the field belonged originally to a potter, and argillaceous clay is still found in the neighborhood. A workman in a pottery which I visited at Jerusalem said that all their clay was obtained from the hill over the val-

8 strangers in. Wherefore that field was called, The field of
9 blood, unto this day. Then was fulfilled that which was
spoken by Jeremy the prophet, saying, " And they took the
thirty pieces of silver, the price of him that was valued, whom
10 they of the children of Israel did value, and gave them for the
potter's field, as the Lord appointed me."
11 And Jesus stood before the governor; and the governor
asked him, saying, Art thou the king of the Jews? And Jesus
12 said unto him, Thou sayest. And when he was accused of
13 the chief priests and elders, he answered nothing. Then saith
Pilate unto him, Hearest thou not how many things they wit-
14 ness against thee? And he answered him to never a word;
15 insomuch that the governor marvelled greatly. Now at that
feast, the governor was wont to release unto the people a pris-
16 oner, whom they would. And they had then a notable pris-
16 oner, called Barabbas. Therefore, when they were gathered
together, Pilate said unto them, Whom will ye that I release
18 unto you? Barabbas, or Jesus, which is called Christ? For
19 he knew that for envy they had delivered him. —— When he

ley of Hinnom." Hackett's Ill. of Scrip., p. 267. 8. **The field of blood, unto this day**] This indicates that the Gospel was written a considerable time afterwards. Matthew says it was called "the field of blood" because it had been bought with the price of blood; while in Acts it is said to have been so called on account of the wretched death of Judas, — not a contradictory, "but a concurrent reason, showing that the ill-omened name could be used with a double emphasis." 9. **Then was fulfilled that which was spoken by Jeremy the prophet**] No such passage as the one here quoted is to be found in Jeremiah. A passage, not identical, but bearing a strong resemblance to it, is found in Zechariah xi. 13, 14. How is this to be accounted for? "The simplest solution of the difficulty," says Olshausen, "is to suppose that the Evangelist mistook the name of the prophet, or that the earliest transcribers might have read some contraction for the name falsely; or perhaps that there was no name at all there at first, and that some transcriber supplied its want erroneously." The passage in Zechariah, very different from that which is here quoted, is thus rendered by Dr. Noyes: " And they weighed for my wages thirty shekels of silver. And Jehovah said to me, Cast it into the treasury, the goodly price at which I was valued by them. And I took the thirty shekels of silver, and cast them into the house of Jehovah, info the treasury." It is impossible for us to see in this account anything more than an incidental similarity to some of the facts connected with the treachery of Judas. It can in no sense be regarded as a prophecy of the events described by Matthew. 16, 17. According to Tischendorf, these verses should read thus: " And they had then a notable prisoner, called Jesus Barabbas. Therefore, when they were gathered together, Pilate said unto them, " Which shall I release unto you, Jesus Barabbas, or Jesus who is called Christ?" The

was set down on the judgment-seat, his wife sent unto him, saying, Have thou nothing to do with that just man; for I have suffered many things this day in a dream because of him.

—— But the chief priests and elders persuaded the multitude 20 that they should ask Barabbas, and destroy Jesus. The 21 governor answered and said unto them, Whether of the twain will ye that I release unto you? They said, Barabbas. Pilate saith unto them, What shall I do then with Jesus, 22 which is called Christ? They all say unto him, Let him be crucified. And the governor said, Why? what evil hath he 23 done? But they cried out the more, saying, Let him be crucified. When Pilate saw that he could prevail nothing, but 24 that rather a tumult was made, he took water, and washed his hands before the multitude, saying, I am innocent of the blood of this just person; see ye to it. Then answered all the peo- 25 ple, and said, His blood be on us, and on our children. Then 26 released he Barabbas unto them; and when he had scourged

---

best critics, however, do not approve of this as the true reading. 19. **when he was set down on the judgment-seat]** This judgment-seat (John xix. 13) was outside of the palace or fortress, on the pavement. The tower or fortress of Antonia, where Pilate sat in judgment, was situated on the north side of the grounds occupied by the temple, and took up a space nearly or quite as large as that which was set apart, within the sacred enclosures, for the temple. The Antonia enclosure measured, south, 975 feet; east, 710; north, 1030; west, 730. Barclay, p. 245. 23. **Let him be crucified]** This punishment was chiefly inflicted on slaves and the worst kind of malefactors. (Juv. VI. 219; Hor. Sat. I. 3. 82.) The criminal, after sentence pronounced, carried his cross to the place of execution; a custom mentioned by Plutarch (De Tard. Dei Vind.) and Artemidorus (Oneir. II. 61) as well as in the Gospels. From Livy (XXXIII. 36) and Valerius Maximus (I. 7) scourging appears to have formed a part of this as of other capital punishments among the Romans. The scourging of our Saviour, however, is not to be regarded in this light, for it was inflicted before the sentence was pronounced, and was done by Pilate with the hope of thus satisfying the vengeance of the Jews without the crucifixion which they had demanded. The criminal was next stripped of his clothes, and nailed or bound to the cross. The latter was the more painful method, as the sufferer was left to die of hunger. The body was not supported by the nails, but by a piece of wood which passed between the legs. Instances are recorded of persons who survived nine days. Smith's Greek and Roman Ant. 24. **he took water, and washed his hands]** " The washing of hands, to betoken innocence from blood-guiltiness, is prescribed Deut. xxi. 6-9, and Pilate uses it here as intelligible to the Jews." Alford. Pilate, having now resided in Judæa seven years, must have become well acquainted with Jewish customs. 26. **Then released he Barabbas]** " One who was moreover guilty of that very crime (treason) of which Jesus was accused; nay, even guilty of a worse crime. However, it was by the death of Him who was the Just One, that those very persons

27 Jesus, he delivered him to be crucified. —— Then the soldiers of the governor took Jesus into the common hall, and gathered
28 unto him the whole band of soldiers. And they stripped him,
29 and put on him a scarlet robe. And when they had platted a crown of thorns, they put it upon his head, and a reed in his right hand; and they bowed the knee before him, and mocked
30 him, saying, Hail, King of the Jews! And they spit upon
31 him, and took the reed, and smote him on the head. And after that they had mocked him, they took the robe off from him, and put his own raiment on him; and led him away to crucify him.

32 And as they came out, they found a man of Cyrene, Simon

who had deserved death are set free." Bengel. **and when he had scourged Jesus, he delivered him to be crucified**] This passage may be taken as a specimen of the manner in which events, which were in fact separated by intervening incidents, are brought together in a condensed narrative, as if one had grown immediately out of the other. Between the scourging of Jesus and his being given up to be crucified, according to John xix. 4 – 16, Pilate had a private interview with Jesus, and more than once tried to persuade the Jews to release him.

27. **the whole band**] σπεῖραν, a cohort, the tenth part of a legion, about 600. The word *whole* is not to be pressed. Alford.

28. **a scarlet robe**] Mark (xv. 17) and John (xix. 2) say *purple*. The two words were probably used indiscriminately to express the color adapted to royalty. In Rev. xvii. 4, the two words are used together. "And the woman was arrayed in purple and scarlet color."

29. **a crown of thorns**] "The *acanthus* itself," says Alford, " with its large succulent leaves, is singularly unfit for such a purpose; as is the plant with very long sharp thorns, commonly known as Spina Christi, being a brittle *acacia*. Some *flexile* shrub or plant must be understood. Hasselquist, a Swedish naturalist, supposes a very common plant, *naba* or *nubka* of the Arabs, with many small and sharp spines; soft, round, and pliant branches; leaves much resembling ivy, of a very deep green, as if in designed mockery of a victor's wreath."

**and mocked him**] This mockery and personal abuse were three times inflicted: 1. at the examination before the Sanhedrim (xxvi. 67); 2. when he was sent to Herod (Luke xxiii. 11); and, 3. here by the Roman soldiers.

32. "Jesus is led towards Golgotha. St. Matthew gives the outline only: *They found a man of Cyrene, Simon by name: him they compelled to bear his cross*. St. Mark (xv. 21) adds to this a word which seems to put the living scene before your eyes: *a man who was passing by* (that very place); and then a particular circumstance which St. Luke (xxiii. 26) adopts from him: *coming out of the country;* finally, another also, which is mentioned by none but St. Mark, and bears upon the person of this Cyrenian: *he was the father of Alexander and Rufus*, men in Mark's time well known in the Church, and particularly in that of Rome. We are not, however, so to understand the matter, as if the cross were taken off our Lord's shoulders and transferred to those of this Simon: much less, as we see it sometimes represented in Bible prints and pictures, as if the men who were leading away Jesus, on seeing him sink under the weight, had therefore thought of laying it on Simon

by name: him they compelled to bear his cross. And when 33 they were come unto a place called Golgotha, that is to say, a

---

as he was passing by. The improbability of this will be perceived at once, by attending to the circumstance, that among the Romans the cross was ordinarily fastened to the shoulders of the condemned person, and could not, accordingly, have been first unloosed by the soldiers, as this supposition requires. No! the Saviour's cross was taken off his shoulders by no one. But the soldiers must in irony have compelled Simon, who in passing had expressed his compassion for the adorable sufferer, to *lift* the cross, and (as St. Luke expresses it) *to bear it after him.* Thus Simon presents us here with an image of the true disciple of our Lord, sharing in his cross and in his ignominy. In perfect accordance with this we find the expressive statement of St. John xix. 17: Jesus, *bearing with pain* (Βαστάζων) his cross, went forth, &c." Da Costa's Four Witnesses, pp. 414, 415. It may have been, nevertheless, that Jesus, bearing his cross with pain, sunk beneath it by the way, and that it was then taken from him and put on Simon, though we prefer Da Costa's view. 33. **And when they were come to a place called Golgotha, that is to say, a place of a skull**] Cranium. Luke, xxiii. 33, says: "And when they were come to the place which is called *Cranium,*" not Calvary. Κρανίον is the Greek word, meaning *a skull,* and Calvary is formed from the corresponding Latin word, Calvaria. The term was probably given in consequence of some natural feature of the place resembling a skull, rather than because the place was used for burial. The situation of the place is unknown. The Church of the Holy Sepulchre, which is five or six hundred yards, in a direction nearly west, from the northern extremity of Mt. Moriah, was built by order of the Emperor Constantine, and dedicated A. D. 335, to commemorate the spot. It has been seriously questioned whether this was really the place where Jesus was crucified. Dr. Robinson has shown, we think, quite conclusively that the site of the Church of the Holy Sepulchre lies within the space which was enclosed by the walls of Jerusalem at the time of the Crucifixion, and it is admitted on all hands that no public execution would at that time have been allowed within the city walls. Dr. Robinson has also shown that there is no historical testimony on the subject which is to be relied upon now, and that there was none when the church was erected, three hundred years after the crucifixion. Stanley, in his able and scholarly work on Palestine, admits the force of the objection to the historical testimony, but does not think Dr. Robinson's view of the topographical question wholly free from difficulties. Barclay, in his City of the Great King, adopts Dr. Robinson's view, and supports it with great earnestness, though with no additional arguments which are entitled to much weight. He even goes so far as to suggest as the scene of the crucifixion a spot lying nearly in the opposite direction from the judgment-hall. After speaking of the name Cranium, as being applicable not only to the head of an animal, but equally so to a head or cape of land, in which we find him sustained by the authority of Tischendorf, he adds, p. 79: "Now there is a kind of head, cape, or promontory of land projecting southeastwardly into the Kedron valley, a short distance above Gethsemane, to which such a term seems quite applicable, just as the low spur of Lebanon on which Beirût reposes is called Cape or Head of Beirût. May not this similar spur of an unnamed ridge be the site of that awful scene, — the crucifixion of the Son of God?" This may have been the spot, but the arguments adduced by Barclay are not sufficient to prove it. Nor do we attach any great importance

34 place of a skull, they gave him vinegar to drink, mingled with gall; and when he had tasted thereof, he would not drink. 35 And they crucified him, and parted his garments, casting lots; that it might be fulfilled which was spoken by the prophet, " They parted my garments among them, and upon my vesture 36 did they cast lots." And sitting down, they watched him there; 37 and set up over his head his accusation written, THIS IS

---

to the question. The grave of Moses was unknown, in order that the people might never have an opportunity to indulge their idolatrous propensity by any superstitious observances connected with it. In the writers of the New Testament we find nowhere the slightest mark of veneration for the places connected with our Saviour's life. They had imbibed too much of the spirit of him to whom Jerusalem and Gerizim were alike unimportant as places of worship, to dwell with reverence on things so purely external. It was not till the spiritual life which he came to awaken and impart had begun to mingle with baser elements, and the worship of the Father " in spirit and in truth " had been alloyed by something very like idolatrous ingredients, that the passion for relics and sacred places was excited in the Church, and pilgrimages began to be performed, and idolatrous substitutes for a devout and holy life began to exercise their degrading and demoralizing influence on the souls of men. Still there is a reasonable curiosity in such matters; and there are associations which ought not to be disregarded. No true follower of Christ could visit the scenes of his earthly ministry, — Nazareth, the Lake of Tiberias, the hills of Galilee, the banks of the Jordan, or the Mount of Olives, — without strong emotion. We even agree with Stanley, when he says, " Granting to the full the doubts which must always hang over the highest claims of the Church of the Sepulchre, no thoughtful man can look unmoved on what has from the time of Constantine been revered by the larger part of the Christian world as the scene of the greatest events of the world's history." Wherever the place was situated, the name of Calvary can never lose its power with the followers of Christ. Among the traditions respecting Golgotha is one that Adam, or at least Adam's skull, was buried there, and the precise spot is still pointed out and believed in as the " entombment of Adam's head " ! 

**34. they gave him vinegar to drink, mingled with gall**] Just before crucifixion the Romans were accustomed to give to the convicts a stupefying drink, wine mingled with myrrh, in order to deaden their sensibility to the awful agonies of this dreadful punishment. Mark (xv. 23) says *wine mingled with myrrh;* Matthew, *vinegar mingled with gall.* But *vinegar* was nothing else than the common sour wine, and the word *gall* was used to denote bitters of any kind. " They gave me also gall for my meat; and in my thirst they gave me vinegar to drink." (Ps. lxix. 21.) It was undoubtedly intended by the Romans as an act of mercy, yet it was here administered in an insulting way. " And the soldiers also mocked him, coming to him, and offering him vinegar." (Luke xxiii. 36.) When Jesus had tasted it, he refused to drink, for " he did not wish to meet death otherwise than in the full possession of his consciousness."

**35. that it might be fulfilled**] These words, and what follow in this verse, are not found in the best manuscripts. They were probably copied in here by transcribers from John xix. 24.

**37. And set up over his head his accusation written, This**

JESUS, THE KING OF THE JEWS. Then were there 38 two thieves crucified with him; one on the right hand, and another on the left.—— And they that passed by reviled him, 39 wagging their heads, and saying, Thou that destroyest the 40 temple, and buildest it in three days, save thyself; if thou be the Son of God, come down from the cross. Likewise also the 41 chief priests, mocking him, with the scribes and elders, said, He saved others, himself he cannot save; if he be the King 42 of Israel, let him now come down from the cross, and we will believe him. He trusted in God; let him deliver him now, 43

---

**is Jesus the King of the Jews**] In Mark it is, THE KING OF THE JEWS; in Luke, THE KING OF THE JEWS THIS; in John, JESUS OF NAZARETH, THE KING OF THE JEWS. " On the difference in the four Gospels as to the words of the inscription itself it is hardly worth while to comment, except to remark that the advocates for the verbal and literal exactness of each Gospel may here find an *undoubted* example of the absurdity of their view, which may serve to guide them in less plain and obvious cases. *A* title was written, containing certain words; not four titles, all different, but one, differing probably from all of these four, but certainly from three of them." Alford. Da Costa, who holds to a literal or verbal exactness, explains the differences thus. According to John xix. 20, the superscription was written in Hebrew, Greek, and Latin. It may therefore have been written with variations, and each of the Evangelists may have given it according to the language and the form best suited to his own plan or style. In St. Luke, he says, it is probably the Latin superscription; in St. Mark, the Hebrew, while St. John gives it to us in the fullest form, which is the Greek, and " *St. Matthew gives us a kind of combination.*" What is this " kind of combination," but a giving up of the literal and verbal exactness?

40. **save thyself.** 42. **He saved others; himself he cannot save**] The word *Jesus* means *Saviour;* and it has been supposed that here in the original Hebrew or Aramaic was a taunting play upon the Saviour's name.

39. **And they that passed by reviled him, wagging their heads**] 41. " *Likewise also the chief priests, mocking him, with the scribes and elders, said,*" 43, " *He trusted in God; let him deliver him now if he will have him; for he said, I am the Son of God.*" The correspondence between this and the seventh and eighth verses of the twenty-second Psalm is very remarkable. " All that see me laugh me to scorn: they shoot out the lip, they shake the head, saying, He trusted on the Lord that he would deliver him: let him deliver him, seeing he delighted in him." In this Psalm are the other expressions: " My God, my God, why hast thou forsaken me?" " They pierced my hands and my feet." " They part my garments among them, and cast lots upon my vesture." Are these accidental coincidences, or were they thrown in through the superintending and prophetic spirit of God, that they might associate themselves with the scene upon the cross as a prediction of that event in some of its minute particulars? Undoubtedly the Psalm, as Dr. Noyes says, is one in which a pious Israelite makes his supplication to God in the midst of great distress, and enumerates the circumstances which aggravate his distress, and the faith by which he may triumph over it. But may it not also be in some of its parts a type of the sufferings of Christ? To this question we would apply

44 if he will have him; for he said, I am the Son of God. The thieves also which were crucified with him cast the same in his 45 teeth.—— Now from the sixth hour there was darkness over 46 all the land, unto the ninth hour. And about the ninth hour

---

the remarks of Dr. Noyes. "As to the typical or mystical sense which has been assigned to this and other psalms, it seems to be beyond the province of the interpreter. There are no human means by which to ascertain it. None but the Divine Spirit can be sure what it is. As has been well observed by Ernesti, in his Principles of Biblical Interpretation, — 'Nor, in searching for this typical sense, is there need of the care and talents of an interpreter. For it is revealed by the information and testimony of the Holy Spirit, beyond whose showing we should not in this matter attempt to advance.'" 44. **The thieves also which were crucified with him cast the same into his teeth**] It may be that *both* at first reviled Jesus, and that afterwards one of them, impressed and subdued by his bearing on the cross, may have spoken as in Luke xxiii. 40-43. It is difficult, however, to suppose that the writer here was acquainted with the facts narrated there. 45. **Now from the sixth hour there was darkness over all the land, unto the ninth hour**] From 12 M. to 3 P. M. This could not have been an eclipse of the sun, for it was then the time of the full moon; nor does the language imply that the darkness extended to any great distance beyond the vicinity of Jerusalem. We know not how close and strong may be the sympathy between the spiritual and the physical universe, nor how far the phenomena of the outward world may be affected by the life and conduct of men. The greatest poets have recognized intimate relations between the two; nor can we "set to the account of accident or imagination all those remarkable coincidences between heaven and earth, all those testimonies which the signs and tokens of heaven have so often yielded, and men taken note of, that the great of this world do not come or go without warning. . . . . . At no time does nature put on a careless, unmeaning face, when aught that intimately concerns her foster-child man is being done, nor make as though this was nothing unto her. On the contrary, her history runs parallel, and is subordinate, to his, — the great moments in the life of nature concurring with the great moments in the life of man, and therefore most of all with the great crises of the kingdom of God, which concerns him the nearest of all. Thus, during all those hours that the Son of God hung upon the cross, there was darkness over the whole earth [land?]; nature shuddered to her very centre, at the moment when he expired; for it was her king, as well as man's, that died." Trench, Star of the Wise Men, p. 23. "The sublimity of this moment seems to have been symbolically solemnized even by nature herself." "How deep lies its foundation in human nature to regard natural events symbolically as manifesting a sympathy between the life of nature and the incidents of humanity, is shown by parallel passages from the profane writers." "In the history of Immanuel appear in their complete and actual truth what were but erroneous, and diversely distracted, suppositions of mankind." Olshausen. "The wise men from the East were led to the Redeemer by the remarkable phenomena which attended his *birth;* and similar wonders accompanied his *death.* As the unity of the world as a whole [the world of nature and of spirit] is seen in natural signs accompanying epoch-making events in history, so we need not marvel to find the greatest event in history — shown as such by its fruits in the spiritual renova-

Jesus cried with a loud voice, saying, Eli, Eli, lama sabachthani? that is to say, My God, my God, why hast thou for-

tion of mankind, even to those who cannot comprehend its internal import — attended by similar manifestations. At the moment of Christ's death there was an earthquake; and at the same time, and perhaps from the same cause, a darkness spread over the sky. The veil of the Holy of Holies in the Temple was rent asunder, signifying that the Holy of Holies in Heaven is opened to all men through the finished work of Christ; the wall of partition between the Divine and the human broken down, and a spiritual worship substituted for an outward and sensible one." Neander, Life of Jesus, pp. 421, 422. "Those whose belief leads them to reflect *who* it was then suffering, will have no difficulty in accounting for these signs of sympathy in nature, nor in seeing their applicability. The consent, in the same words, of all three Evangelists, must silence all question as to the universal belief of this darkness as a fact; and the early fathers (Tertull. Apol. c. 21; Origen c. Cels. 2. 33; Euseb. in Chronicon) appeal to profane testimony for its truth." Alford.

46. **Eli, Eli, lama sabachthani? that is to say, My God, my God, why hast thou forsaken me?**] It is one of the incidental proofs of the genuineness of the Gospels that these extraordinary words should be preserved in the language in which they were spoken. They may be found in the first verse of the twenty-second Psalm. Dr. Noyes says in regard to them: "I cannot agree with those who find in them no expression of anguish or tone of expostulation, and who suppose them to be cited by our Saviour merely in order to suggest the confidence and triumph with which the Psalm ends, but which do not begin before the twenty-second verse. Under the circumstances of the case, the words appear to have had substantially the same meaning when uttered by Christ as when uttered by the Psalmist. They should not be interpreted as the deliberate result of calm reflection, but as an outburst of strong involuntary emotion, forced from our Saviour by anguish of body and mind, in the words which naturally occurred to him, implying *momentary* expostulation, or even complaint. But that the interruption of the consciousness of God's presence and love was only momentary, both in the case of the Psalmist and the Saviour, is evident, first, from the expression, *My God! my God!* repeated with earnestness; secondly, from the expressions of confidence in the course of the Psalm, which might follow in the mind of Christ as well as in that of the Psalmist; and thirdly, from the usage of language, according to which the expression '*to be forsaken by God*' merely means 'not to be delivered from actual or impending distress.' The very parallel line in the verse under consideration, 'Why art thou so far from helping me?' is, according to the laws of Hebrew parallelism, a complete exposition of the language, 'Why hast thou forsaken me?' So Ps. xxxviii. 21, 22." Theological Essays, p. xviii. In confirmation of this view Dr. Noyes quotes Meyer on Matt. xxvii. 46, as follows: "By the words 'Why hast thou forsaken me?' Jesus expressed what he personally felt, his *consciousness* of communion with God having been for a moment interrupted by his sufferings. But this momentary subjective feeling is not to be confounded with an actual objective abandonment by God (against Olshausen and the older commentators), which at least in the case of Jesus would have been a physical and moral impossibility. . . . . . To find, with the older dogmatic theologians, the vicarious feeling of Divine wrath in the cry of anguish, 'Why hast thou forsaken me?' is to go beyond the New Testament view of the atoning

47 saken me? Some of them that stood there, when they heard
48 that, said, This man calleth for Elias. And straightway one
of them ran, and took a sponge, and filled it with vinegar, and
49 put it on a reed, and gave him to drink. The rest said, Let

---

death of Christ, as also that of the agony in Gethsemane. On the other hand, the opinion of some interpreters, that Jesus, when he quoted the first verse of the Psalm, had in his mind the whole of it, is arbitrary, and brings into his condition of immediate feeling the heterogenous element of reflection and citation." For our view of the state of Christ's mind here, and the overpowering nature of his sufferings, we refer to what we have said of the agony in Gethsemane, xxvi. 36-46. His capacity for suffering was on the same vast scale as his other faculties, and therefore far transcending anything that we can know of human anguish. What there may have been beyond this, what relation his sufferings may have had to the redemption of man in the infinite counsels of God, and beyond the limits of this world, has not been revealed in the Scriptures, and therefore cannot be known by us. To assert that they had no such far-reaching influence would be as unauthorized a piece of dogmatism, as to assert that their principal efficacy lies in that direction. We cannot fathom the depth of our Saviour's sufferings, because we cannot comprehend the greatness of his mind, his nature, or his mission. We can no more explain all the sources of his grief, than we can the sources of his knowledge or his power. When we can analyze the process by which he revealed to us the mysteries of the kingdom of heaven, or raised Lazarus from the dead, or talked in open vision, face to face, with Moses and Elias, then we may hope to analyze the sufferings of Gethsemane and Calvary. Undoubtedly his sufferings were terribly aggravated by the intense and perfect sympathy with man, through which he became the representative of the whole race, taking upon himself their sorrows and their sins. We can hardly do more than guess at the amount of anguish thus forced upon him. "An enigma indeed," says Neander, "must this exclamation appear . . . . . to those who forget that Christ suffered and died for mankind, — for mankind laid up in his heart; an enigma to all, in a word, who are strangers to the Christian life. But the Christian sees in this feature of his Master's history a type of the life of individual believers, and of the whole Church; for both must be led through all stages of suffering, and even through moments of apparent abandonment by God, to perfection and glorification." Life of Jesus, p. 420. 47. **Some of them that stood there, when they heard that, said, This man calleth for Elias**] We see no evidence that these words, or those in v. 49, "*Let us see whether Elias will come to save him*," were spoken in derision. The spectators, we suppose, had been deeply impressed by the darkness and the silence, and now that the silence was broken by the remarkable words of Jesus, they misunderstood their meaning, and were waiting with awe to see what the result might be. 48. **And straightway one of them ran, and took a sponge, and filled it with vinegar**] "We have no reason for assuming that the *soldiers offering vinegar* in Luke xxiii. 36, 37 is the same incident as this. Since then the bodily state of the Redeemer had greatly changed; and what was then offered in mockery might well be now asked for in the agony of death, and received when presented, as in our text. The ὄξος is the *posca*, sour wine, or vinegar and water, the ordinary drink of the Roman soldiers." Alford. The

be; let us see whether Elias will come to save him. —— Jesus, 50 when he had cried again with a loud voice, yielded up the ghost. —— And, behold, the veil of the temple was rent in 51 twain from the top to the bottom; and the earth did quake, and the rocks rent; and the graves were opened, and many 52 bodies of the saints which slept arose, and came out of the 53 graves after his resurrection, and went into the holy city, and appeared unto many. Now when the centurion, and they that 54 were with him watching Jesus, saw the earthquake, and those things which were done, they feared greatly, saying, Truly this was the Son of God. —— And many women were there, 55 beholding afar off; which followed Jesus from Galilee, ministering unto him; among which was Mary Magdalene, and 56

---

drink is given in reply to the request of Jesus, "*I thirst*," in John xix. 28. 51, 52. **And, behold, the veil of the temple was rent in twain**] This must have been the veil or curtain before the Holy of Holies. See note on 45. *And many bodies of the saints which slept arose, and came out of the graves after his resurrection, and went into the holy city, and appeared to many.* This passage is rejected by Mr. Norton as an interpolation. But it is found in all the best manuscripts. The events are of a most extraordinary character; but that alone will hardly justify us in excluding the passage from the Gospels. There is nothing in the account which should be incredible to those who believe in the miracles of Jesus. It is only as accessory or dependent incidents arranging themselves around the one great fact of Christ's death and resurrection that these extraordinary events can be regarded in their true aspect and relations. When thus regarded, they may appear as the natural and fitting accompaniments of that death which broke down the powers of the grave, and which became a door or gateway of life to all believers, and thus brought life and immortality to light. But when we undertake to explain the events, and to show precisely how they may have occurred, we find many difficulties in the way, and are obliged to say, with Adam Clarke, that "the place is extremely obscure." There is but one other passage in Matthew (xvii. 27) which seems to us to bear such internal marks of being a *mythical* accretion.

54. **Truly this was the Son of God**] The expression in Luke, xxiii. 47, is, "*Certainly this was a righteous man.*" The two expressions, we suppose, were actually used by the centurion. They may, however, be only different translations of the same words, and meaning substantially the same thing. They were spoken by one who believed in *the Gods*. The exact version of the words recorded by Matthew is, "Truly this was a God's son," i. e. "*a divine*," or, as St. Luke has it, "*a righteous, man.*" It is possible that he used the words in the Jewish sense, as indicated in our common version. 56. **Mary Magdalene**] "See ch. xv. 39. She is not to be confounded with Mary who anointed our Lord (John xii. 1), nor with the woman who did the same, Luke vii. 36; see Luke viii. 2." Alford. There is no evidence except what is indicated by the disease of which Jesus cured her (Luke viii. 2), that she had been a dissolute woman. Her name probably came from Magdala.

**and Mary the mother of James and Joses**] *The mother of*

Mary the mother of James and Joses, and the mother of Zebedee's children.

57 When the even was come, there came a rich man of Arimathea, named Joseph, who also himself was Jesus' disciple. 58 He went to Pilate, and begged the body of Jesus. Then Pilate 59 commanded the body to be delivered. And when Joseph had 60 taken the body, he wrapped it in a clean linen cloth, and laid it in his own new tomb, which he had hewn out in the rock; and he rolled a great stone to the door of the sepulchre, and 61 departed. And there was Mary Magdalene, and the other Mary, sitting over against the sepulchre.

---

*James the less, or the younger,* says Mark, to distinguish him from James the son of Zebedee, and the wife of Alphæus or Clopas; see John xix. 25, and com. on Matt. xiii. 53 – 58.

**and the mother of Zebedee's children**] = *Salome,* Mark xv. 40. 57. **there came a rich man of Arimathea, named Joseph**] "A disciple of Jesus," says John (xix. 38), "but secretly, through fear of the Jews." "A counsellor," i. e. a member of the Sanhedrim, says Luke (xxiii. 50, 51), "and he was a good and righteous man (this man had not consented to their counsel and their deed) from Arimathea, a city of the Jews, who also himself was waiting for the kingdom of God." This is all that is known, nor can it be determined now precisely where Arimathea was. He was evidently a man (Mark xv. 43) of great respectability of character as well as a man of wealth. 58. **He went to Pilate, and begged the body of Jesus**] The Roman custom was to leave the bodies exposed on the crosses till devoured by birds of prey. Horace, Epis. I. 16. 48. The Jewish custom, on the other hand, (Josephus, Jewish Wars, IV. 5. 2,) was to take them down before sunset and bury them. If no one had come to ask for the body of Jesus, it would have been buried in the common place appointed for the burial of executed criminals. He has been "numbered with the transgressors," and now he is to have his grave "with the rich in his death." Had he been placed with others in the common buryingground for malefactors, it would have been impossible to obtain the circumstantial evidence that we now have of his resurrection. The chief priests would not have thought of sealing the stone, or setting a watch there. 59. **Wrapped it in a clean linen cloth**] "The Jews, as well as the Egyptians, added spices to keep the body from putrefaction, and the linen was wrapped about every part to keep the aromatics in contact with the flesh. From John xix. 39, 40, we learn that a mixture of myrrh and aloes, of one hundred pounds' weight, had been applied to the body of Jesus when he was buried. And that a second embalmment was intended, we learn from Luke xxiii. 56 and xxiv. 1, as the hurry to get the body interred before the Sabbath did not permit them to complete the embalming in the first instance." Adam Clarke.

60. **And laid it in his own new tomb**] Matthew alone relates that it was Joseph's own tomb. John relates that it was in a garden, and in the place where he was crucified. "All that we can determine respecting the sepulchre from the data here furnished is: — 1. That it was not a *natural* cave, but an *artificial excavation* in the rock. 2. That it was not cut *downwards,* after the manner of a grave with us, but *horizontally,* or *nearly so,*

Now the next day, that followed the day of the preparation, 62 the chief priests and Pharisees came together unto Pilate, say- 63 ing, Sir, we remember that that deceiver said, while he was yet alive, After three days I will rise again. Command 64 therefore that the sepulchre be made sure until the third day, lest his disciples come by night, and steal him away, and say unto the people, He is risen from the dead; so the last error shall be worse than the first. Pilate said unto them, Ye have 65 a watch; go your way, make it as sure as ye can. So they 66 went, and made the sepulchre sure, sealing the stone, and setting a watch.

---

into the face of the rock. . . . . . 3. That it was *in the spot* where the crucifixion took place." Alford.

**62. the next day, that followed the day of the preparation**] More exactly, On the next day, i. e. the day that came after the preparation. The *preparation* was the day before the Jewish Sabbath. Why should it be mentioned here? Because to Matthew, when he recorded these events, that *preparation day* on which Jesus had been crucified was *the* day from which to reckon even the Sabbath which came immediately after it. It was as if he had said, *The day after the cruci-fixion.*

**Sir**] Κύριε, Lord. The title of respect usually applied to Jesus, and to persons of distinction, but not implying the homage or reverence due to a divine being.

**66. sealing the stone, and setting a watch**] "The sealing was by means of a cord or string passing across the stone at the mouth of the sepulchre, and fastened at either end to the rock by sealing-clay." The watch or guard was probably a small detachment of Roman soldiers which the governor placed at the disposal of the priests, and of course subject to their orders.

# CHAPTER XXVIII.

### The Gospel Narratives of the Resurrection.

"The independence and distinctness of the four narratives in this part," says Alford, "have never been questioned, and indeed herein lie its principal difficulties. With regard to them, I refer to what I have said in the Prolegomena, that supposing us to be acquainted with everything said and done, in its order and exactness, we should doubtless be able to reconcile, or account for, the present forms of the narratives: but not having this key to the harmonizing of them, all attempts to do so in minute particulars must be full of arbitrary assumptions, and carry no certainty with them. And I may remark, that, of all harmonies, those of the incidents of these chapters are to me the most unsatisfactory." After a very careful comparison of the different narratives, without reference to any commentator or harmonist, we do not find the difficulties so great as Alford supposes them to be. The result to which we have been led by our own independent inquiries agrees substantially with the conclusions of Dr. Carpenter, and is in most particulars nearly the same as that in Dr. Robinson's Harmony, which we did not read till after we had satisfied our minds in regard to the true succession of events. In order to study the matter to advantage, it is necessary that the reader should thoroughly master the different accounts, so as to carry clearly and distinctly in his mind all the details as they are given by each separate Evangelist.

In the first place, we have no reason to suppose that all the women mentioned by the Evangelists set out from the same place or at the same moment. It is not improbable that Mary Magdalene and "the other Mary" had spent the Sabbath at Bethany, and there prepared the spices with which to anoint the body of Jesus. Salome, on the other hand, and Joanna, the wife of Chuza (Luke viii. 3), were probably in the city. It would appear also, from Luke xxiv. 33, that the eleven had a place of meeting in the city, and from John xx. 2, that Peter and John at least had their places of abode in Jerusalem.

We may suppose then that "very early in the morning" (Mark xvi. 2), "while it was yet dark" (John xx. 1), Mary Magdalene and the women who were with her set out from Bethany, which was nearly two miles from Jerusalem, talking by the way of what had taken place, and questioning among themselves how they should roll away the heavy stone from the mouth of the sepulchre. When they reached the spot, the sun had already risen (Mark xvi. 2). Mary Magdalene, the moment she saw that the stone had been removed, supposing that the body had been taken away, ran swiftly into the city to Peter and John, who, excited by her words, ran as rapidly as possible to the sepulchre. During this interval, which must have taken up from fifteen to thirty minutes, the other women come nearer to the tomb, see the angel (one angel, Matthew and Mark), and hear from him that Jesus has risen, and that he would meet his disciples in Galilee. They depart to find the disciples, and while on their way are met by Jesus, who has already shown himself to Mary Magdalene at the sepulchre. They tell what they have heard and seen to the disciples, but are not believed. Immediately after they had left the sepulchre, the women from the city, Salome, Joanna, and perhaps others, came with their spices, as by previous agreement, and while they stood there amazed and perplexed (Luke xxiv. 1–7), *two* men stood by them in shining garments, and said, "Why seek ye the living among the dead? He is not here, but is risen" (is raised). They hastily departed, and now, or perhaps before their arrival, Peter and

John reached the spot, and having entered the tomb, and seen precisely how the grave-clothes were laid, they went away, leaving Mary Magdalene behind. She stood weeping by the sepulchre (John xx. 11 – 18) when two angels appeared to her, and afterwards Jesus himself addressed her.

There is no certain evidence that this was the precise order of events. Nor is there any necessity for supposing that any of the women came from Bethany that morning. They may all of them have been spending the Sabbath in Jerusalem, and by a previous agreement may have left their homes in different parts of the city at about the same time to go to the sepulchre. In reading such narratives we should not forget the haste, surprise, and astonishment which must have characterized the transactions of that morning, and prevented any one person from getting at all the details in their precise order of succession or their exact relations to one another. Traces of this state of mind and the apparent inconsistencies growing out of it must be expected, and are to be found, in the Gospels.

THE DIFFERENT ACCOUNTS NOT CONTRADICTORY.

But are there any important contradictions? 1. As to the persons. According to Matthew, Mary Magdalene and the other Mary came very early, &c. Mark mentions Mary Magdalene, Mary the mother of James, and Salome. Luke speaks of Mary Magdalene, Mary the mother of James, and Joanna, and the other women who were with them, while John makes mention only of Mary Magdalene. But no one professes to mention all the women who were there, and it would be natural for each writer to call by name only those who were uppermost in his own mind. John does not say that Mary Magdalene was the only woman. On the contrary, the words which he represents her as using, "*we* know not where they have laid him," imply that others had been with her, especially as after her return to the sepulchre, when she was left alone, she, in the same form of expression (John xx. 13), says, "and *I* know not where they have laid him." This is one of the out-of-the-way coincidences which go to establish the authority of truthful writings, because they cannot be counterfeited.

2. As to the angels. Matthew speaks of one angel, whose appearance was like lightning, and his raiment white as snow, and who was sitting on the stone that had been rolled from the sepulchre. Mark (xvi. 5) says, that when they *entered* or *came to* the sepulchre, for the Greek word may have either meaning, they saw a young man sitting on the right clothed in a long white garment. One of the two writers may speak of an angel outside, and the other of an angel within the sepulchre; but the language of both may equally well apply to the same angel in the same position, i. e. sitting on the right hand, outside of the sepulchre. Luke, who at the end of his account mentions Mary Magdalene, and Joanna, and Mary the mother of James, and the other women with them, as the women who told these things to the Apostles, would naturally confine his narrative of occurrences at the sepulchre to what particularly concerned that portion of the company from whom his information was derived, and they may have been Joanna and the women from Galilee who were with her. These women may have come a little later than the others. They saw not *one*, but *two* angels, and them not *sitting*, but *standing*, and speaking to them in language very different from that which the angel had spoken to the other women (Luke xxiv. 5, 6, 22). According to John, Mary Magdalene saw no angel when she first came to the sepulchre, and Peter and John, who came with her, or rather a little before her, on her return to the sepulchre, saw none, though they entered the sepulchre. But after they had gone, she, stooping down to look into the sepulchre, saw there two angels in white, one at the head and the other at the feet where the body of Jesus had lain. This is plainly a different

transaction from that which is described by the other Evangelists. The inference from all this is, that Matthew and Mark describe one appearance, Luke another to a different party, and John still a third. Where, then, is the contradiction or inconsistency?

3. As to the first manifestation of Jesus. According to John xx. 15 – 17, he appeared first to Mary Magdalene; according to Matthew, he appeared to the women as they were hastening away from the sepulchre. Matthew may have generalized the occurrence which John has given in detail, and represented Jesus as appearing to the women, when as a literal fact he appeared to only one of their number. This is no unusual form of speech. We rather infer, however, from the narrative, that Jesus appeared twice, viz. 1. to Mary Magdalene, and 2. to the women who had been with her when she first came to the tomb.

In the accounts of what occurred in the morning there are no contradictions. The whole period taken up by these events probably was not more than an hour, and may not have been half that time. Yet how have the disclosures of those few moments revolutionized the world, changing its great currents of thought and inaugurating a new and momentous era in its history!

Leaving the events of the morning, the writers go on in very different ways. After a paragraph relating to the soldiers, and without anything to indicate the time or events that had intervened, Matthew. hastens to give an account of the meeting which Jesus had appointed with his disciples in Galilee. Luke details in full the meeting of Jesus with two disciples [not Apostles] on their way to Emmaus in the afternoon, and his appearance to the Apostles in Jerusalem in the evening. This evening appearance of Jesus to the Apostles is mentioned by John (xx. 19 – 23) in a narrative which is remarkably distinct from Luke's account, and yet strikingly corroborates it. Mark, in a passage (xv. 12 – 20) which Tischendorf rejects as not belonging to the Gospel,

says that Jesus appeared in another form to two disciples
as they were going into the country; that they announced it
to the rest, — their associates, and probably not the Apostles,
— and were not believed; and that afterwards he appeared
to the eleven as they were at meat, and reproached them
for their want of faith. This part of Mark's Gospel is very
much condensed, and evidently crowds into a few sentences
sayings and events which were separated by considerable
intervals of time.

### The Different Times of his Appearance.

From all the accounts we gather that Jesus appeared, —
1. to Mary Magdalen (John xx. 13 – 17); 2. to the [other]
women (Matt. xxviii. 9, 10); 3. to Peter (Luke xxiv. 34,
1 Cor. xv. 5); 4. to the two disciples on their way to Emmaus (Luke xxiv. 15), which may possibly have been before
his appearance to Peter; 5. to the Apostles (Thomas being
absent) at supper in Jerusalem (Luke xxiv. 36 – 42, John xx.
19, 20, 1 Cor. xv. 5); 6. on the next Sunday at Jerusalem
to the Apostles, and particularly to Thomas (John xx. 26);
7. to above five hundred of the brethren at once, probably
in Galilee (1 Cor. xv. 6); 8. to James, probably also in
Galilee (1 Cor. xv. 7); 9. to all the Apostles (1 Cor. xv.
7), probably the same meeting as that described in John
xxi.; 10. to the Apostles on a mountain in Galilee (Matt.
xxviii. 16, 17), which may be the same as his appearance
to "above five hundred." 11. There is the charge given to
the Apostles (Matt. xxviii. 18 – 20, Mark xvi. 15 – 18) with
nothing to mark the time or place. 12. There is the last
interview, ending with his Ascension (Luke xxiv. 44 – 50,
Mark xvi. 19, 20, Acts i. 4 – 10). But as Jesus was seen
of the Apostles from time to time for forty days (Acts i. 3),
"speaking to them of the things pertaining to the kingdom
of God," we have no reason to suppose that these were the
only occasions on which he was seen by them.

Matthew (xxviii. 7, 10) says that both the angel and Jesus directed the women to announce a meeting of the disciples with him in Galilee. "Go, tell my brethren that they go into Galilee, and there shall they see me." "Then," verse 16, "the eleven disciples went away into Galilee, into a mountain where Jesus had appointed them. And when they saw him, they worshipped him : but some doubted." If Matthew, one of the Apostles, knew, as he must have known, of the meeting of Jesus with the Apostles more than once in Jerusalem, how could he fail to leave some record of the fact in his narrative ? His Gospel is only a sketch of portions of our Saviour's life, and nowhere professes to give a full account of everything that took place in a single instance. His whole account of the resurrection, and the sayings and events connected with it, contains only a few more words than it requires to fill one of these pages. A dry summary of facts, such as would be required in order to bring the various particulars within such limits, was not at all after his manner of writing. He gives the salient acts and words as they lie most prominent in his mind, often without reference to the intervening or accompanying circumstances. He belonged to Galilee, and may have gone thither before the other Apostles to call the disciples who were there together to meet their risen Lord. In this way the meeting there may, after an interval of some years, have been the one which he remembered most distinctly, and which he therefore selected to be preserved in his brief narrative. The points which he relates are all connected together. On the morning of the resurrection, both the angel and Jesus speak of the meeting which was to take place in Galilee, and after stating this, and inserting by way of parenthesis a short account of the bargain between the elders and the soldiers in regard to the events of that morning, Matthew passes over all that took place in Jerusalem, and hastens on to the meeting in Galilee.

But he says that at the meeting in Galilee "some doubted." If the meetings spoken of as taking place in Jerusalem had really taken place, how could there have been this element of doubt? There is nothing to show that the meeting in Galilee was confined to the Eleven. The direction, " Go, tell my brethren," indicates a wider circle. St. Paul speaks of Jesus being seen by above five hundred at once. And it certainly would not be strange if some of these five hundred came in an unbelieving state of mind. The honesty of the writer who recorded the doubt is more remarkable than that the doubt should exist under such circumstances. The great and important omissions which must, from the nature of the case, belong to so brief a narrative, should make us slow to infer that even important facts connected with the events which he relates either did not take place, or were unknown to the writer, because they are not mentioned by him. This consideration has had too little weight both with those who defend and those who would break down the authenticity of the Gospel narratives. In accounts which from their very nature and design are necessarily so incomplete and fragmentary, the omission of any fact, however important in itself, is no evidence that it did not take place, or that it was unknown to the writer. With so many facts of the greatest significance and weight pressing upon him for admission, and yet obliged as he was by the necessities of the case to exclude most of them from his narrative, it ought not to seem strange to us if we should find wanting in his brief account circumstances as interesting and important as those which he has retained. An accomplished writer in these times would probably fill a hundred pages where St. Matthew did one with the account of what transpired between the Crucifixion and the Ascension. One closely written half-sheet of our letter-paper is more space than he had to spare for his record of all the circumstances connected with the most momentous event in the history of our race.

### Each Account Independent of the Rest.

We have examined in their relation to the Resurrection of Jesus four distinct and independent narratives. Neither of them could have been drawn from one or from all the rest; for each has some characteristic feature of its own,— not only characteristic forms of expression, but statements of fact which are not found in either of the others. Each of the writers must therefore have had his own independent sources of information; and from these separate sources of information they all testify to the same great and wonderful event, not in general terms, but each one in his own way, by facts, and incidental shadings, and colorings of facts, peculiar to himself. These variations are in some cases so great, that superficial or hostile readers have sometimes supposed them to be utterly irreconcilable. But a thorough examination shows, in almost every case, that these apparent discrepancies may be harmoniously adjusted, and thus made to corroborate the truthfulness of the whole account. For example, Mark (xvi. 5) says that the women entered into the sepulchre. Matthew says nothing about their entering into it, but he says (xxviii. 8) "they went quickly out from the sepulchre." Or, to take another of the many instances that might be given, Matthew, Mark, and Luke speak of the women — *more than one* — who came to the sepulchre early on the morning of the resurrection; John speaks of Mary Magdalene alone. Here is an apparent inconsistency. But on looking carefully into John's account, we find Mary saying to Peter and John, "They have taken away the Lord from the sepulchre, and *we* know not where they have laid him," — implying the presence of others with them at the tomb, and thus undesignedly corroborating the accounts of the other Evangelists. Now, unless Jesus did actually rise from the dead, and meet his disciples, and talk with them, how could writings so independent of one another, and apparently so inconsistent with one another, bring forward such a variety of facts, which bear upon the same point, presenting different sides and features of the same case, and which, notwithstanding their apparent inconsistencies, are found, on a minute and exact investigation, to harmonize entirely in their accounts?

### The Resurrection of Jesus.

But we do not like to dwell on this great and life-giving event as critics. It comes to us in a more living form, and has higher lessons to teach.

When the disciples saw that their Master was really dead, their most dearly cherished hopes and expectations died within them. They must have been like men stunned by a violent blow, or walking in some terrible dream, hardly knowing where they went or what they did. The women, less mindful of consequences and more true to the loving instincts of their nature, followed after the body to see where it was laid, when it was hastily embalmed and entombed. They then prepared spices and gums, that, when the Sabbath was ended, they might come back again and complete the rites of burial. There is no word to show how the Sabbath was spent, — that first day of sharp and hopeless grief, whose heavens encircled them like the wall of a tomb out of which all joy and hope were gone, and when there was nothing left to them but a shuddering sense of dreariness and death. The Sabbath interposed its merciful release from care and toil, till they had recovered somewhat from the first benumbing shock of misery. But with the first day of the week, the first Christian Sunday, they are up before the earliest dawn. Their grief must find expression and relief in some act of grateful remembrance, though only to the body of him whom they had followed with such intensity of love and reverence. While it is yet dark, from Bethany, from different parts of Jerusalem, by previous agreement, or with the spontaneous movement prompted by a common impulse, they are on their way, talking sadly as they go, and asking who shall remove for them the heavy stone which had been placed against the mouth of the sepulchre.

But it had been removed. Mary Magdalene, the most ardent and impetuous of their number, having come first within sight of the sepulchre and seen the stone rolled away, ran to Peter and John, with a fresh outburst of grief, to say that even the consolation of paying the last sad rites of burial had been taken from them. "They have taken away the Lord, and we know not where they have laid him." The other women, who were a little behind her, went to the tomb, and saw an angel clothed in white, sitting on the stone which had been rolled away. He asked them, "Why seek ye the living among the dead? He is not here, but is risen." They fly with the intelligence. Other women, from other parts of the city, come, and see two angels. Then Peter and John come running to the tomb, which they enter, and seeing how the grave-clothes are laid, one of them at least believes that he is risen from the dead. Mary Magdalene returns, and, as she stands weeping by the tomb, two angels appear to her. Then, her eyes blinded with tears, she perceives some one whom she supposes to be the gardener. He asks her why she is weeping, and whom she seeks. She says to him, in the sharpness of her grief, "If thou hast borne him hence, tell me where thou hast laid him, and I will take him away." Then, in tones which could not be mistaken, he called her by name. She turned to him with an exclamation of surprise and reverence, and went away bearing with her to the disciples the wonderful intelligence. But it seemed to them as an idle tale, and they believed her not. They ran from one to another, telling and hearing, — not believing what they heard, yet repeating it to others, and impatient with those who did not believe, — thrilled with expectation and wonder.

But the truth breaks upon them. "The Lord *is* risen indeed." It is the creation of a new heaven and a new earth to them. The tomb has given up its dead, and Death himself, discrowned and disarmed, leaves its terrors at the foot of the cross, and through the gate which it has opened points upward to the realms of eternal life. What occurred to Jesus while he was among the dead is unknown, beyond what may be inferred from his words upon the cross: "This day shalt thou be with me in Paradise." If the Evangelists had been unscrupulous men, earnest to make the most of their subject, by ministering to the diseased taste for prying into the things which have been wisely hidden from us, what tales of wonder would they have told of his experience there! But there is nothing of this. And there is the same reserve in regard to all the details which could only serve to excite and gratify an idle or a dangerous curiosity. The great fact of the resurrection of Him who is the resurrection and the life to all who live and believe in him, is set forth in language which cannot be explained away. He came forth, a new sun, from the dark and universal night of death, to throw the radiance of a triumphant morning over the tombs of the world, to drive away the shadows that pressed everywhere so heavily on human hearts, to unfold to them the joy and gladness of the eternal life, to revolutionize the religious ideas of the world, and create a new life in the souls of men. It was so with the Apostles of Jesus Christ. It has been so with his followers since, from generation to generation. New hopes, new principles of thought and life, new aspirations and desires, have been awakened and cherished. No earthly gloom can overshadow the light. They whose plans and expectations here are all broken up, to whom this life, devoted to the highest ends, has sometimes seemed an utter failure, behold now, in that world beyond, a new sphere of activity and power, where plans here broken up shall be renewed, where hopes here dead shall live again, where aspirations doomed here to a perpetual disappointment shall find their fulfilment, and visions of holiness and joy and blessed companionship with others, which were here mocked with a perpetual rebuff, shall embody themselves in the glorious realities which live around them. And most of all, the sinful and rejected, alienated from God and wandering away from their own happiness and rest, dead to all the best hopes and instincts of the soul, may find in him newness of life, reconciliation, atonement through his death and resurrection from the dead, if they come with penitent and trusting hearts to him. "But now is Christ risen from the dead, and become the first-fruits of them that slept." (1 Cor. xv. 20.) "If ye then be risen with Christ, seek those things which are above, where Christ sitteth on the right hand of God." (Col. iii. 1.) "To him that overcometh will I grant to sit with me in my throne, even as I also overcame, and am set down with my Father in his throne." (Rev. iii. 21.) If the Lord is risen within us, we have passed already from death unto life, and death can have dominion over us no more. Let not the greatness of his promises overwhelm and confound and oppress us as revealing too bright a glory and too great a joy for us to bear; but through our faith in him, and our fidelity to him, may his immortal energies unfold themselves within us.

### 19. — THE FORMULA OF BAPTISM.

"Go ye, and make disciples of all nations, baptizing them into the name of the Father, and of the Son, and of the Holy Ghost." Sectarian writers generally maintain that *their peculiar* views of the Trinity, whatever they may be, and they are many and various, are taught in this formula. There can be no doubt, we think, that the words were intended by our Saviour to indicate the broad outlines of Christian belief, as distinguished from every other system of religious faith. They teach not merely a belief in God, but in God as he is revealed to us in Christ, and as he acts upon us by his sanctifying influences, or his Holy Spirit. The religion which Jesus came into the world to teach, and into which those who would be his disciples are to be initiated, is not a more elevated form of Deism, or a refinement on Judaism. It has elements, implied in the baptismal form, which are peculiar to itself, and which deeply affect the character of its disciples, and the nature of their worship. If the New Testament should be divested of all that is said in it about Jesus Christ and the Holy Spirit, leaving to us only what is revealed of the Infinite Father, our religion would lose much of what most commends it to our hearts. God would be thrown back into the distant heavens. Our conceptions of him would become remote, and our feelings towards him chilled. He would not connect himself as he now does with the loving reverence that draws us towards him, and makes us look up to him, not with awe alone, but with tears of trusting gratitude and affection. As we follow Jesus, in the Gospels, through his ministry, and hear his words and imbibe his spirit, we feel that he is to us the manifestation of the Father, that he brings God in all his gentle and endearing attributes home to our hearts, connecting him with our fireside affections, and giving warmth and tenderness, and a sense of trust and nearness to us in our devotions. So likewise our feelings towards God are modified by what is taught of the Holy Spirit, which dwells a sanctifying presence and influence in the soul, subduing our hearts, forming them anew through a divine life into the image of God, till his love pervades all our affections, purges away all bitterness, and is breathed out from us in our daily thoughts and acts.

Here is a type of character and of piety altogether unlike those which proceed from any other religious dispensation. And the influences under which it is formed are in some way or other connected with the formula of Christian baptism. All the agencies — Father, Son, and Holy Ghost —

unite to create in us the highest type of Christian worship
and the Christian life. They who cherish that worship and
that life feel themselves bound together by a powerful bond
of sympathy and union. They are drawn to one another,
and feel that wherever two or three are gathered together
in his name, there is Jesus in the midst of them. They are
brought into communion with him and with heavenly things.
Inward life, strength, peace, is imparted to them, and a
nearer intimacy with heaven.

Now, why cannot the whole Christian world fall back on
the great Scriptural expressions which address themselves
with such power to the imagination and the heart, and feed
the inmost springs of thought and life? Why not be satisfied with the way in which the doctrine has been taught by
Jesus and his disciples? Why refine upon their words, or
cover them over with our metaphysical distinctions, or tie
them up by our definitions, till the simplicity, the power, and
the freedom of the divine revelation is lost? Those living
words, which come to us always in the perennial greenness
of a divine creation, with thought enough to exhaust the
intellect of the profoundest philosopher, while they come
home also to the heart and apprehension of a child, the
moment they are stript of their freedom, and drawn up into
a creed, lose their charm, and become unsatisfactory, barren,
and dead.

Whatever the doctrine of the Father, Son, and Holy
Ghost may be in its last analysis, — a point which no
mind of mortal man will ever be able to reach, — it does
not in the Scriptures offer itself to us under any metaphysical formula. We find a part of it used by Peter as a heartfelt expression of grateful trust: " Thou art the Christ, the
Son of the living God." (Matt. xvi. 16.) It was breathed
out in a promise of unspeakable tenderness: "I will not
leave you comfortless; I will come to you. . . . . Because I
live, ye shall live also." (John xiv. 18, 19.) "I will pray
the Father, and he shall give you another Comforter, that

he may abide with you forever." (John xiv. 16.) And in
the prayer after the last Supper, "And this is life eternal,
that they might know thee, the only true God, and Jesus
Christ whom thou hast sent." (John xvii. 3.) It was uttered
more fully in the baptismal service. It revealed itself to the
first martyr, when at his death he saw the glory of God,
and cried, "Behold, I see the heavens opened, and the Son
of man standing on the right hand of God." (Acts vii. 56.)
It came as a benediction from St. Paul, when, yearning towards his converts with desires which no other language
could express, he said, "The grace of the Lord Jesus
Christ, and the love of God, and the communion of the
Holy Ghost, be with you all." (2 Cor. xiii. 13.) And in
the Apocalypse it appears as a solemn ascription in the triumphal scene, where "a great multitude, which no man
could number, of all nations and kindreds and people and
tongues, stood before the throne, and before the Lamb,
clothed with white robes, and palms in their hands, and cried
with a loud voice, saying, 'Salvation to our God who sitteth
upon the throne, and unto the Lamb.'" (Rev. vii. 9, 10.)
These were the earliest expressions of the doctrine, — not
metaphysical abstractions, or subtile distinctions, or articles
of faith, — but a promise full of tenderness, a prayer, a
benediction, or an anthem. And so it continued to be at
least for three centuries after Christ. The early Christians
had too deep an interest in him, and were bound to him by
affections too strong and full of life, to attempt by any poor
refinements or definitions of theirs to analyze and set forth
the mysteries of his nature. Least of all did they attempt
to bind them up in articles of faith. They were guided by
a higher wisdom than that. And herein let us learn of
them. Man's thoughts respecting God change. Words
lose their power. "The words of that creed, for example,
which we read last Sunday (the Athanasian), were living
words a few centuries ago. They have changed their meaning, and are, to ninety-nine out of every hundred, only dead

words. Yet men tenaciously hold to the expressions of which they do not understand the meaning, and which have a very different meaning now from that they had once, — Person, Procession, Substance; and they are almost worse with them than without them, — for they conceal their ignorance, and *place a barrier against the earnestness of inquiry.*" (Robertson's Sermons, First Series, p. 73.) But worse than this, they oppress humble, sensitive, and conscientious souls, and often either bind them to forms of belief which they cannot accept, or drive them away from a communion which their religious instincts crave, and to which they are bound by the dearest and most sacred associations. "It is a remarkable and indisputable fact, that if Christ were to come on earth unknown, and say anything or everything which he is recorded to have said while on earth, that and no more, it would not be sufficient for his admission into any [so-called] Evangelical church: no bishop could lay hands on him without violating his rubric; no synod ordain him as a preacher." We quote this extraordinary statement from an abstract of a sermon by Rev. George Putnam, D. D. Its truth cannot be denied. And it is a fact of terrible significance to those who hold, as essential to church-membership here and to salvation hereafter, terms of intellectual belief which would exclude from their communion the Saviour himself, unless he should consent to add some new and more explicit articles of faith to those which the Evangelists and Apostles have left on record.

### Concluding Remarks.

The Gospel of St. Matthew begins with an account of the human and the divine parentage of Christ, his earthly humiliation, though descended from patriarchs and kings, and his more than earthly dignity and greatness, though placed in the lowliest walks of life. This twofold aspect of his life appears throughout the Gospel. His humility shows itself amidst his mightiest works, and even when he assumes an authority beyond all that man has ever claimed. And wherever his humiliation and helplessness are most apparent, there his majesty shines forth. This humility and grandeur, the most difficult combination in the life and character, are easily and harmoniously combined and carried out from beginning to end. There is no one act or word to mar the beautiful and always living consistency of the portraiture. Except in the other Gospels, no other such narrative, nor anything which makes any approach to it, is to be found in the literature of the world. Those who have followed us through our work, reading the Gospel itself more than our comments upon it, who have entered into the marvellous depth and elevation of its thought, and of the life in which, more than by any words, its thought is revealed, must, we think, see in them the workings of a power more wonderful than any miracles that were wrought, though on the side of its active manifestation it would find in miracles only its natural forms of expression. But with all this exhibition of power, there is nothing strained, and nowhere any appearance of effort. The language, even when charged with the weightiest burden of meaning, or rising to the sublimest heights, is, in its naturalness and simplicity, fitted to be the reading of a child. When we go into the Epistles, especially those of St. Paul, we are conscious of a change. The same ideas come up to be applied under new circumstances, or carried out into their more distant results. But we feel the strain that is put upon the language, and the efforts that are made by the writer to keep up with the greatness of his theme.

Christ came to establish the kingdom of heaven on earth. Perhaps we may say that this is the central idea of the Evangelist. The Baptist came to announce it, and its near approach was the burden of his preaching. It was the key-note to the ministry of Jesus. "From that time Jesus began to preach, and to say, 'Repent, for the kingdom of

Heaven is at hand.'" In his Sermon on the Mount, he unfolded the nature of that kingdom; and, beginning with the Beatitudes, showed how it was to absorb into itself the Law and the Prophets, and refine their precepts into the principles of a spiritual and divine life. From time to time, as his disciples could bear, and beyond what they could bear, he brought forward the graces and charities which were peculiarly his own, and established a sincere and childlike humility of soul as the one essential condition of pre-eminence in his kingdom. "Whosoever wishes to be great among you, let him be your servant; and whosoever wishes to be first among you, let him be your slave." Only he who, unmindful of his own interests, binds himself by the severest obligations to serve others, can hope for the highest place in the kingdom of God. This heavenly kingdom, or kingdom of Heaven on earth, is explained and illustrated by precept and parable and symbolical act. It is represented as already here, a divine influence and agency in the world. He speaks of the time, then not far removed, when he should "come in his kingdom" (xvi. 28), "on the clouds of heaven with power and great glory" (xxiv. 30). He speaks of it, at other times, as reaching above and beyond this world in its acts and retributions (xvi. 19, xxv. 31 – 46). In the last words of the Gospel, he speaks of its final consummation, — whether on earth or in worlds beyond, he does not say; for time and space are only occasional, and, as it were, accidental accompaniments to his thought, which reaches through and beyond all that belongs to them.

But in the closing words of the Gospel, taken in connection with all that has gone before, we have indicated to us the great Mediatorial office and kingdom of Christ, for which, as its head and king, all authority on the earth and in heaven has been given to him, and for the advancement of which he sends forth his messengers into every land, promising himself to be always with them until the whole shall be fulfilled. Here in this world are its beginnings, and, to a certain extent, its progress with each individual soul, and with the race from generation to generation. It is a spiritual kingdom in which Christ reigns, coming down into this sphere of human interests and souls, dispensing its divine influences more and more, as men are prepared to receive them from age to age, taking up into itself whatever is highest and holiest in man's thought, to infuse into it a diviner life, to lay upon it the hand of a holier ordination, and set it apart for a higher purpose, using present attainments, never as ends, but always as instruments and helps to a further progress, translating its faithful subjects as the ransomed of the Lord from earthly experience to heavenly fruition in what is to each one of them "the end of the world."

Christ came to establish this kingdom among men. He has revealed to us its nature, its agencies, and its design, in words of calmness and power. He has promised to be always with us while we are laboring to unfold its truths, to enforce its precepts, and establish its authority on the earth. His words (xiii. 41, xxv. 34) point also to an influence and a kingly office which he is to have beyond this mortal life and world. But the idea which he introduced is taken up by St. Paul, and carried on into its remote and final results with all the enthusiasm of his fervid and powerful mind.

Perhaps we cannot give a more striking example of the difference between Christ's method of instruction, as shown in the Gospel of St. Matthew, and Paul's, as shown in his Epistles, than is furnished by what they have taught on this subject. The teachings of Christ we have already considered. St. Paul delights to enlarge and expatiate upon them. With him this idea of the Mediatorial kingdom of Christ reaches we know not how high into the realms of light, or how far below into the realms of darkness, extending back in its preparation before the foundation of the world, and forward through we know not what succession of ages upon ages, till at length, working out its mighty evolutions, every opposing rule and authority and power is subdued and overthrown, and it has accomplished its design as one of the æons of eternal love and wisdom, and Christ in triumph shall give back into his Father's hands the kingdom and the authority which are now intrusted to him. In looking to the new worlds of spiritual life and joy which have been created in the advent and progress of that kingdom, through every part of which Christ's influence extends as a redeeming, creative, and sustaining presence, he thus speaks : " Giving thanks unto the Father, who hath made us meet to be partakers of the inheritance of the saints in light; who hath delivered us from the power of darkness, and hath translated us into the kingdom of his dear Son, in whom we have the redemption ["through his blood" is omitted by Tischendorf], the forgiveness of sins ; who is an image of God, first-born of all creation ; because in him were all created that are in the heavens and upon the earth, visible and invisible, whether thrones or dominations or principalities or authorities, — all were created through him and to him, and he is before all, and all stand together in him, and he is the head of the body, the Church, who is first, being first born from the dead, that he might be preeminent in all." (Col. i. 12 – 18.) Carrying his thoughts on into other worlds, respecting which there is a sacred reserve in our Saviour's communications, St. Paul delights to speak of the homage which was there paid to his Redeemer, when God "raised him from the dead and set him at his own right hand among the heavenly ones, far above all principality and power and might and dominion, and every name that is named, not only in this world [æon], but in that which is to come, and hath put all things under his feet, and gave him to be head over all things to the Church, which is his body, the fulness of him that filleth all in all." (Eph. i. 20 – 23.) His language glows with a new intensity, and rises into a more majestic grandeur and a loftier harmony, as he catches from beyond this world glimpses of the active power of Christ, the still advancing progress of his victorious kingdom, or its last and crowning triumph. "Finally," — we quote from the translation of Conybeare and Howson, — "the end shall come, when he shall give up his kingdom to God his Father, having destroyed all other powers which claim rule and sway. For his kingdom must last '*till he hath put all enemies under his feet.*' And last of his enemies, death also shall be destroyed. For '*God hath put all things under his feet.*' But in that saying, '*all things are put under him,*' it is manifest that God is excepted, who put all things under him. And when all things are made subject to him, then shall the Son also subject himself [himself be made subject] to Him who made them subject, that God may be all in all." (1 Cor. xv. 24 – 28.)

There is a singular grandeur and a far-reaching grasp of thought in these views which St. Paul has given of the Mediatorial kingdom and office of Christ. But we see in his language marks of effort and excitement, the strugglings of a mind, however great and inspired it may have been, to master his vast theme, and to find language in which to embody his conceptions. But the words of Jesus come to us as the unexcited and easy utterances of one who is speaking without effort, and by no means above the level of his daily and familiar thought. They lie before us in the calm sunlight of God's truth and the bosom of his love. Great as they are, they plainly come from one who is greater than they, and in whom it is an act of condescension rather than of exaltation to set them forth, and to illustrate, explain, and enforce them, as a Master to his disciples, while an air of divine authority and of unspeakable tenderness distinguishes alike his words to them and all his deportment towards them. Whatever we may find in the language of the Apostles, — and no other writers have ever approached them in richness of spiritual thought or loftiness of conception and of speech, — when we read the words and the life of Jesus, we feel, as did the officers who were sent to apprehend him, that "never man spake [or lived] like this man."

But in studying the Gospels we must beware of placing ourselves too much in the attitude of critics and judges, even though it be to confirm their authority. The word that Christ hath spoken shall judge us, and not be judged by us. Our posture is that of loving, trusting, inquiring, and believing disciples. We come with no theories of our own to establish, but with a single purpose and desire to learn the true meaning of his words of eternal life, and what he would have us to do. It is sad to think with what "a veil upon their hearts" the great majority of the Christian world come when they would study the Gospel of Christ. They can receive from the boundless affluence of his instructions only so much as may be in accordance, not only with their present moral, intellectual, and spiritual culture, but with formulas of faith drawn up and established by the authority of man. Christ speaks to the individual soul, and holds each one of us to a severe and solemn sense of accountability to himself, from which no authority on earth can ever absolve us. The one distinguishing feature of his Gospel is the way in which it addresses itself to the individual consciousness, and demands from each one a direct and personal allegiance to him. The more universal the truths which he proclaimed, the more directly should they come home to each heart and draw it towards himself. Almost every word that he spoke, whether for doctrine, reproof, correction, or instruction and encouragement in righteousness, comes to us, not only as a truth on which our minds should dwell, but as a precept which we should take home to our hearts and carry with us in our lives. In this way his words may become spirit and life to us. And his last directions to his followers, instead of furnishing matter for theological disputations, may be dwelt upon and cherished and obeyed as if addressed to each one of us with all the weight of his commandment, with all the fulness of his instruction, with all the tenderness of his love, and with the certainty that to every one of us his promise will be fulfilled. "All power is given unto me in heaven and on earth. Go ye and make disciples of all nations, baptizing them into the name of the Father, and of the Son, and of the Holy Ghost; teaching them to observe all things whatsoever I have commanded you: and lo, I am with you alway, even unto the end of the world."

---

## NOTES.

IN the end of the sabbath, as it began to dawn toward the first day of the week, came Mary Magdalene, and the other Mary, to see the sepulchre. And, behold, there was a great 2 earthquake; for the angel of the Lord descended from heaven, and came and rolled back the stone from the door, and sat upon it. His countenance was like lightning, and his raiment 3

---

1. **In the end of the sabbath, as it began to dawn toward the first day of the week**] The Jewish Sabbath, it will be remembered, corresponds with our Saturday. The day ended at sunset. The passage may be rendered, *After the Sabbath, as it began,* &c. "No mortal eye," says Dr. Carpenter, "witnessed the glorious moment when the Son of God came forth from the tomb, the first-fruits of a resurrection to an immortal life; and the narratives of the Evangelists merely respect the *disclosures* of the great event. Their close adherence to what alone was *known* is very striking." "The writers of the New Testament," says Olshausen, "make mention of what they saw only, as ' that the sepulchre was already empty.' The creative energies operated in silence and unobservedly, and wove for the sublime person of the Lord, as it were, a raiment of celestial light, worthy of investing the king of the world of light. Even so, no human eye, at that moment when the energies of life flowed into it, beheld how the body of the Holy One arose." "The resurrection was the great act which the Apostles published, and that peculiarly and alone."

2. **And, behold, there was a great earthquake**] "A *shaking* or *commotion* of any kind; probably the word means no more than the *confusion* caused among the guards by the angel's appearance; all this had taken place before the women reached the sepulchre." Adam Clarke. **for the angel of the Lord**] *an* angel of the Lord. "Like the commencement of the Lord's life upon earth, this beginning of his glorified life was also adorned with kindred angel visions." 3. **his countenance**] his *form* or *appearance was like lightning.* The commotion, what-

MATTHEW XXVIII.

4 white as snow. And for fear of him the keepers did shake,
5 and became as dead men. And the angel answered and said
unto the women, Fear not ye; for I know that ye seek Jesus,
6 which was crucified. He is not here; for he is risen, as he
7 said. Come, see the place where the Lord lay. And go
quickly, and tell his disciples that he is risen from the dead;
and, behold, he goeth before you into Galilee; there shall ye
see him : lo, I have told you. And they departed quickly from
the sepulchre, with fear and great joy, and did run to bring his
9 disciples word. And as they went to tell his disciples, behold,
Jesus met them, saying, All hail! And they came and held

---

ever it may have been, and the opening of the tomb by rolling back the stone from the door, must have occurred before the women reached the place. The manifestation of the angel is probably described as it appeared to them in dazzling whiteness and splendor. Whether the angel appeared to their bodily eyes, or only to their spiritual perceptions, is a speculative question which hardly falls within the province of a work like this. The reader who may be curious in such matters will find it ably discussed in " Foregleams of Immortality," by the Rev. E. H. Sears. " All the difficulties, or seeming discrepancies," it is there said, (p. 191,) " in the four narratives, have grown out of the most absurd assumption that the angels appeared in bodies like ours, and to the mortal senses. The variations are just what they would be to the variant perceptions of the half-opened spiritual vision. John and Peter saw nothing, some of the women probably saw nothing, and doubtless none of them saw all. We do not imagine that the divine messengers had been absent from any part of that scene of sorrow and dismay on Friday afternoon, as they certainly were not absent from Gethsemane the night before. True, the Roman soldiers might not know it till the gleaming terrors dispersed them; and the women saw but one or two among the divine powers that engirded and guarded to its sure accomplishment the central fact in the world's history, and heralded the victory of the Son of God over death and the grave." It is well to have the picture of these scenes distinctly before us. We have no doubt of the fact that angels were then seen; but the precise mode of the angelic manifestation, whether by an impression on the bodily senses or a quickening of the spiritual perceptions, is not clearly revealed. The effect produced on the soldiers who were guarding the sepulchre must, we think, have been through the bodily senses. 7. **and, behold, he goeth before you into Galilee**] This was foretold by Jesus (Matt. xxvi. 32) in almost exactly the words here used. The object in going into Galilee may have been to secure retirement, and also that Jesus might show himself to the more numerous body of his disciples who resided there. But while that was to be the scene of his most important interviews with the Apostles after his resurrection, he may have shown himself to them first in Jerusalem, that they might thus be led so far to dismiss their doubts as to go and meet him with the larger company of his followers at the appointed place in Galilee.

8. **with fear and great joy**] " Rejoice with trembling." (Ps. ii. 11.) The two emotions in the proportions here indicated may be united. It is one of those touches of nature which help to bring the whole scene before us. 9. **And they came and held him**

him by the feet, and worshipped him. Then said Jesus unto 10 them, Be not afraid: go, tell my brethren that they go into Galilee, and there shall they see me.

Now when they were going, behold, some of the watch came 11 into the city, and showed unto the chief priests all the things that were done. And when they were assembled with the 12 elders, and had taken counsel, they gave large money unto the soldiers, saying, Say ye, His disciples came by night, 13 and stole him away, while we slept. And if this come to 14

---

**by the feet, and worshipped him**] A not unusual mark of reverence in the East to persons of superior dignity. With what body Christ rose, is a question which it is more difficult than profitable to discuss. The body which was laid in the tomb had risen. But what changes it had undergone is nowhere intimated. From the fact that the women clung to his feet, that Thomas was asked to thrust his hand into his side (John xx. 27), and that he asked the disciples to handle him and see, "for a spirit hath not flesh and bones as you see me have" (Luke xxiv. 39), we cannot well escape the conviction that he rose in a body which acted on those he met, as other bodies do, through the physical organs of sense. On the other hand, his not being recognized by the two disciples with whom he conversed on the way to Emmaus would seem to show that he had then undergone some remarkable change in his personal appearance; and his disappearance from them the moment he was known (Luke xxiv. 31), and his appearance in the midst of the Apostles more than once while they were assembled with closed doors (John xx. 19, 26), seem to imply a facility of movement of which the Gospels furnish no previous instances, unless perhaps in the account of his walking upon water. We cannot tell when his body became spiritual and immortal. Olshausen supposes that "the process of glorification went on during the forty days after the resurrection, and was not thoroughly perfected until the period of his ascension to heaven." It becomes us to be diffident in regard to any specific views that we may entertain in this matter. It is enough for us to know Christ did rise from the dead, whatever may have been the changes which his body underwent in death, and before the ascension.

12. **And when they were assembled with the elders, and had taken counsel**] Here was a meeting, a hasty and probably an informal one, of the Jewish Sanhedrim. It may seem strange that the soldiers should have gone first to the priests, rather than to their own superior officers. But it is plain, from Matt. xxvii. 64, 65, that the guard of soldiers had not only been granted at the request of the priests and Pharisees, but had been placed under their charge. "Ye have a guard," [or watch,] said Pilate; "go, make it as sure as ye know how." It would therefore be proper and natural for them to make their report in the first instance to their immediate employers.

13. **Say ye, His disciples came by night, and stole him away, while we slept**] This whole incident, it is said, is unhistorical and improbable. But the ablest scholars cannot transfer themselves to Jerusalem, as it was during those three days, with such a minute knowledge of the prevailing customs, and all the special interests then acting, as to be able to say precisely what would or what would not be historical in a little incidental occurrence like this. Even in an army under the most

the governor's ears, we will persuade him, and secure you. 15 So they took the money, and did as they were taught. And

rigid discipline, directly before an enemy, there are constantly coming up little exceptional cases, which seem inconsistent with the stately march of history, but of which no man after the lapse of two thousand years can know enough of the attendant circumstances to pronounce them unhistorical or improbable. It would be inconsistent, it is said, with the dignity of the Sanhedrim, to make such a bargain as this with the Roman soldiers. But the history of the world shows plainly enough, that where political or religious bigotry has an important end to gain, it is not accustomed to stand much on its dignity in the means which it uses. They who in their pride assume the loftiest airs, and claim for themselves the greatest show of respect, are often the very persons who stoop to the meanest and most dishonorable arts. But then, how could they know that Jesus had predicted that he should rise from the dead on the third day? Even his own disciples did not understand him; how then could they, his enemies? There is nothing in the world so suspicious as the malignant spirit of such men, when confronted with an ingenuous and powerful mind, that sees through and exposes their subterfuges and pretensions. Having no honesty of their own, they cannot conceive of such a thing as an honest purpose in those who stand in their way. They distrust them at every turn. They subject their acts and words to every unfavorable construction that is possible. They see a plot or an intrigue in the simplest declaration. What wonder, then, if the chief priests should have heard the distinct and reiterated declarations of our Saviour respecting his death and resurrection on the third day? The disciples could not understand the words of their Master, but they must have repeated them again and again, with strange perplexity of heart. And what more natural

than that the Jewish leaders, looking everywhere for a plot, and never quite secure of having accomplished their guilty purpose, even in the death of their victim, should, in calling to mind this declaration, apprehend and provide against some such design as that which is recorded at the close of the previous chapter? And when their precautions, as the most subtle devices of such men often do, had failed, and turned against themselves, what more natural than for them to adopt the only expedient then possible, and bribe the soldiers to misrepresent the facts? But then, it is asked, how would the soldiers dare to confess that they had fallen asleep on their watch? Would it not expose them to the severest punishment for a serious violation of the rules of military discipline? In reply to this, it may be said, that their employers — the very men to whom they were directly accountable for any remissness in their watch, and who alone would have an opportunity to complain of them — were the men who proposed the bargain with them, whose interest it was that no serious accusation should be brought against them, and who promised to interfere in their behalf if by any chance the report of their remissness in duty should reach the ears of the governor. "To affirm," says Davidson, (Introduction to the New Testament, Vol. I. pp. 82, 83,) "that the falsehood could not have escaped Pilate, is to assume that he took more interest in the matter than his whole character justifies. All his anxiety must have coincided with the measures already taken against the person of Christ, in which he had reluctantly involved himself. And as the story told him by the chief priests and scribes must have been more welcome than the real account of the case would have been, he naturally believed it, and took no further trouble. Had he heard the true

this saying is commonly reported among the Jews until this day.

---

circumstances attendant on Jesus's rising from the dead, his fears would have been excited, and his conscience rendered doubly uneasy. Such tidings must have been disagreeable to his agitated spirit. But when he learned that the body had been stolen by the disciples at night, his fears had not to be allayed, nor were his superstitious feelings to be quieted. He felt that the part he had taken in putting Christ to death was unattended by the guilt and impiety in which it must have presented itself, had Jesus proved himself the Son of God by rising from the dead. Thus the information given by the Sanhedrim to Pilate, false though it was, found a welcome reception. Had he even suspected its truth, he would not have instituted a process of inquiry. Whether Joseph of Arimathea, Nicodemus, and Gamaliel were present at the meeting of the Sanhedrim, is a point that cannot be ascertained. . . . . And if they were present, had they the moral courage to object? . . . . . And suppose they *did protest* against the unworthy resolution, was it incumbent on the historian to relate the fact? The decision of the majority is the decision of a council. . . . . Hence the record is perfectly consistent with the idea of a few persons refusing to sanction the open dissemination of a falsehood." On the whole, this little episode, instead of appearing unhistorical and improbable, seems to us to bear upon its face the marks of truth. We agree entirely with what Mr. Norton has said on this matter in his Internal Evidences of the Genuineness of the Gospels (pp. 233, 234): "The remark that the miracles of Christ appear from the Gospels to have been unquestioned, is true of what may be more strictly called *his* miracles. But it is not true of the fact of his resurrection. Respecting this, St. Matthew relates that there was a story in circulation that his disciples came by night and stole his body away while the guards slept. The effect of this single exception is to confirm the argument derived from the general characteristics of the Gospels before mentioned. Here we are told by the Evangelist, that the most important miracle which he records was treated as an imposture. We may fairly conclude, therefore, that with the same honesty, or the same indifference, or the same incapacity for deception, he would, in some way, have given us information of the fact, if the truth of the other miracles recorded by him had been called in question. What he here expressly states confirms most strongly the correctness of those accounts which *imply* that their truth was not disputed. But in what manner does he mention this particular story of the unbelieving Jews? He merely states it, without any attempt at refutation, without even a formal denial of it, without a single remark respecting it. He could not have treated it with more indifference, or with more appearance of regarding it as destitute equally of plausibility and of truth, and wholly unlikely to obtain credit. If the story had been urged with any confidence, if it had been in fact believed by those who brought it forward, it would hardly have been passed over with such slight."

15. **until this day**] i. e. until the time when the Gospel was written. There is no decisive evidence when that was, but the probabilities, we think, rather point to a period eight or ten years after the death of Christ, or about A. D. 42 or 43.

16. **Then the eleven disciples went away into Galilee**] There is no *then* in the Greek. Matthew not unfrequently passes from one event to another, which took place at a different period, without one word to indicate the time that intervened between them. The natural inference from his language here would be that the Apos-

16 Then the eleven disciples went away into Galilee, into
17 a mountain, where Jesus had appointed them. And when

tles went to Galilee immediately after the resurrection. But, in accordance with his method of speaking in other cases, we may suppose a week or a month to have intervened between the two events.

**into a mountain**] to "*the* mountain, where Jesus had appointed."

**the eleven**] Matthew mentions only the eleven; but this does not imply that they were the only persons who met Jesus at the appointed mountain. The "*Go, tell my brethren*," of ver. 10, indicates a larger circle of disciples. Probably notice had been extensively given among the more intimate and trusted followers of Jesus that they should meet him at some particular place which he had specified. The definite article, which our translators omit before mountain, proves this, though Matthew does not mention where it was. This may have been the occasion when he was seen of "above five hundred brethren at once." (1 Cor. xv. 6.) 17. **but some doubted**] Of course, the Apostles who had met Jesus in Jerusalem more than once since his resurrection, could have had no doubts. Either Matthew has transferred to this meeting the doubts which the Apostles had shown in Jerusalem, or, as is more probable, he speaks here of doubts entertained by some of the followers of Jesus who had not met their risen Lord before, and who in the excitement of a first interview could hardly overcome their doubts so as to believe their own eyes. It was precisely the same state of mind which the Apostles had shown when they were first told of the resurrection, and which Thomas persisted in till he had the opportunity to see and examine for himself. It is a strong proof of the truthfulness of the writers, that they should so fearlessly insert this in their narratives, without one word of explanation or apology. Our view of the doubters is that given by Juvencus, a Latin writer who lived in the reign of Constantine. "Nor yet," he says, "did fidelity [virtus] remain equally in the breasts of all [who were assembled to meet him on the Galilæan mountain]; for a part of them doubted." Grotius and some others render the verse, "but some *had* doubted," giving to the aorist the force of the pluperfect. The interpretation that we have adopted is more in accordance with the language of Matthew.

18. **All power is given unto me in heaven and in earth**] Literally *in* heaven and *on* earth. *All power*, or *authority*, indicating the influence which it is given him to exercise over the souls of men in this world and the world to come. In Col. i. 11, St. Paul says, that ye, "*strengthened with all power*," &c. But Christ's authority is not confined to the earth, but diffuses itself through earth and heaven. See Eph. i. 19 – 23; Col. i. 12 – 18; 1 Pet. iii. 22. We suppose that St. Paul (Rom. xiv. 9) explains what is meant by the expression *on earth and in heaven;* "For to this end Christ both died, and rose, and revived, that he might be Lord both of *the dead and living*." The living, and the dead who live in a yet higher sense, make one great community of souls, over whom God has given to Christ all authority or power on earth and in heaven. "Wherefore God also hath highly exalted him, and given him a name which is above every name, that at [literally *in*] the name of Jesus every knee should bow of those in heaven, and those in earth, and those under the earth; and that every tongue should confess that Jesus Christ is Lord, to the glory of God the Father." (Phil. ii. 9 – 11.) It will be observed, that every one of these passages which unite with that before us in ascribing to Jesus such authority, agrees also with his assertion here, and Matt. xi. 27, in declaring that however vast his power may be, it is all *given* to him by the Father. It is a derived, and not an

they saw him, they worshipped him; but some doubted. And 18 Jesus came and spake unto them, saying, All power is given

---

original authority. We must be careful in our dogmatic theology lest we forcibly inject *our* ideas into our Saviour's language, and, by incorporating them into his instructions, give his words a meaning wholly foreign to his intention. *All authority is given to me in heaven and on earth.* "Was there ever a man that dared put himself on the world in such pretensions? — as if all light was in him, as if to follow him, and be worthy of him, was to be the conclusive or chief excellence of mankind! But no one is offended with Jesus on this account, and, what is a sure test of his success, it is remarkable that, of all the readers of the Gospel, it probably never even occurs to one in a hundred thousand, to blame his conceit, or the egregious vanity of his pretensions. . . . . . Come now, all ye that tell us in your wisdom of the mere natural humanity of Jesus, and help us to find how it is, that he is only a natural development of the human; select your best and wisest character; take the range, if you will, of all the great philosophers and saints, and choose out one that is most competent; or if, perchance, some one of you may imagine that he is himself about on a level with Jesus (as we hear that some of you do), let him come forward in this trial and say, 'Follow me,' 'Be worthy of me,' 'I am the light of the world,' 'Ye are from beneath, I am from above,' 'Behold a greater than Solomon is here;' take on all these transcendent assumptions, and see how soon your glory will be sifted out of you by the detective gaze, and darkened by the contempt of mankind! . . . . . Do you not tell us that you can say as divine things as he? . . . . . Are you not in the front rank of human developments? Do you not rejoice in the power to rectify many mistakes and errors in the words of Jesus? Give us then this one experiment, and see if it does not prove to you a truth that is of some consequence; viz. that you are a man, and that Jesus Christ is — more." Bushnell, "Nature and the Supernatural," pp. 289 - 292.

19. **Go ye, therefore, and teach all nations**] *Therefore* does not belong to the text. *Teach;* the original word means *make disciples,* and it is unfortunate that it was not so translated in our common version. "Go ye and make disciples of all nations, *baptizing* them into the name of the Father, and of the Son, and of the Holy Ghost, and *teaching* them to observe all things whatsoever I have commanded you." That is, they are to make all men disciples, baptizing them as the initiatory rite, and teaching them to observe all things whatsoever that Christ had commanded them. **baptizing them in the name of the Father, and of the Son, and of the Holy Ghost**] "After all that has been written," says Davidson, (Introduction to the New Testament, I. 93, 94,) "it is exceedingly difficult to settle the precise meaning of the expression *to baptize into the name of the Father, &c.* Perhaps De Wette assigns it too much meaning, when it is made to involve an express obligation to receive the doctrine of a Triune God as a direct object of faith. The primary idea of it, as far as we can gather from similar phrases in the New Testament, seems to be this, that the person baptized is supposed to adopt the system of religion in which the Father, Son, and Holy Ghost occupy the pre-eminent position, — to come into a state of subordination to the laws of Christianity. . . . . . Those who submitted to baptism virtually professed, by their desire for initiation into a Christian church, to adopt the religious system, and to be subject to the laws of the Son of God. This is probably all that the Apostles and their companions inculcated on the baptized, or that they would have required from them had they reason

19 unto me in heaven and in earth. Go ye, therefore, and
teach all nations, baptizing them in the name of the Father,

to think that any desiring to be admitted within the pale of Christianity were not proper subjects of baptism." It certainly could not have been without design that our Saviour left this form of introduction into his Church with so wide a margin for differences of individual thought and belief. If he had wished to establish the doctrine of a Trinity of three equal persons in the Godhead as a fundamental and essential article of faith, he could easily have so expressed it in this formula as to put his view of the matter beyond all possibility of doubt. He would have only to say, "baptizing them into the name of God the Father, of God the Son, and of God the Holy Ghost, three equal persons, and one God." But if we shrink, as we do almost with a shudder, from putting these words into his mouth, or adding them to those which he has spoken, why should we not also shrink with equal earnestness from imposing upon his words a meaning which he has nowhere expressly authorized, and, contrary to his example, insisting on that as an essential condition of Christian fellowship! Why not be content to let the terms of admission to his Church stand as he and his Apostles left them? It will not do to narrow down a great central statement like this into an expression of any one form of doctrine which man has been able to work out of his own brain. It does not follow that, if any one view of the Divine nature is false, the opposite view is therefore true, and the one which our Saviour meant to teach here. No human mind is able to exhaust his meaning. The more minutely we endeavor to explore and explain the nature of the Father, and of the Son, and of the Holy Ghost, the further we shall be, in all probability, from the truth. We must beware of allowing any human standard of opinions to measure its capacity or extent. "We are all of us, old and young,"
says Stanley in his "Canterbury Sermons," (pp. 111 – 114,) "beset more or less by the sophistries, the systems, the schools, the parties, which time and circumstance, which past ages and our own age, have cast up around us and beside us, before us and behind us. We are involved in their meshes, we walk in the grooves which they have made for us. . . . . Yet still there is encouragement and consolation in the thought, that none of these things of themselves constitute the whole, or the essence of Christianity; that in this respect our Lord is still the pattern of his Church. . . . . There is a true middle way of religion, which not from weakness, not from indolence, not from halting between two opinions, but from sincere love of Christ, and from desire to conform ourselves to his image, we may humbly desire to walk. . . . . No one of us can embrace at a glance the whole of Christian truth. . . . . It is both a confirmation and illustration of this character of Evangelical doctrine, that, if we look into some of the earthly representations of it which have met with most universal acceptance, they also share in this freedom from the bonds in which the world is anxious to confine them. . . . . . Not because their genius is irreligious, not because it is weak and faltering. No; but because it transcends the limits of our ordinary thoughts, because it approaches by another way to something like the loftiness of Him, whose image and superscription it bears." As we stand before a great and comprehensive saying of our Lord, like the baptismal words, we must remember this, and not attempt to measure it by any speculative opinions or dogmatic assumptions of ours. 20. **unto the end of the world**] ἕως τῆς συντελείας τοῦ αἰῶνος. This form of expression occurs five times in the Gospel of Matthew, and nowhere else in the New Testament. A *similar* ex-

and of the Son, and of the Holy Ghost; teaching them to observe all things whatsoever I have commanded you. And, 20

---

pression is found, Heb. ix. 26: " But now once in the end of the world (συντελείᾳ τῶν αἰώνων, *end of the ages*), hath he appeared to put away sin by the sacrifice of himself." In this instance the word αἰώνων, or *æons*, in the plural, refers to a series of dispensations which had their consummation in the religion of Jesus. In Matt. xxiv. 3, " Tell us when these things shall be, and what shall be the sign of thy coming, and of the *end of the world?*" the expression probably has the same meaning. Jesus has been announcing the destructive retribution that is soon to fall upon the Jewish people and their city. The disciples ask when these things shall be, and what shall be the sign of his coming, and of the end of the world? The language has a characteristic of Hebrew poetry, repeating substantially the same idea in different words. *The end of the world* there is the same as the end of the Jewish dispensation, though it may also foreshadow the end of life, i. e. of this present earthly dispensation to each individual soul. This higher meaning of the expression in its more universal application is plainly, we think, implied in Matt. xiii. 39, 40: "The harvest is the end of the world [of this present earthly dispensation]; and the reapers are the angels. As therefore the tares are gathered and burned in the fire; so shall it be in the *end of this world*." This world or dispensation may possibly there, as in chapter xxiv., refer to the Jewish dispensation, and the process by which the good and bad among the Israelites should, like wheat and tares, be separated from one another at the destruction of Jerusalem, and the overthrow of the old religion. But the language, taken in its connection with what goes before and after, seems to us to foreshadow a mightier event, even the retribution which meets every man, when to him this age, i. e. the dispensation of this mortal life, is ended. It is the same at xiii. 49. So in the passage before us, *the end of the world* may possibly refer to the great event which Jesus has described with such prophetic majesty of speech (Matt. xxiv.), and which, while it should destroy the old dispensation as a national religion in the overthrow of the nation itself, was to free the new dispensation and its supporters from a most galling tyranny. In this case he promises his disciples, that during their trials, until that event, he will every day be personally present with them. It is much more probable, however, that his promise has a more universal application, and is for all his followers, in all ages of the world, until to each one of them in the fulness of time *the end of the world* shall come. It is impossible to give in English the precise meaning of the expression. The word translated *world* has nothing to do with the material universe which we call *the world*, but means an *age* or *dispensation*, or *condition of being*. E. g. the care of the *world* (Matt. xiii. 22), i. e. of this present condition of being. The words translated *the end* mean rather the *consummation, completion*, or *fulfilment*. So that *the end of the world* means, as nearly as our language can give its meaning, the *end* or *fulfilment of a dispensation*, as in Heb. ix. 26, and Matt. xxiv. 3, or the *completion* or *consummation* of *our present condition of being*, as Matt. xiii. 39, 40, 49; and xxviii. 20. *The end of the world*, as used by Matthew, in both of its significations, is nearly synonymous with *the coming of the Son of man*. They both imply the passing away of an old, and the coming of a new order of things, the first of which is directly indicated by *the end of the world*, and the second by the *coming of the Son of man*. Both the terms imply far more than they directly express. They have done so much in the development of the

lo, I am with you alway, even unto the end of the world. Amen.

---

Christian consciousness, and have so bound themselves up in the most solemn and endearing associations, that no other words can ever take their place, or have the power which they have over the Christian heart and imagination. No attempt to analyze such words, or to define them precisely, can ever be successful. The fine aroma of sentiment, which fills them as a holy incense, and makes them sacred, escapes in the process, and leaves the words which we use in their stead poor and meagre substitutes. "*And, lo, I am with you alway, even unto the end of the world.*" "For *then* we shall be with the Lord, as he is even now with us. To him, therefore, reader, commit thyself, and remain in him; so will it be best for thee in time and in eternity." Bengel.

# INDEX.

Agony of Gethsemane, 450 – 458, 468, 469.
Ambition, Christian, 359.
Angels, 152 – 156, 327, messengers, 428, 429.
Apostles, 195, 196.
Article, the Greek, 342.

Baptism, 67, 69, 336, 358. Formula of, 515 – 519, 532, 533.
Bearing our infirmities, 143 – 146, 498, 499.
Beatitudes, the, 87, 88.
Bethlehem, 48.
Bethphage, 366.

Centurion, 169.
Church, 289 – 292, 298, 320 – 326, 328 – 330, 359.
Coincidences, 29, 30, 444, 445, 511, 512.
Coming of the Son of Man, 186 – 188, 302 – 304, 346, 347, 399, 400, 407 – 418, 418 – 422, 534.
Conception, miraculous, 35 – 39, 382, 383, 519.
Creeds, 15 – 17, 517 – 519.
Crucifixion, 483 – 488, 492. Place of, 494, 495.

Darkness, outer, 142, 170.
Day, That, 124, 429, 430.
Death, Christ's view of, 174, 175.
Death of Christ, 199, 292 – 294, 357.
Demoniacs, 160 – 168, 172, 212.
Devil, the, 76, 77, 82. *See* Satan.
Discrepancies, 58, 359, 360, 373, 467, 468, 470, 471, 489, 490, 505 – 508, 508 – 510, 511.
Double sense, 79, 140, 144 – 146, 274 – 277, 374, 376, 377, 422, 423.

Elijah, 66, 312, 313, 315, 316.
End of the world, 254, 255, 533 – 535.

Eternal, 229, 254, 255, 344, 443.
Evenings, two, 170, 269, 270.
Existence of evil, 240 – 242.

Faith, 169, 176, 278, 279.
Fasting, 179.
First last and last first, 348 – 354.
Forgiveness of sin, 176, 177.
Fulfilled, that it might be, 43, 44, 252, 366, 367.

Genealogy of Jesus, 34, 35.
Good, One alone, 344.
Gospels, to be studied in their own light, 11 – 14. With preparation of heart, 14, 15. Without preconceptions, 15 – 30.
Guilt, national, cumulative, 394, 395.

Hell, 95, 208, 214.
Herod Antipas, 260 – 264.
Herod the Great, 46, 47, 55.
Herodians, 386.
Holy Ghost, the, 68, 69, 80.
Hypocrites, 282, 295.

Inspiration, 21, 22, 388.

Jerusalem, destruction of, 407 – 418.
Jews, why Jesus confined his ministry to them, 284.
John the Baptist, 60 – 65, 268.
Jonah, 296.
Jordan, 68, 356.
Judas, 444, 445, 458, 465, 480.
Judgment, day of, 437, 438.
Just, righteous or justified, 178, 212.

Kingdom of heaven, or of God, 66, 116, 211, 253, 303, 344, 346, 520 – 526.

Lake of Galilee, 148, 149.

Law fulfilled in Christ's teachings, 88 – 93, 94.
Leprosy, 136 – 138.
Lord, 169.

Marriage, 42, 97, 332 – 335, 342, 343.
Mary, the mother of Jesus, 224 – 226.
Matthew's Gospel, peculiarities of, 32, 34. When written, 31, 32.
Miracles, 35 – 39, 126 – 134, 497, 498, 500.
Murder of the Innocents, 50 – 52.
Mysteries, 251.

Name, 112. My, 197, 329.

Oaths, 97.
Offend, 210, 327.
Olives, Mount of, 466.
Omnipresence of Jesus, 329, 330.

Palm Sunday, 362, 364 – 366.
Parables, 232. Why Jesus taught in, 238 – 240.
Parallelism, 122, 123, 397.
Passover, 464, 465.
Peter's denial, 461, 462, 476 – 478.
Pharisees, 67, 226, 295.
Portents, 426, 427.
Prayer, the Lord's, 102 – 107. Efficacy of, 371.
Predictions made by Jesus, 357, 376, 401 – 406, 407 – 418.
Priests, Chief, 356.
Prophecy, 39 – 41, 43, 44, 52 – 55, 82, 83, 211, 213, 214, 274 – 277, 388 – 390, 401 – 406, 467, 491.
Professions, danger of, 396.
Providence, 107 – 110, 271.
Ψυχή, life or soul, 115, 191 – 193, 199, 301, 302.

Publicans, 99, 196.

Regeneration, the, 346, 347.
Repent, 66.
Resurrection, 379 – 381, 437, 438. Of Jesus, 503 – 508, 512 – 515, 526, 527, 528.
Retribution, 121, 193, 207, 208, 243, 244, 331, 340, 341, 373, 374, 386, 407 – 422, 432, 434 – 436, 440, 441.
Rich, 338, 339.

Sabbath, Christ's view of, 217, 218.
Sadducees, 67, 295.
Salvation, 43.
Sanhedrim, 56.
Satan, 219 – 222, 245 – 250, 255 – 257, 293, 442. *See* Devil.
Scribes, 95, 170, 273.
Self-renunciation, 340.
Sign from heaven, 288.
Spirits, evil, 157 – 168, 230, 442, 456.
Son of David, the, 34, 41. Of God, 35 – 39, 297, 319, 461. Of Man, 170, 171, 226, 227, 296, 519, 520.
Star in the east, 48, 49, 56, 57.
Supper, the Lord's, 445 – 449, 466.
Sword, 471 – 474.
Synagogue, 83.

Temptation, the, 70 – 78, 293.
Tempting God, 81.
Time, Jewish mode of reckoning, 355, 361 – 363.
Tithes, 398.
Tomb of Jesus, 501, 502, 528 – 530.
Transfiguration, 305 – 311, 315, 316.
Trial of Jesus, 479, 480, 481 – 483.
Tribute-money, 318, 386.
Types, 419 – 422.

Wise men, the, 45 – 50.

THE END.

www.ingramcontent.com/pod-product-compliance
Lightning Source LLC
Chambersburg PA
CBHW070259010526
44108CB00039B/1226